financial accounting

canadian edition

financial accounting

canadian edition

a business process approach

Jane L. Reimers
Florida State University, KPMG Professor of Accounting

Leo T. Gallant
St. Francis Xavier University

Kenneth E. MacAulay
St. Francis Xavier University

Toronto

For my mom and my son—for always believing in me.

—J.L.R.

National Library of Canada Cataloguing in Publication

Reimers, Jane L
Financial accounting : a business process approach / Jane L. Reimers, Leo T. Gallant, Kenneth E. MacAulay. — Canadian ed.

Includes index.
ISBN 0-13-123723-3

1. Accounting. 2. Financial statements. I. Gallant, Leo T., 1948– II. MacAulay, Kenneth E. (Kenneth Eugene), 1962– III. Title.

HF5635.R43 2005 657 C2004-902823-5

0-13-123723-3

Vice President, Editorial Director: Michael J. Young
Executive Editor: Samantha Scully
Executive Marketing Manager: Cas Shields
Associate Editor: Rema Celio
Production Editor: Jennifer Handel
Copy Editor: Rohini Herbert
Proofreader: Karen Bennett
Production Coordinator: Andrea Falkenberg
Page Layout: Carolyn E. Sebestyen
Art Director: Julia Hall
Interior and Cover Design: Anthony Leung
Cover Image: Janis Christie/Masterfile

2 3 4 5 08 09 07 06 05

Printed and bound in the United States of America.

Photo credits: page 31, Paul Orenstein; page 396, Dick Hemingway; page 478, Courtesy CoolBrands International

Brief Contents

	Preface	*xi*
Chapter 1	**Business: What's It All About?**	2
Chapter 2	**Qualities of Accounting Information**	44
Chapter 3	**Accruals and Deferrals: Timing Is Everything in Accounting**	82
Chapter 4	**Keeping the Books: The Mechanics of an Accounting System**	124
Chapter 5	**Purchase and Use of Capital Assets**	170
Chapter 6	**Purchases and Payments Cycle: Inventory and Liabilities**	222
Chapter 7	**Sales and Collection Cycle**	280
Chapter 8	**Financing a Business with Debt**	332
Chapter 9	**Financing a Business with Equity**	394
Chapter 10	**Cash Flow Statement: Preparation and Use**	436
Chapter 11	**Financial Statement Analysis**	476
	Appendix A **Annual Report of CoolBrands**	A-1
	Appendix B **Present and Future Value Tables**	B-1
	Appendix C **Check Figures for End-of-Chapter Problems**	C-1
	Glossary	*G-1*
	Index	*I-1*

Contents

Preface xi
Acknowledgments xv

Chapter 1

Business: What's It All About? 2

Purpose of a Business 4
The Nature of Business Operations 5
Ownership Structure of a Business 6
Sole Proprietorships 6
■ UNDERSTANDING BUSINESS
Starting a New Business: The Business Plan 7
Partnerships 7
Corporations 8
Business Activities and the Flow of Goods and Services 11
An Entrepreneur 11
The Acquisition/Payment Process 15
The Sales/Collection Process 16
Information Needs for Decision Making in Business 17
Flow of Information 18
Who Needs Information about Transactions of the Business? 18
Accounting Information: A Part of the Information System 20
The Role of the Information System 20
Overview of the Financial Statements 20
Balance Sheet 20
Income Statement 25
Statement of Retained Earnings 27
Cash Flow Statement 27
Flow of Information and the Financial Statements 28
Business Risks 29
No More Nerd Accountants 30
■ UNDERSTANDING EXCEL 32

Answers to Study Break Questions 33 / Questions 33 / Short Exercises 33 / Exercises 35 / Problems—Set A 37 / Problems—Set B 40 / Issues for Discussion 43 / Internet Exercise: Disney Corporation 43

Chapter 2

Qualities of Accounting Information 44

Information for Decision Making 46
Financial Statement Concepts 47
Objective of Financial Statements 48
Qualitative Characteristics of Accounting Information 48
Elements of the Financial Statements 50
Transactions for the Second Month of Business 50
Assets 55
Liabilities 56
Equity 56
Measurement and Recognition in Financial Statements 57
Measuring Assets 57
Recognizing Revenue and Expenses 57
Accruals and Deferrals 59
Accrual Basis Accounting 59
Cash Basis versus Accrual Basis Accounting 60
Accounting Periods and Cutoff Issues 60
More about the Financial Statements 61
Investors—Owners and Creditors 61
■ UNDERSTANDING BUSINESS
Managing Cash—Planning Inflows and Outflows 62
An Example to Illustrate the Kind of Information Financial Statements Provide 63
Putting It All Together—The Objectives of Financial Statements and the Information in Statements of Clean Sweep and Maids-R-Us 66
Applying Our Knowledge: Ratio Analysis 67
Business Risks 69
Internal Controls—Definition and Objectives 69
Special Internal Control Issues Related to Financial Statements 69
■ UNDERSTANDING EXCEL 71
Summary of Chapters 1 and 2 72

Answers to Study Break Questions 73 / Questions 73 / Short Exercises 73 / Exercises 75 / Problems—Set A 76 / Problems—Set B 78 / Issues for Discussion 80 / Internet Exercise: Globeinvestor.com and High Liner Foods Inc. 81

Chapter 3

Accruals and Deferrals: Timing Is Everything in Accounting 82

Measuring Income 84
Accruals 85
Accruals for Interest Expense and Interest Revenue 85
Receivables with Interest 87
Accruals for Other Revenues and Expenses 88

Deferrals 91
Deferrals Related to Revenue 91
Deferrals Related to Expenses 92

■ UNDERSTANDING BUSINESS
Recognizing Revenue: When Is It the Right Time? 99

Summing Up 99
Applying Our Knowledge: Ratio Analysis 100
Business Risks 101

■ UNDERSTANDING EXCEL 103

Summary Problem 104

Answers to Study Break Questions 111 / Questions 111 / Short Exercises 112 / Exercises 113 / Problems—Set A 114 / Problems—Set B 118 / Issues for Discussion 122 / Internet Exercise: Fairmont Hotels and Resorts 123

Chapter 4

Keeping the Books: The Mechanics of an Accounting System 124

The General Ledger Accounting System 126
Debits and Credits 129
The Accounting Cycle 131
Step 1: Recording Journal Entries 131
Step 2: Posting Journal Entries to the General Ledger 134
Step 3: Preparing an Unadjusted Trial Balance 134
Step 4: Adjusting Journal Entries 134
Steps 5 and 6: Preparing the Adjusted Trial Balance and the Financial Statements 138
Step 7: Closing the Revenue and Expense Accounts 139
Step 8: Preparing a Postclosing Trial Balance 143
Review and Summary of the Accounting Cycle 143
What's Next? The General Ledger System versus Integrated Information Systems 145

■ UNDERSTANDING BUSINESS
Enterprise Resource Planning Systems 146

Business Risks 147

■ UNDERSTANDING EXCEL 148

Summary Problem 149

Answers to Study Break Questions 156 / Questions 157 / Short Exercises 157 / Exercises 159 / Problems—Set A 161 / Problems—Set B 164 / Issues for Discussion 167 / Internet Exercise: Hoover's and Intuit Inc. 168

Chapter 5

Purchase and Use of Capital Assets 170

Acquisition of Long-Term Assets: The Business Process 173
Allocating the Cost of Long-Term Assets 174
Acquisition Costs 175
Basket Purchase Allocation 176
Recording Acquisition Costs 177
Amortization 177
Amortization and the Financial Statements 178
Straight-Line Amortization 178
Recording Straight-Line Method Amortization Expense 180
Units-of-Production Amortization 181
Recording Units-of-Production Method Amortization Expense 181
Declining Balance Method 182
Recording Declining Balance Method Amortization Expense 183
Specific Amortization Formulas 183
Capital Expenditures versus Revenue Expenditures 185
Revising Estimates of Useful Life and Residual Value 187
Depletion of Natural Resources and Amortization of Intangible Assets 188
Depletion of Natural Resources 188
Amortization of Intangible Assets 188
Selling a Long-Term Asset 189
Amortization and Taxes 191
Finding and Using Amortization Information 192

■ UNDERSTANDING BUSINESS
Lease or Buy? 193

Applying Our Knowledge: Ratio Analysis 193
Business Risks 194

■ UNDERSTANDING EXCEL 195

Summary Problem 196

Answers to Study Break Questions 199 / Solution to Summary Problem 201 / Questions 206 / Short Exercises 206 / Exercises 208 / Problems—Set A 209 / Problems—Set B 212 / Recording Transactions 216 / Chapter 5: Comprehensive Financial Statement Preparation Problem 219 / Issues for Discussion 220 / Internet Exercise: Van Houtte Inc. 220

Chapter 6

Purchases and Payments Cycle: Inventory and Liabilities 222

Acquiring Merchandise for Sale 224
Procedures for Acquisition of Goods 224
Merchandise Inventory 225
Purchases 225
Selecting and Accounting for Goods Sold: Inventory Cost Flow 227
Keeping Track of the Inventory: Four Cost Flow Assumptions 228
Record Keeping for the Inventory 229

■ UNDERSTANDING BUSINESS
Selecting Inventory Cost Flow Assumption 229

Example of Cost Flow Assumptions and Timing of Record Keeping 230
Perpetual Inventory 230
Periodic Inventory 231
FIFO Periodic 232
FIFO Perpetual 233
LIFO Periodic 234
Accounting Choices Make a Difference 234
Average Cost Periodic 234
Conclusions about Inventory Cost Flow Assumptions 235
Recording Inventory Purchases and Freight Costs 235
Purchases and Purchase Discounts 235
Purchase Returns and Purchase Allowances 237
Freight-In 237
Inventory and Cost of Goods Sold in Merchandising Operations 237
Recording Inventory and Cost of Goods Sold Transactions 238
Adjustments and Closing under a Perpetual Inventory System 238
Adjustments and Closing under a Periodic Inventory System 239
Inventory Errors 240
Ending Inventory Errors 240
Beginning Inventory Errors 241
Gross Profit Method of Estimating Ending Inventory 242
Valuing Inventory: Lower-of-Cost-or-Market 243
Finding and Using Inventory Information 244
Applying Our Knowledge: Ratio Analysis 244
Paying for Acquisitions: Liabilities 245
Common Types of Liabilities 246
Acquisition of Human Resources and Payroll Liabilities 247
Business Risks 249
Inventory: Risks and Controls 249
Liabilities: Risks and Controls 250

■ UNDERSTANDING EXCEL 250

Summary Problem 251

Answers to Study Break Questions 252 / Solution to Summary Problem 254 / Questions 261 / Short Exercises 261 / Exercises 263 / Problems—Set A 266 / Problems—Set B 270 / Recording Transactions 274 / Chapter 6: Comprehensive Financial Statement Preparation Problem 277 / Issues for Discussion 278 / Internet Exercise: Coca-Cola Company 278

Chapter 7

Sales and Collection Cycle 280

Sales Cycle 282
Timing of Revenue Recognition 283

■ UNDERSTANDING BUSINESS
Managing Accounts Receivable 283

Revenue Recognition: Some Examples 284
Sales Discounts 285
Sales Returns and Allowances 287
Payment for Goods and Services 287
Accounting for Cash 288
Accounts Receivable: Collecting Payment for Sales Made on Account 291
Direct Write-Off Method 291
Allowance Method 292
Credit Card Sales 298
Warranties 299
Finding and Using Information About Sales and Accounts Receivable 300
Using the Financial Statement Information for Analysis 300
Business Risks 302

■ UNDERSTANDING EXCEL 304

Summary Problem 305

Answers to Study Break Questions 306 / Solution to Summary Problem 308 / Questions 316 / Short Exercises 316 / Exercises 319 / Problems—Set A 322 / Problems—Set B 324 / Recording Transactions 327 / Chapter 7: Comprehensive Financial Statement Preparation Problem 330 / Issues for Discussion 330 / Internet Exercise: Intel Corporation 331

Chapter 8

Financing a Business with Debt 332

Long-Term Notes Payable and Mortgages 334

■ UNDERSTANDING BUSINESS
Financing Your Business: Using a Line of Credit 335

Time Value of Money 339
Simple versus Compound Interest 340
Future Value 340
Future Value of an Annuity 343
Present Value 345
Long-Term Liabilities: Raising Money by Issuing Bonds 349
What Is a Bond? 349
More about Bonds 350
Issuing Bonds Payable 351
Getting the Money 351
Paying the Bondholders 352
Accounting for Bonds Payable 353
Issuing Bonds at a Discount or a Premium 353
Amortizing Bond Discounts and Premiums: Effective Interest Method 356
Straight-Line Amortization of Bond Discounts and Premiums 361
Zero-Coupon Bonds 362
Callable and Convertible Bonds 363
Callable Bonds 363
Convertible Bonds 364
Financial Statement Analysis 364
Business Risk 366

■ UNDERSTANDING EXCEL 367

Summary Problem 368

Answers to Study Break Questions 369 / Solution to Summary Problem 372 / Questions 380 / Short Exercises 380 / Exercises 382 / Problems—Set A 383 / Problems—Set B 387 / Recording Transactions 389 / Chapter 8: Comprehensive Financial Statement Preparation Problem 391 / Issues for Discussion 392 / Internet Exercise: Sobeys Inc. and Loblaw Companies Limited 393

Chapter 9

Financing a Business with Equity 394

Owners of a Business 396
Components of Shareholders' Equity in a Corporation: Share Capital 396
Shares: Authorized, Issued, and Outstanding 397

■ UNDERSTANDING BUSINESS
Why Do Companies Have Preferred Shares? 401

Repurchase of Shares 404
Company Buys Its Own Shares 404
Selling Treasury Shares 406
Stock Dividends 407
Stock Splits 408
Components of Shareholders' Equity in a Corporation: Retained Earnings 408
Analysis of Shareholders' Equity 409
Business Risks 411

■ UNDERSTANDING EXCEL 412

Summary Problem 412

Answers to Study Break Questions 415 / Questions 425 / Short Exercises 425 / Exercises 427 / Problems—Set A 428 / Problems—Set B 429 / Recording Transactions 431 / Chapter 9: Comprehensive Financial Statement Preparation Problem 433 / Issues for Discussion 434 / Internet Exercise: Van Houtte Inc. 434

Chapter 10

Cash Flow Statement: Preparation and Use 436

Importance of the Cash Flow Statement 438

■ UNDERSTANDING BUSINESS
It's All about Cash Flow 439

Two Methods of Preparing and Presenting the Cash Flow Statement 440
Review of the Three Sections of the Cash Flow Statement 441
Accrual Accounting versus Cash 442
Preparing the Cash Flow Statement 444
Direct Method of Computing Cash from Operations 444
Indirect Method of Computing Cash from Operations 448
Cash from Investing and Financing Activities 450
Summary of Direct and Indirect Methods 451
Financial Statement Analysis 452

■ UNDERSTANDING EXCEL 455

Summary Problem 456

Answers to Study Break Questions 457 / Solution to Summary Problem 457 / Questions 460 / Short Exercises 460 / Exercises 461 / Problems—Set A 464 / Problems—Set B 467 / Recording Transactions 471 / Issues for Discussion 474 / Internet Exercise: Carnival Corp. 474

Chapter 11

Financial Statement Analysis 476

Financial Information: Looking beneath the Surface 478
A Closer Look at the Income Statement 478
Discontinued Operations 478
Extraordinary Items 479
Changes in Accounting Policy 480

■ UNDERSTANDING BUSINESS
Ordinary Extraordinary Items? 480

Other Financial Statement Items 481
Unusual Items 481
Analysis of Financial Information 482
Horizontal Analysis 482
Vertical Analysis 484
Ratio Analysis 484
Conclusion 489

■ UNDERSTANDING EXCEL 494

Summary Problem 495

Answers to Study Break Questions 497 / Questions 497 / Short Exercises 497 / Exercises 499 / Problems—Set A 501 / Problems—Set B 505 / Issues for Discussion 508 / Internet Exercise: Papa John's International, Inc. 508

Appendix A
Annual Report of CoolBrands A-1

Appendix B
Present and Future Value Tables B-1

Appendix C
Check Figures for End-of-Chapter Problems C-1

Glossary *G-1*
Index *I-1*

Preface

To the Student:

Welcome to your first accounting course! In this course you will learn about the way a business works and how accounting fits into business processes. Our objective is for you to see how accounting relates to and interacts with business.

Financial Accounting: A Business Process Approach, Canadian Edition, attempts to bridge the gap between business and accounting. The text describes what business is all about and emphasizes the basic business processes. This provides a framework in which you can see how accounting relates to and reports on business activity.

This text follows a balanced approach that is useful for financial statement users and preparers. It covers the key concepts and the key procedures that both majors and non-majors in accounting need. You will learn how to record transactions, prepare financial statements, and use financial statements. In addition, you will learn the key accounting concepts underlying these financial statements. More importantly, though, ***Financial Accounting: A Business Process Approach*** allows you to understand what accounting is all about by letting you see how accounting fits into and relates to business processes.

To help you improve your understanding of accounting principles, practise your accounting skills, and see how accounting relates to and interacts with business, we have included the following pedagogical tools to support you.

Tom's Wear: A Running Case Example

In Chapter 1, you are introduced to Tom, an entrepreneur who decides to create a T-shirt business. In subsequent chapters, you will learn financial accounting concepts through Tom's experiences as he grows and expands his business.

Understanding Excel

In every chapter, you can see Tom's Wear's monthly transactions illustrated in Excel—a critical business tool for you to master.

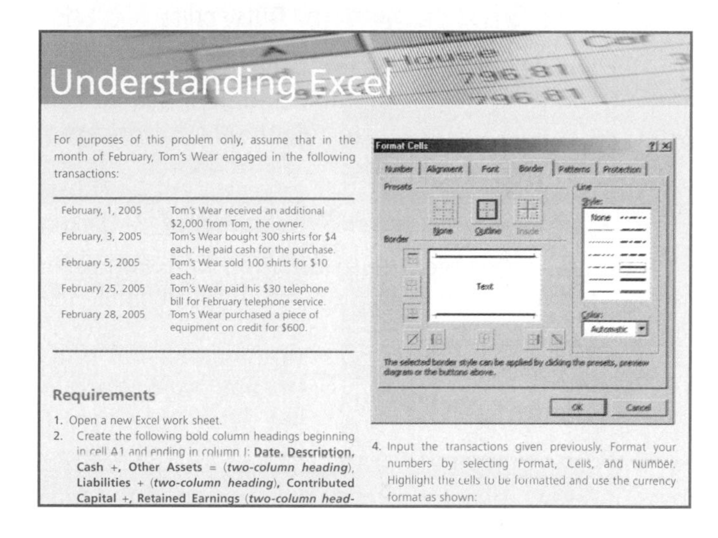
Understanding Excel

For purposes of this problem only, assume that in the month of February, Tom's Wear engaged in the following transactions:

February, 1, 2005	Tom's Wear received an additional $2,000 from Tom, the owner.
February, 3, 2005	Tom's Wear bought 300 shirts for $4 each. He paid cash for the purchase.
February 5, 2005	Tom's Wear sold 100 shirts for $10 each.
February 25, 2005	Tom's Wear paid his $30 telephone bill for February telephone service.
February 28, 2005	Tom's Wear purchased a piece of equipment on credit for $600.

Requirements

1. Open a new Excel work sheet.
2. Create the following bold column headings beginning in cell A1 and ending in column I: **Date, Description, Cash +, Other Assets =** (*two-column heading*), **Liabilities +** (*two-column heading*), **Contributed Capital +, Retained Earnings** (*two-column head-*

4. Input the transactions given previously. Format your numbers by selecting Format, Cells, and Number. Highlight the cells to be formatted and use the currency format as shown:

Understanding Business

Understanding Business boxes appear once in every chapter. Understanding Business boxes relate to the chapter topic and walk you through the various decisions that entrepreneurs make as they prepare to open their businesses. Topics covered include: starting with a business plan, managing cash, and cash flow.

Understanding Business

Starting a New Business: The Business Plan

Starting a new business? In Canada, both the federal and provincial governments are actively involved in supporting the creation of new businesses. Through BusinessGateway.ca the Government of Canada, in co-operation with the provincial governments and territories, makes available information that business owners would find useful.

It all starts with a business plan. A business plan is a recognized management tool used by successful and/or prospective businesses of all sizes to document business objectives and to propose how these objectives will be attained within a specific period of time. It is a written document that describes the nature of the business, the financial management plan, the management plan, and the marketing plan.

The **business description** is the foundation for the rest of the business plan. It should give the form of your

Once the business description is completed, the focus shifts to specific items for the next three sections.

A **financial management** plan, including a startup budget and an operating budget, must be prepared in detail. The financial statements are prepared on the basis of the budgets. The financial statements are a significant part of a business plan.

The **management plan** addresses the functioning of business operations. Strengths and weaknesses of the personnel and the business as a whole should be assessed. Once identified, potential problems can be addressed and solved. To succeed as a business, management's goal should be to keep the employees and customers happy.

Finally, the **marketing plan** must be created. The marketing plan is designed to attract and keep customers. By identifying and getting to know the sector of the mar-

Study Breaks

Study Breaks appear at least once in every chapter and encourage you to pause from reading and immediately apply what you have just learned to solve specific problems.

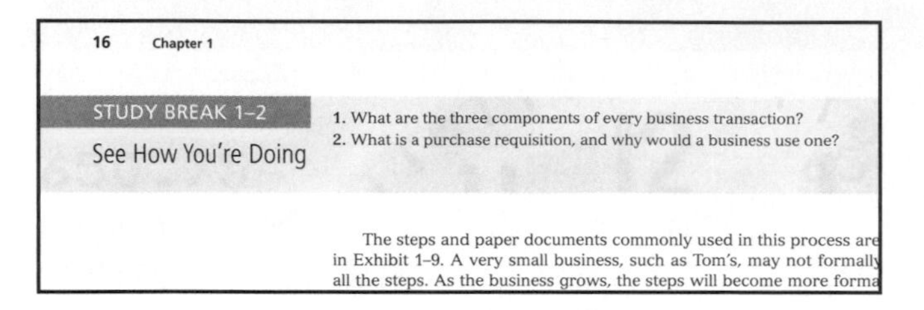
16 Chapter 1

STUDY BREAK 1-2
See How You're Doing

1. What are the three components of every business transaction?
2. What is a purchase requisition, and why would a business use one?

The steps and paper documents commonly used in this process are in Exhibit 1-9. A very small business, such as Tom's, may not formally all the steps. As the business grows, the steps will become more forma

Running Glossary and Margin Notes

Throughout each chapter, the running glossary and margin notes provide definitions and notes to aid your understanding of key terminology and concepts.

Summary Problem with Solution

The Summary Problem with Solution pulls together the chapter concepts with an extensive and challenging review problem.

Summary

At the end of most chapters, a summary, organized by key points, gives a concise description of the material covered in the chapter.

Answers to Study Break Questions

Each chapter provides responses to the Study Break questions that appear throughout the chapter, allowing you to check your understanding of the chapter content.

Questions

The questions at the end of each chapter require short, written answers, often on a single topic.

Short Exercises

We provide short exercises on single topics to allow you to practise what you have learned in the chapter; these exercises reference specific learning objectives.

Exercises

Exercises on single or multiple topics help you to apply in more detail what you have learned in the chapter.

Problems

The end-of-chapter problems, usually based on multiple topics, are presented in two groups that mirror each other, "A" and "B." Many instructors work through one group of problems in class and assign problems from the other group for homework or extra practice.

Recording Transactions

Chapters 5 through 10 include Recording Transactions, which allow you to practise making journal entries and preparing financial statements based on specific end-of-chapter exercises and problems.

Comprehensive Financial Statement Preparation Problem

Chapters 5 through 9 contain a Comprehensive Financial Statement Preparation Problem, which requires you to prepare various financial statements, such as income statements and balance sheets, using skills you have learned so far.

Issues for Discussion

The Issues for Discussion exercises ask you to analyze the financial statements of a company, consider the business risks of that company, and discuss the ethical issues that the business faces.

Internet Exercise

The Internet Exercises ask you to visit a company website and answer questions relating to financial information found on that site.

Media Companion CD-ROM

The Media Companion CD-ROM includes PowerPoint slides and the Accounting Cycle Tutorial, which helps you with concepts like transactions, adjustments, and closing entries. This interactive tool will guide you through every step of the accounting cycle process.

Companion Website

The Companion Website provides a wealth of resources for you and your instructor, including a Study Guide with quizzes and immediate feedback. Go to page xvii to learn more about *Financial Accounting: A Business Process Approach*'s Companion Website.

Good luck with your course!

To the Instructor:

Welcome to ***Financial Accounting: A Business Process Approach***, Canadian Edition.

How Is the Business Process Approach Applied Throughout the Text?

Financial Accounting: A Business Process Approach, Canadian Edition, begins with a description of what a business is all about. This description provides a framework in which students can see how accounting relates to and reports on business activities. We then emphasize how accounting fits into the framework of basic business processes.

Each chapter offers a quick review of what students have just learned (*Here's Where You've Been...*) and a preview of where they're headed (*Here's Where You're Going...*) so that they are prepared to tackle new concepts throughout the rest of the text.

Business Process Model

Every chapter opens with the same image of the business process model. Different parts of the model are highlighted so students can see which part of the model will be discussed in each chapter. The Business Process Icon will appear in the margin whenever the text material refers specifically to the Business Process Model.

Structure of the Text

Chapters 1 through 4 introduce students to business and accounting. In Chapters 5 through 9, business and accounting details are explored in greater depth. Although the text is written in such a way that debits and credits are optional, in these chapters debits and credits are part of the transactions. Study Break questions are designed for solution using debits and credits. The summary problem for Tom's Wear is given in debits and credits. The end-of-chapter material includes a separate section of problems identified to require completion by recording debits and credits. These chapters represent the heart of the business process approach. Chapters 10 and 11 introduce other financial reporting topics. In addition to the integration of cash flows into each chapter (starting with Chapter 1), Chapter 10, "Cash Flow Statement: Preparation and Use," acts as a "wrap-up" chapter at the end of the book.

Instructor Supplements Package: Instructor's Resource CD-ROM

The IRCD includes the following: Instructor's Resource Manual; Instructor's Solutions Manual; TestGen; PowerPoint Slides; and Accounting Cycle Tutorial. (ISBN 0-13-129472-5)

Instructor's Resource Manual Each chapter of this comprehensive resource consists of a list of student learning objectives, a narrative overview of main topics, an outline with teaching tips interspersed, a 10-problem multiple choice quiz cross-referenced to the outline and arranged for easy copying (answers are at the end of the outline and solutions for all quizzes are on separate pages at the end of the manual), suggested readings, examples of ways to integrate the supplements, and transparency masters. (ISBN 0-13-129471-7)

Instructor's Solutions Manual In addition to fully worked-out solutions that have been carefully checked for accuracy for every question, exercise, and problem in the text, the Instructor's Solutions Manual provides suggestions for alternative chapter sequences, a categorization of assignment material, and check figures. (ISBN 0-13-129470-9)

TestGen This test bank consists of over 1,800 questions, including true/false questions, conceptual and quantitative multiple-choice questions, critical thinking problems, and exercises. Each question will identify the difficulty level and the corresponding learning objective. TestGen can create exams and evaluate and track student results. It also provides online testing capabilities. (ISBN 0-13-129469-5)

PowerPoint Slides Each chapter includes dozens of slides that highlight key points and provide the framework for in-class or online lectures. (ISBN 0-13-129468-7)

Accounting Cycle Tutorial An excellent resource for classroom presentation! The Accounting Cycle Tutorial is a six-module interactive CD that guides students through every step of the accounting cycle process.

Acknowledgments

We wish to thank Jane Reimers for providing us with the opportunity to prepare a Canadian edition of the text.

We would also like to thank, in particular, the following people for either reviewing the U.S. edition of this text or the manuscript for the Canadian edition during development:

Lynn Applebaum, Seneca College
Hilary M. Becker, Carleton University
Judy Cumby, Memorial University of Newfoundland
Valorie Leonard, Laurentian University
Doug Ringrose, Grant MacEwan Community College
John D. Russell, University of Saskatchewan
Jan Thatcher, Lakehead University

Special thanks to CoolBrands International for allowing us to use its annual report as the major specimen set of financial statements. Many other companies also granted permission to use portions of their annual reports to illustrate various aspects of financial reporting.

We would also like to acknowledge the people at Pearson Education Canada, in particular: Executive Editor Samantha Scully, Associate Editor Rema Celio, Production Editor Jennifer Handel, Production Coordinator Andrea Falkenberg, and Copy Editor Rohini Herbert.

At the local level in Antigonish we would like to thank our secretary, Anne Marie Durant, for her assistance in the project, as well as our friends and families for their encouragement.

Leo Gallant
Ken MacAulay
Antigonish, Nova Scotia

A Great Way to Learn and Instruct Online

The Pearson Education Canada Companion Website is easy to navigate and is organized to correspond to the chapters in this textbook. Whether you are a student in the classroom or a distance learner you will discover helpful resources for in-depth study and research that empower you in your quest for greater knowledge and maximize your potential for success in the course.

[www.pearsoned.ca/reimers]

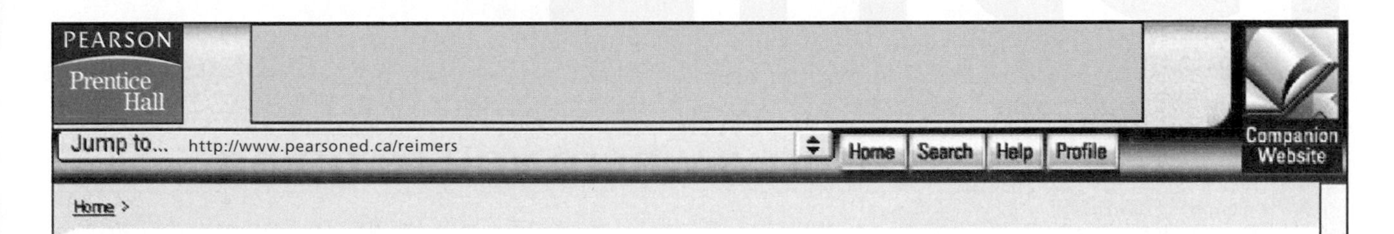

Home >

PH Companion Website

Financial Accounting: A Business Process Approach, Canadian Edition, by Reimers, Gallant, and MacAulay

Student Resources

The modules in this section provide students with tools for learning course material. These modules include:

- Study Guide
- Company URLs
- Glossary

In the Study Guide modules, students can send answers to the grader and receive instant feedback on their progress through the Results Reporter. Coaching comments and references to the textbook may be available to ensure that students take advantage of all available resources to enhance their learning experience.

Instructor Resources

A link to this book on the Pearson online catalogue (vig.pearsoned.ca) provides instructors with additional teaching tools. Downloadable PowerPoint Presentations and an Instructor's Manual are just some of the materials that may be available. The catalogue is password protected. To get a password, simply contact your Pearson Education Canada Representative or call Faculty Sales and Services at 1-800-850-5813.

CHAPTER 1

Business: What's It All About?

Here's where you're going...

When you are finished studying Chapter 1, you should understand what a business does and understand that the financial statements reflect information about the major business processes—the acquisition/payment process and the sales/collection process.

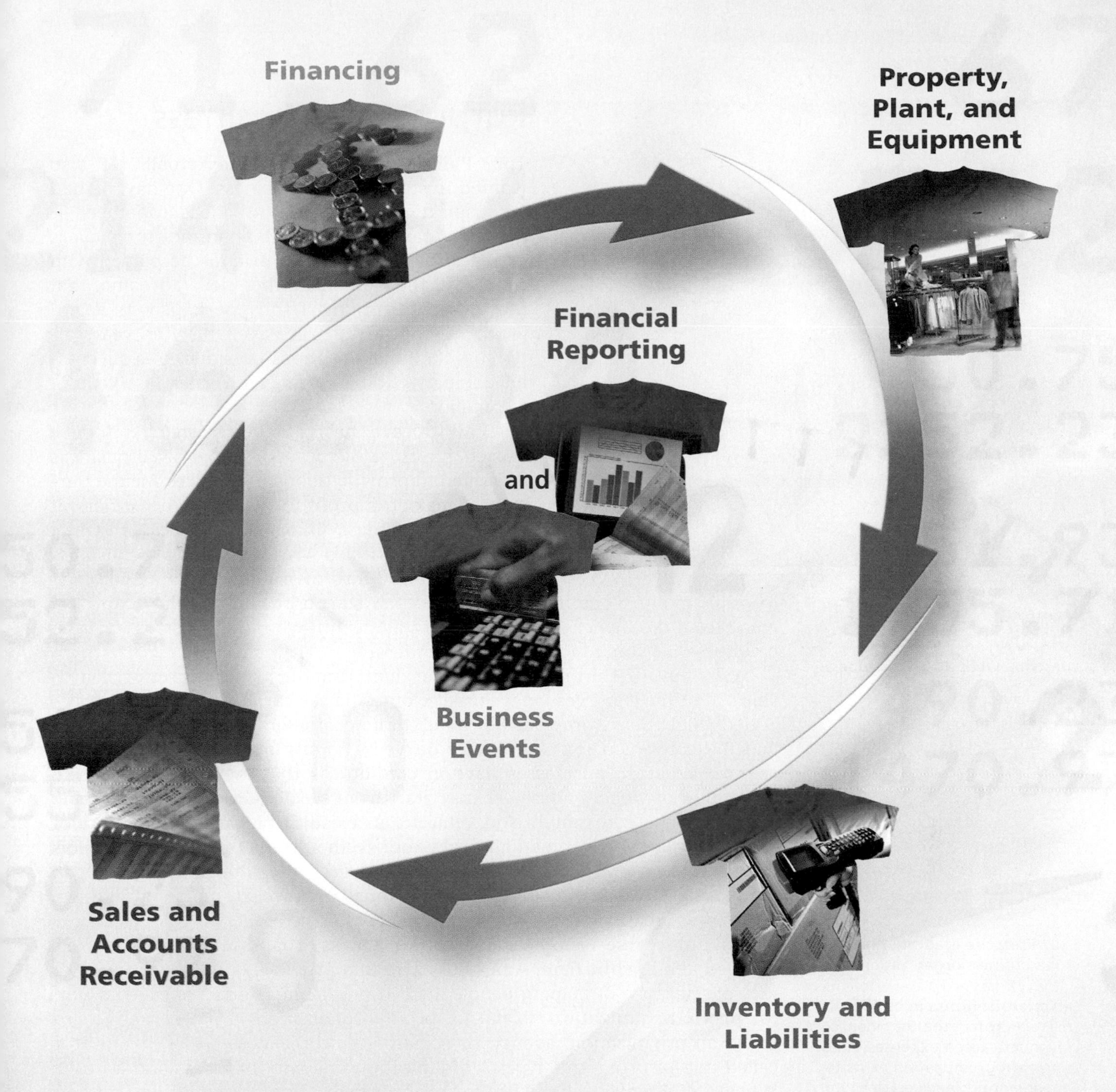

Learning Objectives

More specifically, when you are finished studying this chapter, you should be able to answer these questions:

1. What does a business do, and how is it organized?
2. What are the common business processes?
3. Who needs accounting information, and why?
4. What are the four basic financial statements, and what information does each contain?

Purpose of a Business

Tom Phillips loved to play basketball. He also wanted to start his own business. One day, he had an inspiration that put both ideas together—T-shirts for casual players, like him, not for players on a team. Tom polled the friends he played with regularly; they all liked the idea, agreeing that they would buy such a T-shirt, perhaps with a "no-look" pass on it, if it were available. Ten years after Tom had this idea, he is president of a successful company, Tom's Wear, with sales last year of $12 million.

How does a business get started, and once started, how does it succeed? Generally, a business is formed to provide goods or services for the purpose of making a profit for its owner or owners. It begins by obtaining financial resources—and that means money. Tom's Wear began as a business with $5,000 of Tom's own money and a $500 loan from his mother. The financial resources to start a business—called **capital**—come from the owners of the business (like Tom), who are investors, or from creditors (like Tom's mom), who are lenders.

L.O. 1

Describe what a business does.

Capital is the name for the resources used to start and run a business.

Why buy a T-shirt from Tom, rather than from the manufacturer of plain T-shirts? For the same reason we order clothes from Sears Canada Inc. (Sears)—added value. Sears provides a product to its customers with a certain quality and the convenience of mail-order delivery. Its customers find value in this service. What all businesses have in common is that they provide us with something of value. A business may start from scratch and create something of value, or it may simply add value to an existing product or service. For some customers, the value that Sears adds to the product may be its easy order and delivery procedures. For other customers, the added value may be in the monogram the company will put on shirts or towels to personalize them. Businesses create or add value to earn money for the owners.

An **enterprise** is another name for a business organization.

A **for-profit firm** is in business to make a profit—that is, when revenues exceed expenses. A **not-for-profit organization** exists to provide goods and services to some target group at a reduced cost or no cost.

An **enterprise**—another name for a business organization—with this goal is called a **for-profit firm**. A business firm that provides goods or services for the sole purpose of helping people instead of making a profit is called a **not-for-profit organization**. A not-for-profit organization is more likely to be called an organization, agency, or society than a business. Even though it is called *not-for-profit,* this type of organization does not mind making a profit. What is different is what a not-for-profit organization does with any profit it makes. Instead of distributing it to owners, a not-for-profit organization uses any profit to provide more goods and services to the people it serves. Both for-profit organizations and not-for-profit organizations provide value. Throughout this book, we will be dealing primarily with for-profit organizations—businesses.

To be a viable business, Tom's Wear needed to provide customers with something of value. Tom purchased T-shirts with his special logo and then provided them to his customers at a convenient time and place.

What is business all about?

Adding Value →To Make a Profit

A simple model of the firm is shown in Exhibit 1–1. The inputs in a firm include capital, equipment, inventory, supplies, and labour. The business process of acquiring goods and services and paying for them is called the acquisition/payment process. The firm then does something to add value—that is called

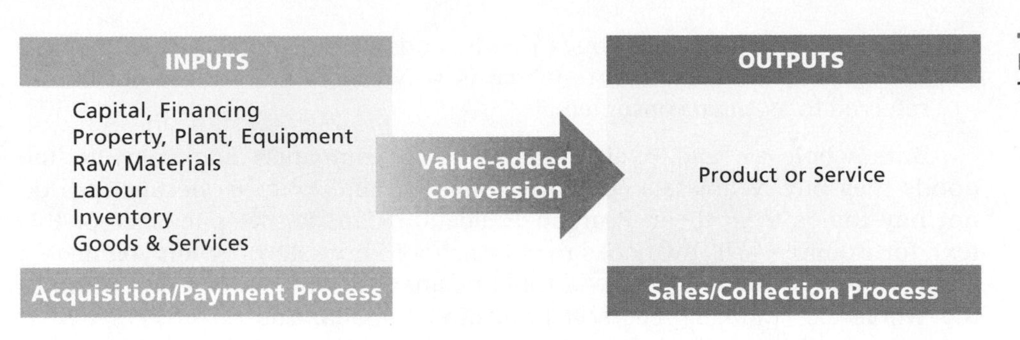

Exhibit 1–1
The Firm

the conversion process. The process is called conversion because the firm takes inputs and converts them into outputs. The outputs of a firm are its products or services. The business process of selling goods and services and collecting payment for them is called the sales/collection process. As the firm carries out these three business processes—acquiring inputs, converting them to outputs, and providing those outputs to customers—information about these activities is recorded in the company's information system. Both insiders (the owners and the firm's employees) and outsiders (the creditors, governmental agencies, and potential investors) use the information.

A business must successfully plan, control, and evaluate its activities. If it does these activities well, the business will survive. If it does them very well, it will make a profit. **Profit** is the difference between the revenue—the amount a business earns for the goods it sells or the services it provides—and the expenses of selling those goods or providing those services. The complexity of a company's planning, control, and evaluation processes depends on the type, size, and structure of the business. You will see this as we look at businesses in two ways: the nature of their operations and who owns them.

Profit is the difference between the revenues and expenses from selling goods or providing services.

The Nature of Business Operations

L.O. 1

Businesses are classified—by type and by organizational form.

The operation of a business depends on what the business has been formed to do. From that perspective, there are four types of businesses: service, merchandising, manufacturing, and financial. Although most businesses can be classified as one of these four types, many large businesses are a combination of two or more.

A **service** company provides a service—it does something for you, rather than selling something to you. Services range from activities you cannot see, such as the advice provided by lawyers or tax consultants, to activities you can see, such as house cleaning or car washing. During the past two decades, our economy has been producing more services than goods.

A **service** company *does* something for its customers; a **merchandising** firm *sells a product* to its customers.

A **merchandising** business buys goods, adds value to them, and then sells them with the added value. It does not *make* the goods, and it does not buy them to *use*. Instead, a merchandising business buys the goods for the purpose of adding its own particular value to them and, after adding value, sells them to another company or person.

> Sears Canada Inc. is an example of a merchandising business. The company buys goods from many different companies and then sells those goods to the final consumer. The added value may be visible, like monograms, or it may be invisible, like good service or fast delivery.

There are two types of merchandising businesses:

- a **wholesale company**, which buys goods, adds value, and sells them to other companies; and

A **wholesale company** is a merchandising company that sells goods to other companies.

A **retail company** is a merchandising company that buys goods, adds value, and sells the goods to consumers.

- a **retail company**, which buys goods, adds value, and sells them to customers who consume them—which is why you will see these customers referred to as "final consumers."

Both wholesale and retail merchandising companies add value to the goods they buy. Wholesale companies are not familiar to us because we do not buy things from them. Pearson Education Canada, the publisher of this text, for example, sells textbooks to your school's bookstore. When you need a book, you go to the bookstore—a retail business—to buy it. You do not go to the wholesale company, Pearson Education Canada. You do not care what business transactions have to take place to get the book from the factory, where it is printed and the covers are put on, to the bookstore. At the bookstore, the books are provided along with thousands of others but in a way that you can immediately and conveniently purchase the one or two books you need. The bookstore is an example of a retailer. *Retail store* is widely used to describe the businesses we find in every shopping mall.

A **manufacturing business** is a business firm that makes the products it sells.

A **financial services company** deals in services related to money.

A **bank** is an institution that provides financial services to customers, such as lending money.

A **mortgage company** is a financial institution that lends money to borrowers to purchase property.

An **insurance company** is a business firm that provides some financial protection in the case of loss of life or property.

A **manufacturing business** makes the products it sells. Manufacturing companies vary in size and complexity. Making clay pots and vases in a space not larger than a garage is a manufacturing business. Automobile giants, such as Ford and General Motors, owned by many thousands of people and employing hundreds of thousands of workers at all levels in enormous factories all over the world, are large, complex, manufacturing businesses.

Financial services companies do not make tangible products, and they do not sell products made by another company. They deal in services related to money. One kind of financial services company lends money, for example, **banks**, which lend money to borrowers to pay for cars and furniture; and **mortgage companies**, which lend money to pay for a house. Another type of financial services company is an **insurance company**, which provides some financial protection in the case of loss of life or property.

Ownership Structure of a Business

L.O. 1

Describe the various structures a business may have.

No matter what type of product or service it provides, a business must have an owner or owners. Governments own some business, but in Canada, an individual or a group of individuals owns most businesses. Business ownership usually takes one of three general forms: a sole proprietorship, a partnership, or a corporation.

Sole Proprietorships

A **sole proprietorship** is a business with a single owner.

If a single person owns a business, like the clay pot maker in his garage, it is a sole proprietorship. A new business often starts as a **sole proprietorship**. A sole proprietorship accumulates financial information—such as cost of materials, equipment, rent, electricity, and income from sales—but is not required by law to make any of that financial information available to the public. That means the average person is not privy to this information. Naturally, some governmental agencies—such as the Canada Customs and Revenue Agency (CCRA)—will receive some of this information from the company's goods and services tax (GST) return.

A business in the form of a sole proprietorship is not separate from its owner in terms of responsibility and liability—the owner is personally responsible for all the decisions made for the business. For example, the income from the business is included as income on the owner's individual income tax return. The business does not have its own tax return. If you are a sole proprietor, you include your business income with any other income you have earned on your individual tax return.

Starting a New Business: The Business Plan

Starting a new business? In Canada, both the federal and provincial governments are actively involved in supporting the creation of new businesses. Through BusinessGateway.ca the Government of Canada, in co-operation with the provincial governments and territories, makes available information that business owners would find useful.

It all starts with a business plan. A business plan is a recognized management tool used by successful and/or prospective businesses of all sizes to document business objectives and to propose how these objectives will be attained within a specific period of time. It is a written document that describes the nature of the business, the financial management plan, the management plan, and the marketing plan.

The **business description** is the foundation for the rest of the business plan. It should give the form of your business enterprise—a sole proprietorship, a partnership, or a corporation. The business description should also describe the nature of your business—manufacturing, merchandising, or service. Then, more specific details should be explained—goals and objectives, operating procedures, location, personnel, marketing, licences and insurance, and financing plans.

Once the business description is completed, the focus shifts to specific items for the next three sections.

A **financial management** plan, including a startup budget and an operating budget, must be prepared in detail. The financial statements are prepared on the basis of the budgets. The financial statements are a significant part of a business plan.

The **management plan** addresses the functioning of business operations. Strengths and weaknesses of the personnel and the business as a whole should be assessed. Once identified, potential problems can be addressed and solved. To succeed as a business, management's goal should be to keep the employees and customers happy.

Finally, the **marketing plan** must be created. The marketing plan is designed to attract and keep customers. By identifying and getting to know the sector of the market you want to serve, you can appeal to its wants and needs. Such characteristics as age, gender, income, and educational levels of potential customers can help you prepare a marketing plan to develop a customer base.

For more information on starting a business visit the website at www.businessgateway.ca/en/hi/.

Also, you are responsible for your company's debts. Your company's bills are your bills; if there is not enough money in your company's "pockets" to pay its bills, then you must pay the bills from your pockets. Moreover, you own the company's assets, and your personal assets are the company's assets—even if those personal assets are the only way of paying your company's bills.

Even though the financial records of a business—the company's books—should be kept separately from the owner's personal financial records, there is no separation of the sole proprietorship's books and its owner's books for tax and legal purposes. For example, your business chequing account should be separate from your personal chequing account, but the income you earn from your business and the income you earn from other sources must both be included on your individual, personal tax return.

Partnerships

A business **partnership** is owned by two or more people, although it is similar to a sole proprietorship in the sense that the income each partner earns (or loses) from the business partnership is included on his or her own personal

A **partnership** is a legal arrangement for a business set up by two or more individuals.

tax return. When two or more people form a business as partners, they often get together with a lawyer to define the specific terms of their business relationship. Such details as how much work each will do and how they will split up the profits from the business are specified in a document called a **partnership agreement**. Like a sole proprietorship, the owners—each of the partners—are responsible for everything the company does. For example, if the company is sued for a negligent act, then the partners are legally liable. The company's assets are the partners' assets, and the company's debts are the partners' debts. Even so, as with a sole proprietorship, the financial records of a partnership should be kept separate from the partners' personal financial records.

A **partnership agreement** is a document that defines the specific terms of a partnership or business relationship.

Corporations

A **corporation** is legally separate and financially separate from its owners. A company must have a corporate charter that describes the business and how the business plans to acquire financing—how many owners it will be allowed to have. Ownership in a corporation is divided into units called **capital shares**, each representing ownership in a fraction of the corporation. An owner of shares in a corporation is called a **shareholder**. In most corporations, many people are owners of the corporation. A corporation whose shares are owned by a very small number of people is called a **closely held corporation**.

A **corporation** is a legal form for a business in which the business is a legal entity separate from the owners. A corporation may have a single owner or a large number of owners.

Capital shares are the units of ownership in a corporation. The owners of the corporation are called **shareholders.**

A corporation whose shares are owned by a very small number of people is called a **closely held corporation**.

As legal entities, corporations may enter into contracts, just like individuals. A corporation pays taxes on its earnings. A corporation's owners do not include their share of the corporation's income in their personal tax returns—unlike the owner of a sole proprietorship or the partners in a partnership. Each individual corporation owner does not have individual legal responsibility for the corporation's actions, as is true for the owners of a sole proprietorship or partnership. For example, a shareholder cannot be sued for the illegal actions of the corporation. The managers are held responsible for the actions of the corporation, and only the corporation's assets are at risk.

Sears Canada Inc. is a corporation. Two of the corporation's financial statements are shown in Exhibits 1–2 and 1–3. There are over 107 million Sears shares, owned by a large number of people. Anyone who wants to invest in Sears Canada Inc. can purchase shares on a **stock exchange**. A stock exchange is a marketplace for buying and selling shares of a **publicly traded corporation**.

A **stock exchange** is a marketplace where buyers and sellers of shares exchange their shares. Buying and selling shares is called **trading.**

A **publicly traded corporation** is a corporation whose shares are traded on the stock exchange.

After the shares are issued—sold for the first time to the public—investors who want to become owners of a corporation may purchase the shares from people who want to sell the same shares. The buyers and sellers get together, usually through a stockbroker or investment dealer, by using a stock exchange.

Stockbrokers represent people who want to buy shares and the people who want to sell shares of a corporation. Stockbrokers work for firms, such as BMO Nesbitt Burns or ScotiaMcLeod. The three major stock exchanges in Canada are the Toronto Stock Exchange (TSX), the Canadian Venture Exchange (CDNX), and the Montreal Exchange (ME). If you wanted to be one of the owners of Sears Canada Inc., you could purchase shares by contacting a stockbroker.

A **stockbroker** is a business person who represents people who want to buy shares and people who want to sell shares of a corporation on the stock exchange.

Another way to buy or sell shares—also known as *trading*—is to use the Internet. Many investment dealers now provide a way for investors to buy and sell stock without a stockbroker. As Internet usage continues to grow at an incredible pace, more and more people are taking advantage of electronic trading in shares.

Exhibit 1–2
Sears Canada Inc.
Courtesy Sears Canada, Inc.

Sears Canada Inc. Consolidated Statements of Earnings
For the 53 and 52 week periods ended
January 3, 2004 (fiscal 2003) and
December 28, 2002, respectively (in millions, except per share amounts)

	2003	2002
Total Revenues	$6222.7	$6535.9
Cost of merchandise sold, operating, administrative and selling expenses	5775.9	6107.9
Depreciation and amortization	146.6	148.7
Interest expense, net	59.5	59.8
Unusual items—expense (Note 12)	5.0	189.1
Earnings before income taxes	235.7	30.4
Income taxes (Note 4)		
Current	7.5	49.3
Future	93.5	(71.1)
	101.0	(21.8)
Net earnings	$ 134.7	$ 52.2
Earnings per share (Note 19)	$ 1.26	$ 0.49
Diluted earnings per share (Note 19)	$ 1.26	$ 0.49

Exhibit 1–3
Sears Canada Inc. Balance Sheets
Courtesy Sears Canada, Inc.

Sears Canada Inc. Balance Sheets
Consolidated Statements of Financial Position

(In millions)	As at January 3, 2004	As at December 28, 2002
Assets		
Current assets:		
Cash and short-term investments	$ 82.6	$ 142.8
Accounts receivable (Notes 2 and 3)	1249.1	1322.5
Income taxes recoverable	11.8	4.1
Inventories	801.3	754.0
Prepaid expenses and other assets	110.6	109.4
Current portion of future income tax assets (Note 4)	149.7	183.1
	2405.1	2,515.9
Investments and other assets (Note 5)	76.8	59.7
Capital assets (Note 6)	1042.8	1036.9
Long-term deferred receivables	229.9	61.7
Deferred charges (Note 7)	293.6	309.3
Future income tax assets (Note 4)	17.5	77.8
	$4065.7	$4061.3
Liabilities		
Current liabilities		
Accounts payable	$ 728.2	$ 799.0
Accrued liabilities	486.4	517.3
Income and other taxes payable	95.9	99.1
Principal payments on long-term obligations due within one year (Note 9)	7.3	6.2
Current portion of deferred credit (Note 4)	—	30.0
	1,317.8	1,451.6
Long-term obligations (Note 9)	763.1	770.2
Deferred credit	—	24.2
Accrued benefit liability (Note 8)	173.9	168.4
	2254.8	2414.4
Shareholders' Equity		
Capital shares (Note 10)	458.8	458.1
Retained earnings	1352.1	1188.8
	1810.9	1646.9
	$4065.7	$4061.3

Regulation. Shareholders usually hire people who are not owners of the corporation to manage the business of the corporation. This separation of ownership and management can create problems. For example, there may be a large number of owners, and they may be far away from the location of the business. How can the owners be sure that the managers are running the corporation the way the owners want it to be run? How do the owners monitor the managers to be sure they are not taking advantage of the power of being a manager of a large company, for example, buying expensive items like country club memberships and luxury cars for the business?

A **securities commission** is a government agency that regulates the sale of securities to the public.

To protect the owners with respect to issues like these, each provincial and territorial government has created a **securities commission** to monitor the activities and financial reporting of corporations that sell shares of their ownership to the public. The Ontario Securities Commission (OSC) and the Commission des valeurs mobilières du Québec (CVMQ) are the two largest in Canada. The degree of regulation for corporations depends on the size and nature of the business. A business that provides an essential product or service, such as electric power generating companies, has more rules to follow than a business that provides something not essential, but discretionary, such as toys. Large companies have more rules than smaller companies because large companies provide more opportunities for managers to take advantage of the owners.

Advantages of the corporate structure of a business organization follow:

- Investors can diversify their financial risk. Being able to buy shares in a variety of corporations means that persons are able to balance the risks they are taking as business owners. For example, an investor may own shares in a soft drink company and also own shares in a coffee company. If coffee companies have a bad year due to a shortage of coffee beans, people will be likely to buy more soft drinks. By owning a little of each type of company, an investor reduces overall risk.

Limited liability is the idea that the owners of a corporation cannot be held personally liable for the actions of the corporation.

- Owners have **limited liability**. Individual owners risk *only* the amount of money they have invested in the company. That is the amount they paid for the shares. If the corporation is found legally responsible for injury to an employee or customer, or if the business fails, only the corporation's assets are at risk—not the owner's personal property. (In contrast, there is no limit to the legal liability of a sole proprietor or a partner. Both the assets of the business and the personal assets of the owners are at risk.)

Disadvantages of the corporate form of ownership include:

- Separation of management and ownership creates a difference in knowledge about the operations of the business. Suppose you own 100 Sears shares. The managers of Sears will know many details of the business that you do not know. For example, the managers are aware of all possible investment options for the company's extra cash. They may select the option that minimizes clerical work, whereas an owner might prefer an option that involves more work but would secure a higher return.
- There are literally thousands of such details that owners do not know,

What is a limited liability partnership (LLP)?

In the past 10 years, a new type of organization has been formed that has some characteristics of a partnership and some characteristics of a corporation. It is a business form mostly of interest to partners in such professions as law, medicine, and accounting. LLP's owners—who are the partners—are not personally liable for the malpractice of any of the partners. They are personally liable for many types of obligations owed to the LLP's creditors, lenders, and landlords. Owners of an LLP report their share of profit or loss on their personal tax returns. The LLP form of business organization is not available in all provinces, and it is often limited to a short list of professions. You may have noticed that some of the major accounting firms have taken this legal form and the letters LLP appear after the firm's name.

many of which they do not even want to know. However, the owners want some assurance that managers are acting in the best interests of the shareholders. Owners need information about how well the business is doing to assess how the actions and decisions of the managers are affecting the business. The owners need some assurance that managers are providing complete and accurate information about the business.

- Corporate income is taxed twice. Here is how: Unlike a sole proprietorship or partnership, a corporation pays income taxes on its income. If the income, after tax (or at least some part of it), is paid out to the shareholders as **dividends**, the shareholders must include the dividend income on their personal tax returns. This amounts to double taxation on the same income. The income of the corporation—which is owned by shareholders—is taxed as corporation income, and what is passed on to owners as dividend income is again taxed, as personal income.

Dividends are the earnings of a corporation distributed to the owners of the corporation. It is a special term for *distributions* that applies only to corporations.

Examples of all types of business are shown in Exhibit 1–4.

STUDY BREAK 1-1

See How You're Doing

1. What do all businesses have in common?
2. What are the different forms of business ownership?

Business Activities and the Flow of Goods and Services

L.O. 2

Describe the common business processes.

An Entrepreneur

A person who starts a business is considered an **entrepreneur**. Let us look at how our entrepreneur, Tom, started his T-shirt business and the sequence of events that followed, analyzing the transactions represented in each event as we go along. Identifying those events is the first step in understanding how a business works. (See Exhibit 1–5.)

We can classify each step in the process of developing a business in terms of **exchanges**—who gets what and who gives what in return. The get portion and the give portion of the exchange are often considered separate transactions.

The first exchange starts the business—Tom invests his own $5,000 in the business. From the perspective of the business, this is called a **contribution**. It

An **entrepreneur** is a person who starts a business firm and takes the economic risk inherent in starting it.

Exchanges are events in the business process that involve getting something and giving something in return.

An owner's investment in a company is called the owner's **contribution** because we are looking at the investment from the point of view of the company.

Exhibit 1–4
Examples of Types of Businesses

	Sole proprietorship	Partnership	Corporation
Service	Jane Doe, CA	Billings, Wren, Childers, and Munns, Barristers & Solicitors	Headhunters, Inc.
Merchandising	Charlie's Hot Dog Stand	Bob and Bill's Autoparts Store	Shoppers Drug Mart
Manufacturing	Custom drapery maker	Jane and John's Pottery Place	Stelco Inc.
Financial services	Joe Dudd, Stockbroker	Mike and Mark's Loan Service	RBC Royal Bank

Exhibit 1–5 How a Business Works

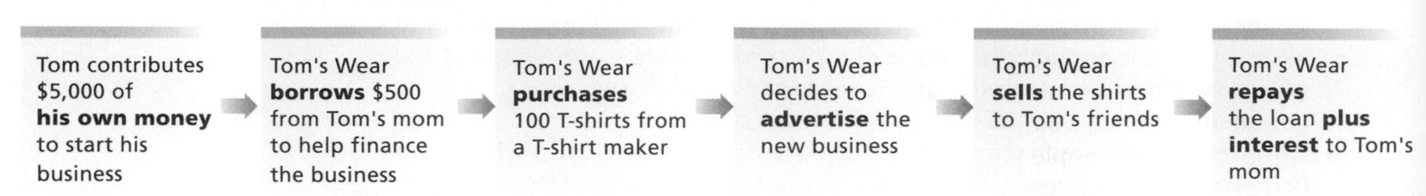

A **transaction** is an exchange or event between entities that has an economic impact on the business firm.

is often called *contributed (share) capital*. As with all **transactions**, we look at this from the point of view of the business entity. The event is the exchange of cash for ownership in the business. This is part of the acquisition/payment process.

You may have to think about it to see the give part of this exchange—it is the business giving ownership to Tom. Because Tom has chosen to organize his business firm as a corporation, a unit of ownership is called a share. For a sole proprietorship or a partnership, the ownership has no special name. Tom has chosen the corporate form of organization because of the limited legal liability of a corporation.

The get part of the exchange is the business getting the $5,000 cash. There is only one agent in this transaction—but Tom actually plays two roles. As an outside agent, Tom, the investor, gives the business cash. As an inside agent of the business, Tom, the manager, gives the outside agent shares of ownership in the business in return. Because Tom is the only shareholder, he owns 100 percent of the shares.

A **cash receipt** is the business event of receiving cash.

The second transaction is between Tom's Wear and Tom's mom. The business borrows $500 from her—the second transaction of the new company. Tom's Wear gets an economic resource—cash—and in exchange Tom's Wear gives an I-owe-you (IOU). From the perspective of Tom's Wear, this event is called a **cash receipt**. In any exchange like this one, there is an outside agent—Tom's mom—and an inside agent—Tom. This cash receipt is part of the acquisition/payment process. Borrowing money to finance a business is the get side of the exchange. The give side is the IOU to Mom—well, it is not really the give side until Tom repays the loan with cash. The IOU is useful for describing the *timing difference* between the time of the get and give sides of the exchange. We will see lots of examples of this type of timing difference in accounting for business events.

The two main business processes we will study in this course are the **acquisition/payment process** and the **sales/collection process.**

The emphasis in financial accounting is on the **acquisition/payment process** and the **sales/collection process**. (The conversion process is the major topic of managerial accounting.) The acquisition/payment process is the group of business activities associated with acquiring and paying for goods and services. The objectives of the acquisition/payment process include purchasing only those goods and services that a company needs and can afford, making sure the goods it orders are received in good condition, properly maintaining them, and providing them to the appropriate people in the company when needed. Although we more often think of companies acquiring and paying for their inventory purchases, companies also acquire human resources, financial resources—that is, money—and property, plant, and equipment. When Tom's Wear borrowed the money from Tom's mom, the company was acquiring financial resources.

Resources, events, and **agents** are the three components of all business transactions.

To understand what happens in a business transaction, it is helpful to know that every business transaction is made up of three components: **resources**, **events**, and **agents** (REA).

- **Resources** are the things that are exchanged in transactions—both tangible and intangible. Examples of resources—called *economic* resources because of their importance in an economy—are money, goods, and services.
- **Events** are the actual transactions—the giving or getting of a resource. Paying someone is an event—a cash disbursement. Other examples of events are making a sale and collecting a payment.
- **Agents** are the people involved in the transaction. Someone actually gives and gets the resources in the exchange. There are inside agents—employees of the company—and outside agents—people involved in the transactions who are not employed by the company.

Resources are the things of economic value exchanged.

Events are the actual giving and getting of the resources.

Agents are the people who actually make the exchange.

All three components—resources, events, and agents—are easy to identify with a little practice. First, the events are identified. Then, the resources and agents related to each event are identified. Let us look at the transactions in Tom's T-shirt business with these three components in mind.

The next transaction is the company's purchase of 100 T-shirts with a unique logo on them. The get part of the exchange is when Tom's Wear gets the shirts for the inventory. The event is a **purchase**. The inside agent is Tom, and the outside agent is the T-shirt manufacturer. The give part of the exchange has the same agents, but the economic resource is cash. The give part of the exchange is when Tom's Wear gives cash to the T-shirt manufacturer, and the event is a **cash disbursement**. All the events are seen through the eyes of Tom's Wear. The transaction would look different if we took the perspective of the T-shirt manufacturer. In business problems, we take one point of view throughout a problem or an analysis. This transaction is part of the acquisition/payment process.

A **purchase** is an event in which the company *gets* goods or services.

A **cash disbursement** is an event in which the company *gives* cash.

We can represent the giving and getting aspects of an exchange in an **REA model** showing the resources, events, and agents comprising the exchange. The exchange consists of two transactions—one part shows what the business is getting, and the other part shows what the business is giving. (See Exhibit 1–6.)

A diagram of the **REA model** shows the resources, events, and agents involved in the economic exchange.

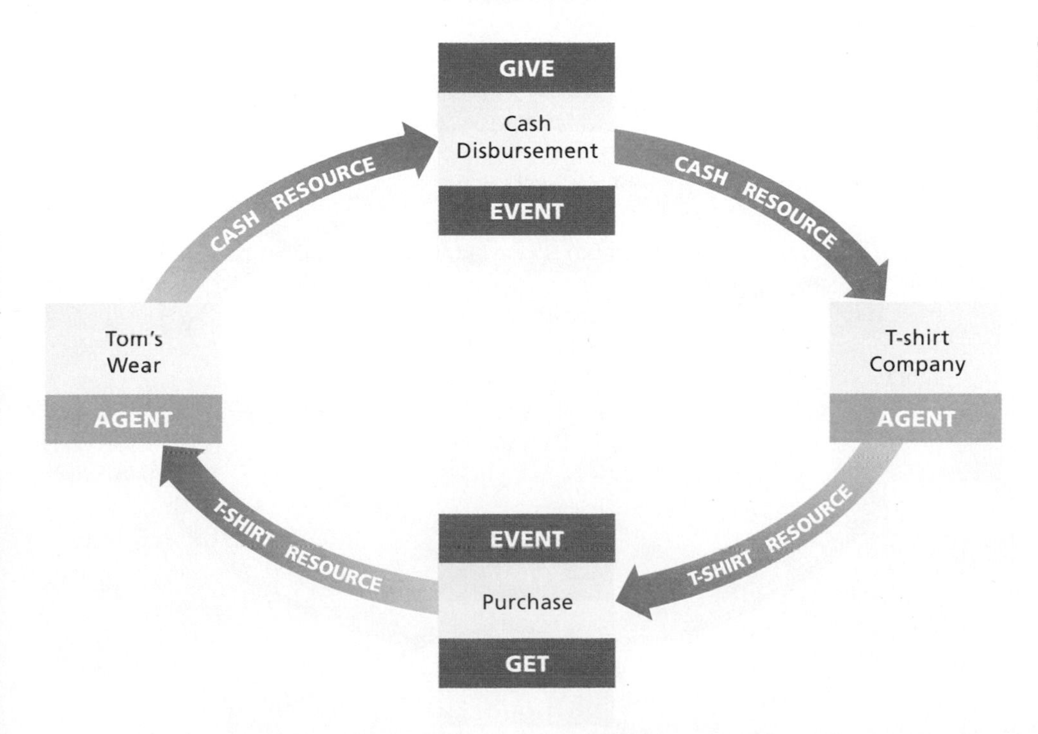

Exhibit 1–6
Acquisition of and Payment for T-Shirts

The next transaction, shown in Exhibit 1–7, is the acquisition of a service. The economic resources in this transaction are advertising and cash. The get part is the acquisition or purchase of advertising. The give part is a cash disbursement transaction; the internal agent is Tom; and the external agent is a person at the advertising company.

Tom's Wear now sells the T-shirts. This is an exchange in the sales/collection process. The get transaction is a cash receipt; the resource is cash. The give transaction is the sale, and the resource is the T-shirt. Tom, the inside agent, sells a T-shirt to a customer, the outside agent. The diagram in Exhibit 1–8 shows these transactions.

Exhibit 1–7
Acquisition of and Payment for a Service

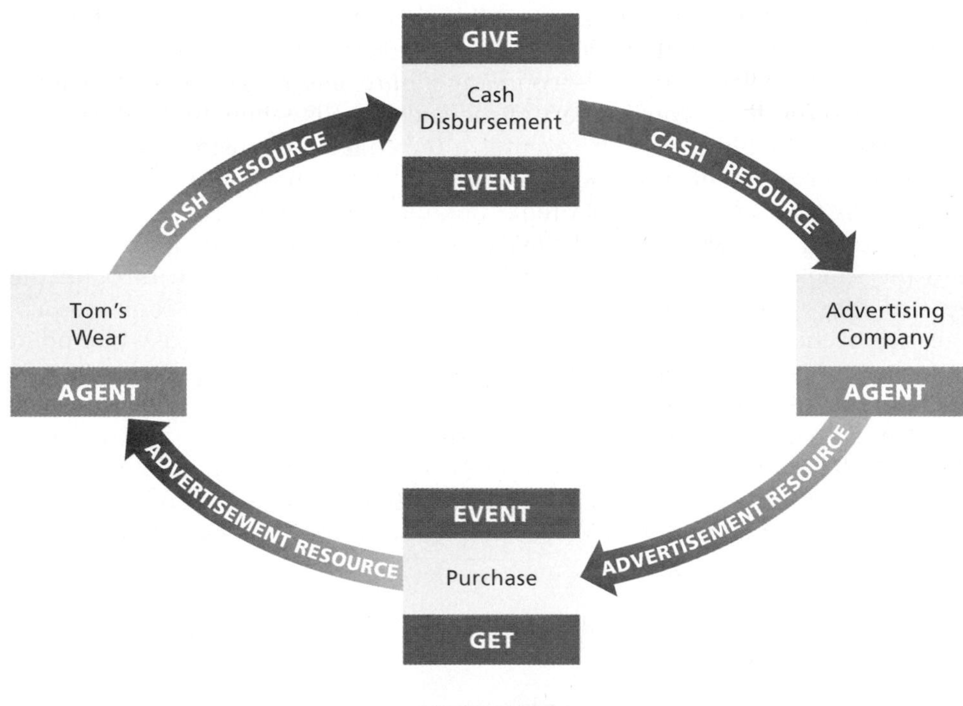

Exhibit 1–8
Sales and Collections

Tom's Wear repays the $500 loan from Tom's mom. The give part is a cash disbursement. That is, the company gives the economic resource of cash (amount of the loan, called the **principal**, plus **interest**, a cost of borrowing the money) to the outside agent, his mom. Recall that the get part of this exchange occurred near the beginning of our story. The second transaction was when Tom's Wear took the cash, as a loan, from his mom. The IOU was a sort of marker, indicating that there would be a timing difference in the get and give parts of this transaction.

Borrowing money is common in business. The amount of money borrowed is called the **principal** of the loan. The cost of borrowing that money—using someone else's money—is called **interest.**

The Acquisition/Payment Process

When a company purchases something, that purchase is classified as part of the acquisition/payment process. When Tom's Wear bought the inventory of T-shirts, the transaction was part of the acquisition/payment process.

There are many steps in the acquisition/payment process. The acquisition—or purchase—part begins when someone in the company identifies the need for something. In many companies, this need is documented on a **purchase requisition**—that is, a record of what is requested. Usually, someone at a level of management must approve this request. Then it is sent to the purchasing department. Modern technology has eliminated the need for paper documents in some businesses. However, whether the request is put on paper or not, the company's information system will record information about this activity.

A **purchase requisition** is a document that is used to request an item or service.

The purchasing department decides on the **vendor**—a business that provides goods and services—on the basis of such factors as price, quality, and terms of delivery. The items, or services, needed are specified to the vendor in a form called a **purchase order (PO)**. This information may be on paper or in a computer file. When filled in with information needed to make the purchase, this purchase order may need approval, usually by someone in the purchasing department, before the order can be placed. Then a copy of the PO goes to the vendor, declaring the intent to purchase. A copy goes to the receiving department so that the personnel there will know what to expect when the goods are delivered.

A **vendor** is the company from whom you buy goods or services. The document used to order items from a vendor is called a **purchase order (PO).**

The next step in the acquisition/payment process is the receipt of the goods or services ordered. The copy of the purchase order that went to the receiving department when the order was placed is considered an open purchase order, also referred to as an unfilled purchase order. Its purpose in the receiving department is to determine if the delivered goods are actually the ones ordered. Receipt of the goods is recorded on a **receiving report**, which is matched with the PO. Both documents are then forwarded to the accounts payable department. There they wait for the **invoice**—the bill—to arrive from the vendor.

A **receiving report** is a document on which the company records the items it gets from the vendor when the items arrive.

An **invoice** is a bill for items that have been purchased.

The last step in the acquisition/payment process is making the payment for the goods or services delivered according to the purchase order. On or before the date that the payment is due to the vendor, the purchasing company begins the process of requesting that payment be made to the vendor. After the accounts payable department has verified, via the receiving report and matched PO, that the ordered goods have been received in satisfactory condition, payment will be made by cheque, debit card, credit card, or electronic funds transfer. The procedures and approvals for the payment process may be more complicated, depending on the size of the business and the number and size of the transactions regularly processed by the accounts payable department. No matter how the payment is made, the vendor will end up getting some of the company's cash. So, the payment to the vendor is called a cash disbursement.

Exhibit 1–9 Steps and Documents in the Acquisition/Payment Process

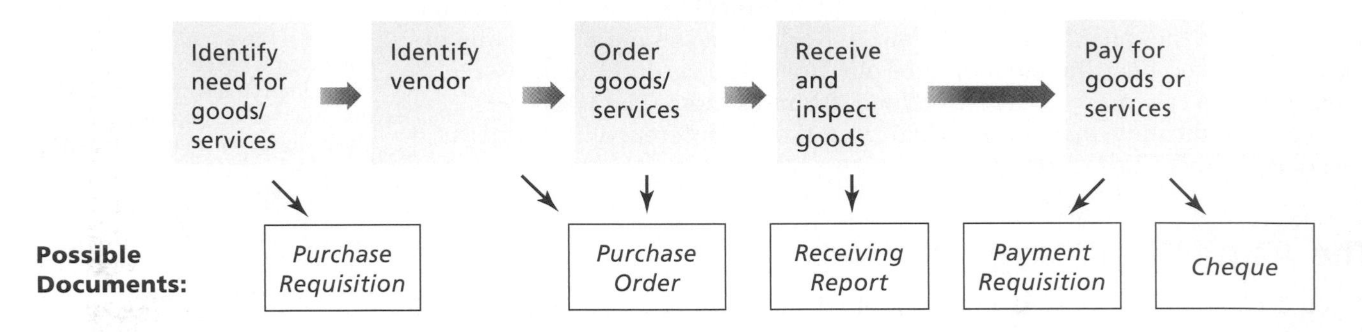

The steps and paper documents commonly used in this process are shown in Exhibit 1–9. A very small business, such as Tom's, may not formally follow all the steps. As the business grows, the steps will become more formalized to make sure that all the transactions are carried out with a minimum of errors.

A business may also purchase labour—hire and pay employees—as well as acquire financing—such as a loan from a bank—to help the business expand. Purchasing labour and acquiring financing are special cases of the acquisition/payment process. We will discuss them in detail in later chapters in the book.

STUDY BREAK 1–2

See How You're Doing

1. What are the three components of every business transaction?
2. What is a purchase requisition, and why would a business use one?

The Sales/Collection Process

Documents that may be involved in the sales process:

Sales order—document with a list of the items a customer wants to buy (the selling company's side of a purchase order).

Picking slip—a document that tells the inventory clerks what items to get from the inventory.

Packing slip—a document included in the shipped order that describes what is in the order.

Accounts receivable are the amounts that customers owe the business for purchases on credit—buy now, pay later.

The sales part of the sales/collection process begins when a customer places an order, called a sales order by the company. Triggered by receipt of the **sales order**, the company examines and approves the customer's credit—if it is a credit sale. A credit sale is a sale for which the customer does not pay cash at the time of the sale but, instead, agrees to pay later. If the customer's credit is approved, the sale information is sent to the warehouse, usually on a document called a **picking slip**, or **stock request**. Another document, the **packing slip**, is then sent to the shipping department signalling that the goods are on the way to be shipped to the customer. One copy of the sales order is then sent to the department that prepares the invoices. Remember, if we sell something on credit, we will have to send an invoice to the customer.

At the warehouse, the goods are selected and sent to shipping. When the goods are shipped, a copy of the shipping notice—specifying what goods were shipped to the customer and when they were shipped—is sent to the billing department. The billing department prepares a sales invoice, which is sent to the customer, and records the transaction in the formal accounting records. In this case, an **accounts receivable** is recorded. That is the written record of all customers who have made credit purchases with the amounts that have not yet been collected.

While many businesses have multiple steps in their sales/collection process (Exhibit 1–10), the retail portion of a business, such as Sears, has a much simpler sales process—the sales portion of the sales/collection process.

Exhibit 1–10 **Steps and Documents in the Sales/Collection Process**

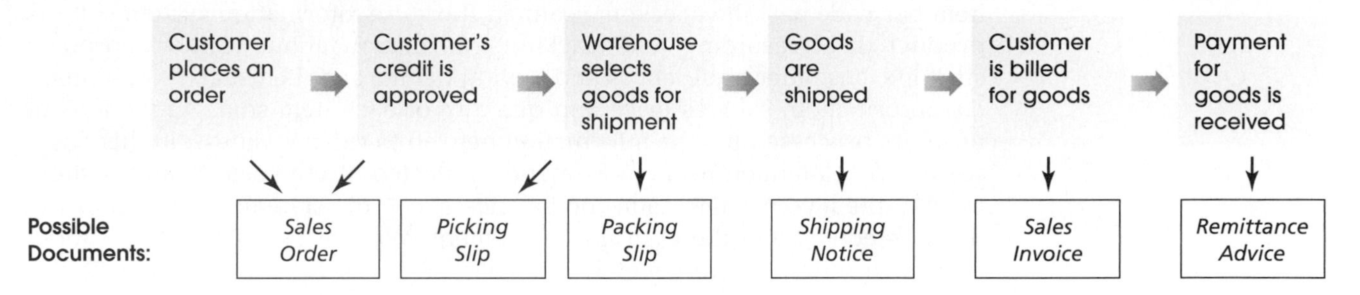

Usually, a wholesale business has a sales/collection process that is more complicated than that of a retail business. On the other hand, the acquisition/payment process is more complicated for a retail business than it is for a wholesale business. How a business makes decisions about vendors, keeps track of purchases, and makes sure there is sufficient inventory—goods on hand for sale—for the planned sales are topics we will examine in subsequent chapters.

Information Needs for Decision Making in Business

L.O. 3

Describe the information used by a business to make decisions.

To start a new business, Tom had lots of decisions to make. First, how would he finance it? What organizational form should it take? How many T-shirts should he buy? From whom should he buy them? How much should he pay for advertising? How much should he charge for the shirts?

After the first complete operating cycle—that is, a period beginning with cash, converting cash to inventory, selling the inventory, and turning inventory sales back into cash—Tom has more decisions to make. Should he buy T-shirts and do the whole thing again? If so, should he buy more T-shirts than he bought the first time and from the same vendor? To make decisions like these, Tom must have information. The kind of information usually provided by accountants will provide the basis for getting a good picture of the performance of his business.

- What was **revenue** from sales during the accounting period? An accounting period is any length of time that a company uses to evaluate its performance. It can be a month, a quarter, or a year.
- What **expenses** were incurred so those sales could be made? (You have probably heard the expression "It takes money to make money.")
- What goods does Tom's company have left at the end of the period?
- Should he increase the price of the T-shirts he sells or lower the price?

Revenue—the amount the company has earned from providing goods or services to customers.

Expenses—the costs incurred to generate revenue.

Besides this kind of financial information, there is other information that can help Tom make decisions about his business. For example, Tom would want information on the reliability of different vendors and the quality of their merchandise to decide which vendor to use next time. Before the advances in computer technology that have enabled us to collect, organize, and report huge quantities of information besides financial information, a company had only the basic financial information to help make its business decisions. Today, financial information is just a part of a firm's information system.

A modern supermarket is a great example of a business that collects a tremendous amount of information. With a simple, swift swipe of the grocery item bar code past the checkout scanner, the store information system collects product data, recording and tracking information about vendors, product shelf life, customer preferences and buying habits, and the usual, typical financial information, such as price and quantity of each item sold. As we look at business processes and the information needed to run a business, in this book, we will pay attention to the information reflected in the basic financial statements—the income statement, the balance sheet, the statement of changes in owner's equity, and the cash flow statement. We will be talking more about each of these statements soon.

STUDY BREAK 1–3

See How You're Doing

1. What are revenues and expenses?
2. What are accounts receivable and why would a company have them?

Flow of Information

Who Needs Information about Transactions of the Business?

L.O. 3

Describe who wants information about a business and why.

The **Canada Customs and Revenue Agency (CCRA)** is the federal agency responsible for collecting income, sales, and excise taxes for the Government of Canada and on behalf of most of the provinces and territories.

Without information, no part of any business can do what it is supposed to do. The functions of the management of a company are to plan, control, and evaluate the operation of the business. To perform these functions effectively, management must have information about what the business has done, what it is currently doing, and where it looks like it is going or should be going. Traditionally, the accounting information system has provided only very general data about the past of a business firm. A business firm used to keep two sets of records, each for specific purposes: one set for financial reporting and one set for internal decision making. Now, with modern computers and software that can organize information in a variety of ways with a few simple commands, one information system can accumulate and organize all the data of a company. The managers of each business area—usually referred to as a department—can obtain and use whatever information is relevant to the decisions they have to make. Accountants, too, can obtain the information they need for preparing the basic financial statements.

In many industries, there are regulatory agencies that require specific information from companies, particularly corporations. For example, public companies are required by provincial and territorial securities commissions to file many different types of reports about the companies' financial transactions.

For all businesses, payroll taxes and sales taxes must be reported and paid to the **Canada Customs and Revenue Agency (CCRA)**. The CCRA requires in-

The language about what an auditor does is very specific. The auditors want to emphasize that they cannot guarantee that the financial statements are error free. The audit opinion—the report the auditors give about a company's financial statements—says whether or not the financial statements present fairly the financial position of the company for the relevant period of time. For example, the auditors' opinion for Sears Canada Inc. says:

> In our opinion, these consolidated financial statements present fairly, in all material respects, the financial position of the Company as at January 3, 2004 and December 28, 2002 and the results of its operations and its cash flows for the 53 weeks and the 52 weeks then ended in accordance with Canadian generally accepted accounting principles.

formation from businesses concerning income and expenses, even if the income from the business flows through to the owners as it does for sole proprietorships and partnerships.

When a company wants to borrow money, creditors—the people and firms who lend money—require information about the company before they will lend money. Banks want to be sure that the loans they make will be repaid. The **creditworthiness**—a term indicating that a borrower has in the past made loan payments when due (or failed to make them when due)—of a business must be supported with information about the business. This information is usually very specific and very detailed.

Who else needs information about the business? Potential investors are information consumers. Suppose Tom wanted to find additional owners for his T-shirt business. That means he would be looking for someone who wanted to invest money in his T-shirt business in return for a portion of ownership in the company. A potential owner would want some reliable information about the business before making a financial investment. Publicly traded corporations—whose shares are traded on the stock exchanges—invite anyone willing and financially able to become an owner by offering for sale shares in the corporation. Buying the shares of a corporation is investing in that corporation. Investors want information about a company before they will buy that company's shares. To ensure that the information contained in a company's financial statements is accurate and reliable, the financial statements are **audited**. Audited information means it has been examined by professional accountants, called **public accountants**, who give an opinion on the fairness with which the financial statements have been presented.

Finally, current and potential vendors, customers, and employees also need useful information about the company. They need to evaluate a company's financial condition to make decisions about working for, or doing business with, the company.

What makes information useful? To be useful, information must be:

- timely
- verifiable
- accurate
- relevant

Usefulness depends on who needs the information and for what purpose it is needed. For example, the market price of a share of a company's shares is useful information to a potential in-

To see how many filings a company must make, go to the website for the System for Electronic Document Analysis and Retrieval (SEDAR). The SEDAR® system and SEDAR.com are maintained by CDS INC. on behalf of the Canadian Securities Administrators. The SEDAR.com website discloses public documents from the database of filings made by public companies and mutual funds across Canada. Here is a list of the filings made by The Forzani Group Ltd. for May of 2003.

Date of Filing	Document Type	File Format	File Size
May 8, 2003	*Annual report—English*	PDF	3214 K
May 8, 2003	*Annual report—French*	PDF	3286 K
May 8, 2003	*Audited annual financial statements—English*	PDF	81 K
May 8, 2003	*Audited annual financial statements—French*	PDF	85 K
May 15, 2003	*Certificate re dissemination to shareholders*	PDF	78 K
May 15, 2003	*Confirmation of mailing*	PDF	78 K
May 15, 2003	*Confirmation of mailing*	PDF	78 K
May 8, 2003	*Form of proxy—English*	PDF	106 K
May 8, 2003	*Form of proxy—French*	PDF	413 K
May 8, 2003	*Management proxy/ information circular— English (BC, ON— Form 30, QC)*	PDF	1908 K
May 8, 2003	*Management proxy/ information circular— French (BC, ON— Form 30, QC)*	PDF	2029 K
May 8, 2003	*MD & A—English*	PDF	53 K
May 8, 2003	*MD & A—French*	PDF	57 K

Used with the permission of CDS INC.

An **audit** is an independent examination of a company's financial statements and the accounting system that produced the statements.

A **public accountant** is someone who has met specific education and exam requirements and is licensed to perform audits. The system of licensing ensures that only individuals who have met these qualifications can perform audits.

The Canadian Institute of Chartered Accountants (CICA) is the organization that has primary responsibility for setting accounting standards in Canada. Accounting standards guide the way business events are reported, and so it makes sense that businesses are very interested in what the CICA does.

vestor, if that market price is current, verifiable, and so on. Even if it is timely and verifiable, the market price of a share is not useful to a manager trying to decide on a delivery schedule. We will spend more time discussing what makes financial information useful in the next chapter.

Accounting Information: A Part of the Information System

The Role of the Information System

L.O. 4

Describe the four basic financial statements and the underlying business processes. Be able to prepare simple financial statements.

Have you ever filed an address change with a company only to find later that one department uses your new address, while another department of that same company continues to use your old address? Even with such common data as customer names and addresses, the information is often gathered and maintained in several different places within the same organization. As computers and databases become more common, central data information systems are replacing departmental systems and eliminating their inefficiencies.

Because accountants have traditionally been the recorders and maintainers of financial information, it makes sense that they have expanded their role as the keepers of business information systems to include more than financial information. The cost of obtaining business information has decreased rapidly in the last few years. The financial accounting information a company reports is now just a small part of the total available business information. The accounting information is provided in four basic **financial statements** and supporting notes.

Financial statements are reports used by a business firm to communicate information to external users.

Overview of the Financial Statements

There are four financial statements a company uses to report its financial condition:

1. balance sheet
2. income statement
3. statement of retained earnings
4. cash flow statement

We will look at each briefly. Later chapters will go into each in detail.

Balance Sheet

The **balance sheet** shows the accounting equation in detail. The statement shows:

A **balance sheet**, also known as the statement of financial position, describes the financial situation of a company at a *specific point in time*. It is a snapshot—a freeze frame—that captures the items of value the business possesses at a particular moment and how it has financed them. A balance sheet has three parts:

- assets
- liabilities
- owner's equity

Assets—economic resources owned by the business,

Assets are things of value owned by a business. Cash and equipment are common assets. When a business has an asset, someone has the rights to, that is, a claim to, that asset. There is a claim on every asset in a business. There are two groups who might have claims to a company's assets—creditors and owners.

The claims of creditors are called **liabilities**. Liabilities are amounts the business owes to others outside the business, those who have loaned money to the company and have not yet been fully repaid for their loan. For example, the amount of a loan—such as your car loan—is a liability.

Liabilities—obligations of the business to creditors,

The claims of the owner are called **owner's equity**. Shareholders' equity is another name for the claims of the owners. Owner's equity is also called net assets because it is the amount left over after the amount of the liabilities is subtracted from the amount of the assets, or liabilities are netted out of assets.

Equity—owners' claims to the assets of the company. There are two types: contributed capital and **retained earnings.**

There are two ways for the owners to increase their claims to the assets of the business. One is by making contributions, and the other is by earning it. When the business is successful, the equity that results from doing business and is kept in the company is called **retained earnings**. We will see the difference between share capital and retained earnings more clearly when we go through the first month of business for Tom's Wear.

Together, assets, liabilities, and owner's equity make up the balance sheet, one of the four basic financial statements. The following relationship, called the accounting equation, is the basis for the balance sheet:

Assets = Claims
Assets = Liabilities + Owner's Equity

Each transaction that takes place in a business can be recorded in the accounting equation, which is actually the balance sheet. In other words, every transaction is changing the balance sheet; but the balance sheet must stay in balance. Let us look at the transactions for Tom's Wear for January and see how each one changes the balance sheet.

Date	Transaction
January 1	Tom contributes $5,000 of his own money to start the business.
January 1	Tom's Wear borrows $500 from Tom's mom for the business.
January 5	Tom's Wear buys 100 T-shirts for $400 cash.
January 10	Tom's Wear pays a company $50 cash for advertising.
January 20	Tom's Wear sells 90 of the T-shirts to Tom's friends for $10 each.
January 30	Tom's Wear repays Tom's mom the $500 plus $5 interest.
January 31	Tom's Wear declares and pays a $100 dividend.

Before the first transaction, there are no assets, no liabilities, and no equity. So, the balance sheet equation is:

Assets	=	Liabilities	+	Shareholders' Equity
0		0		0

Tom starts his company as a corporation. That means the owner's equity will be called shareholders' equity, and his initial contribution will be classified as common shares. We will discuss the details of owners' equity in Chapter 9. This is how the first transaction affects the accounting equation:

Assets	=	Liabilities	+	Shareholders' Equity
+ $5,000 cash		0	+	$5,000 common shares

Also on January 1, Tom's Wear borrows $500. This is how the second transaction affects the accounting equation:

Assets	=	Liabilities	+	Shareholders' Equity
+ $500 cash		+ $500 notes payable		0

A balance sheet can be prepared at any point in time to show the assets, liabilities, and equity for the company. If Tom's Wear prepared a balance sheet on January 2, these two transactions would be reflected in the amounts on the statement. Exhibit 1–11 shows the balance sheet at that time. With every subsequent transaction the balance sheet will change.

There are several characteristics of the balance sheet that you should look at in Exhibit 1–11. First, the heading on every financial statement specifies three things:

- the name of the company
- the name of the financial statement
- the date

A **fiscal year** is a year in the life of a business. It may or may not coincide with the calendar year.

The date on the balance sheet is one specific date. If the business year for Tom's Wear, also known as its **fiscal year**, is from January 1 to December 31, the balance sheet at the *beginning* of the first year of business is empty. Until there is a transaction, there are no assets, no liabilities, and no equity.

The balance sheet in Exhibit 1–11 for Tom's Wear is dated January 2, 2005. Tom's Wear has been in business for only one day. Even though a business would be unlikely to prepare a balance sheet just one day after starting the business, this is what the balance sheet for Tom's Wear would look like on January 2. The balance sheet shows the financial condition—assets, liabilities, and owner's equity—at the close of business on January 2. At this time, Tom's Wear had received $5,000 from owner Tom and borrowed $500 from Tom's mom. The total cash—$5,500—is shown as an asset, and the liability of $500 plus the owner's equity of $5,000 together show who has claim to the company's assets.

Comparative balance sheets are the balance sheets from consecutive fiscal periods for a single company.

Because the balance sheet gives the financial position of a company at a specific point in time, a new, updated balance sheet could be produced after every transaction. That would be data overload. When a company presents its income for a period, that is called an income statement. The company must show the balance sheet at the beginning of that period and the balance sheet at the end of that period. Those two balance sheets are called **comparative balance sheets**. For Tom's Wear, the first balance sheet for the fiscal year is empty. That is, on January 1, 2005, the equation was 0 = 0 + 0. Before we look at the balance sheet at January 31, 2005, we need to see the income statement

Exhibit 1–11
Balance Sheet for Tom's Wear

tom's wear

Tom's Wear, Inc.
Balance Sheet
At January 2, 2005

Assets		Liabilities and Shareholders' equity	
Cash	$5,500	Note payable	$ 500
		Common shares	5,000
		Retained earnings	0
Total assets	*$5,500*	Total liabilities and Shareholders' equity	$5,500

for the month of January 2005. We need the information on the income statement to see what happened during the time between the two balance sheets.

Look at Sears Canada's comparative balance sheets (see Exhibit 1–3). Note the similarities between the real world of Sears Canada and the fictitious world of Tom's Wear—the balance sheets for both actually *balance*. Both companies list assets first, then liabilities and equity. Both companies have used dollars to measure their balance sheet items. There are differences between the balance sheets of the real world and our not-so-real-world examples, which we will discuss in later chapters.

STUDY BREAK 1–4

See How You're Doing

1. What are the two parts of shareholders' equity?
2. What is a fiscal year?

Before we prepare an income statement for Tom's Wear or a balance sheet at January 31, let us look at each transaction that took place in January and see how each affects the accounting equation worksheet. This analysis is shown in Exhibit 1–12.

When a business is started, it begins with an empty balance sheet. For Tom's Wear, there are no assets, and therefore no claims, on January 1. The first two transactions that started the business, Tom's contribution of $5,000 and the loan from Tom's mom for $500, happened on January 1. First, Tom's contribution increases assets by $5,000 and shareholders' equity by $5,000 because the owner, Tom, has claim to the new asset. The company receives its first asset—cash—and the owner has claim to it. Then, Mom's loan increases

Exhibit 1–12 Beginning and Ending Balance Sheets with Transactions for the Month

tom's wear		Assets	=	Liabilities	+	Shareholders' equity	
						Share capital	Retained earnings
Balance sheet at 1/1/05 →		0	=	0	+	0	0
Effect of each transaction on the accounting equation:	January 1	$5,000 cash				$5,000 common shares	
	January 1	500 cash		$500 notes payable			
	January 5	(400) cash 400 inventory					
	January 10	(50) cash					(50) advertising expense
	January 20	900 cash (360) inventory					900 sales revenue (360) cost of goods sold (expense)
	January 30	(505) cash		(500) notes payable			(5) interest expense
	January 31	(100) cash					(100) dividends
Balance sheet at 1/31/05 →		$5,345 cash $ 40 inventory	=	0	+	$5,000 common shares	$385 retained earnings

assets by $500 and liabilities by $500. The company receives an asset—cash—and a creditor—Tom's mom—has claim to it. Following these two beginning transactions, the operations of the business begin. Each transaction that takes place during the month is shown as it affects the balance sheet. Study each transaction in Exhibit 1–12 as you read the following description of each:

An **asset exchange** is a transaction in which one asset increases and another asset decreases.

- On January 5, cash is decreased by $400 and inventory is increased by $400. This is called an **asset exchange** because the company is simply exchanging one asset—cash—for another asset—inventory. Note that the entire effect of this exchange on the accounting equation is on one side of the equation. That is perfectly acceptable. Also note that an asset exchange has no effect on shareholders' equity. Tom still has claim to the same dollar amount of assets.
- On January 10, Tom pays $50 for advertising. This is a cost Tom's Wear has incurred to generate revenue. Assets are decreased, and retained earnings, a component of shareholders' equity, are decreased. Why are retained earnings decreased? Because when assets are decreased by $50, someone's claim must be reduced. Unless we are paying off a debt, the owner's claims are reduced when assets are decreased. Retained earnings are the part of owners' equity that reflects the amount of equity the business has earned. (Throughout this book, as we study the transactions that take place in a business, we will see that all revenues *increase* retained earnings and all expenses *decrease* retained earnings.)
- On January 20, Tom's Wear sells 90 T-shirts for $10 each. This sale increases assets—cash—by $900. Who has claim to this asset? The owner has this claim. Revenues increase retained earnings. At the time of the sale, something else happens. An asset is reduced. The company no longer has 90 of the original 100 T-shirts in the inventory. Because each shirt cost $4 (and we recorded the T-shirts at their original cost), we now must reduce the asset *inventory* by $360. That reduction in assets is an expense and so the owner's claims—via retained earnings—are reduced by the amount of that expense.
- On January 30, Tom's Wear pays off the $500 loan with $5 interest. The repayment of the $500 principal reduces cash and meets the obligation that had been recorded as a liability. In other words, that liability is settled. The $500 reduction in assets is balanced in the accounting equation with a $500 reduction in the claims of creditors. However, the interest expense represents the cost of borrowing money. For a business, that is called interest expense. Like all expenses, it reduces the owner's claims by reducing retained earnings.
- On January 31, Tom's Wear pays a $100 dividend. That reduction in cash reduces the owner's claims to the assets of the firm, shown by the decrease in retained earnings. The $100, after it is distributed, is now part of Tom's personal financial assets, which are entirely separate from his business.

Using the accounting equation to track the transactions of a business is a useful way to see how the financial statements are put together. The actual way a company keeps track of its financial transactions and its records—commonly called its *books*—can vary from a simple manual record-keeping system to a complex computerized system. No matter how a company keeps its records, the financial statements will look the same. The accounting equation is the basis for accumulating accounting information and communicating that information to decision makers. A company starts the year with a balance sheet (only empty at the start of the business firm), engages in business transactions during the year, and ends the year with a new, updated balance sheet. The balance sheet is actually the accounting equation that must be in balance (Exhibit 1–13).

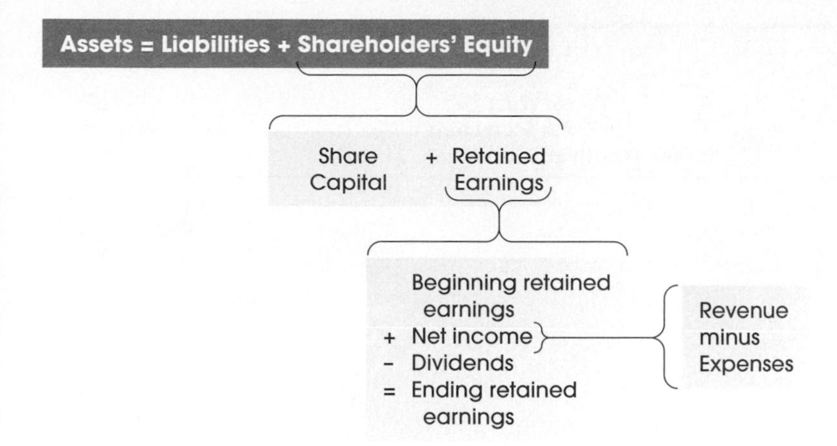

Exhibit 1–13
The Accounting Equation

Income Statement

The most well-known financial statement is the **income statement**, also known as the statement of earnings, or the statement of operations, or the **profit and loss statement (P&L)**. The income statement is a summary of all the *revenues* (income from sales or services) a company earns minus all the *expenses* (costs incurred in the earning process) associated with earning that revenue. It describes the performance of a company during a specific period, which is called a **fiscal period** or an **accounting period**. Most often, *fiscal period* is used to describe the business year, which may or may not coincide with the calendar year. A fiscal year (*not physical* year) for a company may, for example, begin on July 1. That means the fiscal year of the business runs from July 1 of one year to June 30 of the next calendar year.

The **income statement** shows all revenues minus all expenses for an accounting period—a month, a quarter, or a year; also called a **profit and loss (P&L) statement**.

A **fiscal period** or an **accounting period** is a length of time, normally one year, used for preparing financial statements.

Recall that the balance sheet gives the amount of assets, the amount of liabilities, and the amount of shareholders' equity of a business at a specific date. The income statement describes the activity of a company during a period. Look at the income statement for Tom's Wear in Exhibit 1–14. It shows the amount of sales the company made during the month, from January 1, 2005, through January 31, 2005. The expenses shown are also for the same period. The difference between the revenues and expenses is called *net income*, or *net earnings*.

Note several things about the income statement:

- First, only the cost of the T-shirts that were sold is included as an expense—cost of goods sold, also called cost of sales. The cost of the T-shirts *not sold* is shown as an asset called inventory on the balance sheet.
- Second, the repayment of the loan from Tom's mom is *not shown* as an expense. The only expense related to borrowing money is the interest owed to the lender. The repayment of principal is not an expense.

Also note that **dividends** are excluded from the income statement. Tom could have paid himself a salary for running the business. That salary would have been an expense, but he decided not to do that. Instead, he decided to take cash out of the business as a dividend. Dividends are not a *component* of earnings; they are a *distribution* of earnings.

In a corporation, distributions to owners are called **dividends.**

Sears Canada Inc.'s income statement (Exhibit 1–2) looks like the Tom's Wear income statement in many respects. Both have revenues and expenses, but the two companies have presented the data in a different order. Sears presents revenues first and then groups all expenses together. This is called a **single-step income statement**. Tom's Wear lists revenue first and then subtracts the largest expense related to revenue, cost of goods sold, which gives a

A **single-step income statement** groups all revenues together and shows all expenses deducted from total revenue.

Exhibit 1–14
Income Statement for Tom's Wear

tom's wear

Tom's Wear, Inc.
Income Statement
For the Month Ended January 31, 2005

Revenue		
Sales		$900
Cost of goods sold		$360
Gross profit		540
Expenses		
Advertising	50	
Interest	5	
Total expenses		55
Net income		$485

A **multistep income statement** starts with sales and subtracts cost of goods sold to get a subtotal called **gross profit on sales**, also known as gross margin. Then, other revenues are added and all other expenses are deducted.

subtotal called **gross profit on sales**. This is called a **multistep income statement**. Although Sears Canada and Tom's Wear have arranged their revenues and expenses differently, net income for each company is still the difference between all revenues and all expenses. That is what net income always is, no matter how the revenues and expenses are grouped on the statement.

The Difference between the Balance Sheet and the Income Statement. You should get a better idea of the difference between the balance sheet and the income statement by thinking about your own personal finances. If you were asked to prepare a personal balance sheet, you would list all your assets, such as your cash on hand (no matter how little) and the cost of your car, clothes, computer, and CD collection. Then you would list all the people to whom you owe money and how much money you owe to each. This might include some credit card companies and perhaps a bank for a car loan. All these assets and liabilities are measured in dollars. The specific point of time associated with a balance sheet must be given. For example, if you were listing your assets and liabilities on the last day of 2006, your balance sheet date would be December 31, 2006. Remember the accounting equation:

Assets = Liabilities + Owner's Equity

Owner's equity is the amount left over after liabilities are netted out of assets.

If you subtract the amount of your liabilities—what you owe to others—from your assets, the difference is your equity. **Owner's equity** is sometimes called the residual, indicating that it is the amount left over after the claims of creditors are deducted from a company's assets.

Retained earnings is the total of all net income amounts minus all dividends paid in the life of the company. It is descriptively named—it is the earnings that have been kept (retained) in the company. The amount of retained earnings represents the part of the owners' claims that the company has earned and retained (i.e., *not* contributed). Retained earnings is not the same as cash.

If you constructed a personal income statement, it would cover a period of time. For example, what was your net income total during the year 2006? You would list all income you received during the year and then subtract all your expenses during the same year. The difference would be your net income for the year. There is no equation to balance. The income statement lists sources of income and subtracts the related expenses, leaving a difference, hopefully positive, called net income. If the subtraction of expenses from revenues results in a negative number, that amount is called a **net loss**.

Net loss occurs when expenses are greater than revenues.

tom's wear

Tom's Wear, Inc.
Statement of Retained Earnings
For the Month Ended January 31, 2005

Beginning retained earnings	$ 0
Net income for the month	485
Dividends	(100)
Ending retained earnings	$ 385

Exhibit 1–15
Statement of Retained Earnings for Tom's Wear

Statement of Retained Earnings

As its name suggests, the **statement of retained earnings** shows the changes that took place in the amount of retained earnings during a period. The statement starts with the amount of retained earnings at the beginning of a period and then shows the additions (net income) and the deductions (dividends).

The statement of retained earnings is a statement that reports total changes in the amount of retained earnings over a period of time.

The statement of retained earnings for Tom's first month of business is shown in Exhibit 1–15. The statement starts with a beginning balance of zero in retained earnings because January was the first month of operations.

Net income for the period—$485—is shown as an increase in retained earnings. The dividends of $100 are shown as a decrease to retained earnings. The amount of retained earnings at the end of the period is $385.

After preparing the income statement for the month and the statement of retained earnings for the same month, we will be able to prepare the end-of-the-month balance sheet. If we set up the balance sheet horizontally in the accounting equation format, we can view the changes in assets, liabilities, and shareholders' equity from the beginning to the end of the month, with each transaction keeping the accounting equation in balance.

STUDY BREAK 1–5

See How You're Doing

1. What is gross profit?
2. What is the difference between a single-step income statement and a multistep income statement?

Cash Flow Statement

The **cash flow statement** is needed to form a complete picture of the financial position of a company. This statement is, perhaps, the easiest to understand. It is simply a list of all the cash that has come into a business—its cash receipts—and all the cash that has gone out of the business—its cash disbursements—during a specific period. In other words, it shows all the cash inflows and all the cash outflows for a fiscal period. Compare the cash inflows and cash outflows for a specific period with the *revenues and expenses* for the same specific period on the income statement. Accountants *measure revenue* as amounts the company has *earned* during the period, even if it is *not* equal to the amount of cash actually *collected*. Accountants *measure expenses* as the costs *incurred* to generate those revenues, even if they are *not* the same as the amounts actually *paid* in cash. Because this way of measuring revenues and expenses may not have an exact correspondence to the amount of cash collected and disbursed, the cash flow statement is necessary to get a complete picture of the business transactions for the period.

The **cash flow statement** shows all the cash collected and all the cash disbursed during the period. Each cash amount is classified as one of three types:

Cash from operating activities—cash transactions that relate to the everyday, routine transactions needed to run a business.

Cash from investing activities—transactions involving the sale and purchase of long-term assets used in the business.

Cash from financing activities—transactions related to how a business is financed. Examples: contributions from owners and amounts borrowed as long-term loans.

The cash flow statement is divided into three sections:

- **cash from operating activities**
- **cash from investing activities**
- **cash from financing activities**

These represent the three general types of business activities.

Cash inflows and outflows from operating activities pertain to the general activities of the business. For Tom's Wear, purchasing T-shirts is an operating activity. Look at the other cash flows from operations on the cash flow statement in Exhibit 1–16.

Cash inflows and outflows from investing activities are the cash flows related to the purchase and sale of certain assets in a business. If Tom decided to purchase a piece of equipment to silk-screen his own shirts, that purchase would be an investing activity—not an operating activity—because Tom's Wear is not in the business of buying and selling equipment.

Financing activities are related to a company's sources of capital. The two sources of capital, usually cash, for financing a business are contributions from owners and loans from creditors. Both of these transactions are classified as cash inflows from financing activities. Financing outflows include repayment of the principal of loans and distributions to owners. Tom's repayment of the $500 loan is an example of a financing cash outflow.

All four financial statements will be discussed in detail in the chapters to follow. By the time we are finished, you will be able to read and understand what is on most financial statements. You will also be able to analyze business transactions and understand how they affect the financial statements of a business.

Flow of Information and the Financial Statements

A company records and uses a large amount of information about its transactions. The amount of data and the way the information is collected and stored vary widely from company to company. The information contained in the four

Exhibit 1–16
Cash Flow Statement for Tom's Wear

tom's wear

Tom's Wear, Inc.
Cash Flow Statement
For the Month Ended January 31, 2005

Cash from operating activities		
Cash collected from customers	$ 900	
Cash paid to vendors for T-shirts	(400)	
Cash paid for advertising	(50)	
Cash paid for interest	(5)	
Total cash from operations		$445
Cash from investing activities		0
Cash from financing activities		
Proceeds from loan	$ 500	
Repayment of loan (principal)	(500)	
Issue of common shares	5,000	
Dividends paid	(100)	
Total cash from financing		4,900
Net increase in cash		$5,345

financial statements is a specific, well-defined part of the information available from a company's overall information system. The purpose of these four financial statements is to provide the financial information needed to represent and evaluate the transactions of the business. Investors, regulators, vendors, customers, and creditors rely on financial accounting information for decision making.

Business Risks

Starting a business is more than having a good idea about what it should be and obtaining financing to get it going. Both are a good beginning, but they must be followed with sound business planning for acquiring goods and services and selling the company's products or services. Part of that planning is identifying the risks involved. Before we discuss the details of the business activities in the chapters to follow, let us consider the risks of being in business and how we can minimize the negative consequences of those risks.

A **risk** is anything that exposes us to potential injury or loss.

A **risk** may be generally defined as anything that exposes us to potential injury or loss. In business, risks can turn into significant losses, scandals, or total company failure. There are hundreds of risks that any business faces. Some examples follow:

- the risk of product failure that might result in the death of consumers
- the risk that someone will steal assets from the company
- the risk that poor quality inventory will be purchased and sold

What losses could result? For a serious product failure, like the Firestone tires on the Ford Explorers in the early 2000s, the financial losses to the business could amount to millions of dollars in lawsuit settlements. For employee theft, the potential losses range from significant financial losses to the loss of a company secret that could cause a business to fail. Poor-quality inventory could result in the loss of customers and reputation.

Risks relate to all aspects of the business including:

General strategic risks—Should we market our cigarettes to teenagers?
Operating risks—Should we operate without a backup power supply?
Financial risks—Should we borrow the

One in Five Canadians Say Fraud Occurs in Their Workplace

An Ernst & Young-sponsored study also reveals Americans more likely than Canadians to turn in fraudsters at work

(TORONTO, August 8, 2002)—Twenty per cent of Canadians say they are personally aware of people stealing from their employers, according to a poll conducted for professional services firm Ernst & Young LLP by Ipsos-Reid. Of those asked, 38 percent were "very likely," and 39 percent "somewhat likely" to report a co-worker's fraudulent activities. For Americans, the responses were 50 percent and 30 percent, respectively (*see our U.S. press release for more information*).

The types of fraud identified as major problems include inflating expense accounts, "cooking the books," and pocketing money from cash sales.

"The survey results tell us something important," says Nick Hodson, a partner with Ernst & Young's litigation advisory services practice. "If you've got more than five employees, you're a victim of fraud. In effect, all companies are suffering loss through fraud. By knowing what's going on, organizations can work better to deal with it, to identify means to protect themselves, and to encourage the majority of honest employees to join against the fraudsters."

Among other survey findings:

- Sixty-eight percent believe that fraud in the workplace has stayed the same or increased in the past couple of years.
- Respondents believe, on average, that employee fraud robs organizations of 20 percent of every dollar raised.
- Tougher sanctions, improved investigations, and better role models were identified as effective means of reducing workplace fraud.
- Forty-four percent of respondents believe their employer could do more (cost-effectively) to reduce workplace fraud.
- Male, long-term, and junior-level employees are identified as the most likely to be involved in fraudulent activities.
- Thirty-eight percent believe technology makes fraud easier to commit; 36 percent say harder.
- Most differences in survey findings between Americans and Canadians are nearly indistinguishable.

(continued)

(continued)

A strong message coming from the survey is the willingness of employees to report fraud in the workplace. "With 77 percent of employees ready to report fraud, there's a powerful deterrent against those workers who might be thinking about stealing," Hodson says.

The findings also reveal that 44 percent of Canadian employees believe their companies can do more to stop theft—solutions ranging from imposing tougher sanctions for those caught, and conducting better investigations of suspected problems, to improving screening of new employees, and offering better role models and leadership from management. Hodson says this, too, is encouraging news. "Yes, overall the survey tells us that workplace fraud is pervasive. But the majority of employees are honest. Business has a great ally in the war against fraud, and it's right in every company's own back yard—honest employees are part of the solution," he says.

This is the second survey of its kind done in Canada by Ernst & Young, with the initial survey conducted in 2000. This latest poll includes the U.S. marketplace for the first time. Hodson is impressed by the consistency of results from the 2000 survey and the cross-border data, as well as the different categories of respondents. "The findings start to look a lot like a profile of a general human condition—that one in five people in the population may be dishonest. We see that 20 percent figure confirmed in more than one finding over time, across job levels, and between Canada and the United States," he says.

Those answering the survey work in a broad range of employment sectors from retail and health services, to food service and banking and construction and manufacturing. Results are based on surveys conducted in Canada and the United States between June 3 and June 6, 2002. The total sample size in both countries is 1,000, which is reduced based on employment criteria; only those working full or part time qualified for the study. In the United States, the sample is reduced to 617, which has an associated margin of error of ±4.2 percent. The sample size for each question is provided as certain questions have further reduced base sizes.

Source: http://www.ey.com/GLOBAL/content.nsf/Canada/Media_-_2000_-_Workplace_Fraud. Courtesy of Ernst & Young.

money from the bank or get the money by issuing more shares to our shareholders ?

Information risks—Should we use a manual accounting system?

The potential losses may be the loss of reputation, of customers, of needed information, or of assets. All the losses translate into monetary losses that can put the company at risk for total failure.

Why do people take risks? Every risk brings a *potential* reward. The reward is why we are in business. An entrepreneur, such as Tom, puts his money and his reputation at risk to start a T-shirt business. Why? For the potential of developing a successful business. To deal with the risks and increase the chances to reap the rewards, a firm must establish and maintain control over its operations, assets, and information system. A **control** is an activity performed to minimize or eliminate a risk. As we study the business processes that Tom will be engaged in during his first year in business, we will look at how he can control the risk involved in each process.

No More Nerd Accountants

As technology has made financial statement information a part of all the information available to run a business, the role of the accountant has changed. An accountant was once considered someone who records, classifies, and summarizes the business transactions that affect the information that goes on the financial statements. Keeping the books was an accountant's main job.

Accountants do not spend much time recording transactions anymore. Business transactions are captured by a company's information system, and the information is recorded in enough detail to be useful to many people in the company. Accountants are increasingly called on to analyze financial information and provide ways of improving business transactions. What were once known as *accounting firms* are now known as *professional services firms*. Accounting has become a broad and dynamic field, requiring expertise in all aspects of business. As the business world has changed, so has the role of the accountant.

A **control** is an activity designed to minimize or eliminate a risk.

There is a lot of variety in what today's accountant does (see Exhibit 1–17). No more Nerd Accountants!

Exhibit 1–17
Delivering the Goods

Janet Veldhuis knows how to cater to her clients—or, more accurately, to their pets. The 38-year-old CA owns and runs Whiskers & Paws Catering in Erin, Ontario, which provides home delivery of premium pet food.

"It's quite a leap to go from being a CA to delivering dog food," jokes Veldhuis, who has four dogs of her own. But with more than 400 southern Ontario clients from Guelph to Orangeville, it is a successful business with a loyal following. "It has all the elements—it's competitive on price, quality and service," she says.

When Veldhuis started the business two years ago, it was part of a franchise, but she now operates it independently. Since she is running a one-woman show, dealing directly with the pet food manufacturers and making the deliveries, scheduling can be a logistical nightmare. She calculates how much food a cat or dog will need based on its size and activity level and then delivers enough to last four weeks.

Graduating in 1986 with an honours degree in business administration from Wilfrid Laurier University in Waterloo, Ontario, Veldhuis became a CA two years later after articling at PriceWaterhouse in Mississauga, Ontario. "I knew someday I wanted to have my own business, and the CA designation would give me the background I needed," she says.

She worked in industry for 12 years, including eight for Ontario car dealerships in Brampton and Kitchener, and two years with a producer of nutritional supplements in Mississauga. Those years primed her for entrepreneurship. "I picked up a lot from watching successful people who figured out what works," she says.

For Veldhuis, that means attending home and garden trade shows in an attempt to build her client base and, eventually, hiring staff to handle the day-to-day operations so that she can expand the business. "I just want to keep it growing—and keep getting the name out there."

Résumé

1986	articles at PriceWaterhouse
1988	obtains CA designation (Ontario)
1990	becomes controller for Mazda dealership
1998	hired as controller for MuscleTech
2000	opens Whiskers & Paws Catering

Source: http://www.cica.ca/index.cfm/ci_id/6904/la_id/1.htm. Reproduced with permission of *CAmagazine*, published by the Canadian Institute of Chartered Accountants, Toronto, Canada.

Understanding Excel

For purposes of this problem only, assume that in the month of February, Tom's Wear engaged in the following transactions:

February 1, 2005	Tom's Wear received an additional $2,000 from Tom, the owner.
February 3, 2005	Tom's Wear bought 300 shirts for $4 each. He paid cash for the purchase.
February 5, 2005	Tom's Wear sold 100 shirts for $10 each.
February 25, 2005	Tom's Wear paid his $30 telephone bill for February telephone service.
February 28, 2005	Tom's Wear purchased a piece of equipment on credit for $600.

Requirements

1. Open a new Excel work sheet.
2. Create the following bold column headings beginning in cell A1 and ending in column J: **Date, Description, Cash +, Other Assets =** (***two-column heading***), **Liabilities +** (***two-column heading***), **Contributed Capital +, Retained Earnings** (***two-column heading***). Adjust the column widths as needed.

   Hints: The easiest way to resize your column widths is by holding down your left mouse button and dragging when you see the arrow, depicted as follows:

   You may also resize columns by double-clicking your left mouse button when you see the arrow previously depicted. Double-clicking will automatically resize your column based on the longest line.
   Highlight both cells and click the Merge and Center button to centre your two-column headings across both columns. Highlight all your headings and click the Center button to centre all column headings.
3. Underline your heading by selecting Format, Cells, and Border.

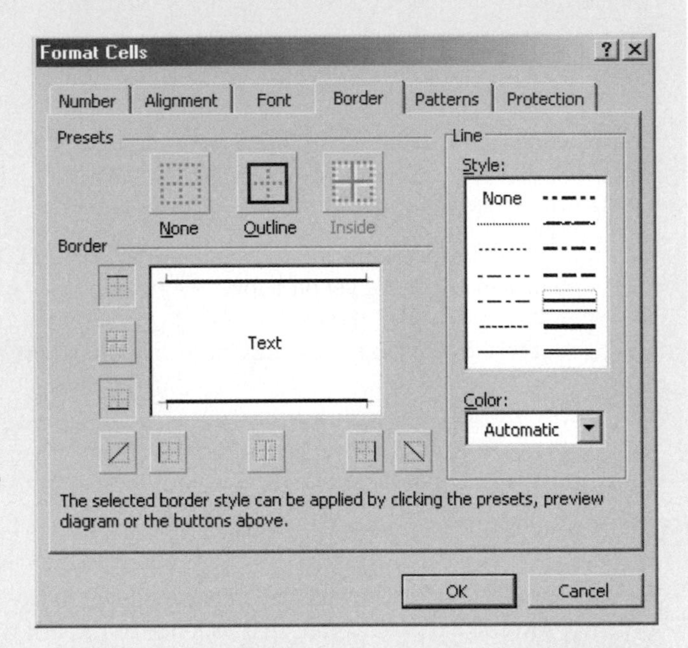

4. Input the transactions given previously. Format your numbers by selecting Format, Cells, and Number. Highlight the cells to be formatted and use the currency format as shown:

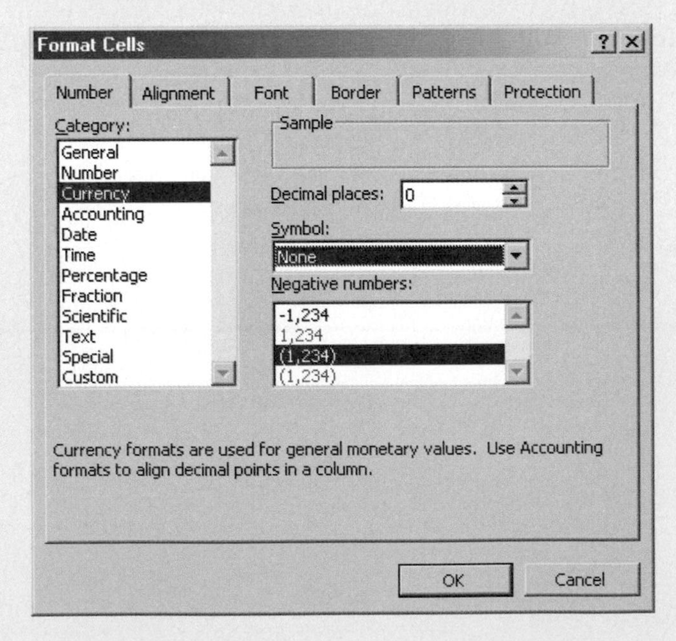

5. Print your file, and save it to disk by clicking the Save button. Name your file TomsWear1.

Answers to Study Break Questions

STUDY BREAK 1–1

1. All businesses have the same goal: to add value or provide value to customers/clients. Typically, they have three processes: acquiring goods (acquisition/payment), conversion (adding value), and selling the goods or services (sales/collection).
2. The different forms of ownership are (1) sole proprietorships, (2) partnerships, and (3) corporations.

STUDY BREAK 1–2

1. Resources, events, and agents are the three components.
2. A purchase requisition is a form on which a request to purchase something is recorded. It is used to document all requests for goods and services.

STUDY BREAK 1–3

1. Revenues are the monetary amounts earned by a company by selling goods or providing services. Expenses are the costs incurred to generate revenues.
2. Accounts receivable are the amounts that customers owe a company for goods and services provided but not yet paid for.

STUDY BREAK 1–4

1. Share capital (also called paid-in capital) and retained earnings are the two parts.
2. It is a *business* year, which may or may not correspond to a calendar year. The word *fiscal* relates to monetary issues (e.g., fiscal policy).

STUDY BREAK 1–5

1. *Gross profit* is the difference between *sales* and *cost of goods sold* (i.e., *sales* minus *cost of goods sold*). It is also known as *gross margin*.
2. A single-step income statement presents all revenues first and then deducts all expenses. A multistep income statement starts with *sales* and subtracts the *cost of goods sold*, giving the subtotal, *gross margin*. Then other revenue and other expenses are itemized.

Questions

1. What is the purpose of a business?
2. Is the goal of all business organizations to make a profit?
3. Name the two main processes that make up most business activities.
4. What are the possible ownership structures for a business?
5. What are the advantages of the corporate form of ownership?
6. What are the disadvantages of the corporate form of ownership?
7. Who are some of the people in need of business information and for what purposes?
8. What is the relationship between the information available to a business and the information provided in financial statements?
9. What are the basic financial statements? Describe the information that each provides.
10. What makes the income statement different from the cash flow statement?

Short Exercises

L.O. 1, 2

SE1-1 For each of the following transactions, identify whether it is better described as part of the acquisition/payment process or the sales/collection process.

a. Merchandise is purchased for resale.
b. Customers buy merchandise on credit.
c. A bank loan is obtained.
d. A cheque is sent to vendor for previous purchase.
e. Customer sends payment for previous purchase.

L.O. 4

SE1-2 Classify the accounts listed below (1 to 7) under the balance sheet headings of:

a. Assets
b. Liabilities
c. Equity

[Use Sears Canada's balance sheet to help you with this exercise.]

1. _____Cash
2. _____Contributions from owners
3. _____Inventory
4. _____Land and buildings
5. _____Prepaid advertising
6. _____Accounts payable
7. _____Retained earnings

L.O. 4

SE1-3 Donkey Doughnut Company shows $125,000 worth of assets on its December 31, 2005, balance sheet. If the company's total liabilities are $35,750, what is the amount of owner's equity?

L.O. 4

SE1-4 Given the following items and amounts on a company's December 31, 2006, balance sheet, how much cash did the company have on hand on December 31, 2006?

Cash	??
Inventory	$100
Equipment	$500
Liabilities	$450
Owner's equity	$650

L.O. 4

SE1-5 Given the following items on a company's December 31, 2007, balance sheet, how much did the company owe its creditors on December 31, 2007?

Cash	$ 1,625	Liabilities	???
Inventory	223		
Equipment	10,647	Contributed capital	$9,300
Other assets	8,235	Retained earnings	5,000
Total	*$20,730*		

L.O. 4

SE1-6 For each of the following, calculate the missing amount:

a. Revenues $560; Expenses $350; Net Income = _______
b. Net Income $500; Expenses $475; Revenues = _______
c. Expenses $600; Revenues $940; Net Income = _______
d. Revenues $1,240; Net Income $670; Expenses = _______
e. Net Income $6,450; Expenses $2,500; Revenues = _______

L.O. 4

SE1-7 Logan Enterprises has $50,000 in cash, $10,000 in prepaid rent, $20,000 balance due to creditors, and $15,000 balance due from customers. What is the amount of owner's equity?

L.O. 4

SE1-8 Given the amounts for the balance sheet on December 31, 2006, how much owner's equity did Greg's Bookstore have on December 31, 2006?

Cash	$200
Inventory	$600
Marketable securities	$300
Accounts payable	$100
Notes payable	$ 50
Salaries payable	$100
Owner's equity	????

SE1-9 After one year of business, Mike's Watch Repair, Inc. had $5,000 in assets, $3,000 in liabilities, and $1,500 in share capital. What is the amount of retained earnings at the end of the corporation's first year of business? L.O. 4

SE1-10 Rex's Camera Store had a retained earnings balance of $1,000 on Decmber 31, 2005. For year 2006, sales were $10,500 and expenses were $6,500. Cash dividends of $2,500 were distributed on December 31, 2006. What was the amount of retained earnings on December 31, 2006? L.O. 4

Exercises

E1-1 Identify the transactions from the following story. For each, identify the *give* and *get* portion of each. Who would be interested in this information? L.O. 1, 2, 3

Tyrone Smith decided to go into business for himself. As a talented computer programmer, he decided to open a small consulting firm with $10,000 of his own money. The company bought a state-of-the-art desktop computer, complete with the accessories and software needed to get the business off the ground, at a total cost of $6,000. The business required a separate phone line put in his house, which cost $350. Then, Tyrone's company hired an Internet company to design and maintain a webpage for the business at a cost of $250 for the design and $45 per month for maintenance. After placing an advertisement in the business section of the local newspaper, at a cost of $50 per month, Tyrone's business was ready to go.

E1-2 Sue King opened a shoe store called "Sue's Shoes" with $10,000 of personal savings and $5,000 from the bank. The company bought $7,000 of shoes from an Italian manufacturer. The rent expense is $450 monthly. Sue's customers liked the shoes, too, as evidenced by the first month's sales. Sue's Shoes sold shoes that cost $4,000 to customers for $6,000. All the transactions were cash. Identify these get/give transactions and determine if there is an increase or decrease to assets, liabilities, or owner's equity. L.O. 1, 2

Use the following format:

Get	Give	Assets	Liabilities	Owner's equity
e.g., cash	Ownership	+$10,000		+$10,000

E1-3 Use the balance sheet for Doggie Dog Company at December 31, 2004, to answer the following questions: L.O. 3, 4

Assets		Liabilities and Owner's Equity	
Cash	$ 3,000	Accounts payable	$ 1,500
Inventory		Notes payable (van)	12,500
Dog bones	30		
Leashes	465	Capital, Kit T. Kat	6,020
Dog collars	725		
Dog food	500		
Mobile grooming van (net)	15,000		
Prepaid insurance	300		
	$20,020		$20,020

1. What assets did the company have on December 31, 2004? List them.
2. Who had claim to these assets?
3. Is this company a sole proprietorship, a partnership, or a corporation? How can you tell?
4. Who are the potential users of this financial information?

L.O. 4

E1-4 Given the following transactions, calculate the (1) amount of assets owned by Charlie's Hot Dogs at the end of his first month of business, and (2) amount of net income for the month. All these transactions took place during the first month of business. Charlie had his hot dog stand open for 20 days during the first month of business.

a. Charlie's Hot Dogs was started with a contribution from Charlie of $2,000 and a loan of $1,000 from the bank.
b. Charlie's Hot Dogs purchased $800 worth of hot dogs and buns (his inventory) for cash.
c. Charlie's Hot Dogs hired a friend with a steamer to cook the hot dogs and deliver a portion of them ready to sell to him at noon each day. For this service, Charlie's Hot Dogs paid $20 each day.
d. Charlie's Hot Dogs sold three-fourths of his hot dog and bun inventory for total cash revenues of $1,600.
e. Charlie's Hot Dogs paid the city a $25 fee, due monthly, for his licence.
f. Charlie's Hot Dogs repaid $200 of the bank loan along with $10 of interest for the first month.

L.O. 2

E1-5 For transactions (b), (c), (d), and (e) in E1-4, what are the resources, events, and agents involved in the give portion of the transaction and what are the resources, events, and agents involved in the get portion of the transaction? Put them in an REA diagram like the one in Exhibit 1–6 that describes the transaction.

L.O. 2

E1-6 For each of the transactions in E1-4, tell whether it is best categorized as part of the acquisition/payment process or part of the sales/collection process.

L.O. 4

E1-7 For each of the transactions given next, tell whether it (1) increases, (2) decreases, or (3) has no effect on owners' equity. Consider both owners' equity components—contributed capital and retained earnings.

a. Two friends get together, each contributing $5,000 to start the Piglet Corporation.
b. Piglet purchases equipment for $1,000 cash.
c. Piglet purchases $6,000 worth of merchandise inventory for cash.
d. Piglet pays rent of $2,000 in advance for store space in a small shopping mall.
e. Piglet makes cash sales to customers of $4,500.
f. Piglet pays employees $300 for hours worked.
g. Piglet declares and distributes $500 dividends to each of its owners.

L.O. 4

E1-8 Assume each transaction below is a cash transaction. Tell how each cash flow would be classified for the cash flow statement: (1) operating, (2) investing, or (3) financing.

a. Dedee makes a contribution of $100,000 to start the Pony D Riding Stables from her personal funds.
b. The company purchases three horses and various equipment for $35,000 in cash.
c. The company purchases $6,000 worth of advertising time on the local radio for cash.
d. The company pays rent of $10,000 for barn and pasture space as well as use of 50 acres of land for riding trails.
e. The company hires several people to clean stables at a cost of $500 for the month.
f. The first customers pay Pony D Riding Stables $3,000 for six months' worth of riding lessons.

L.O. 2

E1-9 Determine if the following would be classified as part of the acquisition/payment process or the sales/collection process of Dog E. Dog Company.

a. Dog E. Dog purchases shares in Kit E. Kat Company.
b. Dog E. Dog issues cheques for the salaries of its employees.
c. Dog E. Dog sells share holdings of Kit E. Kat for a gain.
d. Land held by Dog E. Dog for investment purposes is sold.
e. Dog E. Dog obtains a trademark for the "Doggie Boomerang," its new product.

E1-10 Identify an increase or decrease to assets, liabilities, owner's equity, revenues, or expenses for the following transactions of Blue Box Corp.: L.O. 4

a. Blue Box earned $10,000 in sales revenues.
b. The firm paid $3,000 cash for supplies.
c. Blue Box paid $2,500 of a $5,000 notes payable to creditors.
d. The company paid $1,500 for rent expense.
e. The company's owner provided $8,000 in additional financing.
f. The firm distributed $2,000 in dividends.
g. Blue Box provided $3,000 of cash loan to another company.

Use the following format:

Item	Assets	Liabilities	Owner's equity	Revenues	Expenses
a	+		+	+	

E1-11 For each of the following transactions, determine if there is an increase, decrease, or no change in net income for Fun Movie Productions, Inc. L.O. 4

a. Fun Movie earned $10,000 in monthly sales.
b. The firm recorded a decrease in inventory of $6,000 due to the monthly sales.
c. Monthly rent of $1,500 was paid.
d. Employees were paid $2,500 for work done.
e. The company purchased land for $7,500.
f. Fun Movie invested $4,000 in another company.
g. The firm paid $1,000 in cash dividends.

E1-12 Complete the following amounts—X, Y, and Z—on the balance sheet (retained earnings on 1/1/05 is 0): L.O. 4

	Dec. 31 2005	Dec. 31 2006
Assets	$1,000	$2,500
Liabilities	X	$1,000
Share capital	$ 300	$ 300
Retained earnings	$ 200	Z
Revenue	$ 300	$2,500
Expenses	Y	$1,500

Problems—Set A

P1-1A Use Sears Canada Inc.'s financial statements in Exhibits 1–2 and 1–3 to answer the following questions. For each, tell where you found the information to answer the question. Use the most recent year given for your answers. L.O. 3, 4

Required:

a. What is Sears' form of ownership?
b. What date marks the end of Sears' most recent fiscal year?
c. Did Sears earn a net income or net loss during the year?
d. Did the owners of Sears make any capital contributions during the year?
e. Did Sears buy or sell any major equipment during the year?
f. On the last day of the fiscal year, did Sears have any debts? If so, what was the total amount?

L.O. 4

P1-2A A set of financial statements for Seminole Company follows:

Seminole Company
Income Statement
For the Year Ended December 31, 2006

Sales	$600,000
Cost of goods sold	?
Gross profit on sales	375,000
Administrative expenses	54,000
Operating income	?
Interest expense	6,000
Earnings before income taxes	?
Income taxes (tax rate = 30%)	?
Net income	?

Seminole Company
Balance Sheet
December 31, 2006

Cash	$?	Accounts payable	$ 13,350
Accounts receivable	13,024	Notes payable	9,830
Inventory	43,271		
Equipment	972,684	Share capital	605,000
		Retained earnings	?
Total	*$1,129,780*	*Total*	?

Required: Fill in the missing amounts (indicated with question marks).

L.O. 3, 4

P1-3A The following transactions apply to Tiger Tire Service Company during May 2006.

1. The owner started the business by depositing $4,000 in a business chequing account on May 1.
2. The company provided services to clients and received $3,000 in cash.
3. The company borrowed $1,200 from the bank for the business.
4. The company paid $1,000 of salary expense.
5. A distribution of $1,500 was made to the owner.

Required:

a. What are the total assets of the Tiger Tire at the end of May 2006?
b. Prepare a cash flow statement for May 2006.
c. What was net income for May?
d. Who might find the information on the Tiger Tire financial statements useful?

L.O. 4

P1-4A The following events are for Wolverine Company for the year 2007, the first year of operations:

1. Mitch contributed $15,000 to start the business.
2. Creditors loaned Wolverine Company $7,000.
3. Wolverine Company provided services to its customers and received $32,000.
4. Wolverine Company paid expenses amounting to $18,000.
5. Wolverine Company purchased land for $9,000.

Required: Show the effects of these preceding transactions on the accounting equation. Then prepare the four major financial statements for 2007.

P1-5A What will be the effects (increase, decrease, or no effect) on total assets, total liabilities, and total shareholders' equity in each of the following situations? When owner's equity changes, note whether it is *share capital* or *retained earnings* that changes.

L.O. 3, 4

	Total assets	=	Total liabilities	+	Shareholders' equity: Share capital	Shareholders' equity: Retained earnings
1. Received cash and issued common shares.	________		________		________	________
2. Purchased equipment on credit.	________		________		________	________
3. Received cash from customers for services rendered.	________		________		________	________
4. Billed customers for services rendered on credit.	________		________		________	________
5. Received a utility bill but not yet paid.	________		________		________	________
6. Received cash from the customers in 4.	________		________		________	________
7. Paid the utility bill received in 5.	________		________		________	________

P1-6A You decide to sell T-shirts at a football game during November 2007 at the Vanier Cup to make some extra money. You engage in the following transactions:

L.O. 2, 3, 4

- You (and a couple of family members) invest $3,000 and receive shares in your new company, Vanier Cup T-Shirts, Inc.
- You pay the rent for space during the 2007 Vanier Cup, cash of $300.
- You buy 1,000 T-shirts for $6 each, paying $1,500 cash. You will pay the rest after the football game.
- You sell 1,000 T-shirts for $11 each, all for cash.
- Because you are so successful, you decide to prepay next year's rent (for the 2008 Vanier Cup), to be sure of getting a good location. The amount you pay is $325.
- You rush to your friend who is taking introductory financial accounting to find out where you stand financially.

Required: Prepare the income statement, the statement of changes in shareholders' equity, and the cash flow statement for December 2007. Prepare the balance sheet at December 31, 2007.

P1-7A Given the following information for Pete's Pet Shop:

L.O. 2, 4

1. Retained earnings on January 1, 2005, were $100,000.
2. In January, revenues were $50,000 and expenses were $60,000.
3. In February, revenues were $70,000 and expenses were $65,000.
4. In March, revenues were $90,000 and expenses were $55,000.
5. The only dividends paid were in March for $3,000.

Required: Prepare the retained earnings portion of the statement of changes in shareholders' equity for the three months ended March 31, 2005, for Pete's Pet Shop.

L.O. 4

P1-8A Joe is thinking about starting a new fitness club opening on January 1, 2006. Joe estimates he could sell 300 annual memberships for $400 each. He can get gym equipment for $12,000 and would need to hire an employee for $100 per week. Because the building where the gym would be located is rent free, Joe only has to pay the utilities of $100 per month. He would use his cash savings of $15,000 and obtain a loan from the bank for $50,000. The interest rate would be 10 percent. Regardless of the amount of net income, he would pay $2,000 of dividends the first year.

Required: Create a projected (*pro forma*) income statement, balance sheet, statement of retained earnings, and cash flow statement for the first year of Joe's Fitness Club (assume all transactions are cash). Who would be interested in Joe's *pro forma* financial statements?

Problems—Set B

L.O. 3, 4

P1-1B Use Sears Canada's financial statements (Exhibits 1–2 and 1–3 on page 9) to answer the following questions. For each, tell where you found the information to answer the question. Use the most recent year given for your answers.

Required:

a. What term does Sears use for *owner's equity*?
b. Which financial statement shows revenues and expenses?
c. Which financial statement shows assets and liabilities?
d. Did Sears *buy* more or *sell* more inventory during the year?
e. In which of the two years shown did Sears make the most income?
f. What happened to current liabilities during the year? What does this change mean?
g. What are Sears' total liabilities on January 3, 2004?

L.O. 4

P1-2B A set of financial statements for Shelby's Music, Inc. follows:

Shelby's Music, Inc.
Income Statement
For the Year Ended December 31, 2005

Sales	$1
Cost of goods sold	375,000
Gross profit on sales	525,000
Administrative expenses	2
Operating income	419,000
Interest expense	3
Earnings before income taxes	407,000
Income taxes (tax rate = 35%)	4
Net income	$5

Shelby's Music, Inc.
Balance Sheet
December 31, 2005

Cash	$158,592	Accounts payable	$ 14,070
Accounts receivable	18,621	Notes payable	12,520
Inventory	2		
Equipment	895,895	Share capital	3
		Retained earnings	425,000
Total	$1	*Total*	*$1,231,000*

Required: Fill in the missing amounts.

P1-3B The following transactions apply to Satine's Sewing Service during April 2005: L.O. 3, 4

1. Satine (the owner) started her own business by depositing $6,500 in a business chequing account on April 1.
2. Satine and her assistant Nadine sewed choir robes for a local church choir and received $4,000 cash.
3. Satine's Sewing Service paid Nadine $1,500 for April's salary.
4. Satine's Sewing Service borrowed $1,600 from the local bank.
5. Satine's Sewing Service made a distribution of $2,500 to Satine.

Required:

a. What are the total assets of Satine's Sewing Service at the end of April 2005?
b. Prepare a cash flow statement for April 2005.
c. What was net income for April?
d. Who might be interested in this information, and why?

P1-4B The following events are for Sandra's Sandblasting Company for the year 2006, the first year of operations: L.O. 4

1. Sandra invested $24,000 in the business.
2. Sandra's Sandblasting Company purchased sandblasting equipment for cash of $21,000.
3. Sandra's Sandblasting Company provided sandblasting services to the local community college and received $53,000.
4. Sandra's Sandblasting Company paid expenses amounting to $25,000.
5. Victory National Bank loaned Sandra's Sandblasting Company $18,000.

Required: Show the effects of the preceding transactions on the accounting equation. Then prepare the four major financial statements for 2006.

P1-5B What will be the effects (increase, decrease, or no effect) on total assets, total liabilities, and total shareholders' equity in each of the following situations? When shareholders' equity changes, note whether it is *share capital* or *retained earnings* that changes. L.O. 3, 4

				Shareholders' equity	
	Total assets	=	Total liabilities	+ Share capital	Retained earnings
1. Purchased land on credit.	________		________	________	________
2. Received cash from customers for services performed.	________		________	________	________
3. Received cash and issued common shares.	________		________	________	________
4. Received the insurance bill but not yet paid.	________		________	________	________
5. Billed customers for services performed on credit.	________		________	________	________
6. Purchased equipment on credit.	________		________	________	________

(continued)

			Shareholders' equity	
	Total assets	= Total liabilities	+ Share capital	Retained earnings
7. Received cash from the customers billed in 5.	________	________	________	________
8. Paid the insurance bill received in 4.	________	________	________	________
9. Purchased a building with cash.	________	________	________	________

L.O. 2, 4

P1-6B In August 2005, you decide to sell bonsai trees at a kiosk in Rendezvous Mall to make some extra money. You (and a couple of family members) invest cash and receive shares in your new company. You decide to incorporate your new business. The company engages in the following transactions:

- The company receives $4,800 in cash contributions from you and your family.
- The company pays the rent of $750 for the kiosk to sell the bonsai trees at the mall.
- The company buys 1,500 bonsai trees for $7 each, paying $3,000 cash. The company will pay the rest at the beginning of September.
- During August the company sells 1,500 bonsai trees for $20 each, all for cash.
- Because the business is so successful, the company prepays next month's rent, to be sure of keeping the same kiosk in the mall. The amount is $755.
- You rush to your friend who is taking accounting to find out where you stand financially.

Required: Prepare the four basic financial statements based on the preceding six transactions.

L.O. 4

P1-7B Given the following information for Pete's Pet Shop:

1. Retained earnings on April 1, 2005, were $127,000.
2. In April, revenues were $85,000, and expenses were $72,000.
3. In May, revenues were $16,582, and expenses were $37,000.
4. In June, revenues were $82,000, and expenses were $18,582.
5. Dividends were paid in April for $8,000 and in June for $19,500.

Required: Prepare the statement of retained earnings as of June 30, 2005, for Pete's Pet Shop.

L.O. 2, 3, 4

P1-8B Sunny Susan has decided to open a new tanning salon on July 1, 2005. Sunny Susan estimates she could sell 425 memberships (one year) for $480 each if she had super-tanning beds. She gets a special deal on 10 Wolfe Super-Tanning Beds for only $5,000 each. She hires her brother Gloomy Glen to wash the towels and clean the beds for $150 per week. Because Sunny Susan's grandmother gave her a free remodelled storefront downtown, her rent is free, and she only has to pay the utilities of $125 per month. She invests her cash savings of $27,500 and obtains a loan from the Grover Hills National Bank for $47,000. Regardless of the amount of net income, she has decided to pay $1,750 in dividends the first year.

Required:

1. Create a projected (*pro forma*) income statement, balance sheet, statement of retained earnings and cash flow statement for the first year of the Sunny Susan Tanning Salon. Assume all amounts are cash.
2. Who would be interested in these financial statements?

Issues for Discussion

Financial statement analysis

1. Use the annual report from CoolBrands International Inc. (Appendix A) to answer these questions:
   a. What type of business is CoolBrands, and how is it organized?
   b. Suppose you inherited $10,000 when your great-uncle passed away and you want to invest in a promising company. Would you invest in CoolBrands? What information in the annual report would be useful in your decision? Be specific. What information *not* given in the annual report would you want to have?
   c. What is your opinion of the information in the annual report? For example, do you think it is accurate? Useful? Interesting? Informative? Why, or why not?

Business risk

2. What kinds of risks does CoolBrands face? Use the information in the annual report and your own experience to answer this question.

Ethics

3. Ken Jones wants to start a small business and has asked his uncle to loan him $10,000. He has prepared a business plan and some financial statements that indicate the business could be very profitable. Ken is afraid his uncle will want some ownership in the company for his investment, but Ken does not want to share what he believes will be a hugely successful company. What are the ethical issues Ken must face as he prepares to present his business plan to his uncle? Do you think he should try to emphasize the *risks* of ownership to his uncle to convince him it would be preferable to be a creditor? Why, or why not?

Internet Exercise: Disney Corporation

The Walt Disney Company is a diversified worldwide entertainment company with interests in ABC TV, ESPN, film production, theme parks, publishing, a cruise line, Infoseek, and the NHL Mighty Ducks. By using the Disney website you can explore vacation options and get Disney's latest financial information.
Please go to the Disney website: http://disney.go.com/corporate/investors/

IE1-1 What is the Walt Disney Company key objective?

IE1-2 Go to *Financial Information,* and click on the most recent annual report.

a. What are the *key businesses* of the Walt Disney Company? Identify whether you think the primary business activity is manufacturing, merchandising, or service for each key business segment.
b. Go to *Financial Highlights* (under *Introduction*). Identify the amount of total revenues, operating income, and shareholders' equity for the most recent year. On which financial statement will you find each amount reported? Is the Walt Disney Company a proprietorship, a partnership, or a corporation? How can you tell?
c. Go to *Financial Review* (under *Introduction*). What key business segment earns the greatest proportion of revenues? Identify the proportion of revenues earned by each key business segment, listing them in the order of greatest proportion to least proportion. Does this order surprise you? Explain why or why not.

Please note: Internet websites are constantly being updated. Therefore, if the information is not found where indicated, explore the annual report further to find the information.

CHAPTER 2

Qualities of Accounting Information

Here's where you've been...

In Chapter 1, you learned that a business adds value to make a profit. The acquisition/payment process describes how a business gets the resources it needs and pays for them; and the sales/collection process describes how a business sells its service or product and collects the revenue.

The four basic financial statements—the income statement, the statement of retained earnings, the balance sheet, and the cash flow statement—provide information about these business processes.

Here's where you're going...

When you are finished with Chapter 2, you should understand the qualities of the information contained in the financial statements. You should be able to recognize and explain the difference between accrual basis accounting and cash basis accounting.

Learning Objectives

More specifically, when you are finished studying this chapter, you should be able to answer these questions:

1. What are generally accepted accounting principles, and why are they necessary?
2. What is the objective of financial statements? What qualities are necessary to achieve this objective?
3. What are the elements of the financial statements, and what are their characteristics?
4. What is accrual accounting, and how does it differ from cash basis accounting?

Information for Decision Making

After Tom sold his first batch of T-shirts, he had some decisions to make. The biggest one was whether or not to continue in business. What he needed to know to begin evaluating that decision is—did he make a profit? Profit is the amount left after all expenses of doing business are deducted from all revenues, for a specific period.

For Tom's Wear, this period is his first month of doing business, January 1 through January 31. Information about the month's operations is summarized on the income statement—one of the four basic financial statements. The revenues for the period amounted to $900; that is the total amount the company earned when it sold the 90 shirts. The expenses were the cost of the T-shirts sold, the cost of the advertising, and the interest paid on the loan from Tom's mom. The cost of the 90 T-shirts sold was $360, advertising expense was $50, and the cost of borrowing the money—interest expense—was $5. When those expenses, totalling $415, are deducted from the sales revenue of $900, the remaining $485 is profit. Tom's Wear added value by ordering shirts with the special logo and providing them to Tom's friends at a convenient time and place. And Tom's Wear achieved its goal—to make a profit.

On the income statement in Exhibit 2–1, you will see $485 shown as net income, which is just another name for profit. The term *profit* can be applied to a single sale, a group of sales, or all the transactions for a period of time of business activity, whereas *net income* is a more specific term for describing a company's entire profit for a specific time period. The company made a profit of $540 on the sale, and Tom's Wear's net income for his first month of business activity was $485.

Financial reporting provides information for decision making. An income statement, like the one shown for Tom's Wear, is one source of information. When the second month of business activity is complete, Tom will prepare another income statement and will compare the two statements. To make such a

Exhibit 2–1
Income Statement for Tom's Wear

Tom's Wear, Inc.
Income Statement
For the Month Ended January 31, 2005

Revenue		
Sales		$900
Expenses		
Cost of sales	$360	
Advertising expense	50	
Interest expense	5	
Total expenses		415
Net income		$485

comparison meaningful, Tom needs to use the same rules for preparing the two statements. If Tom wanted to compare his company's performance with the performance of another T-shirt company, he would need to be sure that the other company was using the same rules to prepare its income statement. For financial information to be useful for evaluating the performance of a business across time or for comparing two different companies, the same rules must be used consistently.

L.O. 1

Define generally accepted accounting priniciples and understand why they are necessary.

To enforce this consistency, there is a set of rules called **generally accepted accounting principles (GAAP)** that a company must follow when preparing its financial statements. These rules—usually known as accounting principles—were historically developed through common usage. A principle was acceptable if it was used and acknowledged by most accountants. This is what *generally accepted* means.

Generally accepted accounting principles (GAAP) are the rules set by the accounting profession for preparing financial statements.

As all businesses and their activities became more complex, the need for more consistency became clear. Canada moved to more formal accounting standards with the issuance of the ***Canadian Institute of Chartered Accountants' (CICA) Handbook*** in 1968. Presently the **Accounting Standards Board (AcSB)** of the CICA is responsible for developing and issuing the *Handbook* standards for companies and not-for-profit organizations. The board assigns an accounting standard project to a task force that, in turn, reports back to the board at key points in the process. The Public Sector Accounting Board (PSAB) of the CICA is responsible for developing and issuing standards for the public sector. In addition to formal standards, the AcSB provides guidance (i.e., abstracts) on new or emerging issues through the Emerging Issues Committee (EIC). The EIC allows the CICA to respond faster than would be possible through the more formal standard setting process.

The ***CICA Handbook*** contains statements issued by the AcSB explaining and describing the type of information required from financial reporting.

The **Accounting Standards Board (AcSB)** is the current standards-setting body for companies and not-for-profit organizations.

The activities of both the AcSB and the PSAB are overseen by the Accounting Standards Oversight Council (AcSOC). The AcSOC's purpose is to provide strategic direction to the boards and to support the development of internationally accepted standards. In fact, in light of the increasing internationalization of business, the AcSB has noted that it is unlikely that it will adopt a new standard that differs from the Financial Accounting Standards Board (FASB) in the United States or the International Accounting Standards Board (IASB). The AcSB has and will continue to work extensively with the FASB and the IASB. As a result of the standard setting activities of the CICA in Canada, the terms used to describe accounting rules include principles, standards, guidelines, abstracts, and, in the past, bulletins. All the different expressions to describe the rules in summation are represented by the words *generally accepted accounting principles (GAAP)*.

Financial Statement Concepts

Over the years, as businesses have continued to grow more complex, the number of accounting rules has increased. In the late 1970s, the accounting standard setters in both the United States and Canada decided that some specific guidance was needed to help establish new rules. Until then, there were no written goals or guidelines to help them formulate accounting standards. Although they had been setting accounting principles for years, there was no underlying framework to rely on when creating and evaluating new principles. In Canada, this framework can now be found in Section 1000 of the *CICA Handbook*. The section, titled *Financial Statement Concepts*, defines and describes the kind of information financial reporting should include.

Objective of Financial Statements

L.O. 2

Explain the objectives of financial reporting.

Section 1000 of the *CICA Handbook* defines the objective of financial statements for profit-oriented enterprises. The objective of financial statements is to communicate information that is useful to investors and creditors in making resource allocation decisions and/or assessing management stewardship—or, more simply, to provide useful information for making decisions. The *Handbook* limits the focus of financial statements to investors and creditors because it would not be practical to expect financial statements to satisfy all possible uses of all external users.

Section 1000 also notes that there is a cost to providing information. We have to weigh the costs of providing information with the benefits that can be derived from it. **Cost-benefit analysis**—an economic concept that says we must always stack up the costs of doing something against its *benefits*—is used to decide what financial information a company should include in its financial statements.

A **cost-benefit analysis** is an evaluation of a decision or course of action consisting of comparing all the costs of an action with all the benefits. If the benefits of a course of action exceed the costs, then we would select that course of action.

In addition to the two points noted above, there are two other limits of financial statements that should be noted.

- The information represented in a financial statement is specific to a business enterprise. Financial reporting does not provide industry-wide or economy-wide information. The information in a financial statement relates to a specific business or company. The owner's personal financial records are not part of the financial records and financial statements of a business. This is called the **separate-entity assumption**.
- The information is simplified, summarized, and condensed. There are two reasons for this:

  a. Reporting all transactions in detail would be overwhelming, providing more information than would be useful.

  b. Some of the details of a company's transactions are proprietary—a company wants to keep them secret.

The **separate-entity assumption** means that a company and its owners keep separate financial records.

You should come to realize that many of the measurements in financial statements are approximate. You may see a number and think of it as exact, whereas it is really an estimate of the amount it represents. That is because accountants make many decisions and judgment calls when they are gathering and condensing information for the financial statements.

STUDY BREAK 2–1

See How You're Doing

1. What is the purpose of financial statements?
2. Who sets accounting rules?
3. What is the focus of financial reporting?

Qualitative Characteristics of Accounting Information

L.O. 2

Explain the qualities of accounting information that enable financial reporting to meet its objective of providing useful information to users.

The most important quality of accounting information, **usefulness**, depends on how well the information does what it is supposed to do. To be useful, information must be both **relevant** and **reliable**.

Accounting information should be useful for evaluating the past and predicting the future. **Usefulness** is the most important characteristic of accounting information. What makes information useful depends, like anything else, on how well it does what it is supposed to do. For information to be useful, it must be understandable to users who have a reasonable understanding of business and accounting. Useful information is both **relevant** and **reliable**. For information to be relevant, it needs to be fresh, not so stale that we cannot use it to do what we need to do. We should be able to use the information to evaluate a firm's past performance, to predict where it is going, or both. Reliable

Exhibit 2–2 Characteristics of Accounting Information.

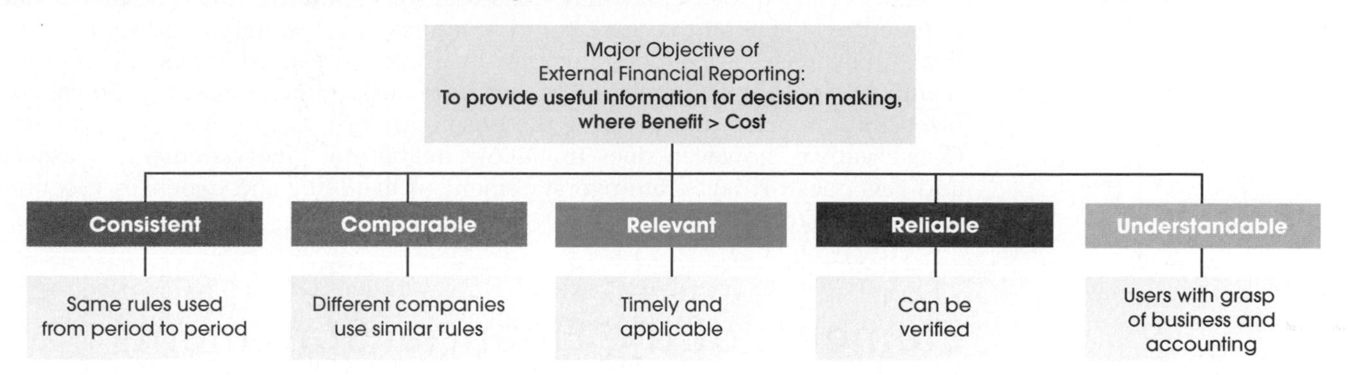

means that you can verify the truthfulness of the information. According to the *Handbook*, the information must have "representational faithfulness," meaning it is accurate and truthful. (See Exhibit 2–2.)

Two more characteristics of useful information are **comparability** and **consistency**. Users of the basic financial statements often want to compare information in one period with the same sort of information in a financial statement for another period. For example, how does the net income for one year compare with the net income for another year? They may want to compare corresponding financial information between two companies—how one company's net income compares with another company's net income. In putting together the financial statements, we must be sure that they allow meaningful comparisons—comparisons across companies, across financial statements, or between individual items on a single financial statement. How does the amount of cash on hand compare with the amount of money customers still owe the company? Consistency is the characteristic that makes comparability possible. Only if we measure financial concepts—for example, *net income*—the same way from period to period are we able to make meaningful comparisons. For example, if we have decided that distributions to owners are not to be included on the income statement as an expense—a rule in GAAP—then we must be sure to exclude them from every income statement. If we changed the rules in the middle of a basketball game, the score from one half would not mean much when compared with the score from the other half. In accounting, keeping the rules the same from period to period makes the information consistent and, thus, comparable.

Comparability is a quality of information based on the idea that it is more useful when related to the same type of information in another period.

Consistency is a quality of useful information requiring accounting methods to be followed in the same manner from period to period, making the information comparable.

Now we come to **materiality**, a very specific term in accounting, addressing whether or not an item or transaction is large enough to have an influence on decisions. If an item that is generally required to be included in a specific place on the financial statements is so small that it is insignificant compared with the amount of either the rest of the transactions or the amount of the company's assets, it may be considered *not material* (immaterial) and included elsewhere. For example, if a company buys a $5 wastebasket and the rest of the company's assets are pieces of equipment that cost over $1,000 each, the balance sheet may omit the $5 wastebasket from the list of assets. The $5 would be counted as an expense for the period instead. In this example, the benefit of treating the wastebasket as an asset and writing it off (i.e., expensing it) over its useful life is smaller than the bookkeeping costs associated with recording it as an asset. There is a lot of judgment in deciding what is material for the financial statements. Materiality is hard to explain because accountants do not agree on exactly how to apply the idea in practice. It is a controversial issue in accounting. All items that are generally required and are considered *material* must be included in the financial statements as the accounting standards direct.

Materiality in accounting refers to the significance of an amount or item on the financial statements. An amount is considered *material* if it would affect someone's interpretation or decision.

The last qualitative characteristic of accounting information that we will address is **conservatism**. When preparing financial information, uncertainty

The **conservatism principle** is an accounting principle explaining that when doubt exists between two reporting alternatives, the user of the information should select the alternative with the least favourable impact on owner's equity.

often exists and this requires us to use professional judgment to make estimates. The use of conservatism means that the estimates should be made that reduce the likelihood that assets and revenues are overstated and that liabilities and expenses are understated. For example, unrealized losses in inventory would be recognized immediately, but unrealized gains would not be recognized until realized (this reduces the possibility of an asset being overstated). Conservatism, however, does not allow deliberate understatement of assets and revenues or deliberate overstatement of liabilities and expenses (Section 1000.21(d), *CICA Handbook*).

Elements of the Financial Statements

L.O. 3

Define a complete set of financial statements and explain the elements contained in those statements.

A complete set of financial statements includes:

- income statement
- balance sheet (sometimes called the statement of financial position)
- statement of retained earnings
- cash flow statement
- notes to the financial statements

Section 1000 of the *CICA Handbook* describes the individual items that are included in the financial statements. To learn what is shown on each financial statement, we will look at the second month of business for Tom's Wear. We will take each of the second month's transactions and see how it affects the accounting equation and the financial statements. Then, we will relate the statements to the items described in Section 1000 of the *CICA Handbook*.

As we begin the second month on February 1, 2005, Tom's Wear has a balance sheet that is identical to the balance sheet dated January 31, 2005. Recall that the company's assets, liabilities, and equity balances roll forward when the new period starts.

Transactions for the Second Month of Business

February 1	Tom's Wear purchases 200 T-shirts at $4 each. They are purchased on credit.
February 5	Tom hires a company to advertise his business. The total cost is $150. Tom pays $100 cash at the time of the service and will pay the remaining $50 later.
February 14	Tom decides to get insurance for his business. On February 14, Tom's Wear pays $150 for 3 months of insurance, with coverage beginning on the date of payment.
February 23	Tom's Wear sells 185 T-shirts for $10 each. 170 of these were sold for cash and the remaining 15 were sold on credit.
February 28	Tom's Wear declares and pays a dividend of $100.

On account means *on credit*. The expression applies to either buying or selling on credit.

The transactions for Tom's second month of business are shown in Exhibit 2–3. The first transaction in February is the purchase of 200 T-shirts, costing $4 each. Last month, Tom's Wear paid cash for the purchase of the T-shirts. This month, the company buys them on credit, also known as **on account**. This means that Tom's Wear will pay for them later. The purchase increases the company's assets—$800 worth of T-shirts—and the $800 claim belongs to the vendor. When a company owes a vendor, what is owed is called

accounts payable. This is the first transaction shown in Exhibit 2–3, where the transactions are presented on a work sheet based on the accounting equation.

Accounts payable are amounts that a company owes its vendors. They are liabilities and are shown on the balance sheet.

Next, Tom hires a company to advertise his business. This cost is $150 for a service. Tom's Wear pays $100 when the service is provided, and so the company still owes $50. Like the first transaction, this one also postpones payment. However, in this transaction, Tom's Wear has incurred an expense. In the first transaction—when the inventory was purchased—Tom's Wear gained an asset. The cost of the shirts will become an expense when the shirts are sold. In contrast, the work done related to the advertising is complete, and that signals an expense. (The timing of recognizing expenses can be tricky; the next chapter will discuss timing in detail.) The $150 expense, like all expenses, reduces the owner's claims to the assets of the firm. Assets decrease by $100, the cash paid for the advertising; and the remaining $50 increases creditors' claims—liabilities—because it will be paid later. This is the second transaction shown in Exhibit 2–3.

As his business grows, Tom decides his company needs some insurance. Tom's Wear pays $150 for three months' worth of coverage, beginning February 14. When a company pays for something in advance, the item purchased is something of future value to the company. Because such an item provides future value, it is classified as an asset. Items purchased in advance may seem like unusual assets, and often have the word *prepaid* with them to provide information about what sort of assets they are. Common prepaid items are insurance, rent, and supplies. In this case, Tom's Wear has purchased an asset called **prepaid insurance**. Cash is decreased by $150, and our new asset—prepaid insurance—is increased by $150. Note that we have not recorded *insurance expense*. Until some of the insurance is used up—and it can only be used up from one point in time to a subsequent point in time—there is no expense.

Prepaid insurance is the name for insurance a business has purchased but not yet used. It is an asset.

Exhibit 2–3 **Effect of Transactions on Accounting Equation**

tom's wear	Assets		= Liabilities		+ Shareholders' equity: Share capital	Shareholders' equity: Retained earnings	
Balance sheet at February 1, 2005	Cash Inventory	$5,345 40		$ 0	$5,000		$385
1- Purchased 200 shirts on account	Inventory	800	Accounts payable	800			
2- Advertising, cost $150, paid cash for $100, owe $50	Cash	(100)	Other payable	50		Advertising expense	(150)
3-Purchased 3 months' worth of insurance for $150	Prepaid insurance Cash	150 (150)					
4-Sold 185 shirts for $10 each, 170 for cash, 15 on account	Cash Accounts receivable Inventory	1,700 150 (740)				Sales Cost of goods sold	1,850 (740)
5- Dividend for $100 paid	Cash	(100)				Dividends	(100)
Balance sheet at February 28, 2005	Cash Accounts receivable Inventory Prepaid insurance	$6,695 150 100 150	Accounts payable Other payable	$800 50	Common shares $5,000	Retained earnings	$1,245

Accounts receivable are amounts customers owe a company for goods or services purchased on credit.

Adjusting the books means to make changes in the accounting records, at the end of the period, just before the financial statements are prepared, to make sure the amounts reflect the financial condition of the company at that date. **Adjusting entries** are the entries necessary at the end of the accounting period to adjust the accounts for accrued revenues and expenses and deferred revenues and expenses.

The company's success continues with the sale of 185 more T-shirts at $10 each. Although transaction 4 shows these sales as a single transaction, they could have been individual sales. They are grouped together here to make the presentation simple. Of the 185 shirts sold, 170 were sold for cash of $1700 (= 170 shirts × $10 per shirt) and 15 were sold on credit for $150 (= 15 shirts × $10 per shirt). When a sale is made on credit, the amount owed by customers is called **accounts receivable**. Accounts receivable are assets—things of value to a business. This is the fourth transaction shown in Exhibit 2–3. Note that the rest of this transaction includes the decrease in inventory of $740 (= 185 shirts × the $4 cost of each) with a corresponding expense—cost of goods sold of $740—which decreases retained earnings by $740.

At the end of the second month of business, Tom's Wear pays a dividend of $100 to its only shareholder, Tom. This transaction reduces assets—cash—by $100, and it reduces retained earnings by $100. This is the fifth transaction shown in Exhibit 2–3.

The financial statements for February can be prepared with the information from these transactions. However, there is still one more step before accurate financial statements can be prepared. This step is called **adjusting the books**. We review the amount that has been recorded for each asset and each claim to make sure every amount correctly reflects the financial situation of the company on the specific date we have chosen for the balance sheet—the last day of the fiscal period (month, quarter, or year). After reviewing the transactions during the month, can you identify any amount that seems incorrect to you? Start at the beginning of the balance sheet work sheet and look at each item that has been recorded. The assets are cash, $6,695; accounts receivable, $150; inventory, $100; and prepaid insurance, $150. Are these amounts accurate at February 28, 2005, the end of Tom's second month of operating his business? Is any asset likely to communicate incorrect information?

Yes—prepaid insurance, as it appears in the company's records, will not express what it should. Because the balance sheet will have the date February 28, 2005, we want the amount of prepaid insurance to be accurate at that date. What is the amount of the asset—insurance that is still unused—at the date of the balance sheet? The $150, paid on February 14, applied to three months. On February 28, half a month, or 15 days, has passed. So, one-sixth (= 15 days/90 days) of the prepaid insurance has been used. An adjustment must be made to make sure the correct amount of prepaid insurance is shown on the balance sheet. Like routine transactions, adjustments must keep the accounting equation in balance. We subtract $25 (=1/6 × $150) from the asset column, reducing the amount of prepaid insurance, and we reduce owner's claims by the same $25 amount. This reduction in the owner's claims is an expense—insurance expense—and so we show it in the retained earnings column. It will be included on the income statement. The correct amount of the asset—the unused portion—will be shown on the balance sheet at $125.

A review of the other items on the balance sheet does not reveal any other problems on this particular balance sheet date. In the next chapter, you will learn there are other situations requiring adjustments before you can prepare the financial statements.

The income statement is prepared first (Exhibit 2–4). It lists the revenues and expenses for the period, and you can find those in the retained earnings column in Exhibit 2–3. All revenues increase retained earnings; all expenses decrease retained earnings. The only item that we regularly find in the retained earnings column that is *not* included in the income statement is a distribution to the owners, dividends in a corporation. Generally accepted accounting principles say that distributions are not expenses.

Revenues and expenses can be found in the retained earnings column of our work sheet. This is all the information we need to prepare the income

Exhibit 2–4
Income Statement for Tom's Wear

tom's wear

Tom's Wear, Inc.
Income Statement
For the Month Ended February 28, 2005

Revenue		
Sales		$1,850
Expenses		
Cost of sales	740	
Advertising expense	150	
Insurance expense	25	
Total expenses		915
Net income		$ 935

statement. Simply go down the list of numbers in the retained earnings column, and group the transactions into revenues and expenses to form an income statement.

The sales revenue, often simply called *sales,* is $1,850.

There are three types of expenses listed. One is the cost of goods sold—also known as cost of sales. Recall, this is the expense associated with selling something purchased from someone else. Tom's Wear has cost of goods sold of $740. The other two expenses are $150 for the advertising and $25 for insurance. Be sure you see and understand that the insurance expense is *not* the amount Tom's Wear actually paid to the insurance company. Instead, it is the cost of the insurance that was *used* during the period. The amount that has not been used as of February 28 remains on the balance sheet as an asset.

The net income for the period is $935—revenues of $1,850 minus expenses of $915.

The statement of retained earnings is prepared next (Exhibit 2–5). This statement provides the details of the changes in retained earnings during the month.

The information for this statement is found in the retained earnings column of the work sheet in Exhibit 2–3. Retained earnings began the month with a balance of $385. Net income of $935 increases retained earnings, and the dividend of $100 decreases retained earnings. The amount of retained earnings at the end of the period is $1,220 (= $385 + 935 – 100).

Next, Tom's Wear prepares the balance sheet. The balance sheet was really prepared as the transactions were put in the accounting equation work sheet—but not in a way to communicate most effectively. The transactions need to be summarized and organized to communicate their information clearly and effectively, in what is often considered the formal balance sheet presentation. Each asset owned at February 28 is listed, along with the claims

Exhibit 2–5
Statement of Retained Earnings for Tom's Wear

tom's wear

Tom's Wear, Inc.
Statement of Retained Earnings
For the Month Ended February 28, 2005

Beginning retained earnings	$ 385
Net income for the month	935
Dividends	(100)
Ending retained earnings	$1,220

to those assets. Note the similarity between the list of transactions on the work sheet in Exhibit 2–3 and the balance sheet in Exhibit 2–6.

The assets are listed at their amounts on February 28, 2005. There is $6,695 cash. (The details of how this number was calculated will be shown on the cash flow statement.) Tom's Wear also has accounts receivable of $150—that is, the amount customers still owe the company for T-shirts purchased during the month but that has not been paid for yet. There are 25 shirts left in the inventory, each costing $4, for a total of $100.

The last asset is prepaid insurance, and the amount shown is $125—the unused portion at February 28. The adjustment reduced prepaid insurance by $25 for the amount used up during the last half of February.

There are two liabilities at February 28, 2005—accounts payable of $800 and other payables of $50. These amounts are still owed by Tom's Wear to creditors.

The last item is the amount of shareholders' equity. The total share capital—in the form of shares—is $5,000. Because we have already prepared the statement of retained earnings, we know that $1,220 is the amount of retained earnings. Together, the liabilities plus shareholders' equity add up to $7,070—the same $7,070 as the total assets.

The cash flow statement (Exhibit 2–7) shows every cash collection and every cash disbursement for the month. Each cash transaction is classified

Exhibit 2–6
Balance Sheet for Tom's Wear

Tom's Wear, Inc.
Balance Sheet
At February 28, 2005

Assets		Liabilities and Shareholders' equity	
Cash	$6,695	Accounts payable	$ 800
Accounts receivable	150	Other payables	50
Inventory	100		
Prepaid insurance	125	Common shares	5,000
		Retained earnings	1,220
Total assets	$7,070	Total liabilities and shareholders' equity	$7,070

Exhibit 2–7
Cash Flow Statement for Tom's Wear

Tom's Wear, Inc.
Cash Flow Statement
For the Month Ended February 28, 2005

Cash from operating activities		
Cash collected from customers	$1,700	
Cash paid to advertising	(100)	
Cash paid for insurance	(150)	
Total cash from operations		$1,450
Cash from investing activities		0
Cash from financing activities		
Cash paid for dividends	$ (100)	
Total cash from financing		(100)
Net increase in cash		$1,350

as one of three types: operating, investing, or financing. To prepare this statement, we need to pick out the cash items from the transactions in the *asset* column of the work sheet in Exhibit 2–3. For each cash amount, ask yourself if it pertains to operating activities, investing activities, or financing activities.

The first *cash* amount in the asset column of Exhibit 2–3 is the payment of $100 in cash for advertising; that was the second transaction. This $100 is an operating cash flow because it is a cash expense related to routine business activities.

The next cash transaction is the $150 paid to the insurance company. The purchase of insurance is an operating cash flow. Note that the cash flow statement shows the cash paid—with *no regard for when* the insurance is used.

Transaction 4 involves cash inflows, for a total of $1,700. This transaction was a sale, which is also an operating cash flow. Note the cash in transaction 4 is $1,700, representing 170 T-shirts sold for cash. Although 185 were actually sold, 15 are not yet paid for. In the cash flow statement, every item must be *cash* only.

The final cash transaction is the distribution of $100 to the owner as dividends. This is classified as a financing cash flow because it relates to how the business is financed.

Be sure you see that the cash flow statement includes *every* cash inflow and *every* cash outflow listed in the asset column of the transaction work sheet. Also note that nothing else is included on this financial statement.

The net amount is the change in the amount of cash during the period. If we add this increase of $1,350 to the beginning cash balance of $5,345, we get the ending cash balance of $6,695, shown on the February 28, 2005, balance sheet.

Notes to the financial statements are not included here for Tom's Wear. As we gain an understanding of the complexity of the choices accountants make in preparing financial statements, we will see the need for notes to give the financial statement users information about those choices.

Assets

Looking at the balance sheet at February 28, 2005, for Tom's Wear, Exhibit 2–6, we see on the left the company's assets, also referred to as economic resources. Assets are those items of value that belong to the company. They are on the balance sheet as a result of past transactions, but they do have value, which they will provide in the future when they will be used to help the business produce revenue.

The first asset on Tom's Wear's balance sheet is cash. The amount has been determined by past transactions, and the money has value because of what it can buy in the future.

Other common assets include accounts receivable (amounts owed to the company by customers) and inventory (items purchased for sale).

The last asset shown is prepaid insurance. This is the *unused* portion of the insurance—it still has value on February 28.

Assets are listed on the balance sheet in order of **liquidity**. Liquidity refers to how easily an asset can be converted into cash. The assets that are expected to be used within a year are called **current assets**. The assets that will not be used within a year are called **noncurrent assets**, or **long-term assets**. So far, Tom's Wear has only current assets. Look at Exhibit 1–3 at the balance sheet of Sears. The asset section of the balance sheet shows both current and long-term assets.

Assets are the economic resources of a company, resulting from past transactions.

Liquidity is a measure of how easily an asset can be converted to cash. The more liquid an asset is, the more easily it can be turned into cash.

Current assets are the assets the company plans to turn into cash or use to generate revenue in the next fiscal year.

Noncurrent, or **long-term, assets** are assets that will last for more than a year.

Assets are one of three classifications of items on the balance sheet. The other two types tell *who*—creditors or owners—has claim to these assets. Recall, the balance sheet *is* the accounting equation:

Assets = Liabilities + Owner's Equity

Liabilities

Liabilities are obligations the company has incurred to obtain the assets it has.

Accounts payable are amounts a company owes to its vendors.

The January 2, 2005, balance sheet, shown in Exhibit 1–11, indicated that Tom's Wear owed $500 to Tom's mom. On February 28, 2005, that is no longer the case. The debt to his mom was paid off in January. On February 28, 2005, the only liabilities Tom's Wear has are accounts payable and other payables. **Liabilities** are amounts that the business owes. They are the claims of creditors. Usually, these claims will be paid to creditors in cash. Liabilities, like assets, are the result of past transactions or events. For example, a purchase of inventory items on credit creates a liability called **accounts payable**. The balance sheet on February 28 was prepared after the purchase of the shirts but before Tom paid for them, and so the balance sheet shows the cost of the shirts as accounts payable. Once incurred, a liability continues as an obligation of the company until the company pays for it. The accounts payable amount for the T-shirts remains on the balance sheet until Tom pays the bill for the shirts. Often, liabilities involve interest—payment of an additional amount for the right to delay payment. When Tom repaid his mom in 2005, he paid $5 interest for the use of her money.

Current liabilities are liabilities the company will settle—pay off—in the next fiscal year.

Noncurrent, or **long-term**, liabilities are liabilities that will take longer than a year to settle.

A **classified balance sheet** shows a subtotal for many items including current assets and current liabilities.

Liabilities can also be current or noncurrent. If a liability will be settled with a current asset, it is called a **current liability**. For practical purposes, you can think of a current liability as a liability that will be paid off in the next year. **Noncurrent liabilities** will be paid off over a period longer than one year. Most balance sheets show the current assets with a subtotal before showing the noncurrent assets. That format is called a **classified balance sheet**. A classified balance sheet will also show the current liabilities with a subtotal before the long-term liabilities. Look at the balance sheet for Sears, shown in Exhibit 1–3. See if you can find the subtotals for current assets and current liabilities. This is a classified balance sheet because it has two classifications of assets and liabilities—short term and long term.

Equity

Equity is the name for owners' claims to the assets of the firm. It includes both **share capital** (or **capital contributions**) and capital *earned* by the business. In a corporation, the earned amount of equity is called **retained earnings.**

Equity, sometimes called net assets, is the owners' claims to the assets of the company. There are two ways owners can create equity in a company. The first way is by making **capital contributions—share capital**. Usually, the capital is cash, but it could be equipment or other items of value. When Tom started his T-shirt business, he invested $5,000 of his own money. Sometimes, this is called the owner's investment in the company. The term *investment* may be confused with investments that the company itself makes with its extra cash. For example, General Motors may invest some of its extra cash in the shares of Sears, which General Motors would call an investment. To avoid that confusion, we will not refer to owners' investments; instead, we will call these amounts owners' *contributions*.

The second way to create equity in a business is to make a profit. (That is the preferred way.) When Tom's Wear sells a shirt, the profit from that shirt increases Tom's equity in the company.

In corporations, the two types of equity are separated on the balance sheet. The first is **share capital**, also known as **contributed capital** or **paid-in capital**; the second is **retained earnings**. In a sole proprietorship or partnership, both types of equity are together called capital. Separating these amounts for corporations provides information for potential investors about how much the owners have actually invested in the corporation.

Share capital is sometimes called **contributed capital** or **paid-in capital**. This is the amount the owners have put into the business.

In a sole proprietorship and partnership, the share capital and earned capital—**retained earnings**—are shown together in one amount called capital.

Measurement and Recognition in Financial Statements

L.O. 3

Recognize how the elements of the financial statements—assets, liabilities, equity, revenue, and expenses—are represented by various items on the financial statements and how they are measured.

Let us take a closer look at the elements on the balance sheet and income statement. Recall, the balance sheet is simply the accounting equation: Assets = Liabilities + Owner's Equity. The three elements are major categories, each divided into subcategories.

Let us start with assets. The most well known asset is cash. It is listed first on the balance sheet. As we noted on the Sears balance sheet, all other assets are listed in order of their liquidity—how easily they can be converted to cash. A monetary value is computed for each asset. Cash, for example, is the total amount of money in chequing and savings accounts. The next asset on the balance sheet is usually accounts receivable—the total amount that customers owe the company for credit sales.

Inventory is another asset, measured at its cost. We saw that Tom's Wear's balance sheet included the cost of the T-shirts still in the inventory on the balance sheet date.

Measuring Assets

So far, we have discussed two characteristics of the way things are measured for the balance sheet.

First, they are measured in monetary units. For us, that means dollars. The actual *number* of T-shirts in the inventory is not shown on the balance sheet. Measuring assets, liabilities, and equity in monetary units is called the **unit-of-measure assumption**. Canadian companies use dollars, Japanese companies use yen, and so on.

The **unit-of-measure assumption** refers to the use of monetary units—dollars in Canada—to measure the financial statement items.

Second, the items on the financial statements are recorded at *cost*—that is, what we paid for them—sometimes called **historical cost**. They are *not* recorded at the amount we hope they will be sold for. The concept behind this is called the **cost principle** and is closely tied to the **going-concern assumption**. We assume the business is not going to quit operating—that it is going to continue as a going concern. If you did not assume a business is a going concern, you could argue that items on the financial statements should be valued at their current value—whatever the company could get for them if it were immediately going out of business. Instead, when a company buys something, it is recorded at the cost at the time of purchase. Some assets continue to be shown at cost on the balance sheet, and others are revalued to a more current amount for each balance sheet. We will learn the details of which assets *are revalued* and which assets *are not revalued* in the chapters to come.

The **historical cost principle**—also called the **cost principle**—refers to measuring the financial statement items at their cost at the time of the transaction.

The **going-concern assumption** means that we will assume a company will continue to be in business in the future.

Recognizing Revenue and Expenses

When should revenue be included on an income statement? GAAP say when it is *earned*, that is when revenue is **recognized**. When Tom delivers a

To **recognize** revenue means to record it so that it will show up on the income statement.

shirt to a customer, Tom's Wear has earned the revenue. This is called the **revenue recognition principle**. When one of Tom's friends says he is going to buy a T-shirt next week, no revenue is recognized. In business, you do not count your chickens before they are hatched. When an exchange actually takes place, or when the earnings process is complete or "virtually complete," that is the time for revenue recognition. When Tom's Wear and a customer exchange the cash and the T-shirt, there is no doubt the transaction is complete. When Tom's Wear delivers the T-shirt and the customer agrees to pay for it later (the sale is on credit), we consider the earnings process virtually complete. Tom's Wear has done its part, and so the sale is included on the income statement.

The **revenue recognition principle** says that revenue should be recognized when it is earned.

What about expenses? When an expense is recognized depends on when the revenue that results from that expense is recognized. Expenses are recognized—included on the income statement—when the revenue they were incurred to generate is recognized. This is called the **matching principle**, and it is the basis of the income statement. Expenses are matched with the revenue they helped generate. An example is the cost of goods sold. Only the cost of the T-shirts *sold* is recognized—included as an expense on the income statement. The expense is matched with the revenue from the sale of those shirts. The cost of the unsold T-shirts is not an expense—and will not be an expense—until those shirts are sold. An expense is a cost that has been used to generate revenue. If a cost has been incurred but it has not been used up, it is classified as an asset until it is used. Prepaid insurance is an example of a cost that is classified as an asset until it is used; and when it is used, it becomes insurance expense.

The **matching principle** says that expenses should be recognized—shown on the income statement—in the same period as the revenue they helped generate.

Does the customer actually have to pay the company in cash before a sale can be counted as revenue? No. Note that the sales of all the shirts are included in the sales total, even though 15 of the shirts have not been paid for yet. When a customer purchases an item on credit, the earnings process is considered virtually complete, even though the cash has not been collected. Similarly, a cost incurred in the generation of revenue does not have to be paid to be included on the income statement. In calculating the revenue and expenses for an income statement, accountants do *not* follow the cash. Instead, they use the time when the "economic substance" of the transaction is complete.

Accountants use the expressions *virtually complete* and *economic substance* to describe the same idea—that a transaction does not have to be technically complete to recognize the resulting revenue. If the transaction is substantially complete, the revenue is recognized. When Tom's Wear sells the T-shirts, delivering them and receiving the customers' promise to pay is considered the economic substance of that transaction. Cash may come before the transaction is complete, or it may come afterward. This way of accounting for revenues and expenses—using the economic substance of the transaction to determine when to include it on the income statement instead of using the exchange of cash—is called **accrual accounting.**

Accrual accounting refers to the way we recognize revenues and expenses. We do not rely on the exchange of cash to determine the timing. We recognize revenue when it is earned and expenses when they are incurred—no matter when the cash is received or disbursed.

When to recognize revenue is easy for some businesses and extremely difficult for others. There is a lot of disagreement among accountants about revenue recognition. They agree that revenue should be recognized when the transaction is virtually complete—but they often cannot agree exactly when that has happened. This is another topic that you will learn more about in later chapters.

Exhibit 2–8 summarizes the characteristics of accounting information, both the qualities and the underlying principles.

Qualities of financial information	Basic assumptions and principles
Relevant	Entity assumption
Reliable	Going-concern assumption
Consistent	Unit-of-measure assumption
Comparable	Cost principle
Understandable	Revenue recognition principle
	Matching principle
	Accrual-based accounting
Benefit > Cost	

Exhibit 2–8
Summary of the Foundation for Accounting Principles

Accruals and Deferrals

Accrual Basis Accounting

L.O. 4

Understand accrual basis accounting and cash basis accounting and the differences between the two. Know that accrual basis accounting is GAAP.

The term *accrual basis accounting* includes two kinds of transactions in which the exchange of cash does *not* coincide with the economic substance of the transaction. The revenues and expenses are recognized at a time other than the time when the cash is collected or paid.

One kind of accrual basis transaction is an **accrual** and the other is a **deferral.** The meaning of each kind of accrual basis transaction is represented graphically in Exhibit 2–9.

An **accrual** transaction is one in which the revenue is earned or the expense is incurred before the exchange of cash.

A **deferral** transaction is one in which the exchange of cash takes place *before* the revenue is earned or the expense incurred.

When the action comes before the cash, it is an accrual. When Tom's Wear made a credit sale, it was an accrual transaction. To accrue means to "build up," or "accumulate." In accounting, we are building up our sales or our expenses even though the cash has not been exchanged. The sale is completed first—merchandise is delivered to the customer—and the cash payment will come later. Instead of receiving the asset *cash* from the purchaser, the company records an asset called *accounts receivable*—meaning cash due from the purchaser. Accounts receivable is the amount owed to the company by customers. Because GAAP are based on accrual accounting, the necessary part of the transaction for recording the revenue is the actual sale of goods or services, *not* the cash receipt from the customers.

When the dollars come before the action, it is called a *deferral.* When Tom's Wear paid for the insurance, it was an advance purchase—as we all have to pay insurance premiums up front, not after the expiration date of the policy. The amount paid for the insurance was not considered an expense until it was actually used. To defer something, in common language, means to put it off—to delay or postpone it. In the language of accounting, a deferral means that the company will postpone recognizing the expense until it is actually used. When Tom's Wear paid the cash in advance of the period covered by the insurance, the company had to record the cash disbursement. In other words, Tom's Wear recorded it in the business records as cash that had been spent. However, the expense was not recognized when the cash was paid. It will be recognized—and remember, that means included on the income statement—when the insurance is actually used.

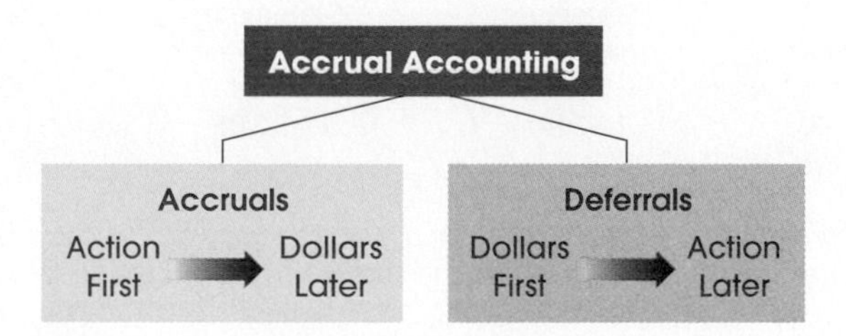

Exhibit 2–9
Accrual Accounting

Cash Basis versus Accrual Basis Accounting

Cash basis accounting is a system based on the exchange of cash. In this system, revenue is recognized only when cash is collected, and an expense is recognized only when cash is disbursed. This is not an acceptable method of accounting under GAAP.

There is another type of accounting called **cash basis accounting**—revenue is only recognized when the cash is collected, and expenses are recorded only when the cash is paid. This is *not* a generally accepted method of accounting according to the CICA. Using the exchange of cash as the signal for recognizing revenue and expense does not communicate the performance of the business in a way that allows us to evaluate its achievements. The cash flows are important, but alone they do not provide enough information for decision makers. This does not stop some businesses from using it as the basis of their own accounting records. Remember, some businesses are not required to follow GAAP. For example, farmers may use cash basis accounting. This means they recognize only the cash they receive as revenue. If they sell a product to an organization that has not yet paid for the product at the time an income statement is prepared, they would not include the expected proceeds as revenue for that income statement. That is not according to GAAP. If the farmers *were* following GAAP, they would count it as revenue and as a receivable (accounts receivable).

Accounting Periods and Cutoff Issues

Why does it matter—for accounting purposes—if there is a difference between the time when the goods or services are exchanged—that is, the economic substance of the transaction—and the time when the cash related to that transaction is received or disbursed? If a company makes a sale on credit and the cash is collected later, why does it matter *when* the sale is recognized—included as revenue on the income statement? Tom's Wear will help you get the answers to these questions.

When Tom began his business in 2005, he chose the calendar year as his company's fiscal year. Each of his annual income statements will cover the period from January 1 to December 31 of a specific year. It is important that what appears on the income statement for a specific year is *only* the revenue earned during those 12 months and *only* the expenses incurred to generate that revenue. What is included as a sale during the period? Accountants have decided to use the exchange of goods and services, not the cash exchange, to define when a sale has taken place. Expenses are matched with revenues, also without regard to when the cash is exchanged. This makes the financial statements of all companies that follow GAAP consistent and comparable.

Exhibit 2–10 shows the relationship between the balance sheet and the income statement and the time periods involved.

Exhibit 2–10
The Balance Sheet and Income Statement

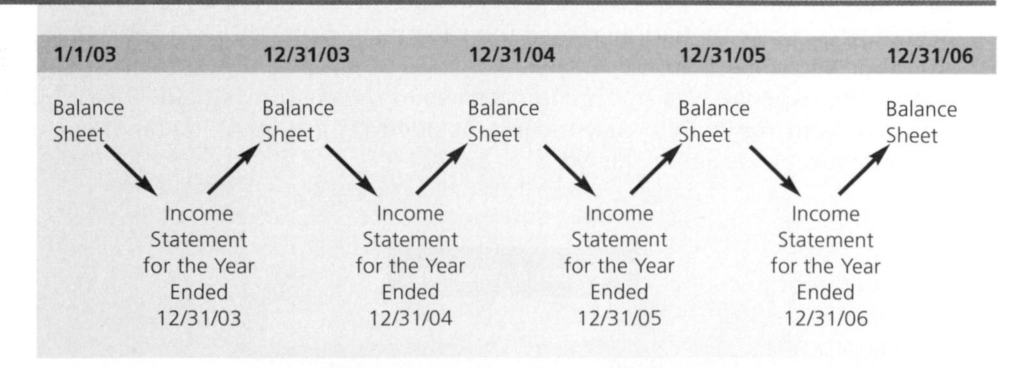

Every balance sheet presents the assets, liabilities, and owners' equity of a business firm at a moment in time. The income statement describes what happened between *two balance sheet dates.*

Recall, the balance sheet is a freeze-frame view of the assets, liabilities, and owner's equity on a specific date. For a company with a fiscal year-end on December 31, that is the date of the balance sheet. Remember, the end-of-the-year balance sheet for one year becomes the beginning-of-the-year balance sheet for the next year. When you are out celebrating New Year's Eve, nothing is happening to the balance sheet. When Tom goes to sleep on December 31, 2005, the cash on the December 31, 2005, balance sheet of Tom's Wear is exactly the amount of cash that the company will have on January 1, 2006. So, the final balance sheet for one year simply rolls forward to the next year.

Then, transactions start happening—exchanges take place. The revenues and expenses for the period of time are shown on the income statement. The income statement covers a period. A company may construct weekly, monthly, quarterly, or annual financial statements. Many companies prepare monthly and quarterly financial statements; *all* companies prepare annual financial statements. The income statement for a specific year gives the revenues and expenses for that year. It gives information about how the balance sheet has changed between the beginning of the year and the end of the year. The revenues increase owner's claims; expenses reduce owner's claims. If the difference between revenues and expenses is positive—if revenues are greater than expenses—the company has a net income. If the expenses are greater than revenues, the company has a net loss. The net income or net loss is sometimes called the *bottom line*.

STUDY BREAK 2-2

See How You're Doing

1. What is the difference between cash basis and accrual basis accounting?
2. What are the three basic elements of the balance sheet? Define each.
3. What is the matching principle?

More about the Financial Statements

Investors—Owners and Creditors

Owners and creditors are both considered investors in a business. Both invest their money to *make* money, and they both take a **risk** in investing their money in the business. *Risk* is the uncertainty associated with *the amount* of future returns and *the timing* of future returns. Some investments are riskier than others. For example, when a bank makes a loan to a company, the banker evaluates the ability of the company to repay the loan amount (the principal) plus interest (the cost of borrowing the money). If the bank makes a loan to a company that does not do well enough to repay the debt, the company may have to sell noncash assets to raise cash to pay off the loan plus interest due. When lending money, the bank must compare the risk with the expected return.

Financial statements provide information about the **risk** related to investing in a company. Will you get a good return on your investment? How long will it take?

Most often, the risk and return of an investment change value in the same direction—we say they are positively correlated. **Positively correlated** means they move in the same direction—higher risk means higher expected return for taking the higher risk; lower risk means lower expected returns. For higher investment risk, the potential for a higher return is needed to attract investors.

The term **positively correlated** describes values or amounts of two items that move in the same direction.

Investing in a company as an owner is riskier than investing as a creditor. A creditor's claim to the assets of a company has priority over an owner's claim. (Creditors have first "dibs" to the assets.) If a company has just enough money either to pay its creditors or to make a distribution to its owner or owners, the creditors *must* be paid, and they *always must be paid* before anything—if there is anything left—is distributed to the owners. That translates into less risk for a creditor. The owner's risk is that the company will go out of business.

However, the owner, who takes more risk, has the right to share the profit. So, the risk for the owner is accompanied by the potential for a higher return.

A creditor, on the other hand, will never receive more than the amount of the loan plus the amount of interest that is agreed on when the loan is made.

Financial information is useful for someone deciding whether or not to invest in a company. Suppose Tom's Wear wanted to borrow money to expand. A bank would want to examine Tom's Wear's income statement, balance sheet, and the cash flow statement. The reason is to evaluate potential risk—the company's ability to make the required principal and interest payments.

The balance sheet shows a company's assets and who has claim to them. A bank loan officer would use the information on the balance sheet to evaluate Tom's Wear's ability to repay the loan. He would want to be sure that the company did not have too many debts. The more debt a company has, the more cash it must generate to make the loan payments.

The information on the balance sheet would not be enough to assure the bank loan officer that Tom's Wear would be able to repay the loan. Because a loan is repaid over several months or years, information about the future earning potential of the business is important. Studying the past performance of a

Managing Cash—Planning Inflows and Outflows

In this chapter, you have learned that financial statements are prepared on an accrual basis, but that does not mean cash is not important. As a matter of fact, cash budgeting is one of the most important activities a company performs. The starting point for avoiding a cash crisis is to develop a comprehensive cash flow budget. Smart business owners develop annual or multi-year cash flow projections to make sure they can meet ongoing business needs. Business owners also prepare and use *historical* cash flow statements to gain an understanding about where all the cash came from and where all the cash went.

By estimating your cash inflows and outflows, you can:

- Make sure you have enough cash to purchase sufficient inventory for planned sales.
- Take advantage of purchase discounts and special offers.
- Plan equipment purchases, repairs, and replacements.
- Be prepared for any financing you may need in periods of cash shortages—short-term credit line, small loans, or long-term debt.
- Increase your chances of success in meeting your obligations.

For a new or growing business, accurate cash flow projections can make the difference between success and failure. For an ongoing business, good cash budgeting can make the difference between moving forward and standing still.

How do you prepare a cash flow budget? According to the Business Owner's Toolkit (www.toolkit.cch.com/text/P06_4300.asp), preparing a cash flow budget involves a number of steps. First, you estimate your cash inflows. Cash is generated primarily by sales. But in lots of businesses, some of the sales are *on account* (charge accounts, term payments, lay-away, trade credit). So, you have to estimate when those credit sales will turn into actual cash inflows. Then, you estimate all the cash disbursements you have to make and *when* you have to make them.

How much detail you include in your cash flow projections depends on the complexity of your business. Using a computerized spreadsheet for your cash flow projections can make the process much faster and more accurate. You can enter formulas for the subtotals and totals to eliminate common addition and subtraction errors. You will also be able to easily develop "what-if" scenarios to help you prepare for variation from your estimates.

The goal of cash budgeting is to always have enough cash to keep your business running smoothly. If it turns out that you have more cash than you need, then you will have to figure out how best to use that extra cash—most likely how best to invest it. That is a cash flow problem that you want!

business helps predict its future performance. That makes the profit the company earned during the past year relevant to the banker. Details about the sales revenue and expenses incurred to generate that revenue would help the bank evaluate the company's potential to generate enough cash to repay a loan.

Still, the information on these two financial statements, no matter how relevant to the bank's evaluation, would not be enough. Another piece of the puzzle is the way the company manages its cash. A company may have little debt and lots of earning potential. However, if the company does not have enough cash, the loan payments cannot be made. Because cash collection is the bank's primary concern, the cash flow statement provides additional information for the bank.

An Example to Illustrate the Kind of Information Financial Statements Provide

Let us compare two companies, each starting its fiscal year with identical balance sheets. Both use GAAP. Then, during the first month of the year, they have very similar transactions. We will only look at a few of the transactions, and we will see that their income statements for the month are the same. As you study the example, try to figure out why their income statements are the same. Their ending balance sheets and cash flow statements are not the same. Where do the differences show up in the financial statements?

The two companies are Clean Sweep and Maids-R-Us. Both are cleaning businesses and both are sole proprietorships. Judy Jones owns Clean Sweep, and Betty Brown owns Maids-R-Us. On January 1, 2006, the two companies have identical balance sheets. Look at each item on the balance sheet in Exhibit 2–11, and be sure you know what it means. Do this before you go on.

Let us take each transaction and look at its effect on the accounting equation. Follow along using Exhibits 2–12 and 2–13.

Exhibit 2–11
Beginning Balance Sheet for Clean Sweep and Maids-R-Us

Balance Sheet
At January 1, 2006

Assets	
Cash	$ 900
Supplies	200
Total assets	$1,100
Liabilities	
Notes payable	$ 400
Owner's equity	
Owner, Capital	700
Total liabilities and owner's equity	$1,100

Exhibit 2–12
Transactions for January 2006 for Clean Sweep and Maids-R-Us

Both Clean Sweep and Maids-R-Us	Clean Sweep	Maids-R-Us
1. Clean 10 houses for a fee of $75 per house.	Collects the fees in cash at the time the services are rendered.	Agrees to extend credit to the customers. Fees will be collected within 30 days.
2. Make a loan payment plus interest.	Pays off the entire loan plus $40 interest.	Pays only $100 of the loan plus $40 interest.
3. Count the supplies on January 31 and find $25 worth left on hand.	Both will make an adjustment to show $175 worth of supplies used.	

Exhibit 2–13 Effects of Transactions on Accounting Equation

	Clean Sweep							
	Assets		=	Liabilities		+	Owner's equity	
Balance sheet at January 1, 2006 →	Cash Supplies	$ 900 200	=	Notes payable	$400	+	Capital	$ 700
	Clean Sweep: Transactions for January:							
1- Performs services for $750, collected in cash	Cash	$ 750					Revenue	$ 750
2- Pays off the note plus interest of $40	Cash	$(440)		Notes payable	$(400)		Interest expense	$ (40)
3- Adjustment for supplies used during the month	Supplies	$(175)					Supplies expense	$(175)
Balance sheet at January 31, 2006 →	**Cash** **Supplies** **Total**	**$1,210** **25** **$1,235**	=		**0**		**Capital**	**$1,235**

(Continued)

Transaction 1: Both companies earn $750 worth of revenue. Clean Sweep collects the cash, but Maids-R-Us extends credit to its customers. Clean Sweep records the asset *cash,* while Maids-R-Us records the asset *accounts receivable.* Both companies have earned the same amount of revenue, so each will show $750 revenue on its income statement for the month.

Transaction 2: Both companies make a loan payment. Clean Sweep pays the entire amount of the note payable, $400, plus interest of $40. Maids-R-Us pays only $100 of principal on the note payable, plus interest of $40. The only expense in this transaction is the interest expense of $40. Both companies have incurred the same amount of interest expense, so each will show $40 expense on its income statement. The repayment of the principal of a loan does not affect the income statement.

Adjustment: At the end of the period, both companies will record supplies expense of $175, leaving $25 as supplies-on-hand on the January 31 balance sheet. Both income statements will show supplies expense of $175.

We can construct an income statement for each company from the numbers in the owner's equity column in Exhibit 2–13. Because there were no distributions to the owner during the period, all the items in that column will be included in the calculation of net income. Revenues for the month of January amounted to $750; expenses were $215; and so net income was $535. This is the case for both companies as shown in Exhibit 2–14. Even though one company extended credit to its customers and the other collected cash for its services, the income statements are identical. The income statement is only concerned with revenues earned and expenses incurred, not with the timing of the related cash flows.

Exhibit 2–13 *(Continued)*

Maids-R-Us		Assets	=	Liabilities		+	Owner's equity	
Balance sheet at January 1, 2006 →	Cash Supplies	$ 900 200	=	Notes payable	$400	+	Capital	$ 700
Maids-R-Us: Transactions for January:								
1- Performs services for $750 on account	Accounts receivable	$ 750					Revenue	$ 750
2- Pays $100 of the note plus interest of $40	Cash	$ (140)		Notes payable	$(100)		Interest expense	$ (40)
3- Adjustment for supplies used during the month	Supplies	$ (175)					Supplies expense	$ (175)
Balance sheet at January 31, 2006 →	Cash Accounts receivable Supplies Total	$ 760 750 25 $1,535	=	Notes payable	$300	+	Capital	$1,235

The balance sheet at January 31 for each company can be constructed by simply organizing the details of the ending equation for each company in Exhibit 2–13. For a sole proprietorship, all owner's equity—shared and earned—is lumped together and called owner's capital. The two balance sheets are shown in Exhibit 2–15. Note the differences. Assets and liabilities are different for the two companies, but the owner's equity amounts are the same.

It is important to understand why both companies have the same amount of owner's equity. Both had beginning equity of $700 plus net income for the month of $535, for a total of $1,235. That is the number we find on the January 31 balance sheet for owner's equity. The timing of cash receipts and disbursements does not affect owner's equity.

Finally, let us look at the cash flow statement. As you have seen, the cash receipts and disbursements for the two companies were *not* the same. This shows up clearly on the cash flow statement. The cash flow statement for each company shows all the cash received and all the cash disbursed for the month. The cash flow statements are shown in Exhibit 2–16.

Exhibit 2–14
Income Statement for Clean Sweep and Maids-R-Us for January

Income Statement for the Month Ended January 31, 2006		
Revenue		
Cleaning fees		$750
Expenses		
Supplies	$175	
Interest	40	
Total expenses		215
Net income		$535

Exhibit 2–15 Balance Sheet for Clean Sweep and Maids-R-Us at January 31, 2006

Clean Sweep Balance Sheet at January 31, 2006

Assets		**Liabilities and Owner's equity**	
Cash	$1,210		
Supplies	25	Capital, Jones	$1,235
Total assets	$1,235	Total liabilities and owner's equity	$1,235

Maids-R-Us Balance Sheet at January 31, 2006

Assets		**Liabilities and Owner's equity**	
Cash	$ 760	Notes payable	$ 300
Accounts receivable	750		
Supplies	25	Capital, Brown	1,235
Total assets	$1,535	Total liabilities and owner's equity	$1,535

Exhibit 2–16 Cash Flow Statements for Clean Sweep and Maids-R-Us

Clean Sweep
Cash Flow Statement
For the Month Ended January 31, 2006

Cash from operating activities		
Cash collected from customers	$750	
Cash paid for interest	(40)	
Total cash from operations		$710
Cash from investing activities		0
Cash from financing activities		
Repayment of loan	(400)	
Total cash from financing		(400)
Net increase in cash		$310

Maids-R-Us
Cash Flow Statement
For the Month Ended January 31, 2006

Cash from operating activities		
Cash paid for interest	$(40)	
Total cash from operations		$ (40)
Cash from investing activities		0
Cash from financing activities		
Repayment of loan	(100)	
Total cash from financing		(100)
Net increase (decrease) in cash		$(140)

Putting It All Together—The Objectives of Financial Statements and the Information in Statements of Clean Sweep and Maids-R-Us

Financial information should be useful. What makes it useful is the way the transactions of the business are organized into the four basic financial statements:

1. The income statement
2. The statement of retained earnings
3. The balance sheet
4. The cash flow statement

The ongoing life of a business is broken down into discrete periods so that performance can be evaluated for a specific period. For our cleaning business, the period we use is a month.

- Income is measured in a way that captures the economic substance of earning revenue and incurring expenses; it is not based on cash collections and cash disbursements. Note that the net incomes for Maids-R-Us and Clean Sweep for January are exactly the same in spite of the differences in when the cash is collected and disbursed. Those timing differences are reflected on the balance sheet by the differences in cash and both receivables and payables; and differences are also shown on the cash flow statement—the statement that provides the details of the timing of cash receipts and disbursements. The four statements have been designed to be relevant, reliable, consistent, comparable, and understandable.

In addition to these qualities, accounting information relies on several basic assumptions and principles, as shown in Exhibit 2–8. Let us relate each of the assumptions and principles to the financial statements of Maids-R-Us.

- The separate entity assumption means that only the business transactions of Maids-R-Us are shown in the financial statements—none of the owner's personal transactions are included.
- The going-concern assumption means that we may assume that Maids-R-Us is an ongoing, viable business. According to GAAP, if it were not ongoing, the company would have to have all its assets appraised and listed at liquidation value.
- The unit of measure assumption means everything shown is measured in monetary units, here dollars.
- The cost principle means that the items on the financial statements are valued at cost. For example, the supplies on the balance sheet are *not* valued at what they might be worth if resold or at the current cost, which might be higher than the amount that Maids-R-Us paid for them. They are valued at the price Maids-R-Us paid when they were purchased.
- The revenue recognition principle means that the revenue on the income statement has been earned. It may not have been collected, but the work of earning it has been completed.
- The matching principle means that related revenues and expenses should be on the same income statement. Only the supplies that are used to earn the revenue during the period are counted as *supplies expense*. The unused supplies are reported on the balance sheet until they are actually used.

Accrual accounting is an accounting system in which the measurement of income is *not* based on cash receipts and cash disbursements. Instead, revenue is included in the calculation of income when it is earned, and expenses are included as they are matched to revenue. Timing differences between the economic substance of a transaction and the related cash flows do not affect income. That is why both companies have the same net income, even though the timing of the cash flows is different.

Applying Our Knowledge: Ratio Analysis

One activity every business must perform is paying its bills. Investors, bankers, and other interested parties often want to evaluate a company's ability to meet its current obligations. Simply looking at how much cash a company has does not provide enough information. There is a financial ratio—a comparison of different amounts on the financial statements—that measures the short-term financial health of a company. It is called the **current ratio**, computed by dividing the total amount of current assets by the total amount of current liabilities. You learned earlier in this chapter that current assets are assets that will be used up or converted to cash in the next year and that current liabilities are obligations that will be settled with current assets. So, the current ratio gives information about the company's ability to pay its bills.

Business Process

The **current ratio** equals *current assets* divided by *current liabilities*, and it measures a company's ability to pay its current bills.

The current ratio provides a way to compare the liquidity of one company—that is, a measure of how easily a company can turn its current assets into cash to pay its debts as they come due—with that of other companies of different types and sizes. It also provides information about the liquidity of a single company over time.

Look at the balance sheet for Danier Leather for the years ending June 28, 2003, and June 29, 2002, shown in Exhibit 2–17.

The current ratio for the fiscal year ending June 28, 2003, is:

$$\frac{46{,}899}{10{,}559} = 4.44$$

The current ratio for the fiscal year ending June 29, 2002, is:

$$\frac{44{,}154}{10{,}552} = 4.18$$

The increase in the current ratio from 2002 to 2003 indicates an increase in the company's liquidity. Looking at the current ratio for two consecutive years gives some information about Danier Leather, but you would need much more information to reach any conclusions. As you learn more about financial statements, you will learn additional ratios and several ways to analyze a company's financial statements.

Exhibit 2–17
Consolidated Balance Sheets for Danier Leather Inc. and Subsidiaries

Courtesy Danier Leather Inc.

(Thousands of Dollars)

Assets	**June 28, 2003**	**June 29, 2003**
Current Assets		
Cash	$ 7,254	$ 3,777
Accounts receivable	600	484
Income taxes receivable	83	—
Inventories (Note 2)	37,029	38,662
Prepaid expenses	889	603
Future income tax asset (Note 8)	1,044	628
	46,899	44,154
Other Assets		
Capital assets (Note 3)	34,246	31,199
Goodwill (Note 4)	342	342
	$81,487	$75,695
Liabilities		
Current Liabilities		
Accounts payable and accrued liabilities	$10,559	$10,472
Income taxes payable	—	80
	10,559	10,552
Deferred lease inducements	2,238	1,837
Future income tax liability (Note 8)	696	784
	13,493	13,173
Shareholders' equity		
Share capital (Note 6)	23,995	23,917
Retained earnings	43,999	38,605
	67,994	62,522
	$81,487	$75,695

Business Risks

Now that we have discussed the general characteristics of accounting information and the four basic financial statements, let us take a look at how companies make sure the information in those statements is reliable from a user's perspective. The risks associated with financial information are often called information processing risks and, like all risks, companies try to minimize them.

Internal Controls—Definition and Objectives

Internal controls are the policies and procedures that the managers of a firm use to protect the firm's assets and to ensure the accuracy and reliability of the firm's accounting records. Internal controls are a company's rules to help it keep its assets safe and to make sure its financial records are accurate. By adhering to those rules, a firm minimizes the risks of being in business. These rules are called *internal* controls because they are put in place and controlled within the company. Controls imposed from outside the firm—laws and regulations, for example—are not internal controls because they are not rules that originated in the company.

Internal controls are a company's policies and procedures to protect the assets of the firm and to ensure the accuracy and reliability of the accounting records.

Special Internal Control Issues Related to Financial Statements

Accountants are particularly concerned with the financial statements. Whether you are involved in preparing them or using them to make decisions, you must have confidence that the information in them is accurate and reliable. When you see *cash* on a company's balance sheet, you should be confident this is actually the amount of cash the company had on the balance sheet date. The *sales* shown on the income statement should be sales that have been completed—goods delivered to the customers.

Inaccurate information creates enormous problems. Regulators have been especially concerned with the information contained in the financial statements. For example, Livent Inc. was investigated by the SEC (Securities and Exchange Commission) in the United States, the OSC (Ontario Securities Commission) in Canada, and the RCMP (Royal Canadian Mounted Police) for fraud and accounting irregularities. One of the main causes of the alleged fraud cited by the SEC was "the absence of adequate internal controls."

Think about a company's accounting information system in terms of inputs, processing, and outputs, as shown in Exhibit 2–18. As you look at this diagram, consider the accounting exercises and problems presented in this book. An end-of-chapter problem provides the transaction data—that is, the input. Your task is to organize and to manipulate—that means to process—the data. You have been using the accounting equation work sheet to help organize and process the data. Then you take the organized information and prepare the four basic financial statements—they are the output of the process. Can you think of any controls to make sure you are processing the information and preparing the output without errors? One control is to check your answer with the answers provided at the end of the book. This would be a detective control—one to help you detect any errors.

Inputs to our information system include data describing the transactions of the business. We want only correct information to get into the system, and we want to be sure it is accurate and complete. Examples of controls (**input controls**) to help manage the risk that the information will be fictitious, erroneous, or incomplete are:

Input controls are controls that help manage risk associated with the possibility that information will be fictitious, erroneous, or incomplete.

Exhibit 2–18
An Accounting Information System

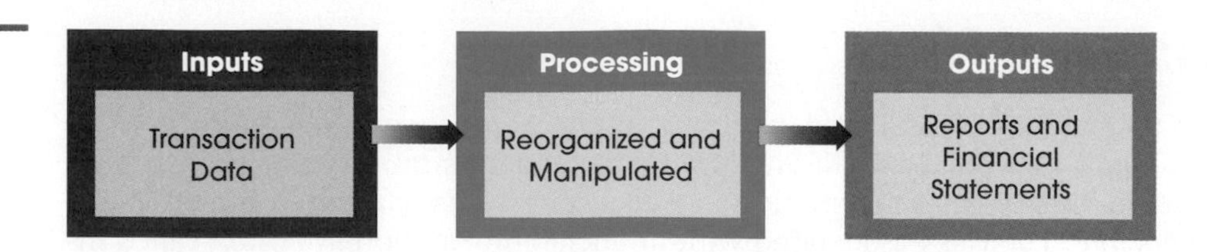

1. *Authorization requirements for certain transactions and for certain inputs*—Have you ever waited at the grocery store to have your cheque approved? Often, a supervisor is required to review the information and put initials on the cheque to indicate approval.
2. *Design and use of adequate documents*—If cashiers have keyed in an incorrect price for an item, they often add it to a correction slip with a list of all the other overcharged or undercharged items erroneously rung up. That corrections slip is one document that helps in keeping accurate information.
3. *Limited access to assets*—To get the cash drawer open, cashiers must enter their personal password, identifying who had access to the cash drawer and when.
4. *Sound personnel policies*—Only certain employees are allowed to run a checkout station. Specific training is necessary.

Processing controls are controls related to the storage and manipulation of data.

Processing controls are related to the storage and manipulation of the data. As you can see from the following examples, some controls apply to more than one area. For example, *sound personnel duties* is a control that is necessary to the input, processing, and the output of any information system. Similarly, *limited access* is necessary in all parts of the system. Examples of processing controls are:

1. *Segregation of duties*—Employees who physically control an asset (like cash) should not keep the records related to that same asset.
2. *Documentation controls* (written guidelines and procedures)—Employees need to know exactly what procedures to follow to do their jobs.
3. *Reconciliation and cross-checking*—When the bank sends a monthly statement, it should be compared with the company's cash account, and any differences should be investigated.
4. *Restrictions programmed into computerized systems*—Computerized systems have the ability to incorporate controls at many levels. Passwords are **access controls**. There are also restrictions on the size of an input into a program. For example, a computer may be programmed to accept only sales amounts under $1,000. For larger sales, a supervisor would need to be called to give direct personal approval.

Access controls are controls related to all business risks associated with protecting the system from unauthorized access.

Output controls are controls related to the accuracy and completeness of a system's output.

Output controls are related to the accuracy and completeness of the system's output. The output will only be as good as the input and processing. If there is something wrong with either the input or the processing, then the output will be unreliable. However, there are specific controls that apply only to the output:

1. *Periodic review of output*—Each week, a sales manager might ask for a list of the previous week's sales for each member of the sales force. The manager would review the output to make sure the system is reporting accurate amounts. One way to catch errors of omission would be to have salespersons review their own individual performance from the prior week.
2. *Internal audit*—A large company will often have a staff of accountants whose only job is to review and evaluate the company's accounting infor-

mation system. They are called internal auditors. Even though they are company employees, their tasks require them to be independent of the daily operations of the accounting information system.

3. *External audit*—External auditors are accountants hired by the company to verify the fairness of the financial statements. The auditors do not guarantee that there are no errors, but they do work hard to make sure that there is nothing misleading on the financial statements. Auditing firms are often hired for special tasks in addition to auditing the financial statements. They may be hired to review and improve a company's internal control system, analyze its inventory management, review its credit and collection policies, or any number of other business consulting jobs.

To be effective, a system of internal control must rely on the people who perform the duties assigned to them. An internal control system is only as effective as the people who execute it. Human error, collusion, and changing conditions can all weaken a system of internal control.

Understanding Excel

The following is a copy of Tom's Wear statement of retained earnings as presented in this chapter.

Tom's Wear, Inc.
Statement of Retained Earnings
For the Month Ended February 28, 2005

Beginning retained earnings	$ 385
Net income for the month	935
Dividends	(100)
Ending retained earnings	$1,220

For purposes of this problem only, assume that in the month of March:

- Tom's Wear issued additional common shares for a $1,000 contribution.
- Total revenue for the month was $2,560.
- Total expenses for the month were $1,150.
- Tom was paid a dividend of $150.

Requirements

1. Open a new Excel work sheet.
2. By beginning in cell A1, input appropriate heading lines for a statement of retained earnings.

   Hint: Highlight the cells to be centred and click the Merge and Center button to centre your heading lines across columns A to C. Each line must be centred separately. (The second line will appear in full after your column widths are increased.)
3. By beginning in cell A5, input the lines of the statement. Adjust the column width of A as needed. (Remember to use the dragging or double-click method from Chapter 1.)
4. Input the appropriate dollar amounts and the appropriate totals in column B. Always use formulas when you calculate totals. For example, ending retained earnings = B5 + B6 – B7.

   Hint: Instead of typing your formulas, try the click method. Click on cell B8 and type "=". Click on cell B5, type "+", click on cell B6, type "–", click on cell B7 and hit enter.
5. Format the appropriate cells with $ by clicking the cells and the Currency Style button. Format the other numbers using the Comma Style button. Highlight all the numbers and click the Decrease Decimal button twice to round the numbers to whole dollars.
6. Underline or double underline the appropriate cells by selecting Format, Cells, and Border.
7. Print your file and save it to disk. Name your file TomsWear2.

Summary of Chapters 1 and 2

- A business is started when investors are willing to risk their money to start a business—to provide something of value for customers and to make a profit. The investors may be owners or creditors.
- Investors, vendors, customers, and governmental agencies require financial information about businesses. There are four basic financial statements that provide the information: the income statement, the balance sheet, the statement of retained earnings, and the cash flow statement.
- The financial statements are based on a set of rules called generally accepted accounting principles (GAAP). These rules are not exact. As you learn more about accounting, you will see that the numbers on the financial statements are not exact.
- To make the financial statements useful, we need to understand the rules and the choices used to construct them.
- The accounting equation,

  Assets = Liabilities + Owner's Equity

  is the basis of the balance sheet. It is a freeze-frame picture of the business at a specific point in time.
- The income statement, statement of retained earnings, and cash flow statement present details about the information on the balance sheet. Each of the other statements covers the period between the dates of two consecutive balance sheets.
- Accounting according to GAAP is accrual based. That means that revenues are recognized when they are earned, not when the cash is collected. Costs are matched to revenues so that they are recognized—put on the income statement as expenses—at the same time as the revenues they helped generate.
- Accrual accounting consists of two types of transactions—accruals and deferrals—in which the exchange of cash takes place at a different time from the exchange of goods or services.
- With accruals, the action takes place before the exchange of cash. An example is a credit sale. The sale is recorded, but the cash will be collected later. Remember, *accrue* means "to build up." When Tom's Wear makes a sale on account, the company *builds up* sales, even though the cash has not been collected yet.
- With deferrals, the dollars are exchanged before the action occurs. An example is paying for something in advance. When Tom's Wear paid for the insurance in advance, that was a deferral. Remember, *defer* means "to postpone." When Tom's Wear's purchases insurance in advance, prepaid insurance, the company postpones recognition of the expense. The action, in this case, is the passing of the time to which the insurance applies.
- Adjustments are made before financial statements are prepared. The amounts recorded throughout the year may need to be adjusted to make sure they accurately reflect the assets, liabilities, owner's equity, revenues, and expenses on the date of the statements. How we actually adjust the amounts to correctly reflect the financial position of a company depends on how we keep track of our business transactions.

Answers to Study Break Questions

STUDY BREAK 2-1

1. The purpose of financial statements is to provide information useful for decision making.
2. The Accounting Standards Board (ACSB) of The Canadian Institute of Chartered Accountants (CICA).
3. The focus of financial reporting is investors and creditors (see top of page 48).

STUDY BREAK 2-2

1. The difference between cash basis and accrual basis accounting is the timing of recognizing revenues and expenses. Cash basis accounting recognizes revenue when the cash is collected and expenses when cash is disbursed. In accrual accounting, revenues are recognized in the period in which they are earned (by the completion of the work) and expenses are matched to the revenues they help create.
2. The basic elements of the balance sheet are:
   - Assets—items of future value to a business, used to produce revenue.
   - Liabilities—creditor's claims to the assets of a company; the company's obligations to creditors.
   - Equity—owner's claims to the assets of the firm.
3. The matching principle is an accounting rule that states that expenses should be included on the income statement in the same period as the revenues they helped generate.

Questions

1. What is the difference between *cash basis* accounting and *accrual basis* accounting?
2. What are the four basic financial statements?
3. Who has the responsibility for setting accounting standards?
4. What is the AcSB? What does it do?
5. Which financial statement pertains to a single moment in time?
6. What is an *asset*? A *liability*?
7. What is the *separate entity assumption*?
8. Explain *materiality,* and give an example.
9. What is a *deferral*?
10. What is an *accrual*?
11. What is the *cost of goods sold*?
12. What does *recognize* mean in accounting?
13. Does a company have to collect the money from a sale before the sale can be recognized?
14. Define the *matching principle* and give an example.
15. What does *representational faithfulness* mean?
16. Describe *cost-benefit* analysis.

Short Exercises

SE2-1 Give the accounting principle, assumption, constraint, or information characteristic that is most applicable to each of the following: L.O. 2

- All items purchased (except inventory) for less than $25 are expensed as incurred—even if they will last longer than a year.
- Personal transactions of the owner are kept separately from business transactions.
- The company uses the same inventory method from period to period.

SE2-2 Give the accounting principle, assumption, constraint, or information characteristic that is most applicable to each of the following: L.O. 1

- Equipment is recorded as an asset and expensed over the periods in which it is used.
- The company prepares financial statements regularly.
- When insurance is purchased in advance, it is recorded as an asset.
- Assets like inventory are valued in dollars, not units, for the financial statements.

L.O. 1

SE2-3 For each of the following, give the accounting principle that is best described:

a. Buffalo Company reports revenue when it is earned instead of when the cash is collected.
b. The land on the Mule Company balance sheet is valued at what it cost, even though it is worth much more.
c. Lion Corp. recognizes amortization expense for a computer over five years, the period in which the computer is used to help generate revenue for the business.
d. The president of Cougar Company thought that it would help the company's balance sheet to include as an asset some land he and his wife personally own. The accountant rejected this idea.

L.O. 2

SE2-4 For each of the following numbered items, select, from the given lettered list, the qualitative characteristics described.

a. Relevance
b. Reliability
c. Comparability
d. Consistency
e. Representational faithfulness

1. It is imperative for providing comparisons of a firm from period to period.
2. Two primary qualities make accounting information useful for decision making.
3. Companies in the same industry often use the same accounting methods.
4. A financial statement should not be biased in what is reported.
5. If combining two assets on the balance sheet would be misleading to users, then they should not be combined.

L.O. 3

SE2-5 For each item that follows, tell whether it is an asset, a liability, or an equity item.

a. Prepaid insurance
b. Accounts receivable
c. Share capital
d. Notes payable
e. Cash
f. Equipment
g. Accounts payable
h. Supplies
i. Inventory

L.O. 3

SE2-6 On which financial statement would you be most likely to see each of the following?

a. Sales revenue
b. Salary expense
c. Prepaid insurance
d. Cash from operations
e. Common shares
f. Inventory

L.O. 3

SE2-7 Cost as a basis of accounting for assets has been severely criticized. Give several pros and cons for this practice.

L.O. 4

SE2-8 Suppose Deer Company performed services for a client on account on March 12, 2006. Deer charged the client $1,500. The client paid for half of the services on March 28, 2006. The remaining balance was paid on April 5, 2006. How did these transactions affect Deer's March 31, 2006 financial statements?

SE2-9 Millie's Moped, Inc. purchased inventory in December 2007 for $60,000 cash. The company sold merchandise that cost $20,000 in December 2007 and the remainder in January 2008. What is the cost of goods sold for December 2007 and for January 2008 if Millie's uses GAAP? What is the cost of goods sold for December 2007 and for January 2008, if Millie's Moped uses cash basis accounting?

L.O. 4

SE2-10 Suppose two companies are identical except for their credit policy. Both use GAAP. One company allows cash sales only, whereas the other sells for cash or credit. Suppose the two companies have the same sales revenue and expenses for the year. The only difference between the two is that the first company has no outstanding accounts receivable, whereas the second has quite a few still outstanding at year-end. Of the four basic financial statements, which one or ones will be different between these two companies? Explain how and why they are different.

L.O. 4

Exercises

E2-1 One of your friends started a business in 2008. At the end of the first year, December 31, 2008, he has prepared the following income statement. Give three examples from the statement that indicate the statement is not prepared according to GAAP.

L.O. 1

Sales	$3,400
Inventory purchases	(2,000)
Rent for 2008 and 2009	(1,000)
Cash on hand	5,000
Due from customers	500
Nct Incomc	$5,900

E2-2 Your car has broken down, so you have decided to look for a replacement. You find an advertisement on the Internet for a used Miata. When you contact the owner, this is what you find:

L.O. 2

1. The car is a 2004 model.
2. The owner said he has used the car only for driving to and from work.
3. The odometer reading is 45,389 kilometres.
4. The owner says that he has had the oil changed every 5,000 to 6,000 kilometres since he bought the car new.
5. The owner says this is the best car he has ever owned.
6. The owner will provide a maintenance record prepared by a licensed mechanic.

Evaluate each item from the preceding list in terms of its *relevance* to the decision about whether to buy this car. Then, evaluate each item with respect to its *reliability*. What additional documentation or supporting evidence would you want for your decision?

E2-3 On which financial statement would you be most likely to see each of the following? Tell whether each is an *asset, liability, owner's equity, revenue,* or *expense*.

L.O. 3

a. Unearned revenue
b. Salary expense
c. Prepaid insurance
d. Share capital
e. Distributions to owners
f. Equipment
g. Sales revenue
h. Cost of goods sold
i. Cash from investing activities
j. Amortization expense
k. Inventory

L.O. 3

E2-4 Ed's Boat Company reported the following information in its records for 2007:

Net income	$ 5,000
Sales	85,000
Beginning balance—retained earnings	26,000
Cost of sales	55,000
Dividends	2,000

a. If the sales revenue given is the only revenue for the year, what were Ed's expenses other than those just listed?
b. Describe what the beginning balance of $26,000 for retained earnings means. Is this useful information for potential investors?
c. What is the balance of retained earnings at the end of 2007?

L.O. 3

E2-5 Listed next are elements of the financial statements discussed in this chapter. Match each element with the descriptions (use each as many times as necessary) that follow:

a. Assets
b. Liabilities
c. Owner's Equity
d. Revenues
e. Expenses

1. ______ Debts of the company
2. ______ Economic resources with future benefit
3. ______ Inflows of assets from delivering or producing goods or services
4. ______ Things of value a company owns
5. ______ The residual interest in the assets of an entity that remains after deducting its liabilities
6. ______ What the company has minus what it owes
7. ______ The owner's interest in the company
8. ______ Probable future sacrifices of economic benefits
9. ______ Outflows or other using up of assets from delivering or producing goods and services
10. ______ Costs that have no future value
11. ______ What the company owes
12. ______ Sales

Problems—Set A

L.O. 2, 3

P2-1A The following cash transactions took place during March, the first month of business for Cats and Dogs Company:

1. D. C. Dawg started a business, Cats and Dogs Company, by contributing $6,000.
2. The Cats and Dogs Company borrowed $2,000 from the bank on March 1. The note is a one-year, 12-percent note, with both principal and interest to be repaid on February 28 of next year.
3. The company earned $900 in revenue.
4. Expenses amounted to $650.
5. Distributions to owners amounted to $25.

Required:

a. Show how each affects the accounting equation.
b. Give one additional piece of information related to the transaction that could be recorded in an information system for a purpose other than the financial statements.
c. Prepare the four basic financial statements for the month of March.

P2-2A Alligator Company started the year with $1,000 in cash and share capital. During 2006, the Alligator Company earned $3,600 of revenue on account. The company collected $2,400 cash from accounts receivable and paid $3,100 cash for operating expenses.

L.O. 3, 4

Required:

a. What happened to total assets (increase or decrease and by how much)?
b. What is the cash balance on December 31, 2006?
c. What is the total owner's equity on December 31, 2006?
d. What is net income for the year?

P2-3A The Brown Bear Company entered into the following transactions during 2009:

L.O. 4

- Brown Bear was started as a corporation with a $5,000 cash contribution from the owners.
- Supplies amounting to $400 were purchased on account.
- Sales on account amounted to $3,200.
- Cash collections of receivables amounted to $2,500.
- On November 1, 2009, the company paid $1,200 in advance for an insurance policy.
- Supplies on hand as of December 31, 2009 amounted to $100.

Required:

a. How would the adjustment to record the supplies expense affect the accounting equation?
b. If the insurance policy covered one year and the policy began on the date of payment, what is the amount of prepaid insurance that would appear in the asset section of the Brown Bear December 31, 2009, balance sheet?
c. What is the amount of cash flow from operations for 2009?
d. What would be the amount of total liabilities appearing on the Brown Bear December 31, 2009, balance sheet?
e. What is the amount of share capital as of December 31, 2009?

P2-4A Use the following information for Elephant Company *for the year ended December 31, 2008,* to answer the following questions. Assume that the shareholders made no new contributions to the company during the year.

L.O. 3, 4

Revenues for 2008 = $350
Net income for 2008 = $110
Beginning balance (*December 31, 2007,* balance) in retained earnings = $140
Ending balance (*December 31, 2008,* balance) in retained earnings = $200
Total liabilities and shareholders' equity at *December 31, 2008* = $600
Total liabilities at *December 31, 2007* = $60
Total liabilities at *December 31, 2008* = $50

Required:

a. What were the Elephant Company's total expenses during 2008?
b. What was the amount of the dividends during 2008?
c. What is the total that owners invested in the Elephant Company as of *December 31, 2008*?
d. What were total assets on the company's *December 31, 2007,* balance sheet?

P2-5A ABC Company was started a year ago by Terry Lions. Early in 2009, when Terry went to the local bank for a loan, the banker asked for the December 31, 2008, financial statements. Terry had no idea how to prepare the statements, but she had heard of income statements and balance sheets. The statements she prepared follow:

L.O. 1, 2, 3

ABC Company Income Statement Prepared on April 1, 2009	
Net revenues	$6,757
Cost of goods sold	4,967
Operating expenses	1,397
Prepaid expenses	930
Accounts payable	300
Salaries payable	100
Accounts receivable	2,345
Net earnings	$ 393

ABC Company Balance Sheet Prepared on April 1, 2009			
Accounts payable	$ 300	Accounts receivable	$ 235
Cash	21,500	Other revenue	1,406
Short-term investments	165	Salary expense	600
Inventories	15,270	Other current assets	990
Other current liabilities	145	Long-term liabilities	1,000
Long-term assets	416		

Required:

a. For each statement, give four examples that indicate Terry has not followed GAAP in the preparation of the statement.

b. What characteristics of financial statements described in the chapter do you think are missing in Terry's statements? If you were the banker, what would you tell Terry?

Problems—Set B

L.O. 2, 3

P2-1B Given the following transactions:

1. Megan Moore's Aunt Myrtle May willed her an old bakery shop. Megan decided to open a pastry shop, Sugar & Spice, by contributing $7,500 on May 1, 2006.
2. The Sugar & Spice Pastry Shop borrowed $6,000 from the bank on May 1. The note is a one-year, 10-percent note, with both principal and interest to be repaid on April 30, 2007.
3. Megan paid $2,000 to rent equipment for the shop for the month.
4. The electricity and water bills for the month were $850, paid in cash.
5. The Sugar & Spice Pastry Shop was a hit and earned $5,500 in revenue the first month, all cash.
6. Since the Sunny Susan Tanning Salon closed, Megan hired her friend to be the customer service specialist for the pastry shop. The salary expense was $425, paid for one month.
7. Learning little from her friend Sunny Susan's business failure, Megan withdrew $560 for a shopping spree to celebrate her business's early success.

Required:

a. Show how each transaction affects the accounting equation.

b. Give one additional piece of information related to the transaction that could be recorded in an information system for a purpose other than the financial statements.

c. Prepare the four basic financial statements for the month of May.

P2-2B Candy Confection Company had $2,500 in cash and share capital when it began its fiscal year on July 1, 2009. During the 2009–2010 fiscal year, the Candy Confection Company earned $6,200 of revenue on account. The company collected $3,700 cash from accounts receivable and paid $2,800 cash for operating expenses. At the end of the year, the company bought a new delivery van for cash of $2,100.

L.O. 3, 4

Required:

a. What happened to total assets (increase or decrease and by how much) during the fiscal year?
b. What is the cash balance on June 30, 2010?
c. What is the total owner's equity on June 30, 2010?
d. What is net income for the year ended June 30, 2010?

P2-3B The Green Emerald Magazine Co. entered into the following transactions during 2008:

L.O. 4

- Green Emerald Magazine Co. was started with a $6,100 cash contribution from the owner.
- There were $750 of supplies purchased on account.
- Magazine sales, all on account, amounted to $7,200.
- Cash collections of receivables amounted to $3,900.
- On March 1, 2008 the company paid $3,600 in advance for an insurance policy.
- Supplies on hand as of December 31, 2008 amounted to $325.
- The owner withdrew $400.

Required:

a. How would the adjustment to record the supplies expense affect the accounting equation?
b. If the insurance policy covered two years and the policy began on the date of payment, what is the amount of prepaid insurance that would appear in the asset section of Green Emerald Magazine on the December 31, 2008, balance sheet; what amount of insurance expense would appear on the income statement for the year ended December 31, 2008?
c. What is the total cash flow from financing activities for 2008?
d. What would be the amount of total liabilities appearing on Green Emerald Magazine's December 31, 2008, balance sheet?
e. What is the amount of capital on December 31, 2008?
f. What would be the amount of total assets appearing on Green Emerald Magazine's December 31, 2008, balance sheet?

P2-4B Use the following information for Monster Mania for the year ended June 30, 2009, to answer the questions below. Assume that the shareholders made no new contributions to the company during the year.

L.O. 3, 4

Revenues for the year ended *June 30, 2009* = $850
Net income for the year ended *June 30, 2009* = $370
Beginning balance (*June 30, 2008,* balance) in retained earnings = $280
Ending balance (*June 30, 2009,* balance) in retained earnings = $360
Total liabilities and shareholders' equity at *June 30, 2009* = $725
Total liabilities at *June 30, 2008* = $80
Total liabilities at *June 30, 2009* = $40

Required:

a. What were Monster Mania's total expenses during the year ended June 30, 2009?
b. What was paid to shareholders during the year ended June 30, 2009?
c. What is the total that owners invested in the Monster Mania as of June 30, 2009?
d. What were total assets on Monster Mania's June 30, 2008, balance sheet?

P2-5B Yakity Yak Company hired a new, inexperienced accountant to prepare its annual income statement. Use the following income statements for the questions below:

L.O. 1, 2, 3

Yakity Yak Company
Income Statement
For the Year Ended December 31

	2008	2007
Sales	$9,723,334	$9,346,911
Cost of goods sold	(6,365,857)	(6,375.651)
Gross margin	3,357,477	2,971,260
General and administrative expenses	(2,460,338)	(2,286,917)
Property, plant, and equipment	23,501	1,740,030
Operating income	920,640	2,424,373
Interest expense	(78,297)	(68,528)
Other income, net	51,037	59,265
Accounts payable	(72,623)	(63,616)
Accounts receivable	11,002	—
Income before income taxes	831,759	2,351,494
Income taxes payable	(371,000)	(305,000)
Net income	$ 460,759	$ 2,046,494

Required:

a. Give four examples that show the statements were not prepared according to GAAP.

b. What characteristics of financial statements described in the chapter do you think are missing in these statements?

Issues for Discussion

Financial statement analysis

1. Use the annual report from CoolBrands to answer these questions:
   - **a.** Does CoolBrands have a single or a multistep income statement? How can you tell?
   - **b.** Does CoolBrands have a classified balance sheet? How can you tell?
   - **c.** Calculate the current ratio for the two most recent fiscal years. What information does this provide?
   - **d.** Is there any evidence that the information in these financial statements is reliable and verifiable?

Business risk

2. In the CoolBrands annual report, find at least two references to the risks that CoolBrands faces.
3. What evidence can you find in the annual report that CoolBrands has controls in place to minimize information processing risks?

Ethics

4. R&R Equipment Company is preparing its annual financial statements in anticipation of applying for a loan. During the last week of the year, R&R received a shipment of inventory but has not paid for it. The invoice indicates R&R owes $5,000 for the purchase. The owner of R&R, Randy Ray, has decided to omit this asset and the related liability from the year-end balance sheet, reasoning that it is acceptable because he is omitting both of them, which means there is no difference in the equity.

   What is your opinion of Randy's reasoning? Discuss circumstances under which Randy's decision would be acceptable under GAAP and circumstances under which it would definitely be unacceptable.

Internet Exercise: Globeinvestor.com and High Liner Foods Inc.

Globeinvestor.com, a part of Bell Globemedia Publishing Inc., offers information about companies, industries, investments, and related news items. For researching a company, this website is a good place to start gathering basic information.

Please go to the Globeinvestor website: http://www.globeinvestor.com
Enter the stock symbol for High Liner Foods Inc. (HLF) and you will be presented with information on the most recent price for the shares of High Liner.

IE2-1 Click on Company Snapshot.

a. What type of company is High Liner?
b. Where are High Liner shares traded?
c. List three of High Liner's competitors.

IE2-2 Scroll down to the Annual Financials.

a. For the most recent year, list the amounts reported for revenue and net income. Does the amount reported for revenue represent cash received from customers during the year? If not, what does it represent?
b. Locate High Liner's most recent financial statements (Click on the link to the company website or click on "News" under "Find Out More"). What does the amount reported for cost of goods sold represent? Is High Liner a profitable company? How can you tell?
c. For the most recent year, list the amount reported for inventories. Does this amount represent cost or market value? This complies with which generally accepted accounting principle (GAAP)?
d. For the most recent year, list the amounts reported for total assets, total liabilities, and total (owner's) equity. Does the accounting equation hold true? Are assets primarily financed with liabilities or equities?
e. Does High Liner use accrual basis or cash basis accounting? How can you tell?

Please note: Internet websites are constantly being updated. Therefore, if the information is not found where indicated, please explore the website further to find the information.

CHAPTER

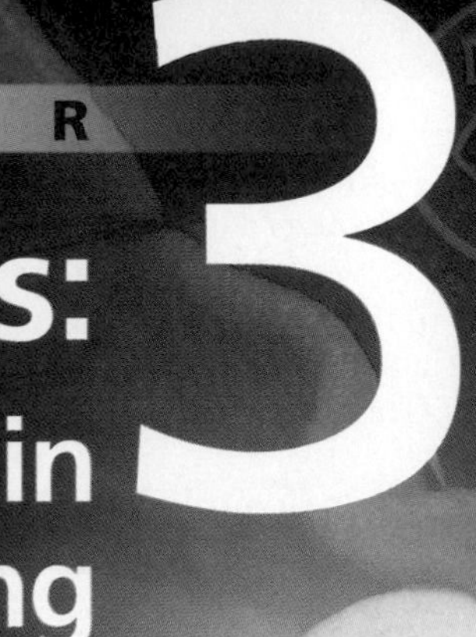

Accruals and Deferrals: Timing Is Everything in Accounting

Here's where you've been...

In Chapter 2, you studied the qualities of the information contained in the financial statements. This information should be *useful*. You also found that GAAP require *accrual basis accounting*—revenues are recognized when earned, and expenses are matched to those revenues.

Here's where you're going...

From Chapter 3, you should be able to understand how the financial statements show transactions in which the exchange of the cash and the exchange of goods and services happen at different times. These are *accruals* and *deferrals*.

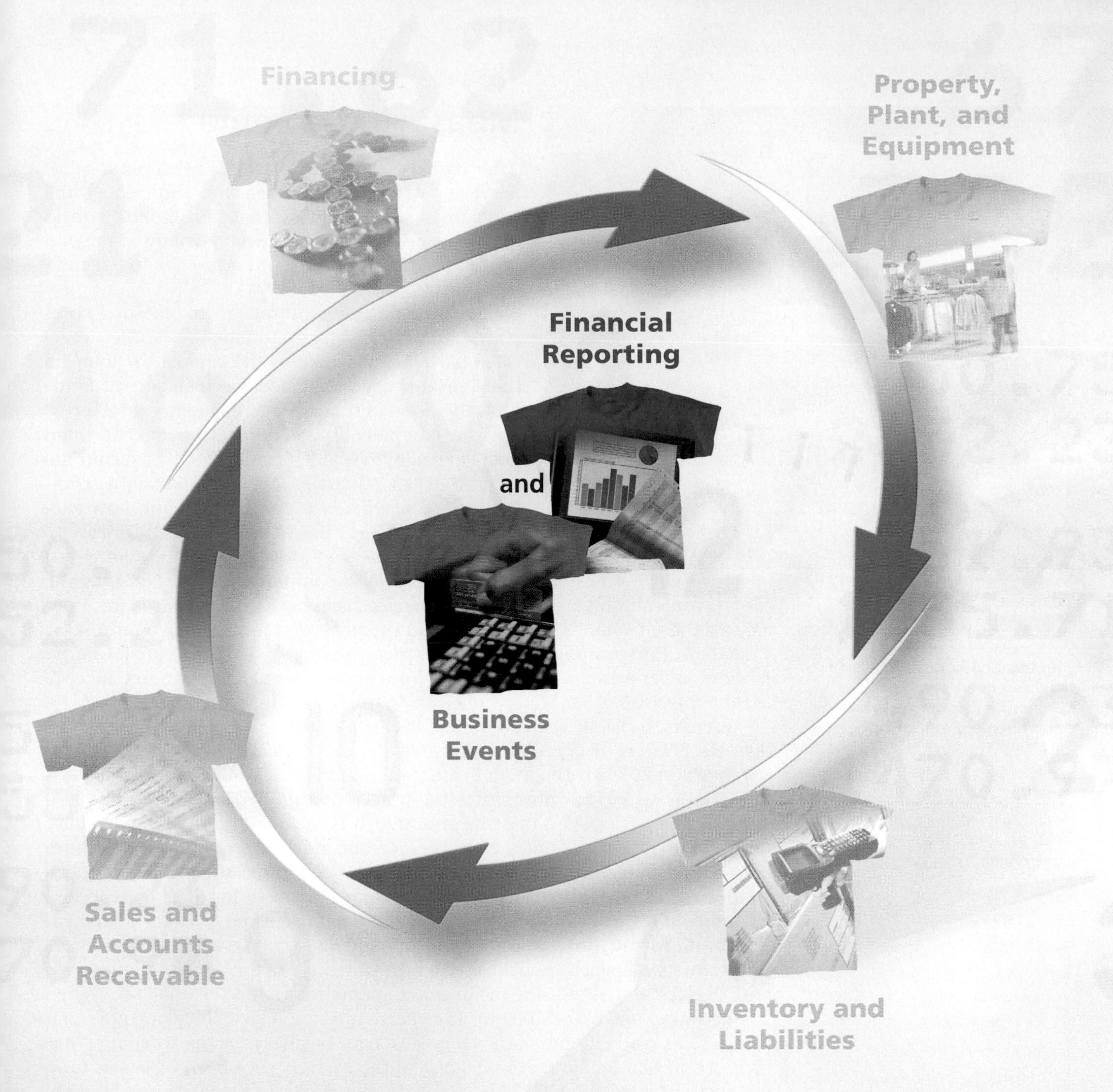

Learning Objectives

More specifically, when you are finished studying this chapter, you should be able to answer these questions:

1. What are accruals, and how do they affect the financial statements?
2. What are deferrals, and how do they affect the financial statements?
3. What are adjustments, when are they made, and why are they necessary?
4. How do you construct the basic financial statements from a given set of transactions that include accruals and deferrals?

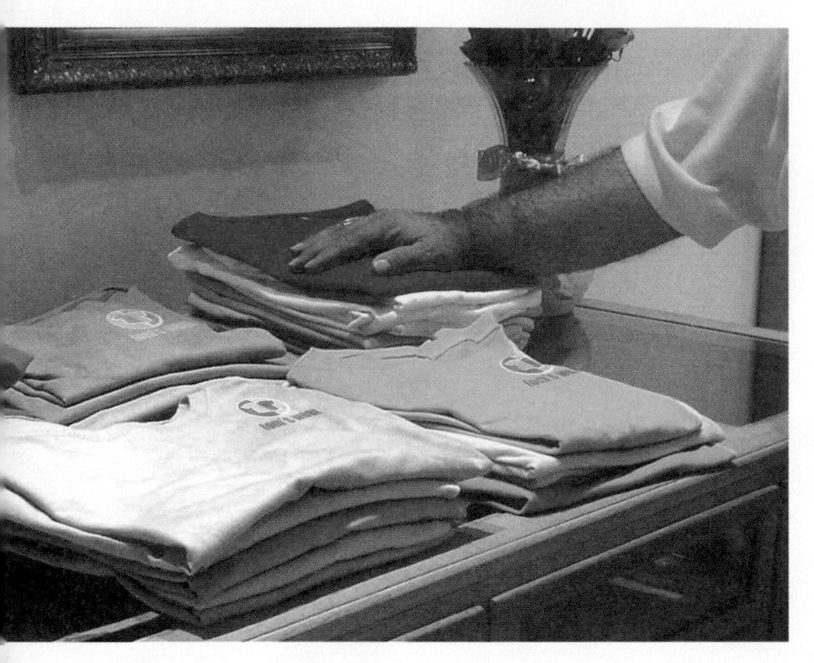

Measuring Income

After its first month, Tom's Wear prepared a set of financial statements to measure and report the company's activity during that first month, and to measure and report its financial position at the end of that month. Tom did both again for the second month.

At different points of time in the life of a company, owners, investors, creditors, and other interested parties want to know the company's financial position and accomplishments—to make all kinds of evaluations and decisions, including whether or not the company is meeting its goals. The main goal is usually to make a profit—so, measuring the profit that the company has made during a specified period plays a big role in evaluating how successfully a company has been doing its business.

L.O. 1, 2

Understand how income is measured, especially how accruals and deferrals affect the measurement of income.

Net income equals all revenues minus all expenses for a given period. Also known as the **bottom line**.

Net income, net profit, or net earnings all mean the same—a company's profit. Net income, the most commonly used term, summarizes revenues and expenses for a period of time, usually a year. It can also be measured for a week, a month, or a quarter. For example, many companies provide quarterly financial information to their shareholders. That information would include net income for the *quarter*.

We can consider the continuous life of a business as being composed of discrete periods of time—months, quarters, or years. The way we divide the revenues and expenses among those time periods is a crucial part of accounting. That is why timing is everything in accounting. If revenue is earned in a certain time period, you must be sure that it is included on the income statement for that period—not the one before and not the one after. If you have used some supplies during a period, then you need to include the cost of those supplies as part of the expenses on the income statement for that same period.

Sometimes, you will see the income statement referred to as the *statement of operations* and other times as the *profit and loss statement*. However it is referred to, it will usually appear as the first statement in a company's annual report. Exhibit 3–1 shows the income statements for Danier Leather Inc. When you see sales of $175,487,000 for the year ended June 28, 2003, you know that *all* the sales made in that fiscal year—a year of business for the company—are included in that amount, even if some of the cash has not been collected from the customers by June 28, 2003. Similarly, the expenses listed are only the expenses incurred in that fiscal year, whether or not the company has paid for those expenses by June 28, 2003. Danier Leather has worked hard to get the amounts right.

The problems created by the differences between

- the time when a company earns revenue by providing a product or service to customers and the time when the cash is collected from the customers, and
- the time when the company incurs an expense and the time when the company pays for the expense

Timing differences refer to the difference between the time a transaction occurs and the time the cash is exchanged.

are referred to as **timing differences**. You will see in this chapter how to identify timing differences and present them on the financial statements.

As discussed in the previous chapter, you can think of the timing problems in accounting in two simple ways:

Exhibit 3–1
Revenue and Earnings
Courtesy Danier Leather Inc.

Danier Leather Inc.
Consolidated Statements of Earnings
For the Years Ended

(thousands of dollars, except per share amounts)	June 28, 2003	June 29, 2002
Revenue	$175,487	$179,977
Cost of sales (Note 7)	88,788	92,098
Gross profit	86,699	87,879
Selling, general and administrative expenses (Note 7)	77,390	69,264
Earnings before interest and income taxes	9,309	18,615
Interest expense—net	66	461
Earnings before income taxes	9,243	18,154
Provision for income taxes (Note 8)		
Current	4,353	7,314
Future	(504)	115
	3,849	7,429
Net earnings	$5,394	$10,725

- action before dollars
- dollars before action

An example of action before dollars is a sale made *on account*. A customer buys on credit and agrees to pay later. The action of making the sale—the economic substance of the transaction—takes place before dollars are exchanged in payment. This type of transaction—action first, dollars later—is called an **accrual.**

An **accrual** is a transaction in which the action comes before the exchange of cash.

An example of dollars before action is when a firm buys insurance. By its nature, insurance must be purchased in advance of the time period to which it applies. Payment—when the dollars are exchanged is made first, and the use of the insurance—the action provided by insurance protection—comes later. Dollars first, action later is called a **deferral.**

A **deferral** is a transaction in which the exchange of dollars comes before the action.

For timing differences, whether accruals or deferrals, we must look at the accounting information on each side of the difference and adjust it before it can be presented on the financial statements.

Accruals

L.O. 1

Understand accruals, how the related adjustments are made, and how they affect the financial statements.

When the substance of a business transaction takes place before any cash changes hands, you include that transaction in the measurement of income. That is, if you have earned it, you must include it as revenue on the income statement. If you incurred an expense to earn that revenue, you must also include that expense on the income statement. Accruals can pertain to both revenues and expenses. There are two types of accruals that need a closer look:

- interest revenue and interest expense
- other revenue and expense

Accruals for Interest Expense and Interest Revenue

The most common timing difference has to do with interest related to borrowing or lending money. When you borrow money, you pay for the use of that money. What you pay is called interest. If you borrowed $500 from a bank on January 1, 2006, and agreed to repay it with 8 percent interest on January 1,

2007, you would have to pay back a total of $540. On January 1, 2006, when you borrow the money, you get the $500 cash, an asset, and you increase your liabilities. The accounting equation is increased on both sides by $500.

Assets	=	Liabilities	+	Shareholders' equity	
				Share capital	Retained earnings
+$500 Cash		+$500 Notes payable			

When you get ready to prepare the financial statements for the year ending December 31, 2006, you see that this liability—notes payable—is still on the books and will be listed on the balance sheet. The reason why is that on December 31, 2006, you still owe the bank the full amount of the loan. What about the $500 cash you received? You may still have it, but it is more likely you spent it during the year to keep your business running. That is why you borrowed it.

What about the cost of borrowing the money—the interest expense? On December 31, 2006, one full year has passed since you borrowed the money. The passing of time has caused interest expense to be incurred.

- Interest expense is the cost of using someone else's money.
- Time passing is the action related to interest expense.

Although the action of using someone else's money during the year has taken place, the dollars have not been exchanged—the interest for using that money. To make the December 31, 2006, financial statements correct, you must show the interest expense of $40 (= $500 × 8%, or $500 × 0.08) on the income statement. Also, you must show—on the balance sheet—the obligation called interest payable. It is a liability, indicating the bank's claim to the $40 as of December 31, 2006. The liability section of the balance sheet will show both the $500 loan and the $40 interest.

Assets	=	Liabilities	+	Shareholders' equity	
				Share capital	Retained earnings
		+$40 Interest payable			$(40) Interest expense

Making an adjustment for a transaction in which the action has occurred but the cash has not yet changed hands is called **accruing** the revenue or expense.

The adjustment increases liabilities and decreases retained earnings in the accounting equation. *Making* this adjustment is called accruing interest expense; the expense itself is called an accrual. Sometimes, a company will label the amount of interest expense accrued as accrued liabilities or accrued expenses instead of interest payable. Each expression means the same thing—interest expense that will be paid in the future.

Suppose you borrowed the $500 on July 1, 2006 (instead of January 1). In this case, you would have use of the money for only half the year and therefore would have incurred only half a year's interest expense as of December 31, 2006. Remember the formula for interest:

Interest = Principal × Rate × Time

Interest = Principal × Rate × Time

Interest rates, like the 8 percent annual interest, always pertain to one year. As of December 31, 2006, the interest payable on the note would be $500 × 0.08 × 6/12 or $20. The last part of the formula gives the time as a percentage of a year, or the number of months out of 12. Whenever you have to accrue interest, you must be careful to count the months that apply. That will help you make sure you put the right amount of interest expense on the income statement for exactly the period of time you had use of the borrowed money.

If you borrowed the $500 on January 1, 2006, for one full year, what would happen when you pay the bank on January 1, 2007? On one side of the accounting equation, you will reduce cash by $540. The equation will be balanced by a reduction of $500 in notes payable plus the reduction of $40 in interest payable. *There will be **no** expense recorded when you actually pay the cash.* Remember, the action has already taken place and the action resulted in interest expense in 2006. There is no interest expense in 2007 because you paid off the loan on January 1, 2007.

This is how timing differences work. The expense is recorded in one period, but the cash is paid in another period.

Assets	=	Liabilities	+	Shareholders' equity	
				Share capital	Retained earnings
$(540) Cash		$(500) Notes payable $(40) Interest payable			

Receivables with Interest

In most of our examples, a company will be borrowing money; however, sometimes, a company lends money to another company or to an employee. A company that lends money accrues interest *revenue* during the time the loan is outstanding. The amount of interest revenue accrued at the time an income statement is prepared is calculated with the same formula used to calculate interest *expense*, I = P × R × T. The amount of interest revenue will increase assets—interest receivable—and will increase shareholders' equity—via interest revenue.

Suppose a company loaned $200 to an employee on October 1 at 10 percent interest, to be repaid on January 1 of the following year. The transaction on October 1 decreases assets—cash—and also increases assets—receivables. Because we use the term *accounts receivable* to describe amounts *customers* owe the company, we call the amounts owed by others—meaning anyone who is not a customer—**other receivables**.

Other receivables are amounts owed to a company by people and companies other than customers.

Assets	=	Liabilities	+	Shareholders' equity	
				Share capital	Retained earnings
$(200) Cash +$200 Other receivables					

On December 31, the company will accrue interest revenue. Why? Because some time has passed and interest revenue has been earned during that period. With interest, the action is the passage of time, and so the action has taken place, but the cash will not change hands until the following January 1. You would record interest revenue of $5 (= $200 × 0.10 × 3/12). You would also record interest receivable of $5. By doing all this, then the financial statements would accurately reflect the following situation on December 31:

- The company has earned $5 of interest revenue as of December 31.
- It has not been received at December 31.

Because all revenues increase retained earnings, the interest revenue will be recorded under retained earnings in the accounting equation:

Assets	=	Liabilities	+	Shareholders' equity	
				Share capital	Retained earnings
+$5 Interest receivable					+$5 Interest revenue

When the company actually receives the cash for the interest on January 1, along with repayment of the $200 principal, it will not be recorded as interest revenue. Instead, the total $205 cash is recorded as an increase in cash and a decrease in the asset other receivables by $200 and the asset interest receivable by $5. The timing difference resulted in recording the interest revenue in one period and the cash collection in another.

Assets	=	Liabilities	+	Shareholders' equity	
				Share capital	Retained earnings
+$205 Cash $(200) Other receivables $(5) Interest receivable					

STUDY BREAK 3-1

See How You're Doing

1. If you borrowed $1,000 at 7 percent (interest rates are always assumed to be ***per year***), how much interest would you pay for having that money for only six months?
2. If you have an outstanding loan and you record interest expense before you actually make the cash payment for the interest, is this an accrual or a deferral? Why?
3. Why would a company record interest expense or interest revenue before any cash is exchanged?

Accruals for Other Revenues and Expenses

There are other types of revenues and expenses that must be accrued at the end of the period so that the financial statements will accurately reflect the business transactions for the period. For example, if you have provided services for a customer during 2008 but have not recorded those services (perhaps because you have not billed the customers yet), you want to be sure to record the revenue on the 2008 income statement. Why record this on the 2008 income statement? Because the action was completed in 2008. You cannot record any cash received for this action in 2008—because you have not received payment in 2008 as a result of your action in 2008. This is a timing difference, recorded as an accounts receivable.

Accrued revenue and receivables are often paired together in accruals. An increase in assets—accounts receivable—and an increase in shareholders' equity—revenue—both in the same amount, balance the accounting equation. Then, when the cash is actually collected, it is not recognized as revenue because it was already recognized in a previous period. That is, receipt of the cash in the following year is not recognized as revenue because the revenue was already recognized in the prior year.

Look at the current asset section of the Van Houtte Inc. balance sheet at March 29, 2003—in Exhibit 3–2. It shows accounts receivable amounting to $33,652,000. This is a significant amount of money! When you see receivables on a company's balance sheet, it means the related revenues have been earned and included on the income statement even though the cash has not been collected yet.

Expenses may also need to be accrued. When you get to the end of an accounting period—that is, when you want to prepare financial statements—you examine your records and business transactions to find any expenses that might have been incurred but not recorded. These are the expenses you have not paid for yet. (If you paid for them, you would have recorded them when you gave the cash to pay for them.) When you receive a bill for some expenses like utilities, you likely will record the expense and the related accounts payable. If you have done that, you will not have to accrue it at the end of the period.

However, there are some typical expenses that companies do not record until the end of the period. These expenses have to be accrued. The most common is salary expense. Typically, you record salary expense when you pay your employees. (In the accounting equation, this transaction would reduce assets—cash—and reduce retained earnings via salary expense.) What do you do if the end of an accounting period does not coincide with payday? What you need to do is record the salary expense for the work that your employees have done since the last time you paid them. *You want to be sure to get the correct amount of salary expense on the income statement for the period.* This accrual will increase liabilities—salaries payable—and decrease retained earnings via salaries expense. The action—the employees performing the work—has already taken place; but the cash will not be exchanged until the next payday, which will be in the next accounting period.

Suppose you are preparing the financial statements for the accounting period ending on December 31, 2008. That date is Wednesday. If you pay your employees every Friday, the last payday of the year is December 26, 2008. As of December 31, 2008, you will owe them for their work done on Monday, Tuesday, and Wednesday, December 29, 2008, through December 31, 2008. You will need to record the salary expense for those three days, even though you will not pay the employees until Friday, January 2, 2009. Recording this salary expense so that it is recognized on the correct income statement is called **accruing salary expense**. This adjustment will increase liabilities—salaries payable—and decrease shareholders' equity—by increasing salary expense.

Recording and recognizing salary expense that will be paid to employees at a later date is called **accruing salary expense.**

Exhibit 3–2
Accounts Receivable
Courtesy Van Houtte Inc.

From the Balance Sheet of Van Houtte Inc. at March 29, 2003

Assets *(in thousands of dollars)*	
Current assets	
Cash	$ 9,148
Accounts receivable	33,652
Income taxes receivable	2,230
Inventories *(Note 8)*	24,402
Prepaid expenses	3,685
Future income taxes *(Note 5)*	1,585
	$74,702

What happens when January 2, 2009, arrives and you actually pay the employees? You will pay them for the week from December 29, 2008, through January 2, 2009. The expense for three of those days—December 29 through December 31—was recorded on December 31, 2008, so that it would be on the income statement for the fiscal year ending December 31, 2008. The expense for the other two days—January 1, 2009, and January 2, 2009—has not been recorded yet. The expense for those two days belongs on the income statement for the fiscal year ending December 31, 2009. When you pay the employees on January 2, 2009, you will reduce liabilities—the amount of the salaries payable you recorded on December 31, 2008, will be taken out of your accounting records—and you will reduce shareholders' equity—by recording salary expense for those two days in 2009.

Putting numbers in an example should help make this clear. Suppose the total amount you owe your employees for a five-day workweek is $3,500. Look at the calendar in Exhibit 3-3—we are interested in the week beginning December 29.

On December 31, you need to accrue three days worth of salary expense. The $3,500 applies to five days, but you need to look at it as $700 per day. To accrue the salary expense for three days, you increase the liability salaries payable and decrease retained earnings via salary expense by $2,100. Why are you recording the salary expense and salaries payable, even though you are not paying your employees until January 2? Because you want to have the expense for those three days on the income statement for the year ending *December 31, 2008*. How does this adjustment affect the accounting equation? Both the income statement and the balance sheet are affected by this accrual.

Assets	=	Liabilities	+	Shareholders' equity	
				Share capital	Retained earnings
		+$2,100 Salaries payable			$(2,100) Salary expense

On January 2, when you actually pay the employees for an entire week, you will give them cash of $3,500. How much of that amount is expense for work done in the year 2008, and how much is expense for work done in 2009? We already know that $2,100 is expense for 2008. The other two days' worth of work done and salary earned—$1,400—applies to 2009. Here is how the transaction on January 2—paying the employees for a full week of work—affects the accounting equation:

Assets	=	Liabilities	+	Shareholders' equity	
				Share capital	Retained earnings
$(3,500) Cash		$(2,100) Salaries payable			$(1,400) Salary expense

Exhibit 3-3
Calendar for Accruing Salaries

Monday	Tuesday	Wednesday	Thursday	Friday
December 22	December 23	December 24	December 25	December 26
December 29	December 30	December 31	January 1	January 2
January 5	January 6	January 7	January 8	January 9

Cash is reduced; salaries payable is reduced; and retained earnings is reduced via salary expense.

Review the example and make sure you know why the adjustment on December 31 was necessary and how the amount was calculated.

STUDY BREAK 3-2

See How You're Doing

Suppose ABC Company pays its employees a total of $56,000 on the 15th of each month for work done the previous month. ABC generally records salary expense when the employees are paid. If the ABC fiscal year-end is June 30, 2008, does any salary expense need to be accrued at year-end? If so, how much?

Deferrals

L.O. 2

Understand deferrals, how the related adjustments are made, and how they affect the financial statements.

The word *defer* means "to put off or to postpone." In accounting, a deferral refers to a transaction in which the dollars have been exchanged before the economic substance of the transaction—the action—has taken place. It can refer to both revenues and expenses. As you read and study the examples that follow, remember that you are taking the point of view of the business.

Deferrals Related to Revenue

A **deferral** is a transaction in which the cash is received before the action takes place. The cash has to be recorded, but the related revenue or expense is deferred. When we adjust that deferral to recognize any portion that may no longer need to be deferred, we are really *undoing* a deferral.

Suppose a company decides to sell items on the Internet. The man who owns the company is a conservative fellow who is not too sure about this new way of doing business, and so he decides that he will not ship the products until he has received a customer's cheque and it has cleared the bank. When the company receives a cheque for $80 for an order, the owner must defer recognition of the revenue until the items are shipped. However, he immediately deposits the cheque. Technically, he does not have claim to the cash until he ships the items he sold. In fact, the claim to the cash belongs to the customer at the time the company receives and deposits the cheque. Here is how this cash receipt affects the accounting equation:

Assets	=	Liabilities	+	Shareholders' equity	
				Share capital	Retained earnings
+$80 Cash		+$80 Unearned revenue			

Unearned revenue is a liability. It represents the amount of goods or services that a company owes its customers. The cash has been collected, but the action of earning the revenue has not taken place.

Unearned revenue is a balance sheet account—a liability. It represents amounts a company owes to others—customers. This is called a deferral because the company is putting off the recognition of the revenue—that is, not showing it on the income statement—until the revenue is actually earned. Note that the name of this liability is a bit unusual. It has the word *revenue* in it, but it is *not* an income statement account.

When the items sold are actually shipped, the company will recognize the revenue. This will be done by decreasing unearned revenue and increasing shareholders' equity via revenue. Here is how the accounting equation will be affected:

Assets	=	Liabilities	+	Shareholders' equity	
				Share capital	Retained earnings
		$(80) Unearned revenue			+$80 Revenue

Note that the claim has changed hands—the claim no longer belongs to the customer. Now that the items have been shipped, the owner has claim to the assets.

Another common example of deferred revenue is magazine subscriptions. Customers pay the company in advance, and so the dollars are exchanged before the action—delivery of the magazine—takes place. When the customers pay, the cash must be deposited, but the revenue is not recognized. If the magazine company prepares a balance sheet after receiving the cash but before the magazines are actually delivered (therefore, the revenue has not been earned), the balance sheet will show the cash and the obligation to the customers—the liability called *unearned revenue*. That obligation will be removed from the balance sheet when the magazines are delivered.

The Thomson Corporation, a large corporation that provides access to information databases to lawyers, accountants, academics, scientists, and business professionals, calls its unearned revenue *deferred revenue*. Their current liabilities are shown in Exhibit 3–4.

STUDY BREAK 3-3

See How You're Doing

Living Time Magazine collected $300,000 for 12-month subscriptions before it published its first issue in June 2004. How much revenue should the magazine company recognize for the fiscal year ending December 31, 2004? Explain what it means to ***recognize revenue*** in this situation.

Deferrals Related to Expenses

Four kinds of expenses are commonly paid in advance. We will first discuss expenses for insurance, rent, and supplies. The other is an advance payment for equipment used by a company for more than one fiscal period. All four expenses have in common that the timing of the cash disbursement precedes the actual use of the product or service purchased.

Insurance. Like any of us when we buy insurance, a company pays for insurance in advance of the service provided by the insurance company. In accounting, the advance payment for a service or good to be received in the future is considered the purchase of an asset. For insurance, accountants call the asset **prepaid insurance**. Remember, assets are items of value that the company will use up to produce revenue. Until it is actually used, prepaid insurance is shown in the current asset section of the balance sheet. Suppose Risky Company paid $2,400 for one year of insurance coverage, beginning on October 1, the date of Risky's payment to the insurance company. Here is how the payment will affect the accounting equation:

Prepaid insurance is an asset representing insurance that has been purchased but not used. The insurance expense has been deferred until the insurance is actually used (expires).

Exhibit 3–4
Unearned Revenue
Courtesy The Thomson Corporation

From the Current Liabilities Section of Thomson Corporation's Balance Sheet At December 31, 2002

Short-term indebtedness *(Note 15)*	$ 87
Accounts payable and accruals	1,542
Deferred revenue	971
Current portion of long-term debt *(Note 15)*	484
Current liabilities of discontinued operations *(Note 6)*	61
Current liabilities	$3,145

Assets	=	Liabilities	+	Shareholders' equity	
				Share capital	Retained earnings
+$2,400 Prepaid insurance $(2,400) Cash					

Purchasing the insurance policy is an asset exchange: cash is exchanged for prepaid insurance. No expense is recorded when the payment is made because the benefit of the cost has not been used. The expense will be recognized when Risky Company actually *uses* the insurance. The signal that the insurance is being used is the passing of time. As time passes, the insurance protection expires and the amount paid for that insurance during that time becomes an expense. You make the adjustment when you prepare the financial statements.

Suppose you want to prepare the financial statements on December 31. How much of the insurance is still *unused*? That is the amount you must show as an asset on the December 31 balance sheet.

How much have you *used* up? That is the amount you must show as an expense on the income statement.

Here is the adjustment Risky Company makes before preparing the December 31 financial statements:

Assets	=	Liabilities	+	Shareholders' equity	
				Share capital	Retained earnings
($600) Prepaid insurance					$(600) Insurance expense

The company has used up three months of the 12-month insurance policy already paid for. Risky paid $2,400 for the 12-month policy, and so the monthly cost of insurance is $200. That means the total insurance expense for three months is $600, and the prepaid insurance remaining—insurance not yet used up—will be on the December 31 balance sheet in the amount of $1,800.

See Exhibit 3–5 on page 94 for another example.

Rent. Rent is also usually paid in advance. In the accounting records, prepaid rent is treated exactly the same way as prepaid insurance. When the company pays the cash for rent in advance, an asset called **prepaid rent** is recorded. The disbursement of cash for prepaid rent is an asset exchange. Suppose Risky paid $9,000 to rent a warehouse for three months, beginning on November 1, the date of the payment. The way it would affect the accounting equation follows:

Prepaid rent is an asset. It represents amounts paid for rent not yet used. The rent expense is deferred until the rented asset has actually been used—when the time related to the rent has passed.

Assets	=	Liabilities	+	Shareholders' equity	
				Share capital	Retained earnings
+$9,000 Prepaid rent $(9,000) Cash					

The asset prepaid rent is increased, and cash is decreased.

Exhibit 3-5
Deferred Expenses—Insurance

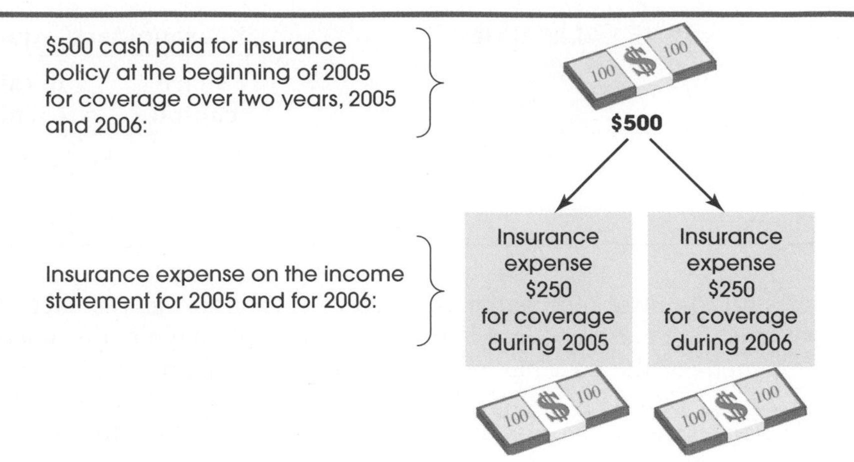

This is an example of a deferral—dollars paid first, action later. The cash payment *for insurance coverage does not happen at the same time the insurance is used and becomes* insurance expense. *In this example, the cash for a two-year insurance policy is paid at the beginning of 2005. The $500* **cash disbursement** *will be on the statement of cash flows for 2005, and the prepaid insurance will be an asset on the balance sheet at December 31, 2005. The* **expense** *will be shown on two different income statements—because the insurance expense applies to two different years. As the cost of the insurance becomes an expense, the amount of prepaid insurance on the balance sheet decreases.*

Note that no expense is recognized when Risky makes the payment for the rent. Until it is actually used, prepaid rent is an asset.

When would the rent expense be recognized, that is, when would it be put on the income statement? When Risky Company prepares financial statements, the company wants to be sure that the rent expense is shown correctly on the income statement. The amount paid was $9,000, for a period of three months, which is $3,000 per month. When Risky prepares the financial statements on December 31, two months of rent has been used—that is, $6,000. To make sure the income statement reflects the expense for the period ending December 31, the company makes the following adjustment:

Assets	=	Liabilities	+	Shareholders' equity	
				Share capital	Retained earnings
$(6,000) Prepaid rent					$(6,000) Rent expense

Note that rent expense is shown as a reduction in retained earnings, like all expenses.

That leaves one month of rent, $3,000, on the balance sheet as prepaid rent. The rent expense for November and December—$6,000—will be shown on the income statement for the year ending December 31.

STUDY BREAK 3-4

See How You're Doing

Advantage Company paid the annual rent on its office space on March 1. The total for a year of rent was $3,600. How much rent expense would be shown on the Advantage December 31 income statement?

Supplies. Supplies are commonly purchased in advance. A company buying supplies is exchanging one asset for another.

The cost of the supplies is not recognized as an expense until the supplies are actually *used*. Suppose Risky Company started March with no supplies on hand and purchased $500 worth of supplies during the month. Here is how the purchase affects the accounting equation:

Assets	=	Liabilities	+	Shareholders' equity	
				Share capital	Retained earnings
+$ 500 Supplies $(500) Cash					

If Risky prepares monthly financial statements, the company will count the amount of *unused* supplies on March 31 to get the amount that will be shown as an asset on the March 31 balance sheet. Only the amount of unused supplies will be an asset on that date. The difference between the amount *available* to use during March and the amount *remaining* on March 31 is the amount of supplies that must have been used. This amount, representing supplies used, will be an expense on the income statement.

Be sure you see **supplies** are *not* called inventory. Supplies are miscellaneous items used in the business. When purchased, supplies are recorded as an asset. Supplies expense is recognized after the supplies are used. Inventory is a term reserved for the items a company purchases to resell.

Exhibit 3–6 Deferred Expenses—Supplies

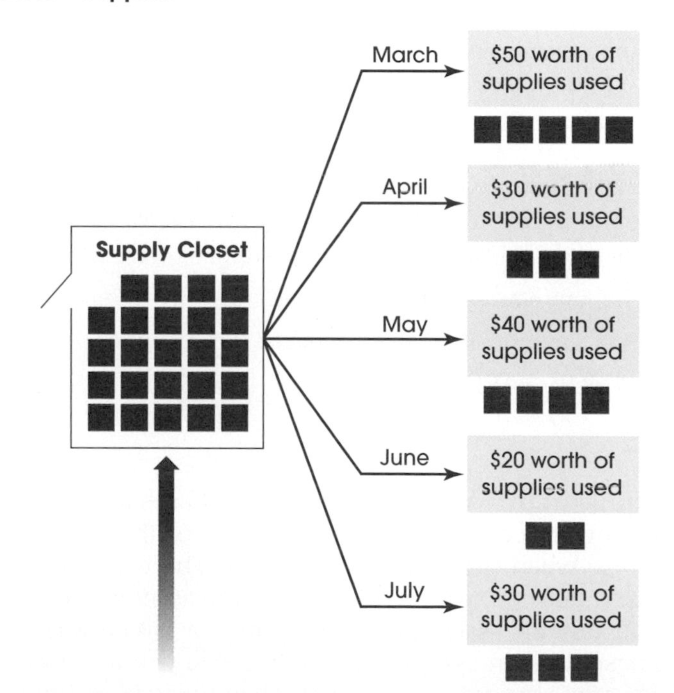

Cost of supplies ***used*** in March will be on the income statement as ***supplies expense of $50*** for the month of March.

Supplies expense for April will be $30.

Supplies expense for May will be $40.

Supplies expense for June will be $20.

Supplies expense for July will be $30.

February 1: Company buys $240 worth of supplies and pays cash. This will be on the **cash flow statement.**

Company puts the supplies in the supply closet. The cost of the supplies is recorded as an asset on the **balance sheet.** The company has something of value. Dollars have been exchanged before the action of using the supplies has taken place. This is a deferral: dollars first, action later.

As supplies are used, the cost of those used becomes supplies expense and will be on the **income statement** as an expense in the period the supplies are used.

There are $70 worth of supplies in the supply closet at the end of July. That amount will remain on the balance sheet as an asset until the supplies are used.

Suppose Risky Company counts the supplies on March 31 and finds that there is $150 worth of supplies left in the supply closet. How many dollars worth of supplies must have been used? $500 – $150 = $350. After supplies have been counted, Risky must make an adjustment to get the correct amounts for the financial statements. Here is the adjustment that must be made:

Assets	=	Liabilities	+	Shareholders' equity	
				Share capital	Retained earnings
$(350) Supplies					$(350) Supplies expense

That will leave $150 for the amount of supplies to be shown on the March 31 balance sheet. The income statement for the month of March will show $350 in supplies expense.

Suppose, during April, Risky purchases an additional $500 worth of supplies. Then on April 30, as Risky is preparing financial statements for April, the supplies left on hand are counted. If $200 worth of supplies are on hand on April 30, what adjustment should be made? Recall that at the end of March, Risky had $150 worth of supplies on hand. That means that April started with those supplies. Then, $500 worth of supplies was purchased. That means that the company had $650 of supplies available to use during April. What dollar amount of supplies was actually used? Because $200 worth of supplies are left, Risky must have used $450 worth of supplies during April. The adjustment at the end of April would reduce the asset supplies by $450 and would reduce retained earnings by $450 via supplies expense.

See Exhibit 3–6 on page 95 for another example.

STUDY BREAK 3–5

See How You're Doing

Konny Company started April with $500 worth of supplies. During the month, Konny purchased $650 worth of supplies. At the end of April, supplies on hand were counted, and $250 worth of supplies were left.

What amount of supplies would Konny put on its balance sheet at April 30?

What amount of supplies expense would appear on its income statement for the month of April?

Equipment. When a company purchases an asset that will be used for more than one accounting period, the cost of the asset is *not* recognized as an expense when the asset is purchased. The expense of using the asset is recognized during the periods in which the asset is used to generate revenue. When you buy an asset—like a computer or office furniture—you record the purchase. It is an asset exchange because you are exchanging one asset—cash—for another asset—equipment. Then you will recognize a portion of that equipment cost each accounting period in which the equipment is used, hopefully to generate revenue.

The matching principle is the reason the cost of equipment is spread over several periods. Expenses and the revenues they help generate need to be on the same income statement—that is the heart of the matching principle. When it is hard to make that precise match, the next best match is to put an expense on the income statement in the *period* in which it is used. That is what you do with equipment—allocate the cost of the equipment to the periods the equipment is used.

Suppose Risky Company purchases a computer for $5,000. When the purchase is made, the company will record the acquisition of the new asset and the cash payment.

Assets	=	Liabilities	+	Shareholders' equity	
				Share capital	Retained earnings
+$5,000 Computer $(5,000) Cash					

If you were to classify the purchase as an expense at this point, you would be doing a very poor job of matching revenues and expenses. In this example, you want to recognize the expense of the computer during the years in which you use the computer. Suppose you expect the computer to last for five years. If the computer has an estimated **residual or salvage value** of zero, you need to recognize $1,000 worth of the computer's cost as an expense in each of the five years.

Residual or salvage value is the estimated value of an asset at the end of its useful life. It is deducted before the calculation of amortization expense.

The terminology accountants use with equipment is different than the terminology used with other deferrals. Instead of calling the expense related to using the computer something logical like "computer expense," it is called **amortization expense**.

Amortizating an asset means to recognize the cost of the asset as an expense over more than one period. Each period's expense is called **amortization expense**.

As the asset is used and you want to reduce its amount in your records, you *do not* subtract the amount of the expense directly from the asset's purchase price. Instead, you show the subtractions separately on the balance sheet. Exhibit 3–7 shows how Salmon Retailers Inc. presents this information.

Using real financial information to learn an accounting concept can be difficult. An example with our fictitious company will help explain the accounting treatment of the cost of equipment and its amortization expense over time. Suppose Risky Company purchased the computer for $5,000 on January 1, 2003, and recorded the asset exchange shown in the preceding accounting equation. Then, when the company prepares its year-end financial statements, amortization expense must be recognized. In the accounting records, the net amount shown for the computer needs to be reduced from the purchase price of $5,000 to $4,000 to reflect its use for one year. The shareholders' claims to the company assets are reduced via amortization expense.

The total reduction in the dollar amount of equipment is called **accumulated amortization**. Each year, accumulated amortization gets larger. Accumulated amortization is not the same as amortization expense. Accumulated amortization is the total amortization taken over the entire life of the asset, and amortization expense is the amount of amortization for a single year.

The reduction to the cost of the asset is called **accumulated amortization**. Accumulated amortization is a contra-asset, deducted from the cost of the asset on the balance sheet.

Exhibit 3–7
Property, Plant, and Equipment

From the Balance Sheet of Salmon Retailers Inc. at December 31, 2005

Property and equipment	
Land	$ 630,000
Building	20,782,000
Leasehold improvements	179,818,000
Furniture, fixtures, and equipment	81,474,000
Construction in progress	4,174,000
	286,878,000
Less accumulated amortization	83,640,000
	$203,238,000

The **book value** of an asset is defined as the cost minus the accumulated amortization related to the asset. **Carrying value** is another expression for the same amount.

A **contra-asset** is an amount that is deducted from an asset.

On the balance sheet, the original cost of the equipment is shown along with the deduction for accumulated amortization—the total amount of amortization that has been recorded during the time the asset has been owned. The resulting amount is called the **book value**, or **carrying value** of the equipment. The book value is the net amount that is included when the total assets are added up on the balance sheet.

Accumulated amortization is called a **contra-asset** because it is the opposite of an asset. It is a deduction from assets. Accumulated amortization is always shown separately on the balance sheet so that the original cost of the equipment is kept intact.

Here is the year-end adjustment to record amortization of the asset after its first year of use:

Assets	=	Liabilities	+	Shareholders' equity	
				Share capital	Retained earnings
$(1,000) Accumulated amortization					$(1,000) Amortization expense

The accumulated amortization is shown on the balance sheet as a deduction from the cost of the equipment. The amortization expense is shown on the income statement. The book value of the asset is $4,000 (cost minus accumulated amortization) at the end of the first year.

After the second year of use, you would again record the same thing—$1,000 more recorded as accumulated amortization and $1,000 as amortization expense. The amount of accumulated amortization will then be $2,000. The amount of amortization expense is only $1,000 because it represents only a single year—the second year—of amortization expense. The accumulated amortization refers to all the amortization expense for the life of the asset through the year of the financial statement. (See Exhibit 3–8 for another example.)

The book value of the computer at the end of the second year is $3,000—that is the $5,000 cost minus its $2,000 accumulated amortization.

Exhibit 3–8
Deferred Expenses—Amortization

Truck purchased on January 1, 2005. The truck will last for seven years. Cost is $49,000. No residual value.

Cost of the truck will be spread over the income statements of the seven years the truck is used as amortization expense. The expense is being ***deferred***, that is, *put off*, until the truck is actually used.

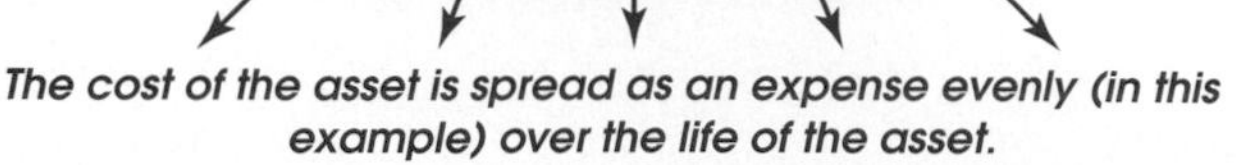

The cost of the asset is spread as an expense evenly (in this example) over the life of the asset.

Year ended December 31	**2005**	**2006**	**2007**	**2008**	**2009**	**2010**	**2011**
Amortization expense	$7,000	$ 7,000	$ 7,000	$ 7,000	$ 7,000	$ 7,000	$ 7,000
Accumulated amortization	$7,000	$14,000	$21,000	$28,000	$35,000	$42,000	$49,000

STUDY BREAK 3-6

See How You're Doing

Tango Company purchased a computer on July 1, 2004, for $6,500. It is expected to last for five years and have a residual value of $500 at the end of the fifth year. How much amortization expense would appear on the Tango December 31, 2004, income statement? What is the book value of the machine at the end of 2005?

Understanding Business

Recognizing Revenue: When Is It the Right Time?

When to recognize revenue is one of the most difficult judgments a company makes when it is getting ready to prepare its financial statements. Earnings—the net income of a company—receive a lot of attention from the financial press, from stock analysts, and from investors. A company will make every effort to meet the earnings forecasts that have been announced by analysts or expected by investors. Why? Because in the stock market, the price of a company's shares often goes down when a company does not meet its earnings forecasts. The timing of revenue recognition is a big factor in the attempt to meet earnings forecasts. In fact, improper revenue recognition is the method of choice for "cooking the books."

The following excerpt explains the practice:

> ... When done on purpose, inflating sales is one of the oldest tricks in the books. It can also help firms raise money.
>
> This kind of trick was perfected by tech companies in the late 1990s, at a time when growth was paramount, and the sales to share price ratio gained acceptance.
>
> Companies like Xerox Corp. were caught prematurely booking equipment sales over a five-year period, while Microstrategy Inc. recognized millions in revenue before it should have and was forced to restate its 1998 and 1999 financials when American regulators issued new reporting guidelines in December 1999.
>
> Canada's Bid.com International Inc. found its own way to present stellar top-line results, booking the total amount sold in its auctions as sales, rather than the sliver of sales that it actually received.
>
> ... More than half of all financial reporting frauds are related to revenue overstatement, according to a March, 1999, study produced by the National Commission on Fraudulent Financial Reporting.
>
> A few of the dirtiest tricks cited in the study include the recording of sales that never took place, shipping products prior to a firm customer agreement.
>
> (*Source:* Ian Karleff, "The fine art of inflating revenue," *Financial Post*, pp. IN1–2, November 12, 2003. Material reprinted with the express permission of: "The National Post Company," a CanWest Partnership.)

There are many examples of how important accounting numbers are to a business. The sales and collection process and how the transactions from that process are reported are closely linked. Customers, investors, owners, and regulators are all watching to see that the timing of revenue recognition follows the rules and that the income statement reflects the revenue that has really been earned during the period.

Summing Up

Accountants want the income statement to reflect the revenues and expenses for the period covered by the statement—none from the period before or the period after. Accountants also want the balance sheet to show the correct amount of assets and liabilities on the date of the statement. To do that, accountants must allocate revenues and expenses to the correct periods. This is done by making adjustments at the end of the accounting period.

Sometimes, a company purchases something and pays for it later. Sometimes, a company earns revenue but collects the cash for that revenue later.

Accountants do not base the recognition of revenues and expenses on the income statement on the collection of cash or on the disbursement of cash. Revenue and expenses are recognized—that is, they show up on the income statement—when the economic substance of the transaction has taken place. The **economic substance** of a transaction is the action of providing or receiving goods and services.

Economic substance refers to part of a transaction that involves an activity other than the exchange of cash, such as providing a service or delivering goods.

When the action has been completed but the dollars have not yet changed hands, it is called an *accrual*. Action comes first, and payment for that action comes later. You accrue—build up, or accumulate—revenue you have earned or expenses you have incurred, even though the cash has not been exchanged.

In some situations, the payment comes first and the action for that payment comes later. Sometimes, you pay *in advance* for goods or services; or sometimes, your customers pay *you* in advance for those goods or services you will provide in a later period. These situations are called deferrals. Dollars are exchanged, but you *defer* recognition of the revenue or expense until the action of the transaction is complete.

Exhibit 3–9 provides a quick view of accruals and deferrals and what comes first, dollars or action.

Applying Our Knowledge: Ratio Analysis

In Chapter 2, you learned about the current ratio and how it helps a company by providing information about the company's ability to meet its short-term obligations. Another measure that helps a company evaluate liquidity is the amount of **working capital** a company has at a particular time. Working capital is defined as current assets minus current liabilities. The current ratio gives a *relative* measure, and the amount of working capital gives an *absolute* measure of a company's ability to finance its operations. Look at the information from the balance sheet of The Forzani Group Ltd. in Exhibit 3–10.

Working capital equals *current assets* minus *current liabilities.*

The working capital for the year ended January 27, 2002, was *$50,112,000* (= $270,233,000 – $220,121,000).

The working capital for the year ended February 2, 2003, was *$100,725,000* (= $318,440,000 – $217,715,000).

Exhibit 3–9
Accruals and Deferrals

	Revenue	Expenses
Action First	**Accrued revenue:** Revenue must be on the income statement even though we haven't received payment. Example: interest on an investment may need to be accrued.	**Accrued expenses:** Expenses must be on the income statement even though we haven't paid for them yet. Example: salaries may need to be accrued.
Dollars First	**Deferred revenue:** Cash has been received from customers, but we haven't done our part to earn it. Example: customers pay in advance for items we will provide later. This results in *unearned revenue*, a liability on the balance sheet.	**Deferred expenses:** Cash has been paid for services or goods we have not used yet, but we have them. Example: supplies purchased but not used must be shown on the balance sheet. The expense is deferred until we use them.

Exhibit 3–10
Finding Current Assets and Current Liabilities on the Balance Sheet
Courtesy The Forzani Group

From the Consolidated Balance Sheet of The Forzani Group Ltd.

(in thousands)	February 2, 2003	January 27, 2002
Assets		
Current		
Cash	$ 523	$ 494
Accounts receivable	38,275	35,988
Inventory	268,519	229,270
Prepaid and other expenses	11,123	4,481
	318,440	270,233
Capital assets (Note 3)	142,236	120,525
Goodwill and other intangibles (Note 4)	38,684	37,394
Other assets (Note 5)	7,452	8,112
	$506,812	$436,264
Liabilities		
Current		
Indebtednesss under revolving credit facility (Note 6)	$ 4,204	$ 17,094
Accounts payable and accrued liabilities	209,873	188,995
Current portion of long-term debt	3,638	14,032
	217,715	220,121
Long-term debt (Note 7)	32,062	35,454
Deferred lease inducements	52,251	46,623
Future income tax liability (Note 10)	1,061	2,021
	303,089	304,219
Shareholders' equity		
Share capital (Note 9)	124,866	83,719
Retained earnings	78,857	48,326
	203,723	132,045
	$506,812	$436,264

This increase is consistent with the overall increase in the net assets of Forzani during this year. Any company considering doing business with Forzani might compute working capital for several years to identify any increases or decreases. This increase would be a positive indication of the company's ability to finance its operations.

Business Risks

In Chapters 1 and 2, we discussed the risks a business faces, particularly those risks associated with financial information. As Tom starts his business operations, he needs to analyze his risks and devise a plan to minimize these risks.

The size of a company has a direct relationship to risk: the larger the company, the more risk it has to deal with. More risk means more controls. A small company like Tom's Wear may not have the risks that General Motors has, but Tom still has to think about the risks in his business and how to deal with them. Small businesses experience a great deal of fraud due to lack of controls, particularly segregation of duties. Let us look at the five components of an internal control system introduced in Chapter 2 and see how Tom might deal with them.

A **control environment** comprises the integrity and ethical values of the entire business organization, management's philosophy, and how the organization treats its employees.

1. *Control environment.* As Tom establishes his business and his business relationships, he must plan to do business with honesty and integrity. Tom must have no tolerance for dishonesty with his vendors, creditors, customers, and employees. When he hires a new employee, for example, Tom's personnel policies need to reflect this commitment. He must be sure

to communicate this to his employees, and then he must be a role model. Tom must set the tone at the top.

2. *Risk assessment.* Tom needs to evaluate his business and information risks. For example, he must assess the risk involved in selling his T-shirts on credit—the risk that his customers will not pay. He needs to evaluate every aspect of his business—when and where he buys the T-shirts, where they are stored, how he keeps records of his inventory and sales, how he controls his cash, and so on. Even a small operation like Tom's Wear has its share of risks.
3. *Control activities.* How will Tom minimize the risks he has identified? For example, selling on credit presents a risk. One control to help minimize that risk would be extending credit to only those customers who have income above a certain level and a good credit rating. That is a common control for companies that sell on credit. There are dozens of other risks that Tom's Wear faces, and Tom will need to put many controls in place. He will have a locked warehouse in which to store his inventory, and he will have a bank account where he keeps most of his cash.
4. *Information system.* Tom's Wear will not need a very complicated information system, but it is still crucial for Tom to keep good records of all business transactions. For example, without them, he would not be able to get the loans he needs to stay in business. As we have discussed, Tom needs more information than what is on his financial statements. He needs a system for keeping track of vendors, customers, and employees. The more complicated the system is, the more controls a company will need to make sure the system is operating correctly.

Monitoring is examining controls to ensure that they are operating properly.

5. *Monitoring.* Making sure that the controls are working is the final item that makes up a company's internal control system. The best controls will not do any good if they are not operating. It is like having rules that no one follows.

Tom needs to monitor the controls he puts in place. For example, if one of Tom's controls is a lock on the warehouse, he needs to check the building periodically to make sure it is locked. If one of Tom's controls is a prenumbered sales document that has a space for the date, the quantity purchased, the customer name and address, and the sales price of each item sold, then Tom needs to be sure that he and his sales people are using the prenumbered documents and recording all that information. Just having such a form is not enough. That is why monitoring is so important. The controls must exist *and* they must be working.

Every part of the business process—sales, collections, purchases, and obtaining financing—needs to have controls to manage the risks associated with the process. As you learn more about these business processes in the chapters to come, think about the risks and the controls needed to make sure that the risks are minimized.

Understanding Excel

The following is a list of accounts for Tom's Wear at March 31, after adjustments:

Cash	$3,995
Accounts receivable	2,000
Prepaid insurance	75
Inventory	300
Computer, net of amortization	3,900
Notes payable	3,000
Interest payable	30
Common shares	5,000
Retained earnings, March 1	1,220
Sales	2,000
Cost of goods sold	800
Amortization expense	100
Insurance expense	50
Interest expense	30

For purposes of this exercise only, assume that the following, additional transactions for Tom's Wear occurred during the month of March:

a. On March 31, Tom paid $150 in cash for two months of advertising in a college newspaper. The ad will appear in the newspaper in the months of April and May.
b. Tom hired a part-time employee who started work on March 26. Tom owes him $80 for wages in March. The wages will be paid on April 2. (Ignore payroll taxes.)
c. On March 31, a customer ordered some special logo T-shirts and gave Tom a deposit of $200. The T-shirts will be delivered to the customer in April.
d. Tom estimates that he will owe $50 in income taxes for the month of March.

Requirements

1. Open a new Excel work sheet.
2. Create the following bold column headings beginning in column A and ending in column D: **Account, Current Balance, Balance Increases, Balance Decreases,** and **Ending Balance.**

   Hint: To minimize the column width of columns that have multi-word headings, select Format, Cells, and Alignment; then check the "Wrap Text" box.)
3. Enter the previous account information in the **Account** and **Current Balance** columns.
4. Complete the process by:
   a. entering the adjustment amounts indicated in items a to d
   b. computing the ending balances

   Hint: Compute the balance for the first account by adding the amount in column B to column A and subtracting column C. For example " = B3 + A3 – C3." Either type in your formulas or use the click method. Use the fill handle to copy the formulas to the remaining accounts. Select the cell you want to copy, and point to the fill handle. When the arrow changes to a thin cross-hair, click your left mouse button, and drag the handle over the range that you want copied. Release the mouse button to finish.

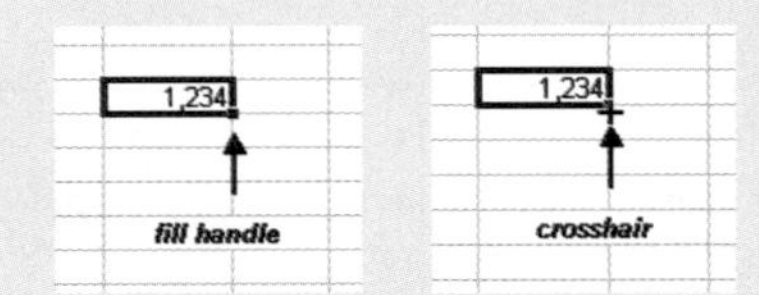

5. Prepare an income statement and balance sheet for the month ended March 31. Use appropriate headings, formats, and borders. Adjust the column widths, as needed. Use the Increase Indent button to indent the totals.

   Hint: Instead of retyping the account names and dollar amounts, input them by referencing cells. For example, "= A4" for the account name or "= E4" for the dollar amount. Remember to use formulas when you add columns of numbers.
6. Print your work sheet, and save it to disk. Name your file TomsWear3.

Summary Problem: Tom's Wear in the Third Month of Business

L.O. 3

Construct a basic set of financial statements with both accruals and deferrals.

In Chapters 1 and 2, Tom's Wear completed its first two months of operations. Exhibit 3–11 shows the company's balance sheet at the end of the second month, which we prepared in Chapter 2.

These are the amounts that are carried over to the next month, and so this is the March 1, 2005, balance sheet, too. Let us take Tom's Wear through the third month of business, with the transactions shown in Exhibit 3–12.

At the end of his third month, Tom wants to prepare his financial statements to see how his business is progressing. Let us see how each transaction affects the accounting equation. Then, prepare the four financial statements for the month of March.

Transaction 1: Purchase of a long-term asset

Tom's Wear purchases a fixed asset that will last longer than one year; therefore, it will be classified as a *long-term* asset. Remember, *current* assets will be used up or converted to cash within one year. If the cost of an asset needs to be spread over more than one year, it is considered long term. The actual purchase of the asset is recorded as an asset exchange, not as an expense. Here is how the purchase of the $4,000 computer with $1,000 down and a note payable of $3,000 with an annual interest rate of 12 percent, due in three months, affects the accounting equation:

Exhibit 3–11
Tom's Wear Balance Sheet at February 28, 2005

Tom's Wear Inc.
Balance Sheet
At February 28, 2005

Assets		Liabilities and Shareholders' equity	
Cash	$6,695	Accounts payable	$ 800
Accounts receivable	150	Other payables	50
Inventory	100		
Prepaid insurance	125	Common shares	5,000
		Retained earnings	1,220
Total assets	$7,070	Total liabilities and shareholders' equity	$7,070

Exhibit 3–12
Transactions for March 2005 for Tom's Wear, Inc.

1 March 1	Purchased computer for $4,000 with $1,000 down and a 3-month, 12% note for $3,000. The computer is expected to last for 3 years and have a residual value of $400.
2 March 10	Paid the rest of last month's advertising bill, $50.
3 March 15	Collected accounts receivable of $150 from customers from February.
4 March 20	Paid for February purchases—paying off the accounts payable balance—of $800.
5 March 24	Purchased 250 shirts @ $4 each for cash, $1,000.
6 March 27	Sold 200 shirts for $10 each, all on account, for total sales of $2,000.

Assets	=	Liabilities	+	Shareholders' equity	
				Share capital	Retained earnings
+$4,000 Computer $(1,000) Cash		+$3,000 Notes payable			

The recognition of the expense related to the cost of the computer will be deferred—put off—until Tom's Wear has used the asset and is ready to prepare financial statements.

Transaction 2: Cash disbursement to settle a liability

Last month, Tom hired a company to do some advertising for his business. On February 28, 2005, Tom's Wear had not paid the full amount. Because the work was done in February, the expense was shown on the income statement for the month of February. In March, Tom's Wear pays cash of $50 to settle—eliminate—the liability. Here is how the cash disbursement affects the accounting equation:

Assets	=	Liabilities	+	Shareholders' equity	
				Share capital	Retained earnings
$(50) Cash		$(50) Other payables			

The action took place during February, and so the expense was shown on that month's income statement. The cash was paid in March, but no expense was recognized in March because that would be double counting the expense. An expense is only recognized *once*.

Transaction 3: Collection of cash to settle a receivable

At the end of last month, Tom's Wear had not received all the cash it was owed by customers. Because the sales were made during February, the revenue from those sales was shown on the income statement for the month of February. Because the cash for the sales was not collected at the time the sales were made, Tom's Wear recorded accounts receivable. Accounts receivable is an asset that will be converted to cash within the next year. When customers pay their bills, Tom's Wear records the receipt of cash and removes the receivable from its records. Here is how the collection of the cash affects the accounting equation:

Assets	=	Liabilities	+	Shareholders' equity	
				Share capital	Retained earnings
+$150 Cash $(150) Accounts receivable					

Revenue is not recorded when the cash is collected because the revenue was already recorded at the time of the sale. To count it now would be double counting.

Transaction 4: Payment to vendor

At the end of last month, the balance sheet for Tom's Wear showed accounts payable of $800. This is the amount still owed to vendors for February purchases. Tom's Wear pays this debt, bringing the accounts payable balance to zero.

Assets	=	Liabilities	+	Shareholders' equity	
				Share capital	Retained earnings
$(800) Cash		$(800) Accounts payable			

Transaction 5: Purchase of inventory

Tom's Wear purchases 250 T-shirts @ $4 each, for a total of $1,000 and pays cash for the purchase.

Assets	=	Liabilities	+	Shareholders' equity	
				Share capital	Retained earnings
$(1,000) Cash +$ 1,000 Inventory					

Transaction 6: Sales

Tom's Wear sells 200 T-shirts at $10 each, all on account. That means the company extended credit to its customers, and they will pay later.

Assets	=	Liabilities	+	Shareholders' equity	
				Share capital	Retained earnings
+$2,000 Accounts receivable					+$2,000 Sales revenue

At the same time sales revenue is recorded, Tom's Wear records the reduction in inventory. The reduction in inventory is an expense called *cost of goods sold.*

Assets	=	Liabilities	+	Shareholders' equity	
				Share capital	Retained earnings
$(800) Inventory					$(800) Cost of goods sold

Note that the sale is recorded at the amount Tom's Wear will collect from the customer. At the same time, the reduction in the inventory is recorded at the cost of the inventory—200 shirts at a cost of $4 per T-shirt. This is a terrific example of the matching principle.

Note that there is no explicit recording of profit in the company records. Instead, profit is a derived amount; it is calculated by subtracting cost of goods sold from the amount of sales. For this sale, the profit is $1,200. It is called the *gross profit*—also called *gross margin*—on sales. Other expenses must be subtracted from the gross margin to get to *net income*, also called *net profit.*

Exhibit 3–13 shows a summary of the routine transactions during the month ending March 31, 2005. At the end of the month, Tom will adjust the company records for any accruals and deferrals needed for the financial statements. Look back over the transactions and see if you can identify the adjustments needed.

Required

Make the adjustments needed, and then prepare the four financial statements for the month of March 2005.

Solution

Adjustments needed at the end of March 2005:
Amortization expense for computer $100
Insurance expense for the month $50
Interest expense on the note payable $30

Adjustment 1: Amortization

The computer purchased on March 1 must be amortized—that is, part of the cost must be recognized as amortization expense during March. To figure out the amortization expense, the residual value is subtracted from the cost of the asset, and then the difference is divided by the estimated useful life of the asset. In this case, the residual value is $400 so that amount is subtracted from the cost of $4,000. The remaining $3,600 is divided by three years, resulting in an amortization expense of *$1,200 per year*. Because Tom is doing a monthly statement, he divides the annual amount by 12 months, giving $100 amortization per month. The adjustment is a reduction to assets and an expense.

L.O. 4

Note that the residual value is deducted only in the calculation of the amount of amortization expense. It is not deducted from the cost of the asset in the company's formal records.

Exhibit 3–13 Work Sheet for March 2005

tom's wear	Assets		=	Liabilities		+	Shareholders' equity: Contributed capital	Shareholders' equity: Retained earnings	
Balance sheet at March 1, 2005 →	Cash	$ 6,695	=	Accounts payable	$ 800	+	Common shares **$5,000**	Retained earnings	**$1,220**
	Accounts receivable	150		Other payables	50				
	Inventory	100			**$850**				
	Prepaid insurance	125							
		$ 7,070							
March 1	Computer	+$4,000		Notes payable	+3,000				
	Cash	(1,000)							
March 10	Cash	(50)		Other payables	(50)				
March 15	Cash	+150							
	Accounts rec.	(150)							
March 20	Cash	(800)		Accounts payable	(800)				
March 24	Cash	(1,000)							
	Inventory	+1,000							
March 27	Accounts rec.	+2,000						Sales	+2,000
	Inventory	(800)						Cost of goods sold	(800)
Balance Sheet at March 31 → before adjustments	Cash	$ 3,995	=	Notes payable	**$3,000**	+	Common shares **$5,000**	Retained earnings	**$2,420**
	Accounts receivable	2,000							
	Inventory	300							
	Prepaid insurance	125							
	Computer	4,000							
	Total assets	***$10,420***		*Total liabilities and shareholders' equity*					***$10,420***

Assets	=	Liabilities	+	Shareholders' equity	
				Share capital	Retained earnings
$(100) Accumulated amortization					$(100) Amortization expense

The reduction to the cost of the computer accumulates each month so that the carrying value of the asset in the accounting records goes down by $100 each month. Tom does not just subtract $100 each month from the computer's cost on the left side of the equation because generally accepted accounting principles (GAAP) require the cost of a specific asset and the total accumulated amortization related to that asset to be shown separately.

The subtracted amount is called accumulated amortization. After the first month, accumulated amortization related to this particular asset is $100. After the second month, the accumulated amortization will be $200. That amount—representing how much of the asset cost we count as used—is a *contra-asset* because it reduces the recorded value of an asset.

The cost of an asset minus its accumulated amortization is called the *book value* or *carrying value* of the asset. Each time amortization expense is recorded, the accumulated amortization increases, and the book value of the asset decreases.

Amortization expense represents a single period's expense and is shown on the income statement.

Adjustment 2: Insurance Expense

In mid-February, Tom's Wear purchased three months' worth of insurance for $150, which is $50 per month. On the March 1 balance sheet, there is a current asset called prepaid insurance in the amount of $125. A full month of insurance expense needs to be recorded for the month of March. That amount will be deducted from prepaid insurance.

Assets	=	Liabilities	+	Shareholders' equity	
				Share capital	Retained earnings
$(50) Prepaid insurance					$(50) Insurance expense

Note that the calculation of the interest expense does *not* take into consideration the length of the note. The interest expense would be the same if this were a six-month note or a two-year note, or a note of any other length of time. Interest expense is calculated on the basis of the time that has passed *as a fraction of a year* because the interest rate used is an **annual rate**.

Adjustment 3: Accruing Interest Expense

On March 1, Tom's Wear signed a three-month note for $3,000. The note carries an interest rate of 12 percent. Interest rates are typically given as an **annual rate.** Because Tom is preparing a monthly income statement, he needs to accrue one month of interest expense. Using the interest rate formula—Interest = Principal × Rate × Time—produces the following interest computation:

$$\text{Interest} = \$3{,}000 \times 0.12 \times 1/12\,(1\,\text{Month out of }12) = \underline{\underline{\mathbf{\$30}}}$$

Assets	=	Liabilities	+	Shareholders' equity	
				Share capital	Retained earnings
		$30 Interest payable			$(30) Interest expense

These are the needed adjustments at March 31, 2005, for Tom's Wear to produce accurate financial statements according to GAAP.

First, Tom prepares the income statement. Revenues and expenses are found in the retained earnings column of the accounting equation work sheet. Organized and summarized, they produce the income statement for Tom's Wear for March. The income statement covers a period of time—in this case, it covers one month of business activity.

tom's wear

Tom's Wear, Inc.
Income Statement
For the Month Ended March 31, 2005

Sales revenue		$2,000
Expenses		
Cost of goods sold	$800	
Amortization expense	100	
Insurance expense	50	
Interest expense	30	980
Net income		$1,020

Second, Tom prepares the statement of retained earnings. Like the income statement, the statement of retained earnings covers a period of time—here, one month.

Tom's Wear, Inc.
Statement of Retained Earnings
For the Month Ended March 31, 2005

Beginning retained earnings	$ 1,220
Net income for the month	1,020
Dividends	0
Ending retained earnings	$ 2,240

Third, Tom prepares the balance sheet—composed of three sections: assets, liabilities, and shareholders' equity, with the amount of each on the last day of the period. The assets are arranged in order of liquidity—that is, how easily the asset can be converted to cash. Current assets will be used or converted to cash sometime during the next fiscal year. Long-term assets will last longer than one year.

Current liabilities are obligations that will be satisfied using current assets. Long-term liabilities are obligations that will *not* be repaid in the next fiscal year.

Shareholders' equity is shown in two parts—share capital and retained earnings.

Because the balance sheet is a summary of all the transactions in the accounting equation, it will balance—assets = liabilities + shareholders' equity.

tom's wear

Tom's Wear, Inc.
Balance Sheet
At March 31, 2005

Assets		Liabilities and Shareholders' equity	
Cash	$ 3,995	Accounts payable	$ 0
Accounts Receivable	2,000	Other payables	0
		Interest payable	30
		Notes payable	3,000
Inventory	300	Total liabilities	3,030
Prepaid insurance	75		
Computer (net of $100 accumulated amortization)	3,900	Common shares	$ 5,000
		Retained earnings	2,240
Total assets	*$10,270*	*Total liabilities and shareholders' equity*	*$10,270*

Fourth, Tom prepares the cash flow statement. Because the first three financial statements—income statement, statement of retained earnings, and the balance sheet—are *accrual based* instead of *cash based,* these three financial statements do not provide detailed information about a company's cash—where it came from and how it was spent. The balance sheet gives only the total amount of cash on hand at the close of business on the last day of the fiscal period, and the income statement—the focus of financial reporting—gives no information about cash. This is why the statement of cash flows is needed. Even though accrual accounting does not base the measurement of income on cash, there is no debate about the importance of the sources and uses of cash to a business. The cash flow statement gives the details of how the cash balance has changed from the first day of the period to the last day.

tom's wear

Tom's Wear, Inc.
Cash Flow Statement
For the Month Ended March 31, 2005

Cash from operating activities		
Cash collected from customers	$ 150	
Cash paid to vendors	(1,800)	
Cash paid for operating expense	(50)	
Total cash from operations		$(1,700)
Cash from investing activities		
Purchase of asset[a]	$(1,000)	(1,000)
Cash from financing activities		0
Net increase (decrease) in cash		$(2,700)

[a]Computer was purchased for $4,000. A note was signed for $3,000 and cash paid was $1,000.

Check it out. Did the cash balance decrease by $2,700 during March? Yes, cash started at $6,695 on March 1 and ended at $3,995 on March 31, a difference of $2,700.

Answers to Study Break Questions

STUDY BREAK 3-1

1. You would pay $\$1,000 \times 0.07 \times 1/2 = \$35$ in interest.
2. This is an accrual—the action of incurring the expense via the passage of time precedes the cash payment.
3. At the end of the accounting period, the books need to be adjusted to get the expense in the correct period (to be shown on the income statement in the right time period).

STUDY BREAK 3-2

Yes, salary expense needs to be accrued. The expense for June would routinely be recorded on July 15 when the payment is made. To get the June salary expense on the income statement for the year ending June 30, ABC Company needs to accrue the expense. A month of salary expense for June is recorded as *salary expense* and *salaries payable* in the amount of $56,000.

STUDY BREAK 3-3

Out of 12 months of magazines, seven months have been delivered at December 31. That means 7/12 of the $300,000 collected in advance has actually been earned by December 31. When the cash was collected, the recognition of the revenue was *deferred*—put off or postponed—because it had not been earned. At December 31, the company recognizes $175,000 worth of revenue. That means it will put $175,000 worth of revenue on the income statement and reduce the liability *unearned revenue* on the balance sheet.

STUDY BREAK 3-4

When Advantage Company made the rent payment on March 1, the company recorded a decrease in cash and an increase in the asset *prepaid rent*. Now, it is 10 months later, and 10 months' worth of rent has been used. That means it should be recorded as *rent expense*. The March 1 payment was $3,600 for one year, which means $300 per month. Now, 10 months $\times$ \$300 per month = \$3,000 must be deducted from *prepaid rent* and added to *rent expense*. Then, $3,000 of rent expense will be shown on the income statement.

STUDY BREAK 3-5

Konny started with $500 worth of supplies and then purchased an additional $650 worth, which makes a total of $1,150 supplies available for the company to use during the month. At the end of the month, there are $250 worth of supplies remaining. That means that the company must have used $900 worth (= $1,150 – $250). Of the supplies remaining, $250 will be on the balance sheet as a current asset, *supplies;* and *supplies expense* of $900 will be shown on the income statement for April.

STUDY BREAK 3-6

1. Because the computer was purchased on July 1, 2004, only half a year of amortization expense, $600, will be shown on the income statement for the year ending December 31, 2004.
2. The book value = cost less accumulated amortization (i.e., all the amortization that has been recorded on the asset during its life) = $6,500 – $600 (for 2004) – $1,200 (for 2005) = $4,700 at December 31, 2005.

Questions

1. How does *accrual accounting* differ from *cash basis accounting*?
2. What is *deferred revenue*?
3. What is *accrued revenue*?
4. What are *deferred expenses*?
5. What are *accrued expenses*?
6. What is *interest*?
7. Explain the difference between *liabilities* and *expenses*.
8. Name two common deferred expenses.
9. What does it mean to *recognize* revenue?
10. How does matching relate to accruals and deferrals?
11. What is *amortization*?
12. Why is amortization necessary?

Short Exercises

L.O. 1

SE3-1 Eve Company pays all salaried employees biweekly. Overtime pay, however, is paid in the next biweekly period. Eve accrues salary expense only at its December 31 year-end. Information about salaries earned in December 2008 is as follows:

- Last payroll was paid on December 26, 2008, for the two-week period ended December 26, 2008.
- Overtime pay earned in the two-week period ended December 26, 2008, was $5,000.
- Remaining workdays in 2008 were December 29, 30, 31, and there was no overtime on those three days.
- The regular biweekly salaries total $90,000.

Using a five-day workweek, what will Eve Company's balance sheet show as a liability—salaries payable—on December 31, 2008?

L.O. 1

SE3-2 Lucky Luke Company purchased equipment on November 1, 2005, and gave a three-month, 9-percent note with a face value of $20,000. How much interest expense will be recognized on the income statement for the year ending December 31, 2005? What effect does this adjustment have on the cash flow statement for 2005?

L.O. 2

SE3-3 The correct amount of prepaid insurance shown on a company's December 31, 2007, balance sheet was $800. On July 1, 2008, the company paid an additional insurance premium of $400. On the December 31, 2008, balance sheet, the amount of prepaid insurance was correctly shown as $500. What amount of *insurance expense* should appear on the company's 2008 income statement?

L.O. 2

SE3-4 The New Start Company collects all service revenue in advance. The company showed an $11,500 liability on its December 31, 2006, balance sheet for service revenue received in advance. During 2007, customers paid $60,000 for future services and the 2007 income statement reported service revenue of $60,700. What amount for the liability *service revenue received in advance* will appear on the 2007 balance sheet?

L.O. 2

SE3-5 Silas Company purchased equipment on November 1, 2005, and gave a three-month, 9-percent note with a face value of $20,000. On maturity, the note plus interest will be paid to the bank. Fill in the blanks in the following chart:

	Interest expense	Cash paid for interest
November 30, 2005	______	______
December 31, 2005	______	______
January 31, 2006	______	______

L.O. 2

SE3-6 Able Company received $4,800 from a tenant on April 1 for one year of rent in advance. *In the Able information system, these cash receipts are coded as revenue.* What adjustment will Able have to make when preparing the December 31 financial statements? Show how the adjustment affects the accounting equation.

L.O. 2

SE3-7 Cain Company paid $3,600 on June 1, 2005, for a two-year insurance policy. *In the Cain information system, these cash disbursements are coded as expenses.* What adjustment will Cain have to make when preparing the December 31 financial statements? Show how the adjustment affects the accounting equation.

L.O. 2

SE3-8 Peter's Pizza started the month with $500 worth of cleaning supplies. During the month, Peter's Pizza purchased an additional $300 worth of supplies. At the end of the month, $175 worth of supplies remained. Give the amounts that would appear on the financial statements for the month for supplies expense and supplies-on-hand.

SE3-9 Mary rented office space for her new business on March 1, 2006. To get a discount, she paid $3,600 for 12 months' rent in advance. How will this appear on the financial statements at December 31? Use the following chart for your answers:

L.O. 2

	Rent expense	Prepaid rent at December 31
2006	________	________
2007	________	________

SE3-10 In November and December 2008, Paul Company, a newly organized magazine publisher, received $60,000 for 1,000 subscriptions (for three years) to a new monthly magazine at $20 per year, starting with the first issue in March 2009.

L.O. 2

Fill in the following chart related to the amount of revenue to be recognized in each of the given years (with fiscal year-end December 31):

	Revenue recognized	Unearned revenue at December 31
2008	________	________
2009	________	________
2010	________	________
2011	________	________

SE3-11 Timothy & Company paid $3,600 on June 1, 2007, for a two-year insurance policy beginning on that date. The company recorded the entire amount as prepaid insurance. By using the following chart, calculate how much expense and prepaid insurance will be shown on the year-end financial statements. The company's year-end is December 31.

L.O. 2

	Cash paid	Insurance expense	Prepaid insurance at December 31
2007	$3,600	________	________
2008	0	________	________
2009	0	________	________

Exercises

E3-1 Thomas Toy Company purchased a new delivery truck on January 1, 2005, for $25,000. The truck is estimated to last for six years and will then be sold, at which time it should be worth approximately $1,000. The company uses straight-line amortization and has a fiscal year-end of December 31.

L.O. 2

- How much amortization expense will be shown on the income statement for the year ending December 31, 2007?
- What is the net book value (also called carrying value) of the truck on the balance sheet for each of the six years beginning with December 31, 2005?

E3-2 On March 1, 2005, Kangaroo Company was formed when the owners invested $35,000 cash in the business. On April 1, 2005, the company paid $24,000 cash in advance to rent office space for the coming year. The office space was used as a place to consult with clients. The consulting activity generated $62,000 of cash revenue during 2005. On the basis of this information alone, prepare an income statement, statement of retained earnings, balance sheet, and cash flow statement as of December 31, 2005.

L.O. 3, 4

E3-3 On January 1, 2006, the law firm of Lions, Tigers, and Bears was formed. On February 1, 2006, the company was paid $18,000 in advance for services to be performed monthly during the coming year. Assuming that this was the only transaction completed in 2006, prepare an income statement, statement of owner's capital, balance sheet, and cash flow statement as of December 31, 2006.

L.O. 3, 4

L.O. 3, 4

E3-4 Best Pest Control was started when its owners invested $20,000 in the business on January 1, 2007. The cash received by the company was immediately used to purchase a $20,000 amortizable asset, which had a $5,000 residual value and an expected useful life of five years. The company earned $13,000 of cash revenue during 2007. On the basis of this information alone, prepare an income statement, statement of retained earnings, balance sheet, and cash flow statement for 2007.

L.O. 3, 4

E3-5 Tell whether each of the following items would appear on the income statement, statement of retained earnings, balance sheet, or cash flow statement. Some items may appear on more than one statement (include all of them in your answer). If an item does not appear on any financial statement, indicate that with *none*.

Interest receivable	Accounts payable
Salary expense	Share capital
Notes receivable	Distributions
Unearned revenue	Total assets
Cash flow from investing activities	Interest revenue
Insurance expense	Consulting revenue
Retained earnings	Amortization expense
Prepaid insurance	Supplies expense
Cash	Salaries payable
Accumulated amortization	Supplies
Working capital	Cash flow from financing activities
Accounts receivable	Land
Debt-to-equity ratio	Service revenue
Operating expenses	Cash flow from operating activities
Total liabilities	Current ratio
Salaries expense	Interest payable
Net income	Office equipment
Interest expense	Notes payable

Problems—Set A

L.O. 1, 2, 3, 4

P3-1A Selected amounts (at December 31, 2007) from The Hay and Barnabas Company's information system appear as follows:

1. Cash paid employees for salaries and wages	$300,000
2. Cash collected from sales to customers	$1,850,000
3. Bonds payable	$500,000
4. Cash	$150,000
5. Common shares	$60,000
6. Equipment	$840,000
7. Prepaid insurance	$30,000
8. Inventory	$250,000
9. Prepaid rent	$140,000
10. Retained earnings	$130,000
11. Salaries and wages expense	$328,000
12. Sales	$2,000,000

Required:
Part A.

There are five adjustments that need to be made before the financial statements can be prepared at year-end. Show the effect of each of the following (a to e) on the accounting equation.

a. The equipment (purchased on January 1, 2007) has a useful life of 12 years with no salvage value. (Straight-line method is used.)
b. Interest accrued on the bonds payable is $20,000 as of December 31, 2007.

c. Unexpired insurance at December 31, 2007, is $7,000.
d. The rent payment of $140,000 covered the four months from December 1, 2007, through March 31, 2008.
e. Salaries and wages of $28,000 were earned but unpaid at December 31, 2007.

Part B.

Indicate the proper balance sheet classification of each of the preceding 12 financial statement items on the December 31, 2007, balance sheet. If the account title would not appear on the balance sheet, indicate the financial statement on which it would be found.

a. Current assets
b. Property, plant, and equipment
c. Current liabilities
d. Long-term liabilities
e. Shareholders' equity

L.O. 1, 2, 3, 4

P3-2A The records of Adam's Apple Company revealed the following recorded amounts at December 31, 2008, before adjustments:

Prepaid insurance	$ 1,800
Cleaning supplies	2,800
Unearned service fees	3,000
Notes payable	5,000
Service revenue	96,000
Wages expense	75,000
Truck rent expense	3,900
Truck fuel expense	1,100
Insurance expense	0
Supplies expense	0
Interest expense	0
Interest payable	0
Wages payable	0
Prepaid rent—truck	0

Before Adam prepares the financial statements for his business, adjustments must be made for the following items:

a. The prepaid insurance represents an 18-month policy purchased early in January for cash.
b. A count of cleaning supplies on December 31 revealed $500 worth still on hand.
c. One customer paid for three months of service in advance on December 1.
d. The truck rent is $300 per month in advance. January 2009 rent was paid late in December.
e. The bank loan was taken out October 1. The interest rate is 12 percent (1 percent per month) for one year.
f. On Wednesday, December 31, the company owed its employees for working three days. The normal workweek is five days with wages of $1,500 paid at the end of the week.

Required:

1. Calculate the correct amount for the preceding financial statement items.
2. Compute *net income before taxes* for the year.

L.O. 1, 2, 3, 4

P3-3A John's Art Shop purchased a machine on January 1, 2006, for $10,000. John expects to use the machine for four years and thinks it will be worth $2,000 at the end of the four-year period. John uses the straight-line method for computing amortization.

Required:

1. Show how the machine will be presented in the asset section of the balance sheet at December 31, 2006, and December 31, 2007, after appropriate adjustments.

2. What amount of amortization expense will be shown on the income statement for 2006? 2007?

L.O. 1, 2, 3, 4

P3-4A The following is a partial list of financial statement items from the records of Twister Company at December 31, 2006.

Prepaid insurance	$10,000
Prepaid rent	18,000
Interest receivable	0
Salaries payable	0
Unearned fee income	30,000
Interest income	10,000

Additional information includes the following:

a. The insurance policy indicates that on December 31, 2006, only five months remain on the 24-month policy that originally cost $18,000.
b. Twister has a note receivable with $2,500 of interest due from a customer on January 1, 2007.
c. The accounting records show that one-third of the fees paid in advance by a customer on July 1 has now been earned.
d. The company purchased $18,000 of prepaid rent for nine months on August 1.
e. At year-end, Twister owed $7,000 worth of salaries to employees for work done in December. The next payday is January 5, 2007.

Required: Describe the needed adjustments, and give the account balances that would be shown on Twister's financial statements for the year ended December 31, 2006.

L.O. 1, 2, 3, 4

P3-5A The following is a list of financial statement items from Chocolate Company as of December 31, 2007.

Prepaid insurance	$ 6,000
Prepaid rent	10,000
Wages expense	25,000
Unearned subscription income	70,000
Interest expense	38,000

Additional information:

a. The company paid a $7,200 premium on a three-year business insurance policy on July 1, 2006.
b. Reese borrowed $200,000 on January 2, 2007, and must pay 11 percent interest on January 2, 2008, for the entire year of 2007.
c. The books show that $60,000 of subscriptions have now been earned.
d. The company paid 10 months of rent in advance on November 1, 2007.
e. Wages for December 31 of $2,000 will be paid to employees on January 3, 2008.

Required: What adjustments must be made prior to the preparation of the financial statements for the year ended December 31, 2007? Give the relevant accounts and the balances that would appear on the financial statements.

L.O. 1, 2, 3, 4

P3-6A The Pickers Packing Company has the following account balances at the end of the year:

Prepaid insurance	$8,000
Rental income	4,200
Wages expense	6,790
Taxes payable	4,168
Interest income	2,475

The company also has the following information available at the end of the year:

1. Of the prepaid insurance, $3,000 has now expired.
2. Of the rental income, $2,200 has not yet been earned.
3. The company must accrue an additional $1,500 of wages expense.
4. The company has earned an additional $500 of interest income, not yet received.

Required: Give the adjustments, and show the income statement and balance sheet account balances after the adjustments.

P3-7A The accounting records for Panda Company contained the following balances as of December 31, 2005:

L.O. 1, 2, 3, 4

Assets		Liabilities and equity	
Cash	$40,000	Accounts payable	$17,000
Accounts receivable	16,500	Share capital	45,000
Land	20,000	Retained earnings	14,500
Totals	*$76,500*		*$76,500*

The following accounting events apply to Panda's 2006 fiscal year:

Jan.1	The company acquired an additional $20,000 cash from the owners.
1	Panda purchased a computer that cost $17,000 for cash. The computer had an estimated $2,000 salvage value and an estimated three-year useful life.
Mar. 1	The company borrowed $10,000 by issuing a one-year note at 12 percent.
May 1	The company paid $2,400 cash in advance for a one-year lease for office space.
June 1	The company made a $5,000 cash distribution to the owners.
July 1	The company purchased land that cost $10,000 cash.
Aug. 1	Cash payments on accounts payable amounted to $6,000.
1	Panda received $9,600 cash in advance for 12 months of service to be performed monthly for the next year, beginning on receipt of payment.
Sept. 1	Panda sold land for $13,000 cash. The land originally cost $16,000.
Oct. 1	Panda purchased $1,300 of supplies on account.
Nov. 1	Panda purchased a one-year, $20,000 certificate of deposit at 6 percent.
Dec. 31	The company earned service revenue on account during the year that amounted to $40,000.
31	Cash collections from accounts receivable amounted to $44,000.
31	The company incurred other operating expenses on account during the year that amounted to $6,000.
31	Salaries that had been earned by the sales staff but not yet paid amounted to $2,300.
31	Supplies worth $200 were on hand at the end of the period.
31	On the basis of the preceding transaction data, there are five additional adjustments that need to be made before the financial statements can be prepared.

Required: Show each transaction and each necessary adjustment in a work sheet with the accounting equation. Then, answer the following questions (all questions pertain to the 2006 financial statements):

a. What is the amount of interest expense that would be shown on the income statement?

b. What is the amount of rent expense that would be shown on the income statement?

c. What is the amount of supplies expense that would be shown on the income statement?

d. What is the amount of total revenues appearing on the income statement?

e. What is the amount of total expenses that would appear on the income statement?

f. What is the amount of the loss from the sale of land that would be shown on the income statement?

g. What is the amount of net income that would be shown on the income statement?
h. What is the amount of total liabilities that would be shown on the balance sheet?
i. What is the amount of unearned revenue that would be shown on the balance sheet?
j. What is the amount of interest payable that would appear on the balance sheet?
k. What is the amount of retained earnings that would appear on the balance sheet?
l. What is the amount of cash flow from financing activities that would be shown on the cash flow statement?
m. What is the amount of net cash flow from investing activities that would be shown on the cash flow statement?
n. What is the amount of net cash flow from operations that would be shown on the cash flow statement?

L.O. 1, 2, 3, 4

P3-8A Given the following transactions for Zebra Company for 2006:

- The owners started the business as a corporation by contributing $30,000 cash.
- The company purchased office equipment for $8,000 cash and land for $15,000 cash.
- The company earned a total of $22,000 of revenue, of which $16,000 was collected in cash.
- The company purchased $550 worth of supplies for cash.
- The company paid $6,000 in cash for other operating expenses.
- At the end of the year, the company owed employees $3,600 for work that the employees had done in 2006. The next payday, however, is not until January 4, 2007.
- Only $175 worth of supplies was left at the end of the year.

The office equipment was purchased on January 1 and is expected to last for five years (straight-line amortization, no salvage value).

Required: Prepare the income statement for the year ended December 31, 2006, and the balance sheet at December 31, 2006.

Problems—Set B

P3-1B Selected amounts (at December 31, 2008) from Ortega Company's accounting records are shown next. No adjustments have been made.

1. Notes payable	$500,000
2. Cash	$150,000
3. Common shares	$60,000
4. Equipment	$840,000
5. Prepaid rent	$120,000
6. Inventory	$250,000
7. Prepaid insurance	$140,000
8. Retained earnings	$130,000
9. Salaries expense during 2008	$328,000

Required:
Part A.

There are five adjustments that need to be made before the financial statements for the year ended December 31, 2008 can be prepared. Show the effect of each of the following (a to e) on the accounting equation.

a. The equipment (purchased on January 1, 2008) has a useful life of 12 years with no salvage value (straight-line method is used).
b. Interest on the notes payable needs to be accrued for the year in the amount of $40,000.
c. Unexpired insurance at December 31, 2008, is $40,000.
d. The rent payment of $120,000 was made on June 1. The rent payment is for 12 months beginning on the date of payment.
e. Salaries of $58,000 were earned but unpaid at December 31, 2008.

Part B.

For each item listed next, give the financial statement on which it would be shown and its amount on the annual financial statements for December 31, 2008.

a. Insurance expense
b. Property, plant and equipment (net of accumulated amortization)
c. Salaries expense
d. Rent expense
e. Interest payable

P3-2B The records of Cabrone Company showed the following amounts at December 31, 2006, before adjustments: L.O. 1, 2, 3, 4

Prepaid insurance	$ 1,500
Supplies	3,500
Unearned service fees	4,000
Notes payable	30,000
Service revenue	106,000
Salary expense	65,000
Prepaid rent	3,900
Insurance expense	0
Supplies expense	0
Rent expense	0
Interest expense	0
Interest payable	0
Wages payable	0

Before Ms. Cabrone prepares the financial statements for her business, adjustments must be made for the following items:

a. The prepaid insurance is for a 12-month policy purchased on March 1 for cash. The policy is effective from March 1, 2006, to February 28, 2007.
b. A count of the supplies on December 31 revealed $400 worth still on hand.
c. One customer paid for four months of service in advance on December 1. By December 31, one month of the service had been performed.
d. The prepaid rent was for 10 months of rent for the company office building, beginning June 1.
e. The bank loan was taken out November 1. The interest rate is 12 percent (1 percent per month) for one year.
f. As of December 31, the company owed its employees $5,000 for work done in 2006. The next payday is not until January 2007.

Required: Calculate the correct amount for the preceding financial statement items. Compute *net income before taxes* for the year.

P3-3B Night's PJ Shop purchased a new piece of office equipment on January 1, 2007, for $20,000. The company expects to use the equipment for three years and thinks it will be worth $2,000 at the end of the three-year period. The company uses the straight-line method for computing amortization. L.O. 1, 2, 3, 4

Required:

1. Prepare the asset section of the balance sheet at December 31, 2007, and December 31, 2008, after appropriate adjustments.
2. What amount of amortization expense will be shown on the income statements for 2007 and for 2008?

P3-4B The following is a partial list of financial statement items from the records of Starnes Company at December 31, 2005. L.O. 1, 2, 3, 4

Prepaid rent	$20,000
Prepaid insurance	12,000
Interest payable	0
Wages payable	0
Unearned service revenue	18,000
Interest expense	5,000

Additional information includes the following:

a. The insurance policy indicates that on December 31, 2005, only five months remain on the 12-month policy that originally cost $12,000.
b. Starnes has a note payable with $2,500 of interest that must be paid on January 1, 2006.
c. The accounting records show that two-thirds of the service revenue paid in advance by a customer on March 1 has now been earned.
d. The company purchased $20,000 of prepaid rent for 10 months on August 1.
e. At year-end, Starnes Company owed $5,000 worth of salaries to employees for work done in December. The next payday is January 3, 2006.

Required: Describe the needed adjustments, and give the account balances that would be shown on the Starnes financial statements for 2005.

L.O. 1, 2, 3, 4

P3-5B The following is a list of financial statement items from Chewy Candy Company as of June 30, 2007. Chewy's fiscal year is from July 1 to June 30.

Prepaid insurance	$ 3,600
Prepaid rent	5,000
Wages expense	12,000
Unearned subscription revenue	30,000
Interest expense	0

Additional information:

a. The company paid a $3,600 premium on a three-year insurance policy on January 1, 2007.
b. Chewy borrowed $100,000 on July 1, 2006, with an interest rate of 11 percent. No interest has been paid as of June 30, 2007.
c. The books show that $10,000 of subscriptions have now been earned.
d. The company paid 10 months of rent in advance on March 1, 2006.
e. Wages for June 30 of $2,000 will be paid to employees on July 3.

Required: What adjustments must be made prior to the preparation of the financial statements for the fiscal year ending June 30, 2007? For the preceding items, give the balances that would appear on the financial statements.

L.O. 1, 2, 3, 4

P3-6B The Delphi Desk Company has the following amounts in its records at the end of the fiscal year:

Prepaid insurance	$5,000
Rental income	4,200
Wages expense	6,790
Accounts payable	4,168
Interest income	2,475

The company also has the following information available at the end of the year:

a. Of the prepaid insurance, $1,000 has now expired.
b. Of the rental income, $3,200 has not yet been earned.
c. The company must accrue an additional $1,250 of wages expense.

d. A bill for $300 from the company that provides the desks that Delphi Desk Company sells arrived on the last day of the year. Nothing related to this invoice has been recorded or paid.
e. The company has earned an additional $300 of interest revenue, not yet received.

Required: Give the adjustments, and show the amounts for the preceding items, as they would appear on the income statement and balance sheet for the year.

P3-7B The accounting records for Bebe Company contained the following balances as of December 31, 2007:

L.O. 3-1, 2, 3, 4

Assets		Liabilities and shareholders' equity	
Cash	$50,000	Accounts payable	$17,500
Accounts receivable	26,500		
Prepaid rent	3,600	Share capital	48,600
Land	10,500	Retained earnings	24,500
Totals	*$90,600*		*$90,600*

The following accounting events apply to Bebe's 2008 fiscal year:

Jan. 1	Bebe purchased a computer that cost $20,000 for cash. The computer had a $2,000 salvage value and a three-year useful life.
Mar. 1	The company borrowed $20,000 by issuing a two-year note at 12 percent.
May 1	The company paid $6,000 cash in advance for a six-month lease starting on July 1 for office space.
June 1	The company paid cash dividends of $2,000 to the owners.
July 1	The company purchased land that cost $15,000 cash.
Aug. 1	Cash payments on accounts payable amounted to $6,000.
1	Bebe received $6,000 cash in advance for 12 months of service to be performed monthly for the next year, beginning on receipt of payment.
Sept. 1	Bebe sold land for $13,000 cash. The land originally cost $15,000.
Oct. 1	Bebe purchased $1,300 of supplies on account.
Nov. 1	Bebe purchased a one-year, $10,000 certificate of deposit at 5 percent.
Dec. 31	The company earned service revenue on account during the year that amounted to $50,000.
31	Cash collections from accounts receivable amounted to $46,000.
31	The company incurred other operating expenses on account during the year that amounted to $6,000.
31	Salaries that had been earned by the sales staff but not yet paid amounted to $2,300.
31	Supplies on hand at the end of the period totalled $200.
31	On the basis of the preceding transaction data, some additional adjustments that need to be made before the financial statements can be prepared. You should make them now.

Required: On the basis of the preceding information, show each transaction and each necessary adjustment in a work sheet with the accounting equation. Then, answer the following questions (all questions pertain to the 2008 financial statements):

a. What is the amount of interest expense that would be shown on the income statement?
b. What is the amount of rent expense that would be shown on the income statement? (Prepaid rent at Dec. 31 was for Jan.–June of 2008.)
c. What is the amount of supplies expense that would be shown on the income statement?
d. What is the amount of total revenues appearing on the income statement?
e. What is the amount of total expenses that would appear on the income statement?
f. What is the amount of the loss from the sale of land that would be shown on the income statement?

g. What is the amount of net income that would be shown on the income statement?
h. What is the amount of total liabilities that would be shown on the balance sheet?
i. What is the amount of unearned revenue that would be shown on the balance sheet?
j. What is the amount of interest payable that would appear on the balance sheet?
k. What is the amount of retained earnings that would appear on the balance sheet?
l. What is the amount of cash flow from financing activities that would be shown on the cash flow statement?
m. What is the amount of net cash flow from investing activities that would be shown on the cash flow statement?
n. What is the amount of net cash flow from operations that would be shown on the cash flow statement?

L.O. 1, 2, 3, 4

P3-8B Given the following transactions for Quackers Company for 2007:

- The owners started the business as a corporation by contributing $50,000 cash.
- Quackers purchased office equipment for $5,000 cash and land for $15,000 cash.
- Quackers earned a total of $32,000 of revenue, of which $20,000 was collected in cash.
- Quackers purchased $550 worth of supplies for cash.
- Quackers paid $6,000 in cash for other operating expenses.
- At the end of the year, Quackers owed employees $3,600 for work that the employees had done in 2007. The next payday, however, is not until January 4, 2008.
- Only $120 worth of supplies was left at the end of the year.

The office equipment was purchased on January 1 and is expected to last for five years (straight-line amortization, no salvage value).

Required: Prepare the income statement for the year ended December 31, 2007, and the balance sheet at December 31, 2007.

Issues for Discussion

Financial statement analysis

1. Use the annual report from CoolBrands International Inc. to answer these questions:
   a. Does CoolBrands have any deferred expenses? What are they, and where are they shown?
   b. Does CoolBrands have accrued expenses? What are they, and where are they shown?
   c. What is the difference between a deferred expense and an accrued expense?
   d. Calculate the amount of working capital for the two most recent fiscal years. What information does this provide?

Business risk

2. What characteristics of CoolBrands' business create risks for the company that would not be experienced by most retailers (i.e., unique risks of its particular business)? Use the entire annual report to answer this question.

Ethics

3. DVD-Online, Inc. is in its second year of business. The company is totally Web-based, offering DVD rental to online customers for a fixed monthly fee. For $30 per month, a customer receives three DVDs each month, one at a time as the previous one is returned. No matter how many DVDs a customer uses (up to three), the fee is fixed at $30 per month. Customers sign a contract for a year, so DVD-Online recognizes $360 sales revenue each time a customer signs up for the service. The owner of DVD-Online, John Richards, has heard about GAAP, but he does not see any

reason to follow these accounting principles. Although DVD-Online is not publicly traded, John does put the company's financial statements on the webpage for customers to see.

a. Explain how DVD-Online would account for its revenue if it did follow GAAP.
b. Explain to John Richards why he should use GAAP, and describe why his financial statements may now be misleading.
c. Do you see this as an ethical issue? Explain.

Internet Exercise: Fairmont Hotels and Resorts

Fairmont Hotels and Resorts is an owner/operator of luxury hotels and resorts in Canada, the United States, Mexico, Bermuda, Barbados, and the United Arab Emirates. Please go to the Fairmont website for investors: http://www.fairmontinvestor.com/

IE3-1 If you were at a Fairmont property, what might you be doing? List two of the Fairmont chains.

IE3-2 Click on *Annual Report* under Investors Tool; then, select the interactive version of the most recent annual report. Find the *Balance Sheets* by clicking *next* or using the "contents" scroll bar. Does Fairmont use a calendar year for its fiscal year? How can you tell?

IE3-3 Refer to the asset section.

a. List the title of one asset account that includes accrued revenue—amounts earned but not yet received in cash.
b. List the title of one asset account that includes amounts that have been paid for in cash but have not yet been expensed.
c. List the title of one asset account that includes amounts that will be amortized.
d. For each account listed in a through c, identify the amount reported for the most recent year. Do these amounts still need adjusting? Explain why or why not.

IE3-4 List the amounts reported for total current assets and total current liabilities for the most recent year. Compute working capital. For Fairmont, what does the amount of working capital indicate?

IE3-5 For the two most recent years, list the amounts reported for total assets, total liabilities, and total shareholders' equity. For each type of account, identify what the trend indicates. Does the accounting equation hold true for both years?

Please note: Internet websites are constantly being updated. Therefore, if the information is not found where indicated, please explore the annual report further to find the information.

CHAPTER 4

Keeping the Books: The Mechanics of an Accounting System

Here's where you've been…

In Chapter 3, you learned:

- *Accruals* are transactions in which the exchange of cash comes after the exchange of the related goods and services.
- *Deferrals* are transactions in which the exchange of cash comes before the exchange of the related goods and services.

Both are part of accrual basis accounting.

Here's where you're going…

From Chapter 4, you should understand the basic accounting cycle—that is, how the traditional general ledger system keeps track of a company's transactions from the beginning of the transaction to the preparation of the financial statements. You will learn about *debits* and *credits* in this chapter.

Learning Objectives

More specifically, when you are finished studying this chapter, you should be able to answer these questions:

1. What is the general ledger system, and how does it work?
2. What are the steps in the accounting cycle?
3. What adjustments are needed before preparing financial statements, and how do you make those adjustments?
4. What is closing, and why is it necessary?
5. What is an ERP? How does that relate to accounting records?

We have been keeping track of Tom's Wear transactions using an accounting equation work sheet. We can do that in a simple world with a small number of transactions. In the real world, that would not work very well. A company in the real world needs a better system to keep track of the large number of transactions represented in the four basic financial statements. A company may have an accounting system that gathers *only* accounting information—just recording the information that applies to the financial statements—and other information systems gathering information for marketing, production, and other parts of the company. Alternatively, a company may have a single, integrated information system in which all company information is recorded—data about suppliers, employees, operations; and the accounting information is simply a small part.

L.O. 1

Define the general ledger system and explain what it is designed to do.

The **general ledger system** is the accountant's traditional way of keeping track of a company's financial transactions and then using those records to prepare the basic financial statements. The debits and credits used in this system are simply a mechanical way to keep track of financial transactions.

An **ERP** is a sophisticated, company-wide information system, of which accounting information is only a small part. The accounting part of an ERP may eventually replace the general ledger system, as we know it.

For years, the accountants have had their own separate record-keeping system—called the **general ledger system**; and the other functional areas of the business—marketing, production, sales, and so on—each have had their own system for keeping track of the information they need. Since the development of computers and software programs that can manage large amounts of information, more and more companies are using a single, integrated information system. Thus, instead of keeping their data separately, accountants may get their information from the company's overall information system—often referred to as an **enterprise-wide resource planning system (ERP).**

The accountants' traditional general ledger accounting system has been used for such a long time that it has become entrenched in the format and organization of the basic financial statements of every business. That is one reason we will discuss the general ledger system in detail in this chapter, even though in many companies it is being absorbed into company-wide information systems. Another reason is that you must be able to understand the output of the general ledger accounting system because the new integrated information systems are designed to produce the financial records in the same format as the general ledger system. The same financial statements are produced with both the general ledger and the integrated types of information systems. We will use the general ledger system, which was designed as a manual system, to demonstrate how transactions are recorded, classified, and summarized for the financial statements.

The General Ledger Accounting System

Business transactions are first recorded in a **journal.** Then they are transferred to accounts in the **general ledger** through a process called **posting.**

Keeping track of financial information with a traditional record-keeping system is often called *bookkeeping.* As transactions occur, they are recorded chronologically by a bookkeeper in a book called a **journal.** When we prepare an accounting equation work sheet—showing the effect of each transaction on the accounting equation—we are doing something similar to what we would record in a journal. The resources exchanged are shown with their dollar amounts. The journal contains a record of each transaction as it occurs. An example is shown in Exhibit 4–1. Most companies use more than one journal; each department may have its own journal. Common journals

Exhibit 4–1
An Example of a Journal

Page 4: General Journal

Ref.	Date	Journal entry	Debits	Credits
J-1	June 1	Cash	$65,000	
		Sales		$65,000
		To record the collection of cash for sales.		
J-2	June 4	Equipment	$20,600	
		Cash		$20,600
		To record the purchase of equipment for sales.		

The journal entries are recorded chronologically. Then, the individual items will be "re-grouped" by account as they are posted to the General Ledger. Trace the cash amounts in the journal entries above to the General Ledger Cash account shown in Exhibit 4–2. The amounts for Sales and Equipment will be posted to their own general ledger accounts.

are the (1) sales journal, (2) cash receipts journal, (3) cash disbursements journal, and (4) general journal. For simplicity, we will use a single, general journal for all our transactions.

Because a company may have thousands of transactions during an accounting period, it would be difficult, probably impossible, to try to gather and use the information from a chronological record, such as the journal. To be useful, the information needs to be reorganized, grouping together transactions that involve the same resource. For example, when all the transactions that involve cash are grouped together, then the company's cash balance can be easily determined. As you can see from that example, it is useful for similar transactions to be grouped together. The transactions from the journal or journals are transferred to another book called the **general ledger**—a process called **posting** the transactions to the general ledger. Posting is done periodically; it could be daily, weekly, or monthly, depending on the size of the company.

The general ledger is the primary record of the financial information of the business. It is organized by what we have called, up to this point, a financial statement *item*. From here on, we will refer to the financial statement items as accounts. Like a financial statement item, an account is the basic classification unit of accounting information. Now we can think of each financial statement item as an account and each account as a page in the general ledger. On the page for a particular account, we record all the additions to and deductions from that account.

For example, one account in the general ledger is Cash. On the Cash page in the general ledger, we find every cash collection and every cash disbursement made by the company. If there are more disbursements or collections than can fit on one page, they will be recorded on as many following pages as needed, all comprising the Cash account. To make it easy to find the amount of cash on hand, the Cash account has a running balance. That means a new balance is calculated after every entry. Think about your own chequebook—that is, the record you keep of each cheque you write—a subtraction; each deposit you make—an addition; and the resulting total remaining in your chequing account—that is, your running balance. If you keep a running balance, it is much faster to find out how much cash you have in your account. (Have you discovered what happens when you fail to keep your chequebook balance current?)

Accounts in the general ledger include Cash, Accounts Receivable, Inventory, Prepaid Insurance, Equipment, Accumulated Amortization, Accounts Payable, Notes Payable, Share Capital, and Retained Earnings. (Note that these are given in the order they appear on the balance sheet.) How many accounts does a company have? Every company is different, and the number of accounts depends on the detail the company wants in its financial records. For example, one company could have an account called Utilities Expenses in which many different utility-related expenses could be accumulated. Another company might prefer to have a separate account for each type of utility expense—a separate page in the general ledger for electricity expense, gas expense, water expense, and so on. The number of accounts is determined by the amount of detail a company wants to be able to retrieve from its records. If a company uses very little gas or water, it would be a waste of time and space to keep a separate account for those expenses. A company that uses water in its production process, on the other hand, would definitely want to keep a separate account for water purchases.

A **subsidiary ledger** is a record that contains detailed information in support of a general ledger account.

Companies also have **subsidiary ledgers**. These are detailed records that support the balances in the general ledger. For example, the *accounts receivable subsidiary ledger* will have details about the customers—sales, receipts, and account balances for every customer. The total dollar amount in the accounts receivable subsidiary ledger will be the total in the general ledger.

Most companies have a large number of accounts, and they combine the similar ones for the financial statements. When we look at the financial statements, we cannot really tell how many individual accounts a company has in its general ledger. Many smaller accounts may be combined for financial statement presentation.

Anyone who wants to know the balance in any account at any time can find it by looking in the general ledger. A list of the balances in all the accounts of a company is called a **trial balance.**

A **trial balance** is a list of all the accounts of a company with the related debit or credit balance.

Before the financial statements can be prepared, adjustments to the records must be made. We discussed those adjustments and how to make them in Chapter 3. Adjustments are needed because of the nature of accrual accounting. On the financial statements, we need to include revenues that have been earned and expenses that have been incurred, even if we have not yet received the cash earned or paid the cash for the expenses incurred during the accounting period. These adjustments are called accruals. The action has taken place, but the dollars have not been exchanged.

We also need to be sure to include on the income statement for the period any revenue we have earned or expenses we have incurred for which the dollars were exchanged at a previous time. These are called deferrals. The dollars were already exchanged, and we recorded the receipt or payment of the cash when we received or paid the cash. However, we did not recognize any revenue or expense at that time. At the end of the accounting period, we have to recognize any revenue we have earned and any expenses that we have incurred.

No matter what kind of accounting system a company uses, the information produced by that system must be adjusted before the financial statements can be prepared. After the adjustments are made, the financial statements are prepared. We have actually done all this—recording the transactions, making the adjustments, and preparing the financial statements—using the accounting equation work sheet. The general ledger system is simply a more feasible way to do it in an actual business.

Debit means the left side of an account. **Credit** means the right side of an account.

To use the general ledger system and to understand the information it makes available, we must learn a bit more accounting language. Do not panic over the terms **debit** and **credit.** You will find them easy to understand, but only if first you get rid of any notions of what you already think debit and credit mean. In accounting, each term has a very specific meaning that should not be confused with its more general meaning.

Debits and Credits

In accounting, when we say *debit,* we mean the left side; when we say *credit,* we mean the right side. (This should be easy to remember.) Left is the only thing we can say about what *debit* means and right, about what *credit* means—unless we apply the terms to specific accounts.

A general ledger has been traditionally composed of a multi-column page, similar to the one shown in Exhibit 4–2. The debit column on the right shows the running balance in the cash account. Note that there would not normally be a credit balance in this account. Now it is often computerized in a similar format.

In the balance columns, the column on the left is called the debit (DR) column, and the column on the right is called the credit (CR) column. As a shortcut to using formal preprinted two-column paper, accountants often draw a **T-account** to represent a page in the general ledger. T-accounts shown in Exhibit 4–3 are our representation of the general ledger shown in Exhibit 4–2.

A **T-account** is a representation of a page in the general ledger with debits on the left side and credits on the right side.

One T-account, such as cash, shown next, represents a single page in the general ledger. The left side of a T-account is the debit side, and the right side of a T-account is the credit side.

Cash	
Debit	Credit

Exhibit 4–2
The General Ledger

Account: Cash					Account No. 1002	
					Balance	
Date	Item	Jrnl. ref.	Debit	Credit	Debit	Credit
2007						
June 1		J–1, p. 4	65,000		**65,000**	
June 4		J–2, p. 4		20,600	**44,400**	

This is the **Cash** account. The cash amounts from all the journal entries are posted here. Trace these amounts back to the journal entries shown in Exhibit 4–1.

Exhibit 4–3 Debits and Credits in T-Accounts

Asset	
Debit increases (normal balance)	Credit decreases

Liability	
Debit decreases	Credit increases (normal balance)

Equity	
Debit decreases	Credit increases (normal balance)

Revenue	
Debit decreases	Credit increases (normal balance)

Expense	
Debit increases (normal balance)	Credit decreases

Numbers we put on the left side of the account are called debits, and *putting* a number in the left column is called *debiting* an account. Debit is a wonderful word that can be an adjective, a noun, or a verb. The same goes for the word credit. The right side of the account is called the credit side; the numbers we put on the right side are called credits; and putting a number in the right column is called *crediting* an account.

In the fifteenth century, a monk named Fra Luca Paccioli wrote about a system that uses debits and credits with the accounting equation. In his system, the accounting equation stays in balance with each transaction *and* the monetary amounts of debits and credits are equal for each transaction. Here is how it works:

1. For the balance sheet equation, the balance in the accounts on the left side of the equation (*assets*) will increase with debits; and the balance in the accounts on the right side of the equation (*liabilities* and *equity*) will increase with credits. It follows that the balance in an asset account will decrease with credits. Liability and equity account balances decrease with debits. Putting that together,

   - Asset accounts are increased with debits and decreased with credits.
   - Liability and shareholders' equity accounts are increased with credits and decreased with debits.

   This means that when we want to add an amount to our cash balance, we put the number of that amount on the left (in the left column of the two columns in the general ledger account for cash)—so, that is a debit. When we disburse cash and want to subtract the amount disbursed from the cash account, we put the number of that amount on the right side—so, that is a credit. The amount in the *increase* side of an account is called its "normal" balance. Cash has a normal debit balance. Because we put the cash we receive on the debit side and the cash we disburse on the credit side, it makes sense that our Cash account will normally have a debit balance. (It is not normal to disburse more cash than you have—it is pretty unusual.)

   In accounting, we do not literally *add* and *subtract* from an account balance—we debit and credit an account to accomplish the same thing. If we make an error, we do not erase the mistake and replace it with the correct answer. Instead, we debit or credit the account to correct the error and make the account balance correct. When accounting records are kept by hand, all entries are made in ink so that no entries can be erased or changed. This has been traditional in accounting to keep the records from being altered. Recording every increase to, and decrease from, an account balance gives a complete record of every change made to the account.
2. Because owner's equity is increased with credits, all accounts that increase owner's equity will increase with credits. Revenue accounts increase with credits and decrease with debits. When we make a sale, we *credit* the Sales account.
3. Because owner's equity is *decreased* with debits, all accounts that decrease owner's equity work in the opposite way as revenue accounts work. For example, expense accounts—where a list of our expenses is kept—increase with debits. As we incur expenses, we put the amounts on the left side of expense accounts.

A summary of the use of debits and credits is shown in Exhibit 4–3. Remember, it is just a clever system to be sure that when we record a transaction, the accounting equation is kept in balance and, at the same time, debits = credits with every transaction. This system is called **double-entry bookkeeping**.

A **double-entry system** is an accounting system that uses debits and credits to record transactions to balance the accounting equation.

STUDY BREAK 4-1

See How You're Doing

Indicate whether each of the following accounts normally has a debit (DR) or credit (CR) balance and what type of account it is:

Account title	Expense	Revenue	Asset	Liability	Owner's equity
Accounts payable				CR	
Accounts receivable					
Advertising expense					
Cash					
Amortization expense					
Furniture and fixtures					
Accumulated amortization					
Unearned fees					
Salary expense					
Common shares					
Rent expense					
Dividends					
Retained earnings					
(Earned) fees					
Land					
Building					

The Accounting Cycle

The process that starts with recording individual transactions, produces the four basic financial statements, and gets our general ledger ready for the next accounting period is called the **accounting cycle.** Some of the steps in the accounting cycle will not make any sense to you yet, but this chapter examines each in detail. By the end of this chapter, you should be able to explain and perform each step. The steps in the accounting cycle follow:

The **accounting cycle** begins with the transactions of a new accounting period. It includes recording and posting the transactions, adjusting the books, preparing financial statements, and closing the temporary accounts to get ready for the next accounting period.

1. Record transactions in the journal, the chronological record of all transactions. These are called journal entries.
2. Post the journal entries to the general ledger.
3. At the end of the accounting period, prepare an unadjusted trial balance.
4. Prepare adjusting journal entries, and post them to the general ledger.
5. Prepare an adjusted trial balance.
6. Prepare the financial statements.
7. Close the temporary accounts.
8. Prepare a postclosing trial balance.

Let us look at each of these steps in detail.

Step 1: Recording Journal Entries

L.O. 2

Identify and perform the steps in the accounting cycle.

In the normal course of business, there are dozens of transactions that must be recorded in the accounting system. Let us look at how the transactions for a company's first year of business would be recorded in a journal. The transactions for the first year of Clint's Consulting Company, Inc. are shown in Exhibit 4–4.

The first transaction in Clint's first year of business is his own contribution of $2,000 to the business. What a journal entry looks like on a journal page follows:

Date	Transaction	Debit	Credit
1/2/05	Cash	$2,000	
	Contributed capital		$2,000
To record owner's contribution			1-1[a]

[a]This is a number we'll use to help us trace journal entries to the general ledger.

The Cash account is increased by $2,000, and so Clint would debit the Cash account for $2,000. Owner's equity is increased, and so Clint would credit Contributed Capital for $2,000. Note that in this case, two accounts are increased—one with a debit and one with a credit. In some transactions, both accounts are increased; in others, one account can be increased and one account can be decreased; or two accounts can be decreased. The only requirement for a journal entry is that the dollar amount of debits must equal the dollar amount of credits.

In the second transaction, Clint's Consulting Company borrows $4,000 from a local bank. Again, two different accounts are increased—one with a debit and one with a credit—in this transaction. Note that debits ($4,000) = credits ($4,000).

Date	Transaction	Debit	Credit
1/10/05	Cash	$4,000	
	Notes payable		$4,000
To record the loan from the bank			1-2

Debits are always listed first; credits are listed after all the debits—sometimes, there is more than one account to debit or credit—and the accounts being credited are indented like the first sentence of a paragraph. Each page of the journal has a page number that is used to trace journal entries to the general ledger. We will see this number again when we post the journal entries to the general ledger.

The third transaction is the purchase of supplies for $400 cash. This is recorded with a debit to Supplies and a credit to Cash.

Exhibit 4–4
Transactions for Clint's Consulting Company, Inc. during 2005

Date	Transaction
Jan. 2	Clint contributes $2,000 of his own money to the business
Jan. 10	Clint's Consulting, Inc. borrows $4,000 from a local bank to begin the business
Feb. 4	Clint's buys supplies for $400 cash
Apr. 10	Clint's hires a company to prepare a brochure for the company for $500 cash
July 12	Clint's provides consulting services and earns revenue of $9,000 cash
Aug. 15	Clint's pays someone to do some typing, which costs $350 cash
Oct. 21	Clint's repays the $4,000 note along with $150 interest
Dec. 10	Clint's Consulting, Inc. makes a distribution to Clint, the owner, for $600

Date	Transaction	Debit	Credit
2/4/05	Supplies	$400	
	Cash		$400
To record the purchase of supplies			1-3

Note that this transaction increases one asset account—Supplies—and decreases another asset account—Cash. Because Supplies is an asset, it is increased with a debit.

The fourth transaction is Clint's hiring a company to prepare a brochure for his new consulting business. He pays $500 for this service.

Date	Transaction	Debit	Credit
4/10/05	Advertising expense	$500	
	Cash		$500
To record the cost of the brochures			1-4

In this transaction, an expense account, Advertising Expense, is increased by $500. Because expense accounts are eventually deducted from owner's equity, they increase with debits, the opposite of owner's equity accounts. Cash, an asset account, is decreased with a credit of $500.

Next, the company provides consulting services for $9,000 cash.

Date	Transaction	Debit	Credit
7/12/05	Cash	$9,000	
	Consulting fees		$9,000
To record consulting revenue			1-5

In this transaction, Cash is increased with a $9,000 debit. Consulting Fees, a revenue account that will eventually be added to owner's equity, is increased with a $9,000 credit.

Clint's Consulting Company has one employee who types for him occasionally, and he pays this person $350 for typing during his first year of business. This is an expense, which Clint categorizes as Salary Expense. Cash is reduced with a credit for $350, and Salary Expense is increased with a $350 debit.

Date	Transaction	Debit	Credit
8/15/05	Salary expense	$350	
	Cash		$350
To record the cost of an employee to type			1-6

Next, the company repays the loan to the bank, with interest. The principal of the loan—the amount borrowed—was $4,000; the interest—the cost of using someone else's money—was $150. The journal entry for this transaction is an example of an entry with more than one debit.

Date	Transaction	Debit	Credit
10/21/05	Notes payable	$4,000	
	Interest expense	150	
	Cash		$4,150
To record the repayment of a note plus interest			1-7

The debit to Notes Payable reduces the balance in that account. Before this transaction, it had a balance of $4,000. Now, when this debit is posted, the account will have a zero balance. The Interest Expense account will increase by $150 because expense accounts increase with debits. Cash is reduced by $4,150.

The final transaction of Clint's Consulting Company's first year of business is a $600 distribution to Clint, the owner. In a sole proprietorship, a distribution is also called a **withdrawal.** Because Clint's Consulting Company is a corporation, the distribution is called a **dividend.** The Dividends account has a debit balance and will eventually reduce Retained Earnings. Paying a dividend reduces the Cash balance. Remember, a dividend payment is not an expense.

A distribution to the owner of a sole proprietorship is called a **withdrawal;** in a corporation, distributions to the owners are called **dividends.**

Date	Transaction	Debit	Credit
12/10/05	Dividends	$600	
	Cash		$600
To record a dividend payment			1-8

Step 2: Posting Journal Entries to the General Ledger

Each of the journal entries a company makes must be posted to the general ledger. How often this is done depends on the number of journal entries a company normally makes. Some computerized systems post every journal entry automatically when it is entered into the system. Other companies post transactions to the general ledger daily or weekly.

The accounts for Clint's Consulting Company, Inc. all begin with a zero balance because this is Clint's first year of business. When an entry is posted in the general ledger, the page number from the journal is also shown. This provides a way to trace every entry in the general ledger back to the original record of the transaction in the journal. After all the journal entries are posted, it is easy to calculate the balance in any account. The accounts, shown in Exhibit 4–5, are listed in the following order: assets, liabilities, owner's equity, revenues, and expenses. Their balances are indicated when there have been more than one transaction in the period.

Step 3: Preparing an Unadjusted Trial Balance

A trial balance is a list of all the accounts in the general ledger, each with its debit or credit balance. The reasons for preparing a trial balance are to confirm that debits equal credits and to have a way to quickly review the accounts for needed adjustments. Exhibit 4–6 shows the unadjusted trial balance for Clint's Consulting at December 31, 2005.

Step 4: Adjusting Journal Entries

L.O. 3

Know why adjustments need to be made and how to make them before the financial statements are prepared.

Recording journal entries as transactions occur and posting them to the general ledger are routine accounting tasks. When a company gets ready to prepare financial statements at the end of the accounting period, there are more journal entries needed. These are not routine journal entries; they are called adjusting journal entries. As we discussed in Chapter 3, there are four situations that require adjustments before the financial statements are prepared. We need to adjust our records for *accrued revenues, accrued expenses, deferred revenues,* and *deferred expenses.* Let us look at an example of each of those adjustments in a general ledger system.

Exhibit 4–5 **Clint's Consulting Company, Inc. T-Accounts**

Cash (asset)

Debit		Credit	
1-1	$2,000	$ 400	1-3
1-2	4,000	500	1-4
1-5	9,000	350	1-6
		4,150	1-7
		600	1-8
	$9,000		

Supplies (asset)

Debit		Credit	
1-3	$400		

Notes payable (liability)

Debit		Credit	
1-7	$4,000	$4,000	1-2
		$0	

Share capital (SC) (owner's equity)

Debit		Credit	
		$2,000	1-1

Consulting fees (revenue)

Debit		Credit	
		$9,000	1-5

Advertising expense (expense)

Debit		Credit	
1-4	$500		

Dividends (owner's equity temporary account)

Debit		Credit	
1-8	$600		

Interest expense (expense)

Debit		Credit	
1-7	$150		

Salary expense (expense)

Debit		Credit	
1-6	$350		

Accruals. **Accrued Revenue.** Suppose Clint's Consulting Company did some consulting for a fee of $3,000, but the company has not been paid yet so the revenue has not been recognized—when it is recognized, it is put on the income statement. At December 31, Clint will adjust the company's records to recognize this revenue, even though he has not collected the cash. First, note the effect of the adjustment on the accounting equation.

Assets	=	Liabilities	+	SC	+	Retained earnings
+3,000 Accounts receivable						+3,000 Consulting fees

The transaction increases assets—Accounts Receivable (AR). That means Clint would debit AR because assets are increased with debits. Clint has also increased a revenue account, Consulting Fees. (The $3,000 is recorded in a revenue account, not directly into the retained earnings account. However, the rev-

Exhibit 4–6
Clint's Consulting Company, Inc. Unadjusted Trial Balance at December 31, 2005

Account	DR	CR
Cash	$ 9,000	
Supplies	400	
Notes payable		$ 0
Share capital		2,000
Dividends	600	
Consulting fees		9,000
Advertising expense	500	
Interest expense	150	
Salary expense	350	
	$11,000	*$11,000*

enue will end up increasing retained earnings on our balance sheet.) Revenue accounts increase with credits, and so we would credit the revenue account Consulting Fees for $3,000. The accounting equation is in balance *and* debits = credits for our transaction. Here is what the journal entry would look like:

Date	Transaction	Debit	Credit
12/31/05	Accounts receivable	$3,000	
	Consulting fees		$3,000
To accrue revenue earned in 2005			A-1

Accrued Expenses. Another situation that requires an adjustment is accrued expenses. If we have incurred an expense (the dollar amount that *will* be paid for an item or a service that has already been used to produce revenue), the matching principle requires us to put it on the same income statement as the revenue it helped generate.

Sometimes, matching an expense with a specific revenue is impossible to do. In that case, we match the expense with the time period when the expense item was used. For example, it is often impossible to match an employee's work with specific revenue the company earns. So, the cost of the work done by an employee is put on the income statement as an expense in the accounting period when the work was done.

Let us look at an example of matching salary expense with the period in which the work was done. When companies pay their employees—on normal paydays during the year—they debit the account Salary Expense and credit the account Cash. The Salary Expense account may have a significant balance at year-end because the company has been recording salary expense as the employees have been paid throughout the year. To make sure we have included *all* the salary expense for the year, we must examine the time our employees have worked near the end of the year. The purpose is to be sure to include the cost of *all* work done during a year in the salary expense on that year's income statement.

If we owe employees for work done in December 2005 but will not pay them until January 2006, we have to accrue salary expense when we are adjusting our accounts at December 31, 2005. Suppose Clint's owes its employee $50 for work done in 2005, but the next payday is in 2006. To get this salary expense on the income statement for the year, Clint must debit Salary Expense for $50 and credit Salaries Payable for $50. The salary expense on the income statement for the year ended December 31, 2005, will now include this $50. Salaries Payable on the balance sheet will show the $50 obligation. Look at the adjustment in the accounting equation, and then look at the journal entry. Note that in the adjusting entry, just like in a routine journal entry, debits = credits. The accounting equation remains in balance.

Assets	=	Liabilities	+	SC	+	Retained earnings
		+$50 Salaries payable				$(50) Salary expense

Date	Transaction	Debit	Credit
12/31/05	Salary expense	$50	
	Salaries payable		$50
To accrue salary expense at year-end			A-2

STUDY BREAK 4-2

See How You're Doing

Suppose a company owes employees $300 on December 31, 2007, the date of the financial statements; and the next payday is January 3, 2008. Give the adjusting journal entry necessary on December 31. How much salary expense will the company recognize when it actually pays the $300 to the employees on January 3, 2008? Give the journal entry for the payment on January 3.

Deferrals. Deferred Revenue. Deferred revenue is revenue that has not been earned yet, and so it is recorded as a liability in a company's records—an obligation—when the cash is collected. Because cash has been collected, it must be recorded; but the goods or services have not yet been provided. The company must defer—put off—recognizing the revenue. When the cash is received, the company increases Cash and increases a liability called Unearned Revenue. In a general ledger system, the amount of cash received is recorded in the Cash account, where it is shown as a debit—that is an increase because assets are increased with debits. The journal entry is balanced with a credit to Unearned Revenue—that is an increase because liabilities are increased with credits.

Suppose Clint had received $4,000 on May 1 for consulting services to be provided over the next 12 months. This is how the receipt of the $4,000 cash for services to be provided in the future affects the accounting equation, followed by the journal entry for the receipt of the $4,000 cash.

Assets	=	Liabilities	+	SC	+	Retained earnings
+$4,000 cash		+$4,000 Unearned consulting fees				

Date	Transaction	Debit	Credit
5/1/05	Cash	$4,000	
	Unearned consulting fees		$4,000
To record the receipt of cash for services to be provided			1-9

Note that this is *not* an adjusting entry; it is a regular journal entry—made when it occurs during the year—to record the receipt of cash. When we look at the T-accounts again, we will see it posted with the transactions we posted previously.

Whenever a company has recorded unearned revenue during the year, an adjustment will be necessary at year-end to recognize the portion of the revenue that has been earned during the time between when the cash was received and year-end. If, on that basis, any of the unearned revenue becomes earned revenue by year-end, the Unearned Revenue account will be decreased and the Revenue account will be increased with an adjustment. In terms of debits and credits, the Unearned Revenue account, which is a liability, will be decreased with a debit. In Clint's case, the credit corresponding to that debit will go to Consulting Fees, which means that the earned revenue will now show up on the income statement with the other consulting fees Clint has earned during the year. This adjustment is necessary to be sure all the earned revenue for the year is recognized—meaning, put on the income statement. Suppose Clint had earned half of the revenue at year-end. The adjustment in the accounting equation and the corresponding journal entry for this adjustment follow:

Assets	=	Liabilities	+	SC	+	Retained earnings
		$(2,000) Unearned consulting fees				+$2,000 Consulting fees

Date	Transaction	Debit	Credit
12/31/05	Unearned consulting fees	$2,000	
	Consulting fees		$2,000
To record earned revenue at year-end			A-3

Deferred Expenses. Deferred expenses may need to be adjusted before the financial statements are prepared. Recall, a deferred expense is something the company paid for in advance. One example is Supplies, discussed in Chapter 3. Clint paid $400 for supplies during the year, and he recorded them as an asset. At the end of the year, he must determine how many supplies are left and how many he used. He counts the supplies on hand and then subtracts that amount from the amount he purchased. Suppose Clint finds that there is $75 worth of supplies left in the supply closet on December 31. Since he purchased $400 worth, that means he must have used $325 worth of supplies during the year. He wants to show supplies expense of $325 on the year's income statement; and he wants the asset Supplies to show $75 on the balance sheet at year end. This is the adjustment to get the accounts to their correct year-end balances, first in the accounting equation and then as a journal entry:

Assets	=	Liabilities	+	SC	+	Retained earnings
$(325) Supplies						$(325) Supplies expense

Date	Transaction	Debit	Credit
12/31/05	Supplies Expense	$325	
	Supplies		$325
To record supplies expense for the year			A-4

The T-accounts with the adjusting entries posted to them are shown in Exhibit 4–7.

Steps 5 and 6: Preparing the Adjusted Trial Balance and the Financial Statements

A **trial balance** is a list of all the accounts, each with its debit balance or its credit balance. An **unadjusted trial balance** is prepared before any adjustments have been made. An **adjusted trial balance** is prepared after adjustments have been made, and it can be used to prepare the financial statements.

After all the adjusting entries have been posted to the general ledger accounts and new balances have been computed in the general ledger, an **adjusted trial balance** is prepared. An **adjusted trial balance** is simply a list of all the general ledger accounts and their balances, to verify that debits = credits for all the company's accounts after all the adjustments have been made. Preparing an adjusted trial balance—and making sure it actually balances—helps ensure the accuracy of the recording process. If the adjusted trial balance *is* in balance—debits = credits—it can be used to prepare the financial statements.

The adjusted trial balance is shown in Exhibit 4–8, and the financial statements are shown in Exhibit 4–9.

Exhibit 4–7 Adjusted T-Accounts for Clint's Consulting Co., Inc.

Cash (asset)

	Debit	Credit	
1-1	$ 2,000	$ 400	1-3
1-2	4,000	500	1-4
1-5	9,000	4,150	1-7
1-9	4,000	350	1-6
		600	1-8
	$13,000		

Supplies (asset)

	Debit	Credit	
1-3	$400	$325	A-4
	$ 75		

Notes payable (liability)

	Debit	Credit	
1-7	$4,000	$4,000	1-2
		$0	

Accounts receivable (asset)

	Debit	Credit	
A-1	$3000		

Salaries payable (liability)

	Debit	Credit	
		$50	A-2

Share capital (SC) (owner's equity)

	Debit	Credit	
		$2,000	1-1

Unearned consulting fees (liability)

	Debit	Credit	
A-3	$2,000	$4,000	1-9
		$2,000	

Consulting fees (revenue)

	Debit	Credit	
		$ 9,000	1-5
		3,000	A-1
		2,000	A-3
		$14,000	

Dividends

	Debit	Credit	
1-8	$600		

Advertising expense (expense)

	Debit	Credit	
1-4	$500		

Interest expense (expense)

	Debit	Credit	
1-7	$150		

Supplies expense (expense)

	Debit	Credit	
A-4	$325		

Salary expense (expense)

	Debit	Credit	
1-6	$350		
A-2	50		
	$400		

After the financial statements are prepared, we are *almost* ready to begin another accounting cycle. First, we must get our general ledger ready for a new fiscal year.

L.O. 4

Describe the closing process and explain why it is necessary.

Step 7: Closing the Revenue and Expense Accounts

Revenue accounts and expense accounts are **temporary accounts**. The balances in those accounts will be transferred to retained earnings at the end of each period; therefore, they will start each new period with a zero balance.

Think about the accounting equation and the work sheet we have been using to record transactions. We have been listing the revenues and expenses in

Temporary accounts are the revenue, expense, and dividends accounts. Their balances are brought to zero at the end of the accounting period, called **closing** the accounts.

Exhibit 4–8
Adjusted Trial Balance for Clint's Consulting Company, Inc. for the Year 2005

Account	DR	CR
Cash	$13,000	
Accounts receivable	3,000	
Supplies	75	
Notes payable		$ 0
Salaries payable		50
Unearned consulting fees		2,000
Share capital		2,000
Dividends	600	
Consulting fees		14,000
Advertising expense	500	
Interest expense	150	
Salary expenses	400	
Supplies expense	325	
	$18,050	$18,050

Exhibit 4–9
Financial Statements for Clint's Consulting Company, Inc. for 2005

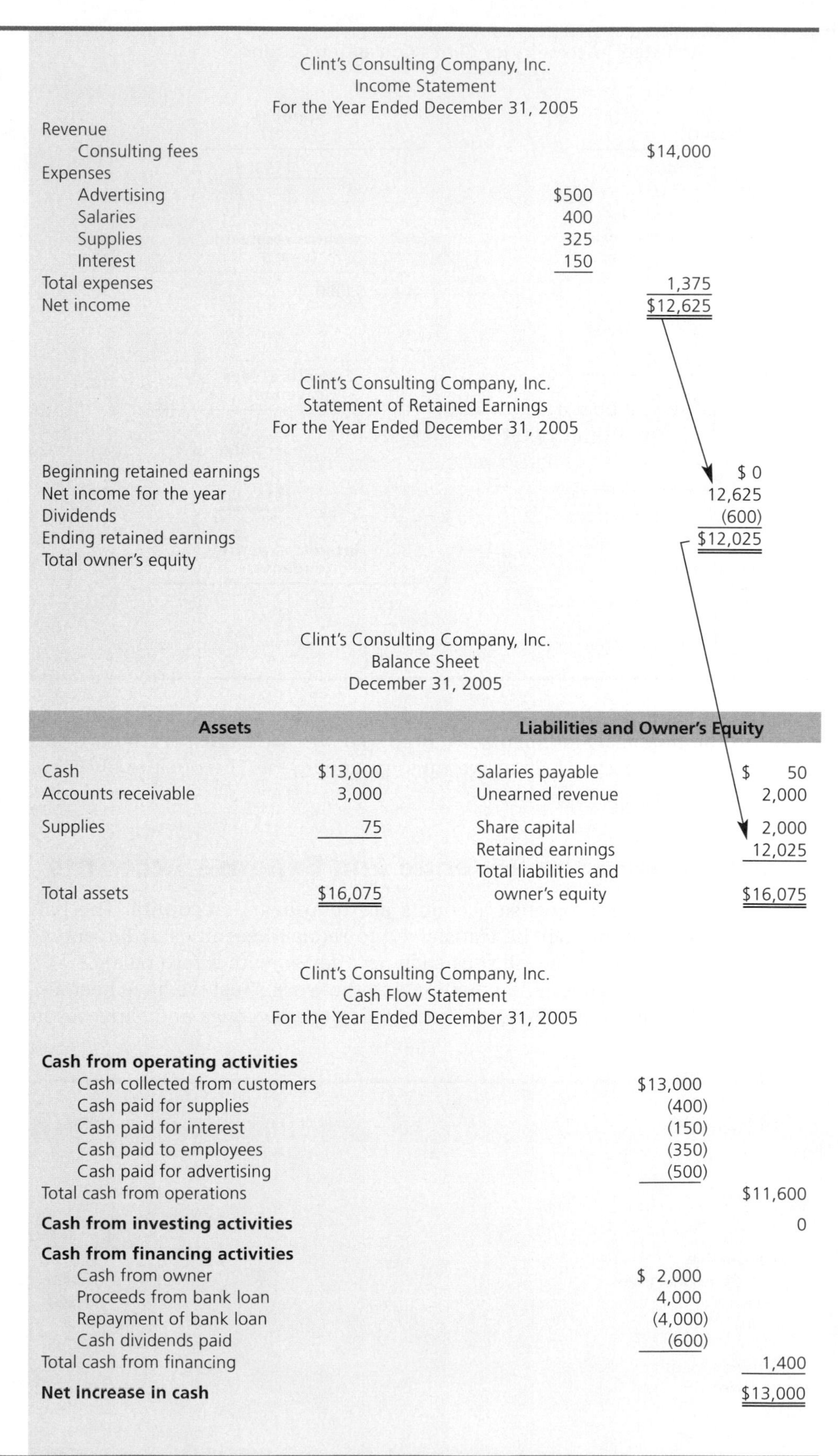

Clint's Consulting Company, Inc.
Income Statement
For the Year Ended December 31, 2005

Revenue		
Consulting fees		$14,000
Expenses		
Advertising	$500	
Salaries	400	
Supplies	325	
Interest	150	
Total expenses		1,375
Net income		$12,625

Clint's Consulting Company, Inc.
Statement of Retained Earnings
For the Year Ended December 31, 2005

Beginning retained earnings	$ 0
Net income for the year	12,625
Dividends	(600)
Ending retained earnings	$12,025
Total owner's equity	

Clint's Consulting Company, Inc.
Balance Sheet
December 31, 2005

Assets		Liabilities and Owner's Equity	
Cash	$13,000	Salaries payable	$ 50
Accounts receivable	3,000	Unearned revenue	2,000
Supplies	75	Share capital	2,000
		Retained earnings	12,025
Total assets	$16,075	Total liabilities and owner's equity	$16,075

Clint's Consulting Company, Inc.
Cash Flow Statement
For the Year Ended December 31, 2005

Cash from operating activities		
Cash collected from customers	$13,000	
Cash paid for supplies	(400)	
Cash paid for interest	(150)	
Cash paid to employees	(350)	
Cash paid for advertising	(500)	
Total cash from operations		$11,600
Cash from investing activities		0
Cash from financing activities		
Cash from owner	$ 2,000	
Proceeds from bank loan	4,000	
Repayment of bank loan	(4,000)	
Cash dividends paid	(600)	
Total cash from financing		1,400
Net increase in cash		$13,000

the retained earnings column because they increase and decrease the owner's claims to the assets of the business. The balance sheet will balance only when the revenue and expense amounts are incorporated into the retained earnings balance. The net amount of revenues minus expenses—net income—is incorporated into retained earnings when we prepare the statement of changes in owner's equity.

From a bookkeeping perspective, the revenue and expense accounts are **closed**—meaning their balances are brought to zero—with journal entries. Each account receives a debit or a credit to close it. For example, if a revenue account has a balance of $300—which would be a credit balance—the account is closed with a debit for $300. The corresponding credit in that closing journal entry is to Retained Earnings. Thus, closing the revenue account increases Retained Earnings. On the other hand, closing an expense account will decrease Retained Earnings. For example, if an expense account has a balance of $100—which would be a debit balance—the account is closed with a credit for $100. The corresponding debit for that closing journal entry is to Retained Earnings. Closing the expense account decreases Retained Earnings.

Keep in mind the reason for having revenue accounts and expense accounts. For a single accounting period, usually a year, the revenues and expenses are recorded separately from Retained Earnings so that we can report them on the year's income statement. Then we want those amounts included in retained earnings, and we want the revenue and expense accounts to be "empty" so they can start over, ready for amounts that will come during the coming year. Remember, the income statement covers a single accounting period. We do not want to mix up last year's revenue with this year's revenue in our revenue accounts or last year's expenses with this year's expenses in our expense accounts. The process of bringing these accounts to a zero balance is called closing the accounts, and the journal entries are called closing entries. We cannot close the revenue accounts and expense accounts until we have prepared the financial statements.

Asset accounts, liability accounts, and shareholders' equity accounts are **permanent accounts**, or **real accounts.** A balance in any of these accounts is carried over from one period to the next. For example, the amount of cash shown in the cash account will never be zero (unless we spend our last cent). The same is true about all balance sheet accounts. Think about your own personal records. If you keep track of your cash (like your checking account), you will have a continuous record of your cash balance. On the date of a personal balance sheet, you would see how much cash you have on that particular date. As the next year begins, you still have that cash. It does not go away because a new year begins.

Permanent accounts or **real accounts** are accounts that are never closed. They are the asset, liability, and equity accounts.

To get a better idea of what we mean by the continuous record in a permanent account, let us consider a simple example of a *temporary* account. Suppose you were keeping a list of your grocery expenses for the year. At the end of the year, after you have reported the amount of those expenses on your annual income statement, you would want to start a new list for the next year. Because an income statement reports expenses for a period of time—a year, in this example—your grocery expenses for one year would be reported on *one* income statement, but those expenses would not apply to the following year. You would want the grocery expense account to be empty when you begin the next year. Expense amounts must apply to a specific time period for them to make sense.

Exhibit 4–10 shows the closing journal entries for Clint's Consulting, which are recorded after the financial statements are prepared.

Exhibit 4–10
Closing Entries

Ref.	Date	Journal entry	DR	CR
C-1	12/31	Consulting fees	$14,000	
		Retained earnings		$14,000
		To close revenue account		
C-2	12/31	Retained earnings	1,375	
		Advertising expense		500
		Salary expense		400
		Supplies expense		325
		Interest expense		150
		To close the expense accounts		
C-3	12/31	Retained earnings	$ 600	
		Dividends		$ 600
		To close dividends		

STUDY BREAK 4-3

See How You're Doing

Simple Company has one revenue account with a balance of $5,000 at year-end and one expense account with a balance of $3,000. Prepare the closing journal entries for Simple Company.

More About Closing Entries and the Relationship Between the Income Statement and the Balance Sheet. The formal way of making the balances zero in the revenue and expense accounts is called closing the accounts. Why do we bother with closing entries? They set the stage for the next accounting period by zeroing out the balances of all the temporary accounts. This is necessary because these accounts keep track of amounts that go to the income statement, which gives us the net income figure for *one specific period.* Without zeroing out the accounts, net income would include revenues or expenses for more than one period. Closing entries transfer the period's net income (or loss) to the retained earnings account (or to the owner's capital account in a sole proprietorship), and so closing entries are the means by which net income flows downstream from the income statement through the statement of changes in owner's equity to the balance sheet.

Here is how the revenue amounts and expense amounts flow through the financial statements:

- *Income statement.* We present the details of net income—the revenues and expenses—on the income statement. The bottom line is net income.
- *Statement of retained earnings.* We show net income as an addition to retained earnings on the statement of retained earnings.
- *Balance sheet.* We present the total amount of owner's equity—which includes retained earnings—on the balance sheet.

After we have used the revenue account balances and the expense account balances to prepare the income statement and after that information has flowed through to the balance sheet, we are ready to close the revenue accounts and expense accounts. That is the formal way of getting the correct balance in Retained Earnings. Here are the steps in detail to record closing entries:

1. Transfer all credit balances from the revenue accounts to Retained Earnings. This is done with a closing entry. The closing journal entry will have a debit to each of the revenue accounts for the entire balance of each—to bring them to a zero balance. The corresponding credit will be to Retained Earnings for the total amount of the period's revenue.
2. Transfer all debit balances from the expense accounts to Retained Earnings. This is done with a closing entry. The closing journal entry will have a debit to Retained Earnings and credits to all the expense accounts for their entire balances to bring them to a zero balance. The debit to Retained Earnings will be for the total amount of the period's expenses.
3. Transfer the Dividends account balance to Retained Earnings. When a distribution is made to the shareholders of a corporation, a special account—Dividends—is often used. This account is a temporary account that carries a debit balance. (When the dividends are paid, Dividends is debited and Cash is credited.) The Dividends account is closed directly to Retained Earnings. The amount of the dividends is not included on the income statement, but it is shown on the statement of changes in shareholders' equity. The journal entry to close this account will have a credit to Dividends and a debit to Retained Earnings.

Look at the closing entries posted to Clint's T-accounts, shown in bold print in Exhibit 4–11. Note how the revenue and expense accounts have a zero balance.

When closing is done, there is one step left to completing our record keeping for the year: That step is preparing a postclosing trial balance.

Step 8: Preparing a Postclosing Trial Balance

The final step in the accounting cycle is to prepare a **postclosing trial balance**. Remember, *post* means *after* (like *pre* means *before*). After the temporary accounts are closed, preparing a trial balance—a list of all the accounts with their debit or credit balances—accomplishes two things:

- It is a final check of the equality of debits and credits in the general ledger.
- It confirms that we are ready to start our next period with only real (permanent) accounts.

The postclosing trial balance for Clint's Consulting is shown in Exhibit 4–12.

A **postclosing trial balance** is a list of all the accounts and their debit balances or credit balances, prepared after the temporary accounts have been closed. Only balance sheet accounts will appear on the postclosing trial balance.

Review and Summary of the Accounting Cycle

To summarize, there are several steps in the process of preparing financial statements using a traditional general ledger system. Together, they are called the *accounting cycle*.

1. Record the transactions in the journal.
2. Post the journal entries to the ledger.
3. Prepare an unadjusted trial balance.
4. Adjust the accounts at the end of the period—record the adjusting journal entries and post them to the general ledger.
5. Prepare an adjusted trial balance.
6. Prepare the financial statements.

Exhibit 4–11 **T-Accounts with Closing Entries for Clint's Consulting Company, Inc.**

Cash (asset)

Ref	Debit	Credit	Ref
1-1	$ 2,000	$ 400	1-3
1-2	4,000	500	1-4
1-5	9,000	4,150	1-7
1-9	4,000	350	1-6
		600	1-8
	$13,000		

Supplies (asset)

Ref	Debit	Credit	Ref
1-3	$400	$325	A-4
	$ 75		

Notes payable (liability)

Ref	Debit	Credit	Ref
1-7	$4,000	$4,000	1-2
		$ 0	

Accounts receivable (asset)

Ref	Debit	Credit	Ref
A-1	$3,000		

Salaries payable (liability)

Ref	Debit	Credit	Ref
		$50	A-2

Unearned consulting fees (liability)

Ref	Debit	Credit	Ref
A-3	$2,000	$4,000	1-9
		$2,000	

Share capital (SC) (owner's equity)

Ref	Debit	Credit	Ref
		$2,000	1-1

Consulting fees (revenue)

Ref	Debit	Credit	Ref
		$9,000	1-5
		3,000	A-1
		2,000	A-3
C-1	**$14,000**		

Advertising expense (expense)

Ref	Debit	Credit	Ref
1-4	$500	**$500**	**C-2**

Retained earnings

Ref	Debit	Credit	Ref
C-2	**$1,375**	**$14,000**	**C-1**
C-3	**600**		
		$12,025	

Interest expense (expense)

Ref	Debit	Credit	Ref
1-7	$150	**$150**	**C-2**

Salary expense (expense)

Ref	Debit	Credit	Ref
1-6	$350	**$400**	**C-2**
A-2	50		

Dividends

Ref	Debit	Credit	Ref
1-8	$600	**$600**	**C-3**

Supplies expense (expense)

Ref	Debit	Credit	Ref
A-4	$325	**$325**	**C-2**

Exhibit 4–12
Postclosing Trial Balance for Clint's Consulting Company, Inc. at December 31, 2005

Account	DR	CR
Cash	$13,000	
Accounts receivable	3,000	
Supplies	75	
Notes payable		$ 0
Salaries payable		50
Unearned consulting fees		2,000
Share capital		2,000
Retained earnings		12,025
Totals	$16,075	$16,075

7. Close the temporary accounts to get ready for the next accounting period.
8. Prepare a postclosing trial balance.

What's Next? The General Ledger System versus Integrated Information Systems

L.O. 5

Define an ERP and describe its purpose.

The general ledger system, with debits and credits, has been in existence for nearly 500 years. It is based on a **chart of accounts**—a list of all the accounts that a company wants in its general ledger. Often, accounts are combined for the financial statements, and so the level of detail in a company's records corresponds to the number of accounts the company includes in its chart of accounts, *not* by what we see on the financial statements. For example, in Clint's Consulting Company, Inc.'s first year of business, discussed earlier in this chapter, the company may combine Advertising Expense and Supplies Expense on its income statement and list the total as Operating Expenses. When Clint designed the company's general ledger, he decided that he wanted to keep track of advertising costs and supplies separately. That is why he made an account for each.

A **chart of accounts** is a list of all the accounts in a company's general ledger.

In the general ledger, each account can be increased or decreased. Debits and credits are combined with the accounting equation to create a system called the double-entry accounting or bookkeeping system. This is a clever system, with checks and balances that help an accountant to minimize errors and to analyze the effects of transactions on the financial statements. Information is stored and organized in a way that provides the information for the four basic financial statements.

However, there is a significant drawback to this traditional system. The problem is that it is dedicated solely to gathering information from business transactions for the financial statements.

In the past 30 years, advancements in technology have made available *computerized* general ledger software, such as ACCPAC® and Great Plains®. These programs are computerized versions of the traditional manual general ledger accounting system we have been studying in this chapter. The biggest advantage of computerized general ledger systems is a reduction in errors in posting journal entries to the general ledger and the ability to program the preparation of the financial statements. Built-in controls will force the system to stay in balance (debits = credits). Computerized software packages are programmed to produce the financial statements automatically with only journal entries as input.

As terrific as these computerized general ledger packages are, they do not solve the basic problem of the general ledger system—the limited amount of information the general ledger system records about the transactions of the business. The functional areas of the company—like the sales department or the marketing department—must each have its own **information system**. The sales department has a list of customers, their credit histories, and a record of their purchases. The sales department may have additional sales information by product or by division. None of this information is recorded as part of a general ledger accounting system. If another department needs any of this information, that department has to keep it in its own information system.

Information systems are computerized systems that enable companies to record, organize, and maintain information.

Only in the past five to 10 years has progress been made in solving the problems associated with multiple information systems. The newest technology allows a company to have one information system that is able to capture enormous amounts of information about every transaction so that the sales department, the marketing department, the payroll department, the advertis-

Understanding Business

Enterprise Resource Planning Systems

Enterprise Resource Planning systems are changing the way businesses manage, process, and use information. ERP systems are computer-based software programs designed to process an organization's transactions and integrate information for planning, production, financial reporting, and customer service. These systems are designed for companies that have computer systems with enormous capabilities. It is estimated that the majority of companies with annual revenues exceeding $1 billion have implemented ERP systems.

Exactly how ERP systems operate varies from company to company, depending on the company's needs.

- ERP systems are packaged software designed for business environments, both traditional and Web based. *Packaged software* means that the software is commercially available—for purchase or lease—from a software vendor, as opposed to being developed in-house. ERP software packages incorporate what the vendors call "best practices." These are supposed to be the best way of doing certain business activities, such as the best practice for inventory management or production management.
- An ERP system is composed of modules relating to specific functions. There are modules for *accounting,* including financial, managerial, and international accounting; *logistics,* including materials requirement planning, production, distribution, sales management, and customer management; and *human resources,* including payroll, benefits, and compensation management.
- All the modules work together with a common database. This creates an enterprise-wide system instead of separate, independent systems for each function of the business.
- ERP systems are integrated in terms of software, but not hardware. So, even though two companies may buy ERP packages from the same vendor, the way the system is used will likely be very different. A company may implement modules from more than one vendor in an attempt to customize its ERP system.
- Because of their popularity and growth, the large ERP vendors are familiar to many of us—SAP, Oracle, PeopleSoft, J.D. Edwards, and BAAN. Together, these vendors hold a major share of the ERP market and provide their system packages along with training to their clients around the world.
- Because the ERP vendors have already sold their systems to most of the large international companies, the vendors are trying to expand their market to slightly smaller (i.e., middle-market) companies.

Companies implement ERP systems to:

- consolidate their systems and eliminate redundant data entry and data storage
- decrease their computer operating costs
- better manage their business processes
- accommodate international currencies and international languages
- standardize policies and procedures
- enhance and speed up financial reporting
- improve decision making
- improve productivity
- improve profitability

In spite of all the potential benefits of ERP systems, there are drawbacks. ERP systems are costly to implement, with total implementation costs running into the millions of dollars. The use of best practices embedded in the software usually requires companies to change the way they conduct their business processes to match the software. This is not always beneficial—especially when companies have business processes that may give them a competitive advantage. Finally, switching to a new system requires extensive and costly training for those who will use the system.

Given the widespread adoption of ERP systems, it is apparent that the market perceives the ERP system benefits to outweigh the costs. Therefore, whether you choose to go into accounting, information technology, finance, marketing, or management, it is likely that you will encounter an ERP system. However, given the speed with which technology changes, the ERP systems that you will encounter will be even more complex with greater capacities than the ones in existence today.

ing department, the production department—any functional area in the company—and the accountants can all use the same database of information.

These information systems are called **enterprise resource planning systems (ERPs);** they are integrated information systems that capture all of a company's information in a single database. Technically, an ERP is a packaged software system that allows a company to:

An **enterprise resource planning system (ERP)** is a company-wide integrated information system.

- automate and integrate many of its business processes, such as purchasing and production;
- share common data across the entire organization, such as customer information or sales data; and
- produce and access information instantaneously.

All the information is recorded without regard for any particular use of the data. Then when someone needs information, it can be retrieved from the database in a variety of ways. For example, sales can be retrieved by date, by customer, by item purchased, just to name a few possibilities.

What are some of the benefits of such a system?

- reduction in inventory and related costs
- faster delivery times
- production problems more easily identified and solved
- improved communication among departments
- decisions can be made faster due to data availability

Because this is a textbook for learning introductory accounting, we are most interested in the data needed for the financial statements. You should be aware that financial data retrieved from an integrated information system like an ERP must be adjusted before the financial statements can be prepared. Most often, the system will produce an unadjusted trial balance; and the accountant goes to work from there to finish the work needed to prepare the financial statements.

STUDY BREAK 4-4

See How You're Doing

How does using an ERP instead of a general ledger system change the information shown on the financial statements?

Business Risks

Record keeping presents a significant risk to a business. This risk—**information processing risk**—is the risk that a company will not properly record the financial information related to its transactions. As we discussed in Chapter 2, we can think of this risk in three parts: inputs, processing, and outputs. In a general ledger system, the input is a journal entry. An accounting system must have controls in place to see that the information in the journal entries is complete and accurate.

The **information-processing risk** is the risk associated with recording, maintaining, or reporting data or information.

Then the input is processed. Journal entries are posted to the general ledger, adjustments are made, and financial statements are prepared. These processing activities need to be monitored for accuracy and completeness. The general ledger system has some built in controls that help minimize errors. The double-entry nature of the debit and credit system is a control for some mathematical errors, and preparing a trial balance at various times is a check to see how that control is working. Many errors in a general ledger accounting system are found and corrected when a trial balance is prepared.

The output of an accounting system is a set of financial statements. The relationship between those statements—net income increases owner's equity and owner's equity is needed to make the balance sheet balance—provides a control for information processing errors. A thorough review of the statements before they are made available to the public is also a necessary control.

Whether the accounting information is processed with a manual general ledger system, a computerized general ledger system, or an enterprise-wide resource planning system, controls should be in place to make sure the input is complete and accurate, the processing is done without errors, and the output is complete and accurate.

Understanding Excel

The following is Tom's Wear, Inc. adjusted trial balance at March 31, 2005.

Tom's Wear, Inc.
Adjusted Trial Balance
March 31, 2005

	Debit	Credit
Cash	$ 3,995	
Accounts receivable	2,000	
Inventory	300	
Prepaid insurance	75	
Computer	4,000	
Accumulated amortization		$ 100
Interest payable		30
Notes payable		3,000
Common shares		5,000
Retained earnings		1,220
Sales		2,000
Cost of goods sold	800	
Insurance expense	50	
Amortization expense	100	
Interest expense	30	
Totals	*$11,350*	*$11,350*

For purposes of this exercise only, assume that Tom's Wear, Inc. is closing the books for the month of March.

Requirements

1. Open a new Excel work sheet.
2. Create the following bold column headings beginning in column A and ending in column E: **Ref., Date, Journal Entry, DR,** and **CR.**
3. Enter the required closing journal entries. Adjust your column widths as needed.
4. Prepare a postclosing trial balance for Tom's Wear, Inc. Use appropriate headings and formatting.

   Hint: To sum the total debits and credits select the appropriate cell and click the Auto Sum Σ button.
5. Print your file and save it to disk. Name your file TomsWear4.

Summary Problem: Tom's Wear Transactions for March 2005 in a General Ledger System

We've already analyzed the transactions for Tom's Wear for the third month of business, and prepared the financial statements for March in Chapter 3. Let us repeat the accounting cycle for the same month, this time using debits and credits. The transactions for March are shown in Exhibit 4–13. Each transaction is recorded as an entry in the general journal, chronologically as it occurs during the company's business activity. Exhibit 4–14 shows the transactions in the accounting equation worksheet. Then, each transaction is posted to the general ledger (we will use T-accounts). At March 31, we will post the adjusting entries needed to prepare the four financial statements. After following along through the adjusted T-accounts, you will prepare the financial statements.

To use a general ledger system, we need to set up the accounts with their balances on March 1, 2005. Exhibit 4–15 shows all the accounts with their beginning balances (indicated with BB). Those accounts, in the Tom's Wear general ledger, will remain with the beginning balances until we post journal entries from the month's transactions.

The first step in the accounting cycle is to record each transaction in chronological order in the journal—as each occurs in the business. Look at each transaction and its journal entry. Note that for each journal entry, there is:

- the date of the transaction
- the account names
- equality between the debits and credits—in every journal entry
- a brief explanation of the transaction

Study each journal entry to make sure you understand how the transaction was recorded.

March 1	Purchased computer for $4,000 with $1,000 down and a 3-month, 12 percent note for $3,000. The computer is expected to last for 3 years and have a residual value of $400.
March 10	Paid the rest of last month's advertising bill, $50.
March 15	Collected accounts receivable of $150 from customers from February.
March 20	Paid for February purchases—paying off the accounts payable balance—of $800.
March 24	Purchased 250 shirts @ $4 each for cash, $1,000.
March 27	Sold 200 shirts for $10 each, all on account, for total sales of $2,000.

Exhibit 4–13
Transactions for March 2005 for Tom's Wear, Inc.

Journal Entries for March 2005

Ref.	Date	Journal entry	DR	CR
3-1	3/01/05	Equipment	$4,000	
		Cash		$1,000
		Notes payable		3,000
		To record the purchase of a computer with a cash down payment of $1,000 and a note payable of $3,000		
3-2	3/10/05	Other payables	50	
		Cash		50
		To record the payment of a liability for last month's advertising expense		
3-3	3/15/05	Cash	150	
		Accounts receivable		150
		To record the collection of accounts receivable		
3-4	3/20/05	Accounts payable	800	
		Cash		800
		To record payment to vendor for last month's purchase		
3-5	3/24/05	Inventory	1,000	
		Cash		1,000
		To record the purchase of 250 T-shirts at $4 each, paid for in cash		
3-6a	3/27/05	Accounts receivable	2,000	
		Sales		2,000
		To record the sale of 200 T-shirts, on account		
3-6b	3/27/05	Cost of goods sold	800	
		Inventory		800
		To record the expense *cost of goods sold* and reduce the inventory by 200 × $4		

Required

1. Post the journal entries for March using the T-accounts shown in Exhibit 4–15.
2. Then prepare an unadjusted trial balance at March 31.
3. Make the necessary adjusting journal entries at March 31, and post them to the T-accounts. For Tom's Wear, three adjustments need to be made before the financial statements can be prepared. The adjustments are:

   a. Amortization expense for the computer
   b. Insurance expense for the month
   c. Interest payable on the note

4. Prepare an *adjusted* trial balance at March 31, 2005.
5. Use the adjusted trial balance to prepare the four basic financial statements.

Exhibit 4–14 **Work Sheet for March for Tom's Wear**

tom's wear	Assets		=	Liabilities		+	Shareholders' equity: Contributed capital	Shareholders' equity: Retained earnings
Balance sheet at March 1, 2005 →	Cash	$ 6,695	=	Accounts payable	$ 800	+	Common shares	Retained earnings
	Accounts receivable	150		Other payables	50			
					$850		**$5,000**	**$1,220**
	Inventory	100						
	Prepaid insurance	125						
		$7,070						
March 1	Equipment	+$4,000		Notes payable	+3,000			
	Cash	(1,000)						
March 10	Cash	(50)		Other payables	(50)			
March 15	Cash	+150						
	Accounts receivable	(150)						
March 20	Cash	(800)		Accounts payable	(800)			
March 24	Cash	(1,000)						
	Inventory	+1,000						
March 27	Accounts receivable	+2,000						Sales +2,000
	Inventory	(800)						Cost of goods sold (800)
Balance sheet at March 31 → before adjustments	Cash	$ 3,995	=	Notes payable	**$3,000**	+	**$5,000** Common shares	**$2,420** Retained earnings
	Accounts receivable	2,000						
	Inventory	300						
	Prepaid insurance	125		Total liabilities and shareholders' equity **$10,420**				
	Equipment	4,000						
	Total assets	**$10,420**						

Solution

1. T-accounts are shown in the answer to part 3.
2.

Tom's Wear, Inc.
Unadjusted Trial Balance
March 31, 2005

Cash	$3,995	
Accounts receivable	2,000	
Inventory	300	
Prepaid insurance	125	
Equipment	4,000	
Accumulated amortization		
Accounts payable		
Other payables		
Interest payable		
Notes payable		$ 3,000
Common shares		5,000
Retained earnings		1,220
Sales		2,000
Cost of goods sold	800	
Insurance expense		
Amortization expense		
Interest expense		
Totals	*$11,220*	*$11,220*

Exhibit 4–15 T-Accounts for Tom's Wear at the Beginning of March

tom's wear

Account	Debit	Credit
Cash	BB 6,695	
Accounts receivable	BB 150	
Inventory	BB 100	
Prepaid insurance	BB 125	
Prepaid rent		
Equipment		
Accumulated amortization		
Other payables		50 BB
Accounts payable		800 BB
Interest payable		
Salaries payable		
Notes payable		
Common shares		5,000 BB
Retained earnings		1,220 BB
Sales (revenue)		
Cost of goods sold		
Salary expense		
Insurance expense		
Amortization expense		
Interest expense		

Note: BB = beginning balance

3. Adjusting journal entries and explanations:

a. The computer has been used for one full month, and so you must record amortization expense. The cost was $4,000, an estimated residual value of $400, and a three-year useful life. Each year the equipment will be amortized by $1,200 (= (4,000 – 400)/3 years). That makes the amortization expense $100 per month.

Date	Transaction	Debit	Credit
3/31/05	Amortization expense	$100	
	Accumulated amortization		$100

To record the depreciation expense for March.

b. Tom's Wear signed a $3,000 note on March 1 to purchase the computer. A month has passed, and Tom's Wear needs to accrue the interest expense on that note in the amount of $30 (= $3,000 × 0.12 × 1/12).

Date	Transaction	Debit	Credit
3/31/05	Interest expense	$30	
	Interest payable		$30

To record the interest expense for March.

c. In mid-February, Tom's Wear purchased three months of insurance for $150, which is $50 per month. On the March 1 balance sheet, there is a current asset called prepaid insurance in the amount of $125. A full month's worth of insurance expense needs to be recorded for the month of March. That amount will be deducted from prepaid insurance.

Date	Transaction	Debit	Credit
3/31/05	Insurance expense	$50	
	Prepaid insurance		$50

To record the insurance expense for the year.

T-Accounts with Adjustments for March 2005 Posted (Balances Shown at the End of Each Account)

Cash

Debit	Credit
BB $6,695	$1,000 1
	50 2
3 150	800 4
	1,000 5
3,995	

Accounts receivable

Debit	Credit
BB $ 150	150 3
6a 2,000	
2,000	

Inventory

Debit	Credit
BB $ 100	
5 1,000	800 6b
300	

Prepaid insurance

Debit	Credit
BB $125	$50 Adj-3
75	

Equipment

Debit	Credit
1 $4,000	
4,000	

Accumulated amortization

Debit	Credit
	$100 Adj-1
	100

(continued)

Other payables

2 $50	$50 BB

Accounts payable

4 $800	$800 BB

Interest payable

	$30 Adj-2
	30

Notes payable

	$3,000 1
	3,000

Common shares

	$5,000 BB
	5,000

Retained earnings

	$1,220 BB
	1,220

Sales (revenue)

	$2,000 6a
	2,000

Cost of goods sold

6b $800	
800	

Insurance expense

Adj-3 $50	
50	

Amortization expense

Adj-1 $100	
100	

Interest expense

Adj-2 $30	
30	

4.

tom's wear

Tom's Wear, Inc.
Adjusted Trial Balance
March 31, 2005

Cash	$ 3,995	
Accounts receivable	2,000	
Inventory	300	
Prepaid insurance	75	
Equipment	4,000	
Accumulated amortization		$ 100
Accounts payable		
Other payables		
Interest payable		30
Notes payable		3,000
Common shares		5,000
Retained earnings		1,220
Sales		2,000
Cost of goods sold	800	
Insurance expense	50	
Amortization expense	100	
Interest expense	30	
Totals	*$11,350*	*$11,350*

5. The financial statements:

tom's wear

Tom's Wear, Inc.
Income Statement
For the Month Ended March 31, 2005

Sales revenue		$2,000
Expenses		
Cost of goods sold	$800	
Insurance expense	50	
Amortization expense	100	
Interest expense	30	980
Net income		$1,020

Tom's Wear, Inc.
Statement of Retained Earnings
For the Month Ended March 31, 2005

Beginning retained earnings	$1,220
Net income for the month	1,020
Ending retained earnings	$2,240

Tom's Wear, Inc.
Balance Sheet
March 31, 2005

Assets		Liabilities and shareholders' equity	
Cash	$ 3,995	Interest payable	$ 30
Accounts receivable	2,000	Notes payable	3,000
Inventory	300	Total liabilities	3,030
Prepaid insurance	75		
		Common shares	5,000
Equipment (net of $100 accumulated amortization)	3,900	Retained earnings	2,240
Total assets	*$10,270*	*Total liabilities and shareholders' equity*	*$10,270*

Tom's Wear, Inc.
Cash Flow Statement
For the Month Ended March 31, 2005

Cash from operating activities		
Cash collected from customers	$ 150	
Cash paid to vendors	(1,800)	
Cash paid for operating expenses	(50)	
Total cash from operations		$(1,700)
Cash from investing activities		
Purchase of asset[a]	$(1,000)	(1,000)
Cash from financing activities		0
Net increase (decrease) in cash		$(2,700)

[a]Computer was purchased for $4,000. A note was signed for $3,000 and cash paid was $1,000.

We have seen these exact financial statements before. When we used the accounting equation to keep track of the transactions in Chapter 3, the results were the same as using the general ledger system here. No matter how we do the record keeping, the financial statements are the same. The mechanics of any accounting system—stand-alone or integrated with an enterprise resource planning system—must be designed to produce the information needed for the basic financial statements.

Answers to Study Break Questions

STUDY BREAK 4-1

Account title	Expense	Revenue	Asset	Liability	Owner's equity
Accounts payable				CR	
Accounts receivable			DR		
Advertising	DR				
Cash			DR		
Amortization expense	DR				
Furniture and fixtures			DR		
Accumulated amortization			(Contra) CR		
Unearned fees				CR	
Salary expense	DR				
Common shares					CR
Rent expense	DR				
Dividends					DR
Retained earnings					CR
(Earned) Fees		CR			
Land			DR		
Building			DR		

STUDY BREAK 4-2

Date	Transaction	Debit	Credit
12/31/07	Salary expense	$300	
	Salaries payable		$300
To accrue salary expense for December 2007.			

No expense will be recognized in January 2008. It was recognized in December 2007 but will be paid in January 2008.

Date	Transaction	Debit	Credit
1/3/08	Salaries payable	$300	
	Cash		$300
To record the cash payment of salaries payable.			

STUDY BREAK 4-3

Date	Transaction	Debit	Credit
12/31/07	Revenue account	$5,000	
	Retained earnings		$5,000
To close the revenue account to retained earnings.			

Date	Transaction	Debit	Credit
12/31/07	Retained earnings	$3,000	
	Expense account		$3,000
To close the expense account to retained earnings.			

STUDY BREAK 4-4

Using an ERP instead of a general ledger system will not change the information shown on the financial statements. The two systems are just ways of keeping track of business information. It does not change the information or the reporting of it.

Questions

1. What is the general ledger system, and what are its advantages?
2. What is an account?
3. What is the trial balance?
4. Which accounts are permanent and which are temporary?
5. What is the normal balance in each of these accounts?

Accounts receivable	Cash
Accounts payable	Supplies expense
Common shares	Distributions (dividends)
Retained earnings	Inventory
Sales revenue	Bonds payable
Salary expense	Cost of goods sold

6. What are the basic steps in the accounting cycle?
7. Can accounting transactions be recorded directly into the general ledger accounts? What is the advantage of using a journal first?
8. Is a *credit* a good thing or a bad thing? Explain.
9. What are adjusting entries and why are they necessary?
10. What is an ERP?
11. What are the advantages of an ERP system?
12. What are the disadvantages of an ERP system?
13. The REA model is a conceptual model, whereas ERPs are operational models. What is the difference?
14. Compare the focus of a general ledger system with the focus of an ERP system.
15. What are some of the specific control issues with an ERP system?
16. Why do accountants care about ERP systems?
17. How does using an ERP change the company's financial statements (compared with those produced in a general ledger (G/L) system)?

Short Exercises

SE4-1 Given the following accounts, tell whether the normal balance of each account is a debit (DR) or credit (CR). L.O. 1

1. ______ Accounts receivable
2. ______ Notes payable
3. ______ Tom Phillips, Capital account
4. ______ Sales
5. ______ Prepaid insurance
6. ______ Supplies inventory
7. ______ Rent expense
8. ______ Salaries payable
9. ______ Retained earnings

SE4-2 Indicate which of the following events would result in recognizing revenue for the year in which the event takes place; indicate the amount and the account. Give the journal entry that would be made in each case. (Take the selling company's point of view.) L.O. 1, 2, 3

a. A used car salesman sells a car for $12,000; the customer financed the purchase because she did not have any cash.
b. Steel Canada is producing three tonnes of steel for Canadian Cans. It costs $3,600 per tonne to produce, but Canadian Cans has promised to pay $5,000 per tonne when it receives the steel. Steel Canada will probably ship it in the near future.
c. Halifax Housers has received $50,000 in advanced ticket sales for next year's basketball games.

d. Reader's Digest collected several accounts that were outstanding from last year. Usually, accounts are collected in advance; but in this case, the customer received the magazine last year but did not pay until this year.
e. Customers paid over $5,000 in advance for services to be rendered next year.

L.O. 1, 2, 3

SE4-3 Indicate which of the following events would result in recognizing expenses for the year in which the event takes place; indicate the amount and the account. (Take the T-shirt company's point of view.)

a. T-Shirt Inc. paid employees $5,000 for work performed.
b. T-Shirt Inc. purchased 20,000 T-shirts for their inventory for $60,000 on account.
c. T-Shirt Inc. paid the factory cash for the 20,000 shirts purchased.
d. T-Shirt Inc. sold 2,000 T-shirts to the FSU Bookstore for $10,000 cash.
e. T-Shirt Inc. received a utility bill for the last month of the year but will not actually pay it until next year.
f. T-Shirt Inc. paid $5,000 for a two-year insurance policy—for the current year and for next year.

L.O. 4

SE4-4 Selected transactions for Red Company that occurred during the month of December follow. For each transaction, tell how it affects the accounting equation. Then tell which accounts will be affected and how. (Ignore adjustments that may be needed on December 31.)

e.g., *Red purchased a new computer for $5,000 for cash. It is expected to last for five years.*

Solution: Assets are increased by $5,000 (equipment) and also reduced by $5,000 (cash): debit (increase) equipment, credit (decrease) cash.

a. The company issued common stock to investors for $10,000 cash.
b. The company rented a warehouse for $1,000 per month, and paid for 3 months' rent on December 1.
c. The company purchased inventory for $3,000 on account.

L.O. 1

SE4-5 The following selected transactions for Blues Company occurred during the month of March. Give the journal entry for each.

a. The firm sold items to customers for $5,000: Half was for cash, and half was on account.
b. Blues paid $2,000 to vendor for inventory purchased on account in February.
c. The company incurred general expenses for $300 cash.
d. Blues purchased supplies for $200 cash.

L.O. 1

SE4-6 How do the following transactions affect Babyland's cash account? (Tell if it would be a debit or a credit.)

a. Babyland purchased $5,000 of baby cribs on account.
b. The company sold one of their buildings for $25,000 cash.
c. The employees were paid $2,000 in sales commissions.
d. The firm gave customers $1,000 for returned merchandise.
e. Babyland issued shares to investors for $5,000 cash.

L.O. 1

SE4-7 How do the following transactions affect the liability and owner's equity accounts for Fast Signs, Inc. during 2005?

a. Fast Signs paid the remainder of a $3,000 loan.
b. The company obtained a loan for $10,000.
c. Fast Signs earned $12,000 in sales for the year.
d. An estimated $2,500 will be due for yearly income taxes, payable in 2006.

L.O. 1

SE4-8 Determine how the accounts would be affected (increase or decrease and debit or credit) for the following transactions occurring in December 2005 for Networking Solutions, Inc.

a. Networking Solutions received $20,000 investment from the owner.
b. The company purchased $8,000 of new office computers on account.
c. The company sold $2,000 of inventory for cash.
d. Networking Solutions paid $3,000 for next year's rent.
e. The company paid $4,000 of the amount owed for the computers.
f. The company declared and distributed $1,000 of dividends.

SE4-9 For each of the following accounts, tell whether it is a permanent account or a temporary account. L.O. 4

1. ______ Cash
2. ______ Accounts payable
3. ______ Jane Smith, Capital account
4. ______ Revenues
5. ______ Prepaid insurance
6. ______ Merchandise inventory
7. ______ Rent expense
8. ______ Income tax expense
9. ______ Income taxes payable
10. ______ Common shares

Exercises

E4-1 Record the following transactions for JG Company in T-accounts and tell how each affects assets, liabilities, or owner's equity. The year-end for JG Company is December 31. L.O. 1, 2, 3

a. On April 1, JG Company issued a $5,000 note at 8 percent, both interest and principal due in 1 year.
b. On June 1, JG Company rented a copy machine and paid 1 year of rent in advance at a rate of $250 per month.
c. On June 30, JG Company purchased an insurance policy for a term of 1 year, beginning immediately. The cost was $960.
d. On July 1, JG Company replenished the supply closet with the purchase of $600 worth of supplies for cash. The company started the year with $100 worth of supplies on hand.
e. Over the course of the year, JG Company earned $35,000 of service revenue, collected in cash.

E4-2 Use the information from E4-1, including your answers to a through e to make the necessary adjustments to JG's accounts in preparation for the year-end financial statements. You may need to use the additional information that follows: L.O. 1, 2, 3

On hand at year-end was $200 worth of supplies.

E4-3 Matt opened his Read A-Lot Bookstore, a sole proprietorship, on April 1, 2006, selling new and used books. The gross profit earned on new book sales is 40 percent. Matt used $4,000 of his own money to start the business. L.O. 1, 2

a. On April 1, the business buys $3,000 of new books from his supplier with cash.
b. On April 30, customers bring in used books and the business buys them for $750.
c. On June 30, new books are sold for $3,000. Half of these sales are on account.
d. On June 30, the business sells all the used books for $1,500 cash.

Record the transactions into T-accounts for Matt.

E4-4 The trial balance of Clevenger's Computer Centre, Inc. on April 1, 2006, lists the company's assets, liabilities, and shareholders' equity on that date. L.O. 1, 2

Account title	Balance Debit	Balance Credit
Cash	$16,000	
Accounts receivable	4,700	
Accounts payable		$ 2,200
Common shares		10,000
Retained earnings		8,500
Total	$20,700	$20,700

During April, Clevenger's completed the following transactions:

a. The company borrowed $5,000 from the bank with a short-term note payable.
b. Clevenger paid cash of $10,000 to acquire land.
c. The company performed services for a customer and collected the cash of $2,500.
d. Clevenger purchased supplies on credit, $175.
e. The company performed services for a customer on account, $1,600.

Required: Set up T-accounts for the accounts given in the April 1 trial balance. Then, post the preceding transactions to the accounts. Calculate the account balances and prepare an unadjusted trial balance at April 30.

L.O. 3, 4

E4-5 By using the information from E4-4, which accounts will likely need to be adjusted before the monthly financial statements are prepared? In each case, explain why or why not. What additional information would you need in each case to make the appropriate adjustment? Which accounts will need to be closed at the end of the accounting period and why?

L.O. 4

E4-6 Given the following adjusted trial balance, record the appropriate closing entries. What is net income for the year?

Climbers Rock Company
Adjusted Trial Balance
December 31, 2009

	Debit	Credit
Cash	$ 13,000	
Accounts receivable	20,000	
Supplies	21,500	
Equipment	20,000	
Accumulated amortization		$ 9,000
Property	64,000	
Prepaid rent	28,000	
Accounts payable		23,000
Notes payable		25,000
Interest payable		2,000
Paid-in capital		51,000
Retained earnings		29,500[a]
Dividends	4,000	
Sales		94,000
Cost of goods sold	45,000	
Amortization expense	3,000	
Salaries expense	15,000	
Totals	*$233,500*	*$233,500*

[a]Retained earnings at January 1, 2009. (No accounts have been closed.)

E4-7 The Brain Trust Consulting Company began business in 2005. The following transactions took place during January: L.O. 1, 2, 3, 4

Jan. 2	Owners invested $50,000 in exchange for shares.
2	The company borrowed $10,000 from a local bank with a 12-percent note and a six-month term. Both the principal and interest will be repaid in six months.
6	Supplies were purchased on account for $500.
8	Office rent of $800 for January was paid in cash.
8	The company purchased computer equipment for $16,000. It should last four years, with no residual value.
20	The company received $2,200 from a customer for services to be performed in February.
5–31	Consulting services performed during January on account totalled $12,000.
31	The company paid salaries of $7,000 to employees.
31	$400 was paid to the supplies vendor as part of the $500 owed to the vendor from the Jan. 6 purchase. The company only used $400 worth of the supplies in January.

Required: Give the journal entry for each transaction. Then make the necessary adjusting entries at January 31, 2005. What else should be done to finish the accounting cycle for the month?

E4-8 Suppose Brain Trust Consulting Company (in E4-7) used an ERP system instead of a general ledger system to record its accounting information. What information about the transactions given in E4-7 would be recorded in the information system that would *not* be recorded in the general ledger? L.O. 5

Problems—Set A

P4-1A The following is account information for Susie's Pottery Barn as of December 31, 2006. L.O. 1, 2, 3, 4

Revenues	$20,000	Equipment	$10,000
Prepaid rent	2,000	Accumulated amortization, equipment	3,000
Capital, Susie	5,000	Accounts receivable	5,000
Accounts payable	2,000	Salaries expense	2,000
Amortization expense	1,000	Cash	1,000
Inventory	8,000	Withdrawal	1,000

Required: Prepare a trial balance, income statement, statement of owner's equity, and balance sheet as of December 31, 2006.

P4-2A Fast Feet Shoe Store has the following account information on its adjusted trial balance. L.O. 3, 4

Fast Feet Shoe Store
Adjusted Trial Balance
December 31, 2007

	Debit	Credit
Cash	$ 18,000	
Accounts receivable	22,000	
Supplies	31,000	
Equipment	15,000	
Accumulated amortization		$ 6,000
Property	34,000	
Prepaid rent	8,000	
Accounts payable		25,000
Notes payable		15,000
Interest payable		2,000
Paid-in capital		21,000
Retained earnings		26,000[a]
Dividends	4,000	
Sales		100,000
Gain on sale of equipment		5,000
Cost of goods sold	50,000	
Amortization expense	3,000	
Salaries expense	15,000	
Totals	*$200,000*	*$200,000*

[a]Balance at January 1, 2007. (No closing entries have been made.)

Required: Prepare the necessary closing entries and a balance sheet as of December 31, 2007.

L.O. 1, 2, 3, 4, 5

P4-3A The Hope Meadows Rental Company has the following accounting balances at the end of the year:

Insurance expense	$ 4,000
Rental income	15,670
Unearned rental income	3,800
Accumulated amortization	7,625
Wages payable	5,550
Taxes expense	4,398
Amortization expense	7,625
Wages expense	10,400

The following information is available at the end of the year:

1. Of the insurance expense, $1,000 has not yet expired.
2. Of the unearned rental income, $1,500 has now been earned.
3. The company currently owes employees $1,200 of wages.
4. The company owes an additional $4,900 in real estate taxes.
5. Amortization expense has been recalculated, and it should be a total of $8,743 for the year.

Required:

a. Prepare the journal entries necessary to adjust the accounts.
b. Use T-accounts to compute and present both the income statement and balance sheet account balances after the adjustments have been prepared.
c. Prepare the closing entries.
d. What information in addition to the information recorded in the general ledger would Hope Meadows want as part of the company's information system?

P4-4A Marcie opened a children's company as a sole proprietorship called Pea-n-Pod.com, selling only via the Internet. During 2007, Marcie's company had the following transactions: L.O. 3, 4

a. It started the online business with $5,000 on January 1, 2007.
b. The company borrowed $10,000 from Quality Bank at 3 percent for 12 months on January 1, 2007.
c. It purchased $9,000 in inventory for cash.
d. The company paid $2,000 to a webmaster for website maintenance fees.
e. It had cash sales of $5,000 for 2003 with cost of goods sold of $2,500.
f. The company paid $1,000 in advertising fees.

Required: From the given information, determine the cash balance on December 31, 2007, and prepare the income statement, statement of owner's equity, and balance sheet. Then prepare the closing entries.

P4-5A A partial list of transactions from Randy's Radiator Repair Shop, Inc. during 2007 follows: L.O. 3, 4

a. On February 1, 2007, the shop paid $12,000 for two years' rent in advance.
b. The shop purchased $10,000 of supplies for cash.
c. On March 15, 2007, the shop obtained necessary repair tools for $2,000 cash. They should last for five years. The company will take a full year of depreciation in 2007.
d. On April 1, 2007, the shop paid an annual insurance premium of $1,000, for coverage beginning April 1.
e. On June 1, 2007, to increase sales, the company paid for one year of advertising for $900.
f. On November 1, 2007, the company obtained a three-month loan for $30,000 at 12 percent from Three Rivers Bank payable on February 1, 2008.
g. As of December 31, 2007, cash revenues totalled $20,000.
h. At the close of business on December 31, the company entered into a contract with a local company to do all their auto repairs in 2008 for $5,000 payable in four installments (beginning on March 1, 2008).
i. On December 31, the company paid $1,000 in cash dividends.

[Note: at the end of the year, remaining supplies totalled $2,000.]

Required: Give the journal entries for the transactions. Then prepare the closing entries and the income statement for Randy's Radiator Repair Shop, Inc. at December 31, 2007.

P4-6A On June 1, Seth Benson started a computer business as a sole proprietorship. Seth opened a bank account for the business by depositing $25,000. He paid two months' rent in advance, totalling $500. On June 3, Seth purchased supplies for $600 and two computers at a total cost of $6,500. Seth expects the computers to last for three years with no residual value. Seth hired an office assistant, agreeing to pay the assistant $1,000 per month, of which he paid $500 on June 15 and June 30. On June 27, Seth paid $200 for an Internet advertisement to announce the opening of the business. Seth earned $4,200 in June, of which he collected $2,800 in cash. At the end of the month, Seth had only $100 worth of supplies on hand. L.O. 1, 2, 3, 4

Required: Show Seth's transactions in the accounting equation. Make the needed adjustments at June 30, and then prepare the four basic financial statements for this company for the month of June. Then prepare the closing entries.

P4-7A This is an exact replica of P3-7A from Chapter 3. In this problem use the general ledger system to keep track of the transactions. L.O. 1, 2, 3

The accounting records for Panda Company, Inc. contained the following balances as of December 31, 2005:

Assets		Liabilities and equity	
Cash	$40,000	Accounts payable	$17,000
Accounts receivable	16,500	Share capital	45,000
Land	20,000	Retained earnings	14,500
Totals	*$76,500*		*$76,500*

The following accounting events apply to Panda's 2006 fiscal year:

Jan. 1	The company acquired an additional $20,000 cash from the owners.
1	Panda purchased a computer that cost $17,000 for cash. The computer had a $2,000 salvage value and a three-year useful life.
Mar. 1	The company borrowed $10,000 by issuing a one-year note at 12 percent.
May 1	The company paid $2,400 cash in advance for a one-year lease for office space.
June 1	The company made a $5,000 cash distribution to the owners.
July 1	The company purchased land that cost $10,000 cash.
Aug. 1	Cash payments on accounts payable amounted to $6,000.
1	Panda received $9,600 cash in advance for 12 months of service to be performed monthly for the next year, beginning on receipt of payment.
Sept. 1	Panda sold land for $13,000 cash. The land originally cost $16,000.
Oct. 1	Panda purchased $1,300 of supplies on account.
Nov. 1	Panda purchased a one-year, $20,000 certificate of deposit at 6 percent.
Dec. 31	The company earned service revenue on account during the year that amounted to $40,000.
31	Cash collections from accounts receivable amounted to $44,000.
31	The company incurred other operating expenses on account during the year that amounted to $6,000.
Also:	Salaries that had been earned by the sales staff but not yet paid amounted to $2,300.
	There was $200 worth of supplies on hand at the end of the period.
	On the basis of the preceding transaction data, there are five additional adjustments that need to be made before the financial statements can be prepared.

Required: Post the journal entries to T-accounts, prepare an unadjusted trial balance, make the appropriate adjustments, and prepare the financial statements (all four) for 2006.

Problems—Set B

L.O. 1, 2, 3, 4

P4-1B The following account information is for Janie's Jewelry Shop as of December 31, 2007.

Sales	$22,000	Other revenue	$13,000
Prepaid advertising	2,000	Equipment	10,000
Capital, Janie	14,000	Accounts receivable	5,000
Accounts payable	4,000	Cost of goods sold	11,000
Operating expense	3,000	Cash	2,000
Inventory	18,000	Distribution to Janie	2,000

Required: Prepare a trial balance, income statement, statement of owner's equity, and balance sheet as of December 31, 2007.

P4-2B Here is an adjusted trial balance from Phillip's Photo Shop:

L.O. 3, 4

Phillip's Photo Shop, Inc.
Adjusted Trial Balance
December 31, 2007

	Debit	Credit
Cash	$ 28,000	
Accounts receivable	2,000	
Prepaid rent	1,000	
Equipment	35,000	
Accumulated amortization		$ 7,000
Land	15,000	
Prepaid insurance	7,000	
Salaries payable		5,000
Notes payable		15,000
Interest payable		2,000
Share capital		20,000
Retained earnings		34,000[a]
Dividends	2,000	
Sales		97,000
Cost of goods sold	52,000	
Rent expense	12,000	
Insurance expense	8,000	
Amortization expense	3,500	
Salaries expense	14,500	
Totals	*$180,000*	*$180,000*

[a]Retained earnings balance on January 1, 2007. (No closing entries have been made.)

Required: Prepare the necessary closing entries and a balance sheet at December 31, 2007.

P4-3B The Hoffman Body Spa, Inc. has the following account balances at the end of the year:

L.O. 1, 2, 3, 4, 5

Service revenue	$34,320
Unearned service revenue	3,250
Wages payable	2,550
Accumulated amortization	2,000
Taxes expense	3,298
Amortization expense	1,625
Insurance expense	1,850
Wages expense	10,400

The following information is also available:

1. The company accountant forgot to depreciate a hot tub that was purchased at the beginning of the year. The hot tub cost $10,400, has a useful life of five years, and has no expected residual value.
2. The Unearned Service Revenue consists of gift certificates sold during the year. Hoffman's has failed to account for the $1,200 worth of certificates that have been used by customers.
3. The company currently owes employees $200 of wages in addition to those given here.
4. The company owes an additional $900 in real estate taxes.

Required:

a. Prepare the adjusting journal entries necessary at year-end.
b. Use T-accounts to compute and present the balances in these accounts after the adjustments have been posted.

c. Prepare the closing journal entries.
d. What information in addition to that recorded in the general ledger would Hoffman Body Spa want as part of the company's information system?

L.O. 3, 4

P4-4B GiGi opened a little shop called Just Apples as a sole proprietorship to sell her applesauce.

a. GiGi started the business with $25,000 on July 1, 2006.
b. On October 1, 2006, the company borrowed $10,000 from Local Bank at 12 percent. The loan was for one year.
c. The company purchased $9,000 worth of apples for cash during the fiscal year and had $1,000 worth left over on June 30, 2007.
d. The company also purchased $1,000 worth of jars, lids, and labels for cash. None was left on June 30, 2007.
e. The company paid $18,000 for rent on the shop for 18 months, beginning July 1, 2006. The shop had a fully equipped kitchen, and electricity costs were included with the rent.
f. Just Apples sold $29,000 worth of applesauce for cash during the first fiscal year.
g. Just Apples paid $1,000 in advertising fees.

Required: From the given information, prepare the income statement, statement of owner's equity, and balance sheet for the fiscal year ending June 30, 2007. Then, prepare the closing entries.

L.O. 3, 4

P4-5B The following information is a partial list of transactions from Mills Hobby Shop.

a. On March 1, 2007, Mills Hobby Shop paid $6,000 cash for a two-year insurance policy.
b. On March 15, the company purchased $10,000 of supplies on account.
c. On April 5, the company purchased some new display shelves for $2,000. They should last for eight years with no residual value. Mills will take a full year of amortization in 2007.
d. On May 1, Mills purchased $1,000 worth of advertising in a local magazine.
e. On September 1, Mills obtained a six-month loan for $10,000 at 12 percent from City National Bank, with interest and principal payable on March 1, 2007.
f. For the year ending June 30, 2007, Mills had cash revenues of $34,000.
g. Mills paid $1,000 in cash dividends on June 29, 2007.

Note: at the end of the fiscal year, remaining supplies totalled $2,000.

Required: From the given information, prepare the income statement for the fiscal year ending June 30, 2007. Then, prepare the closing entries.

L.O. 1, 2, 3, 4

P4-6B On September 1, Irene Shannon started a DVD business on the Internet as a sole proprietorship. Irene opened a bank account for the business by depositing $37,000. The new company paid four months' rent in advance totalling $1,200, for rent beginning on September 1. On September 6, the company purchased supplies for $800 and $6,500 worth of inventory for cash. Irene hired a sales person to help her and agreed to pay the assistant $1,000 per month, payable on the last day of the month. Irene's company paid $200 for an Internet advertisement to announce the opening of the business. The company earned $4,200 in September of which Irene collected $2,800 in cash. At the end of the month, Irene had only $100 worth of supplies on hand, and the inventory on hand on September 30 amounted to $975.

Required: Show the company transactions in the accounting equation. Make the needed adjustments, and then prepare the four basic financial statements for this company for the month of September. Then, prepare the closing entries.

P4-7B (This is the same as P3-7B, but here you will use the general ledger model to keep track of the transactions.) The accounting records for Bebe Company contained the following balances as of December 31, 2007:

L.O. 1, 2, 3

Assets		Liabilities and shareholders' equity	
Cash	$50,000	Accounts payable	$17,500
Accounts receivable	26,500	Capital shares	48,600
Prepaid rent	3,600		
Land	10,500	Retained earnings	24,500
Totals	*$90,600*		*$90,600*

The following accounting events apply to Bebe's 2008 fiscal year:

Jan. 1	Bebe purchased a computer that cost $20,000 for cash. The computer had a $2,000 salvage value and a three-year useful life.
Mar. 1	The company borrowed $20,000 by issuing a two-year note at 12 percent.
May 1	The company paid $6,000 cash in advance for a six-month lease for office space. The lease started immediately.
June 1	The company paid cash dividends of $2,000 to the owners.
July 1	The company purchased land that cost $15,000 cash.
Aug. 1	Cash payments on accounts payable amounted to $6,000.
1	Bebe received $6,000 cash in advance for 12 months of service to be performed monthly for the next year, beginning on receipt of payment.
Sept. 1	Bebe sold land for $13,000 cash. The land originally cost $15,000.
Oct. 1	Bebe purchased $1,300 of supplies on account.
Nov. 1	Bebe purchased a one-year, $10,000 certificate of deposit at 5 percent.
Dec. 31	The company earned service revenue on account during the year that amounted to $50,000.
31	Cash collections from accounts receivable amounted to $46,000.
31	The company incurred other operating expenses on account during the year that amounted to $6,000.
Also:	Salaries that had been earned by the sales staff but not yet paid amounted to $2,300.
	There was $200 of supplies on hand at the end of the period.
	On the basis of the preceding transaction data, there are some additional adjustments that need to be made before the financial statements can be prepared.

Required: Post the journal entries to T-accounts, prepare an unadjusted trial balance, make the appropriate adjustments, and prepare the financial statements (all four) for the year ended December 31, 2008.

Issues for Discussion

Financial statement analysis

1. Use the annual report from CoolBrands International Inc. to answer these questions:
   a. When you look at the financial statements for CoolBrands, can you tell if the company uses a general ledger accounting system? Explain.
   b. Find at least four pieces of quantitative information contained in the CoolBrands annual report that would *not* be found in a general ledger system.

Business risk

2. Who are the auditors for CoolBrands?
3. How does having an audit affect business risk?
4. Compare the reliability of the financial statement information to the information in other parts of the annual report. Defend your opinion.

Ethics

5. Companies often try to manage earnings by recognizing revenue before it is actually earned according to GAAP or deferring expenses that have been incurred. For example, to meet the targeted earnings for a specific period, a company may capitalize a cost that should be expensed. Read the following scenario, and then decide how you would handle this opportunity to manage earnings.

   You are a division manager of a large public company. Your bonus is calculated on your division's net income targets that you must meet. This year that target is $1.5 million. You are authorized to sign off on any decision made within your division. You are faced with the following situation:

   On December 15, your division of the company ordered $150,000 worth of supplies in anticipation for the seasonal rush. Most of them will be used by year-end. These supplies were delivered on the evening of December 27. If you record this supplies expense this year, your net income will be $1.45 million and you will not meet the target and will therefore not receive your bonus of $25,000 that you have worked hard for. (Your company generally expenses supplies when purchased.)

   What would you do and why?

Internet Exercise: Hoover's and Intuit Inc.

The accounting cycle illustrated in this chapter may be simplified with the aid of a computerized general ledger system. Intuit Inc. is a leader in e-finance and develops and supports Quicken®, the leading personal finance software; TurboTax®, the best-selling tax preparation software; and QuickBooks®, the most popular small business accounting software.

To find out more about Intuit Inc. we can use a Web resource such as Hoover's Online.

Hoover's Online, The Business Information Authority, offers information about companies, industries, and related news items. For researching a company, this website is a good place to start gathering basic information.

Please go to the Hoover's website: www.hoovers.com

IE4-1 In the Search For Business Information section, type "INTU," the stock symbol for Intuit Inc., select "by Ticker," and then click Search. Review the information provided, and comment on one item of interest.

IE4-2 In the left-hand column, click on Financials, and select Annual Financials. For the most recent year, list the amounts reported for cash, common shares, total revenues, and interest expense. Note that these amounts are reported in thousands.

a. Which financial statement reports each of these amounts?
b. What was the beginning balance for each of these accounts?
c. Which of these accounts is a real account?
d. Which of these accounts is closed at the end of the accounting period?
e. Which of these accounts has a normal debit balance?
f. Which of these accounts might be affected by an adjusting journal entry? Explain why the account might need to be adjusted.

IE4-3 What are the advantages of a computerized general ledger system such as QuickBooks®, developed by Intuit? Is it important to understand the accounting cycle, even though computerized general ledger systems are available? Explain why or why not.

Please note: Internet websites are constantly being updated. Therefore, if the information is not found where indicated, please explore the website further to find the information.

CHAPTER 5

Purchase and Use of Capital Assets

Financial Reporting

Here's where you've been...

In Chapter 4, you learned about the basic accounting cycle—how the traditional general ledger system is used to keep track of a company's transactions and aids in the preparation of the financial statements. You learned how to use *debits* and *credits,* a tool for organizing and tracking accounting information.

Here's where you're going...

From Chapter 5, you should understand how the financial statements show the purchase, use, and sale of assets that last for longer than one year.

Property, Plant, and Equipment

Learning Objectives

More specifically, when you are finished studying this chapter, you should be able to answer these questions:

1. What are long-term assets—how are they defined, classified, and reported at purchase?
2. How is the use of a long-term asset reflected in the financial statements? What methods are used to write off different assets over their useful life?
3. How are (a) repairs and changes in productive capacity and (b) changes in estimates concerning useful life and residual value of assets reflected in the financial statements?

4. What are depletion and amortization and to what assets are they applied?
5. How is the disposal of an asset reflected in the financial statements?
6. How does amortization for financial statements differ from amortization for taxes?
7. What information about long-term assets is disclosed on the financial statements, and how can we use it to help us evaluate the business?
8. What business risks are associated with long-term assets, and what controls can minimize those risks?

To start his business, Tom used some of his own money.

Then his business, Tom's Wear, borrowed some money from Tom's mom. After the business idea is ready for implementation, a business is always started by acquiring financing. The details related to financing a business—getting capital from owners and creditors—are often more complicated than financing for Tom's Wear. We will discuss those details in later chapters.

In this chapter, we will continue our discussion of the business cycle with the acquisition of property, plant, and equipment. Setting up the infrastructure for a company is often the next big step in starting a business. As we look at the purchase, the use, and the disposal of business assets that will last for more than one year, keep in mind the business processes that result in the accounting information shown on the four basic financial statements. The relationship between the business processes and the accounting information is one of cause and effect in *both* directions. The business activities cause the financial statement effects, and the financial statement information, in turn, influences the business activities.

Long-term assets = capital assets: These terms are used to mean the same thing—assets that will be used for more than one accounting period.

Business Process

The underlying business process of acquiring **long-term assets**—also known as **fixed or capital assets**—requires input and analysis beyond that required in the acquisition of short-term assets. The acquisition of long-term assets requires more than documenting the need for the purchase, selecting the vendor, placing the order, receiving and inspecting the goods, and paying for the goods or services. The investment in long-term assets is typically much greater than the investment in short-term assets.

One of the considerations in the purchase of a typical long-term asset, like a new piece of equipment, is the asset's revenue-generating potential—the primary benefit of purchasing the asset. In the business decision, the cost of a long-term asset must include all the costs incurred to get the asset ready for its use. Long-term assets often require extensive setup and preparation before they become operational, and employees need to be trained to use them. All these costs must be considered in the process of acquiring a long-term asset. As we work through this chapter, you will see that the way we account for the purchases of long-term assets under generally accepted accounting principles (GAAP) reflects the underlying business process.

Acquisition of Long-Term Assets: The Business Process

L.O. 1

Be able to define and identify different types of long-term assets.

Business Process

Factories and machines are considered long-term assets because they are expected to be useful longer than one year. A firm purchases long-term assets because those assets are needed to produce revenue in the normal course of business; a firm does not purchase them for resale. (Assets purchased for resale are called inventory.) Tom's Wear purchased its first long-term asset—a computer—in its third month of business. It is common for a company to purchase long-term assets as one of the first steps in establishing its business.

A company can also purchase long-term assets that *will not* be used in the business. Those assets, such as shares in another firm, artwork, and property expected to increase in value, would be investments that the company plans to keep for longer than one year. However, our focus will be on long-term assets that the company will *use* to produce revenue.

What assets to buy and how to pay for them are important business decisions. The acquisition of assets and payment for them affect the financial statements. If we buy a machine for cash, we have exchanged one asset—cash—for another—a machine. We give cash, and we get a machine. That is a simple exchange. If, instead, we buy a machine and sign a note payable for the purchase, the exchange is more complicated. We *get* the machine, but the *give* portion of the transaction is a *promise* to pay. There is a timing difference between the actual get portion of the exchange—getting the machine—and the actual give portion of the exchange—giving the money to the lender. By now, you know that these timing differences are very important in business decisions. The cost of this type of timing difference is interest expense. The business decision about how to pay for a machine and the accounting related to that business decision are closely linked.

These decisions—what assets to buy and how to pay for them—do not affect the income statement at the time of the purchase. As you saw in Chapter 3, a business defers recognizing the expense of a long-term asset until the asset is actually used in the business. When the asset is used and the expense is recognized, it is called amortization expense. This is another example of a timing difference. We have purchased a machine at one point in time, and we will use that machine over a subsequent period of time. The period of time over which we plan to use the machine is a very important input in the business decision to acquire the asset. The way we subsequently amortize the asset reflects this information. We will discuss the details of amortization later in this chapter.

There are two categories of long-term, or fixed, assets: **tangible assets** and **intangible assets**.

Tangible assets are assets that can be seen and touched. The most common are property, plant, and equipment.

Intangible assets are assets whose true value resides in the rights and privileges given to the owners of the asset. They are often represented by contracts, such as franchises and copyrights.

Tangible assets are assets like Tom's computer—you can see and touch them.

Tangible assets include

- land, such as the property a factory is built on;
- a plant, such as a factory building;
- equipment, such as a machine; and
- natural resources, such as minerals or timber.

Intangible assets have long-term value to the firm, although they are not visible or touchable. Intangible assets give the owner specific rights. Intangible assets include:

- copyrights, such as ownership of the written content of this book;
- patents, such as the rights to the Intel Pentium IV computer chip;

- trademarks, such as Tim Hortons;
- franchises, such as the rights to run and own a McDonalds restaurant; and
- goodwill, the amount a company pays for another business firm *in excess* of the fair market value of the net assets of that business firm.

Allocating the Cost of Long-Term Assets

L.O. 2

Be able to explain how the cost of an asset is allocated to the periods in which the asset is used and how that information is reflected in the financial statements.

Capitalizing a cost means to report it on the balance sheet as an asset.

Amortization is a systematic, rational allocation process to recognize the expense of long-term assets over the periods in which the assets are used.

Writing off = expensing: This means that a cost is put on the income statement as an expense.

Depreciation, depletion, and **amortization**—they all mean to *write off* a cost over more than one accounting period.

The cost of an asset is recorded as an asset at the time of purchase—that is called **capitalizing** the cost. That cost will be recognized as an expense during the periods in which the asset is used. When Tom's Wear bought the computer for $4,000, the transaction was recorded as the acquisition of an asset. Then as the computer is used, Tom's Wear records a portion of the computer cost as an expense on the income statement. Amortization expense is recorded as part of the process of adjusting the accounting records before the financial statements are prepared. The adjustment decreases the value of the asset in the accounting records—via accumulated amortization—and decreases owner's equity—via amortization expense. Allocating the cost of a tangible asset, other than a natural resource, to the accounting periods in which it is used in the operation of the business is called **amortization**. Each year, for the three years the asset is used, Tom's Wear recognizes $1,200 amortization expense on the income statement. That is $100 per month for the monthly financial statements. The cost of the computer is being divided among the periods in which the asset is being used.

There are several expressions used by accountants to communicate the idea of recognizing a cost on the income statement as an expense. In general, doing this is known as **writing off** the cost. It is not unlike the sense of the expression "writing someone off"—it means getting rid of or disregarding someone. In accounting, we get rid of a cost by reporting it on the income statement as an expense. All that actually means is that the cost has been used up. A used-up cost is an expense. (*Not* getting rid of it means keeping it on the balance sheet as an asset.) Taking a portion of the cost of an asset from the balance sheet to the income statement as an expense for the periods in which the asset is used—by making adjustments to the accounting records—is an example of writing off the cost of the asset.

Sometimes, accountants use the term **expensing** to communicate the same idea—recognizing a cost on the income statement as an expense. Expensing most often refers to costs that are written off in one period. For example, when Tom's Wear puts the cost of the shirts he has sold on the income statement as the expense cost of goods sold, it is expensing the cost of those shirts.

When a long-term asset is purchased, the cost is put on the balance sheet as an asset—called *capitalizing* the cost. Expensing and capitalizing a cost are opposites. When a company uses a long-term asset, the capitalized cost is written off over time. The most general expression for writing off the cost of a long-term asset is **amortization**. **Depreciation** is a term that is often used to describe the amortization of certain kinds of property, plant, or equipment. However, in Canada, the term *amortization* is preferred. **Depletion** is the specific word that describes the amortization of a natural resource. There is no specific word for writing off intangible assets, and so accountants use the word *amortization* to describe the writing off of the cost of intangible assets.

The most general word for writing off a long-term asset is amortization. When we refer to writing off an intangible asset, the term *amortization* is used—we amortize a franchise.

When we refer to writing off a piece of equipment, the word *depreciation* or *amortization* is used—we depreciate or amortize a machine.

When specifically referring to a natural resource, the word *depletion* is used—we *deplete* an oil well. All the terms refer to allocating the cost of an asset to more than one accounting period.

STUDY BREAK 5-1

See How You're Doing

For each of the following kinds of long-term assets, give the term or terms used to describe writing off the asset:

1. equipment
2. franchise
3. oil well
4. building

Acquisition Costs

L.O. 1, 2

Understand the costs involved in the acquisition of a long-term asset and how they are reflected on the financial statements.

Consider the purchase of a long-term asset. The **historical cost principle**—part of GAAP discussed in Chapter 2—requires a company to record an asset at the amount paid for it—its **cost**. The cost for property, plant, and equipment includes all expenditures that are reasonable and necessary to get an asset in place and ready for use. This includes:

Cost is the amount paid for an asset. The underlying accounting principle is called the **historical cost principle.**

1. purchase cost
2. freight-in—cost to have the equipment delivered
3. insurance while in transit
4. installation costs including test runs

The acquisition cost of a building may include:

1. architects' or contractors' fees
2. construction costs
3. cost of renovating the building or repairing it

Business Process

This is an example of the relationship between the business process of the acquisition of an asset and the accounting for that acquisition. The accounting treatment of including all these expenditures in the acquisition cost of an asset, shown on the balance sheet, is a reflection of the need to consider all these expenditures when evaluating the potential purchase of an asset. This relationship is an example of the strong link between the acquisition process and the underlying accounting.

When a cost is incurred, there are two possible accounting treatments. Either the cost is recorded as an asset, deferring recognition of the expense, or the cost is immediately recognized as an expense. Remember, reporting the purchase of an asset on the balance sheet and deferring recognition of the expense is called *capitalizing* the asset; and recognizing the expense of a purchase immediately is called *expensing* the cost of the asset.

When you include costs like installation and freight in the *acquisition cost* of an asset, you are capitalizing those costs. They become part of the total cost of acquiring the asset; the total acquisition cost is expensed as part of the periodic amortization expense.

In the case where land is purchased for use as the location of a building or factory, the land is not amortized. Because land typically retains its usefulness and is not used up to produce revenue, accountants have decided it should remain on the balance sheet at cost. This accounting treatment reflects the underlying business implications of the purchase of land. Only if land is purchased to be used in the business, like mining, is it written off over the time it is used by the business. In that case, it would be considered a natural resource, and it would be depleted. The acquisition cost of land may include (1) price paid for the land, (2) real estate commissions, (3) lawyer's fees, (4) costs of preparing the land for use, such as clearing or draining, and (5) costs (less residual value) of tearing down existing structures.

STUDY BREAK 5-2

See How You're Doing

For each of the following expenditures, tell whether it should be capitalized or expensed:

1. payment for employee salaries
2. purchase of a new delivery truck
3. rent paid in advance
4. rent paid in arrears (after the use of the building)

Basket Purchase Allocation

L.O. 1, 2

Understand the costs involved in the acquisition of long-term assets and how they are reflected on the financial statements.

Business Process

The **relative fair market value method** is a way to assign the joint cost of several assets to each of the individual assets purchased together. It is based on the individual values of the assets in the market.

Figuring out the acquisition cost of certain assets can be difficult. Buying a building with the land it occupies is an example of acquiring two assets for a single price. For our accounting records, we need to calculate a separate cost for each asset. Why? The company will need to amortize the building but will not amortize the land. This is another example of an accounting problem that reflects the importance of the underlying factors that should be considered in the related business process. When land and a building are purchased together, the company should consider the individual value of each asset and how their joint purchase should affect those values. The accounting treatment requires that information.

For accounting, the purchase price must be divided between the building and land. The most common method for doing this is called the **relative fair market value method**. Suppose a company purchased a building and its land, together for one price, $100,000. The buyer would obtain a market price, usually in the form of an appraisal, for each item separately. Then, those appraisals would be used to form a ratio to divide the purchase price of $100,000 between the two assets. Suppose the building appraised at $90,000 and the land appraised at $30,000. The ratio you need is the appraisal of each asset as a fraction of the total appraisal amount. The total is $120,000 (= $90,000 + $30,000). The rest is simple ratio math:

For the Building: $90,000 is to $120,000 as x is to $100,000

$$x = (\$90/\$120) \times \$100{,}000 = \$75{,}000$$

Thus, building is recorded at a cost of $75,000. By subtraction, that leaves $25,000 as the cost of the land. If you want to calculate it,

$$\text{Cost of Land} = (\$30/\$120) \times \$100{,}000 = \$25{,}000$$

This same method—using a simple ratio—can be used for any number of assets purchased together for a single price.

Recording Acquisition Costs

When your company buys a long-term asset, the company increases its asset account (e.g., Equipment, Machinery, or Furniture). This means you will debit that asset.

- If you pay cash for the asset, the credit will be to Cash.
- If you sign a note payable for the asset, you will credit Notes payable (a liability).
- All costs incurred to get the asset up and running will be debited to the asset account.

Suppose you purchased a piece of equipment with a $30,000 note and paid $250 in cash for delivery. The journal entry to record the purchase of equipment would be:

Date	Transaction	Debit	Credit
	Equipment	$30,250	
	Notes Payable		$30,000
	Cash		250

STUDY BREAK 5-3

See How You're Doing

Nebo Company paid $480,000 for a building and the land on which it is located. Independent appraisals value the building at $400,000 and the land at $100,000. Prepare the journal entry to record the purchase of the building and land.

Amortization

L.O. 2

Understand how the cost of a long-term asset is allocated to the periods in which the asset is used and how that process is reflected on the financial statements.

Amortization, according to accountants, is "the systematic, rational allocation of the cost (minus its residual value) of a fixed asset to the periods benefited by the asset." That is formal accounting language for dividing the cost of an asset among the accounting periods to which it provides benefits. Amortization does *not* refer to an asset's physical deterioration and does not refer to a decrease in its market value. Amortization is a process of allocating the cost of an asset to the accounting periods it benefits.

If you hear or read, "The asset is worth $10,000 on our books," that does not mean the asset is really *worth* that amount if it were to be sold. To say, "An asset is worth $10,000 on our books" means that $10,000 is the carrying value or book value of the asset in our records—it is the unamortized amount. It is called the *carrying value* because that is the amount we add to our assets on the balance sheet. It is also known as the *book value* because it is the value of the asset on our accounting records, commonly referred to as our books.

To understand more easily what amortizing assets is all about, you should become familiar with the following terms—the vocabulary of amortization:

Terminology for Amortization: Cost is what we pay for an asset.

1. **Cost** or **acquisition cost** is the amount paid for the asset, including all amounts necessary to get the asset up and running.

Estimated useful life is how long we plan to use the asset.

2. **Estimated useful life** is how long the company plans to use the asset; it may be measured in years or in units that the asset will produce. For example, the useful life of a machine may be 5 years or it may be the production of 100,000 units. The estimated useful life of an asset to the company may be less than the actual physical life of an asset. For example, a company may buy a computer and plan to use it for 3 years. The computer may still have some years of useful life after the company is done with it.

Residual value = Salvage value is an estimate of what the asset will be worth when we are done with it.

Amortization base is cost minus estimated residual value.

Book value = carrying value, which is cost minus accumulated amortization.

3. **Residual value,** or **salvage value,** is the estimated value the asset will have when the company is done with it—it is the market value on the disposal date.
4. **Amortization base** is cost minus residual value.
5. **Book value** or **carrying value** of the asset is *cost* less *total amortization* taken to date.

Amortization and the Financial Statements

L.O. 2

Understand how the cost of a long-term asset is allocated to the periods in which the asset is used and how its use is reflected on the financial statements.

Three common methods of amortizing long-term assets used for preparing financial statements are the straight-line method, the activity or units of production method, and the declining balance method. While these methods are acceptable when preparing financial statements for shareholders, they are not acceptable for the purposes of determining income for tax purposes. The Canada Customs and Revenue Agency (CCRA) requires that deductions for the cost of capital assets be made in accordance with the provisions of the *Income Tax Act*. These requirements are referred to as the capital cost allowance system. Our concern here is how to report amortization on the financial statements, although we will also talk briefly about the capital cost allowance system.

Straight-Line Amortization

Straight-line amortization is the method of amortization in which equal amounts of the cost of an asset are written off each year. Amortization expense is the same each year.

Straight-line amortization is the simplest way to allocate the cost of an asset to the periods in which the asset is used. Several steps are needed to calculate the appropriate amount of amortization expense for each accounting period.

First, you must determine the useful life of the asset—an estimate of how long the asset will be useful to the company. This should be considered in the purchase of an asset, and the estimate is subsequently needed to properly account for the cost of that asset.

Second, you estimate the residual or salvage value—the amount you believe the asset will be worth when the company is finished using it. It is the amount you think someone will pay you for the used asset. The estimate of residual value is made by someone who knows a lot about the asset and the relationship between the use of the asset and its market value. This is part of the underlying business process that requires judgment; there is no right answer. Residual value is an estimate, and it is an estimate that may need to be revised more than once during the life of the asset. The useful life and the residual value are related, and these estimates are evaluated during the purchase decision.

Third, to calculate the amount of amortization expense for each accounting period, usually one year, the residual value is deducted from the acquisition cost of the asset. This gives the amortization base.

Fourth, the amortization base—the difference between the asset's cost and its estimated residual value—is divided by the estimate of the number of years of the asset's useful life.

Let us look at a simple example.

Suppose Holiday Hotel purchases a new squeeze-your-own orange juice machine for its self-service breakfast bar. Such a machine is expensive and requires large supplies of fresh oranges. After considering the implications—risks and rewards—of purchasing the machine and evaluating the effect such a purchase would have on the financial statements, Holiday Hotel decides to purchase an $11,500 machine with an estimated useful life of six years. In addition to the invoice price of $11,500, delivery and installation costs amount to $1,000. Recall that these costs must be capitalized as part of the acquisition cost of the asset. Holiday estimates that the machine will have a residual value of $500 when the hotel is done with it. Do you see how both of these estimates are important inputs into the business decision to purchase the asset in the first place? After the judgments about useful life and residual value are made, Holiday will calculate the yearly amortization expense. First, Holiday calculates the amortization base by subtracting the residual value from the cost.

$$\begin{aligned}
&\text{Cost} = \$11{,}500 + \$1{,}000 && = \$\ 12{,}500\\
&\text{Residual value} && = \$\ \ \ \ \ 500\\
&\text{Amortization base} = \$12{,}500 - \$500 && = \$\ 12{,}000
\end{aligned}$$

Then Holiday divides the amortization base by the number of years of useful life:

$$\text{Annual amortization expense} = \$12{,}000 / 6 \text{ years} = \$2{,}000 \text{ per year}$$

Each year the amortization expense on the income statement will be $2,000; and each year the carrying value of the asset will be reduced by $2,000. This reduction in carrying value is accumulated over the life of the asset so that the carrying value decreases each year. The acquisition cost of the asset is always preserved in a company's records and must be presented on the balance sheet, and so Holiday will keep the total accumulated amortization as a separate amount and subtract it from the acquisition cost of the asset on the balance sheet.

If Holiday bought the machine at the beginning of the year 2005 and the company's fiscal year ends on December 31, then the income statement for the year ending December 31, 2005, would show amortization expense of $2,000. The balance sheet would show the acquisition cost, $12,500, and the accumulated amortization at December 31, 2005—$2,000—as a reduction. Here is what it would look like on the balance sheet at December 31, 2005:

Equipment	$12,500
Less accumulated amortization	(2,000)
Net book value	$10,500

The following year, 2006, the income statement for the year would again show $2,000 amortization expense. The straight-line method gets its name from the fact that the same amount is amortized each year, and so the book value of the asset could be graphed as a straight line. The balance sheet at December 31, 2006, would show how the carrying value of the asset is declining because on that date Holiday has used it for two years:

Equipment	$12,500
Less accumulated amortization	(4,000)
Net book value	$ 8,500

Exhibit 5–1 is a table that shows the amortization expense and accumulated amortization amounts for the year-end financial statements during the entire life of the asset.

At the end of the useful life of the asset, the carrying value should equal the residual value. If all the estimates were exactly right—the useful life and the residual value turned out to be exactly what you had estimated when you

Exhibit 5–1
Straight-Line Amortization

Year	Amortization expense on the income statement	Accumulated amortization on year-end balance sheet	Carrying or book value on the year-end balance sheet
2005	$2,000	$ 2,000	$10,500
2006	2,000	4,000	8,500
2007	2,000	6,000	6,500
2008	2,000	8,000	4,500
2009	2,000	10,000	2,500
2010	2,000	12,000	500

began amortizing the asset—you could sell the asset at the end of its useful life for a price equal to its carrying value.

Recording Straight-Line Method Amortization Expense

Holiday Hotel purchased the orange juice machine for $12,500. Its estimated useful life is six years, and expected residual value is $500. The journal entry to record one year's amortization expense on the equipment would be:

Date	Transaction	Debit	Credit
	Amortization expense	$2,000	
	Accumulated amortization, equipment		$2,000

Each year, the amortization expense account is closed to Retained earnings, but the accumulated amortization account, a contra-asset account, is an account that will never be closed. Each year, the balance in the accumulated amortization account will increase by the amount of the annual amortization expense.

For example, after the machine has been used and amortized for two years, here is what the general ledger accounts (we will represent them with T-accounts) look like before closing the revenue and expense accounts for year 2:

Amortization expense

	Debit	Credit	
Year 1	$2,000	$2,000	(closed to retained earnings)
Year 2	$2,000		

Accumulated amortization, equipment

Debit	Credit	
	$2,000	Year 1
	$2,000	Year 2

Do you see that the amortization expense account has a balance of $2,000 and that the accumulated amortization account has a balance of $4,000? Each year, at the end of the year, the amortization expense account will have only one year's amortization expense, while the accumulated amortization account will have all the expense recorded for the asset since it was purchased.

STUDY BREAK 5-4

See How You're Doing

On January 1, 2005, Access Company purchased a new computer system for $15,000. When purchased, the estimated useful life was five years, and the estimate of the residual value was $3,000. Using straight-line amortization, prepare the journal entry to record the amortization expense for the year ending December 31, 2007. What is the net book value at October 31, 2007?

Units-of-Production Amortization

Another way to determine amortization expense is by estimating the productivity of the asset. How many units will the asset produce, or how much work will the asset do during its useful life? This is called the **units-of-production** method of determining amortization expense. Examples of units are *kilometres driven* or *units produced.* If your company buys a car, you may decide to drive it for 100,000 kilometres before you trade it in. The units-of-production method is similar to the straight-line method. The difference is that an estimate of the number of *units of activity* during the asset's useful life is used as the allocation base instead of an estimate of the *number of years* of useful life.

Units-of-production amortization is an amortization method based on the number of units to be produced by an asset as opposed to the years of useful life.

Consider the Holiday Hotel machine and how it was amortized using the straight-line method, but now let us amortize it using the units-of-production method. To use this method, you need to estimate how many units the machine will be able to produce during its useful life. Suppose Holiday estimates the machine will be able to produce 240,000 glasses of juice during its useful life. The amortization base is calculated in exactly the same way when using units-of-production amortization as it is when using straight-line amortization. It is the cost minus the expected residual value. In this example, the amortization base is $12,000 (= $12,500 – $500). You divide that amortization base by the total number of units you expect to produce with the machine during its useful life.

The units-of-production method of amortization can be applied to Holiday's orange juice machine by dividing the amortization base, $12,000, by the estimated number of glasses of orange juice the machine will produce. That gives the amortization *rate:*

$$\$12{,}000/240{,}000 \text{ glasses} = \$0.05 \text{ per glass}$$

This is the rate—$0.05 per glass—by which Holiday will amortize the machine for each glass of juice it produces. Let us say the machine has a counter on it, and suppose it showed that 36,000 glasses of juice were squeezed during the first year. The amortization expense, shown on the income statement, for that year would be 36,000 glasses of juice multiplied by $0.05 per glass.

$$36{,}000 \text{ glasses of juice} \times \$0.05/\text{glass} = \$1{,}800$$

That is the amortization expense for the year, and the book value of the asset would decline by that amount for the year. It is important to keep a cumulative record of how many units the machine produces so that Holiday Hotel does not amortize the asset below its $500 estimated residual value. The residual value will equal the carrying value when the asset has produced 240,000 glasses of juice.

Recording Units-of-Production Method Amortization Expense

No matter which method is used, the journal entry to record the annual amortization expense includes:

- a debit to amortization expense, and
- a credit to accumulated amortization, for the calculated amount of amortization expense.

Each asset has its own accumulated amortization account, which keeps track of how much that asset has been amortizated since it was put into operation. The journal entry to record the amortization expense (activity method) for the year would be:

Date	Transaction	Debit	Credit
	Amortization expense	$1,800	
	Accumulated amortization, equipment		$1,800

STUDY BREAK 5-5

See How You're Doing

Hopper Company purchased equipment on January 1, 2005, for $44,000. The expected useful life is 10 years or 100,000 units of production, and its estimated residual value is $4,000. In 2005, the firm produced 3,000 units. In 2006, Hopper produced 14,000 units. Using units-of-production amortization, prepare the journal entries to record the amortization expense for 2005 and 2006.

Declining Balance Method

L.O. 2

Understand how the cost of a long-term asset is allocated to the periods in which the asset is used and how the use is reflected on the financial statements.

Accelerated amortization methods are ones in which larger amounts of the cost of an asset are written off early in the life of an asset and smaller amounts are written off later in the life of the asset.

The **double-declining balance method** is an accelerated method of amortization that uses 200 percent as the percentage of the straight-line rate.

A third way to amortize an asset is the declining balance method, which is an **accelerated amortization** method. Accelerated methods allow more amortization in the early years of an asset's life and less in the later years. How can this be justified? The matching principle supports the use of such a method. The higher amortization charges will occur in the early, more productive years, when the equipment is generating more revenue. Amortizing more of the asset in the first few years also helps even out the total expenses related to an asset. In later years, the amortization expense is lower, but repair expenses are likely to be increasing.

To use a declining balance method, a company must select a rate of amortization to be applied to the amortization base. Sometimes, a rate equal to twice the straight line rate is used. For example, if the useful life of an asset were five years, the straight-line rate would be 1/5, or 20 percent. That is because 20 percent of the asset would be amortized each year for five years using straight-line amortization. The rate used for declining balance would be 40 percent, which is 200 percent, or twice, the straight-line rate. The most commonly used declining balance rate is 200 percent, and the method is called the **double-declining balance method**.

Here is how it works and why it is called double-declining balance.

Every year, the carrying value, or book value, of the asset is amortized by an amount equal to *2 divided by the useful life in years*. An example will demonstrate that this is an easy way to calculate twice the straight-line rate. Suppose the useful life of an asset is four years. Then the double-declining rate would be 2/4 or 1/2. Alternatively, you could calculate the straight-line rate as:

$$100\% \ / \ 4 \text{ years} = 25\% \text{ per year}$$

That is, using a straight-line rate, you would amortize the asset 25 percent each year for four years. Then, double that amortization rate to get the double-declining balance amortization rate, 50 percent. Thus, 50% = 1/2.

Using this amortization method for the Holiday Hotel orange juice machine, the book value at the beginning of the first year is $12,500—its acquisition cost. Note that any residual value is ignored at this time because book value equals cost minus accumulated amortization. Recall, the useful life of the juice machine is six years. So, the amortization rate is 2/6 years = 1/3, and the amortization expense for the first year is 1/3 × $12,500 = $4,167. The book value of the machine on the balance sheet at December 31, 2005, will be $8,333 (= $12,500 – $4,167).

For the second year, the amount of amortization is again calculated as 1/3 × book value. Thus, for the second year, the amortization expense is 1/3 ×

$8,333 = $2,778. The accumulated amortization at the end of the second year is $4,167 + $2,778 = $6,945. The book value of the machine on the December 31, 2006, balance sheet would be $12,500 – $6,945 = $5,555.

The declining balance amortization method is quite different from the straight-line and units-of-production amortization methods. Although residual value is ignored in the calculation of each year's expense, you must always keep the residual value in mind so that the book value of the asset is never less than its residual value.

Recording Declining Balance Method Amortization Expense

No matter which method of amortization is used, the journal entry looks the same: a debit to amortization expense and a credit to the accumulated amortization account that goes with the asset. Using double-declining balance amortization for the orange juice machine, the amortization expense for the first year is $4,167. The journal entry to record the amortization expense (double-declining balance method) for the year would be:

Date	Transaction	Debit	Credit
	Amortization expense	$4,167	
	Accumulated amortization, equipment		$4,167

Specific Amortization Formulas

Let us look at the calculations involved in amortizing an asset more carefully. Remember, you must make your estimates of useful life and residual value *before* you do any calculations. These estimates are part of the business process of acquiring the asset.

1. Straight line:

$$\text{Amortization expense} = \frac{\text{acquisition cost} - \text{residual value}}{\text{estimated useful life in years}}$$

   Suppose a machine which makes screws costs $50,000. Its estimated useful life is four years, and its estimated residual value is $2,000. Using straight-line amortization, you would calculate a single year's amortization as:

$$\frac{\$50,000 - \$2,000}{4\text{ years}} = \frac{\$48,000}{4\text{ years}} = \$12,000\text{ per year}$$

   Each year for four years, the amortization expense on the income statement will be $12,000. Each year, the carrying value of the asset will decrease by $12,000. The details are shown in Exhibit 5–2.

2. Units of production:

$$\frac{\text{acquisition cost} - \text{residual value}}{\text{estimated activity during useful life}} \times \text{actual activity}$$

   For the same screw machine, cost is $50,000; useful life is four years; and residual value is $2,000. Suppose the machine will produce 100,000 units during its useful life.

Suppose the machine produced 30,000 units during the first year; 25,000 units, the second year; 25,000 units, the third year; and 20,000 units, during the fourth year. The amortization schedule is shown in Exhibit 5–3. See if you can figure out how each number in the table was calculated.

3. Double-declining balance method:

$$\text{Amortization expense} = \text{existing book value} \times (2/\text{estimated useful life in years})$$

The declining balance method has the following features:

a. Residual value is not subtracted from cost.

b. Book value must be recalculated annually.

c. An asset may not be amortized below its residual value (true for all methods).

Using the same asset, let us amortize it using the double-declining balance method.

Using the formula for double-declining balance, you start by multiplying the book value—which is the acquisition cost on the first amortization date—by 2/4. That means the asset will be amortized using a rate of 1/2, or 50 percent.

Each year, amortize the asset at the rate of 50 percent of its book value. (Remember, each year the book value changes.) In the last year of the life of the asset, the amortization expense will be a "plug" figure. That is, plug in for the year's amortization expense whatever number is necessary for the accumulated amortization to equal the total amount of amortization you estimated you would recognize over the life of the asset. In this case (Exhibit 5–4), the last year's amortization needs to be $4,250 to leave the residual value you estimated—$2,000—at the end of the fourth year. Sometimes, amortization expense for the last year is more than the amount calculated by multiplying the

Exhibit 5–2
Straight-Line Amortization

Year of the asset's life	Amortization expense (income statement)	Accumulated amortization (balance sheet at the end of the year)	Book value of the asset (balance sheet at the end of the year)
1	$12,000	$12,000	$38,000
2	12,000	24,000	26,000
3	12,000	36,000	14,000
4	12,000	48,000	2,000

Exhibit 5–3
Units-of-Production Amortization

Year of the asset's life	Amortization rate × screws produced rate: $\frac{\$50,000 - 2,000}{100,000}$ $0.48 per screw	=	Amortization expense (income statement)	Accumulated amortization (balance sheet at the end of the year)	Book value of the asset (balance sheet at the end of the year)
1	$0.48 × 30,000		$14,400	$14,400	$35,600
2	0.48 × 25,000		12,000	26,400	23,600
3	0.48 × 25,000		12,000	38,400	11,600
4	0.48 × 20,000		9,600	48,000	2,000

Exhibit 5–4
Double-Declining Balance Amortization

Year of the asset's life	Amortization rate = 50%	Book value before amortizing the asset for the year	Amortization expense for the year	Accumulated amortization (at the end of the year)
1	0.5	$50,000	$25,000	$25,000
2	0.5	25,000	12,500	37,500
3	0.5	12,500	6,250	43,750
4	0.5	6,250	4,250[a]	48,000

[a]The calculation of (0.5 × $6,250) indicates **amortization** expense of $3,125. Because this is the last year of its useful life and the book value after this year's amortization should be $2,000, the **amortization** expense must be $4,250.

book value by the double-declining rate; sometimes, it is less. When the asset has a large residual value, the amortization expense in the last year is less than the amount calculated using the double-declining amortization rate and the carrying value. When the asset has no residual value, the amortization expense in the last year will be more than the calculated amount.

See Exhibit 5–5 on page 186 for a comparison of straight-line and double-declining balance amortization

STUDY BREAK 5-6

See How You're Doing

An asset costs $50,000, has a residual value of $5,000, and has a useful life of five years. Prepare the journal entry to record the amortization expense for the second year using the double-declining balance method.

Capital Expenditures versus Revenue Expenditures

L.O. 3

Be able to distinguish between a capital and a revenue expenditure.

Any expenditure that will benefit not just the current accounting period but also several more future accounting periods is called a **capital expenditure**. A capital expenditure is recorded as an asset when it is purchased and is amortized over the accounting periods in which it is used.

Any expenditure that will benefit only the current accounting period is called a **revenue expenditure** (also called an *expense*). That sounds like we are saying "an expenditure called a revenue." No, what we are saying is that an expenditure in the current period may be called a revenue expenditure, meaning it is an expenditure related to the current period's revenue. The expenditure is deducted from revenue in the current period—which means it is recognized as an expense—in the current period. We discussed this idea earlier in the chapter when we talked about capitalizing a cost versus expensing a cost.

A **capital expenditure** is one that will be recorded as an asset, not an expense at the time of purchase. This is capitalizing a cost.

A **revenue expenditure** is one that will be recorded as an expense in the accounting period in which it is incurred. It is an expense.

To review, when the concept of capitalizing or expensing a cost is applied to long-term assets and we want to draw a contrast between the two ways a cost can be handled in our accounting records:

- We refer to a cost we put on the balance sheet as an asset as a capital expenditure—capitalizing the cost.
- We refer to a cost we put on the income statement as a revenue expenditure or expense—expensing the cost.

Exhibit 5–5 **Comparison of Straight-Line Amortization and Double-Declining Balance Amortization**

For an asset with a cost of $25,000, estimated residual value of $2,000, and an estimated useful life of 5 years.

Amortization method	Cost	Residual value	Useful Life		Year 1	Year 2	Year 3	Year 4	Year 5
Double-Declining Balance	**$25,000**	**$2,000**	5	Amortization Expense	$10,000	$6,000	$3,600	$2,160	$1,240
				End-of-the-year Book Value	$15,000	$9,000	$5,400	$3,240	$2,000
Straight Line	**$25,000**	**$2,000**	5	Amortization Expense	$4,600	$4,600	$4,600	$4,600	$4,600
				End-of-the-year Book Value	$20,400	$15,800	$11,200	$6,600	$2,000

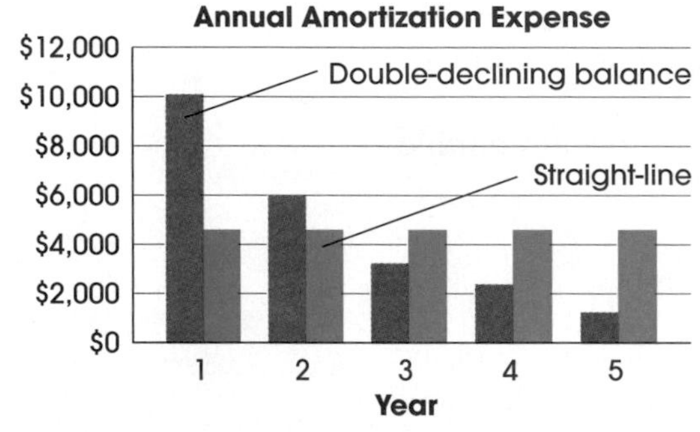

Double-declining balance amortization method will show more amortization expense in the early years of an asset's life and less in the later years.
Straight-line amortization will show an equal amount of amortization expense every year.

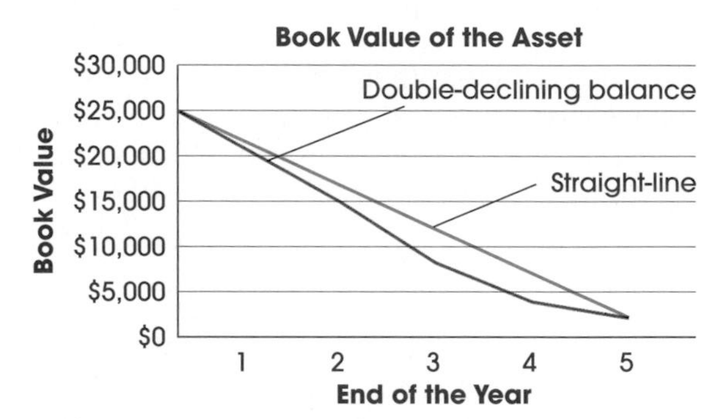

Double-declining balance amortization method shows a rapid decrease in the book value of the asset in the early years of an asset's life and a smaller decrease in the later years.
Straight-line amortization shows a constant decline in the book value of the asset every year—as represented by a straight-line on the graph.

Notice that the graph for **Annual Amortization Expense** shows the amortization expense for 5 years, while the graph of the **Book Value of the Asset** shows 6 amounts. Remember that amortization expense is shown on the *income statement*, which covers a period of time; and the book value of the asset is shown on the *balance sheet*, which shows amounts at a specific point in time. When the asset is purchased at the end of year 0 (= beginning of year 1), there is no amortization expense.

Many companies establish policies, often based on dollar amounts, that categorize purchased items as capital expenditures or revenue expenditures. (What accounting principle applies here? Materiality.) The main rules concerning capital and revenue expenditures are:

1. Remodelling (such as a new wiring system to increase the efficiency of the electrical system of a building) or improvements (such as a more energy-efficient air-conditioning system) are capital expenditures. Because they will offer benefits over a number of years, they are classified as assets. Capital expenditures either increase the useful life of the asset or increase the efficiency or productivity of the asset. They are sometimes referred to as *betterments*.
2. Ordinary repairs (such as painting, tune-ups, and cleaning and lubrication) for vehicles and reshingling a roof are expenditures that are necessary to

maintain an asset in good operating condition. Because these repairs are routine and do not increase the useful life of the asset or its efficiency, they are called revenue expenditures and are recognized as current expenses.

Suppose Tom's Wear's computer needed monthly maintenance and cleaning. The cost of this maintenance would be a revenue expenditure—recognized as an expense in the period the work was done. Let us say Tom's Wear had a new piece of hardware added to the computer to expand its capability or its useful life. This cost would be considered a capital expenditure and capitalized—recorded as part of the cost of the computer and amortized along with the asset over its remaining useful life.

Revising Estimates of Useful Life and Residual Value

Sometimes, the estimates managers make—the useful life and the residual or salvage value of an asset—need to be revised. For example, experience with an asset may provide additional information to help make more accurate estimates of its useful life or residual value. Evaluating estimates related to fixed assets is an ongoing part of the business process related to acquiring those assets. In accounting for long-term assets, revising an estimate is not treated as an error—you do not go back and correct any previous records or financial statements. Those amounts were correct at the time they were prepared—considering that the best estimates *at that time* were used for the calculation. The unamortized balance less the revised estimated residual value is spread over the new estimated (remaining) useful life. This approach is similar to treating the unamortized balance like the *cost* at the time of the new estimates and using the new estimates of useful life and residual value to calculate the amortization expense for the remaining years of the asset's life.

Let us return to the machine that cost $50,000 and see what happens when we change the estimates. Its estimated useful life was four years, and the estimated residual value was $2,000. Using straight-line amortization, a single year's amortization was:

$$\frac{\$50,000 - \$2,000}{4 \text{ years}} = \frac{\$48,000}{4 \text{ years}} = \$12,000 \text{ per year}$$

Suppose that we have amortized the machine for two years. That would make the book value $26,000 (= $50,000 cost – $12,000 amortization, year one – $12,000 amortization, year two). As we begin the third year of the asset's life, we realize that we will be able to use it for three *more* years—instead of two more years as we originally estimated—but we now believe the residual value at the end of that time will be $1,000—not $2,000 as originally estimated.

The amortization expense for the first two years will not be changed. The motto is: the past is past. For the next three years, however, the amortization expense will be different from what it was for the first two years. The unamortized balance of $26,000 (acquisition cost was $50,000 less $24,000 of accumulated amortization) is treated as if it were now the cost of the asset. The estimated residual value is $1,000, and the estimated remaining useful life is three years. The calculation follows:

$$\frac{\$26,000 - \$1,000}{3 \text{ years}} = \frac{25,000}{3 \text{ years}} = \$8,333 \text{ per year}$$

The asset will now be amortized for three years at $8,333 per year. At the end of that time, the book value of the asset will be $1,000 (= $26,000 – ($8,333 per year × 3 years)).

STUDY BREAK 5-7

See How You're Doing

At the beginning of 2005, White Company hired a mechanic at a cost of $2,400 to perform a major overhaul on equipment. The equipment originally cost $10,000 at the beginning of 2001, and the book value of the equipment on the December 31, 2004, balance sheet was $6,000. At the time of the purchase, White Company estimated that the equipment would have a useful life of 10 years and no residual value. The overhaul at the beginning of 2005 extended the useful life of the equipment. White Company's new estimate is that the equipment will now last until the end of 2012—eight years beyond the date of the overhaul. White uses straight-line amortization for all its assets. Prepare the journal entries to record the capital expenditure and amortization expense for 2006.

Depletion of Natural Resources and Amortization of Intangible Assets

Depletion of Natural Resources

L.O. 4

Know how to account for natural resources and intangible assets.

When a company acquires natural resources to use in its business, those resources are assets that are written off in a way that is very similar to the way costs are written off using amortization. When we refer to the process of writing off a natural resource, we say we are depleting that resource.

Depletion is computed in a way similar to the units-of-production amortization calculations, but it applies only to writing off the cost of natural resources. Examples of such natural resources are land being used for farming, oil wells, and mines. A depletion cost per unit is calculated by dividing the cost of the natural resource less any residual value by the estimated units of production or output available from that natural resource. The depletion cost per unit is then multiplied by the units pumped, mined, or cut, per period to determine the total depletion related to the output during the period.

Suppose a company purchases the rights to an oil well in Alberta for $100,000 on January 1, 2005, estimating the well will produce 200,000 barrels of oil during its life. The depletion rate per barrel is ($100,000/200,000 barrels) = *$0.50* per barrel. If 50,000 barrels are produced in the year 2005, then the depletion related to the 50,000 barrels produced in 2005 will be $25,000 (= $0.50 per barrel × 50,000 barrels). The book value of the oil rights will be $75,000 (= $100,000 – $25,000) on the December 31, 2005, balance sheet.

Amortization of Intangible Assets

Writing off an intangible asset is called amortizing the asset. The most common way of writing off an intangible asset is the straight-line method—the cost is divided equally among the periods benefited by use of the asset. An intangible asset is recorded at cost and amortized over its useful life. When the useful life of an intangible asset is unclear, some guidance for the length of its amortization may be provided by GAAP. If an intangible asset has a specific life (e.g., often the legal life of a patent is 20 years), then the asset is amortized over that period of time unless the company plans to keep it for a shorter period of time.

In general, research and development (R&D) costs are expensed and are *not* capitalized as part of the cost of an asset. This is because it is not clear that these costs represent something of value. Software development costs are considered research costs until they result in a product that is technologically feasible; so, these costs must also be expensed as they are incurred. However, once the software is considered technologically feasible, the subsequent costs are capitalized as part of the cost of the software. Deciding when a piece of software is technologically feasible is another example of the judgment required in making accounting decisions.

Selling a Long-Term Asset

L.O. 5

Calculate the gain or loss on the disposal of an asset and understand how that is reflected on the financial statements.

We have bought assets and used them—depreciating, depleting, or amortizing them over their useful lives. Next, let us deal with getting rid of an asset. Disposing of an asset means to sell it, trade it in, or simply toss it out with the trash. When would a company sell an asset? Sometimes, an asset is sold because it is no longer useful to the company. Other times, an asset is replaced with a newer model, even though there is remaining productive capacity in the current asset. Many business decisions must be made before an asset is sold. These decisions are based on judgments that are part of long-term budgeting (called *capital budgeting*) and are examined in detail in managerial accounting. For now, let us look at how we would calculate whether we would have a gain or loss if the asset is sold.

The gain or loss on the disposal of an asset is calculated by comparing the cash received for the asset—also known as **proceeds**—and the asset's book value at the time of disposal. One of three situations will exist:

Proceeds refer to the cash collected from the sale of an asset.

Gain refers to a certain kind of addition to income that is earned outside the normal course of business.

Loss refers to a certain kind of reduction to income that is incurred outside the normal course of business.

- Cash proceeds are greater than the book value of the asset. If cash proceeds are greater than the book value, there is a **gain**.
- Cash proceeds are less than the book value of the asset. If cash proceeds are less than the book value, there is a **loss**.
- Cash proceeds are equal to the book value of the asset. If cash proceeds equal book value, there is no gain or loss.

Suppose you decide to sell an asset that was purchased seven years ago. At the time of the purchase, you estimated it would last 10 years. It cost $25,000, and you used straight-line amortization with an estimated residual value of zero. So, the amortization expense each year was $2,500.

After seven years, you sell the asset for $8,000. Is there a gain or loss on the sale? To determine which, first calculate the book value at the date you sold the asset. Total accumulated amortization is $2,500/year × 7 years = $17,500.

Book Value = $25,000 − $17,500 = $7,500 at the date of sale

Then, subtract the book value from the cash proceeds.

$8,000 − $7,500 = $500

Because the proceeds are larger than the book value, there is a gain on the sale. A gain is a special component of income when shown on the income statement. It is special because it is not a normal part of business operations.

You are not in business to buy and sell the equipment you use in your business. Thus, the income from such a transaction is given the special name *gain*.

The transaction affects the accounting equation as follows:

Assets	=	Liabilities	+	Owner's equity
(25,000) Asset +17,500 Accumulated amortization +8,000 Cash				+500 Gain on sale

To record the journal entries related to the sale, you need to remove the equipment and its accumulated amortization from your accounting records. First, you must calculate the amount of accumulated amortization you have recorded for the equipment. In this case, the amortization expense has been $2,500 per year, and you have amortized the asset for seven years. That means the balance in the accumulated amortization account for this asset is $17,500. To remove the equipment from your records,

1. remove the equipment with a credit to the equipment account;
2. remove the accumulated amortization with a debit to the accumulated amortization—equipment account;
3. record the cash received for the sale; and
4. record the gain or loss to balance the journal entry.

The journal entry to record the sale of equipment for a gain of $500 and to accomplish these four things is:

Date	Transaction	Debit	Credit
	Cash	$ 8,000	
	Accumulated amortization—equipment	$17,500	
	Equipment		$25,000
	Gain on sale of equipment		$ 500

Suppose, instead, you sell the asset after seven years for $5,000. Is there a gain or loss on the sale? You already know the book value is $7,500 at the date of the sale. Subtract the book value from the cash proceeds.

$$\$5,000 - \$7,500 = (\$2,500)$$

Because the proceeds are less than the book value, there is a loss on the sale. A loss is a special component of income when shown on the income statement. For the same reason as for the gain on the sale of equipment, the reduction in income from this transaction is given the special name, *loss*.

Suppose you sold the asset for exactly the book value, $7,500. There would be no gain or loss on the sale. Look at that transaction in the accounting equation to see the effect of selling an asset for its book value.

Assets	=	Liabilities	+	Owner's equity
(25,000) Asset +17,500 Accumulated amortization +7,500 Cash				

The journal entry to record the sale of equipment for its book value of $7,500 would then have no gain or loss:

Date	Transaction	Debit	Credit
	Cash	$ 7,500	
	Accumulated amortization—equipment	$17,500	
	Equipment		$25,000

There is no gain or loss; the transaction only involves assets. As you have learned, when the only effect of a transaction is an increase and a decrease to assets, it is called an asset exchange.

STUDY BREAK 5-8

See How You're Doing

Perry Plants Company owned an asset that originally cost $24,000. The company sold the asset on January 1, 2007, for $8,000 cash. Accumulated amortization on the day of sale amounted to $18,000. Prepare the journal entry to record the asset sale.

Amortization and Taxes

L.O. 6

Distinguish between amortization for accounting records and amortization for tax purposes.

The accounting information related to amortization needed to prepare the financial statements is not the same information needed for income tax determination. The information for the financial statements is prepared according to GAAP for reporting to the company's shareholders—the owners of the company. The information needed for taxes is determined by the legal rules of the *Income Tax Act*. Because GAAP and the *Income Tax Act* require very different information to be reported, managers need an information system that can produce both sets of data.

When calculating income for tax purposes a deduction of capital cost allowance is permitted in place of amortization or depreciation calculated for financial reporting purposes. **Capital cost allowance** is claimed on the cost of assets on a declining balance basis at rates prescribed by CCRA. The rates permitted depend on the type of asset being amortized and vary from 5 percent to 100 percent. Companies need not claim any capital cost allowance, or they may claim up to the maximum allowed. Most would choose to claim the maximum amount available in order to reduce their tax expense.

Capital cost allowance is the deduction permitted in place of amortization when calculating taxable income.

How does more capital cost allowance result in lower taxes? Suppose a company's income before capital cost allowance and before taxes is $10,000. If capital cost allowance for taxes is $2,000, then the company has taxable income of $8,000. Suppose the company's tax rate is 25 percent. Then the company must pay $2,000 (= $8,000 × 0.25) in taxes and will have net income after taxes of $6,000.

Suppose the company can claim $4,000 of capital cost allowance. Income before capital cost allowance and taxes is $10,000, and so income before taxes will be $6,000 (= $10,000 – $4,000). With a tax rate of 25 percent, the company will have to pay $1,500 (= $6,000 × 0.25) in taxes, leaving a net income after taxes of $4,500.

When the amount of capital cost allowance is larger, the amount of taxes a company must pay is smaller. A smaller tax bill means less cash has to be paid in taxes, and so the company's net cash flow for the year will be greater.

However, as we have seen from comparing straight-line amortization and double-declining balance amortization, *over the life of an asset*, the total amortization expense is the same no matter what method is used. The difference between the methods is reflected in the way the total amortization is allocated to the years the asset is used. The reason a company wants to claim the maximum capital cost allowance available for tax purposes is because the largest deductions are taken as soon as possible. Saving tax dollars *this* year is preferred to saving them *next* year—because it is cash the company can use in the business to make money now.

Business Process

L.O. 7

Identify the disclosure requirements related to long-term assets and use them to analyze the performance of a company's long-term assets.

Operational assets are assets with useful lives of more than one year, purchased to generate revenue for the business firm.

Finding and Using Amortization Information

The investment that a company has in long-term assets is useful information and must be disclosed in some detail in the financial statements and the accompanying notes, according to GAAP. Look at the information from Sears Canada Inc. balance sheet in Exhibit 5–6. The amounts shown for land and buildings, fixtures and equipment, and so on are the original cost of those assets. The accumulated amortization is the total amortization that has been taken on all these assets since their purchase. What other information about the **operational assets** would be useful? Details about how the assets have been written off may be of interest to financial statement users. In one of the notes to the financial statements, you can find out the amortization methods used, as well as information about the useful life of the assets. Read the information in the notes in Sears Canada Inc. 2003 financial statements shown in Exhibit 5–7.

Exhibit 5–6
From the Balance Sheet of Sears Canada Inc.
Courtesy Sears Canada, Inc.

(in millions)	2003	2002
Land	$ 73.8	$68.1
Buildings and improvements	964.1	846.5
—held by joint ventures	180.2	178.6
Equipment and fixtures	1,169.3	1,189.5
Gross capital assets	2,387.4	2,282.7
Accumulated amortization		
Buildings and improvements	469.4	389.7
—held by joint ventures	45.3	41.9
Equipment and fixtures	829.9	814.2
Total accumulated depreciation	1,344.6	1,245.8
Capital assets	$1,042.8	$1,036.9

Exhibit 5–7
From Notes to the Financial Statements of Sears Canada Inc.
Courtesy Sears Canada, Inc.

Capital Assets

Capital assets are stated at cost. Depreciation and amortization provisions are generally computed by the straight-line method based on estimated useful lives of 2 to 10 years for equipment and fixtures, and of 10 to 40 years for buildings and improvements.

The Company's proportionate share of buildings held in joint ventures is generally depreciated by the sinking fund method over 20 to 40 years.

The Company capitalizes interest charges for major construction projects and depreciates these charges over the life of the related assets.

Lease or Buy?

Generally accepted accounting principles (GAAP) try to make sure the financial statements reflect the ***substance*** of a company's transactions instead of the ***form*** of the transaction. Because a company's financial statements are so important to investors, creditors, and anyone who wants to evaluate a company's performance, how a transaction is reflected on those statements is very important to the company. Sometimes, recording a transaction on the basis of its substance may not be very appealing. A classic example is buying or leasing assets. When a company ***buys*** an asset, it is shown on the balance sheet, and any amount that the company owes for the purchase of the asset must be shown on the balance sheet as a liability.

Suppose a company does not want to put any additional liabilities on its balance sheet. Then would a company lease an asset instead of buying it? Could the company simply record the expense of leasing the asset as the lease payments are made? If the form of the transaction is a lease but the substance is more like a purchase, the lease is called a ***capital lease,*** and GAAP say the transaction has to be recorded like a purchase. In other words, a company cannot "hide" future financial commitments related to long-term leases by calling the transaction a lease and simply recognizing the expense when the payments are made. That means the company must record the asset on the balance sheet and also record the related long-term obligation of the future lease payments as a liability. Then the asset is amortized, just like any other amortizable asset owned by the company.

The accounting standards have very specific rules about how to account for long-term leases. The criteria for deciding if a lease qualifies as a capital lease are very technical. An accountant comes in handy when this issue comes up.

In the long-term assets section of a company's balance sheet, you will often see items called ***capitalized leases*** or ***leasehold improvements.*** Capitalized leases represent assets a company has, in substance, bought but the ***form*** of the purchase is a lease. Leasehold ***improvements*** are long-term assets in the form of additions and improvements to leased property. For example, if a company remodels the interior of a leased office building, the cost of the remodelling will be called ***leasehold improvements.***

A company decides whether to lease an asset or to purchase an asset on the basis of business factors, such as (1) the type of asset and the risk of obsolescence, (2) the interest rate of the lease payments compared with the interest rate of a purchase, (3) the lease's renewal and purchase options, (4) the acceptable alterations to leased assets, and (5) the estimated useful life of the leased asset to the business. However, the accounting treatment should ***not*** influence the economic decision. It goes the other way—the economic decision influences the accounting treatment.

Applying Our Knowledge: Ratio Analysis

A company purchases assets to help generate future revenue. Remember the definition of an asset—something of value used by a business to generate revenue. A ratio that measures how well a company is using its assets to generate revenue is **return on assets (ROA)**. Like much of the terminology in accounting, the name of this ratio is descriptive. A company's return is what the company is getting back. We want to measure that return as a percentage of assets. So, return on assets is literally return—net income—divided by assets.

$$\text{Return on Assets} = \frac{\text{Net income}}{\text{Average Total Assets}}$$

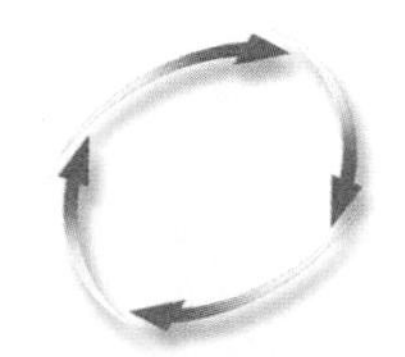

Business Process

Return on assets (ROA) is net income divided by average total assets; a measure of how well a company is using its assets to generate income.

This ratio measures a company's success in using its assets to earn income for the persons who are financing the business. Because interest is part of what has been earned to pay creditors, it is often added back to the numerator. Net income is the return to the owners and interest expense is the return to the creditors. Thus, the numerator is often calculated by adding interest expense back to net income. The denominator is always average total assets.

Using a ratio like ROA gives financial statement users a way to standardize net income across companies. For example, in 2002, High Liner Foods had a net income of $10,242,000. FPI Limited had a net income of $13,771,000. It is useful to compare the dollar amounts, and we can see that FPI had over $3 million more net income than High Liner Foods. One piece of information that would be useful is how well each company is using its assets to make that net income. If we divide net income by average total assets, we'll get the return on assets for the year.

Courtesy High Liner Foods Incorporated, Lunenberg, N.S.

Courtesy Fishery Products International

	High Liner Foods	FPI Limited
Net income 2002	$ 10,242,000	$ 13,771,000
Beginning assets	217,870,000	348,806,000
Ending assets	207,367,000	390,885,000
Return on assets	4.8%	3.7%

It is clear from this comparison that High Liner Foods is earning a better return with its total assets than FPI Limited is earning with its assets.

Sometimes, a return on assets ratio is computed for a single asset. That is often hard to do because the return or net income for that asset has to be measured apart from all other net income. If a company can measure the incremental revenue, net of expenses, provided by a certain asset, that amount can be divided by the investment in that asset. Can you see how this type of calculation might help a company make a decision about purchasing an asset?

Remember, all ratios have this in common: They mean more when they are compared with the ratios from other years for the same company or with the ratio for other companies. Industry standards are often available for common ratios to help investors and analysts evaluate a company's performance using ratio analysis.

Business Risks

L.O. 8

Identify risks and controls associated with long-term assets.

The most significant risk related to long-term assets is that someone will steal one of those assets. It is not a problem with some large assets, such as a factory, but it is a very serious problem with smaller, mobile fixed assets, such as cars, computers, furniture and fixtures, and inventory. Safeguarding all assets, one of the major functions of an internal control system, is necessary in companies of all sizes and types. Controls are necessary to protect the company's assets from theft, as well as damage, whether intentional or unintentional.

Controls to safeguard assets may be as simple as a lock or a security guard. Physical controls are common ways to protect assets. Even when assets are protected in a secure facility with guards, fences, or alarms, the company must be sure that only the appropriate people have access to the assets.

Complete and reliable record keeping for the assets is also part of safeguarding assets. One form of internal control is separation of duties (mentioned in an earlier chapter). That means that the people who are responsible for the record keeping related to the assets should be different from the people who have physical custody of the assets. This is true for all assets—cash, inventory, and long-term assets.

Beyond the record-keeping function related to the company's assets, safeguarding *information* has become a necessary part of a company's risk control. The potential monetary loss from the destruction of information is enormous. The 2001 World Trade Center disaster brought international attention to problems resulting from the loss of information. Hundreds of thousands of documents and computer files were destroyed. For a business to survive the loss of information from physical destruction like fire or flood, the information should be backed up in another location. Many times, this task is outsourced—a firm hires a company that specializes in data backup and recovery.

Monitoring is another control to safeguard assets. That means that someone needs to make sure the other controls—physical controls, separation of duties, and any other policies and procedures related to protecting assets—are operating properly.

From Yahoo News: Business—Reuters

Wednesday September 12, 2001 2:45 PM ET

Key Data Lost in Attack But Soon Regained

NEW YORK (Reuters)—Tuesday's terror attack on New York's financial district destroyed a wealth of important data and documents, but many companies expect to be up and running soon thanks to back-up files in other locations.

Top financial companies such as Morgan Stanley, Deutsche Bank AG, and Cantor Fitzgerald are among those now scrambling to reassure investors and retrieve lost data affecting the flow of hundreds of millions of dollars...

Makers of back-up and recovery software booked $2.7 billion in revenues last year, and that figure is expected to grow to $4.7 billion in 2005, according to research firm IDC.

"My anticipation is that after yesterday's events that figure may increase," said Bill North, an analyst at IDC.

Note: Complete article is not reproduced here.

Understanding Excel

In this chapter, Tom's Wear purchased a new van for $30,000. The purpose of this exercise is to prepare an amortization schedule for each of the three methods of amortization discussed in this chapter. For purposes of this exercise only, assume a five-year or 50,000-kilometre estimated useful life, with a full year of amortization to be taken in the year of purchase and the van to have no salvage value.

Requirements

1. Open a new Excel work sheet.
2. Create the following bold column headings beginning in column A and ending in column E: **Year, Beginning Book Value, Current Amortization Expense, Accumulated Amortization,** and **Ending Book Value.** (Remember to use Format, Cells, Alignment, and "Wrap Text" to minimize the column width of columns that have multi-word headings.) Click the Align Right button to align all the column headings.
3. Prepare amortization schedules for straight-line, units of production, and double-declining balance methods of amortization. Use formulas to calculate current amortization expense, accumulated amortization, and ending book value.

   Hint: Many of the formulas needed may be input once and copied. For example, beginning book value – current amortization expense = ending book value. Input the formula one time for each schedule, and then copy it to the other years either by using the fill handle or by clicking the Copy and Paste buttons.
4. For units of production, assume the following usage breakdown: year 1: 5,000 kilometres; year 2: 15,000 kilometres; year 3: 12,000 kilometres; year 4: 10,000 kilometres, and year 5: 8,000 kilometres. For double-declining balance, assume that the full unamortized book value at the end of year 4 will be taken as amortization expense in year 5.
5. Print your file and save it to disk. Name your file TomsWear5.

Summary Problem: Tom's Wear Expands in April 2005

Since beginning in January 2005, Tom's Wear Inc. has now finished three months of business. Refresh your memory by reviewing Tom's March 31 balance sheet in Exhibit 5–8 before Tom's Wear begins the month of April. Tom's Wear has been struggling along, but Tom believes that he can make a big profit breakthrough if he can expand his business. His research indicates a large demand for his T-shirts, and so he plans a major expansion in April.

Required

Tom's Wear's transactions for April are shown in Exhibit 5–9. Go through the transactions, shown individually, in the accounting equation work sheet to make sure you understand them.

1. Make the month-end adjustments using the accounting equation work sheet.
2. Prepare the four basic financial statements for April.

Exhibit 5–8
Balance Sheet for Tom's Wear at the Beginning of April

Tom's Wear, Inc.
Balance Sheet
At April 1, 2005

Assets		Liabilities and Shareholders' equity	
Cash	$ 3,995	Interest payable	$ 30
Accounts receivable	2,000	Notes payable	3,000
Inventory	300	Total liabilities	3,030
Prepaid insurance	75		
		Common shares	5,000
Equipment (net of $100 accumulated amortization)	3,900	Retained earnings	2,240
		Total liabilities and shareholders' equity	
Total assets	*$10,270*		*$10,270*

Exhibit 5–9
Transactions for April 2005 for Tom's Wear, Inc.

1	April 1	Purchased a delivery van for $25,000 and paid $5,000 for changes to the van's interior to accommodate his T-shirts, and signed a 5-year, 10 percent note payable with the following terms: interest is due each March 31 and $6,000 of principal is repaid each March 31.
2	April 10	Hired an employee, Sam Cubby, for 20 hours per week, to fold, sort, and deliver the shirts. Sam will earn $1,000 per month, payable on the 5th of the following month. Sam will not begin work until May.
3	April 1–15	Collected accounts receivable of $2,000 from customers from March.
4	April 1–15	Purchased 1,000 T-shirts at $4 each, on account.
5	April 15	Rented a warehouse for $1,200 per month, beginning on April 15. Paid a total of $2,400 rent for 2 months.
6	April 15	Contracted with several sporting goods stores to stock Tom's Wear shirts and sold 800 shirts for $10 each, all on account, for total sales of $8,000.
7	April 1–30	Paid $300 for other operating expenses.

Transaction 1

Tom's Wear decided to buy a delivery van for the company. In April, he purchased a van for $25,000. He paid an additional $5,000 to have it equipped with the racks for his T-shirts. Tom's Wear financed the $30,000 at 10 percent per year for five years with a local bank. On March 31 of each year, beginning in 2002, Tom's Wear will pay the bank the interest it owes for the year plus $6,000 of the $30,000 principal. Tom's Wear expects the van to be driven for approximately 200,000 kilometres and have a residual value of $1,000 at the end of its useful life. The company decides to amortize the van using the units-of-production method, based on kilometres.

Assets	=	Liabilities	+	SC	+	Retained earnings
+30,000 Van		+30,000 Notes payable				

Date	Transaction	Debit	Credit
4/1/2005	Equipment—van	$30,000	
	Long-term notes payable		$30,000
To record the purchase of a delivery van.			

Transaction 2

Hiring an employee does not require any formal journal entry. The company information system, however, will certainly record information about Sam Cubby for the payroll records.

No Journal Entry

Transaction 3

Tom's Wear received cash for the prior month of sales on account, settling the $2,000 accounts receivable on the April 1, 2005 balance sheet.

Assets	=	Liabilities	+	SC	+	Retained earnings
+$2,000 Cash $(2,000) Accounts receivable						

Date	Transaction	Debit	Credit
4/1–4/15/2005	Cash	$2,000	
	Accounts receivable		$2,000
To record the collection of accounts receivable			

Transaction 4

Tom has found several sporting goods stores willing to buy his shirts, and so he must dramatically increase the inventory. Tom's Wear purchases 1,000 T-shirts at $4 each on account.

Assets	=	Liabilities	+	SC	+	Retained earnings
+$4,000 Inventory		+$4,000 Accounts payable				

Date	Transaction	Debit	Credit
4/1–4/15/2005	Inventory	$4,000	
	Accounts payable		$4,000
To record the purchase of 1,000 T-shirts at $4 on account			

Transaction 5

Tom's Wear rented a warehouse in which to store its inventory. On April 15, the company paid $2,400 for two months' rent.

Assets	=	Liabilities	+	SC	+	Retained earnings
+$2,400 Prepaid rent						
$(2,400) Cash						

Date	Transaction	Debit	Credit
4/15/2005	Prepaid rent	$2,400	
	Cash		$2,400
To record prepayment of 2 months' rent at $1,200 per month.			

Transaction 6

Tom has arranged the sales of his shirts to a number of sporting good stores in the area. Each month Tom's Wear will deliver 800 shirts for $10 each to several different shops. The delivery will be made on the 15th of each month, and the customer will pay by the 10th of the subsequent month. The first deliveries are on April 15.

Assets	=	Liabilities	+	SC	+	Retained earnings
+$8,000 Accounts receivable						+$ 8,000 Sales
$(3,200) Inventory						$(3,200) Cost of goods sold

Date	Transaction	Debit	Credit
4/15/2005	Accounts receivable	$8,000	
	Sales		$8,000
To record the sale of 800 T-shirts, on account.			
4/15/2005	Cost of goods sold	$3,200	
	Inventory		$3,200
To record the expense cost of goods sold and reduce the inventory by 800 × $4.			

Transaction 7

Tom's Wear paid cash for $300 worth of operating expenses.

Assets	=	Liabilities	+	SC	+	Retained earnings
$(300) Cash						$(300) Operating expenses

Date	Transaction	Debit	Credit
4/1–4/30/2005	Other operating expenses	$300	
	Cash		$300
To record the payment of operating expenses.			

Prepare the adjusting journal entries, post to T-accounts, and prepare an adjusted trial balance. Then, prepare the four financial statements. (Check your answer near the end of the chapter.)

Answers to Study Break Questions

STUDY BREAK 5-1

1. Equipment—Amortization
2. Franchise—Amortization
3. Oil well—Depletion
4. Building—Amortization

STUDY BREAK 5-2

1. Payment for employee salaries—Expensed
2. Purchase of a new delivery truck—Capitalized
3. Rent paid in advance—Capitalized
4. Rent paid in arrears—Expensed

STUDY BREAK 5-3

The total appraised value of the building and land together = $500,000. The percentage of each individual appraisal in the total is calculated. The building was appraised at $400,000. That is 4/5 of the total amount (400,000/500,000 = 4/5). The land was appraised at $100,000. That is 1/5 of the total amount (100,000/500,000 = 1/5).

After the proportions are calculated, they are applied to the cost of the assets, with 4/5 of $480,000 = $384,000 to bc allocated to the Building and 1/5 of $480,000 = $96,000 to be allocated to the land.

The building must be amortized and the land will not be amortized. That is why the amounts have to be separated.

Date	Transaction	Debit	Credit
	Building	$384,000	
	Land	96,000	
	Cash or notes payable		$480,000
To record the purchase of land and building.			

STUDY BREAK 5-4

Using straight-line amortization, the same amount is expensed every year. That amount is calculated as (Cost minus Estimated Salvage Value) divided by the total number of years of useful life: (15,000 – 3,000)/5 = $2,400. *Thus, $2,400 is the annual amortization expense.* Each year, that amount is amortized—added to Accumulated Amortization (a contra-asset) to reduce the value of the asset on the company's books. Amortization of three years means that $7,200 (= 3 × $2,400) has been added to Accumulated Amortization. The cost of the asset, $15,000, minus the total Accumulated Amortization, $7,200, equals the book value at December 31, 2007, $7,800.

Date	Transaction	Debit	Credit
12/31/2007	Amortization expense	$2,400	
	Accumulated amortization		$2,400
To record straight-line amortization expense for 2007.			

STUDY BREAK 5-5

The amortization base is cost minus salvage value; it is $44,000 – $4,000 = $40,000. The total production over its life is estimated to be 100,000 units. Thus, the rate is $40,000 divided by 100,000 units = $0.40 per unit. In 2009, amortization expense is 3,000 units × $0.40 per unit = $1,200. In 2010, amortization expense is 14,000 units × $0.40 per unit = $5,600.

Date	Transaction	Debit	Credit
12/31/2005	Amortization expense	$1,200	
	Accumulated amortization		$1,200
To record activity-based amortization expense for 2009.			
12/31/2006	Amortization expense	$5,600	
	Accumulated amortization		$5,600
To record activity-based amortization expense for 2010.			

STUDY BREAK 5-6

For double-declining balance, we start with 2 divided by the useful life of 5 years. We use that fraction, 2/5, and multiply it each year by the book value. For the first year, the amortization expense is $50,000 × 2/5 = $20,000. For the second year, the amortization expense is ($50,000 – 20,000) × 2/5 = $30,000 × 2/5 = $12,000.

Date	Transaction	Debit	Credit
	Amortization expense	$12,000	
	Accumulated amortization		$12,000
To record double-declining balance amortization expense for year 2.			

STUDY BREAK 5-7

Book value at overhaul date (2005)	$ 6,000
Add overhaul cost	+2,400
Total to be amortized over remaining useful life	$8,400
Divide by remaining useful life	$8,400/8 years
Amortization per year	**$1,050**

Date	Transaction	Debit	Credit
1/2005	Equipment	$2,400	
	Cash		$2,400
To record the cost of overhauling equipment.			
12/31/2006	Amortization expense	$1,050	
	Accumulated amortization		$1,050
To record straight-line amortization expense for 2010.			

STUDY BREAK 5-8

Book value	= $ 6,000
Proceeds	= $ 8,000
Gain of	**$2,000**

Date	Transaction	Debit	Credit
1/1/2007	Cash	$ 8,000	
	Accumulated amortization	18,000	
	Asset		$24,000
	Gain on sale		2,000
To record the asset sale.			

Solution to Summary Problem

1. These are the adjustments that Tom's Wear should make before preparing the financial statements. (The adjustments can be made in any order.)

Adjustment 1

Tom's Wear needs to adjust Prepaid insurance. On April 1, there was $75 worth of prepaid insurance on the balance sheet. Recall, Tom's Wear purchased three months' insurance on February 15 for a total cost of $150, which is $50 per month.

Assets	=	Liabilities	+	CC	+	Retained earnings
$(50) Prepaid insurance						$(50) Insurance expense

Date	Transaction	Debit	Credit
4/30/2005	Insurance expense	$50	
	Prepaid insurance		$50
To record insurance expense for April.			

Adjustment 2

Another item that needs to be adjusted is Prepaid rent. Tom's Wear paid $2,400 for two months' rent, beginning on April 15. On April 30, half a month's rent should be expensed.

Assets	=	Liabilities	+	CC	+	Retained earnings
$(600) Prepaid rent						$(600) Rent expense

Date	Transaction	Debit	Credit
4/30/2005	Rent expense	$600	
	Prepaid rent		$600
To record rent expense for April.			

Adjustment 3

Amortization expense for the computer needs to be recorded. Recall, it is being amortized at $100 per month.

Assets	=	Liabilities	+	CC	+	Retained earnings
$(100) Accumulated amortization						$(100) Amortization expense

Date	Transaction	Debit	Credit
4/30/2005	Amortization expense	$100	
	Accumulated amortization—computer		$100
To record April amortization expense on the computer.			

Adjustment 4

Amortization expense for the new van needs to be recorded. It cost $30,000 and has an estimated residual value of $1,000. It is being amortized using the units-of-production method based on an estimated 200,000 kilometres. During April, the van was driven 5,000 kilometres. The rate is $0.145 per kilometre

(= \$29,000 amortizable base divided by 200,000 kilometres). The amortization expense for the month of April is \$0.145 per kilometre × 5,000 kilometres = \$725.

Assets	=	Liabilities	+	CC	+	Retained earnings
\$(725) Accumulated amortization						\$(725) Amortization expense

Date	Transaction	Debit	Credit
4/30/2005	Amortization expense	\$725	
	Accumulated amortization—van		\$725
To record April amortization expense on the van.			

Adjustment 5

Interest expense on the note for the computer needs to be accrued. The three-month, \$3,000, note at 12 percent was signed on March 1. Interest for April will be \$30 (= \$3,000 × 0.12 × 1/12).

Assets	=	Liabilities	+	CC	+	Retained earnings
		\$30 Interest payable				\$(30) Interest expense

Date	Transaction	Debit	Credit
4/30/2005	Interest expense	\$30	
	Interest payable		\$30
To record the interest expense on the computer for April.			

Adjustment 6

Interest expense on the note for the van needs to be accrued. The \$30,000, note at 10 percent was signed on April 1. Interest for April will be \$250 (= \$30,000 × 0.10 × 1/12).

Assets	=	Liabilities	+	CC	+	Retained earnings
		\$250 Interest payable				\$(250) Interest expense

Date	Transaction	Debit	Credit
4/30/2005	Interest expense	\$250	
	Interest payable		\$250
To record the interest expense on the van for April.			

2. First, the T-accounts are given, with both transactions and adjustments. Then, the adjusted trial balance is presented, followed by the financial statements.

T-Accounts for Tom's Wear with April Journal Entries and Adjustments

Cash

	Debit	Credit	
BB	$3,995	$2,400	5
3	2,000	300	7
	$3,295		

Accounts receivable

	Debit	Credit	
BB	$2,000	$2,000	3
6a	8,000		
	$8,000		

Inventory

	Debit	Credit	
BB	$300	$3,200	6b
4	4,000		
	$1,100		

Prepaid insurance

	Debit	Credit	
BB	$75	$50	Adj-1
	$25		

Prepaid rent

	Debit	Credit	
5	$2,400	$600	Adj-2
	$1,800		

Equipment: computer

	Debit	Credit	
BB	$4,000		
	$4,000		

Accumulated Amortization: computer

	Debit	Credit	
		$100	BB
		100	Adj-3
		$200	

Equipment: van

	Debit	Credit	
1	$30,000		
	$30,000		

Accumulated Amortization: van

	Debit	Credit	
		$725	Adj-4
		$725	

Accounts payable

	Debit	Credit	
		$4,000	4
		$4,000	

Interest payable

	Debit	Credit	
		$30	BB
		30	Adj-4
		250	Adj-6
		$310	

Short-term notes payable

	Debit	Credit	
		$3,000	BB
		$3,000	

Long-term notes payable

	Debit	Credit	
		$30,000	1
		$30,000	

Common shares

	Debit	Credit	
		$5,000	BB
		$5,000	

Retained earnings

	Debit	Credit	
		$2,240	BB
		$2,240	

Sales

	Debit	Credit	
		$8,000	6a
		$8,000	

Cost of goods sold

	Debit	Credit	
6b	$3,200		
	$3,200		

Amortization expense

	Debit	Credit	
Adj-3	$100		
Adj-4	725		
	$825		

Other operating expenses

	Debit	Credit	
7	$300		
	$300		

Insurance expense

	Debit	Credit	
Adj-1	$50		
	$50		

Rent expense

	Debit	Credit	
Adj-2	$600		
	$600		

Interest expense

	Debit	Credit	
Adj-5	$30		
Adj-6	250		
	$280		

Tom's Wear, Inc.
Adjusted Trial Balance
April 30, 2005

	Debits	Credits
Cash	$ 3,295	
Accounts receivable	8,000	
Inventory	1,100	
Prepaid insurance	25	
Prepaid rent	1,800	
Equipment: computer	4,000	
Accumulated amortization: computer		$ 200
Equipment: van	30,000	
Accumulated amortization: van		725
Accounts payable		4,000
Interest payable		310
Short-term notes payable		3,000
Long-term notes payable		30,000
Common shares		5,000
Retained earnings		2,240
Sales		8,000
Cost of goods sold	3,200	
Amortization expense	825	
Other operating expense	300	
Insurance expense	50	
Rent expense	600	
Interest expense	280	
Totals	*$53,475*	*$53,475*

The financial statements follow:

tom's wear

Tom's Wear, Inc.
Income Statement
For the Month Ended April 30, 2005

Sales revenue		$8,000
Expenses		
Cost of goods sold	$3,200	
Insurance expense	50	
Rent expense	600	
Amortization expense	825	
Other operating expenses	300	
Interest expense	280	5,255
Net income		$2,745

tom's wear

Tom's Wear, Inc.
Statement of Retained Earnings
For the Month Ended April 30, 2005

Beginning retained earnings	$2,240
Net income for the month	2,745
Dividends	0
Ending retained earnings	$4,985

Tom's Wear, Inc.
Balance Sheet
At April 30, 2005

Assets		Liabilities and Shareholders' equity	
Cash	$ 3,295	Accounts payable	$ 4,000
Accounts receivable	8,000	Interest payable	310
Inventory	1,100	Short-term notes payable	3,000
Prepaid insurance	25	Total current liabilities	7,310
Prepaid rent	1,800		
Total current assets	14,220	Notes payable	30,000
Equipment (net of $200 accumulated amortization)	3,800	Total liabilities	37,310
		Common shares	5,000
		Retained earnings	4,985
Van (net of $725 accumulated amortization)	29,275		
Total assets	$47,295	Total liabilities and shareholders' equity	$47,295

Tom's Wear, Inc.
Cash Flow Statement
For the Month Ended April 30, 2005

Cash from operating activities		
Cash collected from customers	$2,000	
Cash paid for operating expenses	(2,700)	
Total cash from operations		*$(700)*
Cash from investing activities		0
Cash from financing activities		0
Net increase (decrease) in cash		$(700)

Note: Additional information: Van was purchased for $30,000. A note was signed for the full amount.

Questions

1. What is included in the cost of property, plant, and equipment?
2. What is the purpose of amortization?
3. Does GAAP provide a choice of amortization methods?
4. What is meant by *accelerated amortization*?
5. What is *residual value* (or *salvage* value)?
6. Describe an *intangible* asset.
7. What is the difference between a *capital expenditure* and a *revenue expenditure*?
8. What is a *basket purchase*? What measurement problem does it create?
9. What is the difference between *amortization* and *depletion*?
10. What is the difference between *amortization expense* and *accumulated amortization*?
11. What is meant by the *carrying value* of an asset? How does it relate to the market value of the asset?
12. How is a gain or loss on the disposal of an asset calculated?
13. On which financial statement would we see a gain or a loss on the disposal of an asset?
14. What is the difference between amortization for financial statements and amortization for taxes? What is the method used for taxes?
15. Define the ratio *return on assets*. Describe its usefulness.

Short Exercises

L.O. 1

SE5-1 Gruber Window Fashions bought a new wood-cutting machine as a part of its venture into manufacturing interior shutters. The invoice price of the machine was $90,000. Gruber also had the following expenses associated with purchasing this machine.

Delivery charge	$2,850
Installation	2,500
Power to run the machine for the first year	450

What amount should Gruber record on the books for this equipment?

SE5-2 Settler Company was outgrowing its rented office space fast. The firm decided that it could raise enough capital to buy land and build a new office building. The building was completed on September 15. Consider the following costs incurred for the new building: L.O. 1

Building materials	$110,000
Labour costs (including architect's fees)	205,000
Rental of equipment used in the construction	9,000
Maintenance on the building from September 15 to December 31	14,000

What amount should Settler Company record on the books for the new building?

SE5-3 Tylo Corp. obtained a building, its surrounding land, and a delivery truck in a lump sum purchase for $230,000. An appraisal set the value of land at $80,000, with the building at $145,000, and the truck at $25,000. At what amount should Tylo record each new asset on its books? L.O. 1

SE5-4 Villa Corp. purchased three buildings at a total cost of $960,000. The appraised values of the individual buildings were as follows: L.O. 1

Building 1	$600,000
Building 2	400,000
Building 3	200,000

What amounts should be recorded as the cost for each of the buildings in the Villa Corp. records?

SE5-5 Calculate the annual straight-line amortization expense for an asset that cost $12,000, has a useful life of five years, and has an estimated salvage value of $2,000. L.O. 2

SE5-6 If an asset with no salvage value is being amortized at a rate of $1,000 per year using the straight-line method over a useful life of 10 years, how much did the asset cost? L.O. 2

SE5-7 A machine is purchased on January 2, 2003, for $20,000 and it has an expected life of four years and no estimated residual value. If the machine is still in use five years later, what amount of amortization expense will be reported for the fifth year? (No revision of the estimate was ever made during the asset's life.) L.O. 2

SE5-8 Suppose an asset cost $20,000 and has an estimated salvage value of $2,000. At the end of three years, the carrying value of the asset is $11,000. What is the useful life of the asset? Assume straight-line amortization. L.O. 2

SE5-9 For each of the following, tell whether it should be classified as (1) a revenue expenditure (expensed), (2) a capital expenditure (capitalized), or (3) neither. L.O. 3

a. For routine repairs, $2,000 was paid.
b. $500 cash dividends were paid to shareholders.
c. For repairs that will extend the asset's useful life, $6,000 was paid.
d. A patent for $5,000 cash was purchased.
e. A machine for $10,000 was purchased and the firm signed a two-year note for it.
f. For an addition to a building, $50,000 was paid.
g. For routine maintenance on a machine, $1,000 was paid.

SE5-10 Categorize each of the following as a capital expenditure or a revenue expenditure for Dalton & Sons and explain why. L.O. 3

a. In accordance with the long-term maintenance plan, Dalton & Sons paid for a newly shingled roof.
b. The company built an annex to the building for the executive offices.
c. Dalton improved the ventilation system to increase energy efficiency in the building.
d. The company replaced parts in major equipment as needed.

L.O. 3

SE5-11 On January 1, 2007, the Lance Corp. purchased a machine at a cost of $55,000. The machine was expected to have a useful life of 10 years and no residual value. The straight-line amortization method was used. In 2009, the estimate of residual value was revised from 0 to $6,000. How much amortization expense should Lance Corp. record for 2009?

L.O. 4

SE5-12 CNA Enterprises acquired an oil field that is expected to produce 1,000,000 barrels of oil. The oil field, acquired in January 2005, cost CNA $1.5 million. In 2005, a total of 280,000 barrels were produced. In 2006, production increased to 350,000 barrels. How much depletion should be recorded for each of these years?

L.O. 4

SE5-13 Coppery Mining acquired a copper mine at a total of $3,000,000. The mine is expected to produce 6,000,000 tonnes of copper over its five-year useful life. During the first year of operations, 850,000 tonnes of copper were extracted. How much depletion should Coppery record for the first year?

L.O. 5

SE5-14 A machine is purchased on January 2, 2005, for $50,000. It has an expected useful life of 10 years and no residual value. After 11 years, it sold for $3,000 cash. Will there be a gain or loss on the sale? How much?

L.O. 5

SE5-15 The Crunch Company sold equipment for $35,000. The equipment originally cost $100,000, had an estimated useful life of 10 years and had no estimated residual value. It was amortized for five years using the straight-line method. In the year of the sale, should Crunch report a gain or a loss on its income statement and in what amount?

L.O. 7

SE5-16 Financial ratios are often used to evaluate company performance. What ratio would give information about how efficiently a company is using its assets? Calculate that ratio for CoolBrands and explain what information it provides.

L.O. 8

SE5-17 Write a paragraph describing a specific risk associated with long-term assets and some possible controls that might minimize the risk.

Exercises

L.O. 1, 2

E5-1 Tampa-Cola purchased a building and land for a total cash price of $180,000. An independent appraiser provided the following market values: building—$150,000; land—$50,000.

a. How much of the purchase price should be allocated to each of the assets?
b. If the building has a useful life of 10 years and an estimated residual value of $35,000, how much amortization expense should Tampa-Cola record each year using the straight-line method?
c. By using the double-declining balance method, what would the book value of the building be at the end of 3 years?

L.O. 2

E5-2 Best-Goods Company purchased a delivery truck for $35,000 on January 1, 2006. It had an estimated useful life of seven years or 210,000 kilometres. Best-Goods estimated the truck salvage value to be $5,000. The truck was driven 16,000 kilometres in 2006 and 32,000 kilometres in 2007.

a. Compute the amortization expense for each of these years, first using the straight-line method and then the units-of-production method.
b. In your opinion, which method portrays more accurately the actual use of this asset? Why?

L.O. 2

E5-3 On January 1, 2005, Norris Company purchased equipment for $42,000. Norris was also charged $1,200 for shipping and installation. The equipment is expected to have a useful life of 10 years and a residual value of $3,200.

a. Compute the amortization expense for the years 2005 through 2007, using the straight-line method.
b. Compute the amortization expense for the years 2005 through 2007, using the double-declining balance method.
c. What is the book value of the equipment on December 31, 2005, under each method?

E5-4 Yester Manufacturing Company has had a piece of equipment for six years. At the beginning of the sixth year, it was not performing as well as it should have been. First, Yester relubricated the equipment, which cost $150. Then, it tried replacing some worn-out parts—this cost the firm $520. Finally, at the beginning of the seventh year, the company completed a major overhaul of the equipment that not only fixed the machine but also added new functionality to it and extended the useful life by three years (to a total of 10 years) with no salvage value. The overhaul cost $10,000. (Originally, the machine cost $60,000, had a salvage value of $4,000, and had an estimated useful life of seven years.) The straight-line method of amortization is used. L.O. 3

a. Which of these costs are capital expenditures?
b. Which are revenue expenditures?
c. What amounts will appear on the income statements of years 6 and 7?

E5-5 Zellwiger Plumbing bought a van for $44,000. The van is expected to have a 10-year useful life and a salvage value of $5,000. L.O. 5

a. If Zellwiger sells the van after 3 years for $30,000, would the company have a gain or loss? How much? (Assume straight-line amortization.)
b. What would be the gain or loss if the firm sold the van for $30,000 after 6 years?

E5-6 Troy Wilson Athletic Gear purchased a packaging machine four years ago for $18,000. The machinery was expected to have a salvage value of $2,000 after an eight-year useful life. Assuming straight-line amortization is used, what would be the gain or loss if after four years the machinery was sold for $11,400; for $7,800? L.O. 5

Problems—Set A

P5-1A Pirate Print Shop purchased a new printing press in 2008. The invoice price was $158,500, but the manufacturer of the press gave Pirate a 3 percent discount for paying cash for the machine on delivery. Delivery costs amounted to $2,500, and Pirate paid $900 for a special insurance policy to cover the press while in transit. Installation cost $2,800; and Pirate spent $5,000 training the employees to use the new press. Additionally, Pirate hired a new supervisor at an annual salary of $75,000 to be responsible for keeping the press online during business hours. L.O. 1

Required:

a. What amount should be capitalized for this new asset?
b. To calculate the amortization expense for 2008, what other information do you need? Do you think this information should be gathered before the asset is purchased? Why or why not?

P5-2A On January 1, 2005, the Monticello Manufacturing Company purchased equipment for $130,000. The estimated useful life of the equipment is four years and the estimated residual value is $10,000. The equipment is expected to produce 480,000 units during its service life. Actual units produced were: L.O. 2

Year	Units
2005	100,000
2006	130,000
2007	140,000
2008	105,000

Required: Calculate the amortization expense for each year of the four-year life of the equipment using

a. the straight-line method
b. the double-declining balance method
c. the units-of-production method

L.O. 2

P5-3A Balls and Bats, Inc. purchased equipment on January 1, 2009, at a cost of $100,000. The estimated useful life is four years with a salvage value of $10,000.

Required:

a. Prepare two different amortization schedules for the equipment—one using the double-declining balance method, and the other using the straight-line method. (Round to the nearest dollar.)
b. Determine which method would result in the greatest net income for the year ending December 31, 2009.
c. How would taxes affect management's choice between these two methods for the financial statements?

P5-4A Peps Company purchased a new machine at the beginning of 2006 for $6,400. It is expected to last for five years and have a salvage value of $400. The estimated productive life of the machine is 100,000 units. Yearly production follows: in 2006—28,000 units; in 2007—22,000 units; in 2008—16,000 units; in 2009—14,000 units; and in 2010—20,000 units.

Required: Calculate the amortization expense for each year using each of these amortization methods:

a. straight-line
b. units-of-production
c. double-declining balance

L.O. 3

P5-5A Required: Calculate the gain or loss on the disposal of the following assets:

a. A truck that cost $25,000 had an estimated useful life of five years with no salvage value and was amortized using the straight-line method. After four years, the company sold it for $8,000.
b. A machine that cost $50,000 had an estimated useful life of 12 years and a salvage value of $2,000 and was amortized using the straight-line method. After 10 years, the machine was completely worn out and sold for $500 as scrap.
c. An asset that cost $40,000 had a salvage value of $2,000 and an estimated useful life of four years and was amortized using the double-declining balance method. After three years, it was sold for $10,000.
d. A machine that cost $15,000, with an estimated useful life of six years and no salvage value and was amortized using the straight-line method. After five years, it was deemed to be worthless and hauled to the dump.

L.O. 1, 2, 3, 4

P5-6A During 2008, Umpire's Empire, Inc. had some trouble with its information processing due to an umpire strike, and so several errors were made.

Required: For each situation, describe the effect any error would have on the Umpire 2008 financial statements if it were not corrected. Then, give the adjustment that would need to be made to correct the company accounting records and make the 2008 financial statements accurate. If there is no error, write N/A next to the problem.

a. At the beginning of 2008, a building and land were purchased together for $100,000. Even though the appraisers determined that 90 percent of the price should be allocated to the building, Umpire decided to allocate the entire purchase price to the building. The building is being amortized over 40 years, with an estimated salvage value of $10,000.
b. During the year, Umpire did some R&D on a new gadget to keep track of balls and strikes. The R&D cost $20,000, and Umpire capitalized it. The firm intends to write it off over five years.

P5-7A The Sewing Company purchased a new machine on January 2, 2005, for $48,000. The machine is expected to have a useful life of five years and a residual value of $3,000. The company fiscal year ends on December 31.

L.O. 2, 5

Required:

a. What is the amortization expense for the fiscal years 2005 and 2006 using each of the following methods:
   1. straight-line
   2. double-declining balance
b. Assume that Sewing Company decided to use the straight-line method and that the sewing machine was sold at the end of December 2006 for $27,000. What was the gain or loss on the sale? On which financial statement would the gain or loss appear?

P5-8A In January 2005, Harvey's Hoola Hoop Company purchased a computer system that cost $37,000. Harvey's estimated that the system would last for five years and would have a salvage value of $2,000 at the end of 2009, and the company uses the straight-line method of amortization. Each problem below is independent of the others.

L.O. 3

a. Before the amortization expense is recorded for the year 2007, Harvey is told by his computer experts that the system can be used until the end of 2009 as planned but that it will be worth only $500.

Required: How much amortization expense related to the computer system should Harvey's Hoola Hoop Company show on its income statement for the year ended December 31, 2007?

b. Suppose that before amortization expense is recorded for the year 2007, Harvey's decides that the computer system will only last until the end of 2008. The company anticipates the value of the system at that time will still be $2,000.

Required: How much amortization expense related to the computer system should Harvey's Hoola Hoop Company show on its income statement for the year ended December 31, 2007?

c. Suppose that before amortization expense is recorded for the year 2007, Harvey's decides that the computer system will last until the end of 2010 but that it will be worth only $1,000 at that time.

Required: How much amortization expense related to the computer system should Harvey's Hoola Hoop Company show on its income statement for the year ended December 31, 2007?

d. Before the amortization expense is recorded for the year 2007, Harvey's experts decide that the system can be used until the end of 2011 if the firm spends $4,000 on upgrades. However, the estimated salvage value at that time would be zero.

Required: If the company spends the money on the upgrades, how much amortization expense related to the computer system would Harvey's Hoola Hoop Company show on its income statement for the year ended December 31, 2007?

P5-9A The Cubbie Company purchased a truck three years ago for $50,000. It had an expected useful life of five years with no salvage value. Cubbie has taken three full years of amortization expense.

L.O. 2, 5

Required:

a. Assume that Cubbie uses straight-line amortization. If the truck is sold for $25,000, will there be a gain or loss on the sale? If so, how much? How will it affect the Cubbie financial statements for the year?
b. Assume that Cubbie uses double-declining balance amortization. If the truck is sold for $15,000, will there be a gain or loss on the sale? If so, how much? How will it affect the Cubbie financial statements for the year?

c. Assume Cubbie uses straight-line amortization and sells the truck for $20,000. Would there be a gain or loss on the sale? How would that change if Cubbie had been using double-declining balance amortization? Compare the total effect on income of using and selling the truck during the past three years under the two different methods of amortization.

L.O. 7

P5-10A Use the following information from Harvey's Hardware annual report to answer the questions that follow:

(Numbers are in millions)	January 30, 2003	January 31, 2002
Property and equipment, at cost		
Land	$ 3,248	$2,739
Building	4,834	3,757
Furniture, fixtures, and equipment	2,279	1,761
Leasehold improvements	493	419
Construction in progress	791	540
Capital leases	245	206
	$11,890	$9,422
Less accumulated amortization	1,663	1,262
Net property and equipment	$10,227	$8,160

Note on amortization

The company's buildings, furniture, fixtures, and equipment are amortized using the straight-line method over the estimated useful lives of the assets. Improvements to leased premises are amortized using the straight-line method over the life of the lease or the useful life of the improvement, whichever is shorter. The company's property and equipment is amortized using the following estimated useful lives:

	Life
Buildings	10–45 Years
Furniture, fixtures, and equipment	5–20 Years
Leasehold improvements	5–30 Years
Computer software	3–5 Years

Required:

a. Can you tell how much Harvey's Hardware paid for the buildings it owns? If so, how do you know?

b. Can you tell how much the buildings are worth (i.e., the market value)?

c. What are Leasehold Improvements? (*Hint:* Read the note amortization, and see if you can figure out what they are.)

d. What are Capital Leases? (*Hint:* Read "Understanding Business" in the chapter.)

Problems—Set B

L.O. 1, 2

P5-1B Bikini Bettie's Beach Resort needed some additional land for its resort. The resort decided to buy the adjacent piece of property, which was for sale. Unfortunately, the land came with an old run-down motel. The cost of the land with the old motel was $1,500,000. Real estate commissions and fees including the title search were $317,850. Bikini Bettie's Beach Resort paid its lawyer $15,000 to review the contract and complete the purchase of the land on July 1, 2008. The resort paid $25,750 for the old motel to be demolished and an additional $17,850 for sugar white sand to be hauled in to make the land beautiful for sunbathers. The resort paid $80,000 for some palm trees to make its new sun bathing area attractive. Bikini Bettie hired three new lifeguards at a salary of $35,000 a year each to watch over the expected crowds.

Required:

a. What amount should be capitalized for this new asset?
b. Would there be any amortization expense for land at the end of 2008? Explain your answer.

P5-2B Baseball Company purchased a new pitching machine at a cost of $18,000 at the beginning of January 2007. The machine was estimated to have a salvage value of $2,000 at the end of its useful life of four years. A machine like this is supposed to deliver 160,000 hours of pitching practice. The actual number of hours that the machine was used per year was 2007—40,000 hours; 2008—60,000 hours; 2009—35,000 hours; and 2010—25,000 hours. L.O. 2

Required: Prepare an amortization schedule using the

a. straight-line method
b. units-of-production method
c. double-declining method

For each, make a chart that shows the amortization expense for each year, as well as the book value of the asset at the end of the year.

P5-3B Carla's Candy, Cookies, and More Shop purchased an automated display rack on January 1, 2008, at a cost of $35,000. The estimated useful life is five years with a salvage value of $5,000. L.O. 2

Required:

a. Prepare two different amortization schedules for the equipment—one using the double-declining balance method, and the other using the straight-line method. (Round to the nearest dollar.)
b. Determine which method would result in the greatest net income for the year 2010.
c. How would taxes affect management's choice between these two methods for the financial statements?

P5-4B Clean Water Company purchased a new water filter machine at the beginning of 2010 for $200,000. It is expected to last for eight years and have a salvage value of $32,000. The estimated productive life of the machine is 200,000 units. Yearly production was in 2010—46,000 units; in 2011—28,000 units; in 2012—42,000 units; in 2013—21,000 units; in 2014—26,000 units; in 2015—14,000 units; in 2016—17,000 units; and in 2017—6,000 units. L.O. 2

Required: Calculate the amortization expense for each year using each of these amortization methods:

a. straight-line
b. units-of-production
c. double-declining balance (rounded to the nearest dollar)

P5-5B Calculate the gain or loss on the disposal of the following assets: L.O. 2

a. A company van that cost $32,000 had an estimated useful life of eight years with no residual value and was being amortized using the straight-line method. After six years, the company sold it for $10,000.
b. A copy machine that cost $35,000 had a residual value of $5,000 and an estimated useful life of five years and was amortized using the double-declining balance method. After two years, it was sold for $15,000.
c. A company truck that cost $48,000 had an estimated useful life of seven years and a residual value of $6,000 and was amortized using the straight-line method. After

five years of many kilometres of driving on tough terrain, the truck was completely worn out and sold for $1,050 for spare parts.

d. A state-of-the-art computer that cost $29,000 had a salvage value of $2,000 and an estimated useful life of four years and was amortized using the double-declining balance method. After three years, it was sold for $5,000.

L.O. 1, 2, 3, 4

P5-6B During 2004, Umpire's Empire, Inc. had some trouble with its information processing due to an umpire strike, and so several errors were made.

Required: For each situation, describe the effect any error would have on the Umpire 2004 financial statements if it were not corrected. Then give the adjustment that would need to be made to correct the company accounting records and make the 2004 financial statements accurate. If there is no error, simply write N/A next to the problem.

a. The plumber spent a great deal of time repairing broken toilets in the Umpire building this year. Total cost, which Umpire capitalized, was $5,000. Umpire decided it was best to leave it on the books as an asset and not write it off because the toilets will be used for quite a few more years.

b. Umpire purchased a new van. It cost $20,000 and is expected to last three years. It has a salvage value of $2,000. To properly equip it for all the Umpire gear, the inside was customized at a cost of $6,000. The cost of the van was capitalized, and the cost of the customization was expensed.

L.O. 2, 5

P5-7B The House of Root Beer bought new brewery equipment on January 1, 2008, for $56,000. The machine is expected to have a useful life of seven years and a residual value of $7,000. The company fiscal year ends on December 31.

Required:

a. What is the amortization expense for the fiscal years 2008 and 2009 using each of the following methods?

1. straight-line
2. double-declining balance (round to nearest whole dollar)

b. Assume that House of Root Beer decided to use the double-declining method and that the brewery equipment was sold at the end of December 2009 for $42,000. What was the gain or loss on the sale? On which financial statement would the gain or loss appear?

L.O. 3

P5-8B In July 2005, Henry's Hat Company purchased a computer system that cost $7,000. The company estimated that the system would last for five years and would have a salvage value of $2,000 at the end of June 2010. The company uses the straight-line method of amortization. Henry's Hat Company has a June 30 fiscal year-end. Each problem that follows is independent of the other.

Required:

a. Suppose that before amortization expense is recorded for the year ending June 30, 2007, Henry's decides that the computer system will last until the end of July 2011 but that it will be worth only $500 at that time. How much amortization related to the computer system should Henry's Hat Company show on its income statement for the year ended June 30, 2007?

b. Before the amortization is recorded for the fiscal year ending June 30, 2008, the company computer experts tell Henry that the system can be used until the end of June 2012 if he spends $1,000 on upgrades. However, the estimated salvage value at that time would be zero. If the company spends the money on the upgrades, how much amortization related to the computer system would Henry's Hat Company show on its income statement for the year ended June 30, 2008?

L.O. 2, 5

P5-9B The Queen Grande View Hotel purchased a van three years ago for $62,000. It had an expected useful life of four years and a $10,000 residual value. Queen Grande View has taken three full years of amortization expense.

Required:

a. Assume that Queen Grande View uses straight-line amortization. If the van is sold for $20,000, will there be a gain or loss on the sale? If so, how much? How will it affect the Queen Grande View financial statements for the year?
b. Assume that Queen Grande View uses double-declining balance amortization. If the van is sold for $9,750, will there be a gain or loss on the sale? If so, how much? How will it affect the Queen Grande View financial statements for the year?
c. Assume that Queen Grande View uses double-declining amortization and sells the truck for $23,000. Would there be a gain or loss on the sale? How would that change if Queen Grande View had been using straight-line balance amortization? Compare the total effect on income of using and selling the van during the past three years under the two different methods of amortization.

P5-10B Use the information from the 2003 Greenway Annual Report to answer the following questions: L.O. 7

	Dollars in millions March 31, 2003
Property, plant, and equipment	
Land	$ 1,752
Buildings	7,306
Machinery and equipment	18,444
Construction in progress	875
	$28,377
Less—accumulated amortization	16,532
	11,845
Other Assets	
Intangibles, net	2,061
Goodwill, net	2,772

Property, plant, and equipment and amortization

Property, plant, and equipment is stated at cost. Amortization of property, plant, and equipment is computed on the declining-balance method for Greenway and Japanese subsidiaries and on the straight-line method for foreign subsidiary companies at rates based on estimated useful lives of the assets according to general class, type of construction, and use. Significant renewals and additions are capitalized at cost. Maintenance and repairs, and minor renewals and betterments are charged to income as incurred.

Intangibles and goodwill

Intangibles, which mainly consist of artist contracts, music catalogues, and trademarks, are being amortized on a straight-line basis principally over 16 years, 21 years, and 20 years, respectively.

Goodwill recognized in acquisitions accounted for as purchases is being amortized on a straight-line basis principally over a 40-year period.

Required:

a. What is Greenway's primary method for amortizing its assets?
b. How much did Greenway pay for the machinery and equipment it owns?
c. Are any of the assets listed as Property, Plant, and Equipment not being amortized?
d. Can you tell how much amortization expense Greenway had for the fiscal year ending March 31, 2003?
e. Explain what the $16,532 million of accumulated amortization represents.
f. Can you find a sentence in the notes that summarizes the accounting treatment for major overhaul or additions to assets discussed in Chapter 5?
g. Why would intangible assets be amortized over 16 years, 21 years, and 20 years?

Recording Transactions

R5-1 (SE5-5) Give the journal entry to record the purchase of equipment that cost $12,000 and has a useful life of five years and an estimated salvage value of $2,000. After calculating the annual straight-line amortization expense for the equipment, give the journal entry that would need to be recorded at the end of each of the next five years.

Date	Account	Debit	Credit

R5-2 (SE5-9) For each of the following, give the journal entry to record the transaction. No explanations are required:

- **a.** Paid $2,000 for routine repairs.
- **b.** Paid cash dividends of $500 to shareholders.
- **c.** Paid $6,000 for repairs that will extend the asset's useful life.
- **d.** Purchased a patent for $5,000 cash.
- **e.** Purchased a machine for $10,000 and gave a two-year note.
- **f.** Paid $50,000 for an addition to a building that increases its usefulness.
- **g.** Paid $1,000 for routine maintenance on a machine.

Transaction	Account	Debit	Credit

R5-3 (SE5-14) A machine is purchased on January 2, 2005, for $50,000. It has an expected useful life of 10 years and no residual value. After 11 years, it was sold for $3,000 cash. Give the journal entry needed to record the sale of the asset.

Date	Account	Debit	Credit

R5-4 (E5-2) Best-Goods Company purchased a delivery truck for $35,000 on January 1, 2006. It had an estimated useful life of seven years or 210,000 kilometres. Best-Goods estimated the truck's salvage value to be $5,000. The truck was driven 16,000 kilometres in 2006 and 32,000 kilometres in 2007. Using journal entries, first record the purchase of the asset. Then give the journal entries to record the amortization expense for both 2006 and 2007 using the (1) straight-line method, and (2) the units-of-production method of amortization.

Date	Account	Debit	Credit

R5-5 (E5-5) Zellwiger Plumbing bought a van for $44,000. The van is expected to have a 10-year useful life and a salvage value of $5,000.

- **a.** Suppose Zellwiger sells the van after three years for $30,000. Give the journal entry to record the sale. (Assume the company has used straight-line amortization.)

b. Suppose the van were sold for $30,000 after six years. Give the journal entry to record the sale.

Date	Account	Debit	Credit

R5-6 (P5-1A) Pirate Print Shop purchased a new printing press in 2008. The invoice price was $158,500, but the manufacturer of the press gave Pirate a 3 percent discount for paying cash on delivery for the machine. Delivery costs amounted to $2,500, and Pirate paid $900 for a special insurance policy to cover the press while in transit. Installation cost $2,800, and Pirate spent $5,000 training the employees to use the new press. Additionally, Pirate hired a new supervisor at an annual salary of $75,000 to be responsible for keeping the press on-line during business hours. Give the journal entry to record the purchase of the asset.

Date	Account	Debit	Credit

R5-7 (P5-5A) Required: Give the journal entries for the disposal of the following assets:

a. A truck that cost $25,000 and had an estimated useful life of five years with no salvage value was being amortized using the straight-line method. After four years, the company sold it for $8,000.

b. A machine that cost $50,000, with an estimated useful life of 12 years and a salvage value of $2,000, was being amortized using the straight-line method. After 10 years, the machine was completely worn out and sold for $500 as scrap.

c. An asset that cost $40,000, with a salvage value of $2,000 and an estimated useful life of four years, was being amortized using the double-declining balance method. After three years, it was sold for $10,000.

d. A machine that cost $15,000, with an estimated useful life of six years and no salvage value, was being amortized using the straight-line method. After five years, it was deemed to be worthless and hauled to the dump.

Transaction	Account	Debit	Credit

R5-8 (P5-6A) During 2008, Umpire's Empire, Inc. had some trouble with its information processing because of an umpire strike, and so several errors were made.

Required: For each situation, give the journal entry that would need to be made to correct the company's accounting records and to make the 2008 financial statements accurate. (Use two entries if you prefer.) If there is no error, write N/A next to the problem.

a. At the beginning of 2008, a building and land were purchased together for $100,000. Even though the appraisers determined that 90 percent of the price should be allocated to the building, Umpire's decided to allocate the entire purchase price to the building. The building is being amortized over 40 years, with an estimated salvage value of $10,000.

b. During the year, Umpire's did some research and development on a new gadget to keep track of balls and strikes. The R&D cost $20,000, and Umpire's capitalized it. The company intends to write it off over five years.

Transaction	Account	Debit	Credit

R5-9 (P5-8A) In January 2005, Harvey's Hoola Hoop Company purchased a computer system that cost $37,000. Harvey's estimated that the system would last for five years and would have a salvage value of $2,000 at the end of 2009, and the company uses the straight-line method of amortization. Each problem below is independent of the others.

Required: For each problem, give the journal entry to record the amortization expense for the year ended December 31, 2007.

a. Before the amortization expense is recorded for the year 2007, Harvey is told by his computer experts that the system can be used until the end of 2009 as planned but that it will be worth only $500.

b. Suppose that, before amortization expense is recorded for the year 2007, Harvey's decides that the computer system will only last until the end of 2008. The company anticipates the value of the system at that time will still be $2,000.

c. Suppose that, before amortization expense is recorded for the year 2007, Harvey's decides that the computer system will last until the end of 2010 but that it will be worth only $1,000 at that time.

d. Before the amortization expense is recorded for the year 2007, Harvey spends $4,000 on upgrades that extend the useful life of the system until the end of 2011. However, the estimated salvage value at that time will be zero.

Transaction	Account	Debit	Credit

R5-10 (P5-9A) The Cubbie Company purchased a truck three years ago for $50,000. It had an expected useful life of five years with no salvage value. After three full years of use, the truck is sold.

Required: For each independent case below, give the journal entry needed to record the sale of the truck.

a. Assume that Cubbie Company uses straight-line amortization. The truck is sold for $25,000.

b. Assume that Cubbie Company uses double-declining balance amortization. The truck is sold for $15,000.

c. Assume that Cubbie Company uses straight-line amortization and sells the truck for $20,000.

Transaction	Account	Debit	Credit

R5-Comprehensive

Chapter 5: Comprehensive Financial Statement Preparation Problem

This is the postclosing trial balance for Quality Printing Company, prepared on December 31, 2007.

Account	DR	CR
Cash	$290,000	
Accounts receivable	136,000	
Printing supplies	106,350	
Prepaid insurance	6,000	
Prepaid rental on printing equipment	18,000	
Accounts payable		$ 13,500
Salaries payable		3,500
Long-term note payable		200,000
Common shares		200,000
Retained earnings		139,350
	$556,350	$556,350

Transactions during 2008:

1. The company purchased a new printing press at the beginning of 2008. The invoice price was $158,500, but the manufacturer of the press gave Quality a 3 percent discount for paying cash for the machine on delivery. Delivery costs amounted to $2,500, and Quality Printing paid $900 for a special insurance policy to cover the press while in transit. Installation cost $2,800, and Quality Printing spent $5,000 training the employees to use the new press. Additionally, Quality Printing hired a new supervisor at an annual salary of $75,000 to be responsible for keeping the press on-line during business hours. All payments were made in cash.
2. Collected cash of $134,200 on accounts receivable.
3. Purchased $165,500 worth of printing supplies during the year. Paid cash of $100,000, with the remainder purchased on account.
4. Paid annual insurance premium of $12,000, due every June 30 for insurance coverage from July 1–June 30. Insurance costs were the same for the previous year.
5. Paid accounts payable beginning balance of $13,500.
6. Paid employees total cash for salaries of $72,250. (This includes the amount owed at the beginning of the year.)
7. Performed printing jobs for customers: $354,570. Collected $200,000 in cash, with the remainder on account.
8. On December 31, paid $50,000 to reduce principal of the long-term note and paid interest of $16,000 (8 percent of $200,000 original balance).

Other information:

a. There were supplies that cost $70,250 left on hand at year-end.
b. All prepaid rent for equipment was used up during the year, and the equipment was returned to the leasing company at year-end.
c. Salaries of $6,250 were owed to employees at year-end (earned but not paid).
d. The company estimates that the new printing press will last for 20 years and have a residual value of $2,945 at the end of its useful life. Use the straight-line amortization method.

Required: Prepare T-accounts for the company for the year ending December 31, 2008. Then, post the beginning balances and the transactions for the year. Prepare an unadjusted trial balance at December 31, 2008, make adjusting entries, and prepare the income statement, statement of retained earnings, balance sheet, and cash flow statement for 2008.

Issues for Discussion

L.O. 5-6, 7

Financial statement analysis

1. Use the annual report from CoolBrands International Inc. to answer these questions:
   a. What type of amortizable assets does CoolBrands have? What methods does the company use to amortize these assets?
   b. What can you tell about the age or condition of the CoolBrands long-term assets? Is the company continuing to invest in property, plant, and equipment?
   c. Is the company making good use of its assets? How can you evaluate this?

Business risk

2. What kinds of risks does CoolBrands face with respect to safeguarding its assets? What types of controls do you think it has to minimize these risks? Are any specific controls mentioned in the annual report?

Ethics

3. Rachel works in a real estate office that is equipped with up-to-date copiers, scanners, and printers. She is frequently the only employee working in the office in the evenings and often has spare time to do personal work. She has begun to use the office equipment for her children's school reports and for her husband's business. Do you think Rachel's use of the office equipment is harmless, or is she behaving unethically? Why? If you believe her behaviour is unethical, what controls could be in place to prevent it? Have you ever used office resources for personal tasks? Under what conditions could such use be justified?

Internet Exercise: Van Houtte Inc.

Van Houtte Inc. is one of North America's leading coffee companies, involved in nearly every aspect of the industry. They select and buy beans, roast and package coffees, manufacture state-of-the-art single-cup brewing equipment, and market a wide range of unique products to retail and office customers.
Go to the Van Houtte Inc. website: http://www.vanhoutte.com/

IE5-1 Go to "Investor Relations" under "About Us" and find the most recent annual report. Use the consolidated balance sheets to answer the following questions. At the most recent year-end, examine "Fixed Assets."

a. What is the acquisition cost of these assets?
b. What is the book value (carrying value)?
c. What amount of the acquisition cost has already been expensed?
d. Are any of the assets listed not being amortized?

IE5-2 Use the notes to financial statements to answer the following questions (usually the information can be found in note 1).

a. Find the heading "Fixed Assets." What amortization method does Van Houtte use for fixed assets? What is the range of useful lives for buildings and for equipment? Do these useful lives make sense?

b. Find the heading "Goodwill" on the Consolidated Balance Sheet. What type of an asset is goodwill? How does Van Houtte account for this asset.

c. Identify the amounts reported for revenues and net earnings (net income) for the two most recent years.

d. Compute the return-on-assets (ROA) ratio for the two most recent fiscal years. In which fiscal year did the company make best use of its assets? How can you tell?

Please note: Internet websites are constantly being updated. Therefore, if the information is not found where indicated, please explore the annual report further to find the information.

CHAPTER 6

Purchases and Payments Cycle: Inventory and Liabilities

Property, Plant, and Equipment

Here's where you've been...

In Chapter 5, you learned about how a company accounts for long-term assets—property, plant, and equipment. You learned how assets are amortized and how the information relevant to amortization is presented on the financial statements.

Here's where you're going...

From Chapter 6, you should understand how a company acquires inventory and accounts for payables. You will learn about FIFO and average cost, two popular ways of keeping track of inventory purchases and sales.

Inventory and Liabilities

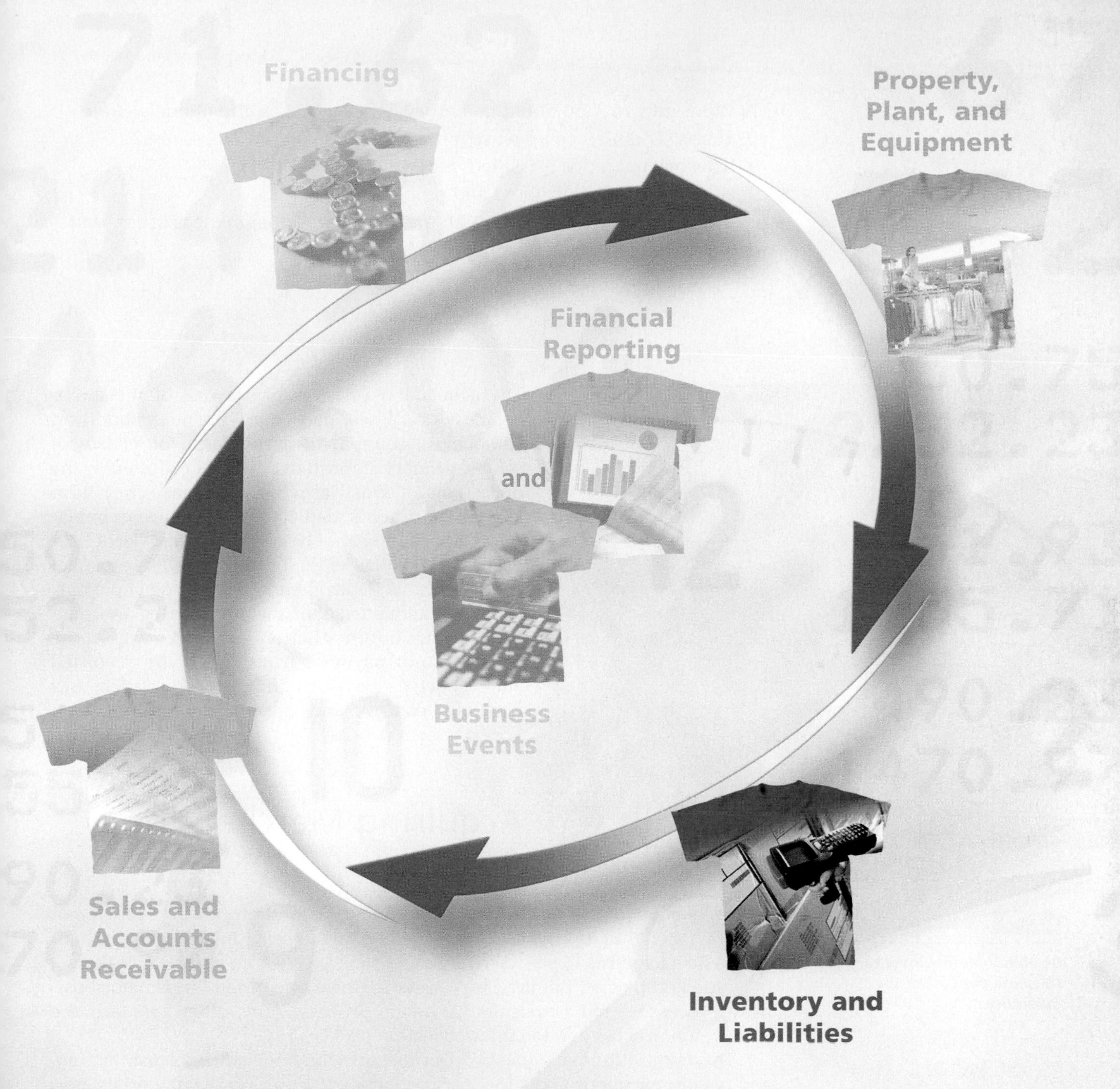

Learning Objectives

More specifically, when you are finished studying this chapter, you should be able to answer these questions:

1. What is inventory, and how is it recorded at purchase?
2. What are the four major inventory cost flow assumptions, and how does each measure and report cost of goods sold and ending inventory?
3. What are the two choices in the timing of updating inventory records?
4. What is the effect of inventory errors on the financial statements?
5. How is inventory estimated using the gross profit method?
6. What is the lower-of-cost-or-market rule?

7. What information about inventory is disclosed on the financial statements, and how can we use it to help us evaluate the business?
8. How are liabilities classified, recorded, and reported?
9. How is payroll calculated and reported?
10. What risks are associated with the acquisition/ payment process, and what controls help minimize those risks?

The acquisition of inventory is one of the major business processes, particularly for merchandising companies. The payment for these purchases is also of primary importance. This is reflected in the operations of most large corporations. They have large departments dedicated to acquiring inventory—the purchasing department—and large departments dedicated to paying the bills—the accounts payable department. Firms, large and small, keep meticulous track of their purchases and payments. The information system—the way these purchase and payment transactions are recorded and reported—provides input for management's planning, control, and evaluation of the acquisition/ payment process.

Acquiring Merchandise for Sale

L.O. 1

Be able to define inventory and calculate the cost of the inventory.

A merchandising firm exists to earn revenue by selling products, but it cannot earn revenue until it purchases the items it plans to sell. The items a merchandising firm acquires to sell, or really to resell, are called inventory; and the acquisition and payment of inventory together form one of the three major business processes—the acquisition/payment process. (The other two are the conversion process and the sales/collection process.)

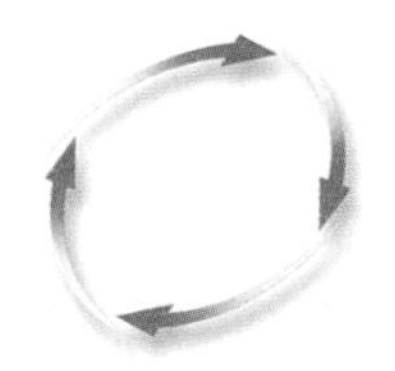

Business Process

The acquisition/payment process includes buying, storing, maintaining, and paying for goods and services. This includes acquiring raw materials, utilities, supplies, insurance, repairs, professional services (such as accounting), and inventory. We will focus on inventory in this chapter.

The objectives of the acquisition/payment process are:

- to purchase from reliable vendors items that meet the firm's standards
- to have resources available when needed
- to receive only those items ordered
- to pay vendors in a timely manner for the items received

Procedures for Acquisition of Goods

A **purchase requisition** is a company's internal record of the request for goods or services.

The acquisition/payment process begins when someone in a company requests goods or services needed by the company. The person requesting the goods or services sends a document, called a **purchase requisition**, to the company's purchasing agent. The purchasing agent selects the vendor on the basis of the vendor's prices, the quality of goods or services needed, and the ability to deliver them in a timely manner. The purchasing agent specifies in a **purchase order**—the company's document where information is recorded—what is needed, prices, and delivery time. A copy of the purchase order is sent to the vendor, and the company keeps several copies for internal records.

A **purchase order** is the record of the company's request to a vendor for goods or services.

One copy is sent to the receiving department for notification that a shipment of goods is expected from the vendor. This copy is slightly different than the one sent to the vendor. It is called a **blind purchase order** because it does not indicate the specific quantity of goods that were ordered. The individuals in the receiving department must count the items when they are received. If the quantity were specified on their copy of the purchase order, the employees in the receiving department might be tempted to use that amount instead of actually counting the goods. Counting the goods helps ensure that all goods requested and ordered were actually received.

A **blind purchase order** is a copy of the purchase order that notifies the receiving department of an expected shipment but does not indicate the quantity of goods ordered.

Another copy of the purchase order is sent to the accounts payable department where it is considered an *open* purchase order until the goods or services have been received.

On arrival of the vendor's truck at the receiving dock, the receiving department accepts the goods delivered on the basis of the authorization implicit in, and information specified in, the blind purchase order sent earlier from the purchasing department. The items are counted and inspected, and the condition and quantity of goods received are recorded in a **receiving report**.

A **receiving report** is the record made by the purchasing company of the details of the goods received.

A copy of the receiving report is also sent to the purchasing department as notification that the goods ordered have been received. Another copy of the receiving report is sent to the accounts payable department to be included in its documentation needed to pay for the goods.

Finally, a copy of the receiving report is sent to the inventory manager, who uses it to update the formal accounting records. After the records are updated for the purchase, the goods may then be transferred to a warehouse or site where they will be stored until they are sold.

Merchandise Inventory

L.O. 1

Understand how inventory is related to cost of goods sold.

All goods owned and held for sale in the regular course of business are considered **merchandise inventory**. Typically, merchandise inventory is simply called **inventory**. Inventory is a current asset. According to the matching principle, inventory should be expensed in the period in which it is sold.

Merchandise inventory is a current asset composed of goods owned and held for sale in the regular course of business. Also simply called **inventory**.

Why does the value of inventory matter? A merchandising firm records the inventory as an asset until it is sold. When it is sold, inventory becomes an expense—cost of goods sold. So, the value of the inventory affects both the balance sheet and the income statement.

Purchases

As was the case for property, plant, and equipment, the costs associated with acquiring inventory and the accounting for those costs are closely related. Gathering all the information to make good decisions is a necessary part of the business process. This information is reflected in the financial statements.

Business Process

The cost of a purchase is not always the amount quoted by the vendor. Often, a company receives a discount for purchasing a large quantity of items or for paying for them early or both. When buying inventory, a company should take advantage of any discounts available. **Purchase discounts** are commonly given for prompt payment. For example, a vendor offering a purchase discount would describe it in terms like this:

A **purchase discount** is a cash discount a company is offered by its vendors to make prompt payments.

2/10, n/30 describes the terms of a purchase discount. This example means the company would receive a 2 percent discount if it paid the invoice within 10 days.

2/10, n/30

read as "two-ten, net-thirty." That means the vendor will give a 2-percent discount if the buyer pays for the entire purchase within 10 days of the invoice date. If not, the full amount is due within 30 days. A vendor may set any discount terms. What would it mean if the terms were 3/15, n/45? The vendor will give a 3 percent discount if payment is made within 15 days. Otherwise, full payment must be made within 45 days.

Taking advantage of such discounts can amount to significant savings. When a vendor offers a sales discount, you should take advantage of it. If you are offered the terms 2/10, n/30, the vendor is actually charging you almost 36 percent annual interest to use the money if *you do not pay* within the discount period and wait until the last day, the 30th day, to pay. You are actually paying 36 percent annual interest for not paying until the last day: if the discount period expires and you have not paid until the 30th day after the invoice date, you are "borrowing" the money from the vendor for an additional 20 days. By your failure to pay within the discount period, the vendor has earned 2 percent in 20 days. Additionally, 2 percent interest on a "loan" over 20 days is the same as a 36 percent annual rate, determined with the help of a simple ratio:

$$\frac{2\%}{20 \text{ days}} = \frac{x}{360}$$

Solve for x and you get $x = 36$ percent annual interest, if you consider a year as having 360 days. Some companies borrow the money from the bank (at 10 or 12 percent annual interest) to take advantage of purchase discounts.

Purchase returns and purchase allowances are amounts that reduce the total cost of purchases of inventory due to returns or reductions related to unsatisfactory merchandise.

Some goods may need to be returned to the vendor because the company ordered too much inventory, ordered the wrong items, or found the goods slightly damaged. The cost of these goods is classified as **purchase returns**. Goods damaged or defective may be kept by the purchaser with a cost reduction—called a **purchase allowance**. Purchase discounts and purchase returns and allowances are deducted from the merchandising firm's *gross purchases* to get *net purchases*.

Freight-in is part of the cost of the purchased merchandise.

Any freight cost paid by the purchasing company to get the goods to the company is also included in the cost of the goods. When a merchandising firm pays for transportation costs on goods purchased, that cost is called **freight-in** and is considered part of the cost of the inventory.

FOB shipping point and **FOB destination** are purchase terms that describe whether the buyer or seller pays the freight related to a purchase. See Exhibit 6-1 for details.

If the terms of purchase are free on board **(FOB) shipping point**, then title to the goods passes to the buyer at the shipping point (the vendor's warehouse), and the buyer is responsible for the cost of the transportation from that point on. If the terms are **FOB destination**, the vendor—the supplier of the goods—pays for the transportation costs until the goods reach their destination, when title passes to the buyer. So, when you're the buyer:

- FOB shipping point ⇒ You pay; the amount is called *freight-in* and is included in the cost of the inventory. (Purchase discounts do not apply to freight charges.)

Exhibit 6–1
Shipping Terms

	FOB shipping point	FOB destination
Buyer	Buyer pays the shipping cost; the cost is recorded in the **inventory** account	Buyer **does not** pay the shipping cost
Seller	Seller **does not** pay the shipping cost	Seller pays the shipping cost, which is recorded as a **selling** expense

- FOB destination ⇒ Seller pays; so, you have no freight-in cost to account for.

When you are the vendor and you pay for goods to be delivered to your customers, the expense goes on your income statement as **freight-out**, or **delivery expense**. Freight-out is an operating expense; freight-in is a part of the cost of the inventory. Exhibit 6–1 shows the relationships among FOB selling point, FOB destination, the buyer, and the seller.

Freight-out, also called **delivery expense,** is an operating expense.

The details of inventory purchases—available discounts and shipping terms—can significantly affect the cost of the inventory. A company must pay attention to these costs because such costs make a difference in the acquisition process. These costs are then reflected in the financial statements.

STUDY BREAK 6-1

See How You're Doing

For each problem, calculate the cost of the inventory purchased.

1. A Company purchased merchandise FOB destination for $10,000. Terms were 2/10, n/30, and payment was made in 8 days. Freight cost was $90.
2. B Company purchased merchandise FOB destination for $10,000. Terms were 2/10, n/30, and payment was made in 29 days. Freight cost was $90.
3. C Company purchased merchandise FOB shipping point for $10,000. Terms were 2/10, n/30, and payment was made in 29 days. Freight cost was $90.
4. D Company purchased merchandise FOB shipping point for $10,000. Terms were 2/10, n/30, and payment was made in 8 days. Freight cost was $90.

Selecting and Accounting for Goods Sold: Inventory Cost Flow

L.O. 2

Be able to use various cost flow assumptions—specific identification, FIFO, LIFO, and average cost—to calculate inventory and cost of goods sold.

Suppose a grocery store buys a truckload of canned corn—1,000 cans—on the first of February for $0.75 per can. Then suppose the store suddenly expects a huge demand for canned corn, and so 1,000 more cans are ordered. The second truckload arrives a few days later. For this second purchase, the unit cost is $0.77 per can. The cans costing $0.77 are indistinguishable from the cans costing $0.75 in the first purchase. Two thousand cans are available to sell during February. There was no beginning inventory at the start of the month because the company had no cans of corn on that date. Suppose the store sells 1,600 cans during February. What is the *cost of goods sold*—also known as *cost of sales*—for the month?

We could figure that out easily if we knew exactly which cans were sold—how many costing $0.75 each and how many costing $0.77 each were sold? The store has no idea. The store simply knows that 1,600 cans were sold for $0.79 per can and that 400 cans are left in the inventory (i.e., not sold). There were 2,000 cans available for sale at a total cost of:

$$\$1{,}520 = (1{,}000 \text{ cans @ } \$0.75 \text{ per can}) + (1{,}000 \text{ cans @ } \$0.77 \text{ per can})$$

How should the store allocate that amount between the 1,600 cans sold (cost of goods sold) and the 400 cans not sold (ending inventory for February)?

The store will have to make an assumption about which cans flowed out of inventory to customers and which cans remain in inventory. That is, the store assumes an order in which the cans were sold, and that assumption makes it possible to calculate the cost of goods sold to go on the income statement and the cost of ending inventory to go on the balance sheet. The actual physical flow of the goods does *not* have to be consistent with the cost flow assumption. The grocery

Inventory flow is the physical movement of goods through a business. **Inventory cost flow** is the flow of inventory costs from the balance sheet to the income statement (inventory to cost of goods sold).

store could know that all the $0.75 cans could not have been sold because of the way shipments are stored in the warehouse; yet, the store is still allowed to use the assumption that the $0.75 cans were sold first in calculating cost of goods sold. **Inventory flow** refers to the physical passage of goods through a business. In accounting, we are generally concerned with **cost flow**—that is, the flow of the costs associated with the goods that pass through a company—instead of *goods* flow, which refers to the actual physical movement of goods.

Keeping Track of the Inventory: Four Cost Flow Assumptions

L.O. 2

Define and explain the four inventory cost flow assumptions: Specific identification, FIFO, LIFO, and average cost.

Specific identification requires keeping track of the specific items sold to calculate cost of goods sold.

Average cost uses the average cost of all the goods on hand to calculate cost of goods sold.

FIFO uses the cost of the oldest goods on hand to calculate cost of goods sold. This will result in a more current inventory value on the balance sheet and a less current value for cost of goods sold on the income statement.

LIFO uses the cost of the most recently purchased goods to calculate cost of goods sold. This will result in a more current value for cost of goods sold on the income statement and a less current value for inventory on the balance sheet.

GAAP allows a company to select one of several inventory cost flow assumptions. Studying several of these methods will help you understand how accounting choices can affect the amounts on the financial statements, even when the transactions are identical. There are four basic inventory cost flow assumptions used to calculate the cost of goods sold and the cost of ending inventory:

1. **Specific identification method**. With this method, each item sold must be identified as coming from a specific purchase, at a specific unit cost. Specific identification can be used for determining the cost of each item of a small quantity of large, luxury items, such as yachts or works of art, but it is almost impossible to use for determining the cost of each item of a large number of identical items. It would take a great deal of time and money to keep track of a large inventory with similar items using specific identification.

   Suppose you first bought two units at $3 each and later bought one unit at $4, and then you sold two units during the accounting period. What is cost of goods sold? To answer that question using the specific identification method, you would need to know exactly which two units were sold. That is, you have to specifically identify the units sold. If you sold both of the $3 units, then cost of goods sold would be $6 and ending inventory would be $4. However, if you sold one of the $3 units and the $4 unit, then cost of goods sold would be $7 and ending inventory would be $3.
2. **Average cost method**. An average unit cost is calculated by dividing the total cost of all the goods a company has available for sale by the total number of units available for sale, resulting in an average cost per unit. This average unit cost is *weighted* because the number of units at each different price is used to weight the unit costs. The calculated average unit cost is applied to all units sold to get cost of goods sold and applied to all units remaining to get a value for ending inventory.

   In the example of three units purchased, two @ $3 and one @ $4, the average cost per unit is $10 (total cost of purchases) divided by three (total number of units purchased). Cost of goods sold is two units × $10/3 = $6.67. Ending inventory would be one unit × $10/3 = $3.33.
3. **First-in, First-out method (FIFO)**. The cost of the first goods purchased is assigned to the first goods sold. The cost of the goods on hand at the end of a period is determined from the most recent purchases.

   By using the same example, two units purchased @ $3 and one unit @ $4, cost of goods sold under FIFO assumes that the two oldest units were sold first. FIFO means the first items purchased are the first *out* of inventory to go to the income statement as cost of goods sold. So cost of goods sold is $6 and ending inventory is $4.
4. **Last-in, First-out method (LIFO)**. The cost of the last goods purchased is assigned to the cost of goods sold, and so the cost of the goods on hand at the end of a period is assumed to be the cost of goods purchased earliest.

Again, using the same example, two units @ $3 and one unit @ $4, cost of goods sold is $7. (The last unit in was the $4 unit, and so it has to be sold first under LIFO. Then, the next most recent unit purchased is one of the $3 units.) Ending inventory is $3.

Note that the same set of facts and economic transactions can result in different numbers on the financial statements, depending on the choice of cost flow methods. It is important to remember this when using and interpreting financial information.

Record Keeping for the Inventory

L.O. 3

Define and use the two choices for inventory record keeping—perpetual and periodic.

In addition to selecting a cost flow assumption, a company must decide *when* to update inventory records and actually calculate cost of goods sold. There are two options. After every sale and purchase, the inventory records

Selecting Inventory Cost Flow Assumption

Inventory Cost Flow and Taxes

Generally accepted accounting principles (GAAP) allow firms considerable latitude in selecting a method of accounting for inventory costs. However, when it comes to income taxes, the Canada Customs and Revenue Agency (CCRA) limits choice to either first-in first-out (FIFO) or average cost. Last-in first-out (LIFO), which in a period of rising prices has the effect of reducing income, is not acceptable for tax purposes in Canada.

Inventory Cost Flow and Record-Keeping Costs

Inventory record-keeping costs are lowest with FIFO, and this, in addition to the acceptability of FIFO for tax purposes, may explain its widespread use. When a business uses FIFO, the dollar value of inventory can be established at any time if the physical quantities of inventory are known (an inventory count may be necessary unless records of inventory quantities are maintained), and these quantities can be priced or valued on the basis of recent invoices. The record keeping for LIFO or average cost is more complicated and, therefore, more costly.

Inventory Cost Flow and Earnings Management

GAAP recommend that the method chosen to determine the cost of inventory should be the one that results in the fairest matching of costs against revenues, regardless of whether or not the method corresponds to the physical flow of goods. In some instances, the choice of a method may have little effect on the financial statements and the income of the business. In other instances, the method chosen could cause income to change considerably. If managers have compensation contracts that are tied to the level of income, a lower income will mean a smaller bonus. In this situation, self-interest may become a factor in the selection of a method of accounting for inventory costs.

A survey of accounting practices reported in *Financial Reporting in Canada* (2001) found that the majority of firms in Canada use FIFO or average cost as their method of determining the cost of inventory. Of the 144 firms that disclosed their inventory cost flow assumption, 55 used average cost, 52 used FIFO, 30 used more than one method, 3 used LIFO, and 4 used other methods. The selection of an inventory cost flow method is an important business decision because of the significant impact it can have on reported financial results.

Perpetual inventory is a method of record keeping that involves updating the accounting records at the time of every sale and purchase.

Periodic inventory is a method of record keeping that involves updating the accounting records only at the end of the accounting period.

Beginning inventory refers to goods on hand (for sale) at the beginning of the accounting period.

Ending inventory is inventory on hand at the end of the accounting period.

can be updated. This is called a **perpetual inventory** system because it requires a continuous updating.

Alternatively, the inventory records can be updated at the end of each accounting period. This is called a **periodic inventory** system because the record keeping is done only at the end of each period.

No matter how the record keeping is done, the relationships between **beginning inventory**, purchases, **ending inventory**, and cost of goods sold are:

$$\left.\begin{array}{l}\text{Beginning Inventory} \\ +\ \text{Purchases}\end{array}\right\} \text{Goods Available for Sale}$$
$$\underline{-\ \text{Ending Inventory}}$$
$$\underline{\underline{\text{Cost of Goods Sold}}}$$

The higher the cost of ending inventory, the lower the cost of goods sold will be, the higher the gross margin will be, and the higher net income will be. From that sequence you should be able to see that the value of the ending inventory has a direct effect on net income.

Let us look at an example to see how these choices—one of the four inventory cost flow methods and one of the two record-keeping methods—affect the values for inventory and cost of goods sold.

Example of Cost Flow Assumptions and Timing of Record Keeping

L.O. 2

Be able to use the two record-keeping choices with several of the cost flow assumptions.

Phil's Photo Shop started the year 2005 with eight cameras in the inventory. Each had a cost of $10. Phil's Photo Shop sells only one kind of camera—a self-focusing, self-forward-winding, easy-to-use model. Exhibit 6–2 shows the record of quantities purchased and at what cost and quantities sold and at what selling price during January 2005.

Perpetual Inventory

Suppose Phil's Photo Shop uses a *perpetual* inventory system. That means each time a sale is made, the cost of goods sold is calculated. Think about what that means in this example. When Phil's sells the three cameras on January 8, the company calculates the cost of goods sold right then—at the time of the sale, on the basis of exactly which goods are owned at that date. The only items in the inventory on January 8 are the eight cameras in the beginning inventory at $10 each. The cost of goods sold for the January 8 sale is $30 (= 3 cameras × $10/camera).

When a company uses a perpetual inventory system, all inventory purchases are debited to the inventory account. When a sale is made, two journal entries are required, one to record the sale and the other to reduce the inventory and record the cost of goods sold. For example, the January 8 sale for

Exhibit 6–2
Inventory Records for January 2005

January 1	Beginning inventory	8 Cameras	@ $10 Each
January 8	**Sales**	**3 Cameras**	**@ $20 Each**
January 16	Purchase	5 Cameras	@ $12 Each
January 20	**Sales**	**8 Cameras**	**@ $22 Each**
January 30	Purchase	7 Cameras	@ $14 Each

Phil's Photo Shop using a perpetual inventory system would require the following two journal entries to record the sale of three cameras—sales price $20 each, cost $10 each:

Date	Transaction	Debit	Credit
1/8/2005	Cash or accounts receivable	$60	
	Sales		$60
	Cost of goods sold	$30	
	Inventory		$30

What about the sale on January 20? On that date, Phil's sells eight cameras. Which ones? Using a perpetual system, Phil's needs to calculate the cost of goods sold at the time of the sale. But there is a problem. Before the company can figure out the cost of goods sold, Phil's has to make a cost flow assumption. If Phil's decides to use FIFO, then the assumption is that the five cameras left from the beginning inventory and three cameras from the January 16 purchase have been sold. If Phil's decides to use LIFO, then the assumption is that the five cameras from the January 16 purchase are sold first and then the other three cameras (to get the total sold of eight) come from the beginning inventory.

Periodic Inventory

Suppose Phil's uses a *periodic* inventory system. *Cost of good sold* is *not* calculated or recorded until the company is ready to prepare financial statements at the end of the period. At that time, Phil would count the cameras in the ending inventory and deduct the number still on hand from the number of cameras available to sell during the period—beginning inventory plus purchases made—to get the number of cameras sold during the period (11 cameras in this example). Then the company would make a cost flow assumption. Which cameras will Phil's assume were sold? If the company uses FIFO, Phil's assumes the earliest purchased cameras were sold first. If the company uses LIFO, Phil's assumes the most recent cameras purchased were sold first. If the company uses average cost, Phil's would calculate the weighted-average cost of a camera and multiply that average unit cost by 11 to get the total cost of goods sold.

If a company does not use specific identification, it must select one of the three remaining inventory cost flow methods. Then, when the company selects FIFO, LIFO, or average cost, a record-keeping method of either perpetual or periodic must be chosen. That produces six possible inventory systems that a company may use, shown in Exhibit 6–3.

When a company uses a periodic inventory system, all inventory purchases are debited to the purchases account. The purchases account is a temporary account used to accumulate the cost of inventory purchased during the period. When a sale is made, only one journal entry is required to record the sale. Cost of goods sold is calculated at the end of the period. The January 8 sale for Phil's Photo Shop to record the sale of three cameras at $20 each using a periodic inventory system would be:

Date	Transaction	Debit	Credit
1/8/2005	Cash or accounts receivable	$60	
	Sales		$60

Exhibit 6–3
Inventory Cost Flow and Record-Keeping Assumptions

	Cost flow assumption		
	FIFO	LIFO	Average cost
Record keeping			
Periodic	1	3	5
Perpetual	2	4	6

1. Cost of the first goods purchased is the first to be included in cost of goods sold, and the record keeping is done at the end of the accounting period
2. Cost of the first goods purchased is the first to be included in cost of goods sold, and the record keeping is done every time a sale is made
3. Cost of the last goods purchased is the first to be included in cost of goods sold, and the record keeping is done at the end of the accounting period
4. Cost of the last goods purchased is the first to be included in cost of goods sold, and the record keeping is done every time a sale is made
5. Cost of all the goods available for sale for the entire accounting period is used to calculate a weighted-average cost; this cost is multiplied by the number of units sold to get cost of goods sold; this is done at the end of the accounting period
6. Cost of all the goods available for sale at the time of the sale is used to calculate an average cost; this cost is multiplied by the number of units sold to get cost of goods sold; a new average cost is calculated and the related record keeping is done every time a sale is made

The January 16th purchases to record the purchase of five cameras at $12 each using a periodic inventory system would be:

Date	Transaction	Debit	Credit
1/16/2005	Purchases	$60	
	Cash or accounts payable		$60

Using the information from Phil's Photo Shop, let us use a sample of these methods to calculate the cost of goods sold and ending inventory for the month of January.

Cost of goods available for sale is the beginning inventory plus all purchases during an accounting period.

No matter which of the six combinations a company selects, the **cost of goods available for sale**—beginning inventory plus purchases—is the same. **Cost of goods available for sale** is determined by:

Beginning Inventory + Net Purchases = Cost of Goods Available for Sale

For Phil's Photo Shop for January, the cost of goods available for sale is $238. The calculation follows:

$$[(8 \text{ cameras} \times \$10 \text{ each}) + (5 \text{ cameras} \times \$12 \text{ each}) + (7 \text{ cameras} \times \$14 \text{ each})] = \$80 + \$60 + \$98 = \$238$$

The inventory cost flow assumption and record-keeping method determine how that dollar amount of *cost of goods available for sale* is divided between *cost of goods sold* and the cost of the *ending inventory*.

Let us start with FIFO.

FIFO periodic means (1) the cost flow assumption is that the oldest goods in the inventory are sold first, and (2) inventory records and cost of goods sold are updated only once, at the end of the accounting period.

FIFO Periodic

Phil's Photo Shop calculates the cost of good sold at the end of the month. At that time the company knows the total number of cameras sold in January was 11. Using FIFO, Phil's counts the oldest cameras in the inventory as *sold*. So, Phil's counts the beginning inventory of eight cameras @ $10 each as the first part of cost of goods sold. On January 16, five cameras were purchased, and so the company will include three of those as part of cost of goods sold, too. That makes 11 cameras Phil's sold during the month.

8 cameras @ $10 per camera	= $ 80
3 cameras @ $12 per camera	= $ 36
Cost of Goods Sold =	$116

What is left in the inventory?

2 cameras @ $12 per camera	= $ 24
7 cameras @ $14 per camera	= $ 98
Ending Inventory =	$122

Note that the cost of goods sold plus the ending inventory equals $238—the cost of the goods available for sale during January.

FIFO Perpetual

FIFO perpetual means (1) the cost flow assumption is that the oldest goods in the inventory are sold first, and (2) inventory records and cost of goods sold are updated at the time of every sale and purchase.

When a perpetual record-keeping system is used, the cost of goods sold for each sale must be calculated and recorded *at the time of the sale*; and only the cameras from the purchases as of the date of a sale—meaning prior and up to the date of a sale—are available to become part of the cost of goods sold. Perpetual record keeping requires you to pay attention to the dates goods are purchased and sold. Phil's first sale is on January 8. Only cameras from the beginning inventory are available to use to calculate the cost of goods sold for the January 8 sale. (The other purchases are in the future, and nothing is known about them on January 8.) The cost of goods sold for the January 8 sale is three cameras × $10/camera = $30.

Next, eight cameras were sold on January 20. Because the cost flow assumption is FIFO, Phil's uses the cameras left in the beginning inventory as part of the cost of goods sold. So, the cost of goods sold for the January 20 sale has to start with the five cameras remaining in the beginning inventory—that will be 5 × $10 each = $50. To get the other three needed to make the total of eight sold, Phil's will count three from the January 16 purchase. That is, three @ $12 = $36. So, the total cost of goods sold for the January 20 sale is $86 (= $50 + $36).

To summarize the cost of goods sold:

3 cameras @ $10 per camera	= $ 30	— Sale on January 8
5 cameras @ $10 per camera	= $ 50	— Sale on January 20
3 cameras @ $12 per camera	= $ 36	
Total	$116	

What is left in the ending inventory?

2 cameras @ $12 per camera	= $ 24
7 cameras @ $14 per camera	= $ 98
Total	$122

Note that all the work to figure out the cost of goods sold using FIFO *perpetual* gives the same amount as using FIFO *periodic*, which is much easier to calculate.

Is this coincidence, or is there a predictable pattern here? Look at the particular cameras that were assumed to be sold under the two methods. You will see that it is more than coincidence. No matter how the company does the actual record keeping, either FIFO method—perpetual or periodic—will give the same dollar amount of cost of goods sold and the same dollar amount of ending inventory for the period.

LIFO Periodic

LIFO periodic means (1) the cost flow assumption is that the newest goods in the inventory are sold first, and (2) inventory records and cost of goods sold are updated only once, at the end of the accounting period.

When you use periodic record keeping, you start by calculating the total number of cameras sold during the month. In January, Phil's Photo sold 11 cameras. Using LIFO, Phil's counts cameras from the latest purchase as those sold first. For LIFO, start at the bottom of the list of purchases in the sequence in which the cameras were purchased.

The purchase on January 30 was seven cameras, and so Phil's counts those as part of cost of goods sold first. (Note that those specific cameras do not have to be sold to treat them "as if" they were sold. In this case, Phil's *could not* have sold them. A cost flow assumption does not have to mimic the actual physical flow of the goods.) The purchase on January 16 was 5 cameras, and so the company will count 4 of them in the cost of goods sold to get the total of 11 cameras sold. The total cost of goods sold will be:

7 cameras @ $14 per camera	= $ 98
4 cameras @ $12 per camera	= $ 48
Cost of Goods Sold =	$146

What is left in the inventory?

1 camera @ $12 per camera	= $ 12
8 cameras @ $10 per camera	= $ 80
Ending Inventory =	$ 92

Note that the cost of goods sold plus the ending inventory equals $238—the total goods available for sale.

Accounting Choices Make a Difference

Compare the cost of goods sold for LIFO periodic with FIFO. Using FIFO, Phil's cost of goods sold is $116. With LIFO periodic, Phil's cost of goods sold is $146. The numbers in this example are small, but the example demonstrates the point that the choice of inventory cost flow assumption makes a difference in the amounts reported on the financial statements—even when the underlying business process and related transactions are identical.

Average Cost Periodic

Average cost periodic means (1) the cost of all the goods available for sale for the entire accounting period is used to calculate an average cost, and (2) the cost of goods sold is calculated at the end of the accounting period.

Let us calculate the cost of goods sold and ending inventory for Phil's Photo Shop using the average cost method to demonstrate the third major cost flow assumption. The computations for this method of keeping track of inventory are the simplest of all methods. Phil adds up beginning inventory and all purchases to get the value of the goods available for sale. Phil previously calculated that amount to be $238. Then, he divides $238 by the total number of cameras available for sale—that is, the number of cameras that comprised the $238—to get an average cost per camera. Phil's Photo Shop had a total of 20 (= 8 + 5 + 7) cameras available for sale. Dividing $238 by 20 cameras gives $11.90 per camera. That average unit cost is used to compute cost of goods sold and ending inventory.

Cost of good sold is the number sold—11 cameras—multiplied by $11.90 per camera, which is $130.90.
Ending inventory is the number in the ending inventory—nine cameras—multiplied by $11.90 per camera, which is $107.10.
These add up to $238 (= $130.90 + $107.10).

Conclusions about Inventory Cost Flow Assumptions

All the combinations of inventory cost flow assumptions and record-keeping methods, shown in Exhibit 6–3, are used in practice. Actually, there are even more methods, derived from these six, in use. These methods are ones that have been modified slightly to meet the needs of specific industries. For now, we have studied enough of these methods to know that the accounting method a company selects to account for inventory can make a difference in the reported cost of goods sold and inventory amounts. A detailed example is shown in Exhibit 6–4.

STUDY BREAK 6-2

See How You're Doing

Jones Saddle Company had the following transactions during August 2006:

- purchased 30 units @ $20 per unit on August 10, 2006
- purchased 20 units @ $21 per unit on August 15, 2006
- purchased 20 units @ $23 per unit on August 21, 2006
- sold 35 units @ $30 per unit on August 30, 2006

Prepare journal entries to record the purchases, assuming that Jones Saddle Company uses a perpetual inventory system. Prepare the journal entries to record the sale using (1) FIFO, (2) LIFO, and (3) weighted average.

Because the inventory cost flow assumption affects the financial statements and because the effect can be quite large, generally accepted accounting principles (GAAP) require a company to include details about inventory cost flow assumptions and related costs in the notes to the financial statements.

Recording Inventory Purchases and Freight Costs

Purchases and Purchase Discounts

When a company takes advantage of a purchase discount, it reduces the cost of its inventory.

- If you are using a perpetual inventory system, the credit for purchase discounts is made to the inventory account.
- If you are using a periodic inventory system, the credit is made to a purchase discounts account.

Assume that you purchase $10,000 worth of inventory on January 5, 2005, with credit terms 2/10, n/30. The purchase is paid for on January 12. The journal entry to record the purchase of inventory, terms 2/10, n/30, would be:

Exhibit 6–4 Two Examples of Cost of Goods Sold Using FIFO versus LIFO

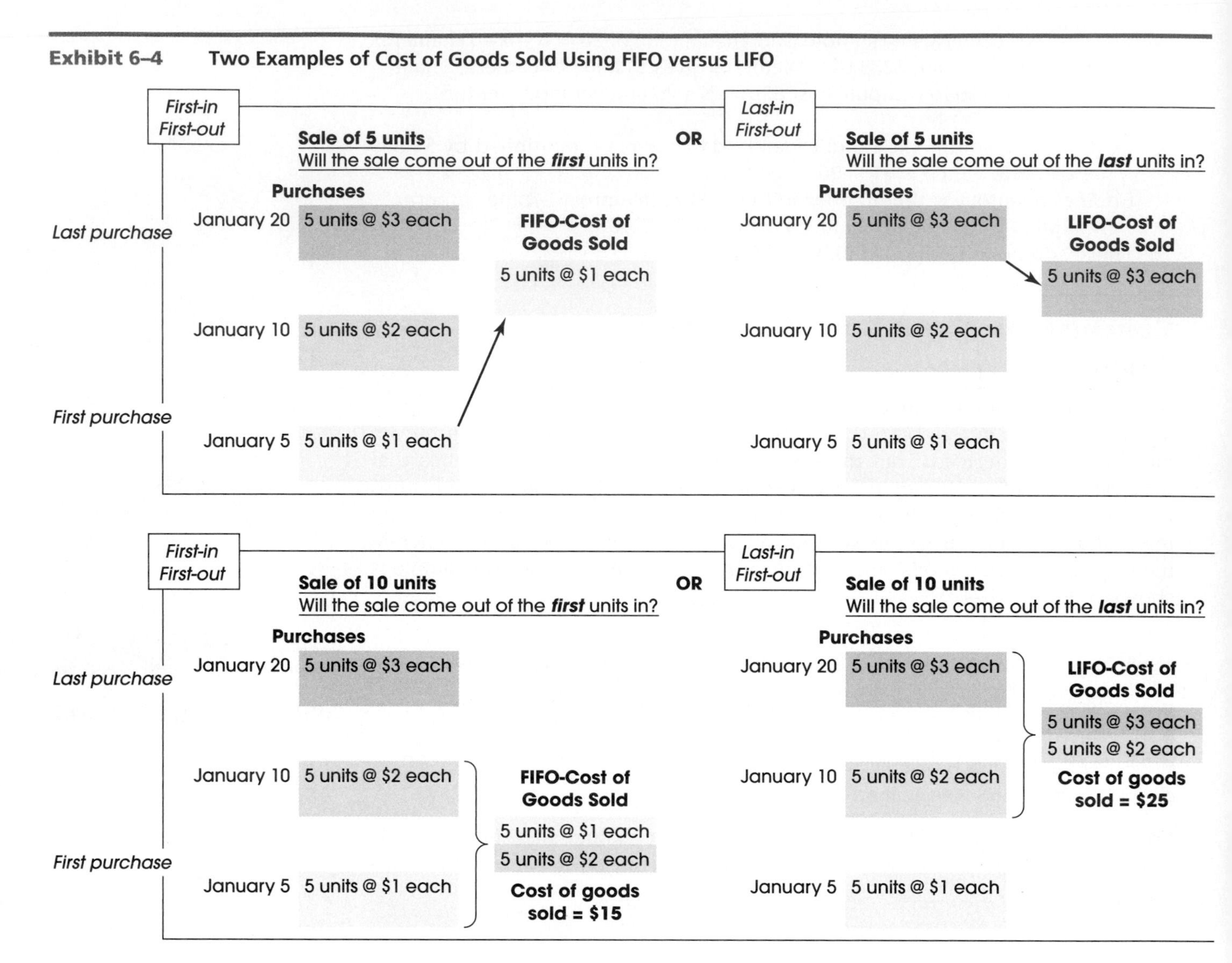

All units are the same inventory item, and the cost is rising sharply during the month of January. Notice that the purchases are listed with the most recent purchase at the top of the list. To calculate FIFO cost of goods sold, the first items purchased are assumed to be sold first. To calculate LIFO cost of goods sold, the last items purchased are assumed to be sold first.

Date	Transaction	Debit	Credit
1/5/2005	Inventory* or purchases	$10,000	
	Accounts payable		$10,000

*The inventory account is debited when using a perpetual record-keeping system, and an account called *purchases* is debited when using a periodic record-keeping system.

The journal entry to record the payment of the 1/5/2005 $10,000 purchase less the discount of $200 ($\$10,000 \times 2\%$) would be:

Date	Transaction	Debit	Credit
1/12/2005	Accounts payable	$10,000	
	Inventory** or purchase discounts		$ 200
	Cash		9,800

**Inventory is used in a perpetual system, and purchase discounts is used in a periodic system.

Purchase Returns and Purchase Allowances

Purchase returns and *purchase allowances* are accounted for much like discounts—the account used for recording the return or the allowance depends on whether you are using a perpetual inventory system or periodic inventory system. With a perpetual system, inventory is credited. With a periodic system, the credit is to purchase returns and allowances. To illustrate: you return $150 of defective merchandise that you have not paid for yet. The journal entry to record the return of $150 of defective merchandise would be:

Date	Transaction	Debit	Credit
	Accounts payable	$150	
	Inventory or purchase returns and allowances		$150

Freight-In

When goods are shipped (FOB) shipping point, the freight cost increases the total inventory cost. With a perpetual inventory system, the freight cost will increase inventory. With a periodic inventory system, a separate freight-in account will be maintained. To illustrate: you receive a bill for $85 to cover the shipping cost of merchandise purchased FOB shipping point. The journal entry to record the shipping cost of inventory would be:

Date	Transaction	Debit	Credit
	Inventory or freight-in	$85	
	Accounts payable or cash		$85

Inventory and Cost of Goods Sold in Merchandising Operations

After cost of goods sold is calculated, that amount is reported on the income statement as an expense. The income statement for a merchandising firm often takes the format shown next. It is called a multistep income statement because it takes an extra step to subtract cost of goods sold and give the subtotal *gross margin from sales.*

Revenues from sales (net sales)
−Cost of goods sold
Gross margin from sales (also known as gross profit)
−Operating expenses
Income before income taxes
−Income taxes
Net income

Cost of goods sold is the largest expense in most merchandising companies. **Operating expenses** are all the other expenses, except interest and taxes. *Income before interest and taxes* is also called **operating income**, *earnings before interest and taxes (EBIT)*, or *income from operations.*

Cost of goods sold, also called **cost of sales,** refers to the company's cost of goods purchased and then sold to its customers.

Operating expenses are all expenses incurred in the normal operations of a business except interest and taxes.

Operating income is income before gains, losses, interest, and taxes. Often, in our examples, we do not include nonoperating items, which means that operating income is the same as net income. Also called **income before interest and taxes, earnings before interest and taxes (EBIT)**, and **income from operations**.

STUDY BREAK 6-3

See How You're Doing

At the end of 2006, the following amounts were shown in the records of Kenny's Sporting Goods, Inc. Place the amount of each account in the proper column to show where it should appear in the income statement.

Account	Amount	Revenue	Cost of Goods Sold	Other expenses
Administrative expenses	$ 57,000			
Income tax expense	9,000			
Sales	617,000			
Purchases	367,000			
Delivery fees (freight-out)	10,900			
Transportation-in	13,000			
Amortization expense	6,000			
Sales salaries	74,000			
Purchase discounts	3,300			
Utilities expense	2,100			

Note: In addition, beginning inventory was $60,000 and a physical count of merchandise showed inventory on hand at December 31, 2006, in the amount of $70,000.

Calculate the following:

Cost of goods available for sale.
Cost of goods sold.
Gross profit.

Recording Inventory and Cost of Goods Sold Transactions

Adjustments and Closing under a Perpetual Inventory System

When a company maintains a perpetual inventory system, the current inventory balance and cost of goods sold are maintained at all times. A physical inventory count at the end of the year is needed to verify the inventory balance and identify shrinkage. Using a perpetual system, the following is what a typical inventory account and a cost of goods sold account would look like before the adjustment and closing process:

Inventory

	Debit	Credit	
BB	$7,500	$372	Purchase discounts
Purchases	26,580	265	Purchase returns and allowances
Freight-in	2,395	27,435	Cost of goods sold
12/31 unadjusted balance	$8,403		

Cost of goods sold

	Debit	Credit
BB	$0	
12/1–12/31	27,435	

A physical count of inventory calculates an ending inventory value of $8,255, indicating shrinkage of $148.

The inventory account and the cost of goods sold account must be adjusted for the shrinkage, and the cost of goods sold account must be closed to income summary, just like all other expense accounts are closed to income summary. To record inventory shrinkage:

Date	Transaction	Debit	Credit
12/31	Cost of goods sold	$148	
	Inventory		$148

To close costs of goods sold ($27,435 sales + $148 shrinkage):

Date	Transaction	Debit	Credit
12/31	Retained earnings (or income summary)	$27,583	
	Cost of goods sold		$27,583

After these two entries are posted, the inventory account will have the correct ending balance of $8,255 (= $8,403 – $148) and the cost of goods sold account will be reset to $0.

Adjustments and Closing under a Periodic Inventory System

Under a periodic system, the same company would have the following T-accounts and balances before adjustments and closing:

Inventory

	Debit	Credit
BB	$7,500	

Purchases

	Debit	Credit
BB	$0	
12/1–12/31	26,580	

Freight-in

	Debit	Credit
BB	$0	
12/1–12/31	2,395	

Purchase discounts

Debit	Credit	
	$0	BB
	372	12/1–12/31

Purchase returns and allowances

Debit	Credit	
	$0	BB
	265	12/1–12/31

Remember that, under a periodic system, no cost of goods sold account is maintained.

Using a periodic system, because cost of goods sold is not recorded at each sale, it must be calculated at the end of each year as follows:

Beginning inventory
\+ Purchases
\+ Freight-in
– Purchase discounts
– Purchase returns and allowances
= Goods available for sale
– Ending inventory (from physical count)
= Cost of goods sold

In a periodic system, shrinkage is automatically absorbed into cost of goods sold because the cost of any items lost or stolen cannot be identified separately from the total of the cost of the goods sold. Closing the temporary accounts and updating the inventory balance transfers the cost of goods sold to retained earnings (or an income summary account). These are the closing entries using a periodic system to close temporary accounts and establish the ending inventory balance:

Date	Transaction	Debit	Credit
12/31	Inventory (ending, per physical count)	$8,255	
	Purchase discounts	372	
	Purchase returns and allowances	265	
	Retained earnings (or income summary)		$8,892

To close temporary accounts and the beginning inventory balance:

Date	Transaction	Debit	Credit
12/31	Retained earnings (or income summary)	$36,475	
	Inventory (beginning balance)		$ 7,500
	Purchases		26,580
	Freight-in		2,395

Note that the difference between the debit made to retained earnings (or income summary) in the second entry ($36,475) and the credit made to retained earnings (or income summary) in the first entry ($8,255) is $27,583, the amount of cost of goods sold.

Inventory Errors

L.O. 4

Calculate and explain the effects of inventory errors on cost of goods sold and net income.

Because inventory indirectly affects cost of goods sold, a major expense, *errors* in the calculation of beginning inventory or ending inventory will affect net income. Tracing the effects of errors requires slow, focused deliberation. To show how inventory errors can affect income, a simple numerical example is given. Read each description that follows and study the related examples.

Ending Inventory Errors

If *ending inventory* is *overstated*, cost of goods sold must be *understated*. Why? It is because ending inventory and cost of goods sold are the two parts of goods available for sale. Cost of goods sold is an expense. If the expense deducted from sales is too small, the result is that net income will be too large. Suppose you have correctly calculated the cost of goods available for sale (beginning inventory + purchases) to be $10. Those goods will either be sold—and become part of cost of goods sold—or they will *not* be sold—and will still be part of the cost of the inventory.

So, goods available for sale consists of two parts—cost of goods sold and ending inventory. Suppose the correct ending inventory is $2 but you erroneously give it a value of $3. If ending inventory is incorrectly valued at $3, then cost of goods sold will be valued at $7. Remember, the ending inventory and cost of goods sold must add up to $10 in this example. What is wrong with cost of goods sold? If ending inventory is actually $2, then cost of goods sold *should* be $8. See what happens? You understate cost of goods sold when you overstate the ending inventory. Anytime you understate an expense, you will overstate net income.

If ending inventory is too small—understated—cost of goods sold must be too large—overstated. The result—net income will be understated. Let us use the same example, in which the cost of goods available for sale was correctly computed at $10. If ending inventory is actually $2 but you erroneously understate it as $1, then cost of goods sold will be valued as $9. It should be $8. Thus, an understatement in ending inventory has caused an overstatement of cost of goods sold. If you overstate an expense, then you will understate net income.

Beginning Inventory Errors

Inventory errors affect the balance sheet—inventory—and the income statement—cost of goods sold.

If ending inventory is overstated in 2005, then *beginning inventory* in 2006 will be overstated. After all, it is the same number. So, errors in the ending inventory will affect two consecutive years—ending inventory one year and beginning inventory the following year.

If beginning inventory is overstated, then cost of goods available for sale is overstated. If ending inventory is then counted correctly, then cost of goods sold will be overstated. So, net income will be understated. Let us continue the previous example. If you value beginning inventory at $3 (and the correct value is $2) and you *correctly* add the purchases for the second year—say, $15 worth—then the cost of goods available for sale will be $18. (Keep in mind, the correct amount is $17.) At year-end, you count the ending inventory correctly at $6. The calculated cost of goods sold would be $12 (ending inventory and cost of goods sold must total $18). However, we know that the true value of goods available for sale is $17. If the correct ending inventory is $6, then the correct cost of goods sold is $11. The calculated cost of goods sold was overstated by $1, as shown in Exhibit 6–5. When an expense is overstated, net income will be understated.

If beginning inventory is understated, then goods available for sale is understated. If ending inventory is counted correctly, then cost of goods sold will be understated. So, net income will be overstated. Try thinking about the example in the format given in Exhibit 6–6.

As you can see, when you understate the beginning inventory, you end up with cost of goods sold understated. This understated expense will result in an overstatement of net income.

Exhibit 6–5
Overstatement Error in Beginning Inventory

	Calculated amounts	Correct amounts
Beginning inventory	$ 3 (Overstated)	$ 2
+ Purchases	+15	+15
Goods available for sale	$ 18	$ 17
− Ending inventory	− 6	− 6
Cost of goods sold	$ 12	$ 11

Exhibit 6–6
Understatement Error in Beginning Inventory

	Calculated amounts	Correct amounts
Beginning inventory	$ 1 (Understated from prior year error)	$ 2
+ Purchases	+15	+15
Goods available for sale	$ 16	$ 17
− Ending inventory	− 6	− 6
Cost of goods sold	$ 10	$ 11

Inventory errors affect net income because they cause cost of goods sold to be wrong. If net income is wrong, then owner's equity will be wrong on the balance sheet and on the statement of retained earnings.

Note that over a period of two years, the errors will counterbalance—they will cancel each other out. However, it is important that the financial statements be correct each year, and so a company will correct **inventory errors** when they are discovered instead of waiting for the errors to cancel each other out.

STUDY BREAK 6-4

See How You're Doing

Berry Corp. miscounted the ending inventory for the year ended December 31, 2007. The balance sheet reported inventory of $3,600,000, but $25,000 worth of items were omitted from that amount. Berry reported net income of $742,640 for the year. What effect did this inventory error have on Berry's cost of goods sold for the year? What is the correct net income for the year ended December 31, 2007?

Gross Profit Method of Estimating Ending Inventory

L.O. 5

Estimate ending inventory using the gross profit method.

There are times when a company might want to *estimate* the cost of the ending inventory instead of counting the units to calculate the exact cost. For example, if a company prepares monthly or quarterly financial statements, GAAP allow ending inventory to be estimated for reporting on those financial statements. This saves a company the trouble of counting the inventory every quarter. Also, if the inventory is destroyed or stolen, a reliable estimate of the cost of the destroyed inventory will be needed for the insurance claim.

Gross profit percentage is gross margin as a percentage of sales.

First, you must know the usual **gross profit percentage** for the company, that is, gross profit divided by sales. You can calculate the gross profit percentage using prior year's sales and cost data. Then, you multiply that percentage by the sales for the period, which gives the estimated gross profit. You then subtract the estimated gross profit from sales to get the estimated cost of goods sold. Because you know (1) beginning inventory (from the last period's financial statements); (2) purchases (from your records); and (3) estimated cost of goods sold, you can estimate ending inventory.

For example, Super Soap Company lost its entire inventory in a flood on April 16. Super Soap had prepared a set of financial statements on March 30, when the inventory on hand was valued at $2,500. During the first part of April, purchases amounted to $3,500; the usual gross margin percentage in this business is 40 percent. If Super Soap had sales of $8,200 during the first 16 days of April, how much inventory was lost?

- If sales were $8,200 and the usual gross profit percentage is 40 percent, then the gross profit would be $3,280.
- If sales were $8,200 and gross profit is $3,280, then cost of goods sold would be $4,920. (Another way to look at that is: if the gross profit percentage is 40 percent, then the other 60 percent must be the cost of goods sold. So, 60 percent of $8,200 = cost of goods sold = $4,920.)
- Beginning inventory + purchases – cost of goods sold = ending inventory, or $2,500 + $3,500 – $4,920 = $1,080. This is our best estimate of the lost inventory.

Valuing Inventory: Lower-of-Cost-or-Market

Inventory is an asset on the balance sheet, recorded at cost. Usually, it is a significant amount. To make sure that inventory is not overstated, GAAP require companies to compare the **cost** of their inventory at the end of the period with the **market** value of that inventory. The company must use the **lower** of either the cost or the market value for the financial statements.

Estimating the **market value** is the difficult part of this procedure. The market value may be measured as either the replacement cost or the net realizable value of the inventory. **Replacement cost** is determined by looking at the cost to buy similar inventory items from a supplier at prevailing prices. Replacement cost is most appropriate for valuing raw materials or inventory items purchased for resale. Net realizable value refers to the net proceeds to be realized from the sale of inventory. It is determined by looking at the selling price for an item of inventory and subtracting from that selling price the costs associated with the selling process (e.g., commissions) or the costs to make the item ready for sale. Net realizable value is most appropriate for valuing partially manufactured goods. In Canada, net realizable value is the most common measure of market value. Using either replacement cost or net realizable value, the company compares the market value of inventory to its cost and uses the lower of the two values for the balance sheet. If the inventory value has to be reduced, the adjustment to reduce the inventory will also reduce net income.

Comparing the cost of inventory to its market value is more than simply an accounting requirement. Information about the market value of inventory is important for formulating sales strategies related to various items in inventory and for inventory purchasing decisions.

Let us look at an example. Suppose a company's ending inventory cost is $150,000 and the market (replacement) cost of that inventory is $145,000. Because the company's records show the cost of $150,000 for inventory and GAAP require the inventory to be valued at the lower of the cost or market value for the year-end balance sheet, the inventory value must be reduced. Accountants call this *writing down* the inventory. Like all adjustments, the adjustment to write down the inventory must keep the accounting equation in balance. Assets are reduced, and there is a corresponding reduction in owner's equity. It will increase cost of goods sold on the income statement. The adjustment would affect the accounting equation as follows:

Assets	=	Liabilities	+	Owner's equity
$(5,000) Inventory				$(5,000) Loss on inventory write-down (cost of goods sold)

The journal entry to record the inventory write-down of the LCM valuation would be:

Date	Transaction	Debit	Credit
	Cost of goods sold	$5,000	
	Inventory		$5,000

Thus, the value of the inventory on the year-end balance sheet will be $145,000, and $145,000 is considered the new cost of the inventory.

If the market value of the inventory later increases, the recorded value of the inventory is not affected. The value of the inventory on the balance sheet is

L.O. 6

Define and use the lower-of-cost-or-market rule for valuing inventory.

Lower of cost or market describes how inventory should be valued on the balance sheet according to GAAP. Inventory is shown at the lower of either cost or market value. Cost is calculated using a cost flow assumption like FIFO or average cost and market value is calculated using replacement cost or net realizable value.

The **market value**, or **market price**, is the price of an asset agreed on between a willing buyer and a willing seller; also, the price an asset could demand if sold on the open market.

The cost that would be incurred if a company had to replace an existing asset is know as the **replacement cost**.

never increased. Continuing the example, suppose the cost of the inventory at the end of the next year is $125,000 and market value is $128,000. It appears that the market value has rebounded from the previous drop. Still, the value of the inventory for the second year's balance sheet would be the lower of the two. No adjustment would be recorded; the inventory would be valued at its cost of $125,000. The bottom line is that inventory is written *down* to the lower of cost or market at every balance sheet date, but it is not written *up*. This is an example of *conservatism*—the idea that accountants are very careful not to overstate assets or income.

STUDY BREAK 6-5

See How You're Doing

At the end of the year, Milner Company had inventory of $345,000. If the replacement cost of the inventory is $350,000, what amount will Milner show on the year-end balance sheet? Suppose the replacement cost were $339,000. In that case, what amount would Milner show on the year-end balance sheet?

Finding and Using Inventory Information

L.O. 7

Identify the disclosure requirements related to inventory and use inventory information to analyze a company's performance.

It is easy to see how important inventory is to a retail company. Inventory is a major asset on the balance sheet, and cost of goods sold is a retail company's largest expense. The method of accounting for inventory must be disclosed. For example, for the fiscal year ended on October 5, 2003, Gildan Activewear had sales of $630 million. The cost of goods sold related to those sales was $440 million. All the other expenses together were less than $113 million.

Merchandise inventory, shown in the current assets section of the Gildan balance sheet, amounts to $138.6 million. That is almost one-quarter of the company's assets. The notes to the financial statements give this additional information: *Inventories are stated at the lower of cost and market value. Cost is established based on the first-in, first-out method. Market value is defined as replacement cost for raw materials and net realizable value for work in process and finished goods.* Note how these sentences about inventory tell us that the company uses a FIFO cost flow assumption and has applied the lower-of-cost-or-market rule to the cost of the ending inventory.

Applying Our Knowledge: Ratio Analysis

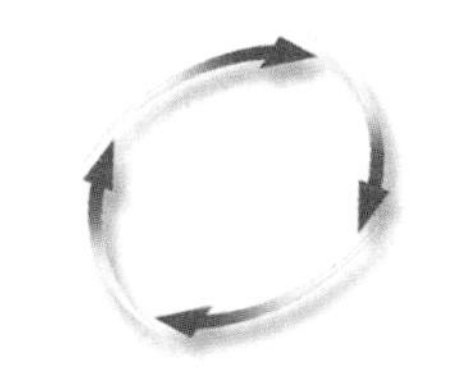

Business Process

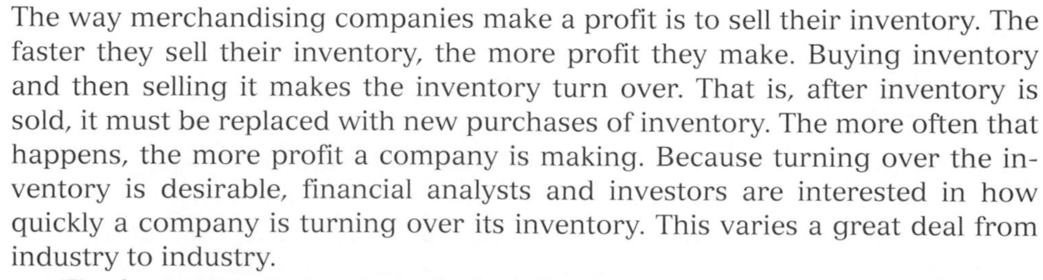

The way merchandising companies make a profit is to sell their inventory. The faster they sell their inventory, the more profit they make. Buying inventory and then selling it makes the inventory turn over. That is, after inventory is sold, it must be replaced with new purchases of inventory. The more often that happens, the more profit a company is making. Because turning over the inventory is desirable, financial analysts and investors are interested in how quickly a company is turning over its inventory. This varies a great deal from industry to industry.

Inventory turnover ratio is cost of goods sold divided by average inventory.

The **inventory turnover ratio** is defined as *cost of goods sold* divided by the *average inventory* on hand during the year. Let us calculate the inventory turnover ratio for Gildan for the fiscal year ended on October 5, 2003. The cost of goods sold for the year, found on the income statement, is $440.3 million. The average inventory can be calculated from the beginning and ending inventory amounts shown on the balance sheet. For Gildan, the average inventory is $112.9 million + $138.6 million divided by 2. The ratio calculation is:

$$\text{Inventory Turnover Ratio} = \frac{\text{Cost of Goods Sold of \$440.3 million}}{\text{Average Inventory of \$125.75 million}} = 3.5 \text{ (rounded)}$$

This means that Gildan turns over its inventory—sells it and replaces it—about three and a half times each year.

Another ratio often computed by both external users—like financial analysts—and internal users—like marketing and sales managers—is **gross margin on sales ratio**. We have already discussed the calculation of the gross margin and its importance to a retail company. The ratio is defined as gross margin divided by sales, and it is one of the most carefully watched ratios by management. It describes the percentage of sales price that is gross profit. A small shift usually indicates a big change in the profitability of the company's sales.

Gross margin on sales ratio is gross margin divided by sales. It is the same as *gross profit percentage*.

Let us calculate the gross margin on sales ratio for two consecutive years for Gildan. That comparison will give us some information about the ongoing performance of the company. Any significant change to this ratio would be a signal to management to investigate the cause of the change. In this case, the ratio has increased, which Gildan would be likely to interpret as good news. A larger percentage of the sale price was profit during the fiscal year ended October 5, 2003, compared with the fiscal year ended September 29, 2002.

For year ended (in millions)	October 5, 2003	September 29, 2002
Sales	$630.1	$600.7
Cost of goods sold	440.3	432.0
Gross margin	189.8	168.7
Gross margin on sales ratio	30.1%	28.1%

Paying for Acquisitions: Liabilities

L.O. 8

Define the major classifications of liabilities.

Inventory is the major acquisition of a merchandising company. After the acquisition, the resulting payment will complete the acquisition/payment process. Although a company may pay cash for its purchases, it is much more common for such purchases to be made on account. We have already discussed shipping terms and purchase discounts; these are important components of the amount of the liability that results from the purchase of inventory. Let us review the steps involved in the acquisition and see how the acquisition portion of the process leads to the payment portion of the process.

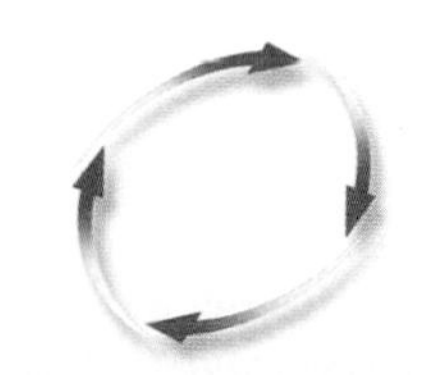

Business Process

When a company buys inventory items on account—on *credit*—an obligation results. Such obligations—*liabilities*—require either future payments of assets or future performance of services. An exchange is not complete until payment to the vendor has been made. However, the company must first receive a bill from the vendor, called a vendor's invoice. When the invoice is received, the accounts payable department reviews the documents it has collected from the various departments involved in the transaction. These documents are the purchase order, the receiving report, and the invoice:

- Reviewing the purchase order confirms that a purchase was actually requested.
- The receiving report is documentation that the goods received are the goods ordered.
- The vendor's invoice helps to confirm the correct amount owed to the vendor. If there is a difference in the quantity or type of items received, the vendor is contacted to resolve the problem. Otherwise, the accounts

payable clerk, who also records a liability on the books, marks the invoice for payment.

A file that contains invoices filed in the order of the date they are due is called a **tickler file**.

Many companies keep invoices filed in order of the date payments are due. This is called a **tickler file**—the name indicates something that will get your attention, like being tickled. If the goods are purchased under the terms 2/10, n/30, the vendor is offering a 2 percent discount on the total amount due if payment is made within 10 days from the date of purchase. The *net* amount, or the total amount is due within 30 days of the date of purchase. A clerk reviews the file every day to locate invoices near their due date and prepares a request for a cash disbursement document, such as a cheque requisition. When payment is made, the invoices will be marked as paid.

There are three issues with respect to liabilities:

- recognition
- valuation
- classification

A liability is recognized—recorded in the accounting records so that it will appear on the balance sheet—when an obligation is incurred. Liabilities are based on past transactions and are generally recognized when incurred. As we have seen with certain liabilities like *interest payable* or *unearned revenue*, end-of-period adjustments may be necessary to make sure the amounts are correct for the financial statements. Liabilities are valued at the amount due or at the fair market value of the goods or services that must be delivered.

On the balance sheet, liabilities are divided into two classifications based on *when* the company must fulfill the obligation. Current liabilities are liabilities that will be satisfied within one year. For example, accounts payable are current liabilities. Vendors typically expect payment within 30 days of receipt of the invoice.

Noncurrent, or long-term, liabilities are liabilities that will be satisfied sometime beyond the next year. Notes payable usually represent an amount borrowed for a period of time longer than a year. If the note were a two-year note, for example, it would be considered a noncurrent liability.

Certain types of noncurrent liabilities—such as mortgage debt—may have a current component and a noncurrent component. The section for current liabilities would include the portion of the debt that will be paid in the next year, and the section for noncurrent liabilities would include the remainder.

Common Types of Liabilities

L.O. 9

Understand how payroll is calculated and reported.

All liabilities—current or long term—can be classified as:

- definitely determinable
- estimated
- contingent

Business Process

Definitely determinable liabilities are obligations that can be measured exactly, like the amount of a note payable.

Definitely determinable liabilities are liabilities that can be measured exactly. Examples are accounts payable, bank loans or lines of credit, or notes payable. Some accrued liabilities, such as dividends payable and unearned revenues, are definitely determinable because we know the amount of the obligation.

Estimated liabilities are obligations whose amount is not certain. Warranty liability is an example. Warranty liability is the estimated future costs for repair and replacement to honour a product's warranty. It is recorded at the time of the sale, and so it has to be estimated. (We will discuss this in the next chapter.) Other estimated liabilities include income taxes, property taxes payable, and vacation pay owed. These are all items that need to be recorded as expenses *before* the company knows the exact amounts.

Estimated liabilities are obligations with some uncertainty in the amount owed, like the cost involved in honouring a warranty.

Contingent liabilities are liabilities that are not currently recorded, but they are looming on the horizon. Past events have led to their potential existence, but a company will not know if they really do exist until *future* events, arising out of *past* transactions, reveal the facts. Lawsuits and tax disputes are two sources of contingent liabilities. For contingencies to be included on the balance sheet, they must meet two criteria:

Contingent liabilities are obligations that have not been recognized at the date of the financial statements but a *potential* liability exists. Disclosure is the important issue.

1. The liability must be likely.
2. The amount can be reasonably estimated.

Talk about judgment. Interpreting the meaning of words like *likely* and *reasonably estimable* as they relate to different circumstances requires professional judgment and expertise. Accountants and lawyers help companies decide when liabilities meet these criteria.

Acquisition of Human Resources and Payroll Liabilities

Acquiring human resources—that is, hiring employees—is similar to acquiring any resource for the company. All companies have employees, and so payroll is a common business expense. Due to government requirements for information (as well as Canada Pension Plan, Employment Insurance, and federal and provincial income taxes), companies have always had to record a great deal more information about payroll than what is needed for accurate and timely financial statements. Hiring and paying employees is a business process that is well suited to the new integrated information systems, and many companies have implemented the part of an enterprise resource planning (ERP) system that handles payroll.

Some of the steps in establishing an effective payroll system include:

- When an employee is hired, information concerning an employee's marital status and number of dependents is recorded for payroll deduction purposes.
- A company may require an employee to use **time cards** to record the amount of time worked each day.
- The payroll department reviews the time cards, verifies the pay rates, and calculates deductions for Canada Pension Plan (CPP) or Quebec Pension Plan (QPP), Employment Insurance (EI) and federal and provincial income taxes. These totals are recorded in a payroll register that is used by the accounts payable department to make a transfer of cash to the payroll chequing account.

A **time card** is a card used by a firm to record the amount of time worked by an employee during each day.

Many companies use a separate bank account from which paycheques are prepared and paid. A single cheque for the entire payroll is transferred to a separate account, and all employee paycheques are written from that account.

Let us look at the details of recording payroll information. We will do it with the accounting equation, but keep in mind that the actual record keeping will be done quite differently. The results on the financial statements will be the same no matter how the record keeping is done.

Suppose Risky Company hired an employee to guard the company's building and that employee is paid $800 per week. That amount is the employee's **gross pay**. As you may know from your work experience, this is not the amount the employee takes home.

The full amount an employee is paid before taxes are deducted is called **gross pay**.

From the gross pay amount, several deductions are made. First, the company is required to deduct CPP and EI premiums from gross pay. The deductions for these two items are determined by a complex calculation but in general the rates at which CPP and EI are deducted are approximately 5 percent and 2 percent, respectively. Employers are also required to make additional payments on behalf of the employee for CPP and EI. Currently, employers must make a payment equal to 100 percent of the amount of CPP deducted from the employee and 140 percent of the EI deducted. The company's payment is classified as payroll tax expense.

Second, income taxes are withheld. To withhold taxes means that the employer, Risky Company, deducts amounts from the employee's pay, withholds those specific amounts in the employee's name, and pays them as income taxes in the employee's name. The government *requires* employers to do this. In doing so, Risky Company is acting as an *agent* for the government. The company simply holds the money back from employees' cheques, and then forwards the payment to the government. The amount forwarded for each employee depends on the specific employee's tax situation (e.g., single or married, number of children, level of income).

With that background, let us continue with the example. First, let us calculate the various amounts that must be withheld from the $800 gross pay of the employee. Assuming 20 percent is withheld for income taxes, Risky Company would deduct $160. We will use 5 percent for CPP, which amounts to $40, and EI at 2 percent, which amounts to $16. So, the amount Risky Company will pay to the employee is $584 ($800 – $160 – $40 – $16). That amount is called net pay or net wages. The disbursement would affect the accounting equation as follows:

Assets	=	Liabilities	+	Contributed Capital	+	Retained Earnings
$(584.00) Cash		+ $160 Income taxes payable (withheld) + $40.00 Canada Pension Plan payable (withheld) + $16 Employment Insurance payable (withheld)				$(800) Salary expense

The journal entry to record salary expense and payroll deductions would be:

Date	Transaction	Debit	Credit
	Salary expense	$800.00	
	Income taxes payable		$160.00
	Canada Pension Plan payable		40.00
	Employment Insurance payable		16.00
	Cash		584.00

When Risky Company makes payment to the government for Canada Pension Plan and Employment Insurance, the company will also pay its share of the cost of these programs. Often, these payments are made by the bank. A company "deposits" its payroll taxes, which actually means the bank makes the payment to the government for the company. The payment to the government, including the company's portion, affects the accounting equation, as shown next:

Assets	=	Liabilities	+	Share Capital	+	Retained Earnings
$(278.40)[a] Cash		$(160) Income taxes payable (withheld) $(40) Canada Pension Plan payable (withheld) $(16) Employment Insurance payable (withheld)				$(62.40) Employer's payroll tax expense

[a] This includes the employers' required contribution for Canada Pension Plan of $40 and for Employment Insurance of $22.40.

The journal entry to record payroll tax expense and the payment of the taxes is:

Date	Transaction	Debit	Credit
	Payroll tax expense	$ 62.40	
	Income taxes payable	160.00	
	Canada Pension Plan payable	40.00	
	Employment Insurance payable	16.00	
	Cash		$278.40

STUDY BREAK 6-6

See How You're Doing

Sandy earned $1,500 at her job at Paula's Bookstore during February. Sandy has 20 percent of her pay withheld for income taxes, 5 percent withheld for Canada Pension Plan, and 2 percent withheld for Employment Insurance. Prepare the required journal entries assuming that Paula's Bookstore will not submit taxes to the government until the end of March.

Business Risks

L.O. 10

Understand the risks and controls associated with the purchase/acquisition process.

Two topics discussed in this chapter present special risks to business: (1) inventory, and (2) payroll. Let us look at each area—both at the risks and at the controls to help minimize those risks.

Inventory: Risks and Controls

Like any of a company's assets, the inventory must be protected from damage and theft. The risks associated with the actual purchase of the inventory—selecting a reliable vendor and making sure the items received are the ones ordered—are minimized by policies and procedures we have discussed in previous chapters. The physical safeguarding of the inventory is accomplished with controls like locked storage rooms and limited access. The policies and procedures for ordering inventory and for providing the inventory to the customer when it is purchased are important and should be designed with risk control in mind.

Separation of duties is a control used by a company to ensure the functions of authorization, recording, and physical custody are not all performed by the same individual.

Separation of duties is a control that is needed to minimize the risk of losing inventory to error or theft. The person who keeps the records related to the inventory should be someone different from the person who has physical control of the inventory. This separation of record keeping and physical control of assets makes it impossible for a single individual to steal the inventory and cover it up with false record keeping. When this control is in place and functioning properly, it would take collusion—that is, two or more people getting together to plan the fraud—to lose inventory in this way.

Liabilities: Risks and Controls

All areas of a company's record keeping are at risk for errors—both intentional and unintentional. We have discussed this information-processing risk in earlier chapters. In the acquisition/payment process, one particular area that faces significant risk is payroll. The payroll policies and procedures need to ensure that only legitimate employees, who have performed the relevant work, are paid. Generally, the person who prepares the payroll cheques should not be the person who distributes the cheques. Controls need to exist to keep a payroll record-keeping clerk from making out cheques to fictitious employees and routing the money to the clerk's own account. Again, separation of duties is a crucial and mandatory control for risk in the payroll area.

In the acquisition/payment process, just as in all business processes, the controls need to be in place, and then those controls need to be tested. When a company is audited by independent auditors, this is one of the jobs the auditors perform. They review the company's internal control system and verify that the existing controls are functioning properly.

Understanding Excel

For purposes of this problem only, assume that in the month of May, Tom's Wear engaged in the following transactions:

May 1, 2005	Beginning inventory was 500 shirts @ $4.00 each.
May 3, 2005	Tom purchased 300 shirts for $4.10 each.
May 5, 2005	Tom sold 600 shirts for $10.50 each.
May 15, 2005	Tom purchased 400 shirts for $4.20 each.
May 18, 2005	Tom sold 400 shirts for $10.50 each.
May 28, 2005	Tom purchased 200 shirts for $4.25 each.
May 30, 2005	Tom sold 100 shirts for $10.50 each.

Tom uses a periodic inventory system.

Requirements

1. Open a new Excel work sheet.
2. By beginning in cell A1, input the following chart based on the information presented previously. Input or calculate the values for the cells highlighted in blue.

   Hints: To sum the total goods available for sale, click on the appropriate cell C7 or E7 and select the Auto Sum Σ button. Select Format, Cells, Number, and Date to format column A.

	A	B	C	D	E
1	Date	Activity	Units	Unit Cost	Total Cost
2					
3	1-May-05	Beginning balance			
4	3-May-05	Purchase			
5	15-May-05	Purchase			
6	28-May-05	Purchase			
7		Total goods available for sale			
8		Shirts sold			
9		Shirts in ending inventory			
10					

3. Calculate cost of goods sold and ending inventory under the FIFO, LIFO, and average cost methods. Remember to use formulas and information entered in cells A1 through E8 to calculate the amounts.

	A	B	C	D
11				
12		FIFO	LIFO	Average
13	Cost of goods sold			
14	Ending inventory			
15				

4. Calculate the gross profit under each of the three methods, by inputting the following schedule. Remember to use formulas where applicable and to copy cost of goods sold from row 13:

	A	B	C	D
16				
17	**Income Statements**	**FIFO**	**LIFO**	**Average**
18				
19	Sales			
20	Cost of goods sold	-	-	-
21	Gross profit			

5. Print your file and save it to disk. Name your file TomsWear6.

Summary Problem: Tom's Wear Faces New Challenges in May

Tom's Wear began in January 2005 and has now completed four months of operating as a business. The April 30, 2005, balance sheet becomes the May 1, 2005, balance sheet as Tom's Wear begins May. Review the balance sheet shown in Exhibit 6–7 before you work your way through the May transactions. The transactions for May are shown in Exhibit 6–8.

Required

1. Make the journal entries for the transactions and the adjusting entries needed for preparation of the financial statements. Post them to T-accounts, and prepare an adjusted trial balance.
2. Prepare the four basic financial statements for the month of May.

   (To complete the problem, you will need to use information from previous chapters.)
   [Solution is provided near the end of the chapter.]

Exhibit 6–7

Tom's Wear, Inc.
Balance Sheet
At May 1, 2005

Assets		Liabilities and shareholders' equity	
Cash	$ 3,295	Accounts payable	$ 4,000
Accounts receivable	8,000	Interest payable	310
Inventory	1,100	Short-term notes payable	3,000
Prepaid insurance	25	*Total current liabilities*	*7,310*
Prepaid rent	1,800		
Total current assets	*14,220*	Long-term notes payable	30,000
		Total liabilities	*37,310*
Computer (net of $200 accumulated amortization)	3,800		
		Common shares	5,000
Van (net of $725 accumulated amortization)	29,275	Retained earnings	4,985
Total Assets	*$47,295*	*Total liabilities and shareholders' equity*	*$47,295*

Exhibit 6–8
Transactions for May 2005 for Tom's Wear, Inc.

1	May 1	Pays cash for insurance premium, $300 for 3 months; coverage starts May 15.
2	May 10	Collects $7,900 on accounts receivable.
3	May 12	Pays accounts payable of $4,000.
4	May 14	Purchases 1,100 shirts @ $4 each for inventory for cash.
5	May 15	Agrees to sell school system 900 shirts @ $11 each; collects cash of $9,900 in advance of delivery. Half the shirts will be delivered by May 30, and the other half will be delivered in June.
6	May 20	Sells 800 shirts @ $11 each to sporting goods stores on account.
7	May 21	Hires Web designers to start a webpage; $200 for design and $50 per month maintenance fee, 6 months paid in advance. A full month of fee will be charged for May due to start-up costs.
8	May 30	Purchases 1,000 shirts @ $4.20 each, on account.
9	May 31	Note issued on March 1 for 3 months is repaid, with interest.

Note: Other information for May: The van was driven 6,000 kilometres in May.

Sam Cubbie started work on May 1 and will be paid for May on June 5. His gross salary is $1,000. Income tax in the amount of $200, and CPP and EI of $77, will be withheld from his pay. Tom's Wear Inc. as the employer will also be required to pay $77 as the employer's contribution to CPP and EI.

Answers to Study Break Questions

STUDY BREAK 6-1

1. A Company took advantage of the discount. (A Company did not have to pay the freight): $9,800.
2. B Company did not take advantage of the discount and did not have to pay the freight: $10,000.
3. C Company did not take advantage of the discount. C Company did have to pay the freight: $10,090.
4. D Company took advantage of the discount, and D Company had to pay the freight: $9,890.

STUDY BREAK 6-2

1. FIFO: units sold were 30 @ $20 and 5 @ $21 for a total cost of goods sold of $705.
2. LIFO: units sold were 20 @ $23 and 15 @ $21 for a total cost of goods sold of $775.
3. Average Cost: average cost is $1,480/70 units = $21.14 (rounded); cost of goods sold is $21.14 × 35 units = $740 (rounded).

Date	Transaction	Debit	Credit
8/10/2006	Inventory	$600	
	Cash or accounts payable		$600
To record the purchase of 30 units @ $20 each.			
8/15/2006	Inventory	$420	
	Cash or accounts payable		$420
To record the purchase of 20 units @ $21 each.			
8/21/2006	Inventory	$460	
	Cash or accounts payable		$460
To record the purchase of 20 units @ $23 each.			

(continued)

(continued)

Date	Transaction	Debit	Credit
8/30/2006	Cash or accounts receivable	$1,050	
	Sales		$1,050
	Cost of goods sold	705	
	Inventory		705
To record the sale of 35 units @ $30 each, using FIFO.			
8/30/2006	Cash or accounts receivable	$1,050	
	Sales		$1,050
	Cost of goods sold	775	
	Inventory		775
To record the sale of 35 units @ $30 each, using LIFO.			
8/30/2006	Cash or accounts receivable	$1,050	
	Sales		$1,050
	Cost of goods sold	740	
	Inventory		740
To record the sale of 35 units @ $30 each, using average cost.			

STUDY BREAK 6-3

Account	Amount	Revenue	Cost of goods sold	Other expenses
Administrative expenses	$ 57,000			$(57,000)
Income tax expense	9,000			Taxes appear below operating expenses on the income statement
Sales	617,000	$617,000		
Purchases	367,000		$(367,000)	
Delivery fees (freight-out)	10,900			(10,900)
Transportation-in	13,000		(13,000)	
Amortization expense	6,000			(6,000)
Sales salaries	74,000			(74,000)
Purchase discounts	3,300		3,300	
Utilities expense	2,100			(2,100)

Beginning inventory	$ 60,000
+ Purchases	367,000
+ Transportation-in	13,000
− Purchase discounts	(3,300)
Goods available for sale	$ 436,700
− Ending inventory	(70,000)
Cost of goods sold	**$366,700**
Sales	$ 617,000
− Cost of goods sold	(366,700)
Gross profit	**$250,300**

STUDY BREAK 6-4

If ending inventory is too low, then cost of goods sold is too high (overstated). In this case, cost of goods sold is overstated by $25,000. That means that net income is too low, because expenses were too high. Thus, net income should have been $767,640 (= $742,640 + 25,000).

STUDY BREAK 6-5

The inventory will be shown on the balance sheet at the *lower* of cost or market.

Cost	Market	Balance sheet
$345,000	$350,000	$345,000
345,000	339,000	339,000

STUDY BREAK 6-6

$1,500.00	Gross pay
(300.00)	Income taxes
(75.00)	CPP
(30.00)	EI
$1,095.00	**Net pay**

The $405.00 withheld from Sandy's paycheque will be recorded as a liability by Paula's Bookstore. Paula's Bookstore owes that amount to the government. Actually, Paula's Bookstore is acting on Sandy's behalf—it is Sandy's money being paid to the government.

Date	Transaction	Debit	Credit
	Salary expense	$1,500.00	
	Income taxes payable		$300.00
	CPP payable		75.00
	EI payable		30.00
	Cash		1,095.00
To record salary expense and payroll deductions.			
	Payroll tax expense	$117.00	
	CPP payable		75.00
	EI payable		42.00
To record employer payroll tax expense.			

Solution to Summary Problem

Transaction 1

Pays $300 cash for an insurance premium. Coverage starts May 15.

Date	Transaction	Debit	Credit
5/1/2005	Prepaid insurance	$300	
	Cash		$300
To record the purchase of insurance.			

Transaction 2

Collects $7,900 on accounts receivable.

Date	Transaction	Debit	Credit
5/10/2005	Cash	$7,900	
	Accounts receivable		$7,900
To record the collection of accounts receivable.			

Transaction 3

Pays accounts payable $4,000.

Date	Transaction	Debit	Credit
5/12/2005	Accounts payable	$4,000	
	Cash		$4,000
To record payment on account.			

Transaction 4

Purchased 1,100 T-shirts at $4 each for cash.

Date	Transaction	Debit	Credit
5/14/2005	Inventory	$4,400	
	Cash		$4,400
To record the purchase of 1,100 T-shirts at $4 for cash.			

Transaction 5

Agrees to sell school system 900 shirts @ $11 each. Collects cash of $9,900 in advance. Half the shirts will be delivered by May 30 and the other half in June.

Date	Transaction	Debit	Credit
5/15/2005	Cash	$9,900	
	Unearned revenue		$9,900
To record the collection of sales revenue in advance.			

Transaction 6

Sells 800 shirts for $11 each on account.

Date	Transaction	Debit	Credit
5/20/2005	Accounts receivable	$8,800	
	Sales		$8,800
To record the sale of 800 T-shirts, on account.			
5/20/2005	Cost of goods sold	$3,200	
	Inventory		$3,200
To record the expense cost of goods sold and reduce the inventory by 800 × $4.			

Transaction 7

Hires Web designers to start a webpage—$200 for design and $50 per month maintenance, six months paid in advance. A full month's fee is being charged in May.

Date	Transaction	Debit	Credit
5/21/2005	Prepaid Web services	$300	
	Other operating expenses	200	
	Cash		$500
To record payment for webpage setup and maintenance.			

Transaction 8

Purchases 1,000 shirts at $4.20 each on account.

Date	Transaction	Debit	Credit
5/30/2005	Inventory	$4,200	
	Accounts payable		$4,200
To record the purchase of 1,000 shirts on account.			

Transaction 9

Repays the three-month note issued on March 1, with interest.

Date	Transaction	Debit	Credit
5/31/2005	Short-term notes payable	$3,000	
	Interest payable	60	
	Interest expense	30	
	Cash		$3,090
To record the repayment of the March 1 note, with interest.			

Adjustment 1

Record insurance expense for May—$25 for the first half of the month (beginning prepaid insurance) and $50 for the second half of the month ($100 month beginning May 15).

Date	Transaction	Debit	Credit
5/31/2005	Insurance expense	$75	
	Prepaid insurance		$75
To record insurance expense for May.			

Adjustment 2

Record rent expense of $1,200 for the month of May.

Date	Transaction	Debit	Credit
5/31/2005	Rent expense	$1,200	
	Prepaid rent		$1,200
To record rent expense for May.			

Adjustment 3

Record Web services expense for May.

Date	Transaction	Debit	Credit
5/31/2005	Other operating expenses	$50	
	Prepaid Web service		$50
To record Web maintenance services for May.			

Adjustment 4

Record amortization expense for the van: 6,000 kilometres × $0.145.

Date	Transaction	Debit	Credit
5/31/2005	Amortization expense	$870	
	Accumulated amortization: van		$870
To record May amortization expense on the van.			

Adjustment 5

Record the $100 monthly amortization expense on the computer.

Date	Transaction	Debit	Credit
5/31/2005	Amortization expense	$100	
	Accumulated amortization: computer		$100
To record May amortization expense on the computer.			

Adjustment 6

Half of the shirts were delivered to the school. Reclassify half of the unearned revenue as earned and record the cost of goods sold.

Date	Transaction	Debit	Credit
5/31/2005	Unearned revenue	$4,950	
	Sales		$4,950
To record delivery of half of the shirts to the school.			
5/31/2005	Cost of goods sold	$1,800	
	Inventory		$1,800
To record the expense cost of goods sold and reduce the inventory by 450 × $4.			

Adjustment 7

Accrue Sam Cubbie's $1,000 salary for May, including the employer portion of payroll taxes and withholding tax.

Date	Transaction	Debit	Credit
5/31/2005	Salary expense	$1,000	
	Employer's payroll tax expense	77	
	Payroll taxes withheld		$277
	Other payables		77
	Salaries payable		723
To record the accrual of Sam Cubbie's salary, withholding, and payroll taxes.			

Adjustment 8

Accrue interest expense on the van note.

Date	Transaction	Debit	Credit
5/31/2005	Interest expense	$250	
	Interest payable		$250
To record the interest expense on the van for May.			

T-Accounts for Tom's Wear with May Journal Entries and Adjustments

Cash

	Debit	Credit	
BB	$3,295	$300	1
2	7,900	4,000	3
5	9,900	4,400	4
		500	7
		3,090	9
	$8,805		

Accounts receivable

	Debit	Credit	
BB	$8,000	$7,900	2
6a	8,800		
	$8,900		

Inventory

	Debit	Credit	
BB	$1,100	$3,200	6b
4	4,400	1,800	Adj-6b
8	4,200		
	$4,700		

Prepaid insurance

	Debit	Credit	
BB	$25	$75	Adj-1
1	300		
	$250		

Prepaid rent

	Debit	Credit	
5	$1,800	$1,200	Adj-2
	$600		

Prepaid Web service

	Debit	Credit	
7	$300	$50	Adj-3
	$250		

Equipment: computer

	Debit	Credit	
BB	$4,000		
	$4,000		

Accumulated Amortization: computer

	Debit	Credit	
		$200	BB
		100	Adj-5
		$300	

Equipment: van

	Debit	Credit	
BB	$30,000		
	$30,000		

Accumulated Amortization: van

	Debit	Credit	
		$725	BB
		870	Adj-4
		$1,595	

Accounts payable

	Debit	Credit	
3	$4,000	$4,000	BB
		4,200	8
		$4,200	

Interest payable

	Debit	Credit	
9	$60	$310	BB
		250	Adj-8
		$500	

Unearned revenue

	Debit	Credit	
Adj-6a	$4,950	$9,900	5
		$4,950	

Payroll taxes withheld

	Debit	Credit	
		$277	Adj-7
		$277	

Other payables

	Debit	Credit	
		$77	Adj-7
		$77	

Salaries payable

	Debit	Credit	
		$723	Adj-7
		$723	

Short-term notes payable

	Debit	Credit	
9	$3,000	$3,000	BB
		$ 0	

Long-term notes payable

	Debit	Credit	
		$30,000	BB
		$30,000	

Common shares

	Debit	Credit	
		$5,000	BB
		$5,000	

Retained earnings

	Debit	Credit	
		$4,985	BB
		$4,985	

Sales

	Debit	Credit	
		$8,800	6a
		4,950	Adj-6a
		$13,750	

Cost of goods sold

	Debit	Credit	
6b	$3,200		
Adj-6b	1,800		
	$5,000		

Amortization expense

	Debit	Credit	
Adj-4	$870		
Adj-5	100		
	$970		

Other operating expenses

	Debit	Credit	
7	$200		
Adj-3	50		
	$250		

Employer's payroll tax expense

	Debit	Credit	
Adj-7	$77		
	$77		

Insurance expense

	Debit	Credit	
Adj-1	$75		
	$75		

Rent expense

	Debit	Credit	
Adj-2	$1,200		
	$1,200		

Interest expense

	Debit	Credit	
9	$30		
Adj-8	250		
	$280		

Salary expense

	Debit	Credit	
Adj-7	$1,000		
	$1,000		

Tom's Wear, Inc.
Adjusted Trial Balance
May 31, 2005

Cash	$ 8,805	
Accounts receivable	8,900	
Inventory	4,700	
Prepaid insurance	250	
Prepaid rent	600	
Prepaid Web service	250	
Equipment: computer	4,000	
Accumulated amortization: computer		$ 300
Equipment: van	30,000	
Accumulated amortization: van		1,595
Accounts payable		4,200
Interest payable		500
Unearned revenue		4,950
Payroll taxes withheld		277
Other payables		77
Salaries payable		723
Long-term notes payable		30,000
Common shares		5,000
Retained earnings		4,985
Sales		13,750
Cost of goods sold	5,000	
Amortization expense	970	
Other operating expense	250	
Employer's payroll tax expense	77	
Insurance expense	75	
Rent expense	1,200	
Interest expense	280	
Salary expense	1,000	
Totals	*$66,357*	*$66,357*

Financial Statements

Tom's Wear, Inc.
Income Statement
For the Month Ended May 31, 2005

Sales revenue		$13,750
Expenses		
Cost of goods sold	$ 5,000	
Insurance expense	75	
Rent expense	1,200	
Amortization expense	970	
Salary expense	1,000	
Employer's payroll tax expense	77	
Other operating expenses	250	
Interest expense	280	8,852
Net income		$ 4,898

Tom's Wear, Inc.
Statement of Retained Earnings
For the Month Ended May 31, 2005

Beginning retained earnings	4,985
Net income for the month	4,898
Dividends	0
Ending retained earnings	$9,883

tom's wear

Tom's Wear, Inc.
Balance Sheet
May 31, 2005

Assets		Liabilities and Shareholders' equity	
Cash	$ 8,805	Accounts payable	$ 4,200
Accounts receivable	8,900	Interest payable	500
Inventory	4,700	Unearned revenue	4,950
Prepaid insurance	250	Salaries payable	723
Prepaid rent	600	Payroll taxes withheld	277
Prepaid Web service	250	Other payables	77
Total current assets	*23,505*	Total current liabilities	10,727
		Long-term notes payable	30,000
Computer (net of $300 accumulated amortization)	3,700	*Total liabilities*	*40,727*
		Common shares	5,000
Van (net of $1,595 accumulated amortization)	28,405	Retained earnings	9,883
Total assets	*$55,610*	*Total liabilities and shareholders' equity*	*$55,610*

Tom's Wear, Inc.
Cash Flow Statement
For the Month Ended May 31, 2005

Cash from operating activities		
Cash collected from customers	$17,800	
Cash paid for operating expenses	(800)	
Cash paid to vendors	(8,400)	
Cash paid for interest	(90)	
Total cash from operations		$8,510
Cash from investing activities		0
Cash from financing activities		
Repaid loan principal		(3,000)
Net increase (decrease) in cash		$5,510
Beginning cash balance (May 1)		3,295
Ending cash balance (May 31)		$8,805

Questions

1. What are the common cost flow methods for accounting for inventory? Describe the differences.
2. If inventory costs are rising, which method results in the lowest net income?
3. Does LIFO or FIFO give the best balance sheet value for the ending inventory? Why?
4. What is the difference between a periodic and a perpetual inventory system?
5. Does the periodic or perpetual choice affect the choice of a cost flow (LIFO versus FIFO) method? Explain.
6. Why would it be necessary to estimate, instead of count, the ending inventory?
7. Does the shipping cost related to inventory affect the recorded inventory cost? Explain.
8. Explain the terms *FOB shipping point* and *FOB destination*. What are the accounting and business implications of the shipping terms? Why is it important to know who owns goods during shipping?
9. Explain the terms of a purchase described as *2/15, n/30*. Would you take advantage of this offer? Why, or why not?
10. What is the *lower-of-cost-or-market* rule, and why is it necessary?
11. If there were an error in the ending inventory, where else would there be an error in the financial statements?
12. What is a contingent liability?
13. According to GAAP, how should likely contingent losses that can be reasonably estimated be treated? What about gains?

Short Exercises

SE6-1 The Woods Company purchased 500 electric saws from Jordan's Equipment Company, FOB shipping point. Each saw cost $300. The saws are to be sold for $650 each. Woods paid $1,550 for freight and $280 for insurance while the saws were in transit. Woods Company also hired two more salespeople for a cost of $4,000 per month. L.O. 1

Calculate the cost of the inventory of saws to be recorded in Woods' accounting records.

L.O. 1

SE6-2 Tone Company acquired 4,000 transformers from the Ochoa Company, FOB shipping point. Each transformer cost $100. Tone will sell them for $125 each. Tone paid $950 for freight and $200 for insurance while the transformers were in transit. Tone Company paid $900 to advertise the transformers in a local real estate magazine.

What is the cost of the inventory of transformers that Tone will record in the accounting records?

L.O. 2

SE6-3 Given the following information, calculate the amount by which income would differ between FIFO and LIFO.

Beginning inventory	5,000 units @ $100
Purchases	7,000 units @ $130
Units sold	6,000

L.O. 2

SE6-4 Calculate the cost of the ending inventory using the average cost flow assumption:

Sales	100 units @ $30 per unit
Beginning inventory	60 units @ $12 per unit
Purchases	80 units @ $13 per unit

L.O. 4

SE6-5 How would each of the following inventory errors affect net income for the year? Assume each is the only error during the year.

a. Ending inventory is understated by $3,000.
b. Ending inventory is overstated by $2,500.
c. Beginning inventory is overstated by $2,000.
d. Beginning inventory is understated by $1,000.

L.O. 4

SE6-6 The Long Company records showed the following at the end of the fiscal year:

Beginning inventory	$ 26,000
Ending inventory	38,000
Cost of goods sold	128,000

A physical inventory was taken and showed that the inventory was actually $39,000. If the Long Company fails to correct the error, what effect will it have on the financial statements for the year?

L.O. 4

SE6-7 The Hawking Company records reported the following at the end of the fiscal year:

Beginning inventory	$ 40,000
Ending inventory	28,500
Cost of goods sold	280,000

A physical count showed that the ending inventory was actually $26,000. If the inventory amount is not corrected, what is the effect on each of the financial statements?

L.O. 5

SE6-8 Guessing Games, Inc. wants to estimate its inventory balance for its quarterly financial statements for the first quarter of the year. Given the following, what is your best estimate?

Beginning inventory	$75,800
Net sales	$92,500
Net purchases	$50,500
Gross margin rate	30%

SE6-9 The following information pertains to item 006A of inventory of the James Company: L.O. 6

	Per Unit
Cost	$180
Replacement cost	150
Selling price	195
Disposal costs	5
Normal profit margin	20%

How much should the balance sheet reflect for this inventory item?

SE6-10 In each case, select the correct amount for the inventory on the year-end balance sheet: L.O. 6

a. Ending inventory at cost $24,500
   Ending inventory at replacement cost $27,000

b. Ending inventory at cost $27,000
   Ending inventory at replacement cost $24,500

What information, in addition to the amounts for the financial statements, does the comparison between cost and market provide to a company's management?

SE6-11 Dayco Company ended its fiscal year with inventory recorded at its cost of $15,679. Dayco believes it will be able to sell the inventory for approximately $20,000. Due to changes in the market, Dayco would be able to replace this inventory for $15,000. How much will the Dayco balance sheet show for inventory on the year-end balance sheet? L.O. 7

Exercises

E6-1 The Ribbon Company began operations on May 1. The following transactions took place in the month of May: L.O. 1

a. Cash purchases of merchandise during May were $300,000.
b. Purchases of merchandise on account during May were $400,000.
c. The cost of freight to deliver the merchandise to Ribbon Company was $25,000, paid in cash by Ribbon during May.
d. Ribbon returned $22,000 of merchandise purchased in part a to the supplier for a full refund.
e. The store manager's salary was $3,000 for the month.

Calculate the amount that the Ribbon Company should record for purchases of merchandise inventory for May.

E6-2 The following information is given related to the purchases of inventory during the month of February: L.O. 1

Invoice price	$5,000
Terms of sale	2/10, n/30
Shipping terms	FOB shipping point
Shipping costs	$250
Salary for inventory stocker	$750
Electricity for storage area	$300

Calculate the amount that would be recorded as the total cost of inventory. All invoices are paid within five days of receipt.

L.O. 1

E6-3 For each of the following situations, calculate the amount that the purchasing company would record as the cost of the inventory purchase:

a. Invoice price of goods is $5,000. Purchase terms are 2/10, n/30 and the invoice is paid in the week of receipt. The shipping terms are FOB shipping point, and the shipping costs amount to $200.
b. Invoice price of goods is $3,000. Purchase terms are 4/10, n/30 and the invoice is paid in the week of receipt. The shipping terms are FOB destination, and the shipping costs amount to $250.
c. Invoice price of goods is $2,500. Purchase terms are 2/10, n/30 and the invoice is paid 15 days after receipt. The shipping terms are FOB shipping point, and the shipping costs amount to $250.
d. Invoice price of goods is $9,000. Purchase terms are 3/10, n/30 and the invoice is paid in the week of receipt. The shipping terms are FOB destination, and the shipping costs amount to $200.

L.O. 1

E6-4 Sonic Corp. uses a periodic inventory system. At December 31, 2006, the end of the company's fiscal year, a physical count of inventory revealed an ending inventory balance of $220,000. The following items were *not* included in the physical count:

Merchandise shipped to a customer on December 30, FOB destination (goods arrived at customer's location on January 5, 2007)	$10,000
Merchandise shipped to a customer on December 29, FOB shipping point (merchandise arrived at customer's location on January 3, 2007)	5,000
Merchandise purchased from a supplier, shipped FOB destination on December 29, in transit at year-end	4,000

What should Sonic correctly report as the amount of inventory on their December 31, 2006, balance sheet?

L.O. 2, 3

E6-5 Given the following information:

January 1	Beginning inventory	20 gallons @ $10 each
February 28	Purchase	50 gallons @ $12 each
April 30	Purchase	40 gallons @ $13 each
September 15	Purchase	60 gallons @ $14 each
December 31	Ending inventory	35 gallons

a. Calculate the cost of goods sold and the cost of the ending inventory using FIFO.
b. Calculate the cost of goods sold and the cost of the ending inventory using LIFO.
c. Are you using perpetual or periodic accounting? Why?

L.O. 2

E6-6 Given the following information, calculate the gross margin under FIFO and under LIFO:

Sales	200 units @ $50 per unit
Beginning inventory	50 units @ $40 per unit
Purchases	175 units @ $45 per unit

L.O. 2, 3

E6-7 Given the following information for March 2005, calculate the cost of goods sold for the month using LIFO periodic.

Inventory, March 1, 2005	10 units @ $5 each
Purchase, March 10	30 units @ $6 each
Sale, March 15	12 units
Purchase, March 20	15 units @ $7

E6-8 Given the following information for March 2005, calculate the cost of goods sold for the month using (1) FIFO periodic, and then using (2) FIFO perpetual. Explain when the two methods will produce a different amount for cost of goods sold. L.O. 2, 3

Inventory, March 1, 2005	10 units @ $5 each
Purchase, March 10	30 units @ $6 each
Sale, March 15	12 units
Purchase, March 20	15 units @ $7

E6-9 Starnes TV Sales and Service began the month of May with two identical TV sets in inventory. During May, six additional TV sets (identical to the two in beginning inventory) were purchased as follows: L.O. 2, 3

two on May 10
one on May 16
three on May 24

The company sold two of the TV sets on May 13, another one on May 18, and two more on May 27.

a. Assume Starnes uses a perpetual inventory system and the FIFO cost flow method:

1. Which two TV sets were booked as cost of goods sold on May 13?
2. Which one was booked as cost of goods sold on May 18?
3. Which two TV sets were booked as cost of goods sold on May 27?
4. The cost of which three TV sets will be included in Starnes' inventory cost calculation at the end of May?

b. If Starnes uses a periodic inventory system and the LIFO cost flow method, the cost of which three TV sets will be included in the inventory at the end of May?

E6-10 Sloppy Company uses a periodic inventory system. On December 31, 2006, at the end of the fiscal year, the clerks miscounted the inventory left on hand. They counted $130,000 worth of inventory, but they forgot to count a stack of goods in the corner with a cost of $20,000. If this error goes undetected, how will it affect the financial statements for the year ending December 31, 2006, and the financial statements for the year ending December 31, 2007? Give the effect on each of the financial statements. L.O. 4

E6-11 The Rim Company records reported the following at the end of the fiscal year: L.O. 4

Beginning inventory	$ 90,000
Ending inventory	60,000
Cost of goods sold	395,000

A physical inventory count showed that the inventory was actually $64,000. If this error is not corrected, what effect will it have on the financial statements for this fiscal year and for the following fiscal year?

E6-12 The following information is available for the Rocklin Office Supply Company: L.O. 5

Inventory, October 1, 2004	$240,000
Net purchases for the month of October	750,000
Net sales for the month of October	950,000
Gross profit ratio (historical)	30%

Estimate the cost of goods sold for October and the ending inventory at October 31.

E6-13 The records of Seattle Ship Products, Inc. revealed the following information related to inventory destroyed in an earthquake: L.O. 5

Inventory, beginning of period	$300,000
Purchases to date of earthquake	160,000
Net sales to date of earthquake	450,000
Gross profit ratio	30%

The company needs to file a claim for lost inventory with its insurance company. What is the estimated value of the lost inventory?

L.O. 7

E6-14 A company calculated its inventory turnover for the past two years. This year the inventory turnover is approximately five, and last year the inventory turnover was approximately four. Will the company view this as good news or bad news? Does it indicate that more or less capital has been tied up in inventory this year compared with last year?

L.O. 8

E6-15 For each item in the list that follows, tell whether it is a definitely determinable liability, an estimated liability, or a contingent liability.

a. Amount owed to vendor for purchase of inventory.
b. Potential loss from a pending lawsuit.
c. Amount of warranty obligations.
d. Amount of loan payment due next year.
e. Amount of vacation pay to accrue for employees for next year.

L.O. 9

E6-16 If a company has gross payroll of $20,000, income tax withheld of $4,000, and CPP and EI withheld of $1,400:

a. How much will the balance sheet show for salaries payable (to employees)?
b. How much will the income statement show for salary expense?
c. What type of liability is salaries payable?

L.O. 10

E6-17 What risks are associated with inventory, and what specific controls minimize those risks?

Problems—Set A

L.O. 1

P6-1A The Battier Company made the following purchases in March of the current year:

March 2	Purchased $5,000 of merchandise, terms 1/10, n/30, FOB shipping point
March 5	Purchased $2,000 of merchandise, terms 2/15, n/45, FOB shipping point
March 10	Purchased $4,000 of merchandise, terms 3/05, n/15, FOB destination

Required:

a. For each of the listed purchases, how many days does the company have to take advantage of the purchase discount?
b. What is the amount of the cash discount allowed in each case?
c. Assume the freight charges are $350 on each purchase. What is the total amount of freight that Battier has to pay?
d. What is the total amount of inventory costs for Battier Company for the month of March, assuming that all discounts were taken?

L.O. 1

P6-2A The Williams Company made the following purchases in May of the current year:

May 3	Purchased $3,000 of merchandise, terms 2/10, n/30, FOB destination
May 12	Purchased $2,800 of merchandise, terms 2/10, n/60, FOB shipping point
May 22	Purchased $6,000 of merchandise, terms 3/05, n/20, FOB destination

Required:

a. For each purchase, when is the payment due assuming the company takes advantage of the discount?

b. For each purchase, when is the payment due if the company does not take advantage of the discount?
c. In each case, what is the amount of the cash discount allowed?
d. Assume the freight charges are $400 on each purchase. For which purchases is Williams Company responsible for the freight charges?
e. What is the total amount of inventory costs for the month of May, assuming that all discounts were taken?

P6-3A Jefferson Company had the following sales and purchases during 2007, its first year of business: L.O. 2

January 5	Purchase	40 units @ $100 each
February 15	Sale	15 units @ $150 each
April 10	Sale	10 units @ $150 each
June 30	Purchase	30 units @ $105 each
August 15	Sale	25 units @ $150 each
November 28	Purchase	20 units @ $110 each

Required: Calculate the ending inventory, the cost of goods sold, and the gross profit for the December 31, 2007, financial statements under each of the following assumptions:

a. FIFO perpetual
b. FIFO periodic
c. LIFO periodic
d. Average cost periodic

P6-4A The following series of transactions occurred during 2006: L.O. 2, 3

January 1	Beginning inventory	50 units @ $10
January 15	Purchase	100 units @ $11
February 4	Sale	60 units @ $20
March 10	Purchase	50 units @ $12
April 15	Sale	70 units @ $20
June 30	Purchase	100 units @ $13
August 4	Sale	110 units @ $20
October 1	Purchase	80 units @ $14
December 5	Sale	50 units @ $21

Required: Calculate the value of the ending inventory and cost of goods sold using the following methods (each case is independent):

a. FIFO perpetual
b. FIFO periodic
c. LIFO periodic
d. Average cost periodic

P6-5A The For Fish Company sells commercial fish tanks. The company began 2006 with 10,000 units of inventory on hand. These units cost $150 each. The following transactions related to the company's merchandise inventory occurred during the first quarter of 2006: L.O. 2, 3

January 20	Purchase	5,000 units @ $160 each
February 18	Purchase	6,000 units @ $170 each
March 28	Purchase	4,000 units @ $180 each
Total purchases		*15,000 Units*

All unit costs include the purchase price and freight charges paid by For Fish. During the quarter ending March 31, 2006, sales in units totalled 17,000 units, leaving 8,000 units in ending inventory. The company uses a periodic inventory system.

Required: Calculate ending inventory at March 31 and cost of goods sold for the quarter using:

a. FIFO
b. LIFO
c. Average cost

L.O. 2, 3

P6-6A Given the following information for Grant's Print Shop, Inc. for the year ending December 31, 2007, at January 1, 2007:

- Cash amounted to $19,375.
- Beginning inventory was $16,000 (160 units @ $100 each).
- Share capital was $15,000.
- Retained earnings was $20,375.

Transactions during 2007 included:

- The company purchased 150 units @ $110 each for cash.
- The company purchased 190 more units @ $120 each for cash.
- Cash sales were $290 units @ $200 each.
- The company paid $11,500 cash for operating expenses.
- The company paid cash for income tax at a rate of 30 percent of net income.

Required:

a. Compute the cost of goods sold and ending inventory using (1) FIFO, (2) LIFO, and (3) average cost. (Are you using perpetual or periodic record keeping?)
b. Compute the net income before taxes and after taxes under each of the three inventory cost flow assumptions.
c. Prepare the 2007 balance sheets, income statements, and cash flow statements for Grant's Print Shop, Inc. using all three inventory methods.

L.O. 2, 3

P6-7A The following merchandise inventory transactions occurred during the month of June for the Furlong Corp.:

June 1	Inventory on hand totalling 3,000 units @ $3.00 each
7	Sold 2,000 units
18	Purchased 4,000 units @ $3.50 each
21	Sold 5,000 units
27	Purchased 4,000 units @ $4.00 each

Required:

a. Calculate ending inventory at June 30 and cost of goods sold for the month using a periodic inventory system under each of the following cost flow methods:

1. Average cost
2. FIFO
3. LIFO

b. Assume that Furlong uses the perpetual inventory system. What would be the *cost of goods sold* for the June 21 sale applying the FIFO inventory system?

L.O. 2, 3

P6-8A Cheny Company buys and then resells a single product. The product is a commodity and is subject to rather severe cost fluctuations. Following is information concerning the inventory activity during the month of June 2007:

June 1	Had 430 units on hand, $3,010
June 4	Sold 200 units
June 6	Purchased 500 units @ $11 per unit
June 10	Purchased 200 units @ $9 per unit
June 15	Sold 300 units
June 20	Purchased 150 units @ $6 per unit
June 25	Sold 400 units
June 29	Purchased 50 units @ $8 per unit

Cheny uses a perpetual inventory system.

Required: Calculate cost of goods sold (units and cost) for the month of June 2007 and ending inventory (units and cost) at June 30, 2007, using FIFO.

P6-9A Stiles Company and Wycoff Company both began their operations on January 2, 2008. Both companies had exactly the same amount of business during 2008. They purchased exactly the same number of units of merchandise inventory during the year at exactly the same cost, and they sold exactly the same number of inventory units at exactly the same selling price during the year. They also purchased exactly the same type and amount of property, plant, and equipment, paying exactly the same amount for those items. At the end of 2008, the two companies prepared income statements for the year. Stiles reported net income of $92,000 and Wycoff reported net income of $65,000.

L.O. 2, 3

What could have caused the reported net income for the two companies to be different?

P6-10A Brickey, Inc. had 800 units of inventory on hand on April 1, 2006, costing $20 each. Purchases and sales of inventory during the month of April were as follows:

L.O. 2, 3, 4

Date	Purchases	Sales
Beginning inventory	800 units @ $20 each	
April 5		500 units
15	400 units @ $21 each	
20	400 units @ $22 each	
27		400 units

Brickey uses a periodic inventory system.

Required:

a. Calculate the ending inventory using FIFO.
b. Calculate the ending inventory using LIFO.
c. Suppose that 100 units were left out of the count of the ending inventory. What effect would that have on the *cost of goods sold* under each of the cost flow assumptions in parts a and b?

P6-11A Beard Company uses a perpetual inventory system, and so both the cost of goods sold is recorded and the inventory records are updated at the time of every sale and purchase. The company's accounting records showed the following related to June 2007 transactions:

L.O. 4

	Units	Cost
Beginning inventory, June 1	200	$ 600
+ Purchases during June	1,700	5,100
= Goods available for sale	1,900	$5,700
− Cost of goods sold	1,500	4,500
= Ending inventory, June 30	400	$1,200

On June 30, 2007, Beard conducted a physical count of its inventory and discovered there were only 375 units of inventory actually on hand.

Required:

a. Correct Beard's records to reflect the results of the physical inventory count.
b. How would this correction change the financial statements for the year?
c. What are some possible causes of the difference between the inventory amounts in the Beard Company's accounting records and the inventory amount from the physical count?

L.O. 5

P6-12A Lewis Company sells blueberries to tourists on Greenwich Road in Prince Edward Island. A hurricane destroyed the entire inventory in late August. To file an insurance claim, Jimmy, the owner of the company, must estimate the value of the lost inventory. Records from January 1 through the date of the hurricane in August indicated that Lewis Company started the year with $4,000 worth of inventory on hand. Purchases for the year amounted to $9,000, and sales up to the date of the hurricane were $16,000. Gross margin percentage has traditionally been 30 percent.

Required:

a. How much should the Lewis Company request from the insurance company?
b. Suppose that several crates of blueberries were spared by the hurricane. The cost of these blueberries was $700. How much was the inventory loss under these conditions?

L.O. 7

P6-13A The following information is given from the financial statements of Music Stores Corp.

Required: Calculate the gross margin ratios and the inventory turnover ratios for the two years shown. What information do these comparisons give?

For year ended (in thousands)	December 31, 2008	December 31, 2007	December 31, 2006
Sales	$1,891,828	$1,846,882	
Cost of goods sold	1,200,993	1,190,582	
Inventory	444,492	446,710	$ 440,890

Problems—Set B

L.O. 1

P6-1B The Winning Lacrosse Company made the following purchases in April of the current year:

April 4	Purchased $6,000 of merchandise, terms 2/15, n/15, FOB shipping point
April 9	Purchased $7,500 of merchandise, terms 3/5, n/30, FOB destination
April 13	Purchased $8,000 of merchandise, terms 1/10, n/45, FOB shipping point

Required:

a. For each of the listed purchases, how many days does the company have to take advantage of the purchase discount?
b. What is the amount of the cash discount allowed in each case?
c. Assume the freight charges are $425 on each purchase. What is the total amount of freight that Winning Lacrosse Company has to pay?
d. What is the total amount of inventory costs for Winning Lacrosse Company for the month of April assuming that all discounts were taken?

L.O. 1

P6-2B Billy Bob's Baseball Barn made the following purchases in March of the current year:

March 1	Purchased $4,500 of baseball gloves, terms 3/15, n/25, FOB shipping point
March 10	Purchased $7,200 of sportswear, terms 2/10, n/20, FOB destination
March 15	Purchased $4,900 of softballs and baseballs, terms 1/5, n/15, FOB shipping point

Required:

a. For each purchase, when is the payment due assuming the company takes advantage of the discount?
b. For each purchase, when is the payment due if the company does not take advantage of the discount?
c. In each case, what is the amount of the cash discount allowed?
d. Assume the freight charges are $275 on each purchase. For which purchases is Billy Bob's Baseball Barn responsible for the freight charges?
e. What is the total amount of inventory costs for the month of May assuming that all discounts were taken?

P6-3B Sandy's Clean Carpet Company sells commercial vacuums. The company began June 30, 2007, with 15,000 units of inventory on hand. These units cost $200 each. The following transactions related to the company's merchandise inventory occurred during the first quarter of the year ended June 30, 2008:

L.O. 2, 3

July 15	Purchased	4,500 units for $210 each
August 28	Purchased	5,750 units for $190 each
September 10	Purchased	6,000 units for $185 each
Total purchases		*16,250 units*

All unit costs include the purchase price and freight charges paid by Sandy's Clean Carpet. During the quarter ending September 30, 2007, sales in units totalled 19,500 units, leaving 11,750 units in ending inventory. The company uses the periodic inventory system.

Required: Calculate ending inventory and cost of goods sold for the quarter ending September 30 using:

a. FIFO
b. LIFO
c. Average cost

P6-4B The following information is given for Nan's Toy Extravaganza, Inc. for the year ended June 30, 2008:

L.O. 2, 3

At July 1, 2007:

- Cash amounted to $25,000.
- Beginning inventory was $32,000 (800 units @ $40 each).
- Share capital was $12,000.
- Retained earnings was $45,000.

Transactions for the year ended June 30, 2008:

- Nan's purchased 700 units @ $41 each for cash.
- The company purchased 300 more units @ $43 each for cash.
- The company had cash sales of 1,000 units @ $56 each.
- Nan's paid $7,500 cash for operating expenses.
- The company paid cash for income taxes at a rate of 40 percent of net income.

The company uses periodic record keeping.

Required:

a. Compute the cost of goods sold and ending inventory using (1) FIFO, (2) LIFO, and (3) average cost. (Round unit cost calculations to the nearest cent.)
b. Compute the net income before taxes and after taxes under each of the three inventory cost flow assumptions.
c. Prepare the balance sheets, income statements, and cash flow statements for the year ended June 30, 2008, under each of the three inventory cost flow assumptions.

L.O. 2, 3

P6-5B The following merchandise inventory transactions occurred during the month of November for Party Heaven, Inc.:

November	5	Inventory on hand, 2,000 units @ $4.00 each
	12	Sold 1,500 units
	16	Purchased 4,000 units @ $4.40 each
	23	Sold 4,300 units
	28	Purchased 5,000 units @ $5.00 each

Required: Calculate ending inventory at November 30 and cost of goods sold for the month using a periodic inventory system and each of the following cost flow methods:

1. Average cost
2. FIFO
3. LIFO

L.O. 2, 3

P6-6B Hillary's Diamonds buys and then resells a single product. The product, a diamond, is a commodity and is subject to rather severe cost fluctuations. Some information concerning Hillary's Diamonds' inventory activity during the month of June 2008 follows:

June 2	Had 860 units on hand, @ $7 per unit
June 6	Sold 400 units
June 8	Purchased 1,000 units @ $11 per unit
June 12	Purchased 400 units @ $9 per unit
June 15	Sold 600 units
June 21	Purchased 300 units @ $6 per unit
June 24	Sold 800 units
June 31	Purchased 100 units @ $8 per unit

Required: Hillary's Diamonds uses a periodic inventory system. Calculate cost of goods sold (in both units and cost) for the month of June 2008 and ending inventory (units and cost) at June 30, 2008, using each of the following cost flow assumptions:

a. FIFO
b. LIFO
c. Which of the two methods resulted in the highest cost of goods sold for June?
d. Which one will provide the highest ending inventory value for Hillary's balance sheet?
e. How would the differences between the methods affect Hillary's income statement and balance sheet for June?

L.O. 2, 3

P6-7B Brutus Company and Gabrielle Company both began their operations on July 1, 2005. Both companies had exactly the same amount of business during the fiscal year ended June 30, 2006. They purchased exactly the same number of units of merchandise inventory during the year at exactly the same cost, and they sold exactly the same number of inventory units at exactly the same selling price during the year. They also purchased exactly the same type and amount of property, plant, and equipment, paying exactly the same amount for those items. At the end of the fiscal year, the two companies prepared income statements for the year. Brutus reported a gross margin of $84,250 and Gabrielle reported a gross margin of $75,680.

Required:

a. If both companies reported $120,000 for sales revenue, what was the cost of goods sold for each?
b. What could have caused the reported gross margin for the two companies to be different? Be specific, and use some numbers to illustrate.

L.O. 2, 3, 4

P6-8B Joe's Medical Supply, Inc. had 750 units of inventory on hand on August 1, 2008, at a cost of $30 each. Purchases and sales of inventory during the month of August were as follows:

Date	Purchases	Sales
Beginning inventory	750 units @ $30 each	
August 4		550 units
12	325 units @ $28 each	
23	275 units @ $26 each	
31		500 units

The company uses a periodic inventory system.

Required:

a. Calculate the ending inventory using FIFO.
b. Calculate the ending inventory using LIFO.
c. Suppose that 50 units were left out of the count of the ending inventory. What effect would that omission have on the *cost of goods sold* under each of the cost flow assumptions in parts a and b?

P6-9B Barney's Flowerpot Company uses a perpetual inventory system, and so the cost of goods sold is recorded and the inventory records are updated at the time of every sale and purchase. The company's accounting records showed the following related to June 2008 transactions:

L.O. 4

	Units	Cost
Beginning inventory, June 1	200	$ 600
+ Purchases during June	1,700	5,100
= Goods available for sale	1,900	$5,700
− Cost of goods sold	1,500	4,500
= Ending inventory, June 30	400	$1,200

On June 30, 2008, Barney conducted a physical count of its inventory and discovered there were actually 425 units of inventory on hand.

Required:

a. Give the adjustment that would correct Barney's Flowerpot Company's records to reflect the results of the physical inventory count.
b. How would this correction change the financial statements for the year?
c. What are some possible causes of the difference between the inventory amounts in Barney's Flowerpot Company accounting records and the inventory amount from the physical count?

P6-10B Cynthia's Cotton Candy Company sells cotton candy to visitors at a travelling county fair. During a drought, a fire destroyed the entire inventory in late July. To file an insurance claim, Cynthia, the owner of the company, must estimate the value of the lost inventory. Records from January 1 through the date of the fire in August indicated that Cynthia's Cotton Candy Company started the year with $4,250 worth of inventory on hand. Purchases for the year amounted to $8,000, and sales up to the date of the fire were $17,500. Gross margin percentage has traditionally been 35 percent.

L.O. 5

Required:

a. How much should the company request from the insurance company?
b. Suppose that one bag of cotton candy mix was spared by the fire. The cost of that bag was $50. How much was the inventory loss under these conditions?

P6-11B The following information is given in the financial statements of Bessy's Salsa, Inc. for 2007 and 2008. Also, the inventory on December 31, 2006, amounted to $528,850.

L.O. 7

Required: Calculate the gross margin ratios and the inventory turnover ratios for the two years shown. What information do these comparisons give?

For year ended	December 31, 2008	December 31, 2007
Sales	$1,732,571	$1,642,352
Cost of goods sold	1,105,725	1,118,745
Inventory	337,781	526,820

Recording Transactions

R6-1 (SE6-1) The Woods Company purchased 500 electric saws from Jordan's Equipment Company. Each saw cost $300. The saws are to be sold for $650 each. Woods paid $1,550 for freight and $280 for insurance while the saws were in transit. Woods Company also hired two more salespeople for a cost of $4,000 per month. Give the journal entry for the purchase of inventory. Assume the company uses perpetual record keeping for inventory.

Date	Account	Debit	Credit

R6-2 (SE6-2) Tone Company acquired 4,000 transformers from the Ochoa Company. Each transformer cost $100. Tone will sell them for $125 each. Tone paid $950 for freight and $200 for insurance while the transformers were in transit. Tone Company paid $900 to advertise the transformers in a local real estate magazine. Give the journal entry for the purchase of inventory. Assume the company uses perpetual record keeping for inventory.

Date	Account	Debit	Credit

R6-3 (SE6-7) The Hawking Company's records reported the following at the end of the fiscal year:

Beginning inventory	$ 40,000
Ending inventory	28,500
Cost of goods sold	280,000

A physical count showed that the ending inventory was actually $26,000. What is the journal entry needed to correct the accounting records?

Date	Account	Debit	Credit

R6-4 (E6-1) The Ribbon Company began operations on May 1. The following transactions took place in the month of May.

a. Cash purchases of merchandise during May were $300,000.
b. Purchases of merchandise on account during May were $400,000.

c. The cost of freight to deliver the merchandise to Ribbon Company was $25,000, paid in cash by Ribbon during May.
d. Ribbon returned $22,000 of merchandise purchased in part a to the supplier for a full refund.
e. The store manager's salary was $3,000 for the month.

Assume Ribbon Company uses periodic record keeping for inventory. Give the journal entry for each transaction described above.

Transaction	Account	Debit	Credit

R6-5 (E6-3) For each of the following situations, give the journal entry that the purchasing company would record for the inventory purchase (including the cost of the freight, where applicable). Assume any freight charges are paid in cash at the time of receipt. Then, record the payment to the vendor for each purchase. Assume the company uses periodic record keeping. Assume discounts are recorded only when the payment is actually made and the purchase discount is taken.

a. Invoice price of goods is $5,000. Purchase terms are 2/10, n/30, and the invoice is paid in the week of receipt. The shipping terms are FOB shipping point, and the shipping costs amount to $200.
b. Invoice price of goods is $3,000. Purchase terms are 4/10, n/30, and the invoice is paid in the week of receipt. The shipping terms are FOB destination, and the shipping costs amount to $250.
c. Invoice price of goods is $2,500. Purchase terms are 2/10, n/30, and the invoice is paid 15 days after receipt. The shipping terms are FOB shipping point, and the shipping costs amount to $250.
d. Invoice price of goods is $9,000. Purchase terms are 3/10, n/30, and the invoice is paid in the week of receipt. The shipping terms are FOB destination, and the shipping costs amount to $200.

Transaction	Account	Debit	Credit

R6-6 (E6-16) For a specific accounting period, a company has gross payroll of $20,000, income tax withheld of $4,000 and CPP and EI withheld of $1,400. Give the journal entry(s) to record the salary expense for the period. Include any related employer expenses, assuming the employer's share is equal to the employees'.

Date	Account	Debit	Credit

R6-7 (P6-1A) The Battier Company made the following purchases in March of the current year:

- March 2: Purchased $5,000 of merchandise, terms 1/10, n/30, FOB shipping point
- March 5: Purchased $2,000 of merchandise, terms 2/15, n/45, FOB shipping point
- March 10: Purchased $4,000 of merchandise, terms 3/5, n/15, FOB destination

Required: Record the journal entries for each purchase. In each case, the freight charges are $350 and are paid in cash. Assume Battier Company records purchases at the full invoice amount and records purchase discounts only when the payment to the vendor is made and the discount is taken. The company uses perpetual record keeping for inventory.

Date	Account	Debit	Credit

R6-8 (P6-5A) The For Fish Company sells commercial fish tanks. The company began 2006 with 10,000 units of inventory on hand. These units cost $150 each. The following transactions related to the company's merchandise inventory occurred during the first quarter of 2006:

January 20	Purchase	5,000 units for $160 each
February 18	Purchase	6,000 units for $170 each
March 28	Purchase	4,000 units for $180 each
Total Purchases		*15,000 units*

The costs shown include all related inventory costs. During the quarter ending March 31, 2006, sales in units totalled 17,000 units, leaving 8,000 units in ending inventory. The company uses a periodic record-keeping system.

Required: Give the journal entry required at March 31 to record the cost of goods sold for the quarter using:

a. FIFO
b. LIFO
c. Average cost

Date	Account	Debit	Credit

R6-9 (P6-8A) Cheny Company buys and then resells a single product. The product is a commodity and is subject to rather severe cost fluctuations. Following is information concerning Cheny's inventory activity during the month of June 2007:

June 1	430 units on hand, $3,010
June 4	Sold 200 units
June 6	Purchased 500 units @ $11 per unit
June 10	Purchased 200 units @ $9 per unit
June 15	Sold 300 units
June 20	Purchased 150 units @ $6 per unit
June 25	Sold 400 units
June 29	Purchased 50 units @ $8 per unit

Cheny uses a perpetual, FIFO inventory system.

Required: Assume Cheny sold each unit for $20 per unit. Give the journal entries to record the sales and reduction in inventory if appropriate:

Date	Account	Debit	Credit

R6-Comprehensive

Chapter 6: Comprehensive Financial Statement Preparation Problem

This is the postclosing trial balance for Tulsa Tire Company, prepared on December 31, 2008:

Account	DR	CR
Cash	$200,000	
Accounts receivable	130,000	
Merchandise inventory	100,000	
Accounts payable		$150,000
Salaries payable		4,000
Long-term notes payable		50,000
Common shares		126,000
Retained earnings		100,000
	$430,000	$430,000

The following events took place during January 2009. Tulsa Tire uses perpetual FIFO as its inventory method. The inventory on hand at 12/31/08 consisted of 10,000 tires that cost $10 each.

1. Purchased 1,000 tires for $12 each, on account.
2. Paid salaries owed to employees at 12/31/08.
3. Sold 500 tires to various tire stores for $20 each, on account.
4. Collected $100,000 from customers.
5. Paid entire accounts payable balance (including purchase in 1 above).
6. Purchased 1,000 tires for $13 each, on account.
7. Sold 5,000 tires to various tire stores for $20 each, on account.
8. To reduce inventory at the end of the month, sold 5,000 tires for $20 each, with terms 2/10, n/30, and FOB destination. Shipping costs, paid in cash, were $250. Sales discounts are recorded if and when the customers take them.
9. Made a payment on the long-term loan of $5,000. Of this amount, $4,500 was principal, and $500 was interest for January.
10. Recorded accrued expenses for January (to be paid in February): utilities $500, salaries $4,500, other expenses $3,000.

Required: Prepare the income statement, balance sheet, and cash flow statement for January 2009.

Issues for Discussion

Financial statement analysis

1. Use the financial statements of CoolBrands International Inc. to answer the following questions:
   a. What inventory methods does the company use?
   b. Compute the inventory turnover ratio for at least two consecutive years. (The company's inventory at year-end for fiscal 2001 was $16,539 thousand.) What information does this provide?
   c. Is cost of goods sold a significant expense for the company? How can you tell?

Business risk

2. A potential control for managing the risk of employee fraud is to require employees to take vacations. Relate that control to the payroll function. Why would it be a good idea to require the payroll clerk, who writes the cheques, to go on vacation?

Ethics

3. Jim's Music Company uses LIFO for inventory, and the company's profits are quite high this year. The cost of the inventory has been steadily rising all year. His accountant has suggested that the company make a large purchase of inventory to be received during the last week in December. The accountant has explained to Jim that this would reduce his income significantly.
   a. Jim does not understand the logic of the accountant's suggestion. Explain how the purchase would affect income.
   b. Is this ethical? Jim is uncertain about the appropriateness of this from a legal and an ethical perspective. Give your opinion and explain the ethical implications of making the purchase.

Internet Exercise: Coca-Cola Company

Coca-Cola Company is the world's largest producer of soft drink concentrates syrups and juices. The firm does no actual bottling but sells more than 230 brands of beverages in 200 nations. Coca-Cola products include Coca-Cola Classic, Diet Coke, Sprite, Fanta, Mr. Pibb, Mello Yello, and Minute Maid.

To find out more about Coca-Cola, go to the Hoover's website: www.hoovers.com

IE6-1 Enter KO, the stock symbol for Coca-Cola, select by ticker and click search. In the left hand column, click on the Financials and select Annual Financials.

a. For the three most recent years, identify the amounts reported for revenue and total net income. Is revenue increasing or decreasing? Is total net income increasing or decreasing? Are these trends favourable or unfavourable? Explain why or why not.
b. For the three most recent years, identify the amount reported for the gross profit margin (gross margin on sales ratio). Is the trend for this ratio increasing or decreasing? Is it considered favourable or unfavourable? What might this trend indicate?
c. For the three most recent years, identify the amount reported for cost of goods sold and ending inventories. For the two most recent years, calculate the inventory turnover ratio. Is Coca-Cola selling inventory more quickly in the most recent year? How can you tell? Is this good for Coca-Cola? Explain why or why not.
d. Review the information gathered in the preceding a through c and comment on the overall profitability of Coca-Cola Company.

IE6-2 Click on the Company URL for Coca-Cola Company: www.cocacola.com.

a. Take the Virtual Plant Tour (look under Our Company and About Bottling) and explore "Ingredient Delivery." What are the ingredients of Coca-Cola? Which ingredient is rigorously filtered and cleansed? Explain why. Can you open the truck door and load the ingredients onto the loading dock? Close the Virtual Plant Tour window.

b. Look under Investors and find the most recent annual report. "Operations Review" reports worldwide unit case volume. Which segment (North American or International operations) is growing faster? Look at the "Operating Segments" note in the "Notes to Financial Statements." Does the global economy impact the Coca-Cola sale of inventory? Explain why or why not.

Please note: Internet websites are constantly being updated. Therefore, if the information is not found where indicated, please explore the website further to find the information.

CHAPTER 7

Sales and Collection Cycle

Inventory and Liabilities

Here's where you've been...

In Chapter 6, you learned about how a company acquires and accounts for inventory and payables. You learned to value inventory with cost flow assumptions, such as LIFO and FIFO, and how that information is shown on a company's financial statements.

Here's where you're going...

When you are finished with Chapter 7, you should understand how a company accounts for *sales, cash,* and *accounts receivable*. You will learn how that information is presented on the financial statements.

Sales and Accounts Receivable

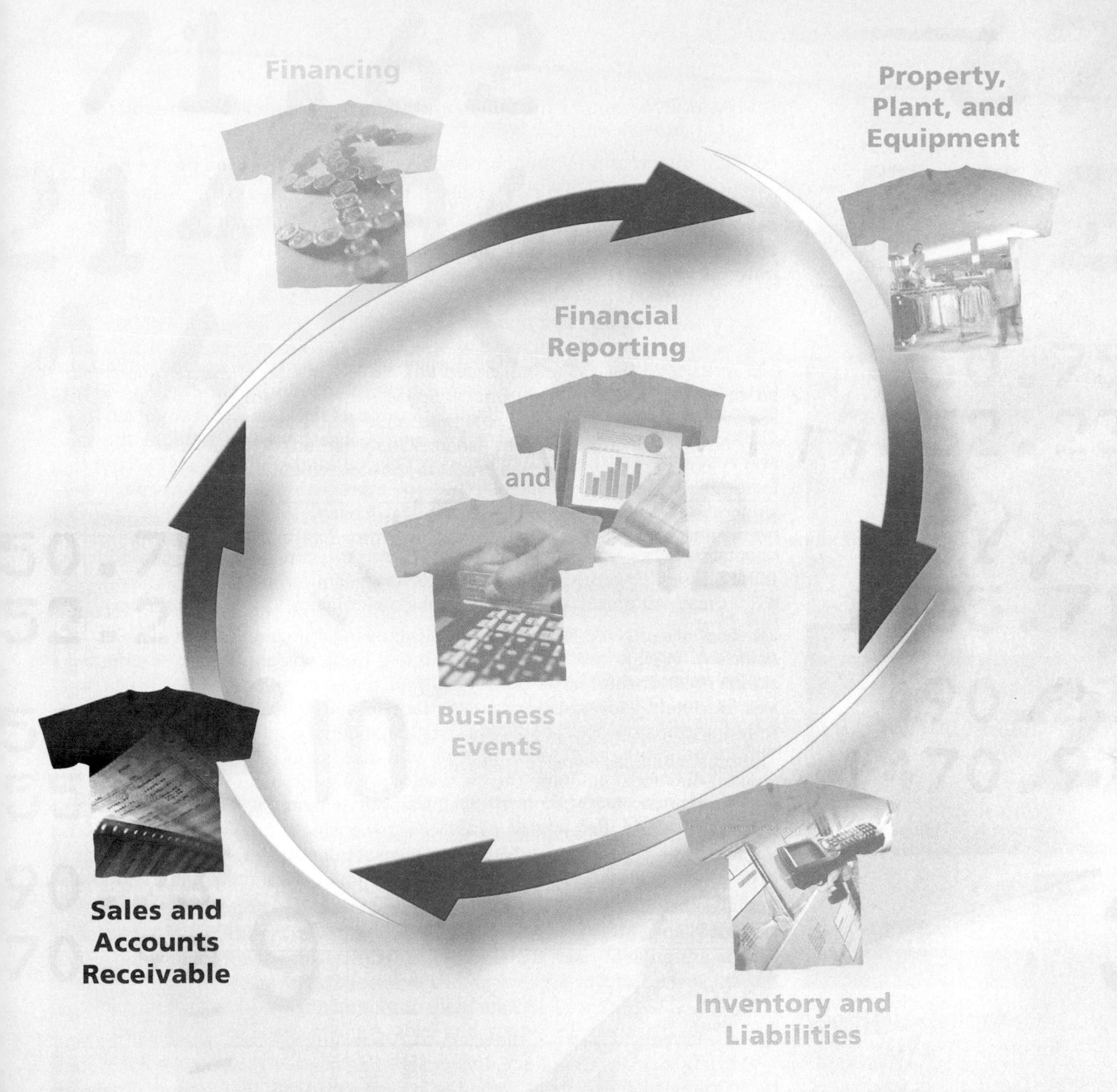

Learning Objectives

More specifically, when you are finished studying this chapter, you should be able to answer these questions:

1. How are sales for cash and sales on account made, recognized, and reported?
2. What is a bank (cash) reconciliation? How is it done? Why is it necessary?
3. How does a company estimate, report, and evaluate the effects of uncollectible accounts?
4. How are credit card sales recorded and reported?

5. How does a company estimate and report warranties and the related expenses?
6. What information about accounts receivable is disclosed on the financial statements? How can we use it to help us evaluate the business?
7. What risks are associated with sales, cash, and accounts receivable?

The two business activities—the purchase of property, plant, and equipment (discussed in Chapter 5) and the acquisition of inventory (discussed in Chapter 6)—are done by a business in preparation for its revenue-generating activities. These activities in the acquisition/payment process set the stage for the sales and collection process. The business process of making a sale and accounting for the sale are closely related. When the managers of a company make decisions about what to sell and how much to charge for it, they use accounting information. Conversely, the accounting information reflects the underlying business process.

Sales, for example, are reported net of sales discounts given to customers. The business decision to give sales discounts will be reflected in the accounting related to those sales, and the accounting information about sales discounts will be an input into the subsequent decisions about sales discounts. A similar relationship exists between the business decision to offer a warranty and accounting for warranties. When a company makes a decision about offering a warranty on a product, it must consider the full cost of that warranty. The accounting treatment, which we will discuss in more detail later in this chapter, includes matching the full cost of a warranty with its related sale. The information needed for the decisions about warranties and the accounting treatment reflect the close link between the business process and accounting for the business transactions. As the transactions in the sales and collection process are discussed, you will see this close link between the underlying business process and the related accounting.

Business Process

L.O. 1

Understand how a business makes cash and credit sales.

Sales Cycle

We discussed the steps in the sales and collection process, shown in Exhibit 7–1, briefly back in Chapter 1. Technology has made it possible for computers to do some of those steps. Whether a firm performs the steps manually or with a computer, the objectives of those steps are the same:

- to ensure that the firm sells its goods or services to customers who will pay
- to ensure that the goods or services delivered are what the customers order
- to ensure that the customers are billed correctly
- to make sure the money received in payment gets deposited into the firm's appropriate bank accounts

Many steps in the sales and collection process—planning, marketing, and production—must take place before a company can make a sale and fill its customers' orders. To prepare the financial statements, we are particularly interested in:

1. recording the sale to make sure the revenue is recognized in the appropriate accounting period.

Exhibit 7–1 Sales and Collection Process

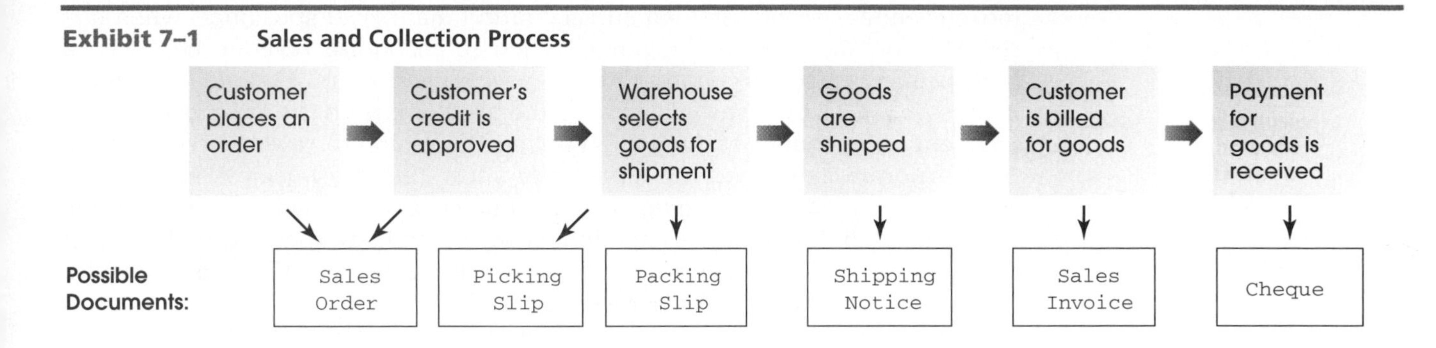

2. collecting the payment for the goods or services and making sure that the payment is properly recorded

Timing of Revenue Recognition

L.O. 1

Explain when revenue should be recognized.

In Chapter 3, you learned that the timing of business transactions and the timing of their appearance on the financial statements are important in account-

Managing Accounts Receivable

Accounts receivable is commonly one of a company's largest current assets. Because current assets support operations, managing the size of those assets and the timing of their use or conversion to cash is a crucial business activity.

How does a company control the size of its accounts receivable? The obvious way is to set credit policies that help achieve the desired level of credit sales and related collections. If the amount of a company's accounts receivable is larger than the company desires, it can tighten credit policies to reduce the amount of credit sales or it can increase collection efforts to speed up the collection of the related cash. If a company has a small amount of accounts receivable and is willing to increase that amount, the company may want to loosen its credit policies. Companies often do that when they want to increase sales.

There are other, less obvious ways for a company to manage its accounts receivable. If a company has a large amount of accounts receivable and it needs cash for operations, the company may sell its accounts receivable to a bank or finance company. This is called *factoring* accounts receivable, and the buyer is called a *factor*. When a company sells accounts receivable to a factor, the factor will keep a percentage of the value of the accounts receivable, similar to a credit card provider. For example, if a company sold $100,000 worth of receivables, the factor would pay the company a percentage of the face value of the receivables—often between 97 percent and 98 percent. The company removes the total accounts receivable from its records and records the remaining 2 percent or 3 percent as factoring expense. The factor takes ownership of the receivables and collects the accounts receivable as they come due.

Managing accounts receivable is an important part of the sales and collection business process. Accounting information—the size and collection time for accounts receivable—provides crucial input for the decisions in this process.

ing. Revenue is *recognized*—in an accounting manner of speaking—when it is reported on the income statement. When to recognize revenue has been a high-profile issue in accounting for the past several years. *Fortune Magazine*'s August 2, 1999, cover story addressed the problems with the attempts of management to "manage" earnings by varying the timing of revenue recognition.

Corporate executives are anxious to show that the business has earned revenue. Sometimes, *managing* earnings becomes *manipulating* earnings. One of the most common ways to manipulate earnings is by cheating with respect to the timing of revenue recognition. For example, the Ontario Securities Commission alleged improper revenue recognition in the prominent cases of Corel Corporation and Livent Inc. Accounting standards setters and security regulators in Canada are very concerned with when a company recognizes revenue.

Consider an information technology company—such as IBM or Hewlett Packard—that provides hardware, software, support, and training for the information systems it sells. Over a period of several years, the company will perform work to earn the revenue for this complicated sale. How should the revenue be recognized? Remember that accrual accounting is not concerned with when the cash is collected. The timing of cash collection does not dictate the timing of revenue recognition. If you do not have an answer to this question, you are not alone. The chief financial officer for IBM wrestles with this problem every day.

Recall from Chapter 2 that according to the accounting standards, revenue is recognized when "the earnings process is virtually complete" and collection is reasonably assured. Whatever a company must do to earn the revenue must be substantially done before the revenue appears on the income statement. Generally accepted accounting principles (GAAP) say that the work must be substantially completed and the cash collection must be reasonably assured. *Virtually, substantially,* and *reasonably assured* are words that leave a lot of room for interpretation and judgment. This is a very complicated problem even for the most experienced accountant.

In practice, revenue for services is recognized when the work is completed. For sales, revenue is typically recognized when the goods are delivered. For example, when Intel sells computer chips to IBM, the time the shipment leaves Intel will most likely be the point at which Intel recognizes the revenue—not when the order is placed and not when IBM pays for the purchase. Note that this step—delivery of the goods—is preceded by many crucial activities in the sales and collection process—planning, marketing, and securing orders, for example. Yet, no revenue is recognized until it is actually *earned*. It is easy to see that in many situations it may be difficult to identify exactly when the earnings process is virtually complete. Does payment have to be received before revenue is recognized? *No!* Remember, GAAP are based on accrual accounting.

Revenue Recognition: Some Examples

Let us look at some examples that illustrate the difficulty in judging the timing of revenue recognition. If you ever travelled by airplane, you probably purchased your ticket well in advance of your actual trip. Airlines usually require payment in advance. When should Air Canada recognize the revenue from your payment for a flight? Air Canada should recognize the revenue only after it has actually provided the service—transported you via the flight you purchased. As you might expect, Air Canada reports a significant liability each year on its balance sheet for *advanced ticket sales,* their term for *unearned revenue.*

Do you buy season tickets to see your favourite sports team? During the winter months, when the Toronto Blue Jays collect hundreds of thousands of dollars for season tickets, they do not recognize any revenue because they have not earned it at that time. As the baseball season progresses and games are played, the revenue is earned and, therefore, recognized. If the financial statements of the Blue Jays were publicly available, we would see a liability reflecting the unearned revenue at certain times of the year, whenever they have collected money for games not yet played. By the time a current year of revenue is earned, the Blue Jays ticket office is collecting money for season tickets for the next year.

If the Blue Jays collected $450,000 in advance ticket sales in March 2005 before the first game is played and 10 percent of the ticket sales related to games played in April, the journal entry to record the receipt of the cash in March to record collection for advance ticket sales would be:

Date	Transaction	Debit	Credit
3/2005	Cash	$450,000	
	Unearned ticket revenue		$450,000

The entry to recognize revenue earned in April from advance ticket sales would be:

Date	Transaction	Debit	Credit
4/2005	Unearned revenue	$45,000	
	Ticket revenue earned		$45,000

Both the airlines selling tickets for future flights and the baseball team selling tickets for games not yet played must make a judgment about when to recognize the revenue from their ticket sales. It is a question of timing. Many other businesses have difficult judgments to make concerning revenue recognition. We will leave those problems to more advanced accounting classes where specific problems with revenue recognition like this will be discussed.

STUDY BREAK 7-1

See How You're Doing

The Rough Riders ticket office has sold $100,000 worth of tickets for the upcoming football season. There are six home games. Prepare the journal entry to record this sale, assuming the tickets have been sold several months before the start of the football season. Prepare the journal entries to record the revenue recognition in September (half the games played) and October (one-third of the games played).

Sales Discounts

L.O. 1

Understand how sales are made and reported.

A **sales discount** is a cash discount provided by companies to encourage their customers to pay their bills promptly.

A company will frequently offer a cash discount as an incentive for customers to pay their bills promptly. This practice is common in wholesale markets. These discounts, called **sales discounts**, are just like purchase discounts, but now we are on the other side. A business decision to offer discounts must include the cost of offering such discounts. The accounting for sales discounts reflects the economic consequences of offering the discounts.

Sales discounts are typically expressed as:

2/10, n/30

Recall that what the first part—2/10—means is this: if the bill is paid within 10 days of the invoice date, then the buyer will receive a 2 percent discount off the invoice price. So, when you see 2/10, think about it as a 2 percent discount

Business Process

for paying the bill in full within 10 days of the invoice date. Recall that the second part—n/30—means: if the bill is not paid within 10 days, then the full amount—no discount—is due within 30 days. So, when you see n/30, think of *n* as meaning *no discount* and the bill must be paid in 30 days. If the bill is not paid within 30 days, it is considered past due. Just as with any bill you do not pay on time, the penalty varies. Often, there is a late fee if a bill is not paid on time.

Sales discounts work like purchase discounts. The only difference is whether you are *offering* the discount to your customers—sales discounts—or whether you are *being offered* the discount by one of your vendors—purchase discounts. As a customer, taking advantage of such discounts can amount to significant savings. As a seller, you would offer the sales discounts as an incentive for customers to buy from you and to pay you early.

A **contra-revenue account** is an account used to record reductions in its related revenue account. The contra-account is used to offset its related account.

Sales discounts are deducted from sales on the income statement. Sales discounts are recorded in a separate account called a **contra-revenue account**. It is called *contra-revenue* because it is deducted from a revenue account. The word *contra* means *opposite*. Recall that a contra-asset, like accumulated amortization, is deducted from an asset account.

Suppose you sold $1,000 worth of merchandise to a customer with the terms 2/10, n/30, and the customer paid within the discount period. The transactions would affect the accounting equation as shown:

Assets	=	Liabilities	+	Shared capital	+	Retained earnings
The sale						
+1,000 Accounts receivable						+1,000 Sales
The collection						
+980 Cash						(20) Sales discounts
(1,000) Accounts receivable						

The journal entry to record the sale of inventory, terms 2/10, n/30 is:

Date	Transaction	Debit	Credit
	Accounts receivable	$1,000	
	Sales		$1,000

The journal entry to record accounts receivable collections is:

Date	Transaction	Debit	Credit
	Cash	$980	
	Sales discounts	20	
	Accounts receivable		$1,000

The sales discount is shown as a reduction in retained earnings because a sales discount reduces net income. The income statement would show sales of $1,000 minus sales discounts of $20, giving a net sales amount of $980.

STUDY BREAK 7-2

See How You're Doing

In March, Good Buy Company sold merchandise for $3,500, terms 3/10, n/30. Customers always take advantage of cash discount offers. Prepare the journal entries to record Good Buy Company's March sales and accounts receivable collections.

Sales Returns and Allowances

L.O. 1

Understand how sales returns and allowances are recorded.

Sales returns and allowances is the account that records the amount for returned goods and allowances for defective goods.

As you may know from standing in line on December 26 to return a Christmas gift you did not like, customers often return merchandise. Most companies accept returns. When goods are returned, sometimes a full refund is issued—in cash or with a credit to the customer's account. Other times, the customer is given a partial refund or some credit toward a replacement purchase. A business typically keeps track of the amount of **sales returns and allowances** because it is useful information for evaluating the performance of its products. This, in turn, is important information for decisions, such as how much inventory to purchase and which suppliers provide high-quality goods. In the accounting records, the amount of returned goods is kept separate from sales. Sales returns and allowances is a contra-revenue account, contra to sales, just like sales discounts. For example, if you sold merchandise for $10,000 and $2,000 of it was returned, you would want to be able to see both numbers. If you simply reduced sales whenever there was a return, you would not be able to identify the amount that was sold and the amount that was returned. There is different information in the fact that sales were $10,000 but that $2,000 worth of merchandise was returned, compared with simply knowing that sales of $8,000 were made. Once again, it is clear that the accounting treatment of a business transaction is important to the underlying business process. The amount of sales returns and allowances is very important information for any merchandising firm. The amount of the returns and allowances—called sales returns and allowances—is deducted from sales to arrive at net sales on the income statement.

The journal entry for the merchandise sale is:

Date	Transaction	Debit	Credit
	Cash or accounts receivable	$10,000	
	Sales		$10,000

The entry for the return of merchandise is:

Date	Transaction	Debit	Credit
	Sales returns and allowances	$2,000	
	Cash or accounts receivable		$2,000

Payment for Goods and Services

L.O. 1

Understand how a company accounts for and collects for sales made.

Customers usually have two choices when paying for goods and services: cash or credit. A company will analyze the risks associated with a method of payment and then put controls in place to minimize them. For example, if a company collects a lot of cash, it may keep large amounts in a locked safe. That is a control that helps protect the firm from robbery. If a company makes sales on credit, it is important that the company keep accurate records so that the customers can be billed for the sales. Millions of dollars of revenue are lost by businesses each year because either they miss capturing revenue they have earned or they miss collecting payment for goods and services they have delivered. By studying cash and the related controls, you will see how a company protects one of its most important assets.

Accounting for Cash

L.O. 2

Understand the purpose of a cash reconciliation.

An important part of properly accounting for cash is comparing a firm's recorded cash balance with the firm's monthly bank statement. A key control, one used in many different business processes, is segregation of duties. For cash that means the person who has the physical custody of cash—anyone who has actual physical access to cash at any time—is not the same person who does the record keeping for cash. For example, the person who makes the daily bank deposit should not be the same person who does the record keeping for cash.

The **cash reconciliation**, or **bank reconciliation**, compares the cash balance on the company's books and the company's cash balance on the bank statement, and identifies any differences between the two amounts.

Making the comparison between the cash balance in the company's records and the cash balance shown on the bank statement is called a **cash** or **bank reconciliation**. This is more than simply part of the record keeping for cash. The cash reconciliation is a crucial part of the collection process, controlling cash. As we all know, the bottom line in our chequebook seldom agrees with the bottom line on our monthly bank statement. It is true for a business, too. The cash balance in a company's records seldom agrees with the cash balance shown on the monthly bank statement. These balances do not agree, and so they have to be reconciled.

Reconciling the bank statement with the company's books is an important element in internal control. It is the process of comparing the company's accounting records with the bank's records and resolving any differences between the two. Reconciliation requires two major steps:

The company's cash account balance reported by the bank as of the bank statement date is called the **balance per bank statement**.

The **balance per books** is the cash account balance on the company's books, and it is used to begin the cash reconciliation.

1. Take the bank's balance—the balance on the periodic bank statement, called the **balance per bank statement**—and adjust that balance for all the transactions that have been recorded in the company's books but not recorded on the bank's balance because the bank did not get the transaction recorded as of the date of its last statement.
2. Take the company's cash balance, called the **balance per books**. Adjust that balance for all the transactions that the bank has reported but that have not been recorded on the company's books.

When the two steps of the reconciliation are complete, both should show the same reconciled cash balance. That will be the actual amount of cash the company had on the date of the bank statement. The actual amount is called the *true cash balance*.

Adjustments to a company's records will always be required for the transactions the bank reported that had not been included in the company's accounting records (from step 2 of the reconciliation). Adjustments will *never* be required for transactions that had already been recorded in the company's books (from step 1 of the reconciliation).

Doing a bank reconciliation enables the company to:

1. locate any errors, whether made by the bank or the company, and
2. make adjustments to the cash account in the company's books for information the bank has reported that the company has not yet recorded in its cash account.

The bank reconciliation begins with the *balance per bank statement* and the *balance per books* as of the bank statement date. Each of these balances is then adjusted to arrive at the true cash balance. Some examples of common adjustments include:

1. Outstanding cheques are deducted from the balance per bank statement.
2. Deposits in transit are added to the balance per bank statement.
3. Service charges by the bank appear on the bank statement and are deducted from the balance per books.

4. A customer's **nonsufficient funds (NSF) cheque** is deducted from the balance per books.
5. Interest earned on a chequing account is added to the balance per books.
6. Miscellaneous charges are deducted from the balance per books; miscellaneous credits are added to the balance per books.

A **nonsufficient funds (NSF) cheque** is a customer's cheque that has been returned by the bank because the customer did not have enough funds in his or her account to cover the amount of the cheque.

The following two items are what the company's books "know"—that is, the information already included in the calculation of the company's cash balance—but the bank has not included these transactions in *its* balance yet:

1. Outstanding cheques are those the company has written but that have not cleared the bank. Deduct the total amount of the outstanding cheques from the balance per bank statement.
2. Deposits in transit are those the company made too late to get them included on the bank statement. Add the total amount of these deposits to the balance per bank statement.

The following six items are what the bank knows—that is, the information already included in the calculation of the bank's balance at the date of the bank statement—but unknown to the company until the bank statement is received:

1. Service charges are those amounts the bank charges for its services. Deduct them from the balance per books.
2. NSF cheques are cheques the bank received in the company's deposits that bounced. Deduct them from the balance per books.
3. Miscellaneous charges, including the cost of printing new cheques, for example. Deduct them from the balance per books.
4. Miscellaneous credits include previous bank charges made by mistake, for example. Add them to the balance per books.
5. Interest earned may be on chequing accounts, for example. Add this to the balance per books.
6. Notes collected by the bank. Add them to the balance per books.

The difficult part of reconciling the company's cash account with the company's bank statement is gathering all the relevant information. In a textbook, where all the information is provided, you can only see and do the easy part—preparing the bank reconciliation—also known as a cash reconciliation.

Let us take the relevant information that follows and prepare the cash reconciliation. Make sure you can identify where each amount is included in the reconciliation.

Low Company	
Balance per bank statement, May 31, 2006	$4,890
Company's books cash balance, May 31, 2006	1,774
Note collected by bank for Low Company in May	1,030
Bank charges for May	10
Deposit made after bank hours by Low Company on May 31, 2006	1,750
Customer cheque marked NSF in May	100
Cheques outstanding on May 31, 2006	
298	1,300
304	456
306	2,358

- The bank statement showed the bank had mistakenly charged Low Company for a $150 cheque that was written by the High Company.
- During May, the Low Company bookkeeper recorded payment of an account payable incorrectly as $346. The cheque was paid by the bank in the correct amount of $364.

Low Company
Bank Reconciliation
May 31, 2006

Balance per bank statement, May 31, 2006	$4,890
Add: **Deposits in transit**	1,750
(Company has made the deposit but it wasn't recorded by the bank as of the date of the bank statement)	
Bank error	150
Deduct: **Outstanding cheques** (298, 304, 306)	(4,114)
Correct (adjusted) balance, May 31, 2006	$2,676
Balance per books, May 31, 2006	$1,774
Add: **Note collected by bank**	1,030
Deduct: **Bank charges**	(10)
NSF cheque	(100)
Correct error	(18)
(+346 − 364 = −18)	
Correct (adjusted) balance, May 31, 2006	$2,676

A bank reconciliation is simply a work sheet—it is not a formal part of the company's accounting system. Nothing on it actually corrects the accounting records. For every item on the bottom half of the reconciliation, the part that started with the balance per books, the accounting records will need to be adjusted to account for the items. For example, the bank charges would be recorded as:

Assets	=	Liabilities	+	SC	+	Retained earnings
$(10) Cash						(10) Operating expenses

Every adjustment to the balance per books requires a journal entry to update the cash account, as well as adjust other accounts as needed. On the basis of the Low Company example, the following journal entries are required:

Date	Transaction	Debit	Credit
5/31/2006	Cash	$1,030	
	Notes receivable		$1,000
	Interest revenue		30

To record collection of a notes receivable by the bank (assuming $1,000 principal and $30 interest).

Date	Transaction	Debit	Credit
5/31/2006	Operating expense	$ 10	
	Accounts receivable	100	
	Accounts payable	18	
	Cash		$128

To record bank service charges and necessary account balance corrections.

STUDY BREAK 7-3

See How You're Doing

ABC Company's unadjusted book balance for cash amounted to $2,400. The company's bank statement included a debit memo for bank service charges of $100. There were two credit memos: one for $300, which represented a collection that the bank made for ABC, and the other for $100, which represented the amount of interest that ABC had earned on its bank accounts during the period. Outstanding cheques amounted to $250, and there were no deposits in transit. Prepare the journal entries that would be required to adjust ABC Company's cash account.

Accounts Receivable: Collecting Payment for Sales Made on Account

L.O. 3

Understand how accounts receivable are recorded and reported.

Accounts receivable, also called *receivables,* are current assets that arise from **sales on credit** to customers. Receivables are a current asset, usually listed just below cash on the firm's balance sheet. Unfortunately, a firm cannot expect to collect 100 percent of its accounts receivable—not all customers will pay what they owe. Some customers go bankrupt or run away to Acapulco without paying. If the amount of collected accounts receivable as a percentage of total accounts receivable is low, the uncollected receivables will be costly to the firm. However, if collected receivables as a percentage of total receivables is high, that could be costly to the firm, too. It could mean that the firm is making it difficult for customers to get credit, and this could mean eliminating potential sales and potential profits. Accounting information is crucial for decisions about credit policies.

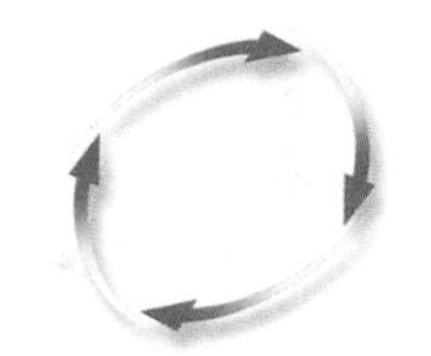

Business Process

A **credit sale** occurs when a customer does not pay cash at the time of the sale but instead agrees to pay later.

When a firm reports accounts receivable on its balance sheet, the amount reported must reflect what the business expects to collect—that is, the real asset. There are two methods of accounting for uncollectible accounts (Exhibit 7–2). The first is called the direct write-off method; the second is called the allowance method.

Direct Write-Off Method

The actual amount of accounts receivable may be reported on the balance sheet without any adjustment—to reflect expected collections—*only if* the amount of total estimated uncollectible receivables is very small—that is, only if it is not *material.* Only when a customer's account is determined to be uncollectible is the balance in Accounts Receivable reduced. The bad account is re-

Exhibit 7–2
Accounting for Uncollectible Accounts

Direct Write-Off Method:

- Not GAAP
- Write off accounts when they are identified as uncollectible and **record bad debt expense.**

Or

Allowance Method:

- Bad debt expense is estimated and matched to sales.
- Bad debt expense is recorded during end-of-period adjustment.
- GAAP

Use SALES to estimate the bad debt expense.

Or

Use ACCOUNTS RECEIVABLE to estimate the bad debt expense.

The **direct write-off method** is used when bad debt expense is recorded only after the specific customer's account is identified as uncollectible.

Bad debt expense is the expense related to the cost of extending credit to customers who do not pay.

moved from the accounting records by subtracting it from accounts receivable. This is the **direct write-off method**. The accounting equation is balanced with an expense called **bad debt expense**.

If you use the *direct write-off method,* no *bad debt expense* is recorded until a specific debt is determined to be uncollectible. For example, if you determine that a $150 account is uncollectible, to record the write-off, the journal entry is:

Date	Transaction	Debit	Credit
	Bad debt expense	$150	
	Accounts receivable		$150

The direct write-off method does *not* provide a particularly good match between the revenue (i.e., the sale) and the expense (i.e., the bad debt expense). A company may make a sale in one period and recognize the bad debt expense in a subsequent period. The direct write-off method can be used only if the amount of bad debt expense is insignificant compared with total sales, either because the company has very strict credit policies (almost everyone pays) or the company has very few credit sales. The direct write-off method is not a generally accepted accounting principle.

STUDY BREAK 7-4

See How You're Doing

Gloria's Glassware uses the direct write-off method to account for bad debts. In 2005, Gloria sold $20,000 on account. She estimated that between $100 and $150 would eventually go uncollected. No specific accounts were identified as uncollectible during 2005. In 2006, a credit customer who owed Gloria $35 filed for bankruptcy. Gloria wants to remove that customer's account from her outstanding accounts receivable. Prepare the journal entries to account for Gloria's bad debt expense that are required in 2005 and 2006.

The **allowance method** is used when bad debt expense is estimated and recognized *before* the specific customers who will not pay are identified in order to match the expense with the sales in a given accounting period.

Because the accounts that will not be collected, called **doubtful accounts**, are unidentified at year-end when the expense is estimated, the amount cannot be directly deducted from accounts receivable. When that amount appears on the balance sheet as a reduction in accounts receivable, it is called the **allowance for doubtful accounts**. The balance in accounts receivable minus the allowance for doubtful accounts gives the amount of receivables the company believes it will collect—that is, the **net realizable value** of accounts receivable.

Allowance Method

Most companies have a considerable amount of credit sales, and, as a result, they have uncollectible accounts. If the amount of those uncollectible accounts is significant, the company cannot use the direct write-off method. When preparing financial statements, the company must determine how much of its recorded accounts receivable it believes will be collected. In other words, the company must value its accounts receivable, where *value* means assigning a value, a dollar amount, to those accounts.

GAAP requires that the financial statements match the *expense* of having customers who do not pay with the *revenue* from sales made to those customers. To do this, a company will estimate the amount it believes it will not collect each period and then the company will expense that amount each period. By making this estimate, the company can go ahead and recognize the expense, and therefore, the company will be matching the expense with the related sales. This method is called the **allowance method**. It is the method required by GAAP.

Let us consider terminology.

The accounts that a company estimates it will not collect are called **doubtful accounts**. Uncollectible accounts and the amount of their losses should be *matched* with the sales that generated them.

The **allowance for doubtful accounts** appears on the balance sheet as a deduction from accounts receivable; it is subtracted from the total amount of accounts receivable. The amount of the allowance for doubtful accounts reduces the amount of accounts receivable to the amount expected to be collected in cash.

The amount expected to be collected in cash from accounts receivable is called the **net realizable value** of accounts receivable, or simply *net* accounts receivable. It is the amount the company expects to realize or, in other words, the amount the company expects to get from credit customers.

The amount remaining when the allowance for doubtful accounts is deducted from the total amount of accounts receivable is called the *book value* or the *carrying value* of accounts receivable. This terminology is used consistently for many different amounts on the balance sheet. Do you recall the name of the remainder when accumulated amortization is subtracted from the cost of equipment? It is called the book value or carrying value of equipment on the balance sheet.

The amount of expense due to **uncollectible accounts** that reduces net income is called *bad debt expense* or *uncollectible accounts expense*. By understanding the meaning of the terms, we can look at the procedures that are expressed in these terms.

Uncollectible accounts are the accounts that a company estimates it will not collect.

Uncollectible accounts expense, also called bad debt expense, is estimated at the end of each accounting period and included on the income statement as an operating expense at the estimated amount.

Uncollectible accounts expense is an expense that recognizes the losses from uncollectible accounts and, therefore, reduces net income.

There are two allowance methods of estimating uncollectible accounts expense. One method of calculating the allowance is the **sales method**; the sales method focuses on the income statement and the amount of the current period sales for which collection will not be made. For the purpose of putting the most meaningful amount on the income statement, the question is: how much of the sales will go uncollected? The bad debt expense is recorded as a percentage of sales. This method is sometimes called the income statement method.

The **sales method** is a method of estimating bad debt expense by focusing on the income statement and the amount of the sale of the current period expected to be uncollectible.

The other method is the **accounts receivable method**; this method focuses on the balance sheet. You start by estimating how much of the year-end balance of accounts receivable you believe will not be collected. This estimate of what will not be collected reduces the amount of accounts receivable on the balance sheet to the amount you *think* you will collect. For the purpose of putting the most meaningful amount on the balance sheet, the question is: how much of the total amount of accounts receivable will not be collected? The bad debt expense equals the amount needed to get the balance in the Allowance for Doubtful Accounts to the amount that needs to be subtracted from Accounts Receivable to make it equal to the net realizable value. This method is sometimes called the balance sheet method.

The **accounts receivable method** is a method of estimating bad debt expense by focusing on the balance sheet and the amount of accounts receivable expected to go uncollected.

Suppose your company had sales of $100,000 during the year. At the end of the year, when you are ready to prepare the financial statements, you need to estimate the portion of those sales for which you will not collect payment. If you knew exactly which customers would not pay, you would never extend credit to them in the first place—but you do not know that. That is why you have to *estimate* the amount of bad debt expense. You base the estimate on past experience.

Sales. Let us start with the sales method. The focus is on the income statement, and the company makes its estimate of uncollectible accounts on the basis of credit sales (or on total sales, when credit and cash sales are not easily separated). Suppose you routinely lose about 5 percent of your sales due to nonpayment. Why do you want to show bad debt expense of $5,000 on your income statement in the same period as the $100,000 worth of sales on which that $5,000 is estimated? You do this to match the expenses with the related revenues. That is why you do not wait until the nonpayers—represented as bad debts—are actually identified to recognize the expense. The adjustment records the bad debt expense that will be reported on the income statement and reduces total accounts receivable in the same period as the sale, long before the specific bad debt customers have been identified. The amount of the adjustment is recorded in a contra-asset account called the Allowance for Doubtful Accounts. The adjustment to recognize bad debt expense would affect the accounting equation as follows:

Assets	=	Liabilities	+	Share capital	+	Retained earnings
(5,000) Allowance for doubtful accounts						(5,000) Bad debt expense

Under the sales method, the bad debt expense estimate is based on a percentage of sales. If sales for the year total $100,000 and you estimate 5 percent of that amount is uncollectible, to record the estimate for bad debts on the basis of the sales method, the journal entry is:

Date	Transaction	Debit	Credit
	Bad debt expense	$5,000	
	Allowance for doubtful accounts		$5,000

A **contra-asset** is the opposite of an asset. It is deducted from its asset partner on the balance sheet.

The allowance for doubtful accounts is a **contra-asset** account. The contra-asset holds the decreases for accounts receivable that represent estimated uncollectible accounts. Those decreases cannot be recorded directly in accounts receivable because you do not know exactly which accounts will go unpaid.

Sometime later, when you eventually identify the specific uncollectible account, you will write it off—remove it from the books—by deducting the amount from accounts receivable (and the customer's outstanding balance from detailed records of the company) and also by removing the amount from the allowance for doubtful accounts. Removing the amount from accounts receivable reduces assets, and removing the amount from the allowance increases assets by reducing the amount deducted from accounts receivable on the balance sheet. There is no bad debt expense recorded when you actually write off an account using the allowance method. That is because you already recognized the bad debt expense when you made your estimate of bad debts at the time you prepared the financial statements. When you actually write off a specific account, you are simply reclassifying an *unnamed* bad debt to a *named* bad debt. You are cleaning up your books.

Suppose your company uses the allowance method and an actual $150 account is determined to be uncollectible, the journal entry reduces the allowance account and accounts receivable. No bad debt expense is recorded at the time of an actual write-off. To record the write-off of an uncollectible account:

Date	Transaction	Debit	Credit
	Allowance for doubtful accounts	$150	
	Accounts receivable		$150

Accounts Receivable. Now let us estimate bad debt expense—still using the allowance method—but this time with the balance in accounts receivable as the starting point—the accounts receivable method. Suppose the balance in accounts receivable for Good Guys Company at December 31, 2007, before any adjustments have been made, is $43,450. Note that this method focuses on the balance sheet. (In this example, we have not even been told the amount of sales.) To use the accounts receivable method, most companies prepare an aging schedule of accounts receivable. An aging schedule is an analysis of the amounts owed to a company by the length of time they have been outstanding. Exhibit 7–3 shows an aging schedule for the accounts receivable in this example.

On the basis of the aging of accounts receivable, management estimates the end-of-year uncollectible accounts receivable to be $2,078. So, the net realizable value—the amount of Accounts Receivable the company thinks it will collect—is $41,372. That amount is what Good Guys Company wants the balance sheet to show—the book value—at December 31, 2007 (Exhibit 7–4). GAAP require the company to show the total accounts receivable and the net realizable value.

In the first year of using the allowance method, Good Guys Company estimated uncollectible accounts of $2,078. Recognizing the expense has the following effect on the accounting equation:

Assets	=	Liabilities	+	Share capital	+	Retained earnings
(2,078) Allowance for doubtful accounts						(2,078) Bad debt expense

The journal entry relating to bad debt expense and the allowance for doubtful accounts for the first year is:

Date	Transaction	Debit	Credit
12/31/2007	Bad debt expense	$2,078	
	Allowance for doubtful accounts		$2,078

Remember, instead of deducting the $2,078 directly from accounts receivable, we will keep it separately in a contra-asset account, show it on the balance sheet as a deduction from accounts receivable. The bad debt expense—also known as uncollectible accounts expense—will be shown on the income statement as an operating expense.

During the following year, specific accounts will be identified as uncollectible and removed from the books. That is when specific accounts are actually written off.

Exhibit 7–3
Aging Schedule of Accounts Receivable

			Number of days past due			
Customer	**Total**	**Current**	**1–30**	**31–60**	**61–90**	**Over 90**
J. Adams	$ 500	$ 300	$ 200			
K. Brown	200	200				
L. Cannon	650		300	$ 350		
M. Dibbs	600				$ 200	$ 400
Others	41,500	25,000	10,000	3,000	2,500	1,000
	$43,450	$25,500	$10,500	$3,350	$2,700	$1,400
Estimated percentage uncollectible		1%	3%	8%	20%	50%
Total estimated bad debts	*$ 2,078*	*$ 255*	*$ 315*	*$ 268*	*$ 540*	*$ 700*

Exhibit 7–4
Balance Sheet Presentation of Accounts Receivable

Balance sheet, December 31, 2007

Current assets	
Accounts receivable	$43,450
Allowance for doubtful accounts	(2,078)
Net accounts receivable	$41,372

One problem with the allowance method of accounting for bad debts is that the bad debt expense is estimated. Suppose the estimate is wrong. When you make an estimate of uncollectible accounts for the *next* year, you adjust it for the overestimate or underestimate for the current year. Writing off the specific accounts, when you know exactly who is not going to pay, involves taking the amount of the bad account out of the allowance and accounts receivable. Because accounts receivable is an asset and the allowance for doubtful accounts is a contra-asset, both can be reduced while keeping the accounting equation in balance.

Only when you use ***the allowance method with accounts receivable as the basis for estimating bad debt expense*** do you "correct" for any inaccuracy in your estimate the previous accounting period.

Suppose M. Dibbs, who owes the company $600, has been identified as an uncollectible account. That means Good Guys has received information that makes it believe this specific account will not be collected. The effect on the accounting equation is a reduction in the allowance and a reduction in accounts receivable. There is no effect on *net* accounts receivable. Writing off a specific account is a matter of cleaning up the company's books. Instead of having only unidentified bad accounts, the company can now associate a name with $600 worth of bad debts. The expense was already recognized with the estimate made at the end of the prior year, and so no bad debt expense is recognized when a specific name is associated with the uncollectible account. Here is how writing off an account affects the accounting equation:

With the allowance method, there is no effect on a company's net accounts receivable when a specific account is written off.

Assets	=	Liabilities	+	Share capital	+	Retained earnings
(600) Accounts receivable (Dibbs) +600 (Allowance for doubtful accounts)						

The journal entry to record the write-off of M. Dibb's account is:

Date	Transaction	Debit	Credit
	Allowance for doubtful accounts	$600	
	Accounts receivable (Dibbs)		$600

There is no net effect on a company's total assets of writing off a specific account.

Suppose that by the end of the year, Good Guys Company has identified and written off $2,000 worth of specific bad accounts. (This is done on an ongoing basis during the year as the bad accounts are identified.) That means last year's estimate of bad debts of $2,078 was $78 too high. For the moment, the company will ignore that and estimate next year's bad debt expense in the same way it did for the prior year. Good Guys Company would prepare an aging schedule and again make an estimate of uncollectible accounts. Suppose the balance in Accounts Receivable was $50,000 and the aging schedule gave an estimate of uncollectible accounts of $2,500. Good Guys Company wants the balance sheet to reflect this estimate, showing the book value or carrying value of Accounts Receivable as $47,500.

At this point, we have to take into consideration that bad debts were overestimated last year. Good Guys Company will record bad debt expense this year of only $2,422 (= $2,500 − $78). The overestimate carried over from last year, $78, is still in the allowance account, and so only $2,422 needs to be added to the allowance for doubtful accounts to get the total $2,500 needed for the balance sheet. Thus, the bad debt expense recognized in the second year would be $2,422; and the allowance for doubtful accounts will be $2,500.

Date	Transaction	Debit	Credit
1/1–12/31/2008	Allowance for doubtful accounts	$1,400	
	Accounts receivable (various)		$1,400
To record the write-off of specific uncollectible accounts during the year.			
12/31/2008	Bad debt expense	$2,422	
	Allowance for doubtful accounts		$2,422
To record the estimate for bad debts based on the accounts receivable aging method ($2,500 estimated uncollectible amount − $78 overestimated amount from 2003).			

When the accounts receivable method for estimating the allowance for uncollectible accounts is used, the balances in the allowance account and the bad debt expense are only guaranteed to be equal in the first year. After that, they would be equal only if the estimate of bad debts for the previous year had been perfect—and that rarely happens. Each year, the expense usually reflects a little adjustment for the misestimate in the previous year. Making the adjustment for the allowance for doubtful accounts is done at the end of the accounting period and is an adjustment to the books.

STUDY BREAK 7-5

See How You're Doing

Suppose, at the end of the year, Pendleton Corp. records showed the following:

Allowance for doubtful accounts (excess from prior year)	100
Bad debt expense[a]	0
Accounts receivable	10,000

[a]Bad debt expense has a zero balance because no adjustments have been made.

On the basis of an aging schedule of current accounts receivable, Pendleton estimated the end-of-year uncollectible accounts receivable to be $500. Prepare the journal entry to record bad debt expense for the year.

Credit Card Sales

L.O. 4

Be able to explain the difference between credit sales and credit card sales and the business implications of the difference.

One way to avoid the risk of extending credit to your customers is to accept payment with their credit cards. Banks or other financial institutions—also known as credit card companies—issue credit cards; and the users often have to pay the issuer a fee to use the card. The credit card companies take the responsibility for evaluating a person's creditworthiness, and they also handle billing the customers and collecting payments. If a company allows customers to use a credit card to pay for their purchases, the company will have to pay the credit card company for these services. This is an important business decision, especially for small companies. The cost of allowing customers to make purchases using credit cards must be compared with the benefits. The most significant cost is the credit card expense. Benefits may include increasing the number of customers and eliminating the risks associated with extending credit to customers, as well as benefiting from the use of the cash at an earlier date. In addition, the company does not have to keep track of customers' credit, payments, and outstanding balances and will not face any problems with late or uncollectible accounts.

Business Process

This is how credit card sales are handled. The company will submit all the credit card sales receipts to the credit card company, and the credit card company will pay the company immediately. The amount the company receives will not be the gross amount of the sales. It will be a smaller amount because the credit card company will deduct a percentage of total sales as its fee for the services it provides. The company classifies the fees withheld by the credit card company as operating expenses.

Suppose that Wally's Tire Company accepts MasterCard, and total credit card sales for the day were $1,000. Suppose the MasterCard fee is 5 percent of sales. Wally's would record the sales for the day in its accounting records as follows:

Assets	=	Liabilities	+	Shareholders' equity	
Accounts receivable—				Sales revenue	+$1,000
MasterCard +$950				Credit card expense	(50)

The journal entry to record the day's credit card sales is:

Date	Transaction	Debit	Credit
	Accounts receivable (MasterCard)	$950	
	Credit card expense	50	
	Sales revenue		$1,000

When the company receives payment from MasterCard—typically daily or weekly, depending on the procedures for submitting credit card receipts to MasterCard—the company will record the increase in cash and the decrease in accounts receivable.

STUDY BREAK 7-6

See How You're Doing

During December, Magic Cow Company made a $5,000 MasterCard sale to a customer. MasterCard charges Magic Cow a fee of 3 percent of sales for its services. Prepare the journal entry to record this transaction.

Warranties

L.O. 5

Understand how a business uses warranties and how the accounting treatment and business implications are related.

A significant amount of a company's time and attention related to the sales and collection cycle is devoted to collections. As we have seen, there are crucial issues related to cash and the collection of accounts receivable for a business to handle. However, there is one more issue related to sales that is very important and has become increasingly important in our customer-service-oriented business world: warranties.

A **warranty** is an obligation of a company to replace defective goods or correct any deficiencies in performance or quality of a product.

Why would a company provide a **warranty** on a product or service? It is a sales and marketing tool, and whether or not to provide a warranty is one of the strategic decisions a company must make. For financial statement purposes, a company wants to recognize warranty expense at the time of the sale of the product. Why? The *matching principle* applies to this situation. Revenues and expenses that go together should be on the same income statement. The company does not know exactly how much it will cost to honour the warranty, and so the cost must be estimated. Because the company is not actually disbursing the cash to fix or replace the item yet—at the time of the sale—a liability is recorded along with the warranty expense. It is an adjustment made either at the time of the sale or when it is time to prepare financial statements. Liabilities are increased by the same amount as warranty expense.

The accounting treatment that requires estimates of future warranty costs reflects the underlying business process. It is crucial for a company to consider and estimate such costs to make sound business decisions. These future costs may be significant, and the accounting rules force companies to record these costs when the sale is made instead of when the warranty is honoured.

What happens when the cash is actually paid to fix a product with a warranty? No expense is recorded. Instead, the liability previously set up is reduced. So, actual expenditures result in a reduction in cash or some other asset (used to fix the item) and an equal reduction in the amount of the liability.

Let us look at an example. Suppose Brooke's Bike Company sold 100 bicycles during June and provided a one-year warranty. The accountant estimated that future repairs and replacement related to the June sales would be approximately $30 per bicycle. (No expenditures were made related to the warranties during the month of June.) What amount of warranty expense would appear on the income statement for the month ended June 30? Brooke's Bike Company would want to show the entire amount, $3,000, as an expense for the month. What is the amount of the June 30 liability (warranty payable or estimated warranty liability)? The total $3,000 would be shown as a liability on the balance sheet.

Assets	=	Liabilities	+	Share capital	+	Retained earnings
		+3000 Estimated warranty liability				(3,000) Warranty expense

The journal entry to record the estimated warranty expense and related liability for June sales is:

Date	Transaction	Debit	Credit
6/30	Warranty expense	$3,000	
	Estimated warranty liability		$3,000

July was a slow month, and Brooke's Bike Company did not sell any bicycles. However, there were several bicycles, from sales in June, which were repaired in July. The repairs cost Brooke's Bike Company $250. What amount of warranty expense would appear on the income statement for the month ended July 31? None. Brooke's Bike Company recognized the expense when the sale was made, and so no expense is recognized when the repairs are made. The cost of the repairs is deducted from the amount "owed" to the customers. So, the amount of the July 31 liability (warranty payable or estimated warranty liability) is $3,000 – 250 = $2,750.

Assets	=	Liabilities	+	Share capital	+	Retained earnings
(250) Cash		(250) Estimated warranty liability				

The journal entry to record the warranty repair costs made in July is:

Date	Transaction	Debit	Credit
7/1–7/31	Estimated warranty liability	$250	
	Cash		$250

STUDY BREAK 7-7

See How You're Doing

August was another slow month for bicycle sales (none were made), but Brooke's Bike Company did some warranty repairs on previous sales. The total spent to make warranty repairs was $500. Prepare the journal entry to record the repairs.

Finding and Using Information About Sales and Accounts Receivable

L.O. 6

Understand the information disclosed on the financial statements about accounts receivable and how to use it.

Because a company's revenue is recognized when it is earned, which is often *before* it is collected, it is important for the financial statement users to have information about the collectibility of the receivables. The way this is done is by reporting accounts receivable at their net realizable value and disclosing the balance in the allowance for doubtful accounts. Some financial statements show only the net realizable value of accounts receivable, whereas others show both the gross and the net amounts. Examples of the disclosure of accounts receivable information are shown in Exhibit 7–5.

Using the Financial Statement Information for Analysis

The **acid-test ratio**, or **quick ratio**, is current assets easily converted into cash (cash, short-term investments, net accounts receivable) divided by current liabilities. It is used to measure a company's ability to meet its short-term obligations.

Business Process

The information about sales and accounts receivable can be used to help measure a company's ability to meet its short-term obligations. When the *current ratio* is computed—that is, *current assets divided by current liabilities*—the numerator includes accounts receivable because it is a current asset. Another ratio similar to the current ratio is called the **quick ratio**, also known as the **acid-test ratio**. Instead of using all of a company's current assets in the numerator, the quick ratio uses only cash, short-term investments, and net accounts receivable. These three assets are the most liquid—easiest to convert to cash—and so they are the most readily available assets for paying off current liabilities. The quick ratio provides a stricter test of a company's ability to meet its short-term obligations.

Exhibit 7–5
Accounts Receivable and Related Disclosures

Courtesy Intrawest Corporation
Courtesy The Thomson Corporation
Courtesy Geac Investors Relations

From the Notes to Consolidated Financial Statements
Intrawest Corporation,
June 30, 2003

7 Amounts Receivable:	2003	2002
Receivables from sales of real estate	$ 54,576	$ 59,679
Ski and resort operations receivables	34,427	23,053
Loans, mortgages and notes receivable (note 20)	89,189	73,408
Funded senior employee share purchase	4,445	4,475
Other accounts receivable	20,930	14,067
	203,567	174,682
Current portion	126,725	109,948
	$ 76,842	$ 64,734

From the Notes to Consolidated Financial Statements
The Thomson Corporation,
December 31,2002

Note 6: Accounts Receivable Allowance

The change in the valuation allowances related to accounts receivable is as follows:

	2002	2001
Balance at beginning of year	381	285
Charged to expense	451	425
Write-offs	(463)	(387)
Other	3	58
Balance at end of year	372	381

From the Notes to Consolidated Statements
GEAC Computer Corporation
April 30, 2003

3. Accounts receivable and other

	April 30, 2003	2002
	$	$
Trade accounts receivable	86,962	83,096
Allowance for doubtful accounts	(8,907)	(8,431)
Other receivables	388	3,702
	78,443	78,367

Another important ratio that involves accounts receivable is the **accounts receivable turnover ratio**. This ratio—net sales divided by average net accounts receivable—measures a company's ability to collect the cash from its credit customers. Let us look at the information from two years of financial statement information for Home Depot. This particular ratio is useful for a company to track over time to make sure receivables are being collected promptly.

The **accounts receivable turnover ratio** helps a company figure out how well it is collecting for its credit sales.

(In millions)	At February 2, 2003	At February 3, 2002	At January 28, 2001
Receivables (net)	$ 1,072	$ 920	$835

	For FYE February 2, 2003	For FYE February 3, 2002
Sales	$58,247	$53,553
Accounts receivable turnover	58.48	61.03

If the average turnover of accounts receivable is 58.48, we can calculate how long it takes for Home Depot, on average, to collect for a sale. If we divide 365—the number of days in a year—by the accounts receivable turnover ratio, we will get the number of days it takes, on average, to collect accounts receivable. For the fiscal year ended (FYE) February 2, 2003, it is 365 ÷ 58.45 = 6.3 days. That is pretty good. One of the reasons it is so low is that Home Depot has a very significant amount of cash sales. Because we do not have credit sales alone to use in the numerator of the ratio, and we have to use total sales, the turnover in days is quite low. It is useful, however, to compare it with last year's turnover. Last year, the accounts receivable turnover ratio was 61.03. If we divide 365 by 61.03, we get 6 days. Home Depot has increased slightly its average time to collect its sales dollars.

If we were to calculate the accounts receivable turnover ratio for a manufacturing firm or a wholesale company, we would expect the turnover ratio to be lower and the average number of days to collect for a sale to be higher than our calculations for a retail company. That is because a wholesale company does not have as many cash sales in its total sales number. For example, look at the following information for Shoppers Drug Mart Corporation.

(Dollars in millions)	Accounts receivable at December 28, 2002	Accounts receivable at December 29, 2001	Sales for FYE December 28, 2002
	\$321	\$312	\$4,019

The accounts receivable turnover ratio is:

$$\frac{\$4,019}{(321 + 312)/2} = 12.70$$

To get the average number of days to collect accounts receivable, we divide 365 by 12.7, which gives 28.7 days. That is quite a bit longer than the average number of days for Home Depot to collect its accounts receivable.

This ratio is quite useful for internal monitoring of receivables. Remember, every day that a dollar is owed to a company—often referred to as being *tied up* in accounts receivable—is a day that the company could have had the dollar to use in the business.

Business Risks

L.O. 7

Identify the risks associated with sales, cash, and accounts receivable.

Control activities are activities intended to prevent, detect, and correct errors and irregularities relating to business risks.

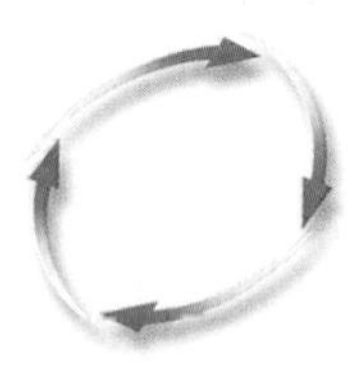

Business Process

The policies and procedures that management establishes to ensure its directions are followed are called the company's control activities. **Control activities** are designed to manage the risks a company identifies. There are three types of control activities, defined by their purpose:

- **Preventive controls** are designed to prevent an error or irregularity. For example, the policy of handling one customer at a time is a control designed to prevent a customer from getting the wrong purchase. (An *error* is an unintended mistake on the part of an employee whereas an *irregularity* is an *intentional* mistake—often fraud.)
- **Detective controls** are designed to identify when an error or irregularity has occurred. Balancing your chequebook with your monthly bank statement is a control designed to detect, or to find, any errors in your records or the bank records.

- **Corrective controls** are directed at recovering from, repairing the damage from, or minimizing the cost of an error or irregularity. Weekly staff meetings to discuss customer complaints are a control designed to correct errors. A corrective control for past errors can become a preventive control for future errors.

Preventive controls try to stop the problem before it starts—to prevent it.

Detective controls are designed to ***find*** errors.

Corrective controls are designed to ***fix*** errors.

Let us identify the specific risks associated with cash and accounts receivable and see how the three control activities discussed here are used to minimize those risks.

First, consider cash. Because it is easy to conceal and difficult to prove who owns it, cash presents a significant risk to a business. Cash is an asset that must be safeguarded with physical controls, such as locked cash drawers and safes. Such controls are preventive. When the cash must be handled, separation of duties is a crucial preventive control. For example, two or more employees should handle cash—*cheques* are considered *cash* in this context—received by mail. Also, the cash reconciliation, discussed earlier in the chapter, should be performed by a person who does not have physical control of the cash either by making deposits or by writing cheques. The purpose of these separation-of-duties controls is to reduce the opportunity for a person to walk away with the company's cash. A cash reconciliation is also a detective control. It is done to detect any errors that may have been made with the cash account. The company may also have a policy of calling the bank if any errors are identified. This would be a corrective control, one in place to ensure that any discovered errors are corrected.

Second, selling on credit creates a business risk for a company. The risk is that the customers will not pay for the purchases they have made on account. The most effective way for a company to minimize this risk is to have credit policies and procedures in place to identify which customers may be bad credit risks *before* allowing those customers to buy on account. This is a preventive control, designed to prevent the business from extending credit to customers who will not pay. The record keeping for accounts receivable should be frequent and thorough. The individual customers' accounts should be reconciled to the total amount of accounts receivable recorded in the company's records. This routine reconciliation is a detective control, designed to detect any errors in records. Finally, a company should have a policy in place to help identify customers who are slow in paying their accounts or who do not pay at all. Denying future credit to these customers may be viewed as a corrective control. This corrects a previous error in extending credit to someone who should not have been given credit and at the same time prevents future risk associated with these customers.

Understanding Excel

In this exercise you create an accounts receivable aging schedule for Tom's Wear, Inc.

Requirements

1. Open a new Excel work sheet.
2. Beginning in cell B1, input the following chart. Resize columns and wrap text as needed. See ***Hint*** that follows for help with formatting.

   Hint: You can improve the appearance of a work sheet by changing the font type and sizes and by adding colour.

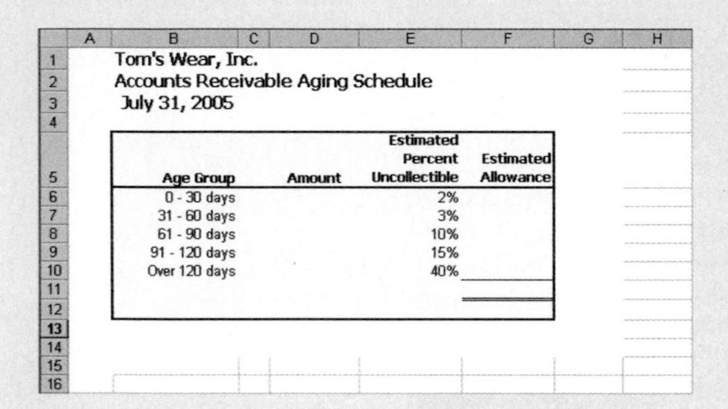

Tom's Wear, Inc.
Accounts Receivable Aging Schedule
July 31, 2005

Age Group	Amount	Estimated Percent Uncollectible	Estimated Allowance
0 - 30 days		2%	
31 - 60 days		3%	
61 - 90 days		10%	
91 - 120 days		15%	
Over 120 days		40%	

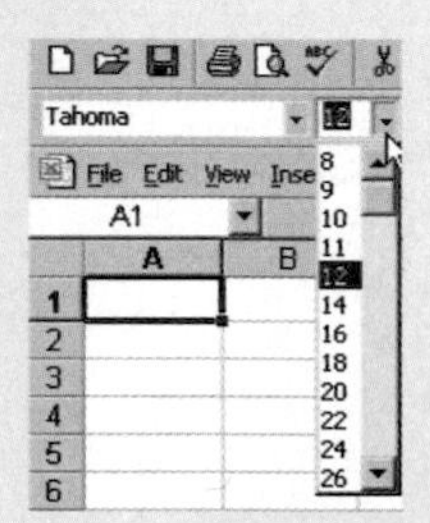

Change the font type and size by using the pull-down menus on the toolbar. To change a large area, highlight the cells you want to change before selecting the font and size. Select Tahoma or any other font you prefer.

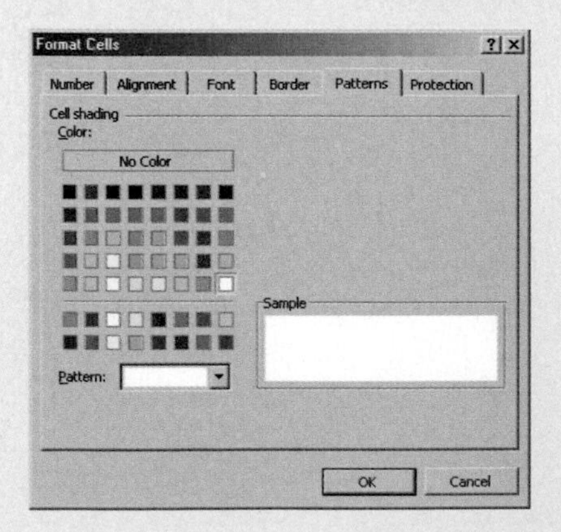

To change the colour of selected areas of a spreadsheet, select Format, Cells, and Patterns. Highlight the areas to be changed and select the colour of your choice. Colours can be layered. In other words, highlight A1 to G15 and choose white. Next, highlight B5 to F12 and choose light yellow.

3. At the end of June, the Tom's Wear, Inc. accounts receivable balance was as follows:

Accounts receivable	$44,100
Less: allowance	(1,320)
Net accounts receivable	$42,780

   Tom's July sales totalled $99,000 (all on account), $37,000 of accounts receivable were collected, and $1,000 was written off as uncollectible. On the basis of this information, calculate the balance of accounts receivable and the allowance account at the end of July before the adjustment for bad debts.

4. Assume for this problem only that Tom has done an aging of his July 31 accounts receivable balance and determined the following:

Accounts Due in	% of Total Accounts Receivable
0–30 days	55
31–60 days	30
61–90 days	10
90–120 days	4
Over 120 days	1
	100

   On the basis of your calculations from step 3, determine the dollar amount for each category in the aging schedule and complete the aging schedule. Remember to use formulas, where appropriate.

5. Beginning in cell B17, input and complete the following information at July 31, 2005:

Accounts receivable	$
Less: allowance	( )
Net accounts receivable	$

   Hint: All these numbers should be calculated using formulas. Use the information from your aging schedule to create a formula for accounts receivable.

6. Print your file and save it to disk. Name your file TomsWear7.

Summary Problem: Tom's Wear Increases Sales in June

When Tom began his T-shirt business, his first customers were a few friends, so collection of accounts receivable was not a problem. Then he branched out to sporting goods stores and local schools. Again, bad debts did not represent a significant problem, and so Tom's Wear did not use the allowance method of accounting for bad debts. However, since hiring Sam to manage the inventory flow, Tom has been able to devote his time to increasing sales. Tom's customer base has now grown to a size that makes it necessary for him to give serious attention to the collectibility of his accounts receivable. The June 1 balance sheet is shown in Exhibit 7–6, followed by the transactions for June (Exhibit 7–7). Study the transactions during June before you prepare the adjustments and the financial statements for June.

As part of the month-end adjustments, Tom has decided to set up an allowance for doubtful accounts. He has decided to use the sales method and, after consulting with some local businesses and some accountants, he will set up an allowance equal to 3 percent of credit sales.

Tom has also decided to offer a warranty against defects in his T-shirts. He estimates that 2 percent of total sales will provide an adequate amount for his warranty obligations.

Both of these decisions are based on the matching principle. Tom wants to match the bad debt and warranty expenses with the sales to which they pertain, even though he does not know how many customers will not pay or how many customers will return a T-shirt.

At the end of the quarter (June 30), Tom's accountant suggests the company classify next year's loan payment as a current liability. So, Tom's Wear will divide the $30,000 long-term note into current and long-term portions.

Exhibit 7–6

tom's wear

Tom's Wear, Inc.
Balance Sheet
June 1, 2005

Assets		Liabilities and shareholders' equity	
Cash	$ 8,805	Accounts payable	$ 4,200
Accounts receivable	8,900	Interest payable	500
Inventory	4,700	Unearned revenue	4,950
Prepaid insurance	250	Salaries payable	723
Prepaid rent	600	Payroll taxes payable	277
Prepaid Web service	250	Other payables	77
Total current assets	23,505	Total current liabilities	10,727
Computer (net of $300 accumulated amortization)	3,700	Notes payable	30,000
Van (net of $1,595 accumulated amortization)	28,405	Total liabilities	40,727
		Common shares	5,000
		Retained earnings	9,883
Total assets	$55,610	Total liabilities and shareholders' equity	$55,610

Exhibit 7–7
Transactions for June 2005 for Tom's Wear, Inc.

tom's wear

1	June 1	Pays cash of $2,400 for 2 months of rent on the warehouse, beginning June 15
2	June 5	Pays Sam Cubby's salary for May; gross pay, $1,000; and also makes payment to CCRA for income tax, CPP, and EI payable.
3	June 10	Delivers the second half of the shirts to the school system—450 shirts—and recognizes revenue of $4,950
4	June 12	Pays accounts payable of $4,200
5	June 14	Signs a contract with the school system to deliver 500 shirts per month for September through December, at a price of $10 per shirt; the shirts will be delivered on the last day of the month with the invoice attached to the delivery; Tom has serious competition for this deal, so he decides to offer the purchase terms, 2/10, n/30, to the school system to secure the contract
6	June 20	Purchases 5,000 T-shirts from a new vendor; the cost of the shirts is only $3.79 each, but the shipping terms are free on board (FOB) shipping point; the shipping costs for the month are $50; Tom's Wear pays cash for the shipping, but makes the purchase on account
7	June 20	Tom's sales efforts pay off with the addition of several sporting goods stores as customers; during June, the company sells 4,000 shirts to various stores for $11 each; all sales are on account
8	June 21	Collects $8,800 on accounts receivable
9	June 30	Pays miscellaneous operating expenses of $600 for the month
10	June 30	Pays a dividend of $1,000

Note: The van was driven 8,000 kilometres in June.

Required:

Make the needed journal entries and adjustments to the accounts, post to T-accounts, prepare an adjusted trial balance, and then prepare the four basic financial statements (solution is provided near the end of the chapter).

Answers to Study Break Questions

STUDY BREAK 7-1

Date	Transaction	Debit	Credit
	Cash	$100,000	
	Unearned ticket revenue		$100,000
To record collection of advance ticket sales.			
9/1–9/30	Unearned revenue	$ 50,000	
	Ticket revenue earned		$ 50,000
To recognize revenue earned from advance ticket sales.			
10/1–10/31	Unearned revenue	$ 33,333	
	Ticket revenue earned		$ 33,333
To recognize revenue earned from advance ticket sales.			

STUDY BREAK 7-2

1. The company will record sales as $3,500 and then deduct the sales discounts on the face of the income statement.
2. Cash collected will be: $\$3,500 \times 0.97 = \$3,395$ (net sales)

Date	Transaction	Debit	Credit
3/1–3/31	Accounts receivable	$3,500	
	Sales		$3,500
To record the sale of inventory, terms 3/10, n/30			
	Cash	$3,395	
	Sales discounts	105	
	Accounts receivable		$3,500
To record accounts receivable collections.			

STUDY BREAK 7-3

Book balance	$2,400
Interest	100
Collection	300
Service charge	(100)
True cash balance	$2,700

Date	Transaction	Debit	Credit
	Cash	$300	
	Miscellaneous operating expenses	100	
	Accounts receivable		$300
	Interest revenue		100
To record bank statement adjustments.			

STUDY BREAK 7-4

With use of the direct write-off method, only the accounts specifically identified and written off are counted as bad debt expense. (Contrast this with the allowance method where the *estimates* are the bad debt expense and the specific write offs have no effect.) In this case, there is no bad debt expense for 2005. Bad debt expense for 2006 is $35.

Date	Transaction	Debit	Credit
2005	No journal entries required		
2006	Bad debt expense	$35	
	Accounts receivable		$35
To record the write-off of an uncollectible account.			

STUDY BREAK 7-5

Date	Transaction	Debit	Credit
12/31	Bad debt expense	$400	
	Allowance for doubtful accounts		$400
To record bad debt expense. $500 estimate less excess from prior year.			

STUDY BREAK 7-6

Sale is $5,000.
Accounts receivable = $5,000 × 0.97 = $4,850.
The remaining 3 percent will be classified as credit card expense.
At the time of the sale, Accounts Receivable increase by $4,850, Sales increase by $5,000, and Expenses (credit card expense) increase by $150. When the cash is received from MasterCard, Accounts Receivable will decrease by $4,850, and cash will increase by $4,850.

Date	Transaction	Debit	Credit
Dec.	Accounts receivable (MasterCard)	$4,850	
	Credit card expense	150	
	Sales revenue		$5,000
To record credit card sales.			

STUDY BREAK 7-7

- This problem is a continuation of the example started in the chapter text.
- There is *no* Warranty Expense. That was previously recorded when the sales were made.
- The Warranty Liability is the amount originally recorded minus any amounts that have been spent on warranty repairs to date; in this case, $2,250.

Date	Transaction	Debit	Credit
8/1–8/31	Estimated warranty liability	$500	
	Cash		$500
To record August warranty repairs.			

Solution to Summary Problem

Transaction 1
Pays cash of $2,400 for two months' rent on the warehouse beginning June 15.

Date	Transaction	Debit	Credit
6/1/2005	Prepaid rent	$2,400	
	Cash		$2,400
To record the prepayment of two months' rent.			

Transaction 2
Pays Sam Cubby's salary for May; gross pay $1,000; also makes the payroll tax deposit, including the employer's matching payroll taxes.

Date	Transaction	Debit	Credit
6/5/2005	Salaries payable	$723	
	Payroll taxes payable	277	
	Other payables	77	
	Cash		$1,077
To record payment of salary and taxes.			

Transaction 3
Delivers the second half of the shirts to the school system (450 shirts) and recognizes revenue of $4,950.

Date	Transaction	Debit	Credit
6/10/2005	Unearned revenue	$4,950	
	Revenue		$4,950
To record delivery of the second half of the shirts to the school.			
6/10/2005	Cost of goods sold	$1,865	
	Inventory		$1,865
To record cost of goods sold (125 @ $4.00 and 325 @ $4.20).			

Transaction 4
Pays accounts payable of $4,200.

Date	Transaction	Debit	Credit
6/12/2005	Accounts payable	$4,200	
	Cash		$4,200
To record payment on account.			

Transaction 5
Signs a contract with the school system to deliver 500 shirts per month for September through December at a price of $10 per shirt. No journal entry is required.

Transaction 6
Purchases 5,000 T-shirts @ $3.79 each; shipping terms—FOB shipping point and shipping costs of $50. Tom's Wear pays cash for the shipping but makes the purchase on account.

Date	Transaction	Debit	Credit
6/20/2005	Inventory	$19,000	
	Cash		$ 50
	Accounts payable		18,950
To record the purchase of 5,000 T-shirts, FOB shipping point at $3.79 each + $50 shipping cost (cost: $3.80 per shirt).			

Transaction 7
Sells 4,000 shirts to various stores for $11 each. All sales are on account.

Date	Transaction	Debit	Credit
6/20/2005	Accounts receivable	$44,000	
	Revenue		$44,000
To record the sale of 4,000 T-shirts on account.			
6/20/2005	Cost of goods sold	$15,470	
	Inventory		$15,470
To record cost of goods sold (675 @ $4.20 and 3,325 @ $3.80).			

Transaction 8
Collects $8,800 in accounts receivable.

Date	Transaction	Debit	Credit
6/21/2005	Cash	$8,800	
	Accounts receivable		$8,800
To record the collection of accounts receivable.			

Transaction 9
Miscellaneous operating expenses for the month are $600.

Date	Transaction	Debit	Credit
6/30/2005	Other operating expenses	$600	
	Cash		$600
To record the payment of miscellaneous operating expenses.			

Transaction 10
Tom's Wear pays a dividend of $1,000.

Date	Transaction	Debit	Credit
6/30/2005	Retained earnings	$1,000	
	Cash		$1,000
To record the payment of a cash dividend.			

Adjustment 1
Record amortization expense for June: $100 for the computer and $1,160 for the van (8,000 kilometres × $0.145).

Date	Transaction	Debit	Credit
6/30/2005	Amortization expense	$1,260	
	Accumulated amortization: computer		$ 100
	Accumulated amortization: van		1,160
To record June amortization expense.			

Adjustment 2
Record interest expense on the van note.

Date	Transaction	Debit	Credit
6/30/2005	Interest expense	$250	
	Interest payable		$250
To record interest expense for June.			

Adjustment 3
Record insurance expense of $100 for the month of June.

Date	Transaction	Debit	Credit
6/30/2005	Insurance expense	$100	
	Prepaid insurance		$100
To record insurance expense for June.			

Adjustment 4
Record rent expense of $1,200 for the month of June.

Date	Transaction	Debit	Credit
6/30/2005	Rent expense	$1,200	
	Prepaid rent		$1,200
To record rent expense for June.			

Adjustment 5
Record Web costs of $50 for June.

Date	Transaction	Debit	Credit
6/30/2005	Other operating expenses	$50	
	Prepaid Web service		$50
To record Web maintenance services for June.			

Adjustment 6
Accrue Sam Cubby's salary for June, including the employer portion of payroll taxes.

Date	Transaction	Debit	Credit
6/30/2005	Salary expense	$1,000	
	Employer's payroll tax expense	77	
	Payroll taxes payable		$277
	Other payables		77
	Salaries payable		723
To record the accrual of Sam Cubby's salary, withholding, and payroll taxes.			

Adjustment 7
Bad debt estimate = 3 percent of credit sales.

Date	Transaction	Debit	Credit
6/30/2005	Bad debt expense	$1,320	
	Allowance for doubtful accounts		$1,320
To record the bad debt estimate for June ($44,000 × 3%).			

Adjustment 8
Warranty liability estimate = 2 percent of total sales.

Date	Transaction	Debit	Credit
6/30/2005	Warranty expense	$979	
	Warranties payable		$979
To record the estimated warranty liability for June ($48,950 × 2%).			

T-Accounts for Tom's Wear with June journal entries and adjustments

Cash

	Debit	Credit	
BB	$8,805	$2,400	1
8	8,800	1,077	2
		4,200	4
		50	6
		600	9
		1,000	10
	$8,278		

Accounts receivable

	Debit	Credit	
BB	$8,900	$8,800	8
7a	44,000		
	$44,100		

Allowance for doubtful accounts

	Debit	Credit	
		$1,320	Adj-7
		$1,320	

Inventory

	Debit	Credit	
BB	$4,700	$1,865	3b
6	19,000	15,470	7b
	$6,365		

Prepaid insurance

	Debit	Credit	
BB	$250	$100	Adj-3
	$150		

Prepaid Web service

	Debit	Credit	
BB	$250	$50	Adj-5
	$200		

Prepaid rent

	Debit	Credit	
BB	$600	$1,200	Adj-4
1	2,400		
	$1,800		

Equipment: Computer

	Debit	Credit	
BB	$4,000		
	$4,000		

Accumulated Amortization: Computer

	Debit	Credit	
		$300	BB
		100	Adj-1
		$400	

Equipment: van

	Debit	Credit	
BB	$30,000		
	$30,000		

Accumulated Amortization: van

	Debit	Credit	
		$1,595	BB
		1,160	Adj-1
		$2,755	

Accounts payable

	Debit	Credit	
4	$4,200	$4,200	BB
		18,950	6
		$18,950	

Interest payable

	Debit	Credit	
		$500	BB
		250	Adj-2
		$750	

Unearned revenue

	Debit	Credit	
3a	$4,950	$4,950	BB
		$ 0	

Payroll taxes payable (withheld)

	Debit	Credit	
2	277	$277	BB
		277	Adj-6
		$277	

Other payables

	Debit	Credit	
2	77	$77	BB
		77	Adj-6
		$77	

Salaries payable

	Debit	Credit	
2	723	$723	BB
		723	Adj-6
		$723	

Warranties payable

	Debit	Credit	
		$979	Adj-8
		$979	

Notes payable

	Debit	Credit	
		$30,000	BB
		$30,000	

Common shares

	Debit	Credit	
		$5,000	BB
		$5,000	

T-Accounts for Tom's Wear with June journal entries and adjustments *(continued)*

Retained earnings

	Debit	Credit	
10	$1,000	$9,883	BB
		$8,883	

Revenue

	Debit	Credit	
		$4,950	3a
		44,000	7a
		$48,950	

Cost of goods sold

	Debit	Credit
3b	$1,865	
7b	15,470	
	$17,335	

Amortization expense

	Debit	Credit
Adj-1	$1,260	
	$1,260	

Employer's payroll tax

	Debit	Credit
Adj-6	$77	
	$77	

Other operating expenses

	Debit	Credit
9	$600	
Adj-5	50	
	$650	

Insurance expense

	Debit	Credit
Adj-3	$100	
	$100	

Rent expense

	Debit	Credit
Adj-4	$1,200	
	$1,200	

Interest expense

	Debit	Credit
Adj-2	$250	
	$250	

Salary expense

	Debit	Credit
Adj-6	$1,000	
	$1,000	

Bad debt expense

	Debit	Credit
Adj-7	$1,320	
	$1,320	

Warranty expense

	Debit	Credit
Adj-8	$979	
	$979	

Tom's Wear, Inc.
Adjusted Trial Balance
June 30, 2005

	Debits	Credits
Cash	$ 8,278	
Accounts receivable	44,100	
Allowance for bad debts		$ 1,320
Inventory	6,365	
Prepaid insurance	150	
Prepaid Web service	200	
Prepaid rent	1,800	
Equipment: computer	4,000	
Accumulated amortization: computer		400
Equipment: van	30,000	
Accumulated amortization: van		2,755
Accounts payable		18,950
Interest payable		750
Payroll taxes payable		277
Other payables		77
Salaries payable		723
Warranties payable		979
Notes payable		30,000
Common shares		5,000
Retained earnings		8,883
Revenue		48,950
Cost of goods sold	17,335	
Amortization expense	1,260	
Employer's payroll tax expense	77	
Other operating expense	650	
Insurance expense	100	
Rent expense	1,200	
Interest expense	250	
Salary expense	1,000	
Bad debt expense	1,320	
Warranty expense	979	
Totals	*$119,064*	*$119,064*

Tom's Wear, Inc.
Income Statement
For the Month Ended June 30, 2005

Sales revenue		$48,950
Expenses		
Cost of goods sold	$17,335	
Insurance expense	100	
Rent expense	1,200	
Amortization expense	1,260	
Salary expense	1,000	
Employer's payroll tax expense	77	
Other operating expenses	650	
Warranty expense	979	
Bad debt expense	1,320	
Interest expense	250	24,171
Net income		$24,779

Tom's Wear, Inc.
Statement of Retained Earnings
For the Month Ended June 30, 2005

Beginning retained earnings	$ 9,883
Net income for the month	24,779
Dividends	(1,000)
Ending retained earnings	33,662

Tom's Wear, Inc.
Balance Sheet
At June 30, 2005

Assets		Liabilities and shareholders' equity	
Cash	$ 8,278	Accounts payable	$18,950
Accounts receivable (net of allowance of $1,320)	42,780	Interest payable	750
		Warranty liability	979
Inventory	6,365	Salaries payable	723
Prepaid insurance	150	Payroll taxes payable	277
Prepaid rent	1,800	Other payables	77
Prepaid Web service	200	Current portion of long-term note	6,000
Total current assets	59,573		
		Total current liabilities	27,756
Computer (net of $400 accumulated amortization)	3,600	Notes payable	24,000
Van (net of $2,755 accumulated amortization)	27,245	Total liabilities	51,756
		Common shares	5,000
		Retained earnings	33,662
Total assets	$90,418	Total liabilities and shareholders' equity	$90,418

Tom's Wear, Inc.
Cash Flow Statement
For the Month Ended June 30, 2005

Cash from operating activities		
Cash collected from customers	$ 8,800	
Cash paid for operating expenses	(4,127)	
Cash paid to vendors	(4,200)	
Total cash from operations		$ 473
Cash from investing activities		0
Cash from financing activities		
Dividends paid to owner		(1,000)
Net increase (decrease) in cash		$ (527)
Beginning cash balance (June 01)		8,805
Ending cash balance (June 30)		$ 8,278

Questions

1. When is revenue recognized?
2. What is the difference between recognizing revenue and realizing revenue?
3. Which asset is extremely easy to steal because there is no common or practical way to identify the owner?
4. What is a major control for safeguarding cash?
5. What are the two methods for accounting for bad debts?
6. What are the main issues in controlling and managing the collection of receivables?
7. How is the net realizable value for accounts receivable calculated? On which financial statement is net realizable value shown?
8. What is the reason for using the allowance method?
9. If a company uses the allowance method, what effect does writing off a specific account have on income?
10. When using the allowance method, what two ways are used to estimate the amount of bad debts?
11. Which method of calculating the allowance provides the best number for the income statement? Explain.
12. Which method of calculating the allowance provides the best number for the balance sheet? Explain.
13. What is the reason for estimating warranty expense? Why not record the expense as it is incurred to actually honour the warranties?

Short Exercises

L.O. 1

SE7-1 Static Company had sales of $100,000 during January. Customers returned $5,000 worth of merchandise for a full refund. Static Company also reduced a customer's invoice balance by $150 due to a minor defect in the product shipped. Static anticipates that in the future, it will spend $1,200 to honour warranties related to January sales. How much should Static report on the January income statement for net sales?

L.O. 2

SE7-2 For each of the following items, indicate whether or not the balance per books should be adjusted. For each item that affects the balance per books, indicate whether the item should be added to (+) or subtracted from (–) the balance per books.

Item	Balance per books adjusted?	+/−
Outstanding cheques	No	N/A
Service charge by bank		
NSF cheque from customer		
Deposits in transit		
Error made by the bank		
Note receivable collected by the bank		

SE7-3 For each item listed next, indicate whether or not the balance per bank should be adjusted. For each item that affects the balance per bank, indicate whether the item should be added to (+) or subtracted from (–) the balance per bank.

L.O. 2

Item	Balance per bank adjusted?	+/−
Outstanding cheques	Yes	—
Service charge by bank		
NSF cheque from customer		
Deposits in transit		
Error made by the bank		
Note receivable collected by the bank		

SE7-4 Datatech's accountant wrote a cheque to a supplier for $1,050 but erroneously recorded it on the company's books as $1,500. She discovered this when she saw the monthly bank statement and noticed that the cheque had cleared the bank for $1,050. How would this be handled in a bank reconciliation? Would Datatech need to make any adjustments to its accounting records?

L.O. 2

SE7-5 On the September bank statement, the ending balance as of September 30 was $9,550.48. The cash balance in the books was $10,053.57. Consider the following information:

L.O. 2

Outstanding cheques	$1,876.67
Interest earned on the account	32.18
NSF cheque from G. Murphy	391.55
Deposits in transit	2,020.39

What is the company's true cash balance on September 30?

SE7-6 Beret and Sons Furniture has a liberal credit policy and has been experiencing a high rate of uncollectible accounts. The company estimates that 5 percent of credit sales become bad debts. Due to the significance of this amount, the company uses the *allowance* method for accounting for bad debts. During 2006, credit sales amounted to $430,000. The year-end accounts receivable balance was $192,000. What was the bad debt expense for the year?

L.O. 3

SE7-7 Quality Autoparts Company sells merchandise to auto repair shops and car dealerships. Quality has always used the direct *write-off method* of accounting for bad debts because of very tight credit policies and predominantly cash sales. During 2007, credit sales were $520,450, and the year-end balance in accounts receivable is $173,500. Quality estimates that about half of 1 percent of the accounts receivable will not be collected. Unfortunately, just prior to the end of 2007, one of Quality's best customers filed for bankruptcy and has informed Quality that it will not be able to pay its outstanding balance of $23,000. That amount is included in the $173,500 accounts receivable balance. How should Quality record this in its accounting records? That is, what amount of bad debt expense will Quality recognize on the income statement for the year ended December 31, 2007?

L.O. 3

L.O. 3

SE7-8 On January 1, 2006, a company's accounts receivable balance was $8,900 and the allowance for doubtful accounts normal balance was $600. This information came from the December 31, 2005, balance sheet. During 2006, the company reported $77,000 of credit sales. During 2006, $400 of specific receivables were written off as uncollectible. Cash collections of receivable were $69,000 for the year. The company estimates that 3 percent of the year-end accounts receivable will be uncollectible. What is the bad debt expense for the year ending December 31, 2006?

L.O. 3

SE7-9 At the end of the year, before any adjustments are made, the accounting records for Raley Company show a balance of $100,000 in accounts receivable. The allowance for doubtful accounts has a normal balance of $2,000. (This means the estimate of bad debt expense last year was too large by $2,000.) The company uses accounts receivable to estimate bad debt expense. An analysis of accounts receivable accounts results in an estimate of $27,000 of uncollectible accounts. What is bad debt expense for the year? What is the net realizable value of accounts receivable on the year-end balance sheet?

L.O. 3, 6

SE7-10 Bett, Inc. had the following balances at year-end prior to recording any adjustments:

Credit sales	$160,000
Accounts receivable	30,000
Allowance for doubtful accounts	100 shortfall[a]

[a]Bett wrote off $100 more accounts during the year than estimated; that is, allowance was too small this year.

Following completion of an aging analysis, the accountant for Bett estimated that $1,100 of the receivables would be Doubtful Accounts. What amount of bad debt expense would Bett show on the year's income statement? What information would be disclosed on the balance sheet?

L.O. 3

SE7-11 The 2005 year-end accounts show the following normal balances: Accounts Receivable (AR), $50,000; Allowance for Doubtful Accounts, $1,000; and Net Sales, $200,000. By using the sales method, the company estimates 2 percent of sales will become uncollectible. What is the bad debt expense for 2005? What will be the net realizable value of AR on the year-end balance sheet?

L.O. 3

SE7-12 The 2007 year-end accounts show the following normal balances: Accounts Receivable (AR), $50,000; Allowance for Doubtful Accounts, $500; and Net Sales, $400,000. By using the accounts receivable method, the company estimates $4,000 of ending accounts receivable will be uncollectible. What is the bad debt expense for 2007? What will be the net realizable value of AR on the year-end balance sheet?

L.O. 4

SE7-13 Selby Company accepts MasterCard from its customers. MasterCard charges Selby Company 4 percent of sales for its services. During 2008, Selby's customers used MasterCard to purchase $43,560 worth of merchandise. How much did Selby show as sales on the income statement for the year ended December 31, 2008? How much cash did Selby actually receive from these sales?

L.O. 4

SE7-14 Harpo, Inc. accepts VISA from its customers. VISA charges Harpo a fixed fee of $100 per month plus 3 percent of VISA sales. If Harpo had VISA sales of $435,500 during 2005, how much did Harpo pay VISA for its services?

L.O. 5

SE7-15 Matt's Rug Company had sales of $100,000 in 2007. The company expects to incur future warranty expenses related to these sales that will amount to 6 percent of sales. There were $4,000 of warranty obligations paid in cash during 2007 related to the 2007 sales. How much warranty expense would Matt's Rug Company show on the income statement for the 2007 fiscal year? What is the amount of the warranty liability on the balance sheet at the end of 2007?

SE7-16 When Handle's Pet Shop sells a puppy, it provides a health warranty for the little critter. If a puppy should become ill in the first two years after the sale, Handle's Pet Shop will pay the vet bill up to $200. Because this is normally a significant expense for the shop, the accountant insists that Handle's Pet Shop record an estimated warranty liability at the end of every year before the financial statements are prepared. On December 31, 2008, the accountant made the appropriate entry to record that liability. On March 30, 2009, the store received a $50 vet bill from one of its customers, who had bought a puppy in 2008. Handle's Pet Shop wrote a cheque for $50 to reimburse the puppy's owner. What effect did this payment have on the financial statements for the year ended December 31, 2009, of Handle's Pet Shop? L.O. 5

Exercises

E7-1 Rachet's Tool Company sells tools to hardware and plumbing supply stores. Mr. Rachet, the owner, has asked you for some advice about the flow of documents in his business. Currently, he has instructed his accounting clerk to prepare an invoice for the customer by using the customer's original sales order. After it is prepared, the accounting clerk promptly mails it to the customer. The customer's sales order is copied and sent to the inventory control clerk, who passes the copy along to the shipping department with the goods. For some reason, Mr. Rachet's customers are continually complaining about inaccurate invoices. To help Mr. Rachet solve this problem, what information would you like to have? What suggestions would you make? L.O. 1

E7-2 The bank statement for David's Landscaping as of February 28 had an ending balance of $38,334.96. Also listed on the statement was a service charge for $16. A cheque that David wrote to pay for equipment purchased February 25 had not cleared the bank yet—the amount was $7,250. Deposits in transit were $4,115.73. David's bank collected a $1,100 note for him in February. After reviewing the bank statement and cancelled cheques, David discovered that the bank mistakenly deducted $297.15 from his account for a cheque that was written by David's Lighting. L.O. 2

Calculate the true cash balance as of February 28.

E7-3 The advertising firm, Carolyn & Company, had the following information available concerning its cash account for the month of July: L.O. 2

Balance per Carolyn & Company books, July 31		$18,280.54
Outstanding cheques		6,440.29
NSF cheque from customer		2,800.00
Note collected by bank		3,000.00
Deposits in transit		5,860.50
Miscellaneous bank fees		
Charge for collection of note	$25.00	
Order for cheques	62.50	
Interest earned on bank account		$ 421.38

Calculate the true cash balance as of July 31.

E7-4 Prepare a bank reconciliation for Jay Gordon's Brake Shop for the month of November using the following information: L.O. 2

Balance per First National Bank statement at November 30	$14,003.90
Outstanding cheques	5,765.44
NSF cheques from customer	366.71
Deposits in transit	3,542.26
Interest revenue earned on chequing account	184.56
Service charge	30.00
Cash balance per Jay Gordon's Brake Shop's books at November 30	$11,992.87

After appropriate adjustments resulting from this reconciliation are recorded in the books, what will be the effect on net income (i.e., will net income be increased or decreased) and by what amount?

L.O. 2

E7-5 Prepare a bank reconciliation for Cheri's Bakery using the following information:

Company's cash account balance, March 31	$5,599.20
Bank statement ending balance, March 31	3,904.37
Deposits in transit	2,504.57
Outstanding cheques	
3941	633.15
3956	194.59

Error found in Cheri's books—cheque 3928 for $142.60 was correctly deducted from the bank account, but was mistakenly recorded in the books as $124.60.

L.O. 3

E7-6 Compute Right uses the allowance method to account for bad debts. Indicate the effect that each of the following transactions will have on gross accounts receivables, the allowance for doubtful accounts, net accounts receivable, and bad debt expense. Use (+) for increase, (–) for decrease, and (0) for no effect.

a. A customer pays his bill.
b. Of $500,000 in sales, 1 percent is estimated to be uncollectible.
c. Of $100,000 in accounts receivable, 5 percent is estimated to be uncollectible. Last year, an excess of $400 beyond what was expected was written off.
d. A specific account receivable previously written off is reinstated.

L.O. 3

E7-7 A company started the year with Accounts Receivable of $20,000 and an Allowance for Doubtful Accounts of $2,500. During the year, sales (all on account) were $80,000 and cash collections for sales amounted to $77,000. Also, $2,400 worth of uncollectible accounts were specifically identified and written off. Then at year-end, the company estimates that 5 percent of ending Accounts Receivable will be uncollectible. (The company tightened up its credit policy this year.) Answer the following questions:

a. What amount will be shown on the year-end income statement for bad debt expense?
b. What is the balance in the allowance after all entries and adjustments have been made?

L.O. 3

E7-8 The Beautiful Bow Company uses the allowance method to account for bad debts. During 2004, the company recorded $800,000 in credit sales. At the end of 2000, before adjustments, account balances were Accounts Receivable, $120,000; and Allowance for Doubtful Accounts, $3,000 (normal balance). If bad debt expense is estimated to be 3 percent of credit sales, how much bad debt expense will be on the year-end income statement?

L.O. 3, 6

E7-9 Havana Honda, Inc. uses the allowance method for bad debts and adjusts the allowance for doubtful accounts to a desired amount on the basis of an aging of accounts receivable. At the beginning of 2004, the allowance for doubtful accounts had a balance of $18,000. During 2004, credit sales totalled $480,000 and receivables of $14,000 were written off. The year-end aging indicated that a $21,000 allowance for doubtful accounts was required. What is the bad debt expense for 2004? What information will be disclosed on the balance sheet at year-end? What information does this provide someone who is evaluating Havana Honda's annual performance?

L.O. 3, 6

E7-10 Western Wear Corp. began 2007 with accounts receivable of $1,240,000 and a normal balance in the allowance for doubtful accounts of $36,000. During 2007, credit sales totalled $5,190,000 and cash collected from customers totalled $5,380,000. Also, actual write offs of specific accounts receivable in 2007 were $33,000. At the end of the year, an accounts receivable aging schedule indicated a required allowance of $32,300. No accounts receivable previously written off were collected.

a. What is the net realizable value of accounts receivable at year-end?
b. What is the bad debt expense for the year 2007?
c. Why would Western Wear use the allowance method?

E7-11 Use the following information from the financial statements of The Thomson Corporation to answer the following questions: L.O. 3, 6

(millions of dollars) December 31 Assets	2002	2001
Cash and cash equivalents	$ 709	$ 532
Accounts Receivable, net of allowance of $ 372 million (2001 – $ 381 million)	1,534	1,700

(Courtesy The Thompson Corporation)

a. Does The Thomson Corporation have significant credit sales? If so, what evidence supports your opinion?
b. Sales for the fiscal year ending on December 31, 2002, were $7,756 million. Compute the accounts receivable turnover ratio and comment on what it tells you about The Thomson Corporation credit and collection policy. What would make the ratio more useful for this assessment?
c. Can you tell what the bad debt expense was for the fiscal year ending December 31, 2002? Explain.

E7-12 An examination of the balance sheet of Toys-R-Us shows no allowance for bad debts. L.O. 3, 6

a. Under what conditions would a company be allowed to omit this account from the balance sheet? Does this make sense for Toys-R-Us?
b. Many of Toys-R-Us customers pay with credit cards. How are those sales reflected on the financial statements?

E7-13 Trane Air Company accepts cash or credit card payment from customers. During July, Trane sold merchandise with a sales price of $100,000 to customers who used VISA to pay for their purchases. VISA charges Trane 4 percent of sales for their services. How will this transaction be recorded in Trane's financial records? Why would Trane accept VISA? L.O. 4

E7-14 The owner of Suzy's Dress Shop is trying to decide whether to extend credit to her customers, to accept MasterCard, or to do both. Suppose Suzy expects to sell approximately $50,000 worth of merchandise each quarter if she offers her customers one of these choices. What costs and benefits should Suzy consider in making her decision? Explain the difference between the alternatives. L.O. 4

E7-15 In June, Hopps, Inc. had sales of $3,500 of its pogo sticks. The company gives a six-month warranty with the purchase of a pogo stick. When Hopps recorded the sales in June, the company also estimated that it will spend $350 to honour those warranties. When the company prepared its June financial statements, no sticks had been brought in for repair. In July, however, five people brought in their broken pogo sticks, and Hopps spent a total of $50 repairing them (at no charge to the customers because the sticks were under warranty). Assume no additional sales were made in July (i.e., no new warranties were given in July). L.O. 5

a. How much warranty expense would Hopps show on an income statement for the month of June?
b. Would Hopps have a warranty liability on the balance sheet at June 30, and if so, how much?
c. How much warranty expense would Hopps show on an income statement for the month of July?
d. Would Hopps have a warranty liability on the balance sheet at July 31, and if so, how much?

Problems—Set A

L.O. 1

P7-1A Consider the following concerning the Computer Tech cash account for the month of April.

- Cash per the Computer Tech records was $85,834.99.
- Customer payments of $16,008.13 were received April 30, but not deposited until May 1.
- Cheques totalling $22,461.87 were issued in April but had not cleared the bank as of the statement date (April 30).
- According to the bank statement, service charges for April were $54.50, and the bank collected a $4,900 note on April 19.

Required: Determine the April 30 cash balance that appears on the Computer Tech bank statement. (*Hint:* compute the true cash balance first.)

L.O. 2

P7-2A The Central Copy Centre (CCC) ending cash balance for October was $9,110.45. The owner deposited $773.14 on October 31 that did not appear on the bank statement. The bank collected a note of $500 for CCC and charged them $25 for the service. The ending balance on the bank statement for October was $9,022.39. After comparing the company's records with the bank statement, cheques totalling $503.65 were found to be outstanding. Besides the collection fee, there was $30 in other service charges. Also, the statement showed that CCC earned $180 in interest revenue on the account and that cheques amounting to $380.57 turned out to be NSF. Finally, a bank error was discovered: cheque number 4320 for $318.04 was paid to one of the CCC vendors. The bank incorrectly deducted $381.04 from the CCC account referencing cheque number 4320.

Required: Using the preceding information concerning the CCC cash account, prepare a bank reconciliation for the month of October.

L.O. 2

P7-3A Given the following errors:

a. The bank recorded a deposit of $200 as $2,000.
b. The company's bookkeeper mistakenly recorded a deposit of $530 as $350.
c. The company's bookkeeper mistakenly recorded a payment of $250 received from a customer as $25 on the bank deposit slip. The bank caught the error and made the deposit for the correct amount.
d. The bank statement shows a cheque written by the company for $255 was erroneously paid (cleared the account) as $225.
e. The bookkeeper wrote a cheque for $369 but erroneously wrote down $396 as the cash disbursement in the company's records.

Required: For each error, describe how it would be shown on a cash reconciliation.

L.O. 3

P7-4A Consider the following:

a. At year-end, Vio Company has accounts receivable of $14,000. The allowance for doubtful accounts has a normal balance prior to adjustment of $300. (Last year, doubtful accounts were overestimated by $300.) An aging schedule prepared on December 31 estimates that $1,100 of the Vio accounts receivable are uncollectible accounts.
b. At year-end, Demato Company has accounts receivable of $25,700. The allowance for doubtful accounts has a negative balance prior to adjustment of $400. (Last year, uncollectible accounts were *underestimated* by $400.) An aging schedule prepared on December 31 indicates that $2,300 of the Demato accounts receivable are uncollectible accounts.

Required: For each of the previously described situations, compute the bad debt expense for the year, the balance in the allowance for doubtful accounts, and the net realizable value of accounts receivable for the year-end financial statements. In both cases, the company uses the accounts receivable balance as the basis for estimating bad debts.

P7-5A Consider the situations that follow:

L.O. 3

a. At year-end, Nash Company has accounts receivable of $84,000. The allowance for doubtful accounts has a normal balance prior to adjustment of $300. (Last year, uncollectible accounts were *overestimated* by $300.) Net credit sales for the year were $250,000 and 3 percent is estimated to be uncollectible.
b. At year-end, Bridges Company has accounts receivable of $83,000. The allowance for doubtful accounts has a negative balance prior to adjustment of $400. (Last year, uncollectible accounts were *underestimated* by $400.) Net credit sales for the year were $250,000 and 3 percent is estimated to be uncollectible.

Required: For each of the preceding situations, compute the bad debt expense for the year, the balance in the Allowance for Doubtful Accounts, and the net realizable value of Accounts Receivable for the year-end financial statements. In both cases, the company uses net credit sales as the basis for estimating bad debts.

P7-6A The following information has been adapted from the annual financial statements of the Dorel Industries Inc.:

L.O. 3, 6

Consolidated Balance Sheet

December 30, 2002 (in thousands of U.S. Dollars)	2002	2001
Assets		
CURRENT ASSETS		
Cash and cash equivalents	$54,450	$18,640
Accounts receivable (Note 4)	98,267	95,445
Inventories (Note 5)	142,157	152,411
Prepaid expenses	10,465	8,743
Funds held by ceding insurer (Note 20)	11,298	-
Income taxes refundable	-	5,156
Future income taxes	11,114	11,195
	327,751	291,590
CAPITAL ASSETS (Note 6)	95,374	98,366
DEFERRED CHARGES (Note 7)	14,111	12,557
GOODWILL (Note 8)	155,669	151,624
INTANGIBLE ASSETS (Note 9)	5,818	4,055
FUTURE INCOME TAXES	-	1,327
OTHER ASSETS (Note 14)	11,400	9,055
	$610,123	$568,574

Consolidated Statement of Income

For the Year Ended December 30, 2002 (in thousands of U.S. dollars, except per share amounts)	2002	2001	2000
Sales	$992,073	$916,769	$757,540
Expenses: Cost of Sales	760,423	718,123	582,741

Note 4 - Accounts Receivable

Accounts receivable consist of the following:	2002	2001
Accounts receivable	$158,006	$146,918
Allowance for anticipated credits	(54,711)	(47,265)
Allowance for doubtful accounts	(5,028)	(4,208)
	$98,267	$95,445

(Courtesy Dorel Industries Inc.)

Required:

1. What are the total amounts of accounts receivable for the two years given *before* considering the possible uncollectible accounts? That is, what are gross accounts receivable?
2. Do you think the company has a significant amount of bad debts? Why, or why not?
3. Calculate the accounts receivable turnover ratio for 2002 and 2001. (Net accounts receivable at the end of 2000 was $126,133 million.) Also, calculate the number of days it takes, on average, to collect an accounts receivable. Explain this information to the company's management.

L.O. 4

P7-7A The following took place during the month of July at Holly's Hoops:

- The company sold $5,000 worth of hoops. Each is guaranteed for 12 months. Any defective hoop will be repaired or replaced free of charge during that period.
- Holly estimated that it will cost $600 during the next year to honour the warranties on the July sales.
- During August, Holly spent $250 to honour warranties related to July sales.
- The company did not sell any hoops in August.

Holly's Hoops prepares monthly financial statements.

Required:

a. What amount of warranty expense would be shown on the July income statement?
b. What amount of warranty liability would be shown on the July balance sheet?
c. What amount of warranty expense would be shown on the August income statement?
d. What effect did recording the warranty expense have on owner's equity?
e. What effect did spending the $250 in August have on owner's equity?

Problems—Set B

L.O. 2

P7-1B Consider the following information concerning Martin Office Furniture for the month of June:

- Deposits in transit as of June 30, were $3,785.15.
- Interest revenue earned was $1,300.
- Bank service charges amounted to $48.
- An error was discovered: The bank deducted from the Martin Office Furniture account a cheque for $161.03 that was written by Morton Office Supply.
- The following cheques were still outstanding as of the bank statement date:

16012	$10,460.60
16006	200.58
16017	532.27

- The Martin Office Furniture accountant recorded a deposit of $332 as $223.
- The bank returned a cheque from a customer as NSF in the amount of $1,059.17.
- Balance per the bank June 30 was $45,020.59.

Required: Given this information, determine the ending cash balance that appears on the Martin Office Furniture books. (*Hint:* compute the true cash balance first.)

L.O. 2

P7-2B Given the following errors:

a. The bank recorded a deposit of $300 as $30.
b. The company's bookkeeper mistakenly recorded a deposit of $240 as $420.
c. The company's bookkeeper mistakenly recorded a payment of $450 received from a customer as $45 on the bank deposit slip. The bank caught the error and made the deposit for the correct amount.

d. The bank statement shows a cheque written by the company for $392 was erroneously paid (cleared the account) as $329.
e. The bookkeeper wrote a cheque for $275 but erroneously wrote down $257 as the cash disbursement in the company's records.

Required: For each error, describe how the correction would be shown on the company cash reconciliation.

P7-3B Information about credit sales and collections for June Company for the fiscal year ending June 30, 2006 follows: L.O. 3

a. June Company had credit sales of $560,000 during the year.
b. June began the year with accounts receivable of $23,500 and an allowance for doubtful accounts of $(800). During the year, the company collected $555,000 cash for payments of accounts receivable. The company also wrote off the balances of two bankrupt customers, totalling $750.
c. June uses the accounts receivable balance to estimate uncollectible accounts.
d. June decides that 4 percent of accounts receivable will be uncollectible.

Required: Calculate the bad debt expense and the net realizable value of accounts receivable for June Company for the year ended June 30, 2006. How does the June estimate of uncollectible accounts for the year compare to the June estimate for the previous year? What factors may have caused this change?

P7-4B Gerard's Merchandising Mart has provided the following information about the company's sales and accounts receivable for the fiscal year ending December 31, 2007. L.O. 3, 6

Accounts receivable at December 31, 2006	$ 42, 500
Allowance for doubtful accounts at December 31, 2006 (after adjustments)	1,275
Credit sales for the year ended December 31, 2007	135,750
Cash collections on accounts receivable during 2007	142,600
Specific accounts written off during 2007	1,050

Required:

1. Suppose Gerard's used the accounts receivable balance to estimate the uncollectible accounts expense at the end of 2006. When 2007 is completed, can you tell if Gerard's over- or underestimated the uncollectible accounts expense at the end of 2006? Explain.
2. If Gerard's used the sales method for estimating the allowance, can you tell what percentage of the sales the company believes will not be collected? Why, or why not?
3. Suppose Gerard's uses accounts receivable to estimate the allowance. The company estimates that 3 percent of ending accounts receivable will be uncollectible. Compute (1) the uncollectible accounts expense for the year ended December 31, 2007, and (2) the net realizable value of accounts receivable on the December 31, 2007, balance sheet.
4. Suppose Gerard's uses the sales method to estimate the allowance for uncollectible accounts, and the company believes 1 percent of credit sales will be uncollectible. Compute (1) the uncollectible accounts expense for the year ended December 31, 2007, and (2) the net realizable value of accounts receivable on the December 31, 2007, balance sheet.
5. Do you have a preference for a method of computing the allowance? Explain why or why not.

P7-5B In July 2004, Jim started a business selling custom bicycle helmets on the Internet. Jim and his staff make the helmets on the basis of measurements provided by the customer. The helmets are guaranteed to fit for two years. When one is returned, Jim and his staff completely rework the helmet to the customer's revised measurements, a very labour-intensive job. The data from Jim's first two years of business follow: L.O. 5

	Fiscal year ended June 30, 2005	Fiscal year ended June 30, 2006
Sales	$252,000	$375,000
Units sold	1,050	1,500
Units returned	100	285
Average cost to repair	$150/unit	$160/unit

Jim estimates that about 20 percent of the helmets will be returned to be reworked during the two years following the sale.

Required:

1. Suppose Jim follows GAAP and matches the warranty cost with the sales. Calculate the estimated warranty liability and the warranty expense for both years. Do you think Jim's estimate of 20 percent is a good one? Explain.
2. Suppose Jim does *not* follow GAAP but, instead, records warranty expense whenever he incurs the repair cost. Calculate the warranty expense for both years.
3. Compare the two methods. If you were a financial statement user (bank loan officer or investor), which method would you prefer? That is, which method do you think gives a better picture of Jim's warranty situation, and why?

L.O. 5

P7-6B The following took place during the month of May at Mega TV Shop:

- Mega sold $50,000 worth of its own brand of television. Each television is guaranteed for 12 months. Any defective television will be repaired or replaced free of charge during that period.
- The company has estimated that it will cost $5,000 during the next year to honour the warranties on the May sales.
- During June, Mega TV Shop spent $1,050 to honour warranties related to May sales.
- The company did not sell any televisions during June.

Mega TV Shop prepares monthly financial statements.

Required:

a. What amount of warranty expense would be shown on the May income statement?
b. What amount of warranty liability would be shown on the May 31 balance sheet?
c. What amount of warranty expense would be shown on the June income statement?
d. What effect does recording the warranty *expense* have on owner's equity?
e. What effect did spending the $1,050 in June have on owner's equity?

L.O. 3, 6

P7-7B On June 1, Evan's Doughnuts, Inc. had a $290,000 balance in Accounts Receivable. During June, the company had credit sales revenue of $758,000. During June, Evan's collected $578,000 of accounts receivable and wrote off specific accounts of $7,200. On June 30, the unadjusted (normal) balance in Allowance for Doubtful Accounts is $2,800 (i.e., after the write-offs, there is still $2,800 in the Allowance). Bad Debt Expense is estimated to be 2 percent of credit sales.

Required:

1. Show all increases and decreases to Accounts Receivable, Allowance for Doubtful Accounts, and Bad Debt Expense for the month of June.
2. What amount of bad debt expense will Evan's Doughnuts, Inc. report on the income statement for the month ended June 30?
3. What amount of *net* accounts receivable will Evan's Doughnuts, Inc. report on its June 30 balance sheet?
4. How would this information about uncollectible receivables help Evan make decisions about the credit policies of his company?

Recording Transactions

R7-1 (SE7-4) Datatech's accountant wrote a cheque to a supplier for $1,050 but erroneously recorded it on the company's books as $1,500. She discovered this when she saw the monthly bank statement and noticed that the cheque had cleared the bank for $1,050. Give the journal entry Datatech needs to make to its accounting records to correct this error.

Date	Account	Debit	Credit

R7-2 (SE7-8) On January 1, 2006, a company's accounts receivable balance was $8,900, and the allowance for doubtful accounts balance was $600. This information came from the December 31, 2005, balance sheet. During 2006, the company reported $77,000 of credit sales, and $400 of specific receivables were written off as uncollectible. Cash collections of receivables were $69,000 for the year. The company estimates that 3 percent of the year-end accounts receivable will be uncollectible. Use T-accounts to analyze the problem, and then make the journal entry to record the bad debt expense for the year ended December 31, 2006.

	Accounts receivable		Allowance for doubtful accounts			Bad debt expense	
1/1	$8,900			$600	1/1		

Date	Account	Debit	Credit

R7-3 (SE7-11) The 2005 year-end unadjusted trial balance shows: accounts receivable (AR) $50,000 debit; allowance for doubtful accounts $1,000 credit; and net sales $200,000. Using the "percent of sales" method, the company estimates 2 percent of sales will become uncollectible. Give the journal entry to record the bad debt expense for 2005.

Date	Account	Debit	Credit

R7-4 (SE7-13) Selby Company accepts MasterCard from its customers. MasterCard charges Selby Company 4 percent of sales for its services. During 2008, Selby's customers used MasterCard for $43,560 worth of purchases. Record the journal entry for these sales.

Date	Account	Debit	Credit

R7-5 (SE7-16) When Handle's Pet Shop sells a puppy, it provides a health warranty for the little critter. If a puppy should become ill in the first two years after the sale, Handle's Pet Shop will pay the vet bill up to $200. Because this is normally a significant expense for the shop, the accountant insists that Handle's Pet Shop record an estimated warranty liability at the end of every year before the financial statements are prepared. On December 31, 2008, the accountant made the appropriate entry to record that liability. On March 30, 2009, the store received a $50 vet bill from one of its customers, who had bought a puppy in 2008. Handle's Pet Shop wrote a cheque for $50 to reimburse the puppy's owner. Give the journal entry for this payment.

Date	Account	Debit	Credit

R7-6 (E7-6) Compute Right uses the allowance method to account for bad debts. Show the journal entry for each item below.

- **a.** A customer pays his bill of $50.
- **b.** 1 percent of $500,000 in sales is estimated to be uncollectible.
- **c.** 5 percent of $100,000 in accounts receivable is estimated to be uncollectible. Last year, an excess of $400 beyond what was expected was written off.
- **d.** A specific account receivable in the amount of $65 is reinstated.

Transaction	Account	Debit	Credit

R7-7 (E7-10) Western Wear Corporation began 2007 with accounts receivable of $1,240,000 and a balance in the allowance for doubtful accounts of $36,000. During 2007, credit sales totalled $5,190,000 and cash collected from customers totalled $5,380,000. Also, actual write-offs of specific accounts receivable in 2007 were $33,000. At end of the year, an accounts receivable aging schedule indicated a required allowance of $32,300. No accounts receivable previously written off were collected. Use T-accounts to show what happened in each of the accounts shown below. Then, give the journal entry to record the bad debt expense for the year ended December 31, 2007.

Accounts receivable		Allowance for doubtful accounts		Bad debt expense	
1/1 $1,240,000			$36,000 1/1		

Date	Account	Debit	Credit

R7-8 (E7-13) Trane Air Company accepts cash or credit card payment from customers. During July, Trane sold $100,000 worth of merchandise to customers who used VISA to pay for their purchases. VISA charges Trane 4 percent of sales for their services. Give the journal entry to record this transaction in Trane's financial records.

Date	Account	Debit	Credit

R7-9 (P7-3A) Given the following errors:

a. The bank recorded a deposit of $200 as $2,000.
b. The company's bookkeeper mistakenly recorded a deposit of $530 as $350.
c. The company's bookkeeper mistakenly recorded a payment of $250 received from a customer as $25 on the bank deposit slip. The bank caught the error and made the deposit for the correct amount.
d. The bank statement shows that a cheque that was written by the company for $255 was erroneously paid (cleared the account) as $225. This was the bank's error.
e. The bookkeeper wrote a cheque for $369 but erroneously wrote down $396 as the cash disbursement in the company's records.

Required: Determine which of the errors would require the company to record a journal entry. Then, record the journal entry.

Transaction	Account	Debit	Credit

R7-10 (P7-4A) Consider the following:

a. At year-end, Vio Company has accounts receivable of $14,000. The allowance for doubtful accounts has a credit balance prior to adjustment of $300. An aging schedule prepared on December 31 indicates that $1,100 of Vio's accounts receivable are uncollectible accounts.
b. At year-end, Demato Company has accounts receivable of $25,700. The allowance for doubtful accounts has a debit balance prior to adjustment of $400. An aging schedule prepared on December 31 indicates that $2,300 of Demato's accounts receivable are uncollectible accounts.

Required: For each situation described above, give the journal entry to record bad debt expense. In both cases, the company uses the accounts receivable balance as the basis for estimating bad debts.

Transaction	Account	Debit	Credit

R7-11 (P7-5A) Consider the following situations:

a. At year-end, Nash Company has accounts receivable of $84,000. The allowance for doubtful accounts has a credit balance prior to adjustment of $300. Net credit sales for the year were $250,000, and 3 percent is estimated to be uncollectible.
b. At year-end, Bridges Company has accounts receivable of $83,000. The allowance for doubtful accounts has a debit balance prior to adjustment of $400. Net credit sales for the year were $250,000, and 3 percent is estimated to be uncollectible.

Required: For each situation described above, give the journal entry to record bad debt expense. In both cases, the company uses net credit sales as the basis for estimating bad debts.

Transaction	Account	Debit	Credit

R7-Comprehensive

Chapter 7: Comprehensive Financial Statement Preparation Problem

Tracy's Service Company started the year with the following trial balance:

Account	Debit	Credit
Cash	$161,000	
Accounts receivable	186,000	
Allowance for doubtful accounts		$ 9,500
Office equipment	50,000	
Accumulated amortization		10,000
Interest payable		7,000
Notes payable		70,000
Common shares		200,000
Retained earnings		100,500
	$397,000	$397,000

During 2008, the company:

1. Paid the $7,000 interest payable. The company pays interest on the note at a rate of 10 percent annually. Interest for the year ending December 31, 2007, was accrued at the end of last year and was remitted to the bank on the second day of January 2008. The principal of the note is due on December 31, 2014.
2. Performed services for customers amounting to $156,800 all on account. Tracy's Service Company decided this year to provide a six-month warranty for its services. The company estimates that it will cost approximately 2 percent of the price of the service to fulfill these obligations.
3. Collected $145,700 cash on accounts receivable.
4. Found out two customers, M. Smith and J. Jones, had both filed for bankruptcy and wrote off their accounts receivable. The total amount the two customers owed was $7,500.
5. Paid cash of $50,000 for employee salaries.
6. Paid consultants $2,700 to provide the warranty service to customers.

Additional information:

1. Office equipment with a useful life of 10 years and no residual value needs to be amortized. Tracy's Service Company uses straight-line amortization.
2. Tracy's estimates that 5 percent of the ending balance of accounts receivable will be uncollectible.

Record the journal entries and adjustments for the year and post them to T-accounts. Prepare an adjusted trial balance, and then prepare the income statement, balance sheet (at December 31, 2008), statement of changes in shareholders' equity, and cash flow statement for the year.

Issues for Discussion

Financial statement analysis

L.O. 6, 7

1. Use the CoolBrands International Inc. financial statements to answer the following questions:

   a. Does CoolBrands have a significant amount of bad debts? How can you tell?

   b. Compute the accounts receivable turnover ratio for two consecutive years. What information does this provide? (Accounts receivable in 2001 was $32,123)

Business risk

2. Consider the following:

   a. Suppose one person opens the cash receipts (cheques received in the mail), makes the bank deposits, and keeps the accounts receivable records. What potential problems could arise from the lack of separation of duties?
   b. Why would a store offer a free purchase to a customer who does not receive a receipt?

Ethics

3. Bargain Books offers a customer discount card for an annual fee of $25. With this card, a customer receives a 10 percent discount on all purchases. One evening a customer was making a purchase of approximately $80, and the cashier asked the customer if she had a discount card. The customer thought she might have purchased one but did not have it with her. The cashier attempted to call the main office to obtain the number of the customer's discount card, but the cashier was put on hold for several minutes. Impatient to complete the transaction, the cashier told the customer that because the main office was so slow, he would use his own discount card and give the customer the 10 percent discount on the purchase. The cashier reached into his own wallet, extracted his discount card, swiped it in the electronic cash register, and proceeded to ring up the customer's order.

   a. Why would a company offer a discount card?
   b. Do you think the cashier acted in an ethical manner? Explain why or why not.

Internet Exercise: Intel Corporation

Intel, by far the world's number one maker of semiconductor chips, commands more than 80 percent of the PC microprocessor market. Compaq and Dell are Intel's largest customers.

To find out more about Intel, go to MSN Money at: http://moneycentral.msn.com/investor/home.asp

IE7-1 Enter the company symbol INTC, the stock symbol of the Intel Corp. Scroll down the left-hand column, and choose Financial Results, Statements to answer the following questions:

a. Identify the amounts reported for total (net sales) revenue for the three most recent years.
b. In general, who are Intel's customers? Who are Intel's two largest customers? Do you think Intel primarily has credit sales or cash sales? Why? Does Intel extend credit to its customers, or do Intel's customers use credit cards to pay the amounts owed?

IE7-2 Find the Annual Balance Sheet to answer the following questions:

a. Identify the amounts reported for trade accounts receivable, net for the three most recent year-ends. Does this represent amounts owed by customers or amounts that the company estimates it will actually collect from customers?
b. Does Intel use the allowance method or the direct write-off method to record uncollectible accounts? How can you tell?

IE7-3

a. Compute the accounts receivable turnover ratio for the two most recent years. In which year did the company collect receivables the quickest? How can you tell?
b. For the most recent year, how long does it take on average for Intel to collect for a sale? Do you think the credit terms might be net/45 or net/60? Explain why.

Please note: Internet websites are constantly being updated. Therefore, if the information is not found where indicated, please explore the website further to find the information.

CHAPTER

Financing a Business with Debt

Sales and Accounts Receivable

Here's where you've been...

In Chapter 7, you learned about how a company accounts for *sales, cash,* and *accounts receivable*. You learned that the amount of accounts receivable shown on the balance sheet has been reduced by the amount the company believes it will not collect. You also learned the importance of collecting accounts receivable in a timely manner.

Here's where you're going...

When you are finished with Chapter 8, you should understand how a company obtains financing from creditors. You should be able to calculate both present and future values of cash flows. You will study long-term notes and bonds—two ways a company borrows money—and interest payments associated with using someone else's money.

Financing

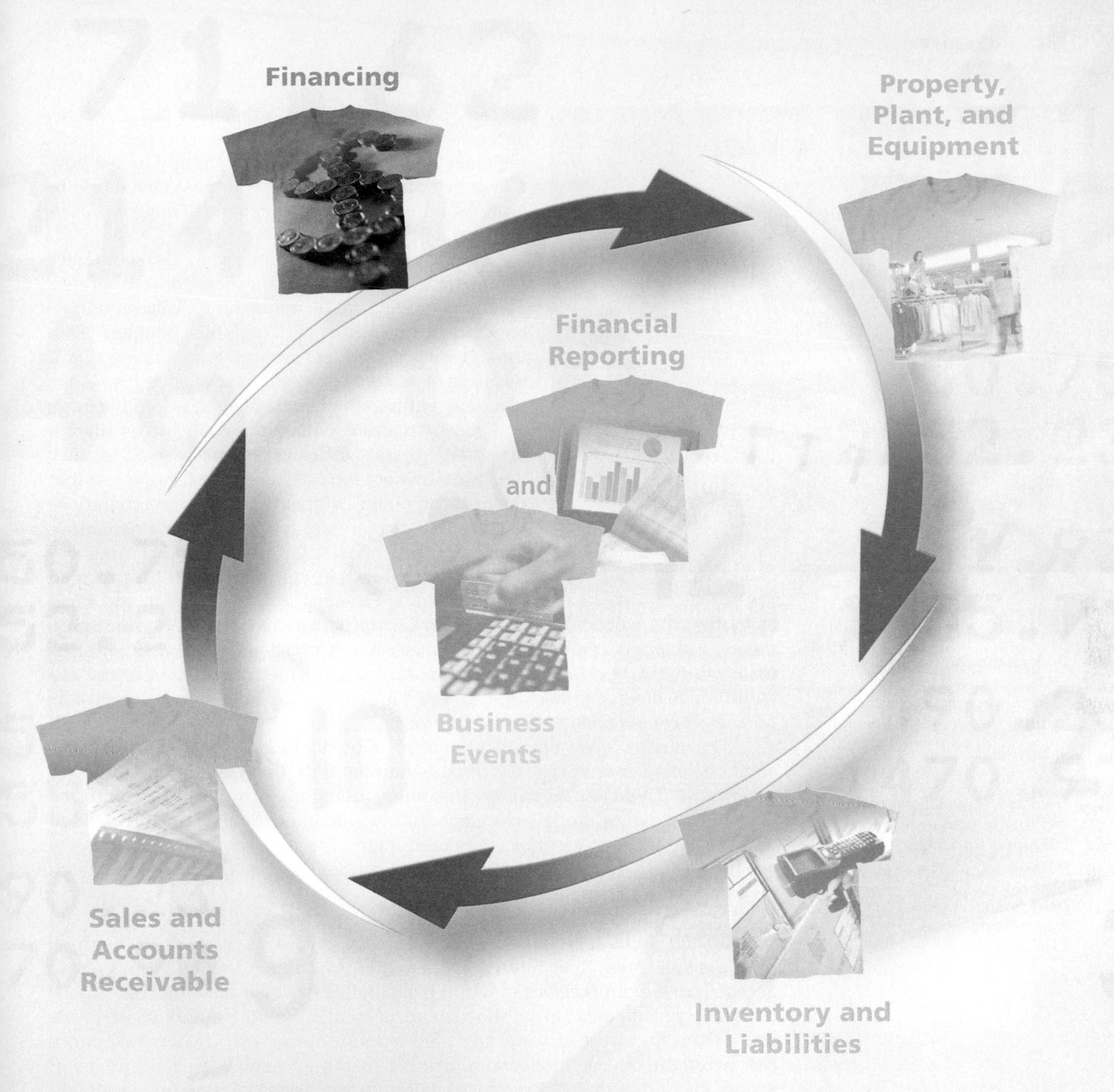

Learning Objectives

More specifically, when you are finished studying this chapter, you should be able to answer these questions:

1. What is a long-term note payable, and how does a company account for this type of debt?
2. What is the time value of money, and how do you calculate the future value and the present value of a lump sum and a series of cash flows?
3. What are bonds payable, and how does a company record and report the transactions associated with bonds?
4. How is information about a company's debt used in financial statement analysis?
5. What risks are associated with long-term debt?

So far, you have seen how a business firm operates and how the firm's operations are reflected in its financial statements. Now, you are ready to see how a firm gets the money it needs to get started, to operate as a business, and to expand. That is what financing a firm is all about.

Financing is easier to understand after you are comfortable with how a business firm operates. That is why we have postponed the discussion of financing a business firm until this chapter, even though it is the *first* concern of someone starting a business firm. Tom could not have started his T-shirt company without financing—the loan from his mom and his own cash. Obtaining financing is always necessary to start a business firm, as well as later when the owners look for sources of money so that the firm can better compete, improve, or expand.

Recall that there are two sources of financing—creditors and owners. **Creditors** lend a company money over a specified duration and for a specified rate of return. **Owners** invest money in the business for an unspecified duration and an *unspecified* return. **Debt financing** means obtaining capital—usually dollars but it could include other assets—from creditors. As we discuss financing as a business process and the accounting related to financing, you will see the close relationship between this business process and the accounting for it.

L.O. 1

Understand the cost of debt.

Creditors are individuals or institutions who lend companies money with a specified rate of return.

Owners are individuals or institutions who invest money in a business for an unspecified return.

Debt financing means a company is borrowing money from creditors.

The most crucial part of obtaining debt financing is the *cost* of using someone else's money. You are already familiar with that cost—it is referred to as *interest*. This chapter will go into more detail about how to calculate the cost of borrowing money. Decisions about obtaining debt financing depend on accurate measurement of the related interest costs. In this chapter, you will see how to measure the cost of borrowing money, as well as how it is reported on a company's financial statements.

Tom's mom is a creditor—when she loaned money to Tom's Wear, she did so with the understanding that she would be repaid the amount of the loan plus a small amount of interest. No matter how much income Tom's Wear earns, Tom's mom receives only the principal of the loan plus interest, details generally specified as part of the loan agreement. Creditors do not share in the profits of a firm beyond some specified amount of interest. Owners take more risk when they invest money in a firm because they stand a greater chance of losing their investment. Creditors' claims to the assets of a company always have priority over owners' claims. Thus, owners are the ones who are rewarded with the potential for a higher return. Owners have a chance to make a lot more money than they have invested in the company, more than they would have made if they had simply been creditors.

Business Process

In this chapter, we will look at ways a business firm *borrows* money. That is, we will look at creditors, sources of funding outside the business, and how these transactions are reported on the financial statements. In the next chapter, we will look at owners using their own money to finance their firms.

A **long-term note payable** is an obligation that occurs when a company borrows money from a financial institution, such as a bank, for longer than one year and is usually repaid with a series of payments of principal and interest over the life of the note.

Long-Term Notes Payable and Mortgages

When a company borrows money for longer than one year, that obligation is called a **long-term note payable**. Long-term notes differ from short-term

Financing Your Business: Using a Line of Credit

Almost every company will need to borrow money during its life—sometimes to maintain a positive cash flow for regular operations and sometimes to expand or make other major changes to the business. Selecting the type of financing to obtain is a major business decision. In this chapter, the focus is on long-term financing. One common way to help a company manage its cash flow *without* long-term borrowing is called a *line of credit.* This is an excellent choice for financing the regular operations of a business.

What is a line of credit? It is an arrangement between a company and its bank, in which the bank allows the company to borrow money for routine operating expenses up to the maximum amount of the credit line. The interest rate charged by the bank for this type of loan is usually much lower than the interest rate for credit card purchases, but it may be a bit higher than a typical bank loan for a specific amount and term. There is typically a very short repayment "window" for a line of credit—60 to 90 days.

What kind of business should use a line of credit? First, the business must be a profitable, established business. Second, the business should have predictable cash flows. A line of credit works best when there is a predictable, temporary, short-term shortage of cash. The amount used—that is, the amount borrowed—needs to be repaid in a short time to make a line of credit a cost-effective financing choice. Having a line of credit is also a good choice for a company that does not have a current cash flow problem but would like a backup in case of a cash flow problem.

When is a line of credit a poor financing choice? If your company needs to make large purchases of major long-term assets, then a loan with a longer term and a lower interest rate would be a better type of financing. If the cash shortage is more than temporary, the company should make a long-term plan for a solution. It is also not a good idea to use a line of credit to pay employees. Payroll is an expense that should be a priority for a company's regular cash inflow. In most cases, a company that must borrow money to meet its payroll needs to rethink its financial situation.

What does a business need to provide to get a line of credit? One of the most important items a company should have is a set of financial statements, particularly a balance sheet and an income statement. In addition to the basic financial statements, a company should have a detailed schedule of projected cash inflows and outflows. Other important items are several years of tax returns, a list of current bank accounts, a current business plan, and appraisals of any assets that might be used as collateral.

Check out the financial statements of some well-known companies. You will find information about their lines of credit in the notes to the financial statements.

notes in several ways. Recall that short-term notes are debt obligations that will be repaid in one year or sooner. Long-term notes are typically repaid with a series of equal payments over the life of the note.

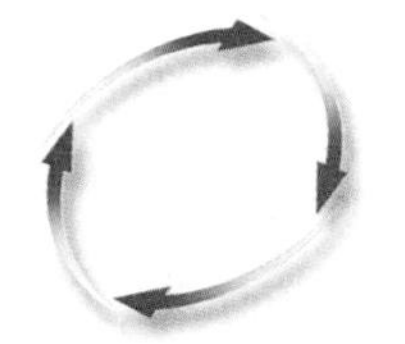

Business Process

A car loan is an example of a long-term note payable. The monthly payments are a combination of interest and principal. With each monthly payment, you are paying that month's interest on the loan as well as a small part of the principal balance due. With each monthly payment, the principal of the note is reduced. Each month when the interest is calculated on the outstanding loan balance, the interest amount becomes a smaller portion of the payment. This is because the total amount of each payment stays the same, but over time the principal decreases and the interest on that declining principal goes down. That leaves a larger part of each monthly payment available to reduce the outstanding principal.

Interest is the cost of using someone else's money. Interest rates are typically given as *annual* rates.

A **mortgage** is a note payable issued for property, such as a house, usually repaid in equal installments consisting of part principal and part interest, over a specified period.

Exhibit 8–1 shows how this works for a loan of $100,000, with a 15-year term, and an **interest** rate of 10 percent per year. The annual payment is the same every year, but the portion of the payment that is interest expense decreases, whereas the portion of the payment that reduces the outstanding principal balance increases.

A **mortgage** is a special kind of note payable—it is a loan to a borrower for the specific purpose of purchasing property and gives the lender a claim against that property if the payments are not made. People often use this type of note payable—commonly referred to as a mortgage loan—to buy a house. Like most long-term notes, mortgage loans are debt obligations commonly repaid in periodic installments—each payment is part principal and part interest.

Exhibit 8–1
Payments Composed of Interest and Principal

	Annual payment	Interest expense (principal balance × 0.10)	Reduction in principal	Principal balance
0				$100,000.00
1	$13,147.38	$10,000.00	$ 3,147.38	96,852.62
2	13,147.38	9,685.26	3,462.12	93,390.50
3	13,147.38	9,339.05	3,808.33	89,582.17
4	13,147.38	8,958.22	4,189.16	85,393.01
5	13,147.38	8,539.30	4,608.08	80,784.93
6	13,147.38	8,078.49	5,068.89	75,716.04
7	13,147.38	7,571.60	5,575.78	70,140.26
8	13,147.38	7,014.03	6,133.35	64,006.91
9	13,147.38	6,400.69	6,746.69	57,260.22
10	13,147.38	5,726.02	7,421.36	49,838.86
11	13,147.38	4,983.89	8,163.49	41,675.37
12	13,147.38	4,167.54	8,979.84	32,695.53
13	13,147.38	3,269.55	9,877.83	22,817.70
14	13,147.38	2,281.77	10,865.61	11,952.09
15	13,147.30	1,195.21	11,952.09	—

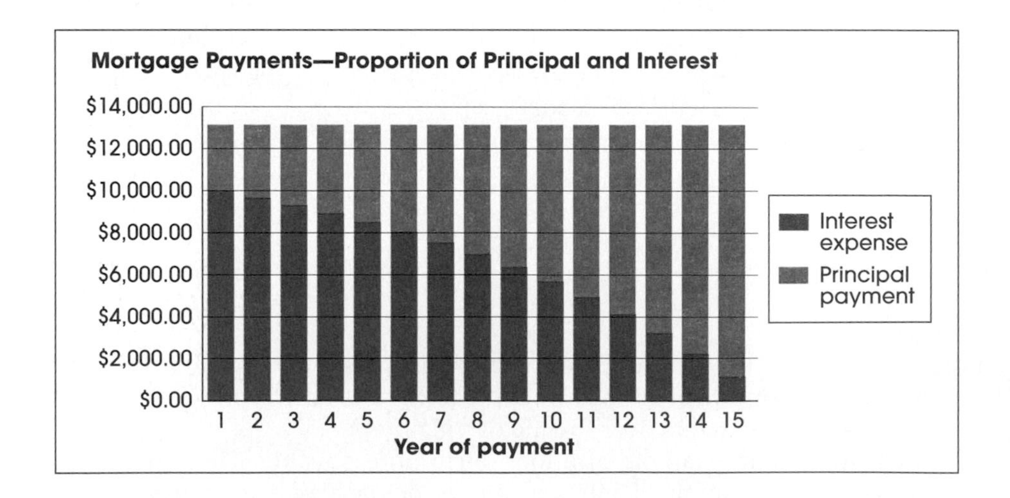

Note: This exhibit shows the payment schedule for a $100,000 loan for 15 years at 10 percent annual interest, with equal annual payments of $13,147.38. Each payment is made up of principal and interest. With each payment, the principal balance is reduced, so there is less interest expense each year. Because the payment stays the same, more of the payment goes toward reducing the principal each year. The graph shows how, over the term of the loan, the proportion of interest in each payment goes down, while the proportion of principal in each payment goes up.

Suppose you sign, on January 1, 2005 a three-year $100,000 mortgage with an 8 percent annual interest rate to buy a piece of land. Payments are to be made annually on December 31 of each year in the amount of $38,803.35. How did the bank figure out the annual payment for the $100,000 loan for three years at 8 percent interest? (Remember, the interest rate is given as an *annual* rate.)

The calculation of the annual payment is based on the time value of money. "Time value of money" means there is value in having money for a period of time. That value is the interest the money can earn. The bank gives you $100,000 today, and so you must repay that amount plus interest for the time you have the borrowed amount or any part of it. The bank figures out what amount, received in three equal annual installments, would give it the same amount of money at the end of three years as it would have if it invested the $100,000 today and it grew at a rate of 8 percent per year. The equivalent value of the sum of those three payments—a $38,803.35 payment at the end of each of the next three years—is called the **present value** of those three payments. Each payment is discounted to an amount equivalent to having the money today. **Discounting** the cash flows strips them of the interest built in for the passage of time, bringing them back to equivalent dollars today. In this example, the dollars today amount to $100,000. The interest rate used in the calculation of present value amounts is also called the discount rate. In this example, the discount rate is 8 percent.

The **present value** is the amount a future amount of money is worth today.

Discounting means finding the present value.

Discount rate is another name for the interest rate in a present value problem.

To get a clearer sense of what is going on here, think about the following:

- A dollar you have today is worth exactly a dollar.
- A dollar you received a year ago is worth more than a dollar today because it has had a year to earn some interest (as long as you put it in the bank instead of spending it).
- A dollar to be received a year from now is worth less than a dollar today, because today's dollar can earn some interest during the year.

Thus, in our example, $100,000 is the present value. What annual payment for three years at 8 percent per year is equivalent to $100,000 today? In this example, this calculation is done for you, but later in this chapter, you will learn how to do it. The concept for you to understand here and now is the *concept* of present value. In this example, the bank has calculated the three payments to be $38,803.35. The present value of those three payments, discounted at the interest rate of 8 percent, equals $100,000. After the three payments are made, both the principal and the interest will be repaid.

When is the first payment due? In this example, the payments are annual, and the first payment will be made at the end of the first year of the loan. (Many loans are repaid monthly or quarterly, but the first payment is usually made after some time has passed.)

How much of the first payment is interest expense, and how much goes toward paying back the principal? Remember, *interest* is the cost of borrowing money. The interest is based on the amount of the principal, the interest rate, and the amount of time for which the money is borrowed. (Interest = principal × rate × time.) The bank lends you $100,000 on day 1 of the note. On day 365, you make a $38,803.35 payment to the bank. The interest on the $100,000 for the year that has just passed is:

$$\text{Interest} = \text{Principal} \times \text{Rate} \times \text{Time}$$
$$\$100{,}000 \times 0.08/\text{year} \times 1\ \text{Year} = \$8{,}000$$

The entire $100,000 was borrowed for a full year, and so you simply multiply principal × the annual rate × the 1-year duration to get the interest expense for the year. Of the $38,803.35 payment, $8,000 is interest, and so the remaining portion of the payment—$30,803.35—is repayment of principal. The first payment affects the accounting equation, as shown next:

Assets	=	Liabilities	+	Share capital	+	Retained earnings
$(38,803.35) Cash		$(30,803.35) Mortgage payable				$(8,000) Interest expense

The journal entry to record the first principal and interest payment on the $100,000, 8-percent, three-year note is:

Date	Transaction	Debit	Credit
12/31/2005	Mortgage payable	$30,803.35	
	Interest expense	8,000.00	
	Cash		$38,803.35

The principal of the mortgage has been reduced. Another way of saying that is, the outstanding balance of the mortgage is lower—meaning you have less of the bank's money at the end of the first year. Therefore, the interest owed the bank for the second year will be smaller than the interest paid for the first year. That is because the interest rate will be applied to a smaller principal, that is, a smaller outstanding balance. Use the interest formula to calculate the portion of the payment that is interest for the second year, and then subtract the interest from the total payment to calculate the amount of the payment that reduces the principal.

- Interest = principal × rate × time.
- Outstanding balance due at the start of the second year: $69,196.65 = $100,000 original principal − $30,803.35 reduction in principal from the first payment.
- Principal of $69,196.65 for year 2 × 0.08 annual interest rate × one year = $5,535.73.
- Principal of $69,196.65 × 0.08 per year × 1 year = $5,535.73.

The journal entry to record the second principal and interest payment on the $100,000, 8 percent, three-year note is:

Date	Transaction	Debit	Credit
12/31/2006	Mortgage payable	$33,267.62	
	Interest expense	5,535.73	
	Cash		$38,803.35

Note that the amount of interest you owe the bank is smaller each year. The reason is because the outstanding balance of the mortgage is smaller each year. At the end of year 2, the bank receives the second payment of $38,803.35. As the preceding calculation shows, $5,535.73 of that payment is interest expense. The rest of the payment—$33,267.62 (= $38,803.35 – $5,535.73)—reduces the outstanding balance. After the second payment, the outstanding balance is $35,929.03. For the third payment of $38,803.35, the interest portion is:

- Interest = principal × rate × time.
- New principal = $35,929.03 = $100,000 original principal – $30,803.35 reduction in principal from the first payment – $33,267.62 reduction in principal from the second payment.

- Interest expense for year 3 = $35,929.03 principal for year 3 × 0.08 annual interest rate × 1 year = $2,874.32.
- Principal of $35,929.03 × 0.08 per year × 1 year = $2,874.32.

The journal entry to record the third principal and interest payment on the $100,000, 8 percent, three-year note is:

Date	Transaction	Debit	Credit
12/31/2007	Mortgage payable	$35,929.03	
	Interest expense	2,874.32	
	Cash		$38,803.35

When you subtract the interest of $2,874.32 from the third payment of $38,803.35, the remaining $35,929.03 reduces the principal—in this case, it reduces it to exactly zero dollars.

Is it just luck that the remaining outstanding balance plus interest is exactly equal to the amount of the last payment? No; the bank did the present value calculations with the principal, interest rate, and length of the loan so that it would come out to exactly zero at the end of the third year. Look at Exhibit 8–2 to see the amortization schedule for this loan.

STUDY BREAK 8-1

See How You're Doing

Tompkins Corp. purchased a building on January 1, signing a long-term, $600,000 mortgage, with monthly payments of $5,500. The interest rate is 9 percent per year. Prepare the journal entry to record the first payment.

Time Value of Money

L.O. 2

Understand the time value of money.

To understand what happens when a company borrows money, it is necessary to learn about the *time value of money*. This is a common expression in business, and it affects the financial life of every business and of every individual. If you have ever bought anything on credit or borrowed money for longer than one year, you have already had experience with the time value of money. The expression means just what it says: money has value over time. That is because invested money can earn interest. A person would prefer to receive a dollar today, rather than a year from now, because the dollar received today can earn interest during the year. Then it will be worth *more* than a dollar a year from now.

Exhibit 8–2
Amortization Schedule for a Mortgage

Mortgage balance		Annual payment	Interest portion of payment (8% × mortgage balance)	Amount of mortgage reduction (annual payment—interest portion)
Beginning balance	$100,000.00	$38,803.35	$8,000.00	$30,803.35
After first payment	69,196.65	38,803.35	5,535.73	33,267.62
After second payment	35,929.03	38,803.35	2,874.32	35,929.03
After third payment	0			

Simple versus Compound Interest

We have calculated the interest on the principal of a loan several times in previous chapters. When interest is computed on the principal only, it is called *simple interest*. Simple interest usually applies to short-term loans, those loans with terms of one year or less.

When interest is computed on the principal of a loan *plus* any interest that has been earned but not collected or paid, it is called *compound interest*. The interest earned during a year is added to the original principal, and that new larger amount is used to calculate the interest earned during the next year. Each year, the interest is calculated on a larger amount—the interest earned each successive year is added to the sum, which includes the initial principal and the interest earned in prior years.

Exhibit 8–3 shows what happens to $1,000 if we invest it today and watch it grow over 10 years. You can easily compare simple interest to compound interest. Compound interest makes your money grow much faster.

When you get familiar with compound interest, you can calculate:

1. the *future* value of an amount of money you deposit today; and
2. the amount of money you need to deposit today, the *present value* of an amount, to grow to a specific amount by some future date.

We will discuss each in detail.

Future Value

If you deposit some money in your savings account today, the amount in your savings account will grow over time because your saved money is earning interest. The amount of money you will have in the future depends on the:

1. amount you have deposited today
2. annual interest rate
3. amount of time your money has to earn interest

To save money for your future, you could deposit a single amount today and watch it grow; or you could make a series of deposits at regular intervals over time.

Single Amount. If you deposit $100 today in your savings account, how much will it be worth a year from today? Suppose the interest rate is 10 percent. You will earn 10 percent interest, or $10, on your $100 principal, one year from today when you will have $110. If you leave it in the bank for another year at 10 percent interest, your $110 will grow to $121, as shown in Exhibit 8–4.

Future Value of $100 in 2 years at 10% per year =
[$100(1.10)] 1.10 = $121

This is the amount you will have after one year.	So you increase this amount by 10% to get the amount you will have at the end of the second year.

If you extend this example to three years, you would multiply the amount at the end of two years, $121, by 1.10, which would give you $133.10. To generalize, you could use the following formula:

Exhibit 8–3 **Simple versus Compound Interest**

Deposit today at 10% annual interest	You'll have this much At the end of year 1	At the end of year 2	At the end of year 3	At the end of year 4	At the end of year 5	At the end of year 6	At the end of year 7	At the end of year 8	At the end of year 9	At the end of year 10
Simple interest										
$1,000	$1,100	$1,200	$1,300	$1,400	$1,500	$1,600	$1,700	$1,800	$1,900	$2,000
Compound interest										
$1,000	$1,100	$1,210	$1,331	$1,464	$1,610	$1,771	$1,948	$2,143	$2,357	$2,593

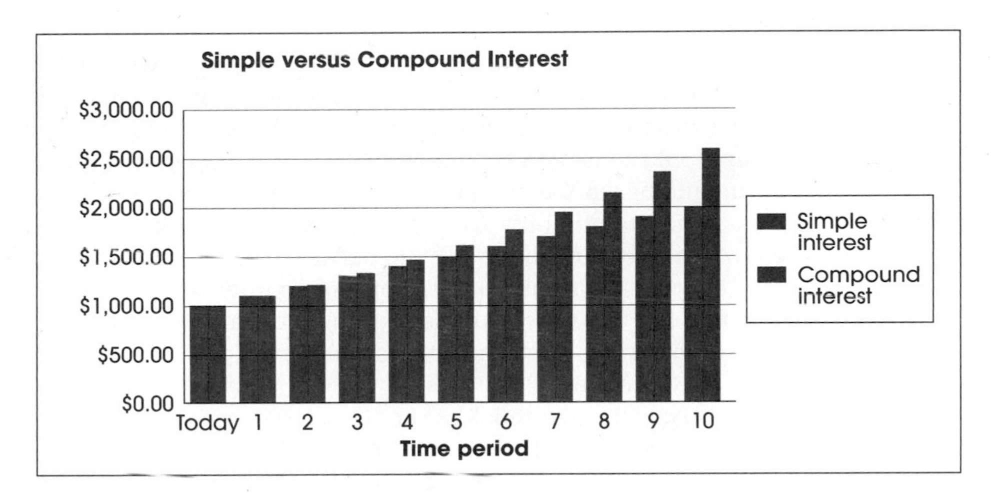

How much money will you have in 10 years if you deposit $1,000 today and it earns 10 percent interest per year?
If the money earns simple interest, you'll have $2,000 at the end of 10 years. Each year, the principal of $1,000 will earn $100.
If the money earns compound interest, you'll have $2,593 at the end of 10 years. Each year, the principal *plus the previously earned interest* will earn interest.

$$FV_n = PV(1+i)^n$$

where

n = Number of periods during which the compounding occurs
i = Interest rate for a single period
PV = Present Value or original amount invested at the beginning of the first period
FV_n = Future Value of the investment at the end of n periods

Exhibit 8–4
Future Value of a Lump Sum

Today	1 Year from today	2 Years from today
$100	$110	$121
Present value		**Future value**

Exhibit 8–5
Partial Future Value of $1 Table

(n) Periods	3%	4%	5%	6%
1	1.03000	1.04000	1.05000	1.06000
2	1.06090	1.08160	1.10250	1.12360
3	1.09273	1.12486	1.15763	1.19102
4	1.12551	1.16986	**1.21551**	1.26248

Try this formula with the $100 invested for two years at 10 percent.

$$\begin{aligned} \text{Future Value} &= 100(1+0.10)^2 \\ &= \$100(1.10)(1.10) \\ &= \$121 \end{aligned}$$

Instead of using a formula to calculate the future value of a single amount, you could do the calculation by using a future value table. Someone did all the multiplication work using various interest rates for many different periods of time and put the factors in a table. The table is based on $1, and so you simply find the number in the table that corresponds to the interest rate and the number of periods that apply to your situation. The interest rates and periods in the table are not labelled as annual because they can be used for any length of time. The important point is that you use an interest rate based on the time period you want to use for compounding. An example will help you understand the relationship between the interest rate and the time period used and how to use future value tables.

Suppose you invested $100 at 10 percent per year with semiannual compounding, instead of the annual compounding we used in the previous example. We would then change the interest rate to a six-month rate of 5 percent and use the number of six-month periods in the problem. If you invested your $100 for two years at 10 percent, compounded semiannually, you would use an interest rate of 5 percent and 4 as the number of periods:

$$\begin{aligned} \text{Future Value} &= \$100(1+0.05)^4 \\ &= \$121.55 \end{aligned}$$

By using the future value of $1 table (shown in Exhibit 8–5), you can find the column with the interest rate of 5 percent and the row with the number of periods equal to 4. That factor is 1.21551. Because you have $100, you multiply the factor by 100. That gives you $121.55.

Note that the more frequently your principal is compounded, the faster it will grow.

In addition to using a formula or a future value table, you could use a financial calculator to do the calculation. To use a financial calculator, put the calculator in financial mode.

- Put in 100, and press the *PV* key. *PV* stands for present value, and $100 is the present value in this problem.
- Then, put in 4, and press the *N* key. *N* means the number of periods, which is 4 in this problem.
- Next, put in 5, and press the *i%* key, the interest rate for each period. It will change to 0.05 automatically on most calculators.
- Then, press the *CPT* key—that means compute—and then press the *FV* key. That is the future value key.
- You should see the answer in the display: 121.55.

Suppose you invested $500 at 12 percent interest per year for 10 years. How much would you have at the end of that time? Use three methods—formula, table (Appendix B), and calculator (if you have one) to determine the amount.

STUDY BREAK 8-2

See How You're Doing

Future Value of an Annuity

Instead of saving a lump sum, you may prefer to make periodic deposits to your savings account. A stream of deposits or payments that are the same amount and made periodically over equally spaced intervals is called an **annuity**. Its name comes from the idea of annual payments because most annuities are annual. There are two types of annuities:

An **annuity** is a series of equal payments over equally spaced intervals of time. With an **ordinary annuity,** a series of payments are made at the end of each interval or period. With an **annuity due,** a series of payments are made at the beginning of each period.

1. An ordinary annuity, also known as an *annuity in arrears*, is a series of payments in which the payments occur at the *end* of each period.
2. An annuity due is a series of payments in which the payments occur at the *beginning* of each period.

If you conclude that the difference between the two types of annuities is the length of time a payment has to earn interest, you are correct. Let us look at an example of an annuity with five deposits of $100 each.

Ordinary Annuity. Exhibit 8–6 shows the annuity as an ordinary annuity, with deposits at the end of each period.

Because the deposits are made at the end of the year, the first deposit would have four years to earn interest; the second deposit, three years; the third, two years; the fourth, one year; and the last deposit would earn no interest. One way to calculate the total you would have at the end of five years is to take each single deposit and calculate the future value of that deposit, and then add all those amounts together. By using an annual interest rate of 10 percent, the calculations for the future value of each deposit follow:

$$\begin{aligned} FV \text{ of } \$100\,(4 \text{ Years}) &= 100\,(1+0.10)^4 \\ FV \text{ of } \$100\,(3 \text{ Years}) &= 100\,(1+0.10)^3 \\ FV \text{ of } \$100\,(2 \text{ Years}) &= 100\,(1+0.10)^2 \\ FV \text{ of } \$100\,(1 \text{ Year}) &= 100\,(1+0.10)^1 \\ \text{Last Deposit}\,(0 \text{ Years}) &= 100\,(1) \end{aligned}$$

Adding the equations gives:

$$FV(\text{Annuity}) = 100(1+0.10)^4 + 100(1+0.10)^3 + 100(1+0.10)^2 + 100(1+0.10)^1 + 100(1)$$

If we factor out the deposit amount of 100, we get:

$$FV(\text{Annuity}) = 100[(1+0.10)^4 + (1+0.10)^3 + (1+0.10)^2 + (1+0.10)^1 + 1]$$

$$FV(\text{Annuity}) = 100(\text{Sum of the factors from the Future Value of a \$1 Table})$$

$$FV(\text{Annuity}) = 100(1.4641 + 1.331 + 1.21 + 1.1 + 1)$$

$$FV(\text{Annuity}) = 100(6.1051) = \$610.51$$

Today | Future value date

Year 1	Year 2	Year 3	Year 4	Year 5
$100	$100	$100	$100	$100

Exhibit 8–6
Future Value of an Ordinary Annuity

Exhibit 8–7
Partial Future Value of an Ordinary Annuity Table

(n) Periods	8%	9%	10%	11%
4	4.50611	4.57313	4.64100	4.70973
5	5.86660	5.98471	**6.10510**	6.22780
6	7.33593	7.52333	7.71561	7.91286
7	8.92280	9.20043	9.48717	9.78327

Once again, just as you saw in problems with the future value of $1, you do not have to use the formulas to calculate the future value of an annuity. There are tables with the factors for the future value of an ordinary annuity. The table is based on a series of payments of $1, and so you simply find the number in the table that corresponds to the interest rate and the number of periods that apply to your situation. Remember, with the future value of an ordinary annuity, the same payment is made at the end of each period.

Let us find the future value of the $100 annuity at 10 percent per year using the table in Exhibit 8–7. Find the row for five periods and the column for 10 percent. The factor from this table is 6.10510. Can you see how the table is just a compilation of the factors from the future value $1 table in Exhibit 8–5? Multiply the deposit amount, $100, by the future value factor from the table to get $610.51. That is just what we calculated with the formula.

Let us do the problem using a financial calculator. With your calculator in the FIN mode:

- Enter 5 for the number of periods (*n*).
- Enter 10 for the interest rate (*i* %).
- Enter $100, and press *PMT* for payment.
- Press *CPT* (for compute) and *FV* (for future value).

You should see $610.51. That is what the deposits would be worth at the end of five years. (Your calculator may give a negative number. This is because it is assuming *payments* instead of *deposits*.)

Annuity Due. Suppose you decided to put away some money for the future in a series of equal payments. Let us say the first deposit is made at the beginning of the year—today when you decided on this savings plan—and each subsequent deposit is made at the beginning of each following year. This annuity would be an annuity *due*. Look at the time line in Exhibit 8–8, and compare it with the ordinary annuity time line in Exhibit 8–6. For the annuity due, the first payment is made today, and the last payment will have a year to earn interest before reaching the future value date. This scenario is more typical when saving money for the future.

Because the deposits are made at the beginning of the year, the first deposit would have five years to earn interest; the second deposit, four years; the third, three years; the fourth, two years; and the last payment, one year. As we have seen with an ordinary annuity, one way to calculate the total you would

Exhibit 8–8
Future Value of an Annuity Due

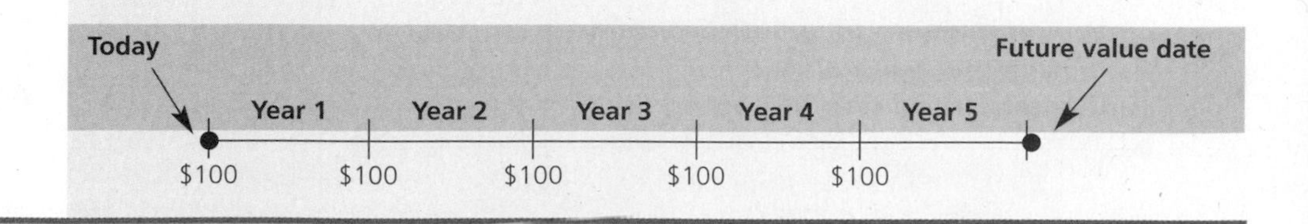

have at the end of five years is to take each single deposit and calculate the future value of that amount, and then add those amounts together.

By using an interest rate of 10 percent per year, the calculations for the future value of each deposit of this annuity due are as follows:

$$FV \text{ of } \$100\,(5 \text{ Years}) = 100(1+0.10)^5$$
$$FV \text{ of } \$100\,(4 \text{ Years}) = 100(1+0.10)^4$$
$$FV \text{ of } \$100\,(3 \text{ Years}) = 100(1+0.10)^3$$
$$FV \text{ of } \$100\,(2 \text{ Years}) = 100(1+0.10)^2$$
$$FV \text{ of } \$100\,(1 \text{ Years}) = 100(1+0.10)^1$$

Adding the equations gives:

$$FV\,(\text{Annuity}) = 100(1+0.10)^5 + 100(1+0.10)^4 + 100(1+0.10)^3 + 100(1+0.10)^2 + 100(1+0.10)^1$$

If we factor out the deposit amount of 100, we get:

$$FV\,(\text{Annuity}) = 100[(1+0.10)^5(1+0.10)^4 + (1+0.10)^3 + (1+0.10)^2 + (1+0.10)^1]$$
$$FV\,(\text{Annuity}) = 100(\text{Sum of the factors from the future value of \$1 table}) \text{ (see Appendix B)}$$

$$FV(\text{Annuity}) = 100(1.6105 + 1.4641 + 1.331 + 1.21 + 1.1)$$
$$FV(\text{Annuity}) = 100(6.7156) = \$671.56$$

Just as with the future value of an ordinary annuity, there is a table to help you calculate the future value of an annuity due. Like all the future value tables, the future value of an annuity due table in Exhibit 8–9 is based on \$1, and so you simply find the number in the table that corresponds to the interest rate and the number of periods that apply to your situation. Remember, with the future value of an annuity due, the same payment is made at the beginning of each period.

Let us find the future value of the \$100 annuity at 10 percent annual interest using the future value of an annuity due table in Exhibit 8–9. Find the row for five periods and the column for 10 percent. The factor from this table is 6.71561. Multiply the regular annual payment amount, \$100, by the future value factor from the table to get \$671.56. That is just what we calculated with the formula.

STUDY BREAK 8-3

See How You're Doing

Find the future value of a series of four deposits of \$200 at the ***end*** of each of the next four years at an annual interest rate of 11 percent. Try using the formula, the future value of an ordinary annuity table, and your financial calculator (if you have one).

Present Value

Sometimes, we want to know how much a future amount is worth today. That is, we want to know the present value of a future amount. That is the opposite

Exhibit 8–9
Future Value of an Annuity Due Table

(*n*) Periods	8%	9%	10%	11%
3	3.50611	3.57313	3.64100	3.70973
4	4.86660	4.98471	5.10510	5.22780
5	6.33592	6.52334	**6.71561**	6.91286
6	7.92280	8.20044	8.48717	8.78327

of the future value of a present amount. In addition to the future value of a single amount ($1) and the future value of an annuity, we will look at the present value of a single amount and the present value of an ordinary annuity.

Single Amount. The present value of a sum of money to be received in the future is the value in *today's dollars*. If you are promised a payment of $100 in one year from today, how much is it worth today? In other words, how much would you have to deposit today to have it grow to be $100 in a year? This is just the reverse of finding the future value of today's dollars. It involves inverse compounding. The difference between finding the present value of a future amount and finding the future value of a present amount comes about from the switch in the investor's point of view.

Earlier, to find the future value of a single amount, we took the present value of the amount and multiplied it by the interest factor. You will recall that:

$$FV_n = PV(1+i)^n$$

where

n = Number of periods
i = Interest rate for a single period
PV = Present Value of the future sum of money
FV_n = Future Value of the investment at the end of n periods

If we solve the equation for PV, we get:

$$PV = FV_n\left(\frac{1}{(1+i)^n}\right)$$

Let us figure out the present value of $100 one year from now—one year *hence*, in the jargon of the finance world—at an annual interest rate of 10 percent.

$$PV = \$100(1/(1+0.10)^1)$$
$$PV = \$100(0.90909)$$
$$PV = \$90.91$$

That means that having $90.91 today is equivalent to having $100 in one year, when the annual interest rate is 10 percent. We can check it out logically.

If we deposit $90.91 today and it earns 10 percent interest per year, at the end of the year we will have $100.

Let us figure out the present value of $100 for two years from now—two years *hence*—at an annual interest rate of 10 percent.

$$PV = \$100(1/(1+0.10)^2)$$
$$PV = \$100(0.82645)$$
$$PV = \$82.65$$

That means that having $82.65 today is equivalent to having $100 in two years, when the interest rate is 10 percent. We can check it out logically.

If we deposit $82.65 today and earn 10 percent interest, we will have $90.91 [= 82.64 (1 + 0.10)] after one year. Then, our $90.91 has a year to earn 10 percent interest, and so at the end of the second year, we will have $99.99—which rounds to $100.

Once again, we do not have to use the formula to calculate the present value of a future amount. We can use a present value of $1 table or a financial calculator. Let us look at a present value table first.

Exhibit 8–10
Partial Present Value of $1 Table

(n) Periods	8%	9%	10%	11%
1	0.92593	0.91743	0.90909	0.90090
2	0.85734	0.84168	**0.82645**	0.81162
3	0.79383	0.77218	0.75131	0.73119
4	0.73503	0.70843	0.68301	0.65873

The present value of $1 table is based on $1. Find the factor from the table in Exhibit 8–10, and multiply it by the dollars in our problem. Find the 10% column and the 2-year row. The factor from the table is 0.82645. Multiply that factor by $100, and the present value is $82.65.

Try it on your financial calculator:

- Enter $100 for the future value (*FV* key).
- Enter 10 for the interest rate (*i* % key).
- Enter 2 for the number of periods (*n* key).
- Press *CPT* and then *PV* to compute the present value.

You should see $82.65 in the display.

Finding the present value of a future amount is called discounting the cash flow, and when discounting a cash flow, the interest rate is called the discount rate.

STUDY BREAK 8-4

See How You're Doing

John wants to have $5,000 in five years. How much should he deposit today to have $5,000 in five years if the annual interest rate is 10 percent? In other words, what is the present value of $5,000 received five years from now? Try using the formula, the present value of $1 table, and your financial calculator (if you have one).

Annuity. In addition to discounting a single amount—often referred to as a lump sum—we may need to calculate the present value of a *series* of payments. The present value of an annuity has lots of practical applications. Most present value problems involving annuities have payments at the end of the period, and so they are *ordinary annuities*. First, let us look at a simple example to see how the formulas work. Then we will look at some examples that should be familiar to you—buying a motorcycle or a car by borrowing money and making payments to repay the loan.

Suppose you are selling your old motorcycle and a friend offers you a series of four payments of $500 each at the end of each of the next four years. How much is the friend actually offering for your motorcycle? It's *not* simply 4 × $500, or $2,000, because of the time value of money. Getting $500 a year from now is *not* the same as getting $500 today. To find out how much a series of four payments of $500 over the next four years is worth today, you need to use an appropriate interest rate and discount the payments to get the present value of each payment. Suppose the interest rate is 8 percent per year.

The first payment, made at the end of one year, will be discounted back one year. The second payment, made at the end of two years, will be discounted back two years, and so on, for the third and fourth payments. The present value of the series of payments will be the sum of the present value of each payment. The formula is as follows:

$$PV = FV_n\left(\frac{1}{(1+i)^n}\right)$$

$$\begin{aligned}
PV &= \$500\,(1/(1+0.08)^1) = 500\,(0.92593) = \$\ \ 462.97\\
PV &= \$500\,(1/(1+0.08)^2) = 500\,(0.85734) = \$\ \ 428.67\\
PV &= \$500\,(1/(1+0.08)^3) = 500\,(0.79383) = \$\ \ 396.92\\
PV &= \$500\,(1/(1+0.08)^4) = 500\,(0.73503) = \underline{\$\ \ 367.52}\\
&\textit{Total}\ \text{PV} \qquad\qquad\qquad\qquad = \underline{\underline{\$1{,}656.08}}
\end{aligned}$$

That means that, if you could deposit $1,656.08 today to earn 8 percent, you would be indifferent to receiving $1,656.08 today and receiving four payments of $500 each at the end of each of the next four years. Another way to express the same idea is that your friend is paying you $1,656.08 for your motorcycle by offering you the four $500 annual payments. The difference between the total payments of $2,000 and the $1,656.08 price of the motorcycle is interest.

Just as the future value of an ordinary annuity table in Exhibit 8–7 is a compilation of factors from the future value of $1 table, the present value of an ordinary annuity table, shown in Exhibit 8–11, has done the work of compiling the individual factors from the present value of $1 table. Use the present value of an annuity table to solve the same problem. Find the column for 8 percent and the row for four periods, and you will see the factor of 3.31213. If you multiply the payment of $500 by the factor 3.31213, you will get $1,656.07. (It is off a cent due to rounding the factors, as shown earlier.)

Try it on your financial calculator.

- Enter $500 as the payment (*PMT* key).
- Enter 4 as the number of periods (*n* key).
- Enter 8 as the interest rate (*i* % key).
- Press the *CPT* key followed by the *PV* key.

You will see $1,656.06 in the display. That is the present value of the series of payments.

Let us look at buying a car as an example. Suppose you have found a car that you want to buy for $23,000. You have $1,000 for a down payment, and you will have to borrow $22,000. If you borrow the money for three years at an annual interest rate of 6 percent, how much will your monthly payments be? Pay special attention to the timing of the payments in this situation. Instead of making annual payments, you will make monthly payments. To accommodate this payment plan, you will need to make sure your time periods, n, and your interest rate, i%, are both expressed with the same time frame. If the period is a month, then the annual interest rate must be changed to a monthly interest rate. You are borrowing money for 36 periods (= 3 years × 12 months per year) at a rate of 1/2% (= 0.5% or 0.005) per month (that is, an annual rate of 6 percent).

Exhibit 8–11
Partial Present Value of an Ordinary Annuity Table

(*n*) Periods	8%	9%	10%	11%
3	2.57710	2.53129	2.48685	2.44371
4 →	**3.31213**	3.23972	3.16987	3.10245
5	3.99271	3.88965	3.79079	3.69590
6	4.62288	4.48592	4.35526	4.23054

Exhibit 8–12
Partial Present Value of an Ordinary Annuity Table

(n) Periods	½%	1%	2%	3%
35	32.03537	29.40858	24.99862	21.48722
36 →	**32.87102**	30.10751	25.48884	21.83225
37	33.70250	30.79951	25.96945	22.16724
38	34.52985	31.48466	26.44064	22.49246

In this case, you have the present value of the loan—that is, the amount you are borrowing for the car. We want to calculate the *series of payments*. Do it using the present value of an ordinary annuity table, shown in Exhibit 8–12, and then try it with a financial calculator.

$$PV(A) = PMT(\text{Factor for 36 Periods, } 0.5\%)$$

where

$PV(A)$ = Present Value of an ordinary annuity
PMT = Amount of each payment in the series of payments and the *factor for* 36 *periods*, 0.5% per period

where period means month, and the factor comes from the present value of an annuity table, like the one shown in Exhibit 8–10.

Instead of knowing the payment and calculating the present value of the payments, we know the present value of the payments and need to compute the amount of the payment.

$$\$22{,}000 = PMT(32.87102)$$

Solving for *PMT*, we get $669.28. Thus, your monthly car payment will be $669.28.

Try it on your financial calculator.

- Enter $22,000 as the present value (*PV* key).
- Enter 36 as the number of periods (*n* key).
- Enter 0.5 as the interest rate (*i*% key).
- Press the *CPT* key followed by the *PMT* key.

You will see $669.28 in the display.

STUDY BREAK 8-5
See How You're Doing

Suppose you want to borrow $50,000 from your rich uncle and he is willing to let you repay him over the next 10 years, with a payment every six months. He has determined that 10 percent is a fair (annual) interest rate. How much will your payments be? Use the present value of an ordinary annuity table, and then check your answer by using your financial calculator, if you have one.

Long-Term Liabilities: Raising Money by Issuing Bonds

What Is a Bond?

L.O. 3

Understand how a company borrows money by issuing bonds and how the company repays the bondholders.

When firms want to borrow large amounts of money, they usually go to the general public to raise the money. They do this by issuing—that is, selling—bonds. Issuing bonds means they borrow money from investors—individuals

> **What Is a Bond?**
>
> The Investor Learning Centre of Canada provides the following insight:
>
> A certificate which is evidence of a debt on which the issuer promises to pay the holder a specified amount of interest for a specified length of time and to repay the loan on its maturity. Bonds are issued by corporations and by federal, provincial, and municipal governments. Bondholders are first in line before shareholders to claim any of a company's assets in the event of liquidation.
>
> *Source:* Investorlearning.ca

like you and me—and companies that want to invest their extra cash. Insurance companies, for example, invest a great deal of money in stocks and bonds. A **bond** is a written agreement that specifies the company's responsibility to pay interest and repay the principal to the bondholders at the end of the term of the bond.

Revisit the discussion of the stock market in Chapter 1. There is a **bond market** that serves a similar function—to bring together buyers and sellers of bonds. Just as there is a stock market, there is also a bond market. The company borrowing the money is sometimes called the seller or, more accurately, the **issuer**. What the company sells or, more accurately, issues is bonds, which are legally binding promises to repay the buyer. The buyer is not really *buying* but is, instead, *lending* the price paid for the bond.

A **bond** is a form of long-term financing in which a company describes in a written agreement its responsibility to pay interest and repay the principal or money it has borrowed from investors.

A **bond market** is a market that facilitates the initial selling and buying and subsequent trading of bonds.

The **issuer** is the company that raises money from investors by issuing bonds or selling equity.

Why would a company borrow money by issuing bonds instead of going to a bank for a loan? There are two reasons.

First, **bondholders** are typically willing to lend money for a longer time period than are banks. Many bonds are 20-, 25-, or 30-year bonds. Most banks will not lend money for such long periods of time. One reason for the willingness of the bondholders to lend money for a long time is that bondholders can convert bonds into cash at any time. The existence of a bond market provides a way for bondholders to sell their bonds to another investor—and get their cash back—without affecting the firm that issued the bond.

Business Process

A **bondholder** is the individual (or institution) who purchases the bond, thus loaning money to the company that issued the bond.

Second, the rate of interest on a bond—that is, the rate the borrower has to pay the bondholder—is commonly lower than the rate on loans charged by banks. Banks pay one rate of interest to people who deposit their money in saving accounts—that is, the savings rate of interest—but charge a higher interest rate to lend money—that is, the borrowing rate of interest. This difference is used to pay the expenses of operating the bank and to pay a return to the owners of the bank. This is one reason why a firm's cost of borrowing money via bonds can be lower than borrowing via bank loans.

Bond convenants are restrictions placed on the bond issuer and stated in the bond agreement, protecting the interest of bondholders.

One disadvantage to borrowing money by issuing bonds is the restrictions placed on a firm that issues bonds. The company may be restricted, by the terms of the bond agreement, from borrowing any additional money from any sources, or the company may need to maintain a certain current ratio—the ratio of current assets to current liabilities. These restrictions, called **bond covenants**, are specified in the bond agreement to protect the interests of the bondholders. Recall that creditors, including bondholders, have priority over the claims of owners.

Exhibit 8–13 shows the information an actual bond will have.

Business Process

More about Bonds

Bondholders are creditors of the company; they are not owners of the company. Bonds require the issuer to make periodic interest payments.

Exhibit 8–13 **What Is on a Bond Certificate?**	**Company name, date of issue, par value, interest rate, payment terms**

Most bonds issued (i.e., sold) in Canada pay the bondholders semiannual interest payments during the life of the bonds. Bondholders are entitled to receive periodic interest payments and, at a specific future date called the maturity date, a lump sum payment equal to the amount given on the face of the bond. Most bonds are issued with a face value in multiples of $1,000.

Bonds can be bought and sold in a secondary market. Just like stock, after the corporation completes the original issue, buyers and sellers get together via the bond market to trade bonds. The price of a bond on the secondary market will be different from the original bond price, depending on whether interest rates have increased or decreased since the date of the original bond issue. Bond prices have an inverse relationship with interest rates: when interest rates increase, bond prices decrease, and vice versa. Because interest payments on a bond are fixed, when the market rate of interest goes down, those fixed rates look better. For example, suppose a $1,000 bond pays 9 percent interest per year. If the market rate of interest is 9 percent, the bond would sell for $1,000. If the market rate of interest goes up to 10 percent, this 9-percent bond of $1,000 is not as attractive as other investments. Thus, the price of this bond will go down. That is the inverse relationship: **market interest rate** goes up, and the bond price goes down. If the market rate of interest goes down to 8 percent, then the 9-percent bond of $1,000 is a very attractive investment; and the price of the bond will go up.

The **market interest rate** is the interest rate in the market for investments with similar risk. It is usually a reference to the interest rate on the date bonds are sold.

The price of a bond when it is issued is stated in terms of a percentage of its face value. If a bond is stated as selling for 98 3/8, that means it is selling for 98 3/8 percent of $1,000 ($1,000 × 0.98375), or $983.75.

A bond that is selling at 100 is selling at par—100 percent of its face value.
A bond selling below 100 is selling at a discount.
A bond selling above 100 is selling at a premium.

Bonds may be secured or unsecured.

- **Secured bonds** give the bondholders a claim to a specific asset of the company in case of default.
- **Unsecured bonds**, also known as debentures, are not linked to specific assets and are issued on the general credit of the company.

Bonds may be **term** or **serial**.

- Term bonds describe bonds that all mature on the same date.
- Serial bonds mature periodically over a period of several years.

A **secured bond** is a bond that gives the bondholder claim to a specific asset of the company in case the company fails to pay the bondholder the interest and principal payments promised.

An **unsecured bond** is a bond that does not give the bondholder a specific claim to a company asset, but, instead, is issued on the general credit of the company.

Term bonds are bonds that mature on a specified date.

Serial bonds are bonds that mature periodically over several years.

STUDY BREAK 8-6

See How You're Doing

If a $1,000 bond is selling for 95 1/2, how much cash does the bondholder pay for the bond? If a $1,000 bond is selling for 102, how much cash does the bondholder pay for the bond?

Issuing Bonds Payable

Getting the Money

L.O. 3

Understand how a company borrows money by issuing bonds and how the company repays the bondholders.

A company may issue bonds at par, at a premium, at a discount. A company's financial statements will show (1) the unamortized discount or premium on the bonds, (2) the periodic payment of interest on these bonds, and (3) the value of the bonds at maturity.

Suppose a company issues a single 10-year bond of $1,000 at 11.5 percent per year, on January 1, 2008. The market rate of interest at the time of issue is 11.5 percent. That means other investments with the same risk are paying an annual return of 11.5 percent. How does this transaction affect the accounting equation?

First, cash is increased by $1,000. Remember, when a company issues bonds, it is borrowing money. The cash receipt is recorded, and a liability is recorded. The $1,000 increase in *cash* is balanced with a $1,000 increase in *bonds payable.*

The journal entry to record the sale of a 10-year, 11.5 percent, $1,000 bond when the market rate of interest is also 11.5 percent is:

Date	Transaction	Debit	Credit
	Cash	$1,000	
	Bonds payable		$1,000

The company must pay the bondholder interest for the use of the $1,000 over the term of the bonds. At the time the bond is issued, the frequency and dates of the interest payments are specified in the contract between the company and the bondholders. Suppose the interest on this bond is paid annually. This means every year the bondholder receives interest from the company. At the end of the term of the bond, the principal—the face amount of the bond—is repaid.

Paying the Bondholders

On December 31, 2008, the company owes its bondholder the first annual interest payment. This payment is calculated with the interest formula:

$$\text{Interest} = \text{Principal} \times \text{Interest Rate} \times \text{Time}$$

In this case:

$$\text{Interest} = \$1,000 \text{ Principal} \times 0.115 \text{ Annual Interest rate} \times 1 \text{ Year} = \$115$$

On December 31, the transaction of paying the interest has the following effect on the accounting equation:

Assets	=	Liabilities	+	Shareholders' equity
$(115) Cash				$(115) Interest expense

The journal entry to record the first interest payment of the 10-year, $1,000, 11.5-percent bond is:

Date	Transaction	Debit	Credit
12/31/2008	Interest expense	$115	
	Cash		$115

Each interest payment will be identical. Remember, the company has to pay the bondholders according to the terms printed on the face of the bond. The cash to be paid at each interest date is determined before the company goes to the market to sell the bond. *Whether the bond is issued at* ***face value****, at a discount, or at a premium, the cash paid to the bondholder is determined by the terms on the face of the bond.* The principal amount, to be repaid at the

Face value is the amount stated on bond or note; the principal.

Exhibit 8–14
Bonds Issued at Face Value, Discount, Premium

Bonds issued at	Interest rates	Bonds will sell for
Par	Stated rate of interest = market rate of interest	Face amount
Discount	Stated rate of interest < market rate of interest	Less than the face amount
Premium	Stated rate of interest > market rate of interest	More than the face amount

end of the term of the bond, is stated on the face of the bond and is used to calculate the interest payments.

It is not difficult to understand how a company reports and makes the payments for bonds issued at face value. However, the real world is often not so simple. Bonds may be issued when the market interest rate is *not* the same as the rate stated on the bonds. Why? Even though the company issuing the bonds tries to pick the market interest rate to use as the stated rate on the face of the bonds, it may not work out as planned. That is because it is not possible to issue bonds on the exact day when the interest for the bond is specified. There is a time delay before the bonds are actually issued. The bond certificates have to be printed and the bond issue filed along with prospective financial statements with the securities commission of the province where the bonds are being issued *before* the issuance date of the bonds. Very often, the market interest rates will change between the time a face interest rate is selected for the bonds and the time the bonds are issued. The market rate of interest is the interest rate that other investments with the same risk are paying on the issue date of the bonds. When the market rate of interest and the stated rate of interest on the bonds are different, the bonds are issued at a premium or a discount. Exhibit 8–14 shows the relationship between the market interest rate and stated interest rate of the bonds as well as the selling price of the bonds.

Accounting for Bonds Payable

Issuing Bonds at a Discount or a Premium

L.O. 3

Understand how a company borrows money by issuing bonds and how the company repays the bondholders.

Suppose a company is offering a $1,000 bond with a stated rate of 10 percent when the market rate of interest is 11 percent. That means that other opportunities exist—with the same risk—that would earn 11 percent. Would you be willing to buy a $1,000 bond of 10 percent if you could invest that same $1,000 in an equivalent investment that pays 11 percent? Of course, you would not. The company issuing the bond will pay $100 in annual interest, whereas other investments—similar to the bond in all respects—are willing to pay $110 in annual interest. Because the issuing company went to a lot of expense to print the bonds and prepare them for issue, it is not possible to simply change the rate of interest stated on the bonds. The company is stuck with what is stated on the bonds—10 percent annual interest payments, that is, $100 annually, and the face of $1,000 to be paid out at maturity.

To make up for the difference between the stated interest rate of 10 percent and the market rate of 11 percent, the company issuing the bonds has to be willing to sell the bonds for *less* than $1,000; that is, sell them at a discount. There is an amount that an investor would pay for a bond that has a $1,000 face value and a stated interest rate of 10 percent when the market rate of interest is 11 percent. That amount is equal to the present value of the future cash flows the bondholder will receive. Bonds sold at less than the face value are sold at a **discount**. We will do the calculations for a bond sold at a discount in the next section of this chapter.

A **discount on bonds payable** is the difference between the selling price and the face amount of a bond when the face amount is greater than the selling price.

On the other hand, if the company were offering a bond that has a face value of $1,000 and a stated interest rate of 10 percent when the market rate of interest is 8 percent, that bond would be a great investment for the investor. If the market rate of return for an investment of equivalent risk were less than the stated interest rate on the bonds, people would flock to buy the bonds, *if* the bonds were issued at the $1,000 face value. However, that will not happen because the market for bonds will respond by bidding up the price of that bond. The rules of supply and demand work well in the bond market. The demand for the bond causes the price of the bond to increase above face value.

Investors should be willing to pay more than $1,000 for that bond because the bond will pay $100 in annual interest when other similar investments only pay $80 for the same $1,000 invested. The extra amount the bondholder is willing to pay for that bond—because the bondholder will collect $100 in interest every year—is called a **premium**. In this case, the bondholder would be willing to pay more than $1,000 for the bond. The bondholder will pay an amount equal to the present value of the future cash flows. The bond still pays $100 interest annually and a lump sum amount for the principal at maturity of $1,000. Later in the chapter, we will look at the calculations.

A **premium on bonds payable** is the difference between the selling price and the face amount of a bond when the selling price is higher than the face amount.

Remember, no matter how much the bondholder pays for the bond—whether the issue price is above or below the price stated on the bond—the series of payments is established by what is printed on the face of the bond. That series of cash flows is what the bondholder is buying. In this example, the cash flows are set at $100 interest annually and a lump sum of $1,000 at maturity.

STUDY BREAK 8-7

See How You're Doing

If Jon-med Company issues a $1,000 bond with a stated interest rate of 9 percent when the market interest rate is 8 percent, will the bond sell for a discount or a premium? How much interest will the bondholders receive each year from Jon-med Company?

Calculating the Proceeds from Bonds Issued at a Premium. Suppose the Biz Corp. issues a $1,000 face value, 10-year, 11.5 percent bond, with interest payable annually. At the time of issue, the market interest rate is 10 percent. How much money will Biz get for the bond?

- First, calculate the bond's annual interest payments of $115 (= $1,000 × 0.115 per year × 1 year). There will be 10 of these payments (one each year for 10 years).
- Next, calculate the present value of an ordinary annuity of $115 for 10 years at an annual interest rate of 10 percent—the market rate of interest. What we need to determine is the equivalent amount of all those interest payments in today's dollars. As you learned earlier in this chapter, tables have been devised and financial calculators have been programmed using interest-compounding formulas to help do this calculation. Recall, the process is called **discounting a series of cash flows**. By using the present value of an ordinary annuity table (Appendix B), the relevant factor is 6.14457, and so the present value of the 10 annual interest payments over 10 years is:

Discounting a series of future cash flows means to calculate the present value of those future cash flows.

$$\$115 \times 6.14457 = \underline{\underline{\$706.63}}$$

Alternatively, you could use your financial calculator to discount the cash flows:

- *PMT* = 115.
- *i* % = 10%.
- *n* = 10 periods.
- Press *CPT* and then *PV*.
- The display will show $706.63 (rounded to the nearest cent).

This means $706.63 today is equivalent to getting 10 payments of $115 over the next 10 years, if the market interest rate is 10 percent per year.

- Determine the present value of the principal repayment. It will be a single $1,000 payment 10 years from now. At the current market rate of interest, how much would you have to invest today to have it grow to be $1,000 in 10 years? To calculate today's value of this $1,000 future payment, use the factor from the present value of $1 table (a single payment instead of a series of payments, in Appendix B)—for 10 years at 10 percent. The factor is 0.38554, and so the present value of the $1,000 principal is:

$$\$1,000 \times 0.38554 = \underline{\underline{\$385.54}}$$

- Alternatively, by using your financial calculator:
- *FV* = $1,000.
- *i*% = 10%.
- *n* = 10 periods.
- The display will show $385.54.
- Today's value—the present value—of the total of the future cash flows is $1,092.17 (= 706.63 + 385.54), even though the face amount of the bond is only $1,000. This bond would be selling today for around 109 1/4, according to the convention of pricing bonds. The way this bond issue would affect the accounting equation is shown next:

Assets	=	Liabilities	+	Shareholders' equity
+$1,092.17 Cash		+$1,000 Bonds payable +$92.17 Premium on bonds payable		

The journal entry to record the issue of a 10-year, $1,000, 11.5-percent bond is:

Date	Transaction	Debit	Credit
	Cash	$1,092.17	
	Bonds payable		$1,000.00
	Premium on bonds payable		92.17

The amount of the face of the bond ($1,000) and the premium ($92.17) are both liabilities. They appear next to each other on the balance sheet. *Premium* on bonds payable is called an adjunct liability. Adjunct means an add-on and describes the relationship between the bonds payable and the premium on bonds payable. The premium is a partner of the bonds payable liability it is matched with, and they are added together on the balance sheet.

Calculating the Proceeds from Bonds Issued at a Discount. Now, suppose the Biz Corp. is issuing a $1,000, 10-year, 11.5-percent bond at a time when the market interest rate is 12 percent. Who would be interested in buying Biz's bond? No one would want to pay $1,000 for the series of payments at the stated 11.5 percent annual interest rate. Biz would have to offer the bond at a discount. What price for the bond will attract buyers?

- First calculate the annual interest payments of $115 (= 1,000 × 0.115 × 1). There will be 10 of these payments.
- Use the factor from the present value of an ordinary annuity table to calculate the present value of the interest payments over 10 years at 12 percent interest per year. The relevant factor is 5.65022, and so the value of the interest payments is:

$$5.65022 \times \$115 = \$649.77$$

Then find the value of the principal repayment. How much is needed today to grow to $1,000 in 10 years at 12 percent per year? The present value is calculated with a factor for 10 periods with 12 percent per period. The present value of $1 gives us a factor of 0.32197, and so the present value is:

$$\$1,000 \times 0.32197 = \$321.97$$

- Biz will sell the bond for a total of $971.74 (= $649.77 + $321.97), even though its face value is $1,000. The bond market would quote a price of approximately 97 1/8, or 97.125, according to the usual way of expressing bond prices.

This bond is being sold at a discount. The transaction has the following effect on the accounting equation:

Assets	=	Liabilities	+	Shareholders' equity
+$971.74 Cash		+$1,000 Bonds payable $(28.26) Discount on bonds payable		

The journal entry to record the issue of the 10-year, $1,000, 11.5 percent bond when the market rate of interest is 12 percent is:

Date	Transaction	Debit	Credit
	Cash	$971.74	
	Discount on bonds payable	28.26	
	Bonds payable		$1,000.00

Contra-liability is an amount deducted from its related liability.

Discount on bonds payable is a **contra-liability** and it is deducted from bonds payable on the balance sheet. It works like the other contra-accounts—accumulated amortization and allowance for doubtful accounts—we have studied in prior chapters. It is shown on the balance sheet with its partner account, and it is deducted from the balance in its partner account. Contra-accounts are valuation accounts. They are used to value the associated asset or liability.

Amortizing Bond Discounts and Premiums: Effective Interest Method

Bond discounts and bond premiums are written off over the life of the bonds. That means the amount of the discount or premium is reduced until it reaches zero.

To show how a discount is written off, let us continue the example of a bond issued at a discount—a $1,000 bond issued for $971.74. The stated rate of interest on the bond is 11.5 percent and the market rate of interest is 12 percent. When the bonds are issued, the value of the net liability, bonds payable minus the discount, is $971.74 (= $1,000 – $28.26). Each time interest is paid to the bondholders, a portion of the discount is written off. The amount of the write off is the difference between the interest expense and the interest payment to the bondholders.

Business Process

Suppose the bond is issued on January 1, 2008. The first interest payment to the bondholders, on December 31, will be in the amount of $115 (= $1,000 × 0.115 × 1 year). The **interest expense**—shown on the income statement—is *not equal* to the **interest payment** to the bondholders. The interest expense is calculated using the usual interest rate formula: $I = P \times R \times T$. In this case, the principal amount borrowed is $971.74. That is the amount the bondholders actually loaned the company on the date of the bond issue. The interest rate is 12 percent—that is the market rate at the date of issue—and the time period is one year.

Interest expense is calculated by multiplying the carrying value of a bond by the market rate of interest at the date of the bond issue.

Interest payment is calculated by multiplying the face value of the bond and the interest rate stated on the bond.

$$\text{Interest Expense} = \$971.74 \times 0.12 \times 1 = \$116.61$$

The difference between the interest payment of $115 and the interest expense of $116.61 is the amount that reduces the discount. After the payment is made, the discount is reduced by $1.61 (= $115 – $116.61). The discount that began with $28.26 at issue is now reduced to $26.65. The same thing happens each time a payment is made. The amount of the discount is reduced. The accounting terminology for that process is called writing off or amortizing the discount, and this method is called the **effective interest method** of amortization.

The value of the bonds payable minus the *un*amortized discount is called the **carrying value** or **book value** of the bonds. Remember, that is the net amount added to the total liabilities on the balance sheet. Over the life of the bonds, the discount is amortized so that the carrying value of the bonds at the date of maturity is exactly the face value. In other words, the amount of the discount is reduced—a portion at each interest payment date—to zero over the life of the bonds. Getting the discount to zero will make the face value of the bond equal to the carrying value. After all, the face value is exactly the amount that must be paid to the bondholders at the maturity date of the bonds.

The **effective interest method** is a method of amortizing bond premiums and discounts that calculates the amount of interest on the outstanding liability, which changes every time a payment is made.

The **book value**, or **carrying value**, of a bond equals bonds payable plus the unamortized premium or the bonds payable minus the unamortized discount.

- Amortizing a bond *discount* will *decrease* the unamortized bond discount and *increase* the carrying value of the bond.
- Amortizing a bond *premium* will *decrease* the unamortized bond premium and *decrease* the carrying value of the bond.

The amortization of bond premiums or discounts is a natural result of calculating the correct amount of interest expense for the period when the company makes an interest payment to the bondholder. Remember, the amount of the cash payments to the bondholders is established before the bond is issued. Consequently, the calculation of the payments to the bondholders is completely independent of the market interest rate at the date of the bond issue. However, the market rate of interest determines the amount of money the bondholders are willing to lend—which is really the amount they are willing to pay for the bonds—to get the fixed payments at specified times in the future.

The demand from the bond market will set the price of the bond so that it will earn exactly the market rate of return. To make the business decision to issue bonds, a company must understand this fact and estimate the cash proceeds when planning the bond issue.

Let us take a closer look at bonds issued at a discount to see how the interest payments to the bondholder and the interest expense to the issuer are different.

Exhibit 8–15
Amortization Schedule for a Bond Issued at a Discount

Period	Annual Interest expense	Interest payment (cash)	Amortization of bond discount	Unamortized bond discount	Carrying value of bond
0				$28.26	$971.74
1		$115			
		115			
		115			
		115			
		Etc.			

Payment of Interest to Bondholders and Amortization of a Discount. Organizing the information about a bond issue in a table like the one shown in Exhibit 8–15 emphasizes the pattern in the calculation of the interest expense related to a bond issued at a discount. The bond is a 10-year, annual interest bond. Note how the details of the bond issue are shown in Exhibit 8–15: cash proceeds amount to $971.74, even though its face value is $1,000. Why wouldn't bondholders pay the full $1,000 for the bond? As stated earlier in the chapter, no one will pay $1,000 because the market rate of interest is 12 percent and this bond has a stated interest rate of only 11.5 percent.

How much interest does the firm that issued the bond owe the bondholder on the first interest date? The bondholder actually loaned the firm $971.74 at the market rate of 12 percent interest. For the first year of the life of the bond, the entire principal balance of $971.74 was outstanding. Thus, the calculation of the interest expense for the first year is:

$$\$971.74 \times 0.12 \times 1 = \$116.61$$

Although the interest expense is $116.61, the firm is going to pay the bondholder only $115—that is, the amount predetermined by the stated rate of interest and face value of the bond. The firm actually owes the bondholder an additional $1.61. Because the payment to the bondholder is fixed, the extra $1.61 will be added to the outstanding principal balance of $971.74. After the first interest payment, the new principal balance is $973.35 (= $971.74 + 1.61). The $1.61—the difference between the interest expense and the interest payment—is amortization of the discount.

The payment to the bondholder of $115 and the discount amortization affects the accounting equation as follows:

Assets	=	Liabilities	+	Shareholders' equity
$(115) Cash		+$1.61 Discount on bonds payable[a]		$(116.61) Interest expense

[a]Remember that the discount is a contra-liability. That is, the discount is subtracted from the bonds payable. As it is amortized, less and less is subtracted, until zero is subtracted from bonds payable. Thus, a reduction in the discount is actually an increase (hence the +) in total liabilities.

The journal entry to record the first interest payment on the bond issued at a discount for the annual discount amortization and cash interest payment is as follows:

Date	Transaction	Debit	Credit
12/31/2008	Interest expense	$116.61	
	Cash		$115.00
	Discount on bonds payable		1.61

Exhibit 8–16
Continuation of the Amortization Schedule for a Bond Issued at a Discount

Period	Annual interest expense (0.12 × carrying value)	Interest payment (cash)	Amortization of discount (interest expense − cash paid)	Unamortized bond discount	Carrying value of bond ($1,000 − unamortized bond discount)
0				$28.26	$971.74
1	**$116.61**	$115	**$1.61**	**26.65**	**973.35**
2	**116.80**	115	**1.80**	**24.85**	**975.15**
3		115			
4		115			

Without getting too technical, let us try to reason out why issuing a bond at a discount results in interest expense that is *greater* than the actual cash payment to the bondholder. Because the interest rate in the market is higher than the interest rate the bond is paying, the difference between the $1,000 face amount to be repaid and the $971.74 issue price may be thought of as some extra interest—in addition to the periodic interest payments—that the bond issuer has to pay to borrow the $971.74.

Each time an interest payment is made to the bondholder, a small portion of the discount is written off as interest expense. At the maturity date of the bond, the discount will be zero.

See if you can fill in the table in Exhibit 8–16 for the first two interest dates. We just calculated the interest expense of $116.61 for the first year. Because the bond annually pays $115, the amount of $1.61 was added to the amount owed to the bondholder. Because a discount is used to reduce the face value of the bonds to the amount actually owed, the discount must get smaller. What is the goal? You want the discount to be zero at maturity. A discount of zero means the book value of the bonds equals the face value of the bonds. See if you can figure out how the numbers for the second interest payment have been calculated.

When you are sure you understand the calculations needed to get the figures for the second interest payment, fill in the numbers for the third and fourth interest payments. (The amortization of discount for the third and fourth years are $2.02 and $2.26, respectively.)

STUDY BREAK 8-8

See How You're Doing

Try this example with semiannual interest payments. Divide the annual interest rate by two and consider each period as a six-month period, and so the number of periods will be the number of six-month periods. Knollwood Corp. issued $200,000 of 6 percent per year, 20-year bonds at 98 on January 1, 2007. Assume the market rate of interest was 6.5 percent. Interest is paid on June 30 and December 31. The company uses the effective interest method of amortization. Prepare the journal entries to record the bond issue and the first two interest payments.

Payment of Interest to Bondholders and Amortization of a Premium. Let us use the same bond but assume it was issued at a premium. Recall, the market rate of interest of 10 percent is lower than the stated rate on the bond of 11.5 percent, and so the bondholder will pay a premium for the bond's series of payments. The format for the amortization schedule is shown in Exhibit 8–17.

Exhibit 8–17
Amortization Schedule for a Bond Issued at a Premium

Period	Annual interest expense	Interest payment (cash)	Amortization of bond premium	Unamortized bond premium	Carrying value of bond
0				$92.17	$1,092.17
1		$115			
		115			
		115			
		115			
		Etc.			

In this example, the amount the bondholder pays—which we should not forget is actually a loan to the firm—is $1,092.17 for the bond. The interest expense incurred is calculated using the market rate of interest. For the first year, the interest expense is:

$$\$1{,}092.17 \times 0.10 \times 1 = \$109.22$$

When the bond issuer makes the cash payment of $115, that amount pays the bondholder the interest for the six months plus a small amount of the principal. The amount of principal paid off is the difference between the interest payment and the interest expense:

$$\$115 - 109.22 = \$5.78$$

This $5.78 is amortization of the premium on bonds payable. The premium of $92.17 will be reduced a little bit each time the bond issuer makes an interest payment to the bondholder, until the premium is zero at maturity. At maturity, the bond issuer pays the bondholder the $1,000 face amount.

The following shows how the interest payment to the bondholder affects the accounting equation:

Assets	=	Liabilities	+	Shareholders' equity
$(115) Cash		$(5.78) Premium on bonds payable		$(109.22) Interest expense

The entry to record the annual premium amortization and cash interest payment is:

Date	Transaction	Debit	Credit
12/31/2008	Interest expense	$109.22	
	Premium on bonds payable	5.78	
	Cash		$115.00

Issuing a bond at a premium results in interest expense (to the bond issuer) that is *less* than the actual cash payment of interest to the bondholder because the 10 percent interest rate in the market is lower than the 11.5 percent interest rate specified on the bond. With that in mind, we can think of the premium the bondholder paid as a payment in advance to the bond issuer to help meet the 11.5 percent payment due the bondholder.

Each time a cash payment for interest is made to the bondholder, a little of the premium is written off. How much? The difference between the interest payment and the interest expense will be the amount of the premium amortization. At maturity, the premium will be zero.

See if you can fill in the table in Exhibit 8–18 for the first two interest rate dates. As calculated previously, the interest expense for the first year is $109.22.

Period	Annual interest expense	Interest payment (cash)	Amortization of bond premium	Unamortized bond premium	Carrying value of bond
0				$ 92.17	$ 1,092.17
1	**109.22**	$115	**5.78**	**86.39**	**1,086.39**
2	**108.64**	115	**6.36**	**80.03**	**1,080.03**
3		115			
4		115			
		Etc.			

Exhibit 8–18
Continuation of the Amortization Schedule for a Bond Issued at a Premium

Because the cash paid as interest to the bondholder each time it is due is $115, there is a difference of $5.78 that will be deducted from the premium. Because the original premium increases the amount owed to the bondholder to an amount *larger* than the face of the bond, the premium must be made smaller over the life of the bond.

The goal is to reduce the premium to zero at maturity so that the bond will have a book value equal to its face value. When you understand the calculations needed to get the figures for the second interest payment, fill in the numbers for the third and fourth interest payments.

STUDY BREAK 8-9

See How You're Doing

Wood Corp. issued $200,000 of 20-year, 10 percent interest bonds at 102 on January 1, 2007. Assume the market rate of interest was 9 percent. Interest is paid annually on December 31. The company uses the effective interest method of amortization. Prepare the journal entries to record the bond issue and the first interest payment.

Straight-Line Amortization of Bond Discounts and Premiums

In addition to the effective interest method of amortizing a bond discount or premium, there is another method sometimes used called the **straight-line method**. Straight-line amortization simply divides the premium or discount equally over the number of interest payment periods. The effective interest method makes logical sense with respect to interest expense being calculated on the outstanding principal, but there is no particular logic to the straight-line method. It is a simple calculation, much easier than the effective interest method, and this simplicity is its only attractive feature. Straight-line amortization often does a poor job of matching, but it is a generally accepted accounting principle (GAAP). However, if the straight-line method and the effective interest method produce similar amounts for interest expense and for net bonds payable, the accounting standards allow the use of the straight-line method of amortization.

Straight-line amortization is a method that expenses an equal amount of amortization for each year of the asset's useful life and that writes off periodic equal amounts of bond premium and discount over the life of the bond.

Let us look at the last example—10-year bonds, 11.5 percent stated rate, $1,000 face value, market rate at issue of 10 percent—and see how straight-line amortization works. Recall, the bond will be issued at a premium, and we calculated the issue price to be $1,092.17. The difference between the face of $1,000 and the issue price of $1,092.17 is a premium. As was shown in Exhibit 8–18, we have already seen how the premium of $92.17 would be amortized using the effective interest method.

To amortize the premium using the straight-line method, divide the premium by the number of interest payments to the bondholders. That means the

Exhibit 8–19
Straight-Line Amortization Schedule for a Bond Issued at a Premium

Period	Annual interest expense	Interest payment (cash)	Amortization of bond premium	Unamortized bond premium	Carrying value
0				$92.17	$1,092.17
1	**$105.78**	$115	**9.22**	**82.95**	**1,082.95**
2	**105.78**	115	**9.22**	**73.73**	**1,073.73**
3	**105.78**	115	**9.22**	**64.51**	**1,064.51**
4		115	Etc.		
		Etc.			

same amount will be amortized each time an interest payment is made. In this example, in which the premium is $92.17, the amount of premium amortized will be $9.22 per year. The amortization schedule for the first three years is shown in Exhibit 8–19.

The journal entry to record the annual premium amortization and cash interest payment using the *straight-line method* of amortization is:

Date	Transaction	Debit	Credit
12/31/2008	Interest expense	$105.78	
	Premium on bonds payable	9.22	
	Cash		$115.00

To use the straight-line method of amortization, you do not have to know the market interest rate to calculate the interest expense. Each period the interest expense is the same; the amortization of the discount or premium is the same; and, of course, the payment is the same. You can see how that makes the calculations easy. However, it is only permissible to use the straight-line method when the interest expense calculated with this method is not significantly different from the interest expense calculated using the effective interest method. The numbers in this example are small, and the difference does not seem to be very significant. When a company has hundreds of thousands or even millions of dollars of bonds outstanding, the two methods can produce very different amounts of interest expense.

Zero-Coupon Bonds

L.O. 3

Understand how a company borrows money by issuing bonds and how the company repays the bondholders.

We have seen that bonds result in two sets of payments to the purchaser. One is the periodic (usually annual or semiannual) payment of interest. The other is the repayment of the principal at maturity.

Certain bonds do *not* make periodic payments of interest. Instead, they make only one payment—the face value of the bond paid to the purchaser at the maturity date. These bonds are known as **zero-coupon bonds**. What is a coupon? At one time it was a little part on a bond that the bondholder tore off and took to the bank to collect the interest periodically. (The bank acts as an agent for the bond issuer.) A zero-coupon bond means the bond has no coupons—and, thus, no interest payments during the life of the bond.

A **zero-coupon bond** is a bond that does not make periodic payments of interest. The full face value of the bond is due at its maturity date.

The purchaser of a $1,000 zero-coupon bond is promised a $1,000 payment when the bond matures. However, the purchaser does not get any periodic interest payments. Because purchasers are only willing to pay for what they get, calculating the price of a zero-coupon bond is easy: it is simply the present value of the future $1,000 payment.

Let us consider the $1,000 bond issued by Biz Corp. Suppose Biz is issuing a 10-year, 10 percent interest (compounded annually) zero-coupon bond. Assume the market rate of interest is also 10 percent. What is the present value of the principal repayment?

From the present value of $1 table, the factor for the present value of a lump sum for 10 years at 10 percent is 0.38554. By using that factor to calculate the present value, the bond's issue price is $385.54 (= 0.38554 × $1,000). This is the *entire* price a purchaser pays for this particular zero-coupon bond. Over the life of the bond, the interest is added to the principal, and it grows to be $1,000 at maturity.

The entry to record the sale of the Biz Corporation 10-percent zero-coupon bond is:

Date	Transaction	Debit	Credit
	Cash	$385.54	
	Discount on bonds payable	614.46	
	Bonds payable		$1,000.00

At each interest payment date, the discount will be amortized on the basis of the outstanding principal balance. For example, the interest due on the first annual payment date would be $38.55 [$385.54 × 0.10 (or 10%)], and the entry to record the annual interest expense on a zero-coupon bond would be:

Date	Transaction	Debit	Credit
	Interest expense	$38.55	
	Discount on bonds payable		$38.55

STUDY BREAK 8-10

Summary Problem

On January 1, 2007, Stanton Corp. issued $100,000 face value of 8 percent interest bonds to yield 10 percent. (That is another way of saying that the market rate of interest on the date of the bond issue was 10 percent.) The bonds are dated January 1, 2007, call for annual interest payments on December 31, and mature on December 31, 2010. Stanton uses the effective interest method for amortizing discounts and premiums.

1. Calculate the proceeds for the bond issue. (Then round the selling price to the nearest whole percentage point to answer the rest of the questions.)
2. Prepare the journal entry to record the bond issue.
3. Prepare the journal entry to record the first interest payment.
4. Prepare the journal entry to record the second interest payment.
5. What is the carrying value of the bonds on the December 31, 2007, balance sheet and on the December 31, 2008, balance sheet?

L.O. 3

Understand how a company borrows money by issuing bonds and how the company repays the bondholders.

Callable and Convertible Bonds

Callable Bonds

Almost all bonds contain a *call* feature, which allows the issuer to buy back and retire the bonds—get rid of the debt—at a given price, usually at a price above face value, before maturity. This allows corporations to save money by refinancing their debt if interest rates drop.

A **callable bond** is a bond containing a call feature giving the issuer the right to buy back and retire the bonds before maturity.

Convertible Bonds

A **convertible bond** is a bond that can be converted into shares at the discretion of the bondholder.

Convertible bonds can be converted into common shares at the option of the investor. This feature can make bonds more attractive because investors can receive interest on the bond and then convert the bond into shares to benefit from future increases in the market price of the shares.

Financial Statement Analysis

L.O. 4

Understand how information about a company's debt is used in financial statement analysis.

The combination of debt and equity that a company chooses is its **capital structure**.

Business Process

Financial leverage refers to using borrowed money to increase earnings.

Debt-to-equity ratio is total liabilities divided by shareholders' equity. It compares the value of claims of creditors with the value of the claims of owners.

A **claim** is the legal right to a company's assets.

Times-interest-earned ratio describes a company's ability to make the interest payments on its debt.

We know that the two ways to finance a business are debt and equity. The combination of debt and equity that a company chooses is called its **capital structure**. That is because debt and equity are the two sources of capital and every company can choose the proportion of each that makes up its total capital.

When should a company borrow money? A very simplistic cost-and-benefit analysis would suggest that when the benefit of borrowing the money (what it can earn for the business) exceeds the cost of borrowing the money (interest expense), then borrowing money is a good idea.

Financial leverage is the concept of using borrowed funds to increase earnings. If a company earns more with the money it borrows than it has to pay to borrow that money, it is called *positive financial leverage*. Suppose Anna Chase has invested $50,000 in her new business and has no debt. If the business earns $5,000 net income, then she has earned a return on her investment of 10 percent. Suppose Anna wants to expand her business. She could earn an additional $5,000 if she borrows an additional $50,000. If the after-tax cost of borrowing the money is 8 percent, then Anna would be taking advantage of financial leverage if she borrows the money. That is because earnings would increase by more than the cost of borrowing the money. The new total income—$5,000 + $5,000 – $4,000 interest = $6,000. Now Anna's return on equity is $6,000/$50,000 = 12%.

Two financial ratios measure a company's debt position and its ability to meet its interest payments. The first is the **debt-to-equity** ratio. This is often calculated as:

$$\frac{\text{Total Liabilities}}{\text{Shareholders' Equity}}$$

This ratio compares the amount of creditors' **claims** to the assets of the firm with owners' claims to the assets of the firm. A firm with a high debt-to-equity ratio is often referred to as a highly leveraged firm.

Another way to express the relationship between debt and equity is to calculate the total liabilities as a percentage of total liabilities plus shareholders' equity. That is just expressing total debt as a percentage of the total claims to the assets of the firm. When you are reading about debt-to-equity ratios, be sure you know how the ratio is defined.

The second ratio related to long-term debt is called the **times-interest-earned** ratio. This ratio measures a company's ability to meet its interest obligations. It is calculated as:

$$\frac{\text{Net Income + interest expense + taxes}}{\text{Interest Expense}}$$

It is important to make sure you have added back the company's interest expense to the numerator. The ratio measures the number of times operating income can cover interest expense. The more interest expense a company has, the smaller the ratio will be. If a company has any trouble covering its interest expense, that company clearly has too much debt.

The details about a company's long-term debt are often found in the notes to the financial statements, instead of the face of the balance sheet. For example, the liabilities section of the Gildan Activewear Inc. balance sheet, shown in Exhibit 8–20, shows only the basic amounts of long-term obligations. The accompanying notes give the details. The more you learn about analyzing financial statements, the more you will come to appreciate the importance of the information in the notes to the financial statements.

STUDY BREAK 8-11

See How You're Doing

Calculate the debt-to-equity ratio for Gildan Activewear Inc. for each of the years shown in Exhibit 8–20. What trend do you see, and how might an investor interpret it?

Exhibit 8–20
Details of Long-Term Debt from the Financial Statements of Gildan Activewear Inc.
Courtesy Gildan Activewear Inc.

From the Balance Sheet	2003	2002
Liabilities and Shareholders' Equity		
CURRENT LIABILITIES:		
Accounts payable and accrued liabilities	$ 90,098,348	$ 82,167,747
Income taxes payable	5,234,699	3,063,050
Current portion of long-term debt (Note 4)	26,089,454	6,249,039
	121,422,501	91,479,836
LONG-TERM DEBT (Note 4)	72,420,923	114,866,404
FUTURE INCOME TAXES	27,743,000	20,385,000
SHAREHOLDERS' EQUITY		
Share capital	111,563,663	104,924,975
Contributed surplus	322,866	322,866
Retained earnings	241,932,198	164,660,258
	353,818,727	269,908,099
	$ 575,405,151	$ 496,639,339
From the Notes to the Financial Statements		
4. Long-Term Debt		
SECURED:		
Senior notes (US$70,000,000)	$ 93,744,000	$ 110,271,000
Obligations under capital leases, bearing interest at rates varying from 5.21% to 16.08%, maturing at various dates through 2005	1,970,941	7,026,062
Term loan, bearing interest at 7.58%, maturing during 2004	34,517	687,951
	95,749,458	117,985,013
Current portion of secured debt	25,375,054	5,570,277
	$ 70,374,404	$ 112,414,736
UNSECURED:		
Term loans, bearing interest at rates up to 6% per annum, maturing at various dates through 2008	$ 2,760,919	$ 3,130,430
Current portion of unsecured debt	714,400	678,762
	$ 2,046,519	$ 2,451,668
Total unsecured and secured long-term debt	$ 72,420,923	$ 114,866,404

Business Risk

L.O. 5

Identify the risks associated with long-term debt.

Business Process

The risks associated with debt are different from the risks associated with assets like cash or inventory. A company must put controls in place to minimize the risk of losing cash and inventory.

The risk associated with debt is risk to both the company and to its creditors. The primary risk for a company associated with long-term debt is the risk of not being able to make the debt payments. The more debt a business has, the more risk there is that the company will not be able to pay the debt as it becomes due. That would result in serious financial trouble, possibly even bankruptcy. This is, of course, a significant risk for the creditors, too. If a company has trouble making its debt payments, you would not like to be one of its creditors.

There are two steps a company can take to minimize the risk associated with long-term debt.

1. Be sure a thorough business analysis accompanies any decision to borrow money. This is where the concept of positive financial leverage comes in. The company must make sure there is a high probability of earning a higher return with the borrowed funds than the interest costs associated with borrowing the funds. How high should the probability be? That is an individual business decision. The point is that this should be a consideration. The more the amount of money involved, the higher the probability should be.
2. Study the characteristics of various types of debt—terms, interest rates, and ease of obtaining the money—and evaluate their attractiveness in your specific circumstances, given the purpose of the debt and the financial situation of the company. For example, bonds are more flexible—the terms and cash flows can be varied, whereas a bank loan can be arranged much more quickly.

Understanding Excel

In this exercise, you create an amortization schedule for the loan Tom's Wear has taken to pay for its new building.

Requirements

1. Open a new Excel work sheet.
2. Beginning in cell B1, input the following chart. Resize columns, wrap text, and add colour and borders, as required. You may also choose the font type and size, as desired. (See Chapter 7 Excel Exercise for formatting hints.)

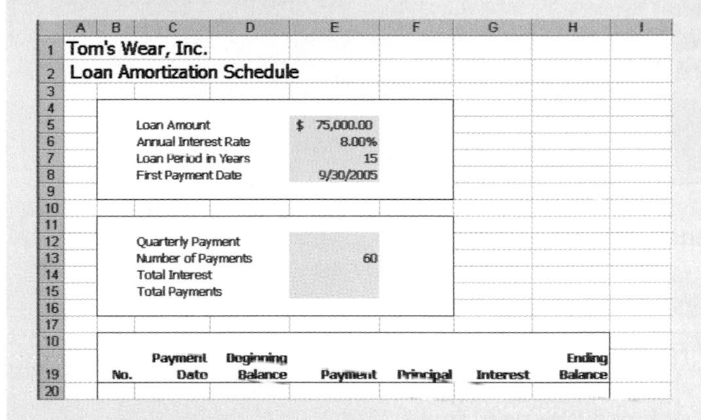

3. To calculate the quarterly payment amount, click the Paste Function button and then select Financial and PMT.

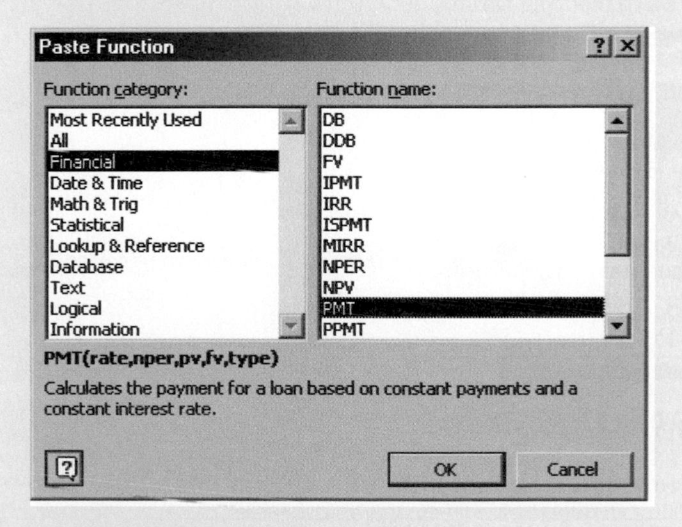

4. Select cell E12, and input the information that follows to calculate the quarterly payment. Note that when entering formulas, the "=" sign is not required.

   Hint: To remove the negative sign, multiply your results by −1.

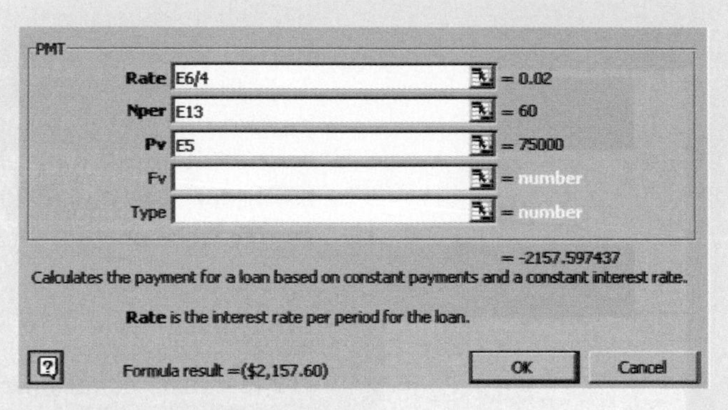

5. By using appropriate formulas, calculate the total interest and the total payments to be made on the loan.
6. Complete the amortization table as follows:

   ■ Input the number and date of each payment.

   Hint: Input the first three numbers (1 to 3) or the first four payment dates, and Excel will complete the series if you use the fill handle and drag over the rest of the range.

No.	Payment Date
1	9/30/2005
2	12/31/2005
3	3/31/2006
4	6/30/2006
5	

   ■ Input the beginning balance and payment amount using the appropriate cell reference.

   Hint: Input the payment amount as = E12. The dollar signs allow you to copy the payment without the cell reference changing.

   ■ Use appropriate formulas and cell references to calculate the interest, principal, and ending balance for payment 1. Copy the formulas and cell references to complete the schedule.

   Hint: To copy the beginning balance, you must enter the correct cell reference for payment 2: "= **H20.**"

7. Print your file and save it to disk. Name your file TomsWear8.

Summary Problem: Tom's Wear Obtains Debt Financing in July

When Tom started his T-shirt business in January, he borrowed a small amount of money from his mom. Now that he has the business up and running, Tom decides he needs more space for inventory and for the actual business operations. This is crucial if he wants to take advantage of the demand for his shirts. Tom finds an excellent deal on a small office complex with a large warehouse; and so he goes to his local bank and secures a mortgage loan for $75,000, the cost of the office complex. The balance sheet from June 30 is shown in Exhibit 8–21, and the transactions for July are shown in Exhibit 8–22.

Additional information needed to make the month-end adjustments:

1. The van was driven 10,000 kilometres this month.
2. Bad debt expense and warranty expense are calculated on the basis of the same percentages as Tom's Wear used in June: 3 percent of credit sales for bad debts and 2 percent of sales for warranties.

Required:

Record the journal entries and the needed adjustments. Post the entries to T-accounts, and prepare an adjusted trial balance. Then, prepare the four basic financial statements for Tom's Wear for the month of July. Ignore income taxes. (Solution provided near the end of the chapter.)

Exhibit 8–21

Tom's Wear, Inc.
Balance Sheet
At June 30, 2005

Assets		Liabilities and shareholders' equity	
Cash	$ 8,278	Accounts payable	$18,950
Accounts receivable (net of allowance of $1,320)	42,780	Interest payable	750
Inventory	6,365	Warranty liability	979
Prepaid insurance	150	Salaries payable	723
Prepaid rent	1,800	Payroll taxes payable	277
Prepaid Web service	200	Other payables	77
		Current portion of long-term note	6,000
Total current assets	59,573	*Total current liabilities*	27,756
Equipment (net of $400 accumulated amortization)	3,600		
Van (net of $2,755 accumulated amortization)	27,245	Notes payable	24,000
Total assets	$90,418		
		Total liabilities	51,756
		Common shares	5,000
		Retained earnings	33,662
		Total liabilities and shareholders' equity	$90,418

Exhibit 8–22
Transactions for July 2005 for Tom's Wear, Inc.

1	July 1	For a new office complex, Tom borrows $75,000 at an annual interest rate of 8 percent for a term of 15 years. The terms of the loan call for quarterly payments of principal and interest. The first payment will be made on September 30. (The principal portion of the quarterly payments due in 2005 of $2,710 will be shown as the current portion of the mortgage payable.) As part of his decision to buy the office complex, Tom had an appraisal done on the land and building. Recall, we discussed "market basket" purchases in Chapter 5. Tom has to separate the cost of the land and building, so he can amortize only the building. The land was appraised at 10 percent of the purchase price and the building at 90 percent. The building has an estimated useful life of 40 years and an estimated residual value of $5,100. The company will use straight-line amortization.
2	July 5	Pays Sam's June salary and deposits the related payroll taxes.
3	July 10–30	Collects cash on accounts receivable of $37,000.
4	July 12	Pays accounts payable of $18,950.
5	July 14	Tom has been concentrating on increasing sales, so he must increase inventory purchases as well. Tom has found a supplier who will give him a significant discount with a large quantity purchase, so the company purchases 10,000 T-shirts. The cost is $3.60 each. The shipping terms are FOB destination. Tom's Wear makes the purchase on account.
6	July 20	Tom finds out that Big Bend Sports has closed and filed for bankruptcy. He writes off their account, which has a balance of $1,000.
7	July 15–30	Tom's sales efforts continue to pay off with the addition of several more sporting goods stores as customers. During July, Tom sells 500 shirts for $11 each to 18 different stores. All sales are on account.
8	July 15–30	During July, 200 shirts are returned with defects. Tom replaces all of them with new shirts.
9	July 15–30	Pays other operating expenses of $2,600 for the month.
10	July 30	Tom has hired a firm to handle his payroll because he has hired several new employees. He sends the payroll company a cheque for $3,500 by the 30th of each month to cover the monthly payroll and payroll tax expenses. The payroll company pays the employees, the payroll taxes, and charges a fee based on the number of employees. Tom's Wear records the total expense as salary expense for financial statement purposes.
11	July 30	Pays a dividend of $2,000.

Answers to Study Break Questions

STUDY BREAK 8-1

Interest expense = $600,000 × 0.09 × 1/12 (1 month) = $4,500 interest per month.

Total payment = $5,500, and so $4,500 is interest, and the remaining $1,000 is principal.

Date	Transaction	Debit	Credit
2/1	Mortgage payable	$1,000	
	Interest expense	4,500	
	Cash		$5,500

To record the first principal and interest payment on the $600,000, 9% note.

STUDY BREAK 8-2

Future value = *PV* × (factor of *FV* of a single amount table)
= 500 × 3.10585
= $1,552.92

STUDY BREAK 8-3

FV ordinary annuity = *PMT* × (factor from *FV* of an ordinary annuity table)
= 200 × (4.70973)
= $941.95

STUDY BREAK 8-4

PV = \$5,000 × (factor from PV of \$1 table)
PV = \$5,000 × 0.62092
PV = \$3,104.60

STUDY BREAK 8-5

$PV = PMT\,(n, i\%)$
$50{,}000 = PMT\,(20, 5\%)$
$50{,}000 = PMT\,(12.46221)$
PMT = \$4,012.13

STUDY BREAK 8-6

\$1,000 × 0.955 = \$ 955
\$1,000 × 1.02 = \$1,020

STUDY BREAK 8-7

- The bond will sell for a *premium* because the bond's stated interest rate is higher than the market rate of interest.
- The interest payment is calculated by the information on the face of the bond: \$1,000 × 0.09 = \$90 per year.

STUDY BREAK 8-8

Interest *expense* (as opposed to interest *payment*) is calculated by multiplying the bond's carrying value (the loan) by the market rate of interest. The amount of proceeds (selling price of the bonds) equals the carrying value of the bonds on the date of the first interest payment. Thus, \$196,000 × 0.065 × 1/2 = \$6,370 is the interest expense for the first six months. Because the payment (fixed by the face value of the bond and the stated interest rate) for the six months is \$6,000 (= \$200,000 × 6% × 1/2), the difference of \$370 will be subtracted from the discount on bonds payable. That will increase the carrying value of the bonds to \$196,370 after the first interest payment. Then, at December 31, 2007, Knollwood will accrue interest expense for the last half of the year; the expense is \$196,370 × 0.065 × 1/2 year = \$6,382. The payment is \$6,000, and so the difference of \$382 will be subtracted from the discount. The carrying value of the bonds on December 31, 2007, will be \$196,752. The total interest expense for the year is \$6,370 + \$6,382 = \$12,752.

Date	Transaction	Debit	Credit
1/1/2007	Cash	\$196,000	
	Discount on bonds payable	4,000	
	Bonds payable		\$200,000
To record the issue of \$200,000, 6% bonds at 98			
6/30/2007	Interest expense	\$6,370	
	Cash		\$6,000
	Discount on bonds payable		370
To record the first semi-annual interest payment on bonds (expense = \$196,000 × 0.0325)			
12/31/2007	Interest expense	\$6,382	
	Cash		\$6,000
	Discount on bonds payable		382
To record the second semi-annual interest payment on bonds (expense = \$196,370 × 0.0325)			

STUDY BREAK 8-9

Interest *expense* (as opposed to interest *payment*) is calculated by multiplying the bond's carrying value (the loan) by the market rate of interest. The amount of proceeds (selling price of the bond) equals the carrying value of the bonds on the date of the first interest payment.

Thus, \$204,000 × 0.09 = \$18,360 is the first year's interest expense.

The interest payment (fixed by the face value of the bonds and the stated interest rate) for the first year is \$20,000 (= \$200,000 × 0.10), the difference of \$1,640 will be deducted from the premium on bonds payable. That will decrease the carrying value of the bonds to \$202,360 (\$204,000 – \$1,640) after the first interest payment. (Remember, the carrying value will decrease over the life of these bonds to go from $204,000 to the face amount of $200,000 by maturity.)

Date	Transaction	Debit	Credit
1/1/2007	Cash	$204,000	
	Bonds payable		$200,000
	Premium on bonds payable		4,000
To record the issue of $200,000, 10% bonds at 102.			
12/31/2007	Interest expense	$18,360	
	Premium on bonds payable	1,640	
	Cash		$20,000
To record the first annual interest payment on bonds (expense = $204,000 × 0.09).			

STUDY BREAK 8-10

1. For computing bond price *PV* = present value.
Principal: $100,000 × *PV* of $1 for 4 periods at 10% = $100,000 × 0.68301[a] = $68,301
Interest: $8,000 × *PV* of an ordinary annuity of $1 for 4 periods at 10% =
$8,000 × 3.16987[b] = $25,359

Total price (PV) $93,660 This means that the bonds were issued for approximately 94, which means 94 percent of the face value. Use 94 to answer these questions:

[a]Where 0.68301 is from *PV* of $1 table.
[b]Where 3.16987 is from *PV* of an annuity table.

2. Show how the actual issue of these bonds affects the accounting equation:

Assets	=	Liabilities	+	Share capital	+	Retained earnings
+$94,000 Cash		+100,000 Bonds payable (6,000) Discount on bonds payable				

Date	Transaction	Debit	Credit
1/1/2007	Cash	$94,000	
	Discount on bonds payable	6,000	
	Bonds payable		$100,000
To record the issue of $100,000, 10% bonds at 94.			

3. Show how the payment of interest on December 31, 2007, affects the accounting equation:

Assets	=	Liabilities	+	Contributed capital	+	Retained earnings
$(8,000) Cash		+1,400 Discount on bonds payable				$(9,400) Interest expense

Date	Transaction	Debit	Credit
12/31/2007	Interest expense	$9,400	
	Cash		$8,000
	Discount on bonds payable		1,400
To record the first annual interest payment on bonds (expense = $94,000 × 0.10).			

Note: Interest expense: $94,000 × 0.10 = $9,400. Because the payment is fixed at $8,000, you amortize the discount (it becomes interest expense) by the difference, $1,400. Deducting $1,400 from the discount actually increases the carrying value of the bonds to $95,400. (You are working up to the face.)

4. Show how the payment of interest on December 31, 2008, affects the accounting equation:

Assets	=	Liabilities	+	Share capital	+	Retained earnings
$(8,000) Cash		+$1,540 Discount on bonds payable				(9,540) Interest expense

Date	Transaction	Debit	Credit
12/31/2008	Interest expense	$9,540	
	Cash		$8,000
	Discount on bonds payable		1,540
	To record the second annual interest payment on bonds (expense = $95,400 × 0.10).		

Note: $95,400 × 0.10 = $9,540 interest expense. Because the payment is $8,000, you amortize $1,540 as additional interest expense. So, the new book value for the bond and the premium = $96,940.

5. The carrying value of the bonds on the December 31, 2007, balance sheet is $95,400; and on the December 31, 2008, balance sheet, $96,940.

STUDY BREAK 8-11

Debt to equity:

2003 $$\frac{\$221,586,424}{\$353,818,727} = 0.626$$

2002 $$\frac{\$226,731,240}{\$269,908,099} = 0.840$$

The company has reduced its debt-to-equity ratio. An investor would likely see this as good news.

Solution to Summary Problem

Transaction 1

Tom borrows $75,000 for a new office complex (land and building).

Date	Transaction	Debit	Credit
7/1/2005	Buildings	$67,500	
	Land	7,500	
	Mortgage payable		$75,000
	To record the purchase of a building and land.		

Transaction 2

Pays Sam Cubby's salary for June and deposits the related payroll taxes.

Date	Transaction	Debit	Credit
7/5/2005	Salaries payable	$723	
	Payroll taxes withheld	277	
	Other payables	77	
	Cash		$1,077
	To record payment of salary and taxes.		

Transaction 3
Collects cash on accounts receivable of $37,000.

Date	Transaction	Debit	Credit
7/10–7/30/2005	Cash	$37,000	
	Accounts receivable		$37,000
To record the collection of accounts receivable.			

Transaction 4
Pays accounts payable of $18,950.

Date	Transaction	Debit	Credit
7/12/2005	Accounts payable	$18,950	
	Cash		$18,950
To record payment on account.			

Transaction 5
Purchases 10,000 T-shirts @ $3.60 each, FOB destination.

Date	Transaction	Debit	Credit
7/14/2005	Inventory	$36,000	
	Accounts payable		$36,000
To record the purchase of 10,000 T-shirts at $3.60 each.			

Transaction 6
Writes off accounts receivable of Big Bend Sports, $1,000.

Date	Transaction	Debit	Credit
7/20/2005	Allowance for doubtful accounts	$1,000	
	Accounts receivable (Big Bend)		$1,000
To record the write-off of Big Bend Sports' account.			

Transaction 7
Sells 500 shirts to 18 stores for $11 each, for a total of 9,000 shirts. All sales are on account.

Date	Transaction	Debit	Credit
7/15–7/30/2005	Accounts receivable	$99,000	
	Sales revenue		$99,000
To record the sale of 9,000 T-shirts on account.			
7/15–7/30/2005	Cost of goods sold	$32,735	
	Inventory		$32,735
To record cost of goods sold = [(1,675 × $3.80) + (7,325 × $3.60)].			

Transaction 8
During July, 200 shirts are returned with defects. Tom replaces them all with new shirts.

Date	Transaction	Debit	Credit
7/15–7/30/2005	Warranties payable	$720	
	Inventory		$720
To record the replacement of 200 defective shirts (200 × $3.60).			

Transaction 9
Other operating expenses for the month are $2,600.

Date	Transaction	Debit	Credit
7/30/2005	Other operating expenses	$2,600	
	Cash		$2,600
To record the payment of other operating expenses.			

Transaction 10
Records salary expense of $3,500.

Date	Transaction	Debit	Credit
7/30/2005	Salary expense	$3,500	
	Cash		$3,500
To record the payment of payroll, related taxes, and fees.			

Transaction 11
Tom's Wear pays a dividend of $2,000.

Date	Transaction	Debit	Credit
7/30/2005	Retained earnings	$2,000	
	Cash		$2,000
To record the payment of a cash dividend.			

Adjustment 1
Record operating expenses: $1,200 for rent, $100 for insurance, and $50 for Web services.

Date	Transaction	Debit	Credit
7/31/2005	Rent expense	$1,200	
	Insurance expense	100	
	Other operating expenses	50	
	Prepaid rent		$1,200
	Prepaid insurance		100
	Prepaid Web service		50
To record July's operating expenses.			

Adjustment 2
Record amortization expense for June: $100 for the computer, $1,450 for the van (10,000 kilometres × $0.145), and $130 for the building ($62,400 ÷ 40) ÷ 12.

Date	Transaction	Debit	Credit
7/31/2005	Amortization expense	$1,680	
	Accumulated amortization: computer		$ 100
	Accumulated amortization: van		1,450
	Accumulated amortization: building		130
To record July amortization expense.			

Adjustment 3
Record interest expense on the notes: van—$250 ($30,000 × 10%) ÷ 12; mortgage—$500 ($75,000 × 8%) ÷ 12.

Date	Transaction	Debit	Credit
7/31/2005	Interest expense	$750	
	Interest payable		$750
To record interest expense for July.			

Adjustment 4
Bad debt estimate = 3 percent of credit sales.

Date	Transaction	Debit	Credit
7/31/2005	Bad debt expense	$2,970	
	Allowance for doubtful accounts		$2,970
To record the bad debt estimate for July (3% × $99,000).			

Adjustment 5
Warranty liability estimate = 2 percent of total sales.

Date	Transaction	Debit	Credit
7/31/2005	Warranty expense	$1,980	
	Warranties payable		$1,980
To record the estimated warranty liability for July (2% × $99,000).			

T-Accounts for Tom's Wear with July journal entries and adjustments

Cash

	Debit	Credit	
BB	$8,278	1,077	2
3	37,000	18,950	4
		2,600	9
		3,500	10
		2,000	11
	$17,151		

Accounts receivable

	Debit	Credit	
BB	$44,100	$37,000	3
7a	99,000	1,000	6
	$105,100		

Allowance for doubtful accounts

	Debit	Credit	
6	$1,000	$1,320	BB
		2,970	Adj-4
		$3,290	

Inventory

	Debit	Credit	
BB	$6,365	$32,735	7b
5	36,000	720	8
	$8,910		

Prepaid insurance

	Debit	Credit	
BB	$150	$100	Adj-1
	$ 50		

Prepaid Web service

	Debit	Credit	
BB	$200	$50	Adj-1
	$150		

Prepaid rent

	Debit	Credit	
BB	$1,800	$1,200	Adj-1
	$ 600		

Equipment: computer

	Debit	Credit	
BB	$4,000		
	$4,000		

Accumulated amortization: computer

	Debit	Credit	
		$400	BB
		100	Adj-2
		$500	

Equipment: van

	Debit	Credit	
BB	$30,000		
	$30,000		

Accumulated amortization: van

	Debit	Credit	
		$2,755	BB
		1,450	Adj-2
		$4,205	

Buildings

	Debit	Credit	
1	$67,500		
	$67,500		

Accumulated amortization: buildings

	Debit	Credit	
		$130	Adj-2
		$130	

Land

	Debit	Credit	
1	$7,500		
	$7,500		

Accounts payable

	Debit	Credit	
4	$18,950	$18,950	BB
		36,000	5
		$36,000	

Interest payable

	Debit	Credit	
		$750	BB
		750	Adj-3
		$1,500	

Payroll taxes withheld

	Debit	Credit	
2	$277	$277	BB
		$ 0	

Other payables

	Debit	Credit	
2	77	$77	BB
		$ 0	

Salaries payable

	Debit	Credit	
2	723	$723	BB
		$ 0	

Warranties payable

	Debit	Credit	
8	$720	$979	BB
		1,980	Adj-5
		$2,239	

T-Accounts for Tom's Wear with July journal entries and adjustments

Notes payable

Ref	Debit	Credit	Ref
		$30,000	BB
		$30,000	

Mortgage payable

Ref	Debit	Credit	Ref
		$75,000	1
		$75,000	

Common shares

Ref	Debit	Credit	Ref
		$5,000	BB
		$5,000	

Retained earnings

Ref	Debit	Credit	Ref
11	$2,000	$33,662	BB
		$31,662	

Sales revenue

Ref	Debit	Credit	Ref
		$99,000	7a
		$99,000	

Cost of goods sold

Ref	Debit	Credit
7b	$32,735	
	$32,735	

Amortization expense

Ref	Debit	Credit
Adj-2	$1,680	
	$1,680	

Miscellaneous operating expenses

Ref	Debit	Credit
9	$2,600	
Adj-1	50	
	$2,650	

Salary expense

Ref	Debit	Credit
10	$3,500	
	$3,500	

Insurance expense

Ref	Debit	Credit
Adj-1	$100	
	$100	

Rent expense

Ref	Debit	Credit
Adj-1	$1,200	
	$1,200	

Interest expense

Ref	Debit	Credit
Adj-3	$750	
	$750	

Bad debt expense

Ref	Debit	Credit
Adj-4	$2,970	
	$2,970	

Warranty expense

Ref	Debit	Credit
Adj-5	$1,980	
	$1,980	

Tom's Wear, Inc.
Adjusted Trial Balance
For the Month Ended July 31, 2005

	Debits	Credits
Cash	$ 17,151	
Accounts receivable	105,100	
Allowance for doubtful accounts		$ 3,290
Inventory	8,910	
Prepaid insurance	50	
Prepaid Web service	150	
Prepaid rent	600	
Equipment: computer	4,000	
Accumulated amortization: computer		500
Equipment: van	30,000	
Accumulated amortization: van		4,205
Buildings	67,500	
Accumulated amortization: buildings		130
Land	7,500	
Accounts payable		36,000
Interest payable		1,500
Warranties payable		2,239
Notes payable		30,000
Mortgage payable		75,000
Common shares		5,000
Retained earnings		31,662
Revenue		99,000
Cost of goods sold	32,735	
Amortization expense	1,680	
Other operating expense	2,650	
Salary expense	3,500	
Insurance expense	100	
Rent expense	1,200	
Interest expense	750	
Bad debt expense	2,970	
Warranty expense	1,980	
Totals	*$288,526*	*$288,526*

Tom's Wear, Inc.
Income Statement
For the Month Ended July 31, 2005

Sales revenue		$ 99,000
Less cost of goods sold		32,735
Gross profit		$ 66,265
Expenses		
Salary expense	$3,500	
Rent expense	1,200	
Insurance expense	100	
Amortization expense	1,680	
Interest expense	750	
Bad debt expense	2,970	
Warranty expense	1,980	
Other operating expenses	2,650	
Total expenses		14,830
Net income		**$51,435**

Tom's Wear, Inc.
Statement of Retained Earnings
For the Month Ended July 31, 2005

Beginning retained earnings	$33,662
Net income for the month	51,435
Dividends	(2,000)
Ending retained earnings	$83,097

Tom's Wear, Inc.
Balance Sheet
July 31, 2005

Assets		**Liabilities and shareholders' equity**	
Cash	$ 17,151	Accounts payable	$ 36,000
Accounts receivable (net of allowance of $3,290)	101,810	Interest payable	1,500
		Warranty liability	2,239
Inventory	8,910	Current portion of long-term note	6,000
Prepaid insurance	50	Current portion of mortgage	2,710
Prepaid rent	600	Total current liabilities	48,449
Prepaid Web service	150		
Total current assets	128,671	Notes payable	24,000
Computer (net of $500 accumulated amortization)	3,500	Mortgage payable	72,290
		Total liabilities	144,739
Van (net of $4,205 accumulated amortization)	25,795	Common shares	5,000
		Retained earnings	83,097
Land	7,500		
Building (net of $130 accumulated amortization)	67,370		
Total assets	**$232,836**	Total liabilities and shareholders' equity	**$232,836**

Tom's Wear, Inc.
Cash Flow Statement
For the Month Ended July 31, 2005

Cash from operating activities		
Cash from customers	$ 37,000	
Cash paid to vendor for T-shirts	(18,950)	
Cash paid for operating expenses	(7,177)	
Total cash from operations		$10,873
Cash from investing activities		0
Cash from financing activities		
Dividends	$ (2,000)	(2,000)
Net increase in cash		**$ 8,873**
Opening cash balance (July 01)		$8,278
Closing cash balance (July 31)		$17,151

Note: Building and land purchased with a mortgage payable of $75,000.

Questions

1. What are the two main sources of financing for a business?
2. What is a mortgage?
3. What does the expression *time value of money* mean?
4. What is an annuity?
5. What are bonds?
6. How are the interest payments associated with a bond calculated?
7. What is the difference between the stated rate of interest and the effective rate (market rate) of interest on a bond?
8. What is another name for the face value of a bond?
9. When is a bond issued at a discount?
10. When is a bond issued at a premium?
11. What does it mean to amortize a discount or premium?
12. What is a convertible bond?
13. What does it mean to "call" a bond?
14. How is the carrying value of a bond computed?
15. At maturity, what is the carrying value of a bond that was issued at a premium?
16. What is the difference between the straight-line method and the effective-interest method of amortizing a bond discount or premium?
17. What advantage is there to obtaining financing using bonds as opposed to getting a loan from a bank?
18. What is the difference between term bonds and serial bonds?
19. What is a debenture?
20. When installment loan payments (on a mortgage) are made, the amount paid reduces cash. What other two items (financial statement amounts) are affected?

Short Exercises

L.O. 1

SE8-1 Nunez Company has arranged to borrow $25,000 for five years at an annual interest rate of 8 percent. The annual payments will be $6,261.41. When Nunez makes its first payment at the end of the first year of the loan, how much of the payment will be interest?

SE8-2 Feathers and Furs borrowed $75,000 to buy a new fur storage facility. The company borrowed the money for 10 years at 12 percent per year, and the monthly payment is $1,076.03. When the company makes the first monthly payment, by how much will that payment reduce the principal of the loan? L.O. 1

SE8-3 Curtain Company borrowed $10,000 at 9 percent for seven years. The loan requires annual payments of $1,986.91. When Curtain Company makes the first annual payment, how much of the payment will be interest, and how much will reduce the principal of the loan? L.O. 1

SE8-4 On July 1, 2004, Maxine's Equipment Company signed a long-term note with the local bank for $50,000. The term of the note was 10 years, with an annual interest rate of 8 percent. If Maxine's makes annual payments of $7,451.47, beginning on June 30, 2005, how much of the first payment will be interest? L.O. 2

SE8-5 GuGa's Shirt Company wants to borrow $35,000, and the bank has quoted an interest rate of 8 percent for five years. If GuGa's makes equal annual payments at the end of each year, how much will each payment be? L.O. 2

SE8-6 Suppose you want to have $100,000 in five years and you know the interest rate is approximately 10 percent. If you are willing to make a deposit of the same amount at the beginning of every month, what will your deposit be?

SE8-7 If a $1,000 bond is selling at 95, how much cash will the issuing company receive? If a $1,000 bond is selling at face value, how much cash will the issuing company receive? If a $1,000 bond is selling at 101, how much cash will the issuing company receive? L.O. 2

SE8-8 If $100,000 of 8 percent bonds are issued (sold) for $95,000, to result in an effective yield of 9 percent, how much interest will be paid in cash during the first year? How much interest expense will be incurred for the first year, using effective interest amortization? L.O. 3

SE8-9 For each of the following situations, tell whether the bond described will be issued at a premium, at a discount, or at face value. L.O. 3

a. Colson Company issued $200,000 worth of bonds with a stated interest rate of 10 percent. At the time of issue, the market rate of interest for similar investments was 9 percent.
b. Dean Company issued $100,000 worth of callable bonds with a stated rate of 12 percent. At the time of issue, the market rate of interest for similar investments was 9 percent.
c. Liddy Company issued $200,000 worth of bonds with a stated rate of 8 percent. At the time of issue, the market rate of interest for similar investments was 9 percent.

SE8-10 For each of the following, compute the proceeds from the bond issue: L.O. 3

- Haldeman Hair Systems issued $20,000 worth of bonds at 106.
- Erlichman Egg Company issued $100,000 worth of bonds at 99.
- Carl's Cutlery Company issued $500,000 worth of bonds at 96 1/2.

SE8-11 Altoona Company was able to issue (sell) $200,000 of 9 percent bonds for $220,000 because their credit rating is excellent and market interest rates have fallen. The resulting effective yield on these bonds is 8 percent. L.O. 3

a. How much interest will be paid in cash during the first year?
b. What will interest expense be for the first year, using effective interest amortization?

Exercises

L.O. 1

E8-1 Stephen's Storage Company needed some long-term financing and arranged for a 20-year, $100,000 mortgage loan on December 31, 2005. The stated interest rate is 9 percent per year, with $11,000 payments made at the end of each year.

a. What is the amount of interest expense related to this loan for the year ended December 31, 2005?
b. What amount of liability should appear on the December 31, 2005, balance sheet?
c. What is the amount of interest expense related to this loan for the year ended December 31, 2006?
d. What amount of liability should appear on the December 31, 2006, balance sheet?

L.O. 1

E8-2 Grace's Gems purchased some property on December 31, 2004, for $100,000, paying $20,000 in cash and obtaining a mortgage loan for the other $80,000. The interest rate is 8 percent per year, with $2,925 payments made at the end of March, June, September, and December.

a. What amounts should appear as interest expense on the quarterly income statements and as a liability on the quarterly balance sheets during 2005?
b. What amount of interest expense should appear on the income statement for the year ended December 31, 2005?

L.O. 2

E8-3 For each of the following, calculate the payment each loan would require. Assume the payments are made at the end of the period in each case. Interest rates are annual rates.

a. Principal = $30,000; interest rate = 5%; term = 5 years; payments = annual.
b. Principal = $30,000; interest rate = 8%; term = 5 years; payments = annual.
c. Principal = $30,000; interest rate = 8%; term = 10 years; payments = annual.
d. Principal = $30,000; interest rate = 8%; term = 10 years; payments = semi-annual.
e. Principal = $30,000; interest rate = 12%; term = 5 years; payments = monthly. [Note: Financial calculator required.]

L.O. 2

E8-4 For each of the following, how much would you need to save today (a single amount) to have the amount needed in the future?

a. In five years $40,000, interest rate = 8%.
b. In 10 years $25,000, interest rate = 8%.
c. In two years $25,000, interest rate = 10%.
d. In eight years $100,000, interest rate = 5%.
e. In 20 years $500,000, interest rate = 6%.

L.O. 3

E8-5 On December 31, 2004, Bert's Batteries, Inc. issued $10,000 worth of 10 percent bonds at 94. The market rate of interest at the time of issue was approximately 11 percent. These are 10-year bonds with interest paid annually on December 31. By using the effective interest method to amortize the discount, calculate the following:

a. Interest payments for the first two years
b. Interest expense for the years ending December 31, 2005, and December 31, 2006
c. Carrying value of the bonds on the balance sheet at December 31, 2005, and December 31, 2006.

L.O. 3

E8-6 On December 31, 2004, Carl's Cartons, Inc. issued $100,000 worth of 9 percent bonds at 104 because the market rate of interest at the time of issue had fallen to 8 percent. The interest on these bonds is paid annually on December 31. By using the effective interest method to amortize the premium, calculate the following:

a. Interest payments for the first two interest payment dates
b. Interest expense for the years ended December 31, 2005, and December 31, 2006
c. Carrying values of the bonds on the balance sheets at December 31, 2005, and December 31, 2006

E8-7 On December 31, 2007, Dave's Delivery Service issued $10,000 worth of 10-percent bonds at approximately 89. The market rate of interest at the time of issue had risen to 12 percent. These are 10-year bonds with interest paid semi-annually on June 30 and December 31. By using the effective interest method to amortize the discount, calculate: L.O. 3

a. Interest payments for the first four interest payment dates
b. Total interest expense for the years ending December 31, 2008, and December 31, 2009
c. Carrying values of the bonds on the balance sheets at December 31, 2008, and December 31, 2009

E8-8 On June 30, 2007, Ellie's Electronics issued $20,000 face value of 10 percent bonds at 105. The market rate of interest at the time of issue was approximately 9 percent. They were 10-year bonds with interest paid semi-annually, on December 31 and June 30. By using the effective interest method to amortize the premium, calculate: L.O. 3

a. Interest payments for the first three payments
b. Total interest expense for the years ended December 31, 2007, and December 31, 2008
c. Carrying values of the bonds on the balance sheets at December 31, 2007, and December 31, 2008

E8-9 On June 30, 2005, Fred's Fudge Company issued $50,000 worth of 10-percent bonds for $50,000. The interest is paid annually on June 30. Calculate: L.O. 3

a. Interest payments for the first two interest payment dates
b. Total interest expense for the fiscal years ending December 31, 2005, and December 31, 2006
c. Long-term liability reported on the December 31, 2005, and December 31, 2006 balance sheets
d. Interest payable on December 31, 2005 and December 31, 2006

E8-10 On September 30, 2005, Gene's Garden Shop, Inc. issued $100,000 worth of 9 percent bonds at 100. The interest is paid semiannually on March 31 and September 30. Calculate: L.O. 3

a. Interest payments for the first four interest payment dates
b. Total interest expense for the fiscal years ending December 31, 2005, and December 31, 2006
c. Long-term liabilities reported on the December 31, 2005, and December 31, 2006, balance sheets
d. Interest payable on December 31, 2005, and December 31, 2006

E8-11 On January 1, 2008, John's Electronics issued $10,000 worth of 10 percent bonds at 96. The market rate of interest at the time of issue was approximately 10.66 percent. They were 10-year bonds with interest paid semi-annually. John's uses the effective interest method for amortizing any bond discounts or premiums. Calculate: L.O. 3

a. Interest payments for the first four interest dates
b. Total interest expense for the fiscal years ending December 31, 2008, and December 31, 2009
c. Carrying value of the bonds on the balance sheet at December 31, 2008, and December 31, 2009

Problems—Set A

P8-1A The SD Company engaged in the following transactions related to long-term liabilities during 2007. L.O. 1

a. On March 1, the firm borrowed $25,000 for a machine. The loan is to be repaid in equal annual payments at the end of each of the next five years (beginning February 28, 2008); and the interest rate SD is paying for this loan is 8.5 percent.
b. On October 1, the company borrowed $120,000 from Suwannee Local Bank at an interest rate of 7.25 percent. The loan is for 10 years, and SD Company will make annual payments on September 30 of each year.

Required: [Note: Financial calculator required.]

a. For each loan described, prepare an amortization schedule for the first four payments. Be sure to show the reduction in principal and the interest expense for each payment.
b. What total interest expense related to these two loans would SD Company show on its income statement for the year ended December 31, 2007?
c. How much interest payable would be shown on the SD balance sheet at December 31, 2007?

L.O. 2

P8-2A Joe Brinks is making plans to finance a series of projects. Several projects he is considering are described next.

a. He will purchase a truck for $30,000 to be repaid in equal monthly payments over the next five years. The bank has quoted an interest rate of 7.5 percent. [Note: Financial calculator required.]
b. He will purchase a piece of land, whose owner is offering to sell it to Joe for $25,000. The seller would accept five annual payments at 10 percent.
c. He will sell old equipment for $4,000. Joe is willing to accept quarterly payments for the next two years at an interest rate of 8 percent.
d. He will purchase land and building for $50,000, with a down payment of $5,000 and a semi-annual payment for the next 10 years at an interest rate of 6.5 percent. [Note: Financial calculator required.]

Required: For each situation, calculate the amount of the payment involved. Assume all payments are made at the end of the period.

L.O. 2

P8-3A Given the following situations, what annual interest rate is implied in the transaction?

a. Sam borrowed $10,000, and the annual payments are approximately $2,571 at the end of each of the next five years.
b. Don purchased a piece of land for $120,000. He made a down payment of $20,000, and he is making semi-annual payments of $7,358.18 at the end of each six-month period for the next 10 years.
c. Abbie borrowed $30,000 from the local bank. She will repay the money in a lump sum at the end of two years. The banker told her that the payment would be $36,300.
d. Tommy bought a new stereo system and the store will provide financing. The total purchase came to $8,634. Tommy will make semi-annual payments for the next three years of $1,647.04 each.

Required: For each situation, calculate the annual interest rate implied by the principal amount and the payment schedule.

L.O. 3

P8-4A Hewitt's Paints issued $1,000,000 worth of five-year bonds with a stated interest rate of 8 percent and interest payable annually on December 31. The bonds were issued when the market interest rate was 10 percent. Hewitt's issued the bonds on January 1, 2009. The fiscal year-end for Hewitt's Paints is December 31.

Required: Calculate the proceeds from the bond issue. Then, by using the effective interest method of amortization, calculate the interest payments, interest expense, and year-end carrying value for each of the five years.

P8-5A Julie's Jewels issued $20,000 worth of 10-year bonds at 102 1/2. The bonds have a stated rate of 8 percent. L.O. 3

Required:

a. Was the market interest rate at the time of issue higher or lower than 8 percent? How do you know?
b. What were the proceeds from the bond issue?
c. If the bonds were issued on January 1 and the interest is paid annually on December 31, what is the carrying value of the bonds at the end of the first year? Julie's uses the effective interest method of amortization. (Assume the interest rate at the time of issue was 7.63 percent.)
d. If the bonds were issued on July 1 and the interest is paid semi-annually on December 31 and June 30, what is the amount of interest expense at the date of each interest payment in the first year? Julie's uses the effective interest method of amortization.
e. Calculate the interest expense each period if Julie's Jewels used the straight-line method of amortizing discount or premiums. Assume interest is paid semi-annually.

P8-6A Matrix Construction issued $1 million of its 10 percent bonds on July 1, 2006, at 98. The bonds mature on June 30, 2011. Interest is payable semi-annually on June 30 and December 31. L.O. 3

Required:

a. What were the proceeds from the bond issue?
b. Was the market interest rate at the time of issue higher or lower than 10 percent?
c. The Matrix fiscal year-end is December 31. The company uses the straight-line method for amortizing discounts and premiums. Calculate the interest expense for each year, 2006 through 2011.

P8-7A Newman Corp. issued $100,000 of bonds on January 1, 2006. The bonds mature on January 1, 2016. Interest is payable annually on December 31. The stated rate of interest is 8 percent, and the market rate of interest was 10 percent at the time of issue. L.O. 3

Required:

a. Calculate the proceeds for the bond issue. How would issuing the bonds affect the financial statements for Newman (on the date of issue)?
b. Prepare an amortization schedule for the first three years of the life of the bonds, showing the interest expense and the carrying value at the end of each interest period. Newman uses the effective interest method for amortizing discounts and premiums.
c. How much interest expense related to these bonds would Newman show on its income statement for the year ended December 31, 2007? (Assume effective interest method.)
d. Calculate the interest expense for the year ended December 31, 2007, using the straight-line method of amortization. Then, compare that amount to the amount calculated using the effective interest method. Which method do you think Newman should use and why?

L.O. 3

P8-8A The following information comes from annual report of The Forzani Group Ltd.:

Consolidated Balance Sheets (in thousands) (audited)

As at	February 2, 2003	January 27, 2002
ASSETS		
Current		
Cash	$523	$494
Accounts receivable	38,275	35,988
Inventory	268,519	229,270
Prepaid and other expenses	11,123	4,481
	318,440	270,233
Capital assets (Note 3)	142,236	120,525
Goodwill and other intangibles (Note 4)	38,684	37,394
Other assets (Note 5)	7,452	8,112
	$506,812	$436,264

Consolidated Balance Sheets (in thousands) (audited)

As at	February 2, 2003	January 27, 2002
LIABILITIES		
Current		
Indebtedness under revolving credit facility (Note 6)	$4,204	$17,094
Accounts payable and accrued liabilities	209,873	188,995
Current portion of long-term debt	3,638	14,032
	217,715	220,121
Long-term debt (Note 7)	32,062	35,454
Deferred lease inducements	52,251	46,623
Future income tax liability (Note 10)	1,061	2,021
	303,089	304,219
SHAREHOLDERS' EQUITY		
Share capital (Note 9)	124,866	83,719
Retained earnings	78,857	48,326
	203,723	132,045
	$506,812	$436,264

(Courtesy The Forzani Group)

Required:

a. Calculate the debt-to-equity ratio for the years ended February 2, 2003, and January 27, 2002.

b. Who would be interested in this information, and why?

c. Suppose you were considering investing in some Forzani Group shares. What do you think of the change in this ratio from 2002 to 2003?

d. If Forzani Group has bonds payable, where do you think they might be included on the balance sheet?

e. What risks are associated with the long-term debt on Forzani Group's balance sheet?

Problems—Set B

P8-1B The McIntyre Company engaged in the following transactions related to long-term liabilities during 2006: L.O. 8-1

a. On July 1, the firm borrowed $50,000 for a new piece of office equipment. The loan is to be repaid in equal annual payments at the end of each of the next eight years (beginning June 30, 2007); and the interest rate McIntyre is paying for this loan is 8 percent.
b. On October 1, McIntyre borrowed $200,000 from Shell Point Local Bank at an interest rate of 9.5 percent. The loan is for 10 years, and the company will make annual payments on September 30 of each year. [Note: Financial calculator required.]

Required:

a. For each loan described, prepare an amortization schedule for the first four payments. Be sure to show the reduction in principal and the interest expense for each payment.
b. What total interest expense related to these two loans would McIntyre Company show on its income statement for the year ended 2006?
c. How much interest payable would be shown on the McIntyre balance sheet at December 31, 2006?

P8-2B Don Black is making plans to finance a series of projects. Several projects he is considering are described next. L.O. 8-2

a. He will purchase a boat for $50,000 to be repaid in equal *monthly* payments over the next six years. The bank has quoted an interest rate of 12 percent. [Note: Financial calculator required.]
b. He will purchase property for $125,000. The seller would accept 10 semi-annual payments at 8 percent.
c. He will sell old equipment for $8,000. Don is willing to accept quarterly payments for the next two years at an interest rate of 8 percent.
d. He will purchase land and building for $250,000, with a down payment of $50,000, and semi-annual payments for the next 10 years at an interest rate of 10 percent.

Required: For each situation, calculate the amount of the payment. Assume all payments are made at the end of the period.

P8-3B Given the following situations, what annual interest rate is implied in the transaction? L.O. 8-2

a. Robert borrowed $10,000, and the annual payments are approximately $2,439 at the end of each of the next five years.
b. Marc purchased a piece of land for $240,000. He made a down payment of $40,000, and he is making semi-annual payments of $13,443.14 at the end of each six-month period for the next 10 years.
c. Carol borrowed $25,000 from the local bank. She will repay the money in a lump sum at the end of three years. The banker told her that the payment would be $30,198.74.
d. Joan bought a new big screen television; the store will provide financing. The total purchase came to $5,450. Joan will make quarterly payments for the next two years of $760.10 each.

Required: For each situation, calculate the annual interest rate implied by the principal amount and the payment schedule.

L.O. 8-3

P8-4B Glassworks, Inc. issued $150,000 worth of six-year bonds with a stated interest rate of 7.5 percent and interest payable annually on December 31. The bonds were issued when the market interest rate was 8 percent. The bonds were issued on January 1, 2007. The fiscal year-end for Glassworks, Inc. is December 31.

Required: Calculate the proceeds from the bond issue. Then, by using the effective interest method of amortization, calculate the interest payments, interest expense, and year-end carrying value for each of the six years.

L.O. 8-3

P8-5B Venus Rug Company issued $80,000 worth of 10-year bonds when the market rate of interest was 8.5 percent. The bonds have a stated interest rate of 9 percent.

Required: [Note: Financial calculator required.]

a. What were the proceeds from the bond issue, assuming interest is paid annually?
b. If the bonds were issued on January 1 and the interest is paid annually on December 31, what is the carrying value of the bonds at the end of the first year? Venus Rugs uses the effective interest method of amortization.
c. If the bonds were issued on July 1 and the interest is paid semi-annually on December 31 and June 30, what is the amount of interest expense at the date of each of the first two interest payments? Venus Rugs uses the effective interest method of amortization.
d. Calculate the interest expense each period if Venus Rugs used the straight-line method of amortizing discount or premiums. Assume semi-annual interest payments.

L.O. 8-3

P8-6B Slam Racquet Company issued $1 million of its 6 percent bonds on July 1, 2007, at 98. The bonds mature on June 30, 2011. Interest is payable annually on June 30. Slam uses the straight-line method of amortizing discounts and premiums.

Required:

a. What were the proceeds from the bond issue?
b. Was the market interest rate at the time of issue higher or lower than 6 percent?
c. The Slam Racquet Company fiscal year-end is December 31. Calculate the interest expense for each year, 2007 through 2011.

L.O. 8-3

P8-7B Morgan Corp. issued $1,000,000 of bonds on January 1, 2008. The bonds mature on January 1, 2016. Interest is payable annually each December 31. The stated rate of interest is 11 percent, and the market rate of interest was 10 percent at the time of issue.

Required:

a. Calculate the proceeds for the bond issue. How would issuing the bonds affect the accounting equation for Morgan (on the date of issue)?
b. Prepare an amortization schedule for the first four years of the life of the bonds, showing the interest expense and the carrying value at the end of each interest period. Morgan uses the effective interest method for amortizing discounts and premiums.
c. How much interest expense related to these bonds would Morgan show on its income statement for the year ended December 31, 2009? (Assume effective interest method.)
d. Calculate the interest expense for the year ended December 31, 2009, using the straight-line method of amortization. Then, compare that amount to the amount calculated using the effective interest method. Which method do you think Morgan should use, and why?

P8-8B The following information comes from annual report of Danier Leather Inc.: L.O. 8-3

Consolidated Balance Sheets (thousands of dollars)

	June 28, 2003	June 29, 2002
ASSETS		
Current Assets		
Cash	$7,254	$3,777
Accounts receivable	600	484
Income taxes recoverable	83	-
Inventories (Note 2)	37,029	38,662
Prepaid expenses	889	603
Future income tax asset (Note 8)	1,044	628
	46,899	44,154
Other Assets		
Capital assets (Note 3)	34,246	31,199
Goodwill (Note 4)	342	342
	$81,487	$75,695
LIABILITIES		
Current Liabilities		
Accounts payable and accrued liabilities	$10,559	$10,472
Income taxes payable	-	80
	10,559	10,552
Deferred lease inducements	2,238	1,837
Future income tax liability (Note 8)	696	784
	13,493	13,173
SHAREHOLDERS' EQUITY		
Share capital (Note 6)	23,995	23,917
Retained earnings	43,999	38,605
	67,994	62,522
	$81,487	$75,695

(Courtesy Danier Leather Inc.)

Required:

a. Calculate the debt-to-equity ratio for the years ending June 28, 2003, and June 29, 2002.
b. Who would be interested in this information, and why?
c. Suppose you were considering investing in Danier Leather. What do you think of the change in the debt-to-equity ratio from 2002 to 2003?
d. If Danier Leather has bonds payable, where might they be included on the balance sheet?
e. What risks would be associated with the long-term debt on Danier Leather balance sheet if there was such a long-term debt?

Recording Transactions

R8-1 (SE8-3) Curtain Company borrowed $10,000 at 9 percent for seven years. The loan requires annual payments of $1,986.91. Give the journal entry to record the first annual payment.

Date	Account	Debit	Credit

R8-2 (SE8-8) $100,000 of 8 percent bonds are issued (sold) for $95,000, to result in an effective yield of 9 percent. Give the journal entry to record the first annual interest payment.

Date	Account	Debit	Credit

R8-3 (SE8-10) For each of the following, give the journal entry to record the bond issue:

Transaction	Account	Debit	Credit

- Haldeman Hair Systems issued $20,000 worth of bonds at 106.
- Erlichman Egg Company issued $100,000 worth of bonds at 99.
- Carl's Cutlery Company issued $500,000 worth of bonds at 96 1/2.

R8-4 (SE8-11) Altoona Company was able to issue (sell) $200,000 of 9 percent bonds for $220,000 because their credit rating is excellent and market interest rates have fallen. The resulting effective yield on these bonds is 8 percent. Give the journal entry to record the first annual interest payment.

Date	Account	Debit	Credit

R8-5 (E8-5) On December 31, 2004, Bert's Batteries, Inc. issued $10,000 worth of 10 percent bonds at 94. The market rate of interest at the time of issue was approximately 11 percent. These are 10-year bonds with interest paid annually on December 31. The company uses the effective interest method to amortize bond premiums and discounts. Give the journal entries to record the first two interest payments.

Date	Account	Debit	Credit

R8-6 (E8-8) On June 30, 2007, Ellie's Electronics issued $20,000 face value of 10 percent bonds at 105. The market rate of interest at the time of issue was approximately 9 percent. They were 10-year bonds with interest paid semi-annually on December 31 and June 30. The company uses the effective interest method to amortize bond premiums and discounts. Give the journal entries for the first three interest payments.

Date	Account	Debit	Credit

R8-7 (E8-11) On January 1, 2008, John's Electronics issued $10,000 worth of 10 percent bonds at 96. The market rate of interest at the time of issue was approximately 10.66 percent. They were 10-year bonds with interest paid semi-annually. Give the journal entries for the interest payments for the first four interest dates. John's Electronics uses the effective interest method for amortizing any bond discounts or premiums.

Date	Account	Debit	Credit

R8-8 (P8-1A) The SD Company engaged in the following transactions related to long-term liabilities during 2007: [Note: Financial calculator required.]

1. On March 1, borrowed $25,000 for a machine. The loan is to be repaid in equal annual payments at the end of each of the next five years (beginning February 28, 2008), and the interest rate SD is paying for this loan is 8.5 percent.
2. On October 1, borrowed $120,000 from Suwannee Local Bank at an interest rate of 7.25 percent. The loan is for 10 years, and SD Company will make annual payments on September 30 of each year.

Required: For each loan described, give the journal entries for the first two interest payments.

Transaction	Account	Debit	Credit

R8-9 (P8-7A) Newman Corporation issued $100,000 of bonds on January 1, 2006. The bonds mature on January 1, 2016. Interest is payable annually on December 31. The stated rate of interest is 8 percent, and the market rate of interest was 10 percent at the time of issue.

Required:

a. Calculate the proceeds for the bond issue. Give the journal entry to record the issue of the bonds.
b. Give the journal entries to record the first two interest payments. Newman uses the effective interest method for amortizing discounts and premiums.
c. Assume, instead, that Newman uses the straight-line method for amortizing discounts and premiums. Give the journal entries to record the first two interest payments.

Transaction	Account	Debit	Credit

R8-Comprehensive

Chapter 8: Comprehensive Financial Statement Preparation Problem

Ultra Corporation began operations on January 1, 2009, when it issued bonds with a face value of $100,000, a term of 10 years, and a stated interest rate of 9 percent. At the time of issue, the market rate of interest was 10 percent. Interest will be paid annually on December 31. Jeff Ultra, the founder of the corporation, also contributed $100,000 to start the company and received ownership in the form of common shares. After receiving the proceeds from these transactions, Ultra Corporation completed the following transactions during 2009 and 2010.

In 2009, Ultra Corporation:

1. Purchased land and building for $60,000. An independent appraisal valued the land at 10 percent of the total purchase price. The building will be amortized using straight-line amortization, and Ultra estimates it will be useful for 20 years and have a residual value of $1,600 at the end of that time. Ultra will take a full year's amortization in 2009.
2. Purchased office and store equipment for $20,000, with a useful life of 10 years and an estimated residual value of $2,000. Ultra will take a full year's amortization on a straight line basis in 2009.
3. Purchased inventory of $70,000 for cash and sold all of it for $140,000 on account. Ultra Corporation estimates that 3 percent of the ending balance in accounts receivable will be uncollectible.
4. Paid cash expenses of $20,000.
5. Paid interest on the bonds (on December 31).

In 2010, Ultra Corporation:

1. Purchased inventory of $100,000 for cash and sold 90 percent of it for $180,000, all on account.
2. Collected $200,000 from customers on accounts receivable.
3. Paid cash expenses of $25,000.
4. Paid interest on bonds (on December 31).
5. Wrote off L. James's account in the amount of $3,000 after finding out that this customer had filed for bankruptcy.

Prepare the four basic financial statements for Ultra Corporation for both years (ended December 31, 2009, and December 31, 2010). Do not forget to make the appropriate adjustments each year for amortization and the allowance for doubtful accounts.

Issues for Discussion

Financial statement analysis

L.O. 4, 5

1. Use the CoolBrands International Inc. financial statements to answer the following questions:
   a. What types of debt does CoolBrands have? Where did you find this information?
   b. Compute the times-interest-earned ratio and the debt-to-equity ratio for the last two years. What information do these ratios provide?

Business risk

2. Consider the following:
   a. By using the level of long-term debt and the ratios calculated in 1, how would you describe the level of risk for the creditors of CoolBrands?
   b. Are there any indications that the level of the CoolBrands long-term debt presents a serious risk to the company?

Ethics

3. Lucy Shafer wants to borrow $100,000 to expand her dog-breeding business. She is preparing a set of financial statements to take to the local bank with her loan application. She currently has an outstanding loan from her uncle for $50,000. Lucy's uncle is allowing her to borrow the money at a very low interest rate, and she does not have to make any principal payments for five years. Due to the favourable terms of the loan from her uncle, Lucy has decided that it is not significant enough to disclose on her financial statements. Instead, Lucy has classified the $50,000 as share capital (ownership), and the interest payments are included in miscellaneous expenses on Lucy's income statement.

a. What are the effects of Lucy's classifications on the financial statements?
b. Are there any ratios that might be of concern to the local bank that will be misstated by Lucy's actions?
c. Do you think Lucy's actions are unethical? Suppose Lucy's uncle agrees to be a partner in the company until Lucy can afford to buy his share by repaying the $50,000 with interest. Does that change your opinion?

Internet Exercise: Sobeys Inc. and Loblaw Companies Limited

Sobeys Inc. and Loblaw Companies Limited are major players in the Canadian grocery industry. In order to finance their operation both companies rely on capital provided by lenders and shareholders.

IE8-1 Go to the Sobeys Inc. website: http://www.sobeys.com/

a. Under "Investor Centre," find the most recent annual report. Identify amounts reported for total long-term debt at the two most recent year-ends. For the most recent year-end, how much of the debt does Sobeys have to pay back? Do these amounts reflect the future value of the debt? Explain why or why not.
b. Identify amounts reported for interest expense for the two most recent years. Did interest expense increase or decrease? What might cause this change? Is this the amount of interest paid during the year? Which financial statement reports this information?
c. Identify amounts reported for total liabilities and total equity at the two most recent year-ends. Calculate the debt-to-equity ratio (total liabilities to total equity) for each year-end. Is Sobeys primarily financing assets with liabilities or equities? How can you tell? Is the ratio increasing or decreasing? Is this trend favourable or unfavourable? Explain why.

IE8-2 Go to the Loblaw Companies Limited website: http://www.loblaw.com/

a. Under "Investor Zone" find the most recent Annual Report. Identify amounts reported for total liabilities and total equity at the two most recent year-ends.
b. Calculate the debt-to-equity ratio (total liabilities to total equity) for each year-end.
c. Do owners or creditors have more claims on the Loblaw's assets? How can you tell?

IE8-3 Review the information recorded earlier. Which corporation has a higher level of financial risk? Explain why.

Please note: Internet websites are constantly being updated. Therefore, if the information is not found where indicated, please explore the website further to find the information.

C H A P T E R 9

Financing a Business with Equity

Financing

Here's where you've been...

In Chapter 8, you learned how a company obtains financing from creditors. Two common ways are long-term notes and bonds. You learned how the debt is repaid and how interest on debt is calculated and paid to the creditors.

Here's where you're going...

When you are finished with Chapter 9, you should understand how a company obtains financing from owners. You will learn how the money that a corporation receives from its owners—shareholders—and how the money the corporation earns are shown on the financial statements. You will also learn about how the corporation pays a return to its owners with dividends.

Financing

Learning Objectives

More specifically, when you are finished studying this chapter, you should be able to answer these questions:

1. How does a corporation account for owners' contributions to a company? What are the major types of share capital?
2. What are dividends—for common and preferred shareholders? How are they computed, recorded, and reported?
3. Why would a company purchase its own shares?
4. What are stock dividends and stock splits?

5. What are retained earnings? How are they valued, recorded, and reported?
6. How is information about a company's equity used in financial statement analysis?
7. What risks are associated with equity financing?

Owners of a Business

Every business firm has owners. As you know from Chapter 1, there are three common forms of business organization:

- sole proprietorships
- partnerships
- corporations

No matter which form a firm takes, the firm always needs contributions from owners. We refer to them as contributions because we are looking at them from the point of view of the firm. As you know from earlier chapters, owners' contributions are called share capital and shown on the firm's balance sheet.

For sole proprietorships and partnerships, acquiring money is a personal matter. The individual owners may use their own money, or they may borrow money from family, friends, or banks.

L.O. 1

Understand how a company finances its business with equity.

For a corporation, there are more options. There are more opportunities to acquire funds—that is one of the advantages of the corporate form of business organization.

You learned about financing a company with debt in Chapter 8. In this chapter, you will learn about acquiring funds from owners of the corporation.

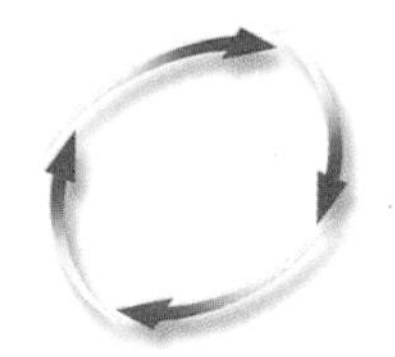

Business Process

Components of Shareholders' Equity in a Corporation: Share Capital

The owners' claims to the assets of the firm are called shareholders' equity. Recall, there are two parts to shareholders' equity in a corporation—share capital and retained earnings. Each part is recorded and reported on the balance sheet as a separate amount. We will spend most of the chapter discussing share capital.

Share capital and **paid-in capital** are both names for the same thing—owners' contributions to the firm.

The term **investment** is sometimes used to describe an owner's contribution to a company.

Share capital is the amount owners have invested in the corporation. From an individual owner's point of view, a share of ownership in a corporation is an **investment**. From the firm's point of view, the amount paid for a share of ownership is a contribution to the firm. Another name for these contributions is **paid-in capital** because these contributions are literally paid into the firm by the owners.

The form of capital contributions is usually cash, but contributions of other assets are possible. For example, an owner may contribute an asset in the form of land or a machine in return for ownership in the corporation. Whether the capital contribution is cash or another asset, the owner who makes the contribution receives shares equal to the value of the contribution. As you learned at the beginning of this textbook, a share represents ownership in a corporation.

Shares: Authorized, Issued, and Outstanding

Business Process

In return for their contributions, the owners receive shares, representing ownership equal to the value of those contributions. When a corporation is initially formed, it is formed under either federal or provincial law. Depending on the appropriate statute, there may be an unlimited or limited number of shares **authorized** for issuance. If there is a limited number of shares authorized, then this number of shares is the maximum number of shares a corporation is allowed to issue. The number of shares actually **issued** will be less than the total number of shares authorized. It is common that shares are offered—made available for sale to potential owners—in batches, during times when a company needs capital.

The number of **authorized shares** is the maximum number of shares that a corporation is allowed by its articles of incorporation to issue.

After a share has been issued, it does not have to remain outstanding. **Outstanding shares** are ones that are currently owned by investors. Often, the managers of the company will buy back—not as individuals but for the company itself—the company's own shares from other investors who own shares through prior purchase in the stock market. There are several reasons why a firm would buy its own shares. For example, a firm may purchase its own shares to bolster the market price of its shares. If a share is repurchased and cancelled, it is no longer issued or outstanding.

Issued shares are the actual number of shares currently classified as issued—comprises all the shares given in return for ownership in the corporation less any shares that have been retired.

Outstanding shares are the amount of shares issued and currently owned by investors.

Common Shares. As the name suggests, **common shares** are the most common type of shares representing ownership of a corporation. All corporations have common shares. The owners of common shares have specific rights:

1. To vote for members of the board of directors.
2. To share in the corporation's profits.
3. To share in any assets left if the corporation has to dissolve (e.g., if the company has to go out of business due to bankruptcy).
4. To acquire more shares when the corporation issues new shares if the corporation provides such a right.

Common shares represents the most common form of ownership in a corporation. Common shareholders have a vote in running the company.

Common shares are what most people mean when they refer to a corporation's shares. When common shares are issued, the accounting is straightforward. An asset account, cash, and an equity account, share capital, are increased by the proceeds from the sale of the shares. Assume a company issues 100 shares for $10 per share. How would this be shown on the financial statements? The balance sheet would show cash of $1,000 under current assets and common shares of $1,000 in the share capital section under shareholder's equity. The equity section would appear as follows:

Share Capital	
Common shares	$1,000

We would describe the company as having 100 shares issued and outstanding with a stated value of $1,000.

Preferred Shares. Corporations may also have **preferred shares**. They are called *preferred* because the owners of this type of shares have a preference over common shareholders when the corporation pays dividends. The pre-

Preferred shares represent a special type of ownership in a corporation. Preferred shareholders do not get to vote in running the company, but they do get their dividends first.

ferred shareholders must receive their dividends before any of the common shareholders are paid. They also have a preferred claim on assets. That means if a firm goes out of business, the preferred shareholders will receive leftover company assets—left after the creditors have been paid—before the common shareholders. However, the owners of preferred shares do not have many of the rights common shareholders have. For example, preferred shareholders usually do not have voting rights.

Par value of shares is a monetary value assigned to, and printed on, each share. For common shares, par value has little relevance to the company or the shareholders. For preferred shares, par value is commonly the basis for calculating the dividend payment.

Par Value of Common and Preferred Shares. In Canada, most shares issued do not have a par value. The use of par value shares was common in the past in Canada and is still common in some states in the United States. Par value is a fixed per share amount printed on the share certificate. The par value of common shares does not have any relationship to the market value of the shares. For preferred shares, par value can serve as the basis for calculating the dividends that preferred shareholders receive. Given that par value shares are rarely used in Canada, the accounting for shares will focus on no-par value shares. The remainder of this section briefly shows how par value common shares are presented in a set of financial statements.

If par value shares are issued, they are usually sold for more than the par value of the shares. Suppose the par value of a company's share is $2, and the market price of the share on the date the share is originally issued is $10. If the company issues 100 shares, the par value multiplied by the number of shares issued—$2 par × 100 shares = $200—will be shown on the balance sheet as common shares, and the excess contributions amount—$8 excess over par × 100 shares = $800—is reported on the balance sheet as **contributed surplus**, (sometimes also called premium on common shares, share capital in excess of par, or additional contributed capital). Suppose the corporate charter of the company authorizes 1,000 common shares at par value $2. How would the issuance of 100 shares at $10 per share be shown on the financial statements? The owner's equity section of the balance sheet would show this information in the section representing share capital.

Contributed surplus is the capital from the sale of stock that is above par value of the shares.

Share capital	
Common shares (Par value $2; 1,000 shares authorized; 100 shares issued and outstanding)	$200
Contributed surplus	800

Exhibit 9–1 shows the shareholders' equity section of the January 3, 2004, balance sheet and part of note 6 from the annual report of High Liner Foods. For now, focus on the information given for the preferred and common shares. For both classes of shares, the number of shares authorized and issued is given in note 6. For the preferred shares, several different types or classes are described and the par value of each is given in note 6. The annual dividend for Class C and Class D preferred shares (before they were redeemed) was 27.5 cents which can be calculated by multiplying 5.5 percent by the par value of $5 (.055 × 5.00 = 0.275). For the common shares, note that 200,000,000 no-par value shares are authorized and 10,794,455 are outstanding. The foreign currency translation account will be addressed in more advanced accounting courses, but retained earnings is an item that you should recognize. You will read more about retained earnings later in the chapter.

Exhibit 9-1 **Shareholders' Equity from High Liner Foods**

Excerpts from Consolidated Balance Sheets
(in thousands of dollars)

	January 3, 2004	December 28, 2002
Shareholders' Equity		
Preference Shares (Note 6)	20,000	21,246
Common Shares (Note 6)	34,030	28,361
Retained earnings	75,259	37,080
Foreign currency translation account (Note 7)	(7,893)	2,341
	121,396	89,028

Excerpt from Note 6
Share Capital
The share capital of the Company is as follows:

	January 3, 2004	December 28, 2002
Authorized		
Cumulative Redeemable Convertible Preference Shares of $5 each		
5 1/2% Class C	600,000	600,000
5 1/2% Class D	400,000	400,000
Cumulative Redeemable Second Preference Shares value of $100 each	200,000	200,000
Preference Shares of $25 each, issuable in series	9,999,944	9,999,944
Subordinated Redeemable Preference Shares of $1 each, redeemable at par	1,025,342	1,025,542
Common Shares	200,000,000	200,000,000

	January 3, 2004		December 28, 2002	
	Shares	$000s	Shares	$000s
Issued				
Preference				
Class C and D Preference Shares (i)	-	-	249,007	1,246
Second Preference Shares (ii)	200,000	20,000	200,000	20,000
		20,000		21,246
Common				
Common Shares (iii)	10,794,455	34,030	9,835,944	28,361

(i) During the year the Class C and D Preference Shares were redeemed plus accrued and unpaid dividends. In 2002 the Class C and D Preference Shares are shown net of 142,868 shares which were owned by a subsidiary company.
(ii) On June 30, 2003, all dividends in arrears in the amount of $6.3 million were paid. There are no further arrears.
(iii) Common Shares issued are shown net of 171,500 shares (2002; 171,500 shares) in the amount of 2,558,200 (2002; $2,558,2000) which are owned by a subsidiary company.

Courtesy High Liner Foods Incorporated, Lunenberg, N.S.

STUDY BREAK 9-1

See How You're Doing

Use the following information from the equity section of these comparative balance sheets to answer the question that follows:

Shareholders' equity	December 31, 2005	December 31, 2004
Common shares	$373,000	$353,000
Retained earnings	55,000	51,000
Total shareholders' equity	*$428,000*	*$404,000*

If 1,000 common shares were issued during the period from January 1, 2005 through December 31, 2005, what was the average issue price of the shares?

L.O. 2

Define cash dividends and know who decides whether dividends will be paid. Understand the allocation of dividends between common and preferred shareholders.

Distributions are cash or other assets given by a company to its owners.

Dividends are distributions of a corporation's earnings to the shareholders—usually in the form of cash.

Cash Dividends. People buy shares in a corporation—that is, they buy partial ownership in the corporation—because they hope the value of the corporation—and therefore, their part of the ownership—will increase in value. Selling shares for more than their cost is one way the shareholder can make money on the investment.

Shareholders also receive **distributions** from the earnings of the corporation called **dividends**. Dividends are distributions of a corporation's assets—usually cash—to its shareholders. The board of directors decides the amount of dividends to be paid and when they will be paid to the shareholders. The directors are also free *not* to pay dividends at any time they believe it is in the best interests of the corporation. For example, the board of directors may want to reinvest the available cash in the business by buying more equipment or inventory.

When the board of directors decides that a cash dividend will be paid, there are three important dates relating to that dividend: the declaration date, the date of record, and the payment date.

The **declaration date** is the date on which the board of directors makes the official decision to pay a dividend.

Declaration Date. The dividend **declaration date** is the date on which the board of directors decides a dividend will be paid. On this date, a legal liability is created. This particular liability is called *dividends payable*. The amount of this liability is balanced in the accounting equation by a reduction in retained earnings.

Remember, dividends are not included as an expense on the income statement because they are not related to generating revenue. Instead of a *deduction* from a company's earnings, dividends are considered a *distribution* of a company's earnings to owners in proportion to their share of ownership. Dividends are not deducted from share capital because they are a distribution of earnings, not a distribution of an owner's original share capital.

Assets	=	Liabilities	+	Share capital	+	Retained earnings
		+Dividends payable				−Dividends

The **date of record** is the date used to determine which shareholders are to receive declared dividends.

Date of Record. The **date of record** is used to determine exactly who will receive the dividends. Anyone owning the shares on this date is entitled to the dividend. After a corporation originally sells shares to its investors, who become owners of the company, these owners are free to trade—sell and buy—shares with other people. Whoever owns the shares on the *date of record* will receive the dividend. A shareholder may own the shares for only one day and receive the full dividend amount. After this date, shares are said to be ex-dividend. That is, if it is traded after the date of record, the new owner will not get the dividend.

Payment Date. The third date of importance for a dividend is the payment date. This is when the cash is actually paid to the shareholders. This payment has the same effect on the accounting equation as the payment of any liability: assets (cash) are reduced and liabilities (dividends payable) are reduced.

Preferred Share Dividends. Preferred shares have preference over common shares for dividends. The holders of preferred shares must receive, from the corporation, a certain amount of dividends before common shareholders can receive any dividends. Dividends on preferred shares are usually fixed.

Why Do Companies Have Preferred Shares?

One way a firm can obtain needed funds is to issue preferred shares. Just like issuing common shares, issuing preferred shares is a source of financing. Preferred shares are a special class of shares that has certain features that common shares do not have. These features can include shareholders' rights: to receive dividends before the common shareholders receive any dividends, to receive a share of the assets in the event of bankruptcy before common shareholders get any, and to exchange their preferred shares for common shares under certain conditions. Preferred shares may be bought back by the issuing corporation directly from the shareholders (this means they are "callable" preferred shares), and preferred shareholders do not get a vote in running the company. Because of the features of the shares, preferred shareholders may seem more like creditors than owners. In fact, as you will see in a more advanced accounting course, depending on the features attached to the preferred shares, these shares may be treated for accounting purposes as debt and their dividends as related interest. This is an example of accounting looking to the economic substance of the event and not the legal form (substance over form) to determine the appropriate accounting treatment.

Because the holders of preferred shares are more like creditors, preferred shares may be used as a weapon in a hostile takeover attempt—that is, when someone tries to buy enough of the target company's shares to get the majority of shares so that the person (or a company), the new buyer, will be able to take over and run the target company. This could happen when a corporation is formed initially, and the corporate charter authorizes a certain number of shares to be issued over the company's life. At the same time, the corporate charter may also give the board of directors (BOD) complete discretion about when and how to offer preferred shares. If necessary, the BOD can issue a very large number of preferred shares to make a takeover more difficult. The newly issued preferred shares will be issued to the current shareholders at a reduced rate, and the shareholders will convert them to common shares. This way to defend against a hostile takeover has been called a ***poison pill***.

Of the total amount of all shares issued, the BOD will set a maximum amount that a single outside party may acquire. If an outsider acquires a number of shares of the firm's shares exceeding that amount, the BOD will activate the poison pill. Poison pills became a great defence in the 1980s when they were devised to prevent hostile takeovers that were prevalent at that time. The poison pill is a trigger point that, once activated, means the BOD uses the blank cheque proviso to issue preferred shares at a reduced rate to current shareholders. This, in turn, increases the price of taking over to an outside party and in most cases kills the takeover efforts by the outside party.

For example, a $10 preferred share will pay a dividend of $10 in any year the corporation's board of directors declares a dividend. The preferred shareholders must get their $10 per preferred share before the common shareholders receive any dividends. The board of directors has discretion about whether to pay dividends to the preferred shareholders, but the board does not decide on the amount of the dividend for the preferred shareholders. The dividend for preferred shareholders is typically shown on the face of the preferred share certificate and is often used to describe the preferred shares.

There are two types of preferred shares—cumulative and noncumulative—identified by a characteristic of their dividends.

Cumulative preferred shareholders must receive any past, unpaid dividends before a company can pay any current dividends.

Noncumulative preferred shareholders do *not* receive past, unpaid dividends. Past dividends do not accumulate.

Dividends owed to holders of cumulative preferred shares but not yet declared are called **dividends in arrears.**

- **Cumulative preferred shares** mean the fixed dividend amount accumulates from year to year, and the entire amount of all past unpaid dividends must be paid to the preferred shareholders before any dividends can be paid to the common shareholders.
- If the shares are **noncumulative preferred shares**, it is up to the board to determine whether it will make up any missed dividends to the preferred shareholders.

Any dividends on cumulative preferred shares from past years but undeclared and unpaid are called **dividends in arrears**. Such dividends are not considered liabilities. Only after a dividend is actually declared is it considered a liability.

Example of Dividend Payment. Suppose JG Company has outstanding 1,000 $9 cumulative preferred shares and 50,000 common shares. The company last paid dividends in December 2004.

With the 2004 payment, JG paid all dividends through December 31, 2004. There were no dividends in arrears. No dividends were declared in 2005.

On October 1, 2006, the board of directors declares a total of $30,000 in dividends for its shareholders to be paid on December 15 to all shareholders of record on November 1.

How much will go to the preferred shareholders and how much to the common shareholders?

First, calculate the annual dividend for the preferred shareholders—1,000 shares × $9 = $9,000. Because the preferred shares are cumulative and no dividends were paid to the preferred shareholders in 2005, JG must first pay the 2005 dividend of $9,000 to the preferred shareholders. Then, JG has to pay the current year dividend of $9,000 to the preferred shareholders. Thus, a total of $18,000 must be paid to the preferred shareholders, and the remaining $12,000 will be paid to the common shareholders.

On the date of declaration, October 1, the legal liability for the dividend payment is incurred. The company must record the transaction, which has the following effect on the accounting equation:

Assets	=	Liabilities	+	Shareholders' equity	
				SC	RE
		+$18,000 Dividends payable to preferred shareholders +12,000 Dividends payable to common shareholders			$(30,000) Retained earnings

The journal entry to record the declaration of dividends to shareholders is:

Date	Transaction	Debit	Credit
	Retained earnings	$30,000	
	Dividends payable to preferred shareholders		$18,000
	Dividends payable to common shareholders		12,000

On the declaration date, the company records the liability. If JG were to prepare financial statements between October 1 and the payment of the dividends on December 15, the balance sheet would show a current liability called *dividends payable*. This liability is a debt owed to the shareholders for dividends. A corporation may list the liability to common shareholders separately from the liability to preferred shareholders, as shown in the preceding example; or the corporation may combine the preferred and common dividends into one amount for total dividends payable.

The date of record, November 1, has no significance in the accounting records. It is simply the date that indicates who will get the dividend. The shareholders as of November 1 will receive this dividend.

Why Do Companies Buy Their Own Shares?

October 1, 2003

Fairfax Financial Holdings Ltd. (TSX: FFH) has renewed efforts to acquire its own issued subordinate voting shares in a bid to boost shareholder value in the company's listed equity. Fairfax says that, pending regulatory approval, it will purchase about one million subordinate voting shares that have been issued by the company from between September 22 of this year to September 21 of 2004.

The latest share repurchase bid follows a similar action taken last year to acquire the company's subordinate voting shares in response to a perceived under-valuation of the issued paper.

Source: From the *Canadian Underwriter*, "Fairfax renews share buyback to boost shareholder value." Courtesy *Canadian Underwriter* Magazine.

On December 15, when JG actually pays the cash to the shareholders to fulfill the obligation, cash is reduced and the liability—dividends payable—is removed from the records. How that looks is shown in the following accounting equation:

Assets	=	Liabilities	+	Shareholders' equity	
				Share capital	Retained earnings
$(30,000) Cash		$(18,000) Dividends payable to preferred shareholders (12,000) Dividends payable to common shareholders			

The journal entry to record the payment of the dividends is:

Date	Transaction	Debit	Credit
	Dividends payable to preferred shareholders	$18,000	
	Dividends payable to common shareholders	12,000	
	Cash		$30,000

Suppose the preferred shares were noncumulative. Then JG would only have to pay the current year dividend of $9,000 to the preferred shareholders, and the remaining $21,000 would go to the common shareholders.

STUDY BREAK 9-2

See How You're Doing

A corporation has 10,000 shares of $8 cumulative preferred shares and 20,000 common shares outstanding. No dividends were paid last year, but this year $200,000 of dividends will be paid to shareholders. Prepare the journal entry required on the date of the dividend declaration.

Repurchase of Shares

Company Buys Its Own Shares

L.O. 3

Explain why a company would purchase its own shares.

Treasury shares are a company's own shares that the company has purchased via the stock market. It is shown on the balance sheet as a **contra-equity** account—a reduction in total shareholders' equity.

Companies are allowed to buy their own shares on the open market like anyone else. In Canada, a company buying its own shares is usually required to retire the shares that it acquired. On retirement, the shares cease to exist. In some provinces, however, shares are not required to be retired and these shares are called **treasury shares**. Treasury shares are shares that have been issued but are no longer outstanding. Companies purchase their own shares for several reasons:

1. To increase the company's earnings per share.
2. To reduce the chance of a hostile takeover.
3. To signal to the market that the shares are undervalued.
4. If acquired as treasury shares, to have shares to distribute to employees as compensation.

Some important facts about share repurchases include:

- The repurchase of shares reduces a company's assets (cash) and shareholders' equity.
- No gains or losses are ever recorded in the company's financial records when a company purchases its own shares or, if allowed, later resells them.

The accounting for share repurchases that are immediately retired is straightforward. If the company pays less on the open market than the average price paid by the company's investors for the shares, then the cash and common share accounts are reduced and any apparent gain is credited to the contributed surplus account (recall that no gains or losses can be recorded when a company buys or sells its own shares; therefore, we make an adjustment directly to the equity section). For example, suppose that a company repurchased 100 of its own shares at $30 on the open market and the average price that had been paid by investors to purchase the shares from the company was $40. Cash would decrease by $3,000, common shares would decrease by $4,000 (the average cost of the shares being retired), and the apparent gain of $1,000 would be credited to contributed surplus. The repurchase of the company's shares affects the accounting equation as follows:

Assets	=	Liabilities	+	Shareholders' equity	
				Share capital	Retained earnings
$(3,000) Cash				$(4,000) Common shares $1,000 Contributed surplus	

The journal entry to record the purchase of 100 shares for $30 per share is:

Date	Transaction	Debit	Credit
	Common shares	$4,000	
	Cash		$3,000
	Contributed surplus		$1,000

If the company pays more on the open market than the average price paid by the company's investors for the shares, then the cash and common share accounts are reduced; any apparent loss is first debited to the contributed surplus account, and any remaining balance is debited to retained earnings. For example, suppose that a company repurchased 100 of its own shares at $30 on the open market and the average price paid by investors to purchase the shares from the company was $20. Cash would decrease by $3,000, common shares would decrease by $2,000 (the average cost of the shares being retired), and the apparent loss of $1,000 would be debited to retained earnings (assuming that the contributed surplus had a zero balance). The repurchase of the company's shares affects the accounting equation as follows:

Assets	=	Liabilities	+	Shareholders' equity	
				Share capital	**Retained earnings**
$(3,000) Cash				$(2,000) Common shares	$(1,000)

The journal entry to record the purchase of 100 shares for $30 per share is:

Date	Transaction	Debit	Credit
	Common shares	$2,000	
	Retained earnings	$1,000	
	Cash		$3,000

Exhibit 9–2 shows the changes to Shoppers Drug Mart Corporation's common shares during 2003 and 2002. Note that when the company repurchased 8,772 shares for cancellation in 2003, the apparent loss (or premium) of $82 was charged against (reduced) retained earnings.

Accounting for treasury shares can take several forms, but the most common is to account for it at cost. That means when the shares are repurchased, the company records the treasury shares—a contra-shareholders' equity account—at the amount the company paid for them. How much the shares were previously issued for does not matter. Treasury shares are simply recorded at cost. Suppose a company repurchased 100 of its own shares at $30 per share. Cash would decrease by $3,000, and treasury shares—a contra-equity account that decreases equity—is increased by $3,000. When the financial statements are prepared, treasury shares are listed at the end of the owner's equity section of the balance sheet and are subtracted from total equity. The repurchase of the shares affects the accounting equation as follows:

Assets	=	Liabilities	+	Shareholders' equity	
				Share capital	**Retained earnings**
$ 3,000 Cash				$3,000 Treasury share	

Exhibit 9–2 Shares Issued and Repurchased by Shoppers Drug Mart

From the Shoppers Drug Mart Annual Report
for the 53 weeks ended January 3, 2004
and the 52 weeks ended December 28, 2002
(in thousands of dollars)
Excerpt from Note 12

12. Share Capital

Authorized
Unlimited number of common shares
Unlimited number of preferred shares, issuable in series without nominal or par value

Outstanding

	2003		2002	
	Number of Common Shares	Stated Value	Number of Common Shares	Stated Value
Beginning balance	209,703,488	$1,419,783	209,671,705	$1,418,605
Shares issued	29,691	377	210,045	2,384
Shares repurchased	(8,772)	(59)	(178,262)	(1,206)
Share purchase loans, net	—	(8,223)	—	—
Ending balance	209,724,407	$1,411,878	209,703,488	$1,419,783

During the period ended January 3, 2004 the Company issued 29,691 common shares (2002 – 210,045) with a stated value of $377, net of tax of $21 (2002 – $2,384, net of tax of $145), inclusive of 17,250 common shares (2002 – 14,037) with a stated value of $91 (2002 – $74) issued upon the exercise of options. In addition, 8,772 common shares (2002 – 178,262) were repurchased for cancellation for $141 (2002 – $3,552), which includes an $82 premium (2002 – $2,346) over the stated capital, which has been charged against retained earnings.

Courtesy Shoppers Drug Mart Corporation

The journal entry to record the purchase of 100 treasury shares when they have a market value of $30 per share is:

Date	Transaction	Debit	Credit
	Treasury shares	$3,000	
	Cash		3,000

Selling Treasury Shares

If treasury shares are resold at a later date, the shares sold will be removed from treasury shares at the price paid for the shares when they were repurchased. If the treasury shares are sold at a price higher than their cost, the excess will be classified as contributed surplus from treasury share transactions.

If the treasury shares are sold at a price lower than their cost, the deficit will reduce the contributed surplus from treasury share transactions. If the amount of the contributed surplus from treasury share transactions were insufficient to cover the deficit, then retained earnings would be reduced by the amount needed to balance the accounting equation.

Always remember, there are never any gains or losses from treasury share transactions. Exchanges between a company and its owners—issue of shares, payment of dividends, purchase or sale of treasury shares—do not affect the income statement. Recall, the separate entity assumption requires a company and its owners *not* to mix their financial records. A company and its owners are separate entities, *not* the same entity—and so there may be transactions between the owners and the company. However, these transactions are never shown on the income statement.

STUDY BREAK 9-3

See How You're Doing

Surety Corp. started the year 2006 with 125,000 common shares issued and outstanding. The issue price of these shares averaged $6 per share. During 2006, Surety purchased, for cancellation, 1,000 of its own shares at an average price of $7 per share. Prepare the journal entry to record the purchase.

Stock Dividends

L.O. 4

Be able to define stock dividends and stock splits.

A **stock dividend** is a company's distribution of new shares to the company's current shareholders.

A corporation may want to pay a dividend to its shareholders but not have sufficient cash on hand to do so. Instead of a cash dividend, the corporation may issue a **stock dividend**. When this happens, the corporation seems to be giving a shareholder something of value, but is it really? Stock dividends are not a distribution of assets, such as cash. Instead of giving the shareholders cash, the corporation gives the shareholders additional shares in the company. The accounting equation is affected only by the way in which the amounts in the different equity accounts are distributed. The corporation that pays a stock dividend converts retained earnings to share capital, thereby giving the shareholders a more direct claim to that portion of equity. Suppose a company issued $150,000 worth of new common shares (market value) by distributing it to its current shareholders as a stock dividend. That transaction would affect the accounting equation as shown next:

Assets	=	Liabilities	+	Share capital	+	Retained earnings
				+$150,000 Common shares		$(150,000) Retained earnings

The journal entry to record the stock dividend of $150,000 would be:

Date	Transaction	Debit	Credit
	Retained earnings	$150,000	
	Common shares		$ 150,000

When considering stock dividends, remember:

1. There are no income tax effects for the corporation.
2. *Stock dividends do not increase any shareholder's percentage of ownership in the company.* If you owned 5 percent of the company before the stock dividend, you own 5 percent of the company after the stock dividend. After the dividend, your 5 percent includes more shares—but every shareholder's share increases proportionally.
3. As with cash dividends, three dates are important:
   - date of declaration
   - date of record (specifically, who is going to receive the shares)
   - date of distribution

Stock Splits

A **stock split** is the division of the current shares by some multiple, to increase the number of shares. For example, a 2-for-1 stock split means every share becomes two shares.

Stock splits occur when a corporation increases the number of shares authorized, issued, and outstanding. It is different from a stock dividend. There are no *new* shares issued, but instead, the outstanding shares are "split" into two or more shares. Suppose you own 100 shares of Micromoney, Inc. It has a market value of $80 per share. Micromoney's board of directors votes to split the stock 2 for 1. After the split, instead of having 100 shares, you have 200 shares. Of course, the stock market does not get fooled by the split. It seems logical that your 200 shares would now have a market value of $40 per share, and so your total Micromoney stock after the split would continue to be worth $8,000.

Why does a corporation split its shares? Financial analysts have different opinions.

One reason a corporation splits its shares is to lower the price of a share. If a single share has a high price—over $100, for example—it may be a barrier to the share's trading. An investor may believe the price is too much to pay for one share, that too much money is at risk for a single share.

Business Process

Another reason is that a stock split may be a signal to the stock market concerning some future "good news." This rationale for stock splits comes from many observations that when a share is split, a split share trades for proportionally more than the share was trading for before the share was split. For example, let us say your shares that are trading for $80 per share are split 2 for 1. After the split, the shares are likely to trade at some price *higher* than $40 per share—even though they are theoretically only worth half of the presplit price. No formal recording is necessary for stock splits. Instead, the details of the stock split are shown parenthetically in the owners' equity part of the financial statements.

STUDY BREAK 9-4

See How You're Doing

1. Compare a stock split and a stock dividend.
2. Suppose you own 1,500 common shares, which is 3 percent of the ABC Company outstanding shares. If ABC declares a 2-for-1 stock split, how many shares will you own? What percentage ownership will your shares now represent?

Components of Shareholders' Equity in a Corporation: Retained Earnings

L.O. 5

Understand the meaning of retained earnings and how they are recorded and reported.

Shareholders' equity includes share capital (which itself is made up of common shares and contributed surplus) and **retained earnings**. Retained earnings are the amount of all the earnings of the firm—since its beginning—that have not been distributed to the shareholders. Retained earnings may also be called **earned capital**.

Retained earnings, also known as **earned capital**, are the total amount of net income minus all dividends paid since the company began.

Retained earnings equal:

1. Profits since the day the company began, minus
2. Losses since the day the company began, minus
3. Dividends paid to shareholders since the company began, minus
4. Stock dividends distributed to shareholders since the company began.

A complete set of financial statements includes a statement of changes in retained earnings.

STUDY BREAK 9-5

See How You're Doing

Suppose B&B Company started the year with retained earnings of $84,500. During the year, B&B had net income of $25,600 and paid dividends of $12,200. What was the ending balance in retained earnings?

Analysis of Shareholders' Equity

L.O. 6

Understand how information about a company's equity can be used in financial statement analysis.

The shareholders' equity of a firm, expressed in several different ratios, can provide information useful for the financial statement analysis of that firm. We will discuss three ratios using shareholders' equity:

1. Return on equity
2. Earnings per share
3. Book value per share

Return on equity is net income divided by average shareholders' equity.

Business Process

Return on equity (ROE) is a measure of how well a company produces income with the amount of investment the common shareholders have made in the company. It is calculated exactly as it sounds: return (net income) divided by average shareholders' equity. To calculate this ratio, we need the amount of common shareholders' equity at the beginning and at the end of the period. We will get those amounts from two comparative balance sheets and use the average of those amounts in the denominator. Common shareholders' equity will be all the equity *except* the preferred shareholders' equity. The ratio uses common shareholders' equity because common shareholders are considered the *true* owners of the firm. Then we use the net income, reduced by the amount of preferred dividends paid, for the numerator. The reason for deducting preferred dividends from net income is that we are calculating the return to the *common* shareholders. The ratio takes the claims of preferred shareholders' out of both the numerator and denominator. You may recall from our discussion earlier in the chapter that common shareholders are entitled to the earnings of the firm only after preferred dividends are paid. Return on equity provides information about how well the company is using the owners' contributions and earnings retained in the business.

Exhibit 9–3 shows the information needed to calculate the ROE for Loblaw Companies Limited for two consecutive years. The ratio should be compared with other similar companies or with industry standards for a meaningful analysis. We will discuss in Chapter 11 how to make the most of the information provided by financial statement ratios. For now, note that Loblaw's ROE has increased, which is favourable, and that changes in either net income or total equity will affect the ratio. Potential investors are interested in this information.

Earnings per share (EPS) is the most well-known accounting number because financial analysts use it to evaluate a company's performance. It is a company's net income on a per-share basis.

Earnings per share (EPS) is perhaps the most well-known and most used ratio derived from the information on the basic financial statements. The earnings in the numerator of this ratio begins with net income. Because EPS is designated as the earnings for the common shareholders, preferred dividends must be deducted from net income, just as in the calculation of the numerator of return on (common) shareholders' equity. The denominator is the average number of common shares outstanding during the year. To calculate this average, you need to know if and when any new shares were issued during the year and if and when any shares were repurchased. Then, you calculate a weighted average for the denominator of the EPS ratio.

Fortunately, all financial statements provide EPS. Often, two different EPS ratios are shown. One is called basic EPS and is calculated as just described: net income for the common shareholders divided by the weighted average number of common shares outstanding. The other is called diluted EPS and is calculated as if all outstanding securities that could be converted into common shares and would reduce the basic ratio actually *were* converted. This would make the denominator—the weighted average number of shares outstanding—larger. Calculations for diluted EPS can be complicated and are done often by a company's accountant when the annual financial statements are prepared.

EPS is the most common indicator of a company's overall performance. Earnings are forecast by financial analysts, anticipated by investors, managed by business executives, and announced with great anticipation by major corporations. Gildan's income statements, in Exhibit 9–4, show both basic and diluted EPS.

Book value per (common) share is total shareholders' equity (minus any equity represented by preferred shares) divided by the average number of outstanding shares.

Book value per (common) share is another ratio whose name says what it means. We have referred to the accounting records as "books," even though these records may not actually be kept in a book in modern businesses. The ratio, book value per common share, simply tells us how much of the shareholders' equity is associated with each share. The numerator is common shareholders' equity and the denominator is average number of common shares outstanding.

The financial information from Loblaw Companies Limited provided in Exhibit 9–5 is used to compute the book value per share for two consecutive years. The usefulness of this ratio, like all others, depends on how it compares with the same ratio for similar companies or how it changes over time. The increase in the book value per share is positive information.

STUDY BREAK 9-6

See How You're Doing

If you were considering making an investment in a firm, would you be more interested in the firm's earnings per share ratios for the past few years or in its book value per share for the past few years? What factors would influence your opinion? Explain the information provided by each ratio.

Exhibit 9–3
Return on Equity for Loblaws

(In millions)	For the 52 weeks of 2002[a]	For the 52 weeks of 2001
Net income	$728.0	$ 563.0
Average equity	$3,846.5	$3,346.5
Return on equity	18.9%	16.8%

[a] The Loblaws fiscal year ends on the Saturday nearest December 31.

Business Risks

L.O. 7

Explain the risks associated with equity financing.

As discussed in Chapter 1, owners of a company take a risk that the company will not be successful. Owners invest their money in hopes of making more money, and there is always the risk it will not actually happen. In the history of the stock market, there have been many shareholders who have risked their money and lost it. The risk associated with a share of ownership in a company and the potential return on that investment are the two most important characteristics of share ownership. Investors are often willing to take significant risks for the potential of earning a corresponding significant return. The evaluation of personal financial investments in the shares of corporations is the topic of many finance texts and courses. There are also many websites that address personal finance and investing.

Exhibit 9–4
Earnings per Share Reported after Net Income
Courtesy Gildan Activewear

Gildan Activewear 2003 Annual Report
Consolidated Statements of Earnings
Years ended October 5, 2003, September 29, 2002 and September 30, 2001

	2003	2002	2001
Sales	$630,139,018	$600,660,380	$504,867,353
Cost of sales (note 10)	440,293,451	431,996,459	398,566,740
Gross profit	189,845,567	168,663,921	106,300,613
Selling, general and administrative expenses (note 10)	71,153,448	63,926,673	76,074,745
Earnings before the undernoted items	118,692,119	104,737,248	30,225,868
Depreciation and amortization (note 10)	23,614,704	17,591,885	16,208,560
Interest	9,463,475	13,341,823	13,628,350
	33,078,179	30,933,708	29,836,910
Earnings before income taxes	85,613,940	73,803,540	388,958
Income taxes (recovery) (note 9)	8,342,000	7,312,000	(427,000)
Net earnings	$77,271,940	$66,491,540	$815,958
Earnings per share (note 11):			
Basic	$2.64	$2.33	$0.03
Diluted	2.60	2.26	0.03

Exhibit 9–5
Book Value per Share for Loblaw

(In millions)	For the year 2002[a]	For the year 2001
Total equity	$4,124	$3,569
Average common shares outstanding	276.2	276.2
Book value per share	$ 14.93	$ 12.92

[a]The Loblaw fiscal year ends on the Saturday nearest December 31.

Understanding Excel

The following is a copy of the Tom's Wear, Inc. shareholders' equity section of the balance sheet at August 31, 2005:

Common shares (50,000,000 shares authorized, 750,000 shares issued and outstanding)	$ 1,255,000
Retained earnings	136,616
Total shareholders' equity	*$1,391,616*

For purposes of this problem only, assume that in the month of September:

- Tom was authorized to sell 10,000 shares of $6 preferred shares.
- Tom sold 1,000 of the preferred shares at $100 per share.
- A cash dividend of $6.00 per share was paid to the preferred shareholders.
- Tom declared and issued a 5 percent stock dividend on the common shares when the market value of each share was $2.25.
- Net income for the month was $54,345.

Requirements

1. Open a new Excel work sheet.
2. Beginning in cell A1, input the shareholders' equity section of the Tom's Wear, Inc. balance sheet. Use appropriate formatting. Complete requirement 3 before inputting any numerical data.
3. Calculate the appropriate balances of the shareholders' equity accounts as of September 30, 2005, on the basis of the preceding information. Show all work and use formulas, as appropriate. Place your calculations under the shareholders' equity section. Use appropriate labels, formatting, and formulas.
4. Input the numbers into the equity section using formulas, as appropriate.
5. Print your file and save it to disk. Name your file TomsWear9.

Summary Problem: Tom's Wear Goes Public

When a privately owned company decides it wants to offer ownership to the public to raise a significant amount of capital, the form of the business organization must be a corporation. (A sole proprietorship or a partnership wanting to offer ownership to the public must first change its form to a corporation.) The first public offering of shares on one of the stock exchanges is called an initial public offering (IPO). Much like the work done before a company issues bonds, a company must do a great deal of work to prepare for an IPO. The securities regulators require the company to provide many reports, including a set of financial statements contained in a report called a **prospectus**. Remember, the job of the securities regulator is to protect the public.

A **prospectus** is a report detailing a future share offering containing a set of financial statements. These are required by securities regulators from a company that wishes to make an initial public offering of its shares.

In August, Tom decides his company could raise a great deal of capital by "going public." The company has a substantial amount of debt, and Tom decides it would be a good long-term strategy to increase the company's equity.

As you know, a company's creditors and owners have claim to the company's assets, and the relationship between the amount of debt and the amount of equity in a company is called the company's *capital structure*. Tom decides that his company's capital structure is weighted too heavily toward debt, and he wants to increase the cash available to pay off some of that debt. To increase his company's equity, Tom will offer the opportunity to the general public to become part owners in Tom's Wear.

Exhibit 9–6 shows the balance sheet for Tom's Wear at the beginning of August. This is the July 31 balance sheet you prepared at the end of Chapter 8.

The first transaction for August is the Tom's Wear IPO. Although the form of the company has been a corporation, Tom's Wear has a lot of work to do to prepare to go public. The requirements for this initial public offering are extensive, and we will let the investment bankers do the work behind the scenes. These are finance, accounting, and legal experts in the area of IPOs. The accounting changes in the balance sheet depend on the characteristics of the debt and equity of the company and the agreements the creditors and owners make. We will make it very simple for Tom's Wear, but in a real-world IPO, transactions could be much more complicated.

Tom works with an investment banking firm and an accounting firm to prepare the share offering—the IPO. The investment bankers do the legal work and essentially buy the shares and then offer them to the public. The accountants prepare extensive financial information, required by the securities regulator, in a document called a prospectus. Tom's Wear's corporate charter has 50,000,000 common shares authorized. Tom's personal ownership, which we have simply referred to as common shares without any details of the number of shares, is actually 500,000 shares. (Recall, his contribution was $5,000.) Tom wants to retain a majority of the shares so that he can retain control of the company, and so Tom's Wear decides to issue 250,000 additional common shares in this initial offering. The shares are issued at $5 per share.

Tom's Wear, Inc.
Balance Sheet
At August 1, 2005

Exhibit 9–6
Balance sheet for Tom's Wear, Inc. at August 1, 2005

Assets		Liabilities and Shareholders' equity	
Cash	$ 17,151	Accounts payable	$ 36,000
Accounts receivable (net of allowance of $3,290)	101,810	Interest payable	1,500
		Warranty liability	2,239
Inventory	8,910	Current portion of long-term note	6,000
Prepaid insurance	50		
Prepaid rent	600	Current portion of mortgage	2,710
Prepaid Web service	150	Total current liabilities	48,449
Total current assets	128,671	Notes payable	24,000
Computer (net of $500 accumulated amortization)	3,500	Mortgage payable	72,290
		Total liabilities	144,739
Van (net of $4,205 accumulated amortization)	25,795	Common shares	5,000
		Retained earnings	83,097
Land	7,500		
Building (net of $130 accumulated amortization)	67,370		
Total assets	$232,836	Total liabilities and shareholders' equity	$232,836

Assets	=	Liabilities	+	Share capital	+	Retained earnings
$1,250,000 Cash				+$1,250,000 Common shares		

The rest of the transactions for Tom's Wear follow. Record the transactions in the accounting equation work sheet, and then check your work with the work sheet provided in the solution before you continue.

Transactions for August 2005 for Tom's Wear, Inc.

1	August 1	Tom's Wear issues shares for $1,250,000
2	August 10	Collects cash on accounts receivable of $96,000
3	August 12	Pays accounts payable of $30,000
4	August 14	Tom has been concentrating on increasing sales, so he must increase inventory purchases as well. With the new inflow of cash from the share offering, Tom decides to buy 25,000 shirts. He gets a quantity discount from the vendor, paying $3.50 for each shirt. He pays cash for the purchase.
5	August 20	Tom finds out that Play Ball Sports Shop has closed and filed bankruptcy. He writes off the account, which has a balance of $3,000.
6	August 15–30	Tom's sales efforts continue to pay off with the addition of several more customers. He lowers the price slightly, and he is able to dramatically increase sales. During August, Tom's Wear sells 20,151 shirts at $10 each. All sales are on account.
7	August 15–30	During August, 300 shirts are returned with defects, and Tom replaces them with new shirts.
8	August 15–30	Other operating expenses amount to $42,500 for the month.
9	August 30	The payroll has grown considerably because Tom has hired several new employees, including an on-site manager to run the warehouse. He has also put himself on the management payroll. He sends the payroll company a check for $22,000 by the 30th of the month to cover the payroll and payroll tax expenses for the month.
10	August 30	Tom's Wear pays for insurance to cover the business from August 15 to December 31, for a total of $675.
11	August 31	By the end of the month, Tom sees that he needs to increase the number of delivery vans and purchase some new office equipment. Tom buys two vans for a total cost of $100,000 and new office equipment for $100,000.

Additional information for August includes the following: Tom's Wear drove the van 20,000 kilometres in August; Tom also decided to reduce the warranty liability from 2 percent to 1 percent of sales because he noticed that the liability appeared to be larger than needed. Due to the huge increase in sales, Tom decided to keep the allowance for doubtful accounts at 3 percent of credit sales.

Required:

Prepare the journal entries and adjustments, and post them to T-accounts. Prepare an adjusted trial balance. Then, prepare the four basic financial statements.

Answers to Study Break Questions

STUDY BREAK 9-1

$373,000 – $353,000 = $20,000 (increase in common shares account)
$20,000/1000 shares = $20 average issue price per share

STUDY BREAK 9-2

Because the preferred shares are cumulative, the preferred shareholders must receive from the corporation all the dividends in arrears (those from the past that were not paid to preferred shareholders) plus the current year dividends before any dividends can be paid to the common shareholders.

The annual dividend to preferred shareholders is 80,000 (10,000 shares × $8). The company owes preferred shareholders for last year and the current year, for a total of $160,000; that will leave $40,000 for the common shareholders.

Date	Transaction	Debit	Credit
	Retained earnings	$200,000	
	Dividends payable to preferred shareholders		$160,000
	Dividends payable to common shareholders		40,000
	To record the declaration of a dividend.		

STUDY BREAK 9-3

Assets are decreased by $7,000 (cash outflow). Owner's equity is also reduced by $7,000.

Date	Transaction	Debit	Credit
2006	Common shares	$6,000	
	Contributed surplus	$1,000	
	Cash		$7,000
	To record the purchase of shares for cancellation.		

STUDY BREAK 9-4

1. A company would issue a stock dividend to give its shareholders *something*, even though the company may be short of cash. Distributing shares as dividends involves recording a transfer of retained earnings to share capital. A stock split involves increasing the number of shares by turning a single share into two or more shares. There is no formal recording of a stock split in the accounting records. A stock split is most often done to lower the trading price of a company's shares.
2. You will now own 3,000 shares but you will still own 3 percent, just as you did before the split.

STUDY BREAK 9-5

Beginning retained earnings	$84,500
+ Net income	25,600
– Dividends paid	(12,200)
Ending retained earnings	$97,900

STUDY BREAK 9-6

Earnings per share (EPS) is the more relevant of the two numbers; EPS is extremely important to investors. It is very current because it is based on the current year's income. Book value per share, on the other hand, may have a numerator that is less current. Its relevance is influenced by the age of the company's assets and by any differences between the market value of the assets and the historical cost of those assets.

Solution to Summary Problem

Transaction 1
Tom's Wear issues shares for $1,250,000.

Date	Transaction	Debit	Credit
8/1/2005	Cash	$1,250,000	
	Common shares		$1,250,000
To record the issue of 250,000 common shares at $5.00 per share.			

Transaction 2
Collects cash on accounts receivable of $96,000.

Date	Transaction	Debit	Credit
8/10/2005	Cash	$96,000	
	Accounts receivable		$96,000
To record the collection of accounts receivable.			

Transaction 3
Pays accounts payable of $30,000.

Date	Transaction	Debit	Credit
8/12/2005	Accounts payable	$30,000	
	Cash		$30,000
To record payment on account.			

Transaction 4
Purchases 25,000 T-shirts @ $3.50 each for cash.

Date	Transaction	Debit	Credit
8/14/2005	Inventory	$87,500	
	Cash		$87,500
To record the purchase of 25,000 T-shirts @ $3.50 each.			

Transaction 5
Writes off the $3,000 accounts receivable for Play Ball Sports.

Date	Transaction	Debit	Credit
8/20/2005	Allowance for doubtful accounts	$3,000	
	Accounts receivable		$3,000
To record the write-off of Play Ball Sports' account.			

Transaction 6
Sells 20,151 shirts for $10 each. All sales are on account.

Date	Transaction	Debit	Credit
8/15–8/31/2005	Sales revenue	$201,510	
	Accounts receivable		$201,510
To record the sale of 20,151 T-shirts on account.			
8/15–8/31/2005	Cost of goods sold	$70,776	
	Inventory		$70,776
To record cost of goods sold [(2,475 @ $3.60) + (17,676 @ $3.50)].			

Transaction 7
During August, 300 T-shirts are returned with defects. Tom replaces them all with new T-shirts.

Date	Transaction	Debit	Credit
8/15–8/31/2005	Warranties payable	$1,050	
	Inventory		$1,050
To record the replacement of 300 defective shirts (300 × $3.50).			

Transaction 8
Miscellaneous operating expenses for the month are $42,500.

Date	Transaction	Debit	Credit
8/15–8/31/2005	Other operating expenses	$42,500	
	Cash		$42,500
To record the payment of other operating expenses.			

Transaction 9
Records salary expense of $22,000.

Date	Transaction	Debit	Credit
8/30/2005	Salary expense	$22,000	
	Cash		$22,000
To record the payment of payroll, related taxes, and fees.			

Transaction 10
Pays $675 for insurance coverage for the period August 15 to December 31.

Date	Transaction	Debit	Credit
8/30/2005	Prepaid insurance	$675	
	Cash		$675
To record insurance payment.			

Transaction 11
Purchases two new vans and some new office equipment.

Date	Transaction	Debit	Credit
8/31/2005	Office furniture and fixtures	$100,000	
	Equipment: van	100,000	
	Cash		$200,000
To record the purchase of equipment and two vans.			

Adjustment 1
Records rent expense of $600 for the month of August.

Date	Transaction	Debit	Credit
8/31/2005	Rent expense	$600	
	Prepaid rent		$600
To record rent expense for August.			

Adjustment 2
Records insurance expense of $125 for the month of August.

Date	Transaction	Debit	Credit
8/31/2005	Insurance expense	$125	
	Prepaid insurance		$125
To record insurance expense for August.			

Adjustment 3
Records Web costs of $50 for August.

Date	Transaction	Debit	Credit
8/31/2005	Other operating expenses	$50	
	Prepaid Web service		$50
To record Web maintenance services for August.			

Adjustment 4
Records amortization expense of $2,900 on the van (20,000 kilometres @ $0.145).

Date	Transaction	Debit	Credit
8/31/2005	Amortization expense	$2,900	
	Accumulated amortization: van		$2,900
To record August amortization expense on the van.			

Adjustment 5
Record amortization expense of $100 on the computer.

Date	Transaction	Debit	Credit
8/31/2005	Amortization expense	$100	
	Accumulated amortization: computer		$100
To record August amortization expense on the computer.			

Adjustment 6
Records amortization expense of $130 on the building.

Date	Transaction	Debit	Credit
8/31/2005	Amortization expense	$130	
	Accumulated amortization: building		$130
To record August amortization expense on the building.			

Adjustment 7
Records interest expense on the van note.

Date	Transaction	Debit	Credit
8/31/2005	Interest expense	$250	
	Interest payable		$250
To record interest expense on the van for August.			

Adjustment 8
Records interest expense on the mortgage.

Date	Transaction	Debit	Credit
8/31/2005	Interest expense	$500	
	Interest payable		$500
To record interest expense on the mortgage for August.			

Adjustment 9
Bad debt estimate = 3% of credit sales.

Date	Transaction	Debit	Credit
8/31/2005	Bad debt expense	$6,045	
	Allowance for doubtful accounts		$6,045
To record the bad debt estimate for August ($201,510 × 3%).			

Adjustment 10
Warranty liability estimate = 1% of total sales.

Date	Transaction	Debit	Credit
8/31/2005	Warranty expense	$2,015	
	Warranties payable		$2,015
To record the estimated warranty liability for August ($201,510 × 1%).			

T-Accounts for Tom's Wear with August journal entries and adjustments

Cash

	Debit	Credit	
BB	$17,151	$30,000	3
1	1,250,000	87,500	4
2	96,000	42,500	8
		22,000	9
		675	10
		200,000	11
	$980,476		

Accounts receivable

	Debit	Credit	
BB	$105,100	$96,000	2
6a	201,510	3,000	5
	$207,610		

Allowance for doubtful accounts

	Debit	Credit	
5	$3,000	$3,290	BB
		6,045	Adj-9
		$6,335	

Inventory

	Debit	Credit	
BB	$8,910	$70,776	6b
4	87,500	1,050	7
	$24,584		

Prepaid insurance

	Debit	Credit	
BB	$50	$125	Adj-2
10	675		
	$600		

Prepaid Web service

	Debit	Credit	
BB	$150	$50	Adj-3
	$100		

Prepaid rent

	Debit	Credit	
BB	$600	$600	Adj-1
	$ 0		

Equipment: computer

	Debit	Credit	
BB	$4,000		
	$4,000		

Accumulated amortization: computer

	Debit	Credit	
		$500	BB
		100	Adj-5
		$600	

Equipment: van

	Debit	Credit	
BB	$30,000		
11	100,000		
	$130,000		

Accumulated amortization: van

	Debit	Credit	
		$4,205	BB
		2,900	Adj-4
		$7,105	

Buildings

	Debit	Credit	
BB	$67,500		
	$67,500		

Accumulated amortization: buildings

	Debit	Credit	
		$130	BB
		130	Adj-6
		$260	

Land

	Debit	Credit	
BB	$7,500		
	$7,500		

Office furniture and fixtures

	Debit	Credit	
11	$100,000		
	$100,000		

Accounts payable

	Debit	Credit	
3	$30,000	$36,000	BB
		$6,000	

Interest payable

	Debit	Credit	
		$1,500	BB
		250	Adj-7
		500	Adj-8
		$2,250	

Warranties payable

	Debit	Credit	
7	$1,050	$2,239	BB
		2,015	Adj-10
		$3,204	

Notes payable

	Debit	Credit	
		$30,000	BB
		$30,000	

Mortgage payable

	Debit	Credit	
		$75,000	BB
		$75,000	

Common shares

	Debit	Credit	
		$5,000	BB
		1,250,000	1
		$1,255,000	

Retained earnings

	Debit	Credit	
		$83,097	BB
		$83,097	

Sales revenue

	Debit	Credit	
		$201,510	6a
		$201,510	

Cost of goods sold

	Debit	Credit
6b	$70,776	
	$70,776	

Amortization expense

	Debit	Credit
Adj-4	$2,900	
Adj-5	100	
Adj-6	130	
	$3,130	

Other operating expenses

	Debit	Credit
8	$42,500	
Adj-3	50	
	$42,550	

Salary expense

	Debit	Credit
9	$22,000	
	$22,000	

Insurance expense

	Debit	Credit
Adj-2	$125	
	$125	

Rent expense

	Debit	Credit
Adj-1	$600	
	$600	

Interest expense

	Debit	Credit
Adj-7	$250	
Adj-8	500	
	$750	

Bad debt expense

	Debit	Credit
Adj-9	$6,045	
	$6,045	

Warranty expense

	Debit	Credit
Adj-10	$2,015	
	$2,015	

Tom's Wear, Inc.
Adjusted Trial Balance
For the Month Ended August 31, 2005

	Debits	Credits
Cash	$ 980,476	
Accounts receivable	207,610	
Allowance for doubtful accounts		$ 6,335
Inventory	24,584	
Prepaid insurance	600	
Prepaid Web service	100	
Equipment: computer	4,000	
Accumulated amortization: computer		600
Equipment: van	130,000	
Accumulated amortization: van		7,105
Buildings	67,500	
Accumulated amortization: buildings		260
Land	7,500	
Office furniture and fixtures	100,000	
Accounts payable		6,000
Interest payable		2,250
Warranties payable		3,204
Notes payable		30,000
Mortgage payable		75,000
Common shares		1,255,000
Retained earnings		83,097
Sales revenue		201,510
Cost of goods sold	70,776	
Amortization expense	3,130	
Other operating expense	42,550	
Salary expense	22,000	
Insurance expense	125	
Rent expense	600	
Interest expense	750	
Bad debt expense	6,045	
Warranty expense	2,015	
Totals	*$1,670,361*	*$1,670,361*

Tom's Wear, Inc.
Income Statement
For the Month Ended
August 31, 2005

Sales revenue		$201,510
Less: cost of goods sold		70,776
Gross margin		130,734
Expenses[a]		
Salary expense	$22,000	
Rent expense	600	
Insurance expense	125	
Amortization expense	3,130	
Bad debt expense	6,045	
Warranty expense	2,015	
Interest expense	750	
Other operating expenses	42,550	
Total expenses		*77,215*
Net income		$ 53,519

[a] It is unlikely that a company would itemize the expenses at this level of detail. However, they are detailed here to make it easy for you to follow the numbers.

Tom's Wear, Inc.
Statement of Retained Earnings
For the Month Ended
August 31, 2005

Beginning retained earnings	$ 83,097
Net income	53,519
Dividends paid to shareholders	0
Ending retained earnings	136,616

Tom's Wear, Inc.
Balance Sheet
August 31, 2005

Assets		Liabilities and shareholders' equity	
Cash	$ 980,476	Accounts payable	$ 6,000
Accounts receivable (net of allowance of $6,335)	201,275	Interest payable	2,250
		Warranty liability	3,204
Inventory	24,584	Current portion of long-term note	6,000
Prepaids	700	Current portion of mortgage	2,710
Total current assets	1,207,035		
Land	7,500	Total current liabilities	20,164
Equipment (net of accumulated amortization of $600)	103,400	Notes payable	24,000
		Mortgage payable	72,290
Van (net of accumulated amortization of $7,105)	122,895	Total liabilities	116,454
Building (net of accumulated amortization of $260)	67,240	Common shares (50,000,000 shares authorized, 750,000 shares issued and outstanding)	1,255,000
		Retained earnings	136,616
Total assets	$1,508,070	Total liabilities and shareholders' equity	$1,508,070

Tom's Wear, Inc.
Cash Flow Statement
For the Month Ended August 31, 2005

Cash from operating activities		
Cash collected from customers	$ 96,000	
Cash paid for salaries	(22,000)	
Cash paid to vendors	(117,500)	
Cash paid for other expenses	(43,175)	
Total cash from operating activities		*$ (86,675)*
Cash from investing activities		
Purchase of fixed assets		(200,000)
Cash from financing activities		
Proceeds from common shares issue		1,250,000
Net increase in cash		**$963,325**
Cash opening balance (August 01)		17,151
Cash closing balance (August 31)		$980,426

Questions

1. What is share capital?
2. What are retained earnings?
3. What is the difference between common shares and preferred shares?
4. What is the relationship between the par value of common shares and their market price?
5. Are dividends expenses of a corporation? Explain why or why not.
6. Who gets their dividends first: common or preferred shareholders?
7. What is the difference between cumulative and noncumulative preferred shares?
8. Why would a company purchase its own shares?
9. Who decides the amount and timing of dividend payments?
10. What are stock dividends?
11. What are dividends payable?

Short Exercises

SE9-1 The Delta Corp. corporate charter authorizes the company to sell one million common shares. As of December 31, 2006, the company had issued 575,000 shares for $5 each. Delta has not repurchased any shares for cancellation. How many common shares will be disclosed as authorized, issued, and outstanding on the December 31, 2006, balance sheet? L.O. 1

SE9-2 Sunshine Corp. began operations on July 1, 2007. When the first fiscal year of Sunshine ended on June 30, 2008, the balance sheet showed 300,000 common shares issued and 300,000 common shares outstanding. During the second year, Sunshine repurchased 10,000 shares for the treasury. After the purchase, how many shares would be classified as issued? How many shares are outstanding? L.O. 1

SE9-3 If Vest Corp. sells 100 of its common shares at $11 per share, how will the transaction be reflected in the accounting equation? L.O. 1

SE9-4 Ice Video Corp. issued 5,000 of its common shares for $6.55 per share. How will the proceeds be shown in the equity section of the balance sheet? L.O. 1

SE9-5 If 10,000 of $1 par common shares are issued for $10 per share, what is the effect on total share capital? What is the effect on contributed surplus (also known as paid-in capital in excess of par)? L.O. 1

SE9-6 Stockton Company reported total shareholders' equity of $58,000 on its December 31, 2006, balance sheet. During 2006, it reported a net income of $4,000, declared and paid a cash dividend of $2,000, and issued additional capital shares of $20,000. What was total shareholders' equity at the beginning of the year, on January 1, 2006? L.O. 1

SE9-7 On December 15, 2005, the board of directors of Seat Corp. declared a cash dividend, of $2 per share on the 100,000 common shares outstanding, payable January 8, 2006. The accounting period ends December 31. How will this be reflected on the balance sheet at December 31, 2005? L.O. 2

SE9-8 In 2004, the board of directors of Best Bakery Corp. declared total dividends of $50,000. The company has 2,000 of $8 preferred shares. No dividends are in arrears. How much of the $50,000 will be paid to the preferred shareholders? How much will be paid to the common shareholders? L.O. 2

SE9-9 Cab Company paid $30,000 to its preferred shareholders this year. The preferred shares have a par value of $100 and a dividend rate of 6 percent. If there were no L.O. 2

dividends in arrears, how many shares of preferred shares were outstanding (on the date of record)?

L.O. 2

SE9-10 Bates Corp. has 7,000 of $5 cumulative, preferred shares outstanding and 50,000 common shares outstanding. If the board of directors declares $100,000 of total dividends and the company did not pay dividends the previous year, how much will the preferred shareholders receive (in total)?

L.O. 3

SE9-11 Fitness and Fashion Corp. decided to buy back some of its own shares for cancellation. If there were 30,000 shares issued and outstanding before the share repurchase and the company bought 250 shares, how many shares were issued and outstanding after the share purchase?

L.O. 3

SE9-12 If Fitness and Fashion Corp. paid $10 per share for 250 of its own shares when the average price paid by investors was $8, how would the transaction affect the accounting equation? How would the transaction be reflected in the shareholders' equity section of the balance sheet?

L.O. 3

SE9-13 Suppose Fitness and Fashion Corp. paid $6 per share for 250 of its own shares. How would the transaction affect the accounting equation?

L.O. 4

SE9-14 Borax Company declared and paid a 10 percent stock dividend on June 1, 2008. Before this dividend was declared and distributed, there were 120,000 of common shares outstanding. After the stock dividend, how many shares are outstanding?

L.O. 4

SE9-15 Romax Company announced a 2-for-1 stock split on its common shares. Before the announcement, there were 120,000 of common shares outstanding. After the stock split, how many shares will be outstanding?

L.O. 5

SE9-16 On January 1, 2007, Netto Inc. started the year with a $22,000 balance in retained earnings. During 2007, the company earned net income of $40,000 and declared and paid dividends of $10,000. Also, the company received cash of $15,000 from a new issue of common shares. What is the balance in retained earnings on December 31, 2007?

L.O. 5, 6

SE9-17 Details Corp. had a return on shareholders' equity of 12 percent in 2008. If average shareholders' equity for Details Corp. was $500,000 and the company has no preferred shares, what was net income for 2008?

L.O. 5, 6

SE9-18 Gildan Activewear reported the following information on the financial statements for 2003. Were any new common shares issued between 2002 and 2003? Did the company report net income for the year ended October 5, 2003?

(Dollars are in millions.)

Class A Common ahares Authorized: unlimited	**October 5, 2003**	**September 29, 2002**
Issued and outstanding		
22,826,964 shares at September 29, 2002		
23,425,966 shares at October 5, 2003	$ 106.5	$ 99.8
Retained earnings	241.9	164.7

L.O. 6

SE9-19 Spikes, Inc. started and ended the year with 400,000 common shares issued and outstanding. Net income was $35,000. Calculate earnings per share for the year.

Exercises

E9-1 The ABC Company corporate charter allows it to sell 200,000 common shares. To date, the company has issued 50,000 shares for a total of $125,000. Last month, ABC repurchased 1,000 shares for $3 per share for cancellation. L.O. 2

a. If ABC were to prepare a balance sheet, how many shares would it show as (1) authorized, (2) issued, and (3) outstanding?
b. In addition to the owner's equity previously described, ABC Company also has $350,000 in retained earnings. Using this information, prepare the owner's equity section of the ABC Company balance sheet.

E9-2 DEF Company had a net income of $250,000 for the year ended December 31, 2007. On January 15, the board of directors met and declared a dividend of $0.50 per share for each of the 300,000 outstanding common shares. The board voted to distribute the dividend on March 1 to all shareholders of record as of February 1. L.O. 2

What is (1) the date of declaration, (2) the date of record, and (3) the date of payment? If DEF Company were to prepare a balance sheet on January 30, how would the dividends be shown (if at all)?

E9-3 G-Hi Company has 4,000 of $9.00 cumulative preferred shares outstanding and 10,000 common shares outstanding. The company began operations on January 1, 2007. The cash dividends declared and paid during each of the first three years of G-Hi's operations are shown next. Calculate the amounts that went to the preferred and the common shareholders each year. L.O. 2

Year	Total dividends paid	Dividends to preferred shareholders	Dividends to common shareholders
2007	$60,000		
2008	20,000		
2009	60,000		

E9-4 JKL Company had the following shareholders' equity section on the December 31, 2008, balance sheet: L.O. 1, 2, 3

Preferred shares, $100 par, 8% cumulative	$1,250,000
Common shares, $2 par value	800,000
Contributed surplus, common shares	3,500,000
Retained earnings	3,467,000
Total	*$9,017,000*

a. How many common shares are issued?
b. How many common shares are outstanding?
c. How many preferred shares are outstanding?
d. What was the average selling price of a common share?
e. If $150,000 of dividends were declared and no dividends were in arrears, how much of that amount would go to the common shareholders?

E9-5 The following balances were shown on the year-end balance sheets for 2007 and 2008 for MNO Company. For each item, give the most likely reason for the change from one year to the next. L.O. 1, 2, 3, 5

	12/31/07	12/31/08	Explanation?
Common shares	$ 245,000	$ 280,000	
Retained earnings	182,500	200,000[a]	
Treasury shares	(3,450)	(5,450)	

[a]Net income for the year was $20,000.

Problems—Set A

L.O. 1, 2, 3

P9-1A The following information pertains to the shareholders' equity section of the December 31, 2005, balance sheet of Sammie's Soap Company, Inc:

a. Share capital on January 1, 2005, was made up of 70,000 issued and outstanding common shares with a stated value of $385,000 and retained earnings of $500,000.
b. During January 2005, Sammie's issued an additional 10,000 common shares for $7 per share.
c. On the December 31, 2004, balance sheet, Sammie's noted that there were 150,000 common shares authorized.
d. Net income for 2005 was $49,500.
e. Sammie's paid shareholders a dividend of $0.25 per share on October 1.
f. During November, Sammie's CEO decided the company should buy 1,000 of its own shares for cancellation. At that time, the shares were trading for $6 per share in the stock market.

Required: Prepare the equity section of the balance sheet at December 31, 2005.

L.O. 4

P9-2A As of December 31, 2008, Ginger's Snap Company had 100,000 common shares issued and outstanding. The retained earnings balance was $125,000. On January 15, 2009, Ginger's issued a 5 percent stock dividend to its common shareholders. At the time of the dividend, the market value of the shares was $15 per share, and so the dollar amount of the stock dividend was $75,000 (100,000 shares × 5% = 5,000 shares; 5,000 shares × $15 per share = $75,000).

Required:

a. What effect did the stock dividend have on the accounting equation?
b. How many shares are outstanding after the stock dividend?
c. If you owned 3 percent of the outstanding common shares of Ginger's Snap Company before the stock dividend, what is your percentage of ownership after the stock dividend?

L.O. 1, 2, 3

P9-3A The following information is from the shareholders' equity sections from comparative balance sheets for Wildwood Company:

	At December 31,	
	2005	2004
Common shares ($10 par)	$420,000	$400,000
Contributed surplus	326,000	306,000
Retained earnings	55,000	51,000
Total shareholders' equity	*$801,000*	*$757,000*

Note: Net income for the year ended December 31, 2005, was $70,000.

Required:

a. How many common shares were issued to new shareholders during 2005?
b. What was the average issue price of the shares issued during 2005?
c. What was the amount of dividends declared during 2005?
d. Did the company have any treasury shares at the end of 2005?

P9-4A Use the information from the High Liner Foods annual report in Exhibit 9–1 to answer the following questions: L.O. 1, 5

a. How many new common shares did the company issue during the fiscal year ended January 3, 2004?
b. What was the approximate (average) issue price of the shares issued during the year?
c. Did High Liner Foods earn net income during the year?
d. If High Liner Foods paid dividends of $0.60 per share, what would you estimate net income for the year to be?

P9-5A Use the information from the Shoppers Drug Mart annual report in Exhibit 9–2 to answer the following questions: L.O. 1, 3, 5

a. How many common shares were outstanding at January 3, 2004 (end of 2003 fiscal year)?
b. How many common shares were outstanding at December 28, 2002?
c. What was the average issue price per share of the common shares classified as "issued" at January 3, 2004? (Round the answer to the nearest cent.)
d. How many shares did the company purchase during 2003?
e. What was the average price per share paid for the shares purchased during the fiscal year ended January 3, 2004?
f. What was the average issue price of the common shares issued during the fiscal year ended January 3, 2004?
g. Examine the average issue price for shares issued upon the exercise of options. Why does the average issue price differ from your answer in **f**?

Problems—Set B

P9-1B The following information pertains to All Batteries Company, Inc: L.O. 1, 2, 3

a. Share capital on October 1, 2004, was composed of 50,000 issued and outstanding common shares with a stated value of $300,000 and retained earnings of $400,000.
b. During October 2004, All Batteries Company issued an additional 20,000 common shares for $8 per share.
c. On the September 30, 2005, balance sheet, the company showed 500,000 common shares authorized.
d. Net income for the year ended September 30, 2005, was $87,500.
e. All Batteries Company paid its shareholders a dividend of $0.50 per share on August 1.
f. During November, the All Batteries Company CEO decided the company should buy 600 of its own shares for cancellation. At that time, the shares were trading for $7 per share.

Required: Prepare the equity section of the September 30, 2005, balance sheet.

P9-2B At December 31, 2007, Robby's Shoe Company had 200,000 common shares issued and outstanding. The retained earnings balance was $165,000. On January 15, 2008, Robby's issued a 3 percent stock dividend to its common shareholders. At the time of the dividend, the market value of the shares was $20 per share, and so the dollar amount of the stock dividend was $120,000 (200,000 shares × 0.03 = 6,000 shares; 6,000 shares × $20 per share = $120,000). L.O. 4

Required:

a. What effect did the stock dividend have on the accounting equation?
b. How many shares are outstanding after the stock dividend?
c. If you owned 5 percent of the outstanding common shares of Robby's Shoe Company before the stock dividend, what is your percentage of ownership after the stock dividend?

L.O. 1, 2, 3

P9-3B The following information was shown on the recent comparative balance sheets for Paul's Dot-Com Company:

	At December 31, 2006	At December 31, 2005
Common shares ($1 par)	$520,000	$400,000
Contributed surplus	326,000	296,000
Retained earnings	65,000	50,000
Total shareholders' equity	*$911,000*	*$746,000*

Note: Net income for the year ended December 31, 2006, was $75,000.

Required:

a. How many common shares were issued to new shareholders during 2006?
b. What was the average issue price of the shares issued during 2006?
c. What was the amount of dividends declared during 2006?
d. Did the company have any treasury shares at the end of 2006?

L.O. 1, 5

P9-4B At June 30, 2007, High Quality Mining Company reported the following on its comparative balance sheets (amounts in millions):

	June 30	
	2007	2006
Common shares		
Authorized: 2,500 shares		
Issued		
1,450 shares in 2007	$18,850	
1,400 shares in 2006		$16,890
Retained earnings	15,500	14,300

Required:

a. Did the company issue any new shares during the fiscal year ended June 30, 2007?
b. What was the approximate (average) issue price of the shares issued during the year?
c. Did High Quality Mining Company earn net income during the year?
d. Assume no dividends were paid this year. What would you estimate net income for the year to be?

L.O. 1, 3, 5

P9-5B This information is from the equity section of the comparative balance sheets of Tick Tock, Inc.

Consolidated Balance Sheets
(in thousands, except share data)

Shareholders' equity	September 30, 2006	September 30, 2005
Common shares, $0.10 par value; 450,000 shares issued and ________ shares outstanding at September 30, 2006; and 425,000 shares issued and ________ shares outstanding at September 30, 2005	$ 45.0	$ 42.5
Contributed surplus	9,475	8,925
Retained earnings	25,237	21,450
Treasury shares, at cost, 21,340 shares at September 30, 2006, and 17,148 shares at September 30, 2005	(448)	(343)

Required:

a. What was the average issue price per share of the 450,000 shares classified as "issued" at September 30, 2006? (Round the answer to the nearest cent.)
b. What was the average issue price of the 25,000 common shares issued during the fiscal year ending September 30, 2006?
c. How many shares were outstanding at September 30, 2006? How many shares were outstanding at September 30, 2005?
d. How many shares did the company buy back during the year? What was the average cost of a share of the treasury shares purchased during the year?
e. If no dividends were paid, what was net income for the year ending September 30, 2006?

Recording Transactions

R9-1 (SE9-3) If Vest Corporation sells and issues 100 of its common shares at $11 per share, what is the journal entry needed to record the transaction?

Date	Account	Debit	Credit

R9-2 (SE9-7) On December 15, 2005, the board of directors of Seat Corporation declared a cash dividend, payable January 8, 2006, of $2 per share on the 100,000 common shares outstanding. The accounting period ends December 31. Give the journal entry to record the December 15 transaction.

Date	Account	Debit	Credit

R9-3 (SE9-10) Bates Corporation has 7,000 shares of $5, cumulative preferred shares outstanding and 50,000 common shares outstanding. If the board of directors declares $100,000 of total dividends and the company did not pay dividends the previous year, what is the journal entry that Bates should record?

Date	Account	Debit	Credit

R9-4 (SE9-13) Suppose Fitness and Fashion Corporation paid $6 per share for 250 of its own shares when the average price paid by investors was $8. Give the journal entry for this transaction.

Date	Account	Debit	Credit

R9-5 (SE9-15) Romax Company announced a 2-for-1 stock split on its common shares. Before the announcement, there were 120,000 common shares outstanding. After the stock split, how many shares will be outstanding? What is the journal entry needed to record this transaction?

Date	Account	Debit	Credit

R9-6 (E9-2) DEF Company had a net income of $250,000 for the year ended 12/31/07. On January 15, the board of directors met and declared a dividend of $0.50 per share for each of the 300,000 outstanding common shares. The board voted to distribute the dividend on March 1 to all shareholders of record as of February 1. Give the journal entry for the declaration of the dividend.

Date	Account	Debit	Credit

R9-7 (E9-3) G-Hi Company has 4,000 shares of $9.00, cumulative preferred shares outstanding and 10,000 common shares outstanding. The company began operations on January 1, 2007. The cash dividends declared and paid during each of the first three years of G-Hi's operations were: $60,000 in 2007, $20,000 in 2008, and $60,000 in 2009. Give the journal entry for the dividend declaration for each of the three years.

Date	Account	Debit	Credit

R9-8 (P9-1A) The following information pertains to the equity section of the December 31, 2005, balance sheet of Sammie's Soap Company, Inc.

- **a.** Share capital on January 1, 2005, consisted of 70,000 issued and outstanding common shares with a stated value of $385,000 and retained earnings of $500,000.
- **b.** During January 2005, Sammie's issued an additional 10,000 common shares for $7 per share.
- **c.** Sammie's paid shareholders a dividend of $0.25 per share on October 1.
- **d.** During November, Sammie's CEO decided the company should buy 1,000 of its own shares for cancellation. At that time, the shares were trading for $6 per share in the stock market.
- **e.** Net income for 2005 was $49,500.

Required: Use the following T-accounts to record the beginning balances in the equity accounts and to record the transactions described in parts b–e.

Common shares		Retained earnings	

R9-9 (P9-2A) As of December 31, 2008, Ginger's Snap Company had 100,000 common shares issued and outstanding. The retained earnings balance was $125,000. On January 15, 2009, Ginger's issued a 5 percent stock dividend to its common shareholders. At the time of the dividend, the market value of the shares was $15 per share, and so the dollar amount of the stock dividend was $75,000 [100,000 shares × 5% = 5,000 shares; 5,000 shares × $15 per share = $75,000]. Give the journal entry for the stock dividend.

Date	Account	Debit	Credit

R9-Comprehensive

Chapter 9: Comprehensive Financial Statement Preparation Problem

Shelby's Pet Mart, Inc. began operations in January 2007. The company's corporate charter authorizes the company to issue up to 500,000 common shares and 100,000 of $10, cumulative preferred shares. The company completed the following transactions during its first two years of operations.

In 2007, Shelby's Pet Mart, Inc.:

1. Issued 50,000 common shares for $3 per share on January 1.
2. Issued 10,000 preferred shares for $120 per share on January 20.
3. Issued 20,000 common shares for $5 per share on March 30.
4. Earned and collected $320,000 revenue during the year.
5. Paid cash expenses of $121,000 during the year.
6. Declared dividends of $50,000 on December 31. The dividend will be paid on February 1, 2008, to shareholders of record at January 15, 2008.

In 2008, the company completed these transactions:

1. On February 1, paid the cash dividend declared on December 31, 2007.
2. On March 30, issued 10,000 preferred shares for $130 per share.
3. On July 1, purchased 1,000 of its own common shares at $6 per share for cancellation.
4. Earned $400,000 of revenue; collected $300,000 of it in cash during the year.
5. Paid cash expenses of $150,000 during the year.
6. Declared dividends of $15,000 on December 31. The dividend will be paid on February 1, 2009, to shareholders of record at January 15, 2009.

Record the transactions in T-accounts. Then, prepare the four basic financial statements for both fiscal years.

Issues for Discussion

Financial statement analysis

1. Use the annual report of CoolBrands International Inc. to answer the following:
   a. CoolBrands issued shares during 2003. Where is this disclosed in the financial statements? What was the dollar amount of shares issued? Describe how this is reflected in the comparative balance sheet amounts. On what other statement will the dollar amount of shares be found? Where?
   b. Compute the return-on-equity for the two consecutive years ending in 2003 and 2002. What information do these ratios provide? The shareholders' equity at the end of fiscal 2001 was $132,237,000.

Business risk

2. a. What kinds of risks do the owners of CoolBrands face?
   b. Would you prefer to be a creditor or an owner of CoolBrands? Explain why.

Ethics

3. AVX Electronics is very close to bringing a revolutionary new computer chip to the market. The company fears that it could soon be the target of a takeover by a giant telecommunications company if this news were to leak before the product is introduced. The current AVX management intends to redistribute the company's stock holdings so that its managers will have a larger share of ownership. Thus, management has decided to buy back 20 percent of the company's common shares while the price is still quite low and distribute it to the managers—including themselves—as part of the company's bonus plan. Are the actions of AVX management ethical? Explain why this strategy would reduce the risk of a hostile takeover. Was any group hurt by this strategy?

Internet Exercise: Van Houtte Inc.

Van Houtte Inc. is one of North America's leading coffee roasters. The company is involved in nearly every aspect of the industry. They select and buy their beans, roast and package coffees, manufacture state-of-the-art single-cup brewing equipment, and market a range of unique products to retail and office consumers.

Go to the Van Houtte website: www.vanhoutte.com

IE9-1 Explore the "About Us" link to find out more about Van Houtte's business operations. Look under "Investor Relations" for the current stock quote (market price) of Van Houtte's shares. Is this market price reflected on Van Houtte's balance sheet? If it is, where?

Access the most recent annual report and find the consolidated balance sheets to answer the following questions:

IE9-2 How many types of shares have been authorized and issued? For the most recent year, how many shares are issued and are outstanding?

IE9-3 For the most recent year-end, identify total shareholders' equity. Of this total, how much was contributed by shareholders for issued shares? On average, how much did shareholders pay per issued share? Is the average issue price more or less than the current market price? Give an explanation for this difference.

IE9-4 For the most recent year-end, what amount of shareholders' equity is earned capital? What is the name of the earned capital account? Did earned capital increase or decrease compared with the previous year? What might cause this change?

IE9-5 Has the company reacquired any of its common shares? How can you tell? How were these shares acquired? When a company reacquires shares, does total shareholders' equity increase or decrease? Why might a company want to reacquire issued shares?

Please note: Internet websites are constantly being updated. Therefore, if the information is not found where indicated, please explore the website further to find the information.

CHAPTER 10

Cash Flow Statement: Preparation and Use

Here's where you've been...

In Chapter 9, you learned about how a company obtains financing from its owners. You learned that shareholders' equity is made up of *share capital* and *retained earnings*. You studied how the financial statements reflect that information and how the company pays a return—dividends—to its owners.

Here's where you're going...

Chapter 10 will give you a better understanding of the cash flow statement that we have been discussing throughout this book. You will learn two ways to prepare and present the cash flow statement. You will get a clearer understanding of the difference between cash basis accounting and accrual basis accounting.

Learning Objectives

More specifically, when you are finished studying this chapter, you should be able to answer these questions:

1. Why is the cash flow statement so important to a business?
2. What are the three types of cash flows shown on the cash flow statement, and what transactions are included in each?
3. How is the cash flow statement prepared using the direct method?
4. How is the cash flow statement prepared using the indirect method?
5. What are the important elements of the cash flow statement for financial statement analysis?

Importance of the Cash Flow Statement

The cash flow statement—one of the four financial statements a company must prepare as part of generally accepted accounting principles (GAAP)—shows all the cash the company has received and all the cash the company has disbursed during the accounting period. Each cash flow relates to one of three business activities—operating, investing, or financing activities. The statement explains the details of the change in the cash balance—that is, the net increase or decrease in cash—during the accounting period.

L.O. 1

Explain the importance of the cash flow statement.

Business Process

Thousands of companies go bankrupt each year because they fail to plan their cash flows effectively. When the time comes to pay their bills, they do not have enough cash on hand. They do not manage their cash very well. Preparing a cash budget is a crucial activity for all companies. It is more complicated than just estimating cash inflows and outflows for the accounting period. The sources of cash and the uses of cash must be estimated in detail—both the amounts of cash and when cash is needed. Each month, projected cash inflows and outflows must be budgeted by source. With this level of detail, a company can plan ahead for any cash shortage by (1) securing a line of credit from a local bank, (2) borrowing the money, or (3) altering the timing of its receipts (tightening up credit policies) or disbursements (postponing purchases).

A cash budget is a detailed plan of a company's estimated cash receipts and estimated cash disbursements, with very specific forecasts of the sources, uses, and the timing of the cash flows. The budgeted cash flows in the cash budget can then be compared with actual cash flows, and the comparison is the basis for planning and evaluating performance. In that sense, a budget is a tool for planning and evaluating performance.

To compare the actual cash flows for an accounting period with the period's cash budget, a company has to produce details about the actual sources of cash and actual uses of cash from the company's records. Comparing actual cash flows with budgeted cash flows gets a company ready to prepare the next period's budgeted cash flows. Even though the focus of financial reporting is financial statements for shareholders and investors, the information about cash flows is equally useful to managers of a company.

Since Tom started his T-shirt business in January 2005, we have prepared the four basic financial statements for his business every month, including the cash flow statement. The way we have prepared the cash flow statement has been to:

1. identify every cash transaction from the asset column on our accounting equation work sheet, and then
2. classify each cash amount into one of three categories: operating, investing, or financing.

When we use a separate column in the accounting equation work sheet for cash transactions, we simply take each addition of cash and each subtraction of cash; then we classify each cash flow as cash from operations, cash from investing, or cash from financing activities. Because a real company has a much more complex accounting system, needed to handle thousands or millions of transactions, examining each transaction is not a feasible way for a company to prepare the cash flow statement.

Exhibit 10–1 shows a summary of the information presented on the cash flow statement—the sections of a cash flow statement and the questions the statement is designed to answer. Next, we will discuss how the statement is actually prepared.

Exhibit 10–1
Sources and Uses of Cash

CASH
Where did we get it? Examples:

From customers	**From selling fixed assets**	**From a bank loan**
Operating Activities	Investing Activities	Financing Activities

How did we spend it? Examples:

To pay vendors	**To purchase fixed assets**	**To repay loan principal**

It's All about Cash Flow

A business firm must have cash when it needs it. This is true for all kinds of firms in all kinds of businesses.

Some companies are almost short of cash to pay dividends

Taken from *Financial Post (National Post)*, "Brascan cash won't solve Noranda's dividend dilemma: Shares likely to take hit unless Noranda's cash flow improves," January 30, 2003, by Steve Maich.

> Noranda Inc. sent a wave of relief through the market yesterday with its assurance that it remains committed to paying its dividend. But some analysts still wonder how long the company can afford its generous yield, with commodity prices stuck in the doldrums.
>
> Desjardins Securities analyst Michael Fowler laid out the numbers in a report to clients yesterday, and came to a stark conclusion. "Noranda's problem is one of low commodity prices, too much debt and a lack of cash flow," he said. "Clearly, this situation cannot go on forever."

Farmers need cash

Taken from Canadian Press Newswire in the *Halifax Chronicle-Herald*, "N.S. task force says $11 million needed for farmers hurt by mad cow scare," October 29, 2003.

> The United States border was closed to Canadian beef after it was revealed in May that one cow in Alberta had tested positive for the disease, formally known as bovine spongiform encephalopathy, earlier in the year. Cattle still are not moving freely over the border.
>
> Farmers have seen market prices fall, and those who chose to wait for a better price now find themselves overstocked and have no cash flow.

Two Methods of Preparing and Presenting the Cash Flow Statement

L.O.2

Know the different classification of various types of cash flows on the cash flow statement.

The **direct method** shows every major cash inflow and every major cash outflow.

The **indirect method** starts with net income and makes adjustments for all the items that are not cash.

Cash from operations includes all cash receipts and cash disbursements for routine sales and purchases made in the course of doing business.

GAAP describe two ways of preparing the cash flow statement: the **direct method** and the **indirect method**. These two methods are named for the way in which the operating section of the cash flow statement—**cash from operations**—is prepared, either directly (by converting every number on the income statement to its cash amount) or indirectly (by starting with net income and adjusting it until you have the cash from operations). For the other two sections, investing and financing, there is only one way to compute the cash flows: the transactions are directly identified. Thus, in any discussion about different methods of preparing a cash flow statement, the difference between the direct method and the indirect method applies only to cash from operations.

Before we discuss the two different methods in detail, let us look at a simple example of the difference between these methods of preparing the cash flow statement.

We will start with the first month of business for a simple company, with the following transactions:

1. purchase of inventory for $250—paid cash of $200 to vendor with the remaining $50 on account (accounts payable)
2. sales of all inventory for $600—$500 for cash and $100 on account (accounts receivable)
3. paid $30 for supplies and used $20 worth of them, with $10 worth of supplies remaining for next month

Net income is calculated as follows:

Sales $600 – Cost of goods sold ($250) – supplies expense ($20) = $330 Net Income

You can easily calculate the amount of cash the company collected and disbursed:

$(200) Inventory + $500 Cash Sales – $(30) Supplies = $270 Net Cash Inflow

Exhibit 10–2 shows how the cash flow statement would be presented using the direct and indirect methods. Note that the only cash flows in this example are cash flows from operations; and both methods produce the same amount of cash from operations.

Both methods of preparing the operating section of the cash flow statement require information about the underlying transactions so that the cash can be separated from the accrual accounting numbers. For example, the

Exhibit 10–2
Example of Direct versus Indirect Methods for the Cash Flow Statement

Direct method		Indirect method	
Cash from operations		Cash from operations	
Cash collected from customers	$500	Net income	$330
Cash paid for supplies	(30)	+ Or – change in accounts receivable	(100)
		+ Or – change in supplies	(10)
Cash paid to vendors for inventory	(200)	+ Or – change in accounts payable	50
Net cash from operations	*$270*	*Net cash from operations*	*$270*

amount of sales has to be examined to get the actual cash collected from making those sales. Supplies expense has to be examined to get the actual cash paid for supplies.

This change from accrual basis numbers to cash basis numbers can be done in the two ways shown in Exhibit 10–2—direct or indirect. The direct method examines each item on the income statement, one by one. The indirect method is more mechanical: net income is adjusted for all the changes in the current assets and current liabilities, excluding cash, that relate to the items on the income statement.

Before we discuss each in detail, let us quickly review the three sections of the cash flow statement and the items contained in each section.

Review of the Three Sections of the Cash Flow Statement

The three sections of the cash flow statement are operating, investing, and financing.

- The first section of the cash flow statement is the *operating* section, also known as **cash from operating activities**, where the cash inflows and cash outflows from the firm's normal, day-to-day operations of the business are included—cash flows such as:

Cash from operating activities includes cash transactions that relate to the everyday, routine transactions needed to run a business.

Cash inflows	*Cash outflows*
Cash collected from customers	Cash paid to employees
Cash collected for interest	Cash paid for inventory
	Cash paid for expenses
	Cash paid for interest
	Cash paid for taxes

- The second section of the cash flow statement is the *investing* section, also known as **cash from investing activities**, where the cash flows related to investments are shown. GAAP define investing activities as activities that involve buying and selling assets that the company plans to keep for at least a year, such as:

Cash from investing activities includes all cash receipts and all cash disbursements for long-term business assets.

Cash inflows	*Cash outflows*
Cash proceeds from the sale of property, plant, and equipment	Cash paid to buy property, plant, and equipment
Cash from the sale of certain securities	Cash paid for long-term investments
	Cash loaned to others

- The third section is the *financing* section, also known as **cash from financing activities**, where the cash flows related to all financing activities are included, such as:

Cash from financing activities includes all cash receipts and all cash disbursements for loans (principal only), contributions from owners, and distributions to owners.

Cash inflows	*Cash outflows*
Cash proceeds from the sale of the company's shares	Cash paid to repurchase shares
Cash received from borrowing	Cash paid to retire debt principal
	Cash payment of dividends

STUDY BREAK 10-1

See How You're Doing

What are the three classifications of cash flows? Give an example of a cash inflow and a cash outflow in each category.

Accrual Accounting versus Cash

L.O. 3

Know how to convert accrual numbers to cash.

Companies that follow GAAP maintain their accounting records using the accrual basis. Preparing the cash flow statement is actually converting the records of the business to cash basis. That is what we did in Exhibit 10–2. There are many reasons why accrual basis accounting and cash basis accounting are not generally the same.

For example, a company will record a sale and recognize the revenue on the income statement when the merchandise is shipped or delivered. Does the company always receive the cash at that time? No. Thus, the amount of revenue earned from sales for an accounting period may not be the same as the amount of cash collected during the period. At the end of the accounting period, when the company is preparing its financial statements, customers may still owe the company some money—there may be outstanding accounts receivable. That is one reason the cash collected from sales might not equal the amount of the sales for a specific accounting period.

Also, the company may have collected cash during the current period from sales made during the prior accounting periods—accounts receivable from the prior year may have been collected. Thus, to calculate the cash collected from customers for the cash flow statement, we have to consider and make an adjustment for the change in accounts receivable.

Suppose a company began 2007 with accounts receivable of $500. These accounts receivable were recorded during 2006, when the revenue from the sales was recognized. All sales are made on credit; and during 2007, the company had sales of $3,000. At the end of 2007, the balance in accounts receivable was $600. How much cash was collected from customers during 2007? Because accounts receivable started with a balance of $500 and ended with a balance of $600, the increase represents sales that have not been collected from the customers. Therefore, while sales amounted to $3,000, only $2,900 worth of those sales must have been collected in cash. Using the T-account approach, we can trace the transactions through the accounts receivable account:

	Accounts Receivable		
BB	$ 500		
Credit Sales	3,000	**2,900**	**Cash collections**
EB	600		

Another way to think about it is first to suppose that customers paid off their old accounts of $500. If total sales were $3,000 and if an ending accounts receivable balance were $600, then $2,400 of the current sales must have been collected. The beginning balance of $500 was collected plus current sales of $2,400 have been collected—making the total cash collected from customers during the period of $2,900. This is the sort of reasoning that must be applied to each item on the income statement to prepare the cash flow statement using the direct method.

The number for every item on the income statement is potentially different from the cash related to it. For example, sales is potentially different from cash collected from customers. Cost of goods sold is potentially different from cash paid for inventory. Insurance expense is potentially different from the cash paid to the insurance company and so on, for all items on the income statement.

The change in a current asset or a current liability will reflect the difference between the accrual-based income statement amount and the cash amount. Consider an expense on the income statement. Suppose salary expense is shown on the year's income statement as $75,000. For the cash flow statement, we want to have cash paid to employees as an operating cash outflow. What could make salary expense different from cash paid to employees? First, we could have paid some employees cash that we owed them from last year. The cash payment would reduce the liability salaries payable. If we did pay some salaries we owed at the beginning of the year, that cash paid would be in addition to any current year's salary paid to employees. What else could make cash paid to employees different from salary expense? We could have incurred salary expense that will not be paid until next year. In other words, we recognized some salary expense that did not get paid to the employees. We must have recorded it as salaries payable. In both cases, the difference between salary expense and cash paid to employees is reflected in the change in salaries payable from the beginning of the year to the end of the year. This is the sort of reasoning that must be applied to each current asset and each current liability on the balance sheet to prepare the cash flow statement using the indirect method.

Suppose we started the year with salaries payable of $690. Our salary expense for the year, as shown on the income statement, is $75,000. If the balance in salaries payable is $500 at year-end, how much cash was actually paid to employees? First, we must have paid off the amount we owed at the beginning of the year, $690. Then, because the ending balance in salaries payable is $500, we must have paid only $74,500 (= $75,000 – $500) of the current year's salary expense. Thus, the total cash paid to employees is $75,190 (= $690 + $74,500). Another way to interpret what happened is to say that we paid the full $75,000 of this year's expense in cash and we paid down our salaries payable by $190 ($690 down to $500). That total is $75,190.

	Salaries Payable		
		$ 690	BB
Cash payments	**75,190**	75,000	Salaries expense
		500	EB

With those simple examples in mind, let us prepare an entire cash flow statement.

STUDY BREAK 10-2

See How You're Doing

Robo Company began the year with $25,000 in accounts receivable. During the year, sales totalled $50,000. The year-end accounts receivable balance was $15,000. Using a T-account, determine the amount of cash collected from customers during the year.

Preparing the Cash Flow Statement

L.O. 3

Know how to prepare a cash flow statement using the direct method.

First, the cash from operations section of the cash flow statement is prepared using one of the following two methods we have already discussed:

1. Direct method: Each item on the accrual-based income statement is converted to cash; or
2. Indirect method: Net income is the starting point, and adjustments are made by adding and subtracting amounts necessary to convert net income into cash.

After you have determined the cash flows from operations, you determine the cash flows from investing activities and cash flows from financing activities. These two sections of the cash flow statement are prepared by examining the noncurrent assets and noncurrent liabilities in the company's balance sheets at the beginning and the end of the year, and by examining the company's financial records to identify any investing and financing related transactions.

Direct Method of Computing Cash from Operations

The direct method of computing cash flows from operations begins with the income statement. Item by item, every amount on the statement is analyzed to determine how much cash was actually collected or disbursed related to that item.

The first item on the income statement is usually revenue. What makes revenue on the income statement different from cash collected from customers? Any cash collected for sales in previous periods—that is, accounts receivable—must be counted as cash collected even though it is not included as revenue. Conversely, any sales for the period for which cash has *not* been collected must be excluded from cash collections. Both cash collected but not counted as revenue and cash not collected but included in revenue can be identified by looking at the change in accounts receivable during the period.

Let us use Tom's Wear's third month of business—March—to see how this works. We start at the beginning of the income statement, shown in Exhibit 10–3, for the month and analyze each amount to change it from accrual to cash.

Sales on the income statement for March amounted to $2,000. What we need to know for the cash flow statement is how much cash was collected from customers during March. We need to see how accounts receivable changed during the month. On March 1, 2005, the beginning of the month,

Exhibit 10–3
Income Statement for Tom's Wear, Inc. for the Month Ended March 31

Tom's Wear, Inc.
Income Statement
For the Month Ended March 31, 2005

Sales revenue		$2,000
Expenses		
Cost of goods sold	800	
Amortization expense	100	
Insurance expense	50	
Interest expense	30	980
Net income		$1,020

Exhibit 10–4 Comparative Balance Sheets for Tom's Wear, Inc.

tom's wear

Tom's Wear, Inc.
Balance Sheet
At March 1 and March 31, 2005

	March 31	March 1		March 31	March 1
Cash	$ 3,995	$ 6,695	Accounts payable	$ 0	$ 800
Accounts receivable	2,000	150	Other payables	0	50
Inventory	300	100	Interest payable	30	0
Prepaid insurance	75	125	Notes payable	3,000	0
Prepaid rent	0	0	*Total liabilities*	*$ 3,030*	*$ 850*
Equipment (net of $100 accumulated amortization)	3,900	0	Common shares	5,000	5,000
			Retained earnings	2,240	1,220
Total assets	*$10,270*	*$7,070*	*Total liabilities and shareholders' equity*	*$10,270*	*$7,070*

Tom's Wear had $150 worth of accounts receivable, and ended the month with $2,000 worth of accounts receivable. By comparing the balance sheet at the beginning of the month with the balance sheet at the end of the month, both shown in Exhibit 10–4, we can see accounts receivable increased by $1,850. The amount of the change in accounts receivable came from the current period's sales not collected.

One way to compute cash collected from customers is to analyze what happened to accounts receivable. It started with $150. Then during the month, credit sales of $2,000 were made. (That is *sales* on the income statement.) The ending balance in accounts receivable is $2,000. Thus, the cash collected from customers must have been $150 (= $2,000 – $1,850). If you go back and look at the transactions for Tom's Wear during March (in Chapter 3), you'll find *$150 was exactly the amount of cash the company collected from customers.*

Using the T-account approach, start with accounts receivable, where the beginning balance is $150 and the ending balance is $2,000. During the month, $2,000 of credit sales were made. That means total cash collected must have been $150:

	Accounts receivable		
BB	$ 150		
Credit sales	2,000	150	Cash collections
EB	2,000		

Continuing down the March income statement, the next item is cost of goods sold of $800. This is the cost of the merchandise sold during the month. How does that compare with the amount of cash paid to vendors during the month? Did Tom's Wear sell anything it bought the previous month from the beginning inventory; or did the company buy more goods in March than it actually sold in March? We need to look at what happened to the amount of inventory during the month. The beginning inventory balance was $100. The ending inventory balance was $300. That means Tom's Wear bought enough inventory to sell $800 worth and to build up the inventory by an additional $200. Thus, purchases of inventory must have been $1,000.

Here is the analysis using T-accounts:

	Inventory		
BB	$ 100	$800	Cost of goods sold
Purchases	1,000		
EB	300		

Did Tom's Wear pay cash for these purchases of inventory?

To see how the purchase of $1,000 worth of inventory compares with the cash paid to vendors, we have to look at the change in accounts payable (to vendors). The beginning balance in accounts payable was $800, and the ending balance was zero. That means Tom's Wear must have paid $1,000 to vendors for the month's purchases *and* the $800 owed from February. Thus, the total paid to vendors was $1,800.

Here is the analysis using the accounts payable T-account:

	Accounts payable		
		$ 800	**BB**
Cash paid	**1,800**	1,000	Purchases
		0	**EB**

The next expense on the March 31 income statement is amortization expense. Amortization expense is a noncash expense. That means we do not have any cash outflow when we record amortization expense. The cash we spend to buy equipment is considered an investing cash flow, and our periodic amortization does not involve cash. Amortization is one expense we can skip when we are preparing the cash flow from operations using the direct method.

Insurance expense of $50 is shown on the March 31 income statement. How much cash was actually paid for insurance? When a company pays for insurance, the payment is generally recorded as prepaid insurance. Examining the change in prepaid insurance will help us figure out how much cash was paid for insurance during the month. Prepaid insurance started with a balance of $125 and ended with a balance of $75. Because the decrease in prepaid insurance is exactly the same as the insurance expense, Tom's Wear must not have paid for any insurance this month. All the expense came from insurance that was paid for in a previous period.

The T-account analysis confirms that no cash was paid this period.

	Prepaid insurance		
BB	$125	$50	Insurance expense
Insurance purchased	0		
EB	75		

The last expense we need to consider is interest expense. On the income statement for March, we see interest expense of $30. Did Tom's Wear pay that in cash? On the balance sheet, the company began the month with no interest payable and ended the month with $30 interest payable. If it started the month without owing any interest and ended the month owing $30, how much of the $30 expense did the company pay for with cash? None. Tom's Wear must not have paid any cash for interest because it owes the entire amount of the expense at year-end.

Again, the T-account analysis confirms that no cash was paid for interest.

Interest payable

	Debit	Credit	
		$ 0	BB
Cash paid	0	30	Interest expense
		30	EB

Tom's Wear paid out one more amount of cash related to operations during the month. Can you find it? On the March 1 balance sheet, there is $50 that Tom's Wear owed; it is called *other payables*. By the end of March, that payable has been reduced to zero. Only one thing could have caused that reduction: a cash payment to settle the obligation related to advertising. Thus, we will also have to put that on the cash flow statement.

Here is the T-account analysis. The beginning balance was $50, and the ending balance was $0. No expense was recorded for the month. That means cash paid must have been $50.

Other payables

	Debit	Credit	
		$50	BB
Cash paid	50		
		0	EB

To summarize, we have "translated" the accrual amounts found on the income statement to cash amounts for the cash flow statement. The cash collected from customers was $150. Tom's Wear paid its vendors cash of $1,800. It also paid $50 of other payables. Net cash flow from operations was $(1,700). The operating section of the cash flow statement is shown in Exhibit 10–5.

Remember, Exhibit 10–5 shows only the cash flow from operations. To explain the entire change in cash from March 1 to March 31, the investing and financing cash flows must be included.

STUDY BREAK 10-3

See How You're Doing

Flex Company began the year 2007 with $350 in prepaid insurance. For 2007, the company's income statement showed insurance expense was $400. Flex Company ended the year with $250 of prepaid insurance. Using a T-account, determine the amount of cash paid for insurance during the year.

Exhibit 10–5
Cash from Operations—Direct Method

Tom's Wear, Inc.
Partial Cash Flow Statement
For the Month Ended March 31, 2005

Cash from operations	
Cash collected from customers	$ 150
Cash paid to vendors	(1,800)
Cash paid for other expenses	(50)
Net increase (decrease) in cash from operations	**$(1,700)**

Indirect Method of Computing Cash from Operations

L.O. 4

Know how to prepare a cash flow statement using the indirect method.

Even though the Canadian Institute of Chartered Accountants (CICA) suggests that "(t)he direct method provides information which may be useful in estimating future cash flows and which is not available under the indirect method" (paragraph 1540.21, *CICA Handbook*), the vast majority of companies in Canada still use the indirect method. Preparing the cash flow statement using the indirect method—applied just to the operating section of the cash flow statement—starts with net income. Following net income, any amounts on the statement that are noncash must be removed to leave only cash amounts. The logic and reasoning we use to prepare the cash flow statement using the indirect method are not too different from the reasoning we use with the direct method.

Let us start with net income for Tom's Wear for March. Exhibits 10–3 and 10–4 show the numbers we need to prepare the cash flow statement using the indirect method.

The net income for March was $1,020.

The first adjustment we make is to add back any noncash expenses, such as amortization. For Tom's Wear, we add back to net income the $100 amortization expense. When we calculated the net income of $1,020, we subtracted $100 that was not a cash outflow. Thus, we have to add it back to net income to change net income to a cash number.

Then, just as we do when we prepare the cash flow statement using the direct method, every amount on the income statement has to be evaluated for its relationship to cash flows. Recall that in the direct method, we use changes in accounts receivable to convert sales revenue into cash collected from customers, and we use changes in inventory and accounts payable to convert cost of goods sold to cash paid to vendors. For the indirect method, if we adjust net income for every change in each current asset—with the exception of cash—and every change in each current liability, we will make every adjustment we need to convert net income into net cash from operations. Let us continue preparing the cash flow statement using the indirect method with Tom's Wear for March.

We start with net income of $1,020 and add back any noncash expenses. Amortization of $100 is added back. Then, using Exhibit 10–4, we examine each current asset account and each current liability account for changes during the month.

Accounts receivable increased by $1,850. That increase represents sales for which we did not collect any cash yet. Thus, we need to subtract this increase in accounts receivable from net income to convert net income into a cash number.

The next change in a current asset is the increase in inventory of $200. This $200 represents purchases made that have not yet been reported as part of cost of goods sold on the income statement because the items have not been sold. Still, we did pay cash for them (or we will assume cash was paid and make any adjustment when we examine accounts payable), and so the amount needs to be deducted from net income because it was a cash outflow.

Prepaid insurance decreased from $125 to $75. This decrease of $50 was deducted as insurance expense on the income statement, but it was not a cash outflow this period. This amount will have to be added back to net income because it was not a cash outflow.

The last changes in current assets and current liabilities are the changes in payables. Tom's Wear started the month with $800 of accounts payable and $50 of other payables. Tom's Wear ended the month with a zero amount of each of these. The other current liability is interest payable. It started the month with no interest payable but ended the month with $30 of interest payable. The total change in current liabilities is a net decrease of $820. This

$820 amount was not included on the income statement—*not* deducted in the calculation of net income. Because the amount was a cash outflow, we need to deduct an additional $820 from net income to finish converting net income into cash from operations.

Following the example in the text, you can use the indirect method of preparing a cash flow statement with a spreadsheet as follows:

A Spreadsheet Approach to Computing Cash from Operations with the Indirect Method

	A	B	C	D	E	F	G	H
1	**Tom's Wear, Inc.**							
2	**Spreadsheet for Operating Activities Cash Flow Statement**							
3	**(Indirect Method) For the month ended March 31, 2005**							
4								
5			March 1,		Analysis of Changes			March
6			2005		Debit		Credit	31, 2005
7	**Balance Sheet: Debits**							
8	Cash		$6,695				$2,700	$3,995
9	Accounts receivable		150	(b)	$1,850			2,000
10	Inventory		100	(c)	200			300
11	Prepaid insurance		125			(d)	50	75
12	Equipment		0		4,000			4,000
13			$7,070					$10,370
14	**Balance Sheet: Credits**							
15	Accumulated amortization		$0			(e)	$100	$100
16	Accounts payable		800	(f)	$800			0
17	Other payables		50	(g)	50			0
18	Interest payable		0			(h)	30	30
19	Notes payable		0				3,000	3,000
20	Common shares		5,000					5,000
21	Retained earnings		1,220			(a)	1,020	2,240
22			$7,070					$10,370
23								
24	**Operating Activities**							
25	Net income			(a)	$1,020			
26	Increase in accounts receivable					(b)	$1,850	
27	Increase in inventory					(c)	200	
28	Decrease in prepaid insurance			(d)	50			
29	Amortization expense			(e)	100			
30	Decrease in accounts payable					(f)	800	
31	Decrease in other payables					(g)	50	
32	Increase in interest payable			(h)	30			
33					$8,100		$9,800	
34	Net increase (decrease in cash from operations)						(1,700)	
35					$8,100		$8,100	
36								

Exhibit 10–6
Cash from Operations—Indirect Method

tom's wear

Tom's Wear, Inc.
Partial Cash Flow Statement
For the Month Ended March 31, 2005

Net income	$ 1,020
+ Amortization expense	100
− Increase in accounts receivable	(1,850)
− Increase in inventory	(200)
+ Decrease in prepaid insurance	50
− Decrease in payables	(820)
Net cash from operations	**$(1,700)**

Look at the operating section of the cash flow statement for Tom's Wear for March in Exhibit 10–6. The statement starts with net income and makes all the adjustments we discussed. Compare the operating section of this cash flow statement prepared using the indirect method with the operating section we prepared using the direct method shown in Exhibit 10–5. The net cash flow from operations is the same, no matter how we prepare it—when we prepare the statement by examining every cash transaction, as we did in Chapter 3, when we prepare it using the direct method; as we did earlier in this chapter; and when we prepare it using the indirect method, as we just did in this chapter. Which way is easier to understand? The presentation produced by the direct method—the presentation shown in Exhibit 10–5—gives details about cash that are easier to understand than the details provided by the indirect method. Still, almost all companies today use the indirect method. A change in this practice could be a real benefit to users of financial statements.

STUDY BREAK 10-4

See How You're Doing

What is the major difference between the direct and indirect methods of presenting the cash flow statement? What are the similarities?

Cash from Investing and Financing Activities

In addition to cash from operations, there are two other sections of the cash flow statement: cash from investing activities and cash from financing activities. No matter which method you use to prepare the cash flow statement, direct or indirect, the cash from investing activities and cash from financing activities sections are prepared the same way—by reviewing noncurrent balance sheet accounts. The primary amounts on the balance sheet to review are property, plant, and equipment; notes payable; bonds payable; common shares; and retained earnings.

For Tom's Wear during March, start in the noncurrent assets section of the balance sheet. The balance sheet at March 31 shows equipment with a cost of $4,000. The carrying value is $3,900 and the accumulated amortization is $100, for a total cost of $4,000. The asset representing this equipment *was not* on the March 1 balance sheet, and so Tom must have purchased $4,000 worth of equipment during March. The purchase of equipment is an investing cash flow. When we see that a company purchased a noncurrent asset, we must investigate how the company paid for the asset. In this case, we find that Tom paid cash of $1,000 and signed a note for $3,000. We include only the $1,000 cash outflow in the cash flow statement, but we must disclose in the financial statements the amount of the loan and its purpose. All investing and financing activities must be disclosed, even if there was no cash involved.

Next, we review the liability section of the balance sheet for changes in non-current liabilities. Note that on the balance sheet at March 1, Tom's Wear shows no notes payable. On the balance sheet at March 31, notes payable shows a balance of $3,000. That means Tom borrowed $3,000 during March. Again, when we discover such a change, we must find out the details of the transaction before we can decide how the transaction affects the cash flow statement. Generally, borrowing money using a long-term note would result in a financing cash inflow. However, in this case, the note was given in exchange for equipment.

Note that the loan is disclosed, even though the amount is not included on the cash flow statement. Whenever a company engages in a financing or investing activity, it must be disclosed on the cash flow statement, even though the company never actually received or paid out any cash. The cash is considered *implicit* in the transaction. It is *as if* Tom's Wear received the cash from the loan and immediately turned around and purchased the equipment with it.

Other transactions we should look for when preparing the financing section of the cash flow statement include any principal payments on loans, any new capital contributions—such as shares issued or dividends paid to the shareholders. For Tom's Wear for March 2005, none of these transactions took place.

When we put the information about investing activities and financing activities with the cash from operations we have already prepared, we have all the information we need to complete the cash flow statement. Look at the two statements in Exhibits 10–7 and 10–8. Then look back to Chapter 3 and find the cash flow statement in the solution to the summary problem. We used different methods to prepare the statements, but they are similar in form and amounts.

Check it out. The balance sheets in Exhibit 10–4 show that cash went from $6,695 on March 1 to $3,995 on March 31. The difference is a $2,700 decrease in cash. Explaining that change in the cash balance is the purpose of the cash flow statement.

Summary of Direct and Indirect Methods

There are two ways, both ways acceptable using GAAP, to prepare and present the cash flow statement: the direct method and the indirect method. The

Exhibit 10–7
Cash Flow Statement (Direct)

tom's wear

Tom's Wear, Inc.
Cash Flow Statement
For the Month Ended
March 31, 2005

Cash from operations		
Cash collected from customers	$ 150	
Cash paid to vendors	(1,800)	
Cash paid for other expenses	(50)	
Net cash from operations		$(1,700)
Cash from investing activities		
Purchase of equipment	$(1,000)[a]	
Net cash from investing activities		(1,000)
Cash from financing activities		0
Net increase (decrease) in cash		$(2,700)
Opening cash balance (March 01)		$6,695
Closing cash balance (March 31)		$3,995

[a] Equipment was purchased for $4,000. A note was signed for $3,000 and cash paid was $1,000.

Exhibit 10–8
Cash Flow Statement (Indirect)

tom's wear

Tom's Wear, Inc.
Cash Flow Statement
For the Month Ended
March 31, 2005

Cash from operations		
Net income	$ 1,020	
+ Amortization expense	100	
− Increase in accounts receivable	(1,850)	
− Increase in inventory	(200)	
+ Decrease in prepaid insurance	50	
− Decrease in payables	(820)	
Net cash from operations		$(1,700)
Cash from investing activities		
Purchase of equipment	(1,000)[a]	
Net cash from investing activities		(1,000)
Cash from financing activities		0
Net increase (decrease) in cash		$(2,700)
Opening cash balance (March 01)		$ 6,695
Closing cash balance (March 31)		$ 3,995

[a]Machine was purchased for $4,000. A note was signed for $3,000 and cash paid was $1,000.

direct method provides more detail about cash from operating activities. It shows the individual operating cash flows.

The indirect presentation of the cash flow statement is easier to prepare from the income statement and the beginning and ending balance sheets for the period, but the presentation of the information is not easily understood.

Keep in mind that the investing activities and the financing activities sections for the two methods are identical; and the total net cash flow is the same for both methods.

Financial Statement Analysis

L.O. 5

Know how to do a simple analysis of the cash flow statement.

Look at the cash flow statement for Gildan Activewear Inc., shown in Exhibit 10–9. First, note the organization of the statement. The statement has the three required parts: (1) cash provided by operations, (2) cash flows from financing activities, and (3) cash flows from investing activities. Second, note the first section—cash provided by operations—is prepared using the indirect method. The statement starts with the amount for *net earnings*—another name for *net income*—and makes several adjustments to that amount. Look at the adjustments and see if you understand what information they provide. For example, depreciation and amortization are added back to net income to work toward cash from operations because the amounts for depreciation and amortization were *subtracted* in the original computation of net income but they were not cash expenditures. That subtraction is *undone* by adding the amounts back to net income. Investors are looking for a positive cash flow from operations. In the long run, this is crucial for the continuing success of any business.

The cash flows from financing activities section of the cash flow statement shows the cash flows related to the way the company is financed. Some of the items should be recognizable—proceeds from sale of shares and long-term borrowings. Other items are beyond the scope of an introductory course. However, all of them relate to the Gildan financing. This information, when combined with the information on the balance sheet, gives the financial statement user a complete picture of the way the company is financing the business.

The cash flows from investing activities section of the statement shows net purchases of fixed assets as the first entry. Those are items such as property, plant, and equipment. Recall the discussion in Chapter 5 about capital versus revenue expenditures—capitalizing a cost versus expensing a cost. These are costs that have been capitalized by Gildan. The cash flows from investing activities section include cash inflows and outflows related to the purchase and sale of assets *not* related to the normal operations of Gildan. (When Gildan buys the items that it resells in the normal course of business, the cash flows are included in the first section—cash provided from operations.) The cash flow from the investing activities section of the cash flow statement gives information about the company's plans for the future. Investments in property, plant, and equipment may indicate an expansion or, at the very least, a concern about keeping the company's infrastructure up to date. Over time, a company's failure to invest in the infrastructure may indicate a problem.

We should consider three more characteristics of the statement. First, following the calculation of the net cash flow for the year, the reconciliation from the year's beginning cash balance to the year's ending cash balance is shown. Second, the statement uses cash and cash equivalents where cash equivalents are "...short-term, highly liquid investments that are readily convertible to known amounts of cash and which are subject to an insignificant risk of changes in value" (Section 1540.06, *CICA Handbook*). Third, there is supplementary information disclosed concerning the cash paid for interest. This is required by GAAP.

When analyzing the cash flow statement, managers and analysts often calculate one more amount called **free cash flow**. Free cash flow is defined as *cash flows from operations minus dividends and capital expenditures.* This gives a measure of a firm's ability to engage in long-term investment opportunities. It is sometimes seen as a measure of a company's financial flexibility.

Free cash flow is net cash from operations minus dividends and minus capital expenditures.

The net change in cash, $21.9 million, can be traced back to the comparative balance sheets for Gildan. At the beginning of the year, the cash balance was $70.9 million. At the end of the year, the cash balance was $92.8 million. The purpose of the cash flow statement is to describe in detail this change in the cash balance.

The cash flow statement is a crucial part of the financial reporting for any company. Often, creditors and investors will look at this statement first when they are analyzing the financial condition of a firm. For the firm, however, the importance of the cash flow statement is tied to the cash budget and how the actual sources and uses of cash compare with the budgeted amounts. This analysis is an important function of **managerial accounting.**

Managerial accounting is the study of how managers use accounting information that is internal to the firm—that information is generally not shown on the financial statements.

The cash flow statement provides important information for managers, creditors, and investors. In corporate annual reports, the cash flow statement is presented with the other three basic financial statements—the income statement, the balance sheet, and the statement of changes in retained earnings—to provide information needed to evaluate a company's performance and to provide a basis for predicting a company's future potential.

Exhibit 10–9 Consolidated Cash Flow Statement for Gildan Activewear Inc.

Consolidated Cash Flow Statements for Gildan Activewear Inc.
Years ended October 5, 2003, September 29, 2002 and September 30, 2001
(In Canadian dollars)

	Fiscal Year Ended		
	2003	2002	2001
Cash Flows from Operating Activities			
Net earnings	$77,271,940	$66,491,540	$815,958
Adjustments for:			
Depreciation and amortization	23,614,704	17,591,885	16,208,560
Future income taxes	6,116,000	5,013,000	(268,000)
Loss on disposal of fixed assets	321,043	949,092	7,534
Foreign exchange (gain) loss	(44,279)	3,443,038	(416,640)
Net changes in noncash working capital balances:			
Accounts receivable	(11,222,582)	38,170,839	(13,129,676)
Inventories	(25,640,632)	65,380,407	(56,636,049)
Prepaid expenses and deposits	(1,648,912)	599,018	(225,444)
Accounts payable and accrued liabilities	19,072,679	(21,026,308)	39,545,292
Income taxes payable	2,294,728	1,488,272	1,755,409
	90,134,689	178,100,783	(12,343,056)
Cash Flows from Financing Activities			
(Decrease) Increase in revolving bank loan	–	(35,083,026)	35,083,026
Repayment of capital leases	(5,007,368)	(5,119,718)	(5,164,290)
Increase in other long-term debt	390,422	2,974,000	–
Repayment of other long-term debt	(1,411,227)	(6,433,817)	(2,209,780)
Proceeds from the issuance of shares	6,638,688	4,563,338	986,726
Increase in deferred financing charges	(40,521)	(1,086,020)	(405,514)
	569,994	(40,185,243)	28,290,168
Cash Flows from Investing Activities			
Purchase of fixed assets, net of disposals	(58,576,710)	(65,764,900)	(49,149,541)
Decrease (Increase) in other assets	6,178	(1,395,301)	(133,199)
	(58,570,532)	(67,160,201)	(49,282,740)
Effect of exchange rate changes on cash and cash equivalents	(10,179,584)	150,158	(156,753)
Net increase (decrease) in cash and cash equivalents during the year	21,954,567	79,905,497	(33,492,381)
Cash and cash equivalents, beginning of year	70,905,497	–	33,492,381
Cash and cash equivalents, end of year	$92,860,064	$70,905,497	$ –
Supplemental disclosure of cash flow information (note 12 (b))			
See accompanying notes to consolidated financial statements.			

Excerpt from Note 12
(b) Supplemental cash flow disclosure:

	2003	2002	2001
Cash paid during the year for:			
Interest	$9,499,215	$13,587,113	$13,172,660
Income taxes	1,548,967	795,141	1,196,166
Noncash transactions:			
Acquisition of fixed assets through the assumption of debt and settement of amounts due to the Company	–	–	6,800,000
Additions to fixed assets included in accounts payable and accrued liabilities	3,145,138	6,470,616	1,337,900
Cash and cash equivalents consist of:			
Cash balances with banks	$67,860,064	$45,700,697	$ –
Short-term Investments	25,000,000	25,204,800	–
	$92,860,064	$70,905,497	$ –

Courtesy Gildan Activewear

Understanding Excel

In this exercise, you prepare a cash flow statement for Tom's Wear, Inc. for the month of August, 2005 (indirect method).

Requirements:

1. Open a new Excel work sheet.
2. Beginning in cell A1, input the following chart. Resize columns and wrap text, as required. You may also choose the font type and size, as desired. Use appropriate formulas to calculate the change in the balances.
3. Beginning in cell F1, prepare a cash flow statement for Tom's Wear, Inc. for the month ended August 31. Use appropriate headings, formats, and formulas.

   Hint: To change a negative number to a positive, multiply your formula or input cell by "–1."
4. Print your file and save it to disk. Name your file TomsWear10.

	July 31, 2005	August 31, 2005	Change
Assets			
Cash	$ 17,151	$ 980,476	
Accounts receivable	105,100	207,610	
Allowance for doubtful accounts	(3,290)	(6,335)	
Inventory	8,910	24,584	
Prepaids	800	700	
Land	7,500	7,500	
Equipment	4,000	104,000	
Accumulated amortization, equipment	(500)	(600)	
Van	30,000	130,000	
Accumulated amortization, van	(4,205)	(7,105)	
Building	67,500	67,500	
Accumulated amortization, building	(130)	(260)	
Total assets	$232,836	$1,508,070	
Liabilities and Equity			
Accounts payable	$ 36,000	$ 6,000	
Interest payable	1,500	2,250	
Warranty liability	2,239	3,204	
Notes payable*	105,000	105,000	
Common shares	5,000	1,255,000	
Retained earnings	83,097	136,616	
Total liabilities and shareholders' equity	$232,836	$1,508,070	

**Note:* Current and long-term notes and mortgages did not change and are combined here to simplify the presentation.

Summary Problem: Tom's Wear for April 2005 Revisited

The income statement for Tom's Wear for April is shown in Exhibit 10–10 (and is also given in the solution to the summary problem for Chapter 5). The comparative balance sheets at March 31 and April 30 are shown in Exhibit 10–11.

Required

Use this information to prepare the cash flow statement for April, first using the direct method and then the indirect method.

Exhibit 10–10
Income Statement

Tom's Wear, Inc.
For the Month Ended
April 30, 2005

Sales revenue		$ 8,000
Expenses		
Cost of goods sold	$3,200	
Insurance expense	50	
Rent expense	600	
Amortization expense	825	
Other operating expenses	300	
Interest expense	280	5,255
Net income		$ 2,745

Exhibit 10–11 Comparative Balance Sheets

Tom's Wear, Inc.
Balance Sheet
At April 30 and
March 31, 2005

	April 30	March 31		April 30	March 31
Cash	$3,295	$ 3,995	Accounts payable	$ 4,000	$ 0
Accounts receivable	8,000	2,000	Other payables	0	0
Inventory	1,100	300	Interest payable	310	30
Prepaid insurance	25	75	Currrent portion of notes payable	3,000	3,000
Prepaid rent	1,800	0			
Total current assets	*14,220*	*6,370*	Total current liabilities	7,310	3,030
Equipment (net of $200 and $100 accumulated amortization)	3,800	3,900	Notes payable	30,000	0
			Total liabilities	37,310	3,030
Van (net of $725 accumulated amortization)	29,275	0	Common shares	5,000	5,000
			Retained earnings	4,985	2,240
Total assets	*$47,295*	*$10,270*	*Total liabilities and shareholders' equity*	*$47,295*	*$10,270*

Answers to Study Break Questions

STUDY BREAK 10-1

The three classifications are (1) operating cash flows (e.g., payment from customers is an inflow, and payment to employees is an outflow); (2) financing (e.g., owners contributing cash to a business is an inflow, and the company paying dividends is an outflow); and (3) investing cash flows (e.g., the sale of a long-term asset is an inflow, and the purchase of equipment that will be used for more than one year is an outflow).

STUDY BREAK 10-2

Robo probably collected the beginning accounts receivable first during the year, for a cash collection of $25,000. Then, sales of $50,000 were made. Because the accounts receivable balance at year-end was $15,000, $35,000 worth of the sales has been collected. Thus, total cash inflow from customers = $25,000 + 35,000 = **$60,000**. Another way to look at the problem is to take sales of $50,000 and adjust that for the change in accounts receivable. Because the change is a $10,000 decrease in accounts receivable, that would be $10,000 of collections, making the cash inflow from customers $50,000 + 10,000 = **$60,000**. Cash collected from customers should be reported in the cash from operations section of the cash flow statement.

	Accounts receivable		
BB	$25,000		
Sales	50,000	60,000	Cash collected
EB	$15,000		

STUDY BREAK 10-3

Start by thinking about the expense as a cash outflow and then adjusting it for why it is not all cash. Insurance expense is $400. Then, look at the change in prepaid insurance. It started at $350 and ended at $250. That means $100 of prepaid insurance was used. That reduction in prepaid insurance must be part of the $400 expense shown on the income statement. Thus, the cash paid for insurance must have been **$300** (= $400 – $100).

	Prepaid insurance		
BB	$350		
Cash paid	**300**	400	Insurance expense
EB	$250		

STUDY BREAK 10-4

The major difference between the two is the way the cash from operations section is presented. Even though the amount of cash from operations is the same, the method used to calculate the number is different. The other parts—cash from investing activities and cash from financing activities—are exactly the same.

Solution to Summary Problem

Tom's Wear, Inc.
Cash Flow Statement
For the Month Ended April 30, 2005

Cash from operating activities (direct)		
Cash collected from customers	$ 2,000	
Cash paid for rent	(2,400)	
Cash paid for other operating expenses	(300)	
Total cash from operations		$ (700)
Cash from investing activities		0
Cash from financing activities		0
Net increase (decrease) in cash		(700)
Opening cash balance (April 01)		3,995
Closing cash balance (April 31)		$3,295

Note: A long-term note for $30,000 was issued to purchase a van.

(If the company had received the cash and then purchased the van, there would be a $30,000 outflow from investing activities for the purchase of the van, and a $30,000 inflow from financing activities from the note payable.)

Solution details for the direct method follow.

Cash collected from customers	
Sales	$ 8,000
− Increase in accounts receivable	(6,000)
	$2,000
Cash paid to vendors	
Cost of goods sold	$ 3,200
+ Increase in inventory	800
− Increase in accounts payable	(4,000)
	0
Cash paid for insurance	
Insurance expense	$ 50
− Decrease in prepaid insurance	(50)
	0
Cash paid for rent	
Rent expense	$ 600
+ Increase in prepaid rent	1,800
	$2,400
Cash paid for other operating expenses	
Other operating expenses	$ 300
No balance sheet items related to this expense	0
	$ 300
Cash paid for interest expense	
Interest expense	$ 280
− Increase in interest payable	(280)
	0

Solution for indirect method follows.

Tom's Wear, Inc.
Cash Flow Statement
For the Month Ended April 30, 2005

Cash from operating activities (indirect)		
Net income	$ 2,745	
+ Amortization expense	825	
− Increase in accounts receivable	(6,000)	
− Increase in inventory	(800)	
+ Decrease in prepaid insurance	50	
− Increase in prepaid rent	(1,800)	
+ Increase in accounts payable	4,000	
+ Increase in interest payable	280	
Net cash from operations		$ (700)
Cash from investing activities		0
Cash from financing activities		0
Net increase (decrease) in cash		(700)
Opening cash balance (April 01)		3,995
Closing cash balance (April 30)		$3,295

Note: A long-term note for $30,000 was issued to purchase a van.

Solution details for indirect method follow:

	A	B	C	D	E	F	G	H
1	**Tom's Wear, Inc.**							
2	**Spreadsheet for Cash Flow Statement (Indirect Method)**							
3	**For the month ended April 30, 2005**							
4								
5			March 31,		Analysis of Changes			April 30,
6			2005		Debit		Credit	2005
7	**Balance Sheet: Debits**							
8	Cash		$3,995			(j)	$700	$3,295
9	Accounts receivable		2,000	(b)	$6,000			8,000
10	Inventory		300	(c)	800			1,100
11	Prepaid insurance		75			(d)	50	25
12	Prepaid rent		0	(e)	1,800			1,800
13	Equipment		4,000					4,000
14	Van		0	(i-1)	30,000			30,000
15			$10,370					$48,220
16	**Balance Sheet: Credits**							
17	Accumulated amortization		$100			(f)	$825	$925
18	Accounts payable		0			(g)	4,000	4,000
19	Other payables		0					0
20	Interest payable		30			(h)	280	310
21	Current portion of notes payable		3,000					3,000
22	Notes payable		0			(i-2)	30,000	30,000
23	Common shares		5,000					5,000
24	Retained earnings		2,240			(a)	2,745	4,985
25			$10,370					$48,220
26								
27	**Statement of Cash Flows**							
28	Operating activities							
29	Net income			(a)	$2,745			
30	Increase in accounts receivable					(b)	$6,000	
31	Increase in inventory					(c)	800	
32	Decrease in prepaid insurance			(d)	50			
33	Increase in prepaid rent					(e)	1,800	
34	Amortization expense			(f)	825			
35	Increase in accounts payable			(g)	4,000			
36	Increase in interest payable			(h)	280			
37	**Non-cash investing and financing activities**							
38	Purchase of a van with a note			(i-2)	30,000	(i-1)	30,000	
39					$76,500		$77,200	
40	Net increase (decrease) in cash					(j)	(700)	
41					$76,500		$76,500	
42								

Questions

1. What is the purpose of the cash flow statement?
2. Define the three types of cash flows shown on the cash flow statement.
3. Why is the cash flow statement so important to a company?
4. Explain how modern technology could enable a company to prepare the cash flow statement using a *very* direct method—identifying each cash flow, as we have done with Tom's Wear.
5. What are the two traditional ways of preparing and presenting the cash flow statement? Which is easier for a reader to interpret?
6. Give three examples of transactions that would be classified as cash flows from operations.
7. Give three examples of transactions that would be classified as cash flows from investing activities.
8. Give three examples of transactions that would be classified as cash flows from financing activities.
9. How is amortization expense treated when using the direct method of preparing the cash flow statement? How is this expense treated when using the indirect method?

Short Exercises

L.O. 1

SE10-1 One common reason for small business failure is the lack of planning concerning cash flows. Explain this problem and why cash planning is so important to the successful operation of a business.

L.O. 2

SE10-2 Given the following cash transactions, classify each as a cash flow from (1) operating activities, (2) investing activities, or (3) financing activities:

a. payment to employees for work done
b. dividends paid to shareholders
c. payment for new equipment
d. payment to vendor for inventory
e. interest payment to the bank related to a loan

L.O. 2

SE10-3 Given the following cash transactions, classify each as a cash flow from: (1) operating activities, (2) investing activities, or (3) financing activities:

a. principal payment to the bank for a loan
b. collection from customers to whom sales were previously made on account
c. collection from customers for cash sales
d. collection for sale of land that had been purchased as a possible factory site
e. cash used to pay for doughnuts for staff

L.O. 3

SE10-4 College Television Company had supplies worth $20,000 on its balance sheet at December 31, 2007. The income statement for 2008 showed a supplies expense of $50,000. The balance sheet at December 31, 2008, showed supplies of $25,000. If no supplies were purchased on account (all were cash purchases), how much cash did College Television Company spend on supplies during 2008? How would that cash outflow be classified on the cash flow statement?

L.O. 3

SE10-5 Jill Corp. reported sales of $950,000 for 2005. Jill's accounts receivable from sales were $40,000 at the beginning of 2005 and $50,000 at the end of 2005. What was the amount of cash collected from customers in 2005?

L.O. 3

SE10-6 A building cost $55,000 and had accumulated amortization of $15,000 when it was sold for a gain of $5,000. It was a cash sale. Where would the cash from this transaction appear on the cash flow statement?

SE10-7 Sales for 2005 were $50,000; cost of goods sold was $35,000. If accounts receivable increased by $2,000, inventory decreased by $1,300, accounts payable decreased by $2,000, and other accrued liabilities decreased by $1,000, how much cash was paid to vendors and suppliers during the year? L.O. 3

SE10-8 During 2008, Cameron Company had $300,000 in cash sales and $3,500,000 in credit sales. The accounts receivable balances were $450,000 and $530,000 at December 31, 2007 and 2008, respectively. What was the total cash collected from all customers during 2008? L.O. 3

SE10-9 The income statement for Lilly's Company for the year ended June 30, 2008, showed sales of $50,000. During the year, the balance in accounts receivable increased by $7,500. What adjustment to net income would be shown in the operating section of the cash flow statement prepared using the indirect method related to this information? How much cash was collected from customers during the fiscal year ended June 30, 2008? L.O. 4

SE10-10 The income statement for Sharp Inc. for the month of May showed insurance expense of $250. The beginning and ending balance sheets for the month showed an increase of $50 in prepaid insurance. There were no payables related to insurance on the balance sheet. What adjustment to net income would be shown in the operating section of the cash flow statement prepared using the indirect method related to this information? How much cash was paid for insurance during the month? L.O. 3, 4

SE10-11 During 2007, Cable Direct Inc. incurred salary expense of $37,500, as shown on the income statement. The January 1, 2007, balance sheet showed salaries payable of $10,450; and the December 31, 2007, balance sheet showed salaries payable of $15,200. What adjustment to net income would be shown in the operating section of the cash flow statement prepared using the indirect method related to this information? How much cash was paid to employees (for salary) during 2007? L.O. 3, 4

SE10-12 Havelen's Road Paving Company had an amortization expense of $43,000 on the income statement for the year. How would this be shown on the cash flow statement prepared using the indirect method? Why? L.O. 4

SE10-13 Beta Company spent $40,000 for a new delivery truck during the year. Amortization expense of $2,000 related to the truck was shown on the income statement. How are the purchase of the truck and the related amortization reflected on the cash flow statement prepared using the indirect method? L.O. 4

SE10-14 If you were interested in investing in a company, what item or items on the cash flow statement would be of most interest to you? Why? L.O. 4

Exercises

E10-1 For each of the following items, tell whether it is a cash inflow or a cash outflow and the section of the cash flow statement in which the item would appear.

Item	Inflow or outflow	Section of the statement
(a) Cash collected from customers		
(b) Proceeds from issuing shares		
(c) Interest payment on loan		
(d) Principal repayment of loan		
(e) Cash paid for advertising		
(f) Cash paid to purchase shares for cancellation		
(g) Money borrowed from the local bank		
(h) Cash paid to employees (salaries)		
(i) Purchase of equipment		
(j) Cash paid to vendors for inventory		
(k) Taxes paid		

L.O. 2

E10-2 For each of the following transactions, give the section of the cash flow statement prepared using the direct method in which the item would be found:

a. issued 100 common shares at $12 per share
b. borrowed $5,000 from a local bank to expand the business
c. purchased supplies for $400 cash
d. paid a carpenter $500 cash to build some bookcases for the office
e. earned revenue of $9,000 cash
f. hired a student to do some typing and paid him $300 cash
g. repaid $1,000 of the bank loan along with $150 interest
h. paid dividends of $400

L.O. 3

E10-3 Use the income statement for Clark Corp. and the information from the comparative balance sheets shown for the beginning and the end of the year to prepare the operating section of the cash flow statement using the direct method.

Sales		$100,000
Cost of goods sold		35,000
Gross margin		$65,000
Operating expenses		
Wages	$ 2,500	
Rent	1,200	
Utilities	980	
Insurance	320	5,000
Net income		$60,000

Account	Beginning of the year	End of the year
Accounts receivable	$10,000	$12,000
Inventory	21,000	18,500
Prepaid insurance	575	400
Accounts payable	9,000	10,400
Wages payable	850	600
Utilities payable	150	0

L.O. 4

E10-4 Use the information from E10-3 to prepare the operating section of the cash flow statement using the indirect method. Then compare it with the statement you prepared for E10-3. What are the similarities? What are the differences? Which do you find more informative?

L.O. 3

E10-5 Given the following information, calculate the change in cash for the year:

Cash received from sale of equipment	$ 20,000
Cash paid for salaries	8,250
Amortization expense for the year	12,450
Cash received from issuing shares	150,000
Cash collected from customers	87,900
Cash received from sale of land	14,500
Cash paid for operating expenses	2,000
Cash paid to vendor for inventory	32,480

L.O. 3

E10-6 Use the information for Sharp Company to calculate:

a. cash paid for salaries
b. cash paid for income taxes
c. cash paid for inventory
d. cash collected from customers

From the financial statements for Sharp Company	Income statement amount for the year	Balance sheet	
		Beginning of the year	End of the year
Sales revenue	$95,600		
Accounts receivable		$8,700	$10,000
Salary expense	31,400		
Salaries payable		2,300	2,100
Cost of goods sold	24,300		
Inventory		4,800	9,000
Accounts payable		2,500	3,000
Income tax expense	28,500		
Income taxes payable		7,400	8,200

E10-7 The following events occurred at Gadgets, Inc., during 2008: L.O. 3, 4

January	Issued bonds for $250,000
February	Purchased new machinery for $80,000
March	Sold old machinery for $30,000, resulting in a $10,000 loss
April	Paid interest of $20,000 on bonds issued in prior years
May	Borrowed $5,000 from a local bank
June	Purchased a new computer for $3,000
July	Paid cash dividends of $4,600

Compute Gadgets' net cash flow from (1) investing activities, and from (2) financing activities for the year ended December 31, 2008.

E10-8 The following information applies to Computer Company: L.O. 3

Income Statement for the Year Ended 2006

Sales	20,000
Cost of goods sold	(15,200)
Gross margin	4,800
Rent expense	(1,000)
Net income	$ 3,800

- Accounts receivable started the year with a balance of $1,000 and ended the year with a balance of $3,300.
- The beginning balance in accounts payable (to vendors) was $2,000, and the ending balance was zero. Inventory at the end of the year was the same as it was at the beginning of the year (i.e., there was no change in inventory).
- The company started the year with $5,000 of prepaid rent, and ended the year with $4,000 of prepaid rent.

For 2006, give the amount of cash that was

a. collected from customers for sales
b. paid to vendors for inventory
c. paid for rent

E10-9 The following information has been taken from the most recent cash flow statement of Expansion Company: L.O. 5

Net cash used by operating activities	$ (932,000)
Net cash provided by investing activities	1,180,500
Net cash provided by financing activities	2,107,000

a. What information do these subtotals from the cash flow statement tell you about Expansion Company?
b. What additional information would you want to see before you analyze the ability of Expansion Company to generate positive operating cash flows in the future?
c. Can you tell if Expansion had a positive net income for the period? What information would you like to see to help you predict next year's net income?

Problems—Set A

P10-1A The Samsula Service income statement for the year ended December 31, 2009 and the balance sheets at December 31, 2008, and December 31, 2009, follow:

Samsula Service Company
Income Statement
For the Year Ended December 31, 2009
(In Thousands, Except Earnings per Share)

Service revenue		$92,000
Expenses		
Wages and salaries	$60,000	
Advertising	10,000	
Rent	4,800	
Amortization	3,600	
Miscellaneous	5,200	
Total expenses		83,600
Income before taxes		8,400
Income taxes		2,940
Net income		$ 5,460
Earnings per share		$ 0.55

Samsula Service Company
Comparative Balance Sheets
($ in Thousands)

	December 31, 2009		December 31, 2008	
Assets				
Current assets:				
Cash		$ 6,910		$ 3,500
Accounts receivable		12,000		14,000
Supplies		200		370
Prepaid advertising		800		660
Total current assets		$19,910		$18,530
Property, plant, and equipment				
Equipment	$ 44,000		$ 40,000	
Less: Accumulated amortization	(21,600)		(18,000)	
Total property, plant, and equipment		22,400		22,000
Total assets		$42,310		$40,530
Liabilities and shareholders' equity				
Current liabilities				
Wages and salaries payable		$ 2,700		$ 3,300
Taxes payable		1,900		1,780
Total current liabilities		4,600		5,080
Shareholders' equity				
Common shares	$30,000		$ 30,000	
Retained earnings	7,710		5,450	
		37,710		35,450
Total liabilities and shareholders' equity		$42,310		$40,530

Required:

a. Prepare a cash flow statement for the year ended December 31, 2009, using (1) the direct method, and (2) the indirect method.
b. Why is this information important to the company and to parties outside the company?
c. As a user, which format would you prefer, and why?

P10-2A The following information is from the comparative balance sheets of Reba's Record Company at December 31, 2007 and 2006:

L.O. 4

	At December 31	
(In thousands)	**2007**	**2006**
Current assets		
Cash	$3,500	$2,990
Accounts receivable	1,825	2,200
Inventory	2,150	1,380
Prepaid rent	320	270
Total current assets	*$7,795*	*$6,840*
Current liabilities		
Accounts payable	$1,890	$1,050
Salaries payable	2,500	3,800
Total current liabilities	*$4,390*	*$4,850*

Net income for 2007 was $356,000. Amortization expense of $135,000 was included in the operating expenses for the year.

Required: Prepare the cash from operations section of the cash flow statement using the indirect method for Reba's Record Company for the year ended December 31, 2007.

P10-3A The following information comes from the balance sheets of TCB Company at June 30, 2008 and 2007:

L.O. 4

TCB Company
Information from Balance Sheets
June 30, 2008, and June 30, 2007
Current Assets and Current Liabilities Only

(In thousands)	**2008**	**2007**
Current assets		
Cash	$2,110	$2,650
Accounts receivable	1,254	977
Inventory	730	856
Prepaid insurance	127	114
Total current assets	*$4,221*	*$4,597*
Current liabilities		
Accounts payable	$1,054	$1,330
Wages payable	2,100	1,750
Total current liabilities	$3,154	$3,080

Net income for the year ended June 30, 2008, was $86,900. Included in the operating expenses for the year was amortization expense of $102,000.

Required: Prepare the cash from operating activities section of the TCB Company cash flow statement for the year ended June 30, 2008. Use the indirect method.

L.O. 4

P10-4A Ridge Oak Land Corp. had the following information available for 2005:

	January 1	December 31
Accounts receivable	$78,000	$71,000
Prepaid insurance	48,000	36,000
Inventory	56,000	75,000

Ridge Oak Land Corp. reported net income of $270,000 for the year. Amortization expense, included on the income statement, was $24,200.

Required: Assume this is all the information relevant to the cash flow statement. Prepare the cash flow from the operating activities section of the Ridge Oak Land Corp. cash flow statement.

L.O. 3, 4

P10-5A To prepare its cash flow statement for the year ended December 31, 2007, Myers Company gathered the following information:

Loss on sale of machinery	$ 8,000
Proceeds from sale of machinery	50,000
Proceeds from bond issue (face value $100,000)	80,000
Amortization of bond discount	1,000
Dividends declared	25,000
Dividends paid	15,000
Purchase of shares for cancellation	30,000

Required: Prepare the cash from investing section of the cash flow statement for Myers Company for the year ended December 31, 2007.

L.O. 3, 4

P10-6A To prepare its cash flow statement for the year ended December 31, 2005, Martin Company gathered the following information:

Gain on sale of equipment	$ 4,000
Proceeds from sale of equipment	10,000
Purchase of equipment	80,000
Dividends declared	5,000
Dividends paid	2,000
Proceeds from issuance of shares	90,000
Repayment of loan principal	21,000
Payment of interest on loan	210

Required:

a. Prepare the cash from investing section of the cash flow statement.
b. Prepare the cash from financing section of the cash flow statement.

L.O. 3, 4

P10-7A To prepare its cash flow statement for the year ended December 31, 2006, Repass Company gathered the following information:

Dividends paid	$ 18,500
Purchase of shares for cancellation	50,000
Proceeds from bank loan	150,000
Gain on sale of equipment	7,000
Proceeds from sale of equipment	20,000
Proceeds from sale of common shares	260,000

Required: Prepare the cash from financing section of the cash flow statement for Repass Company for the year ended December 31, 2006.

P10-8A Use the cash flow statement for the Matlock Company to answer the following questions:

L.O. 1, 2, 5

Matlock Company
Cash Flow Statement
For the Year Ended December 31, 2006

		(In thousands)
Cash flows from operating activities		
Net income		$1,500
Amortization expense	$ 210	
Decrease in accounts receivable	320	
Increase in inventory	(70)	
Increase in prepaid rent	(10)	
Increase in accounts payable	150	600
Net cash provided by operating activities		2,100
Cash flows from investing activities		
Purchase of equipment	(1,000)	
Proceeds from sale of old equipment	200	
Net cash used by investing activities		(800)
Cash flows from financing activities		
Repayment of long-term mortgage	(1,350)	
Proceeds from sale of common shares	500	
Payment of cash dividends	(200)	
Net cash used by financing activities		(1,050)
Net increase in cash during 2006		250
Cash balance, January 1, 2006		346
Cash balance, December 31, 2006		$ 596

Required:

a. How did Matlock Company use the majority of its cash during 2006?
b. What information does this give you about Matlock Company?
c. How did Matlock Company obtain the majority of its cash during 2006?
d. Is this an appropriate source of cash for the long run? Explain.

Problems—Set B

P10-1B The following income statement for the year ending December 31, 2007, and the balance sheets at December 31, 2006, and December 31, 2007, are given for Oviedo Oil:

Oviedo Oil Company
Income Statement
For the Year Ended December 31, 2007

Sales revenue		$150,000
Cost of goods sold		63,000
Gross margin		87,000
Other expenses		
Wages and salaries	$ 32,000	
Amortization	4,500	
Miscellaneous	12,400	
Total other expenses		48,900
Income before taxes		$ 38,100
Income taxes		8,200
Net income		$ 29,900

Oviedo Oil Company
Comparative Balance Sheets

(In thousands)	2007		2006	
Assets				
Current assets				
Cash		$ 0		$ 6,400
Accounts receivable		2,900		2,700
Inventory		60,000		42,000
Total current assets		$ 62,900		$51,100
Property, plant, and equipment				
Equipment	$82,300		$39,000	
Less: accumulated amortization	(20,100)		(15,600)	
Total property, plant, and equipment		62,200		23,400
Total assets		$125,100		$74,500
Liabilities and shareholders' equity				
Current liabilities				
Accounts payable	$ 6,400		$ 5,700	
Salaries payable	1,500		1,300	
Taxes payable	1,900		2,100	
Total current liabilities	9,800		9,100	
Notes payable	30,000		10,000	
Total liabilities		39,800		19,100
Shareholders' equity				
Common shares	$40,000		$40,000	
Retained earnings	45,300		15,400	
		85,300		55,400
Total liabilities and shareholders' equity		$125,100		$74,500

Required:

a. Prepare a cash flow statement for the year ending December 31, 2007, using (1) the direct method, and (2) the indirect method.
b. Why is this information important to the company and to parties outside the company?
c. As a user, which format would you prefer, and why?
d. Evaluate the way the company spent its cash during the year. Do you think the company is in a sound cash position?

L.O. 4

P10-2B The information shown below is from the comparative balance sheets of Faith's Music Company at December 31, 2005 and 2004:

(In thousands)	At December 31 2005	2004
Current assets		
Cash	$2,500	$2,990
Accounts receivable	3,725	2,080
Inventory	1,050	1,300
Prepaid insurance	520	470
Total current assets	*$7,795*	*$6,840*
Current liabilities		
Accounts payable	$2,890	$1,650
Salaries payable	1,500	3,200
Total current liabilities	*$4,390*	*$4,850*

Net income for the year ended December 31, 2005, was $206,000. Amortization expense of $85,000 was included in the operating expenses for the year.

Required: Prepare the cash from operations section of the cash flow statement for Faith's Music Company for the year ended December 31, 2005. Use the indirect method.

P10-3B Information that follows comes from the balance sheets of Walker Corp. at September 30, 2008 and 2007: L.O. 4

From the Balance Sheets of Walker Corp.
September 30, 2008, and September 30, 2007

(In thousands)	2008	2007
Current assets		
Cash	$2,110	$1,650
Accounts receivable	1,254	1,977
Inventory	700	656
Prepaid insurance	157	314
Total current assets	*$4,221*	*$4,597*
Current liabilities		
Accounts payable	$2,000	$2,330
Wages payable	1,154	750
Total current liabilities	*$3,154*	*$3,080*

Net income for the year ended September 30, 2008, was $146,000. Included in the operating expenses for the year was amortization expense of $112,000.

Required: Prepare the cash from the operating activities section of the Walker Corp. cash flow statement for the year ended September 30, 2008.

P10-4B Treasures Corp. had the following information available for 2005: L.O. 4

	January 1	December 31
Accounts receivable	$70,000	$76,000
Prepaid insurance	58,000	36,000
Inventory	86,000	65,000

Treasurers Corp. reported net income of $130,000 for the year. Amortization expense, included on the income statement, was $20,800.

Required: Assume this is all the information relevant to the cash flow statement. Prepare the cash flow from operations section of the Treasures Corp. cash flow statement.

P10-5B To prepare its cash flow statement for the year ended December 31, 2006, Wright's Company gathered the following information: L.O. 2, 3, 4

Proceeds from bond issue (face value $100,000)	$120,000
Amortization of bond premium	1,000
Dividends declared	15,000
Dividends paid	12,000
Purchase of shares for cancellation	50,000
Loss on sale of machinery	18,000
Proceeds from sale of machinery	30,000

Required: Prepare the cash from investing section of the cash flow statement for Wright's Company for the year ended December 31, 2006.

L.O. 2, 3, 4

P10-6B To prepare its cash flow statement for the year ended December 31, 2005, Bowden Company gathered the following information:

Dividends declared	$15,000
Dividends paid	12,000
Proceeds from issuance of shares	70,000
Repayment of loan principal	32,000
Payment of interest on loan	320
Gain on sale of equipment	3,500
Proceeds from sale of equipment	11,000
Purchase of equipment	75,000

Required:

a. Prepare the cash from investing section of the cash flow statement.
b. Prepare the cash from financing section of the cash flow statement.

L.O. 2, 3, 4

P10-7B To prepare its cash flow statement for the year ended December 31, 2008, Mango Company gathered the following information:

Proceeds from bank loan	$257,000
Gain on sale of equipment	17,500
Proceeds from sale of equipment	45,000
Proceeds from sale of common shares	160,000
Dividends paid	15,400
Purchase of shares for cancellation	75,000

Required: Prepare the cash from the financing section of the cash flow statement for Mango Company for the year ended December 31, 2008.

L.O. 1, 2, 5

P10-8B Use the cash flow statement for the SS&P Company to answer the following questions:

SS&P Company
Cash Flow Statement
For the Year Ended December 31, 2006

	(In thousands)	
Cash flows from operating activities		
Net income		$ 2,500
Amortization expense	$ 510	
Decrease in accounts receivable	720	
Increase in inventory	(90)	
Increase in prepaid rent	(20)	
Decrease in accounts payable	(150)	970
Net cash provided by operating activities		3,470
Cash flows from investing activities		
Purchase of equipment	$(3,000)	
Proceeds from sale of old equipment	900	
Net cash used by investing activities		(2,100)
Cash flows from financing activities		
Repayment of long-term mortgage	$(7,500)	
Proceeds from sale of common shares	2,100	
Payment of cash dividends	(1,200)	
Net cash used by financing activities		(6,600)
Net increase in cash during 2006		(5,230)
Cash balance, January 1, 2006		10,580
Cash balance, December 31, 2006		$ 5,350

Required:

a. How did SS&P Company use the majority of its cash during 2006?
b. What information does this give you about SS&P Company?
c. How did SS&P Company obtain the majority of its cash during 2006?
d. Is this an appropriate source of cash in for the long run? Explain.

Recording Transactions

R10-1 (SE10-5) Jill Corporation reported credit sales of $950,000 for 2005. Jill's accounts receivable from sales were $40,000 at the beginning of 2005 and $50,000 at the end of 2005. Use the T-account approach to determine the amount of cash from customers collected in 2005.

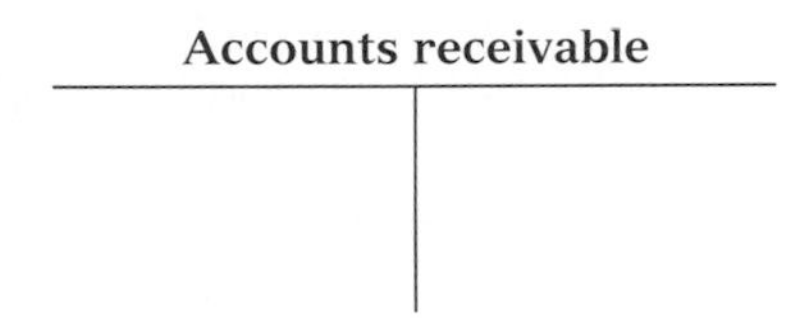

R10-2 (SE10-11) During 2007, Cable Direct, Inc. incurred salary expense of $37,500. The January 1 balance in salaries payable was $10,450, and the December 31 balance was $15,200. Use the T-account approach to determine the amount of cash paid to employees during 2007.

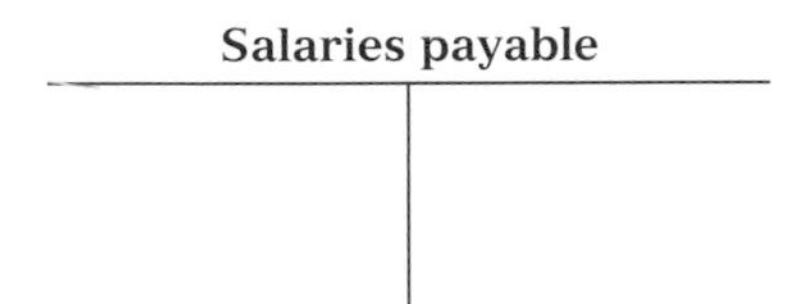

R10-3 (SE10-13) Beta Company spent $40,000 for a new delivery truck during the year. Amortization expense of $2,000 related to the truck was shown on the income statement. Give the journal entries to record the purchase of the asset and the amortization expense. What effect do these transactions have on the cash flow statement?

Date	Account	Debit	Credit

R10-4 (E10-2) Suppose Kianna's Company completed the following cash transactions during the year ended June 30, 2008. For each transaction, give the appropriate journal entry and the effect on the cash flow statement. Then, prepare a cash flow statement for the year ended June 30, 2008.

a. Issued 100 common shares for $12 per share.
b. Borrowed $5,000 from a local bank to expand the business.
c. Purchased supplies for $400 cash.
d. Hired a carpenter to build some bookcases for the office for $500 cash.
e. Earned revenue of $9,000 cash.
f. Hired a student to do some typing and paid him $300 cash.
g. Repaid $1,000 of the bank loan along with $150 interest.
h. Paid dividends of $400.

Date	Account	Debit	Credit

R10-5 (E10-3) Given the income statement for Clark Corporation for last year and selected information from the comparative balance sheets shown for the beginning and the end of the year, give a journal entry that would explain the change in each balance sheet account balance. The first one is done as an example.

Sales		$100,000
Cost of goods sold		35,000
Gross margin		$65,000
Operating expenses		
Wages	2,500	
Rent	1,200	
Utilities	980	
Insurance	320	5,000
Net Income		$60,000

Account	Beginning of the year	End of the Year
Accounts receivable	$10,000	$12,000
Inventory	21,000	18,500
Prepaid insurance	575	400
Accounts payable	9,000	10,400
Wages payable	850	600
Utilities payable	150	0

Item	Accounts	Debit	Credit
Change in AR	Accounts receivable	$2,000	
	Sales revenue		$2,000
Change in inventory			
Change in prepaid insurance			
Change in accounts payable			
Change in wages payable			
Change in utilities payable			

R10-6 (E10-7) The following events occurred at Gadgets Inc. during 2008:

January	Issued bonds for $250,000
February	Purchased new machinery for $80,000
March	Sold old machinery for $30,000, resulting in a $10,000 loss
April	Paid interest of $20,000 on the bonds
May	Borrowed $5,000 from a local bank
June	Purchased a new computer for $3,000
July	Paid cash dividends of $4,600

Required: Give the journal entry for each transaction as well as the effect on the cash flow statement. Suppose Gadgets began the year with $10,000 cash. Determine the ending cash balance, and prepare the cash flow statement for 2008.

Date	Account	Debit	Credit
January			
February			
March			
April			
May			
June			
July			

R10-7 (P10-1A) Use the information about Samsula Service Company from Problem 10-1A.

Required: Prepare a cash flow statement for the year ending December 31, 2009, using the indirect method with spreadsheet analysis.

Issues for Discussion

L.O. 1, 5

Financial statement analysis

1. Use the annual report of CoolBrands International Inc. to answer the following:
   a. What were the major sources and uses of cash during the fiscal year ended August 31, 2003? What do these indicate about the company's cash position?
   b. Is there any evidence on the cash flow statement that CoolBrands is expanding its business?

Business risk

2. To be successful, a company must anticipate its cash flows. What evidence can you find in the CoolBrands annual report that this company does adequate cash planning? Is there any information not available in the annual report that would help you make this evaluation?

Ethics

3. After two years of business, the Lucky Ladder Company decided to apply for a bank loan to finance a new store. Although the company had been very successful, it had never prepared a cash budget. The owner of Lucky Ladder used the information from the first two years of business to reconstruct cash forecasts, and presented them with his financial statements as though they had been prepared as part of the company's planning. Do you think this behaviour was ethical? What would you do in similar circumstances? Why?

Internet Exercise: Carnival Corp.

Carnival Corp. prides itself on being "The Most Popular Cruise Line in the World®"— a distinction achieved by offering a wide array of quality cruise vacations.
Please go to the Carnival website: http://www.carnival.com/

IE10-1

a. Select "About Us" and "World's Leading Cruise Lines" and watch the introduction. List three of the six cruise lines operated by the Carnival Corp. Close the "World's Leading Cruise Lines" window.
b. Go to Carnival's "News" and select "Virtual Press Kit" and then "Carnival Cruise Lines' Fleet Information." Within the past five years, how many new ships has Carnival put into service?
c. Are the payments for ships considered capital expenditures or revenue expenditures? On the cash flow statement, which business activity category will report these payments?

IE10-2 Under "Investor Relations," find the most recent annual report for Carnival. Find the annual cash flow statement to answer the following questions:

a. Does Carnival use the direct or the indirect method to prepare the cash flow statement? How can you tell? Which activity section is affected by this choice of method?
b. For the most recent year, list the amount of net cash inflow or outflow from each of the three major types of activities reported on the cash flow statement. Which type of activity is providing the most cash? Is this considered favourable or unfavourable?
c. For the most recent year, what amount is reported for net income and total cash from operating activities? Are these amounts the same? Explain why or why not.
d. For the most recent year, did Carnival report cash inflows or outflows for capital expenditures? Is this considered favourable or unfavourable? Explain why. What

do you think these capital expenditures are primarily for? What was the net amount of the capital expenditure? Which activity section reports this information?

e. For the most recent year, what amount of cash dividends did Carnival pay out? For the most recent year, did Carnival issue or retire more common shares? What was the net amount issued or retired? For the most recent year, did Carnival issue or retire more debt? What was the net amount issued or retired? Which activity section reports this information?

f. Does this cash flow statement indicate a strong or weak cash position? Explain why.

Please note: Internet websites are constantly being updated. Therefore, if the information is not found where indicated, please explore the website further to find the information.

CHAPTER 11

Financial Statement Analysis

Here's where you've been...

In Chapter 10, you learned the details involved in preparing the statement of cash flows. You learned that there are two ways to prepare and present the statement: the direct method and the indirect method. You learned the importance of planning cash flows and what can be learned from an analysis of the cash flow statement.

Here's where you're going...

When you are finished with Chapter 11, you will be able to recognize two new items on the financial statements—discontinued operations and extraordinary items. You should be able to do horizontal analysis, vertical analysis, and ratio analysis of a set of financial statements.

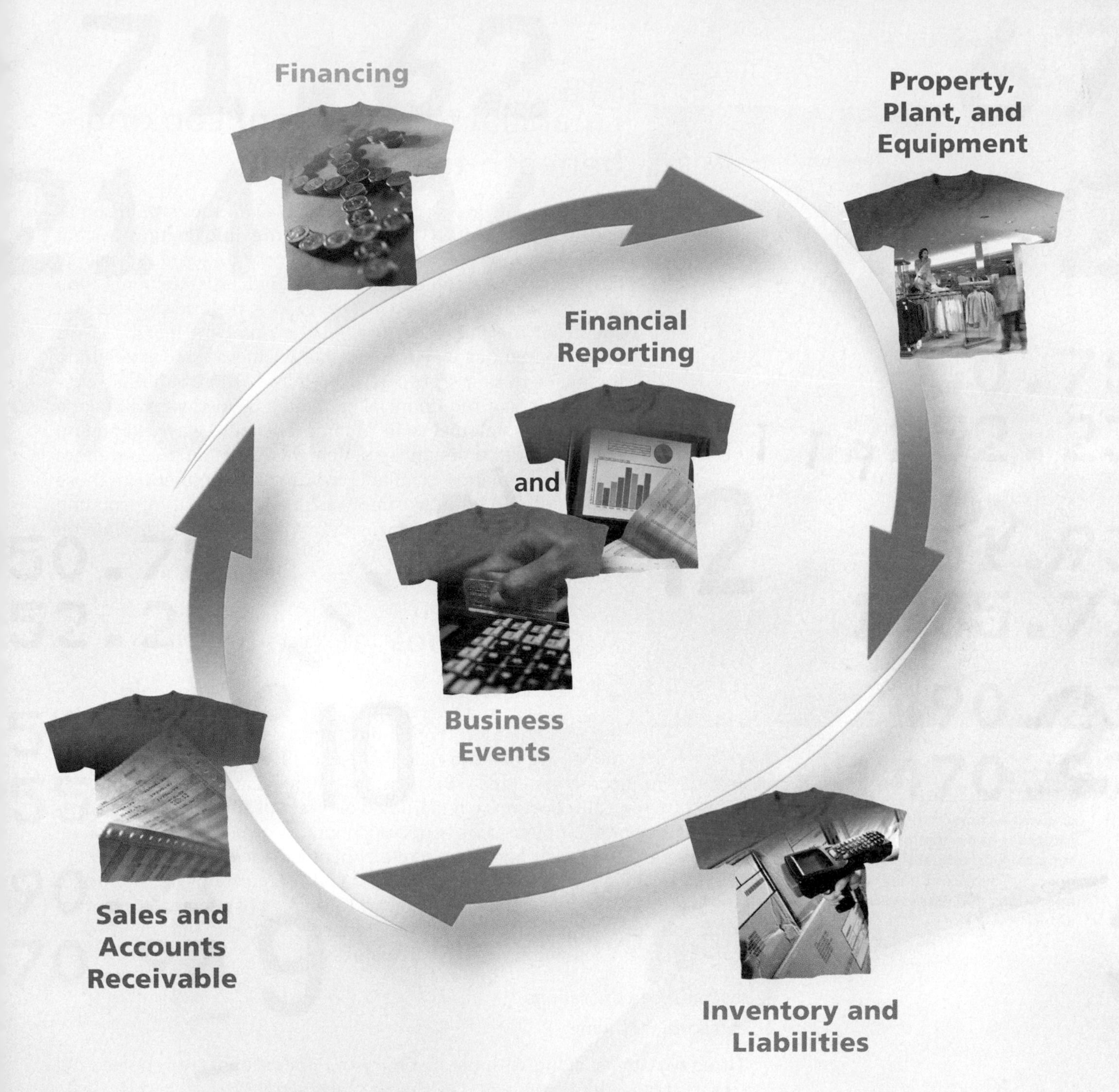

Learning Objectives

More specifically, when you are finished studying this chapter, you should be able to answer these questions:

1. What items are shown separately from *income from operations* on the income statement, and why?
2. What are vertical and horizontal analyses?
3. How are ratios used to analyze financial statements?

Financial Information: Looking beneath the Surface

You can easily see some information from the data in the financial statements. There is still more information in that same data, but you have to look harder to see it. To use all the information contained in the financial statements, you have to get beneath the surface, to look beyond the size and source of the numbers to what the numbers mean. As we have worked our way through the business cycle, examining the major business processes, we have been examining individual parts of the financial statements. Now, we will take a look at the statements in a comprehensive way, examining parts of the four financial statements together to find more of the information available within the numbers in those statements. To put it as simply as possible: What information do financial statements provide? What does the information mean? How can we use it?

A Closer Look at the Income Statement

L.O. 1

Know the components of net income that are disclosed separately, after net income from operations: discontinued operations and extraordinary items.

Before beginning the detailed analysis of the financial statements, we need to take a closer look at some of the characteristics of the income statement. Because earnings—that is, net income—is the focus of financial reporting, companies worry about the effect their earnings will have when announced. It is not uncommon for companies to be accused of manipulating their earnings to make them appear better than they actually are. In an effort to make the components of earnings clear and to communicate exactly what they should mean to financial statement users, accounting standard setters in Canada have defined two items that need to be separated from the regular earnings of a business:

1. discontinued operations
2. extraordinary items

These two items, along with net income from operations, are reported net of taxes, that is, with the related taxes already subtracted.

Discontinued Operations

If you pay attention to the financial news, you are bound to hear about a company selling off a division or disposing of one of its business segments. Firms are always evaluating the contribution that a firm's various business segments make to the profits of the firm. A part of a company's operations that is eliminated is referred to as **discontinued operations.**

Discontinued operations are those that a company has gotten rid of, usually by selling a segment or division. The related gain or loss is shown net of taxes after income from continuing operations.

When a segment's operation is discontinued, the financial implications related to that segment are separated from the regular operations of the firm. Why would this separation be useful? Earnings, or income, is an important number because it is used to evaluate the performance of a firm and to predict its future performance. To make those evaluations and predictions more meaningful, it is important for one-time occurrences to be separated out. In this way, investors see them as exceptions to the normal operations of the firm. The financial implications of discontinuing a business segment—the gain or loss on the disposal—are nonrecurring, and so those items are reported separately. The income or loss for the accounting period for the discontinued operations must also be shown separately.

Let us look at an example of a firm with discontinued operations. Containers, Inc. sold off a major business segment, the package mailing division, during 2007. Whenever a business segment is discontinued, the income or loss from that segment for the year of disposal must be shown separately. Doing this will make the firm's income from continuing operations more useful for predicting the firm's future performance. Both the current year's income or loss from the discontinued operations and the gain or loss from the sale of those operations are shown separately. Suppose:

1. The Containers income from continuing operations before taxes was $400,000.
2. Taxes related to income from continuing operations were $160,000.
3. The discontinued segment contributed income of $12,400 during the year.
4. Taxes related to that income were $2,300.
5. The discontinued segment was sold for a profit of $60,000.
6. The taxes related to the profit from that sale were $25,000.

Exhibit 11–1 shows how this information would be presented on the income statement for Containers, Inc.

Extraordinary Items

Events that are unusual in nature, infrequent in occurrence, and not determined by management are considered extraordinary items. To qualify as extraordinary, the events must not typify the normal business activities of the entity, must not be expected to occur frequently over several years and must not depend primarily on the decisions or determinations of management or owners. Examples of occurrences that have been considered extraordinary include eruptions of a volcano, takeover of foreign operations by a foreign government, and effects of new laws or regulations that result in a one-time cost for compliance. Each situation is unique and must be considered in the environment in which the business operates.

Extraordinary items are events that are both unusual, infrequent and beyond management control. The gain or loss related to them is shown separately on the income statement after income from continuing operations and after any discontinued operations.

Suppose Containers, Inc. lost a factory in a foreign country, when the government of that country expropriated (took possession of) all foreign busi-

Exhibit 11–1
Discontinued Operations

Containers, Inc.
Partial Income Statement
For the Year Ended December 31, 2007

Income before taxes		$400,000
Income tax expense		160,000
Income from continuing operations		240,000
Discontinued operations		
Income from discontinued operations, net of taxes of $2,300	$10,100	
Gain on disposal of segment, net of taxes of $25,000	35,000	45,100
Net income		$285,100

nesses in the country. The book value of the lost factory was $105,000. Because a loss like this is tax deductible, there is a tax saving that must be deducted, and so the extraordinary loss is reported net of tax. Suppose the applicable tax saving is $35,000. Exhibit 11–2 shows how the information would be shown on the Containers, Inc. income statement for the year.

Changes in Accounting Policy

Generally accepted accounting principles (GAAP) are constantly evolving. Some of the changes are additions of new disclosures and new ways of valuing financial statement items. There are instances in which a company may change accounting methods simply to benefit from the resulting financial statement changes—something that securities regulators refer to as "cooking the books." When the accounting profession changes one of its principles or when a company chooses a different principle from the available choices (e.g., change in

Ordinary Extraordinary Items?

You have seen that managers separate the income statement into sections, such as gross profit, operating income, income before income taxes, and net income. Occasionally, something unusual and infrequent happens in a company, and the company must report it separately as an extraordinary item. Different companies could experience the same or similar events but choose to classify them differently. For example, hurricanes are common in Florida, where they would probably not be classified as extraordinary items. However, if a hurricane struck a company in Halifax, Nova Scotia, and damaged its assets, that company would probably classify the loss as an extraordinary item.

On September 18, 2001, eight airlines in the United States wrote a letter to the Financial Accounting Standards Board (FASB) requesting that a number of costs associated with the September 11, 2001, terrorist attacks be classified as extraordinary items. Such costs would include costs associated with increased airport security, costs associated with laying off workers due to the decreased demand for air travel, and cost of employee benefits (such as long-term disability and workers' compensation related to the attacks).

Initially, in a news release on September 28, 2001, the FASB indicated it tentatively agreed that many of the incremental losses attributable to the events of September 11 should be classified as extraordinary and agreed on guidance as to what kinds of losses should be included. However, after considerable debate, the FASB decided to reject its original tentative position. The Chairman of the Emerging Issues Task Force of the FASB, Tim Lucas, said, "The task force understood that this was an extraordinary event in the English language sense of the word, but in the final analysis, we decided it wasn't going to improve the financial-reporting system to show it" (as an extraordinary item). The FASB believed it would be impossible to come up with clear, objective guidelines for all companies in all affected industries. The main problem was how to value the losses of assets not physically damaged in the attack. The airline industry was in the midst of economic problems before the terrorist attacks, and the FASB determined that it would be impossible to disentangle those economic problems and the effect of the terrorist attacks.

Company managers will still be allowed to deduct losses from operating income and also be able to give their opinions about how the attack affected their firms. However, this extraordinary event, in any sense of the word, will be given an ordinary treatment in the financial statements. It will be up to the financial statement users to determine how earnings were affected by the terrorist attacks of September 11, 2001.

Exhibit 11–2
Extraordinary Items

Containers, Inc. Partial Income Statement For the Year Ended December 31, 2007		
Income before taxes		$400,000
Income tax expense		160,000
Income from continuing operations		240,000
Discontinued operations		
Income net of taxes of $2,300	$10,100	
Gain on disposal net of taxes of $25,000	35,000	
		45,100
Income before extraordinary item		285,100
Extraordinary item		
Loss from expropriation of foreign operation, net of tax savings of $35,000		70,000
Net income		$215,100

amortization method), the effect of such a change must be reflected in the opening retained earnings and disclosed in the notes to the financial statements. Comparative statements for prior years must also be restated to give effect to the change. As you can see, this disclosure is meant to discourage companies from trying to manipulate income by changing accounting principles they use for financial reporting. Because the change has to be singled out and identified, the company cannot "hide" the change from financial statement users.

Let us look at Mega Bloks for an example of a change in accounting principle. For Mega Bloks, the statement of retained earnings is called the consolidated statements of deficit because they have net accumulated losses. The statement is shown in Exhibit 11–3. The effect of a change in accounting policy by the CICA has decreased the deficit (i.e., increased retained earnings) by $544,000. Note 2 explains that a mandated change in how to account for foreign exchange gains and losses resulted in the credit to the beginning deficit balance.

STUDY BREAK 11-1
See How You're Doing

Why are discontinued operations and extraordinary items shown *net* of tax? What is the alternative?

Other Financial Statement Items

Unusual Items

L.O. 2

Be able to recognize unusual items and understand what they mean when you see them.

Before we discuss the overall analysis of the financial statements, there is one more set of items commonly found on a set of financial statements. Although we will not discuss all the details here, you should be able to recognize **unusual items** and understand what they mean when you see them.

Unusual items are items on the income statement that result from transactions that are either not typical of normal business activities or are infrequent in nature.

As mentioned in the previous section, income from operations is presented as a distinct line item in the income statement. Incomes from discontinued operations and extraordinary items are presented separately, below income from operations. To further aid users of financial statements, standard setters in Canada require that within income from operations, items that are unusual in nature should be disclosed separately. Unusual items are items that do not meet the definition of an extraordinary item. Unusual items result from transactions that are either not typical of normal business activities or are infrequent in nature. The designation of an item as unusual requires considerable judgment as

Exhibit 11-3
Change in Accounting Principle
Courtesy Mega Bloks Inc.

From the Consolidated Financial Statements of Mega Bloks
Consolidated Statements of Deficit

(In thousands of U.S. dollars)	Years ended December 31. 2002	2001
Balance, beginning of period	$(126,504)	$(132,552)
Net earnings	20,166	6,048
Change in accounting policy (Note 2)	544	–
Related party transaction adjustment (Note 9)	(220)	–
Balance, end of period	$(106,014)	$(126,504)

See accompanying notes to consolidated financial statements.

2. Significant accounting policies (cont'd)

Revenue recognition
Revenue is recognized upon shipment of products to customers. Accruals for customer discounts, rebates, and defective allowance are recorded as the related revenues are recognized.

Foreign currency translation
Monetary assets and liabilities denominated in foreign currencies are translated at the rates of exchange at the balance sheet date. Other balance sheet items denominated in foreign currencies are translated at the rates prevailing at the respective transaction dates. Revenue and expense items arising from transactions in foreign currencies and from the foreign exchange are recorded in the consolidated statements of earnings.

Effective January 1, 2002, the Company adopted the recommendations of the *Canadian Institute of Chartered Accountants (CICA) Handbook* Section 1650, "Foreign Currency Translation." The amended recommendations require that all unrealized translation gains and losses on assets and liabilities denominated in foreign currencies be included in earnings for the year, including gains and losses on long-term monetary assets and liabilities, such as long-term debt, which were previously deferred and amortized on a straight-line basis over the remaining lives of the related items. On January 1, 2002, included in deferred credits was $544,000 relating to unrealized foreign currency gains, which was credited to opening deficit.

what is unusual for one business may not be unusual for another business. According to the 2003 edition of *Financial Reporting in Canada,* the most common unusual losses are asset write-downs and restructuring costs and the most common unusual gains are gains on disposal of capital assets and investments. Unlike extraordinary items, unusual items are not presented net of tax. An example of unusual items can be found in Exhibit 11–4 where Note 10 to the financial statements for Mega Bloks is presented. The presentation of unusual items on the income statement of Mega Bloks can be found in Exhibit 11–5.

Analysis of Financial Information

Now that you are prepared to recognize some new items—extraordinary items and discontinued operations, for example—that may appear on financial statements, you are ready to analyze an entire statement or set of statements. We will discuss three ways to approach the analysis of financial information: horizontal analysis, vertical analysis, and ratio analysis.

Horizontal Analysis

L.O. 4

Perform and interpret a horizontal analysis of financial statement information.

Horizontal analysis is a technique for evaluating a series of financial statement data over a period of time. The purpose of a horizontal analysis is to express the changes in an item in percentages, on the basis of a specific past year chosen as the base year. Suppose we wanted to analyze the change in the capital expenditures of Sears over the past six years.

Exhibit 11-4
From Notes to the Financial Statements for Mega Bloks Inc.
Courtesy Mega Bloks Inc.

(in thousands of U.S. dollars)

10. Unusual items

	2002	2001
Liquidity event award(1)	$2,567	$ –
Cancellation of previous credit facility(2)	2,309	–
Charges incurred to settle CCRA's tax audit(3)	720	–
Manufacturing facility move	–	1,715
Refinancing credit facility	–	1,389
Write-off of deferred charges	–	229
Others	220	383
	$5,816	$3,716

(1) The Company granted selected executives and other key employees a Liquidity Event Award that entitles the holder to receive a bonus based upon the occurrence of certain future corporate events ("Liquidity Event"). These future events have been identified as a change in control or a public offering that would result in an active market of at least 25% of Common Stock. The amount of the liquidity bonus would be payable upon the date on which stock options become vested and exercisable pursuant to the Initial Stock Option Plan. On May 9, 2002, the Initial Public Offering constituted a Liquidity Event under the Liquidity Event Award and accordingly, the Company recorded a provision of $2.6 million, of which $2.2 million was paid during 2002.

(2) See Note 5 for a description regarding the cancellation of the previous credit facility.

(3) See Note 11 for a description of the Canada Customs and Revenue Agency's ("CCRA") tax audit and its outcome.

Exhibit 11-5
Vertical Analysis
Courtesy Mega Bloks Inc.

From the Consolidated Financial Statements of Mega Bloks Inc.
Consolidated Statements of Earnings

(in thousands of U.S. dollars, except per share amounts)	2002		2001	
Net sales	$ 188,807	100.0%	$ 150,043	100.0%
Cost of sales	98,816	52.3%	80,021	53.3%
Gross profit	89,991	47.7%	70,022	46.7%
Marketing, research and development, and advertising expenses	21,701	11.5%	16,502	11.0%
Other selling, distribution and administrative expenses	30,047	15.9%	23,623	15.7%
(Gain) loss on foreign currency translation	(223)	(0.1)%	1,609	1.1%
Unusual items (Note 10)	5,816	3.1%	3,716	2.5%
Earnings from operations	32,650	17.3%	24,572	16.4%
Interest expense				
Long-term debt	4,516	2.4%	10,218	6.8%
Other	340	0.2%	130	0.1%
	4,856	2.6%	10,348	6.9%
Earnings before income taxes	27,794	14.7%	14,224	9.5%
Income taxes (Note 11)				
Current	9,854	5.2%	4,082	2.7%
Future	(2,226)	(1.2)%	4,094	2.7%
	7,628	4.0%	8,176	5.4%
Net earnings	$ 20,166	10.7%	$ 6,048	4.1%

Sears Canada, Inc.
Capital Expenditures—Base Year 1997
(In Millions)

2002	2001	2000	1999	1998	1997
$184	$143	$447	$231	$142	$160

The difference between each year and the base year is expressed as a percentage of the base year. In this example, 1997 has been chosen as the base year and is assigned 100 percent. Then, 1997 capital expenditures are subtracted from 1998 expenditures. That difference is then expressed as a percentage of the base year.

$$\frac{142 - 160}{160} = \frac{-18}{160} = -11.3\% \text{ (The negative sign means decrease.)}$$

During 1998, the company reduced capital expenditures by over 11 percent of the base year expenditures.

See if you can figure out the calculations for the other percentages for Sears.

Sears Canada, Inc.
Capital Expenditures—Base Year 1997
(In Millions)

2002	2001	2000	1999	1998	1997
$184	$143	$447	$231	$142	$160
15.0%	–10.6%	179.4%	44.4%	–11.3%	100%

It is often difficult to understand the significance of a single number or to interpret a trend when looking at the absolute amounts in dollars. It may be useful to express the change in percentage form in order to make the magnitude of the change more apparent.

Vertical Analysis

L.O. 4

Perform and interpret a vertical analysis of financial statement information.

Vertical analysis is a technique similar to horizontal analysis, but it involves items for a single year of a financial statement. Each item in a financial statement is expressed as a percentage of a selected item on the statement. For example, a common income statement analysis uses *sales* as the base amount and then expresses the other income statement items as a percentage of sales. This type of analysis can point out areas in which the costs might be too large or growing without an obvious cause. This analysis is shown in Exhibit 11–5 for Mega Bloks income statements for the years ended December 31, 2002 and 2001.

The analysis for a single year provides some information, but the comparison of two years reveals more about what is going on with Mega Bloks. What item stands out in the analysis? The unusual items are worth further investigation. The notes to the financial statements would be the first place to look for additional information whenever an analysis reveals something interesting.

L.O. 5

Understand the information provided by ratio analysis and perform a basic ratio analysis of a set of financial statements.

Ratio Analysis

Throughout the previous chapters, you have seen financial statement ratios that apply to the various topics we have discussed. You have learned that ratio analysis uses information in the financial statements to calculate specific values that give some measure of a company's financial performance. Most ratios can be classified as one of four types. You have already been introduced to the first three types in the previous chapters; we will briefly recap each here. The fourth type is new and will be described in detail following the review of the first three.

The basic ratio classifications and the questions each ratio helps answer are:

1. *Liquidity:* Can a company pay the bills as they come due?
2. *Solvency:* Can the company survive over a long period of time?
3. *Profitability:* Can a company earn a satisfactory rate of return?
4. *Market indicators:* Is the company a good investment?

A summary of the ratios is shown in Exhibit 11–6; we will discuss each ratio next.

Liquidity Ratios. Liquidity ratios measure the ability of the company to pay its maturing obligations and to meet unexpected needs for cash in the short run. These are of special interest to bankers and suppliers who want to assess a company's ability to meet its short-term obligations.

The following are several common liquidity measures:

1. Current ratio:

$$\frac{\text{current assets}}{\text{current liabilities}}$$

2. Acid-test ratio (sometimes called the quick ratio):

$$\frac{\text{cash + short-term investments + net accounts receivable}}{\text{current liabilities}}$$

3. Working capital:

$$\text{current assets} - \text{current liabilities}$$

4. Inventory turnover ratio:

$$\frac{\text{cost of goods sold}}{\text{average inventory}}$$

5. Accounts receivable turnover ratio:

$$\frac{\text{net sales}}{\text{average (net) accounts receivable}}$$

Although working capital is not a ratio, it is often included in the analysis of financial statements as a measure of liquidity.

STUDY BREAK 11-2

See How You're Doing

A corporation pays off a current liability with cash. What effect would this have on the company's current ratio and on the company's working capital?

Exhibit 11–6 Common Ratios

Ratio	Definition	Uses	Chapter
Liquidity			
Current Ratio	$\frac{\text{current assets}}{\text{current liabilities}}$	This ratio measures a company's ability to pay current liabilities with current assets. Creditors want to know if a company can meet its short-term obligations.	2
Acid-test Ratio (also known as the quick ratio)	$\frac{\text{cash + short-term investments + net accounts receivable}}{\text{current liabilities}}$	This ratio is similar to the current ratio. However, by limiting the numerator to very liquid current assets, it is a stricter test of a company's ability to meet its short-term obligations.	11
Working Capital	current assets − current liabilities	Although technically not a ratio, working capital is often measured as part of financial statement analysis. It is another measure of a firm's ability to meet its short-term obligations.	3
Inventory Turnover Ratio	$\frac{\text{cost of goods sold}}{\text{average inventory}}$	This ratio measures how quickly a company is turning over its inventory.	6
Accounts Receivable Turnover Ratio	$\frac{\text{net sales}}{\text{average net accounts receivable}}$	This ratio measures a company's ability to collect the cash from its credit customers.	7
Solvency			
Debt to Equity	$\frac{\text{total liabilities}}{\text{total shareholders' equity}}$	This ratio compares the amount of debt a company has with the amount the owners have invested in the company.	8
Times Interest Earned	$\frac{\text{net income + interest expense + taxes}}{\text{interest expense}}$	This ratio compares the amount of income that has been earned with the interest obligation for the same period.	8
Profitability			
Return on Assets	$\frac{\text{net income}}{\text{average total assets}}$	This ratio measures a company's success in using its assets to earn income for the persons who are financing the business. Average total assets are the average of beginning assets and ending assets for the year.	5
Return on Equity	$\frac{\text{net income − preferred dividends}}{\text{average common shareholders' equity}}$	This ratio measures how much income is earned with the common shareholders' investment in the company.	9
Gross Margin Ratio	$\frac{\text{gross margin}}{\text{sales}}$	This ratio is used to measure a company's profitability. It is one of the most carefully watched ratios by management. It describes the percentage of sales price that is gross profit. A small shift usually indicates a big change in the profitability of the company's sales.	6

Exhibit 11-6 (continued)

Earnings per Share	$\frac{\text{net income} - \text{preferred dividends}}{\text{average number of outstanding common shares}}$	This gives the amount of net income per common share	9
Market Indicators			
Price-Earnings (PE) Ratio	$\frac{\text{market price per share}}{\text{earnings per share}}$	This ratio indicates the market price for $1 of earnings.	11
Dividend Yield	$\frac{\text{dividend per share}}{\text{market price per share}}$	This ratio gives the percentage return on the investment in a share via dividends.	11

Solvency Ratios. Solvency ratios measure the ability of the company to survive over a long period of time. Long-term creditors and shareholders are interested in these ratios as a measure of long-term expectations. They want to be sure that a company can meet its interest obligations and repay any debts at maturity. Two common ratios that measure solvency are:

1. Debt to equity:

$$\frac{\text{total liabilities}}{\text{total shareholders' equity}}$$

2. Times interest earned:

$$\frac{\text{net income} + \text{interest expense} + \text{taxes}}{\text{interest expense}}$$

Profitability Ratios. Profitability ratios measure the operating success of a company for a given period of time. Some financial statement users see these ratios as a measure of management's performance. These ratios are important for a company's ability to obtain debt and equity financing. These ratios also provide information to management about specific areas of the business that need attention. There are many different profitability ratios that measure different aspects of profitability. Following are four of the most common:

1. Return on Assets:

$$\frac{\text{net income}}{\text{average total assets}}$$

2. Return on equity (sometimes called return on investment):

$$\frac{\text{net income} - \text{preferred dividends}}{\text{average common shareholders' equity}}$$

3. Gross margin ratio:

$$\frac{\text{gross margin}}{\text{sales}}$$

4. Earnings per share (EPS):

$$\frac{\text{net income} - \text{preferred dividends}}{\text{average number of common shares outstanding}}$$

STUDY BREAK 11-3

See How You're Doing

Company A has a gross margin ratio of 30 percent, and Company B has a gross margin ratio of 60 percent. Can you tell which company is more profitable? Explain why or why not.

Market Indicator Ratios. There are two ratios that use the current market price of a share to indicate the return an investor might earn by purchasing that share. Because the share price is what an investor would pay for the share, the market price is the investment on which the shareholder earns a return.

Price-earnings (PE) ratio equals the market price of a share divided by that share's earnings per share.

One ratio is the **price-earnings (PE) ratio**. This ratio is defined by its name: it is the price of a share divided by the current EPS. Investors and financial analysts believe this ratio gives an indication of the future earnings. A high PE ratio means investors believe that the company has the potential for significant growth. If the PE ratio is extremely large (50 or greater), some analysts believe the share is overpriced. A share with a very low PE ratio may be underpriced.

1. Price-earnings ratio (PE ratio):

$$\frac{\text{market price per share}}{\text{earnings per share}}$$

Dividend-yield ratio equals dividend per share divided by the current market price per share.

The other ratio is the **dividend-yield ratio.** It is the dividend per share divided by the market price per share. You may find that the values for the dividend-yield ratio are quite low compared with the return an investor would expect. Investors are willing to accept a low-dividend yield when they anticipate an increase in the price of the shares. On the other hand, shares with low-growth potential may offer a higher dividend yield to attract investors.

2. Dividend-yield ratio:

$$\frac{\text{dividend per share}}{\text{market price per share}}$$

Exhibit 11–7 shows the EPS, the dividends per share, and the market price per share for ATI Technologies and for the Royal Bank of Canada for their fiscal years ending in 2003. Which shares would be a better buy for long-run growth? Which would be better if you needed regular dividend income?

The types of shares that will appeal to an investor depend on the investor's preferences for income and growth. If an investor does not need dividend income (e.g., a young investor may have a retirement fund invested in shares) and has plenty of time to realize growth, the investor would prefer to invest in companies with high-growth potential, no matter what the dividend yield. ATI Technologies may be more attractive, with its high PE ratio, than the Royal Bank. (The extremely high PE ratio could, on the other hand, indicate that the shares are overpriced. Check out what happened to ATI Technologies' share price and earnings in 2002. It indicates the caution needed regarding shares with enormous PE ratios.) Investors who need dividend income for living expenses (e.g., a retiree may be using dividend income for food and rent) will be more concerned with the size of the dividend yield of an investment and less concerned with the investment's long-term growth. The Royal Bank would be better than ATI Technologies for dividends.

Exhibit 11–7
Price-Earnings and Dividend-Yield Ratios

For fiscal years ending in 2003	ATI Technologies	Royal Bank
Earnings per share	$ 0.15	$ 4.44
Dividends per share	0.00	1.72
Ending market price per share	15.10	63.48
Price-earnings ratio	100.6	14.3
Dividend-yield ratio	0%	2.7%

These market-related ratios are very important to management and to investors. If you examine a company's annual report, you are likely to see these ratios reported, usually for the most recent two or three years.

Understanding Ratios. A ratio by itself does not give much information. To be useful, a ratio must be compared with other ratios from previous periods, ratios of other companies in the same industry, or industry averages. Keep in mind that with the exception of EPS, the calculations to arrive at a specific ratio may vary from company to company. There are no "standard" or required formulas to calculate a ratio. One company may calculate a debt ratio as *debt* to *equity*, whereas another company may calculate a debt ratio as *debt* to *debt plus equity*. When regarding and using any company's ratios, be sure you know how those ratios have been computed. When you are computing ratios, be sure to be consistent in your calculations so that you can make meaningful comparisons among them.

Even though the only ratio that must be calculated and presented as part of the financial statements is EPS, managers typically include in their company's annual report many of the ratios we have discussed in this chapter. If these ratios are not shown as part of the financial statements, they may be included in other parts of the annual report, often in graphs depicting trends of the ratios over several years.

Any financial statement analysis requires more than a cursory review of ratios. The analyst must look at trends, components of the values that make up the ratios, and other information about the company that may not even be contained in the financial statements. Financial statements are only one source of information for investors, and ratio analysis is only one tool for analyzing financial statements.

Using Ratio Analysis. Let us compute the ratios shown in Exhibit 11–6 for Dorel, using its 2002 Annual Report. The income statements for three years are shown in Exhibit 11–8, and the balance sheets for two years are shown in Exhibit 11–9.

Other information needed for the analysis include market price per share at the close of business on December 30, 2002 = $35.25 and dividends paid during the 12 months of the year ended December 30, 2002 = $0.00 per share.

All the ratios shown in Exhibit 11–6 are calculated for Dorel for the fiscal year ending December 30, 2002. Even though one set of ratios does not give us much information, use this as an opportunity to become familiar with how the ratios are calculated. The computations for each ratio are shown in Exhibit 11–10.

Conclusion

You have probably noticed at the end of every financial statement, "The accompanying notes to the financial statements are an integral part of these fi-

Exhibit 11-8
Income Statements for Dorel Industries Inc.
Courtesy Dorel Industries Inc.

Dorel Industries Inc.
Consolidated Statement of Income
For the Year Ended December 30, 2002
(In thousands of U.S. dollars, except per share amounts)

	2002	2001	2000
Sales	$992,073	$916,769	$757,540
Expenses			
Cost of sales	760,423	718,123	582,741
Operating	106,969	97,164	83,189
Amortization	24,850	21,168	21,041
Research and development costs	3,698	2,569	2,876
Product liability (Note 20)	–	20,000	2,300
Restructuring costs (Note 21)	–	–	9,737
Interest on long-term debt	9,987	17,643	14,968
Other interest	452	819	574
	906,379	877,486	717,426
Income from Operations before Income Taxes and Amortization of Goodwill	85,694	39,283	40,114
Income taxes (Note 22)			
Current	19,388	(973)	9,389
Future	4,711	5,704	(3,957)
	24,099	4,731	5,432
Income from Continuing Operations before Amortization of Goodwill	61,595	34,552	34,682
Amortization of goodwill	–	7,990	4,708
Income from Continuing Operations	61,595	26,562	29,974
Loss from Discontinued Operatings (note 23)	–	1,058	12,668
Net income	$61,595	$25,504	$17,306
Earnings per share (Note 24)			
Basic			
Income from continuing operations before amortization of goodwill	$ –	$1.23	$1.23
Income from continuing operations	$ –	$0.94	$1.07
Net income	$ 2.05	$0.91	$0.62
Fully diluted			
Income from continuing operations before amortization of goodwill	$ –	$1.21	$1.22
Income from continuing operations	$ –	$0.93	$1.05
Net income	$ 2.00	$0.89	$0.61
See accompanying notes.			

Notes to the financial statements refers to information provided along with the four basic financial statements, considered to be an integral part of the statements. The notes describe the accounting methods used to prepare the statements and explain various aspects of the financial condition of the company.

nancial statements." Some analysts believe there is more real information about the financial health of a company in the **notes to the financial statements** than in the statements themselves. Look at the notes that accompany the statements of CoolBrands in Appendix A. The notes are extensive and detailed. The more you learn about analyzing and evaluating a company's performance, whether in subsequent courses or in actual business experience, the better you will understand the information in the notes to the financial statements.

We have seen what a business firm does and why it does it. To be successful in adding value and making a profit, a firm must be able to record the details of its transactions in a way that makes the information available to the people inside and outside the firm when they need it. To better appreciate the importance of the role of accounting information, look at a business plan. A business plan is a detailed analysis of what it would take to start and maintain the operation of a successful business firm. Financial information is a large and crucial component of a business plan. Sales must be forecast, and ex-

Exhibit 11-9
Balance Sheets of Dorel Industries Inc.
Courtesy Dorel Industries Inc.

Dorel Industries Inc.
Consolidated Balance Sheet
December 30, 2002
(in thousands of U.S. dollars)

Assets		
Current Assets	2002	2001
Cash and cash equivalents	$ 54,450	$ 18,640
Accounts receivable (Note 4)	98,267	95,445
Inventories (Note 5)	142,157	152,411
Prepaid expenses	10,465	8,743
Funds held by ceding insurer (Note 20)	11,298	–
Income taxes refundable	–	5,156
Future income taxes	11,114	11,195
	327,751	291,590
Capital assets (Note 6)	95,374	98,366
Deferred charges (Note 7)	14,111	12,557
Goodwill (Note 8)	155,669	151,624
Intangible assets (Note 9)	5,818	4,055
Future income taxes	–	1,327
Other assets (Note 14)	11,400	9,055
	$610,123	$568,574

Liabilities		
Current Liabilities	2002	2001
Bank indebtedness (Note 10)	$ 8,346	$ 7,911
Accounts payable and accrued liabilities (Note 11)	131,805	104,873
Income taxes payable	11,721	–
Current portion of long-term debt	2,061	2,680
	153,933	115,464
Long-term debt (Note 12)	83,301	225,246
Post-retirement benefit obligation (Note 14)	13,213	12,879
Future income taxes	5,670	3,073
Shareholders' Equity		
Capital shares (Note 15)	138,446	63,023
Retained earnings	212,660	153,223
Cumulative translation adjustment (Note 17)	2,900	(4,334)
	354,006	211,912
	$610,123	$568,574

penses must be estimated. A full set of forecasted financial statements must be prepared. These are "what if" financial statements, forecasts that fit the business plan.

Because accounting is such an integral part of business, accounting principles will continue to change as business changes. Each year, the Canadian Institute of Chartered Accountants (CICA) adds to and changes the rules for including, excluding, and valuing items on the financial statements. Further, because accountants are concerned with the continued usefulness and reliability of the accounting data, the accounting profession will be increasingly concerned with new developments, such as electronic transactions, e-business, and real-time access to financial data. As competition takes on new dimensions, particularly due to new technology, and the strength of the economy is uncertain, the financial information needed for good decision making will be more important than ever.

Exhibit 11–10 Ratio Analysis of Dorel

Ratio	Definition	Computation	Interpretation
Liquidity			
Current Ratio	$\frac{\text{current assets}}{\text{current liabilities}}$	$\frac{\$327,751}{\$153,933} = 2.13$	This is a good current ratio. A value over two is considered good for this industry.
Acid-Test Ratio (also known as the quick ratio)	$\frac{\text{cash + short-term investments + net accounts receivable}}{\text{total current liabilities}}$	$\frac{\$54,450 + 98,267}{\$153,933} = 0.99$	This is a good acid-test ratio. If this ratio is too low, a company could have problems meeting current obligations.
Working Capital (technically not a ratio, but still a measure of liquidity)	current assets – current liabilites	$327,751 – 153,933 = $173,818	The dollar amount of working capital doesn't give much information alone. It certainly should be positive!
Inventory Turnover Ratio	$\frac{\text{cost of goods sold}}{\text{average inventory}}$	$\frac{\$760,423}{\$(142,157 + 152,411)/2} = 5.16$	The company is turning over its inventory more than 5 times each year. It would be useful to compare this with previous years and with other companies in the industry.
Accounts Receivable Turnover Ratio	$\frac{\text{net credit sales}}{\text{average net accounts receivable}}$	$\frac{\$992,073}{\$(98,267 + 95,445)/2} = 10.24$	The company is turning over its receivables about 10 times each year. If you divide 365 days by 10, you'll see that it takes the company about 36 days to collect its receivables. To evaluate the ratio for Dorel, you would need more information.
Solvency			
Debt to Equity	$\frac{\text{total liabilities}}{\text{total equity}}$	$\frac{\$153,933 + 83,301 + 13,213 + 5,670}{\$354,006} = 0.72$	The company has different types of debt. To evaluate the ratio, you would need ratios from other periods or other companies for comparison.
Times Interest Earned	$\frac{\text{net income + interest expense + taxes}}{\text{interest expense}}$	$\frac{\$61,595 + 9,987 + 452 + 24,099}{9,987 + 452} = 9.21$	The larger this number, the better. Its value should be compared with previous year ratios and with ratios of other companies in the industry.

Exhibit 11-10 (continued)

Ratio	Definition	Computation	Interpretation
Profitability			
Return on Assets	$\frac{\text{net income}}{\text{average total assets}}$	$\frac{\$61,595}{\$(610,123 + 568,574)/2} = 0.10 = 10\%$	This is a good return on assets, but it should be compared with previous period ratios and to the ratios of other companies in the industry.
Return on Equity	$\frac{\text{net income} - \text{preferred dividends}}{\text{average common shareholders' equity}}$	$\frac{\$61,595 - 0}{\$(354,006 + 211,912)/2} = 0.22 = 22\%$	Most investors would be happy to earn a 22% return on their investment. Again, a comparison with previous periods or other companies would be informative.
Gross Margin Percentage	$\frac{\text{gross margin}}{\text{sales}}$	$\frac{\$(992,073 - 760,423)}{\$992,073} = 0.234 = 23.4\%$	The gross margin percentage is interesting (for every dollar of sales, $0.77 was the cost of the item to Dorel), but it doesn't mean much by itself. For this ratio, a comparison to others in the same industry would be very useful.
Earnings per Share	$\frac{\text{net income} - \text{preferred dividends}}{\text{average number of common shares outstanding}}$	$\frac{\$61,595}{\$30,097^{a}} = \$2.05$	By itself, this ratio is not very informative (at least we know that a positive number is good). It is the *trend* in EPS that gives the most information about the company.
Market Indicators			
Price-Earnings Ratio	$\frac{\text{market price per share}}{\text{earnings per share}}$	$\frac{\$35.25}{\$2.05} = 17.2$	This PE ratio is high, indicating a company that is growing (as opposed to being a stable low-growth firm).
Dividend-Yield Ratio	$\frac{\text{dividend per share}}{\text{market price per share}}$	$\frac{\$0.00}{\$35.25} = 0.00 = 0\%$	The dividend yield also indicates a growth firm. Many high-growth firms don't pay any dividends.

Note: As you evaluate the ratios, keep in mind that a single ratio is not very useful. Ratios from the previous year would provide a useful comparison.
[a]Weighted average, disclosed in the notes to the consolidated financial statements.

Courtesy Dorel Industries Inc.

Understanding Excel

In this exercise, you perform ratio analyses for Tom's Wear, Inc. for the third quarter of the year.

Requirements

1. Open a new Excel work sheet.
2. Beginning in cell A1, input the following chart that details Tom's Wear, Inc.'s financial statement information at the end of the second quarter, as given in the chapter. For this problem only, assume the numbers given in the chart are Tom's results at the end of the third quarter. Use formulas, as appropriate, to calculate totals. You may also choose the font type and size, as desired.
3. Beginning in column F, calculate the following ratios for Tom's Wear, Inc. for the third quarter of 2005:
   a. Current
   b. Acid test
   c. Working capital
   d. Debt to equity
   e. Times interest earned
   f. Return on assets
   g. Return on equity
   h. Gross margin percentage
   i. Inventory turnover
   j. Accounts receivable turnover

   Hint: All the ratios can be calculated using your table input and formulas. Use parentheses as needed to ensure the correct calculation.
4. Beginning in column H, comment on each ratio. (Use the comments for the first and second quarters as your guide, and do not forget to consider the change from the earlier quarters.)

   Hint: Widen column H to 50 and then wrap text, as needed, for your comments.
5. Print your file and save it to disk. Name your file TomsWear11.

Income statements for the	**Second quarter**	**Third quarter**
Sales revenue	$70,700	$ 522,171
Cost of goods sold	(25,535)	(177,826)
Gross margin	45,165	344,345
Interest expense	(810)	(2,250)
Other expenses	(11,933)	(185,603)
Net income	$32,422	$ 156,492
Balance sheets at	**June 30, 2005**	**September 30, 2005**
Assets		
Cash	$ 8,278	$ 921,249
Accounts receivable	42,780	331,611
Inventory	6,365	30,269
Prepaid insurance	150	450
Prepaid Web service	200	50
Prepaid rent	1,800	1,800
Total current assets	59,573	1,285,429
Land	0	7,500
Building, net	0	67,110
Equipment, net	3,600	101,715
Van, net	27,245	110,970
Total assets	$90,418	$1,572,724
Liabilities		
Accounts payable	$18,950	$ 18,711
Other payables	2,806	4,359
Current portion of long-term debt	6,000	8,710
Total current liabilities	27,756	31,780
Notes payable	24,000	96,290
Total liabilities	51,756	128,070
Equity		
Common shares	$ 5,000	$ 1,255,000
Retained earnings	33,662	189,654
Total shareholders' equity	38,662	1,444,654
Total liabilities and shareholders' equity	$90,418	$1,572,724

Summary Problem: Analysis of the Financial Statements of Tom's Wear

Even though we do not have several years of Tom's Wear financial statements needed to perform a typical analysis, we do have several months of financial statements to examine. Publicly held corporations—those that trade on the stock exchanges—provide quarterly statements to their shareholders, and investors and financial analysts often analyze those quarterly statements. First, we will put the January, February, and March financial statements together to give us the first quarter financial statements; and then we will combine the April, May, and June statements together for the second quarter. Exhibit 11–11 shows the financial statements for the first two quarters.

Required

Calculate the following ratios using the financial statements for Tom's Wear for the first two quarters of 2005.

1. Current ratio
2. Acid-test ratio
3. Working capital
4. Debt-to-equity ratio

Exhibit 11–11
Financial Statements for Tom's Wear for First and Second Quarters of 2005

Income statements for the	First quarter	Second quarter
Sales revenue	$ 4,750	$ 70,700
Cost of goods sold	(1,900)	(25,535)
Gross margin	2,850	45,165
Interest expense	(35)	(810)
Other expenses	(375)	(11,933)
Net income	$ 2,440	$ 32,422

Balance sheets at	March 31, 2005	June 30, 2005
Assets		
Cash	$ 3,995	$ 8,278
Accounts receivable	2,000	42,780
Inventory	300	6,365
Prepaid insurance	75	150
Prepaid Web service		200
Prepaid rent		1,800
Total current assets	6,370	59,573
Equipment (net)	3,900	3,600
Van (net)		27,245
Total assets	$10,270	$ 90,418
Liabilities		
Accounts payable	$ 0	$ 18,950
Other payables	30	2,806
Notes payable (current)	3,000	6,000
Total current liabilities	$ 3,030	27,756
Notes payable (long-term)	0	24,000
Total liabilities	3,030	51,756
Equity		
Common shares	$ 5,000	$ 5,000
Retained earnings	2,240	33,662
Total shareholders' equity	7,240	38,662
Total liabilities and shareholders' equity	$10,270	$ 90,418

5. Times interest earned
6. Return on assets
7. Return on equity
8. Gross margin percentage

Comment on the meaning and interpretation of each ratio.

Solution

These are the ratios for Tom's Wear for the first two quarters of 2005.

Selected Ratios for	First Quarter	Second Quarter	Comments
Current ratio	2.10	2.15	The current ratio is in line with many businesses. (Current ratio of 2 or higher is considered good.) We would need an industry average or another couple of quarters to interpret this ratio.
Acid test	1.98	1.84	The closer the acid test to the current ratio, the more liquid Tom's current assets are.
Working capital	$3,340	$31,817	This does not give us much information yet. We need many more quarters to get a feeling for the amount of working capital that Tom needs.
Debt to equity	0.42	1.34	The change in this ratio indicates Tom's Wear's increasing amount of debt. The second quarter value is quite high.
Times interest earned	70.71	41.03	Even with a large amount of debt, Tom's Wear is having no trouble covering its interest payments.
Return on assets	48%	64%	This ratio is a good sign, indicating that Tom's Wear is earning an excellent return on its assets.
Return on equity	67%	141%	This return on equity is very, very good. Only a small number of companies have a return on equity over 100%. Check it out on the Internet. See if you can find any companies that earned a return on equity over 100% last year.
Gross margin %	60%	64%	This ratio does not tell us very much because we have little basis for evaluation. The ratio has increased slightly, a positive change. Tom's Wear is earning more money on every sale in the second quarter than it did the first quarter. Can you recall anything in the transactions that would account for this?

Answers to Study Break Questions

STUDY BREAK 11-1

These items are shown net of tax; thus, the tax effect is shown along with the accounting effect. If they were not shown net of tax, the tax effect would have to be included in the taxes for the period. Including the tax effects of these items in the current tax expense would distort the tax expense of the period.

STUDY BREAK 11-2

If a company pays off a current liability with cash, the current ratio would go up. Equal numbers would be subtracted from the numerator and from the denominator. Try it — see what happens. Suppose the current ratio equals $5/$4 or 1.25. Then, if current assets and current liabilities were each reduced by 1, the new current ratio would be $4/$3 or 1.33.

Working capital would not change. In the example, it is $5 – 4 = $1 before the debt is paid off, and it is $4 – 3 = $1 after the debt is paid off.

STUDY BREAK 11-3

No, you cannot tell how profitable a company is from a gross margin percentage. For the comparison to be useful, you would have to know whether the companies are in the very same business. Otherwise, you can tell nothing about the profitability of one company relative to the profitability of the other. If a company has a very low gross margin percentage, it could still make a significant profit by turning over the inventory rapidly. Grocery stores are a good example of an industry with low margins but very high turnover. Furthermore, gross profit is not net income. Two companies may have very different selling and administrative expenses, which will have an impact on net income.

Questions

1. What items are required to be shown separately on the income statement, after income from operations, and why?
2. Why would a company want to change an accounting principle? Do the accounting requirements encourage or discourage such changes? Why?
3. What does it mean to show an item *net of tax*?
4. What is horizontal analysis?
5. What is vertical analysis?
6. What ratios are useful for measuring liquidity?
7. What ratios are useful for measuring solvency?
8. What ratios are useful for measuring profitability?

Short Exercises

L.O. 1

SE11-1 In 2007, Earthscope Company decided to sell its satellite sales division, even though the division had been profitable during the year. During 2007, the satellite division earned $54,000, and the taxes on that income were $12,500. The division was sold for a gain of $750,000, and the taxes on the gain amounted to $36,700. How would these amounts be reported on the income statement for the year ended December 31, 2007?

L.O. 1

SE11-2 In 2008, Office Products, Inc. decided to sell its furniture division because it had been losing money for several years. During 2008, the furniture division lost $140,000. The tax savings related to the loss amounted to $25,000. The division was sold for a loss of $350,000; and the tax savings related to the loss on the sale amounted to $50,000. How would these amounts be reported on the income statement for the year ended December 31, 2008?

L.O. 1

SE11-3 Sew and Save Company suffered an extraordinary loss of $30,000 last year. The related tax savings amounted to $5,600. How would this be reported on the income statement?

L.O. 1

SE11-4 LaFluentes Electronics, Inc. purchased an asset for $30,000 at the beginning of 2004. The asset was expected to last for four years with no residual value. The company used double-declining balance amortization for the first two years; but for 2006, the company decided to switch to straight-line amortization. How would this change in accounting principle be reflected in the financial statements? Give both financial statement line items and amounts. Assume a 30-percent tax rate.

L.O. 1

SE11-5 Often a change in accounting principle is the result of a change in GAAP. Suppose Hasty Company had been correctly capitalizing the costs associated with a certain type of software development. At December 31, 2007, costs worth $50,000 had been capitalized as a long-term asset. Suppose that during 2008, the Accounting Standards Board (AcSB) decided the costs of this particular type of development should be expensed as incurred. What effect would this have on the income statement for Hasty Company for the year ended December 31, 2008? Assume a 30-percent tax rate.

L.O. 2

SE11-6 Olin Copy Corp. reported the following amounts on its 2008 comparative income statement:

(In thousands)	2008	2007	2006
Revenues	$6,400	$4,575	$3,850
Cost of sales	3,900	2,650	2,050

Perform a horizontal analysis of revenues and gross profit in both dollar amounts and in percentages for 2008 and 2007, using 2006 as the base year.

L.O. 2

SE11-7 Use the following information about the capital expenditures of Andes Company to perform a horizontal analysis, with 2005 as the base year. What information does this provide about Andes Company?

(In millions)	2008	2007	2006	2005
Capital expenditures	$41,400	$45,575	$43,850	$50,600

L.O. 2

SE11-8 Bessie's Quilting Company reported the following amounts on its balance sheet at December 31, 2008:

Cash	$ 5,000
Accounts receivable, net	40,000
Inventory	35,000
Equipment, net	120,000
Total assets	$200,000

Perform a vertical analysis of the assets of Bessie's Company. Use *total assets* as the base. What information does the analysis provide?

L.O. 2

SE11-9 Perform a vertical analysis on the following income statement, with sales as the base amount. What other information would you need to make this analysis meaningful?

Sales	$35,000
Cost of goods sold	14,000
Gross margin	21,000
Other expenses	7,000
Net income	$14,000

L.O. 3

SE11-10 Fireworks, Inc. reported current assets of $720,000 and a current ratio of 1.2. What were current liabilities? What was its working capital?

SE11-11 A five-year comparative analysis of the Low Light Company current ratio and quick ratio follows: L.O. 3

	2005	2006	2007	2008	2009
Current ratio	1.19	1.85	2.50	3.40	4.02
Acid-test ratio	1.15	1.02	0.98	0.72	0.50

a. What has been happening to the liquidity of Low Light Company over the five years from 2005 through 2009?
b. Does the trend in the two ratios give any information about what has happened to the makeup of the Low Light current assets over the five-year period?

SE11-12 A company's debt-to-equity ratio has been increasing for the past four years. Give at least two steps the company might have taken during this time that would have resulted in this increase. L.O. 3

SE11-13 The following is a five-year comparative analysis of the Accent Company return on assets and return on equity: L.O. 3

	2005	2006	2007	2008	2009
Return on assets	8%	7.5%	7.12%	6.54%	6%
Return on equity	20%	21%	21.8%	22.2%	23%

a. What does this analysis tell you about the overall profitability of Accent Company over the five-year period?
b. What does this analysis tell you about what has happened to Accent's amount of debt over the past five years?

SE11-14 Earnings for Archibold Company have been fairly constant over the past six months, but the price-earnings ratio has been climbing steadily. How do you account for this? What does it tell you about the market's view of the future of the company? L.O. 3

Exercises

E11-1 Use the following information to construct the part of an income statement beginning with income from continuing operations: L.O. 1

Income from continuing operations	$230,000
Loss during the year from discontinued operations	50,000
Tax benefit of loss	8,500
Loss from sale of discontinued operations	138,500
Tax savings from loss on the sale	1,900

E11-2 CFI, Inc. began operations in 2004 and selected FIFO periodic as its inventory method. In 2007, before preparing the financial statements, CFI decided to change to average cost. Use the following information—net income under each of the inventory methods for the years from 2004 to 2007—to prepare the statement of retained earnings for the year ended December 31, 2007. Ignore tax considerations. L.O. 1

	FIFO	Average cost
2004	$26,000	$24,000
2005	30,000	25,000
2006	28,000	27,000
2007	34,000	30,000

L.O. 2

E11-3 Jones Furniture, Inc. reported the following amounts for its sales during the past five years. By using 2004 as the base year, perform a horizontal analysis. What information does the analysis provide that was not apparent from the raw numbers?

2008	2007	2006	2005	2004
$30,000	$28,400	$26,300	$23,200	$25,400

L.O. 2

E11-4 Use the income statement from Colour Copy, Inc. to perform a vertical analysis with sales as the base.

Colour Copy, Inc.
Income Statement
For the Year Ended September 30, 2008

Sales revenue		$10,228
Cost of goods sold		5,751
Gross profit on sales		4,477
Operating expenses		
Amortization on equipment	$ 100	
Other selling and administrative	2,500	
Total expenses		*2,600*
Income before interest and taxes		1,877
Interest expense		350
Income before taxes		1,527
Income taxes		150
Net income		$ 1,377

L.O. 3

E11-5 Calculate the current ratio and the amount of working capital for Albert's Hotels, Inc. for the years given in the following comparative balance sheets. Although a period of two years is not much of a trend, what is your opinion of the direction of these ratios?

Albert's Hotels, Inc.
Balance Sheet
December 31, 2007 and 2006

	2007	2006
Current assets		
Cash	$ 98,000	$ 90,000
Accounts receivable, net	110,000	116,000
Inventory	170,000	160,000
Prepaid expenses	18,000	16,000
Total current assets	396,000	382,000
Equipment, net	184,000	160,000
Total assets	$580,000	$542,000
Total current liabilities	$206,000	$223,000
Long-term liabilities	119,000	117,000
Total liabilities	325,000	340,000
Common shares	90,000	90,000
Retained earnings	165,000	112,000
Total liabilities and shareholders' equity	$580,000	$542,000

E11-6 Use the balance sheets from Albert's Hotels, Inc. given in E11-5 to compute the debt-to-equity ratio at December 31, 2007 and 2006. Suppose you calculated a debt ratio using debt plus equity as the denominator. Which ratio—*debt-to-equity* or *debt-to-debt plus equity*—seems easier to interpret? As an investor, do you view the "trend" in the debt-to-equity ratio as favourable or unfavourable? Why?

L.O. 3

Problems—Set A

P11-1A Each of the following items was found on the financial statements for Hartsfield Company for the year ended December 31, 2004:

L.O. 1

Effect of a change in accounting principle, net of taxes of $10,000	$ 49,500
Net income from operations	136,500
Gain on the sale of a discontinued segment	140,000
Taxes due on the gain on the sale of discontinued segment	14,000

Required: For each item, give the financial statement and section, where applicable, where the item would appear. Describe the item and give as many details of each item's financial statement presentation as possible.

P11-2A The following income statements are from the annual report of Gildan Activewear Inc.:

L.O. 2

		Years ended	
(In Canadian Dollars)	**October 5, 2003**	**September 29, 2002**	**September 30, 2001**
Sales	$630,139,018	$600,660,380	$504,867,353
Cost of sales (Note 10)	440,293,451	431,996,459	398,566,740
Gross profit	189,845,567	168,663,921	106,300,613
Selling, general and administrative expenses (Note 10)	71,153,448	63,926,673	76,074,745
Earnings before the undernoted items	118,692,119	104,737,248	30,225,868
Depreciation and amortization (Note 10)	23,614,704	17,591,885	16,208,560
Interest	9,463,475	13,341,823	13,628,350
	33,078,179	30,933,708	29,836,910
Earnings before income taxes	85,613,940	73,803,540	388,958
Income taxes (recovery) (Note 9)	8,342,000	7,312,000	(427,000)
Net earnings	$77,271,940	$66,491,540	$815,958

(Courtesy Gildan Activewear)

Required:

a. For each of the years shown, prepare a vertical analysis, using sales as the base. Write a paragraph explaining what the analysis shows.

b. By using 2001 as the base year, prepare a horizontal analysis for sales and cost of goods sold. What information does this analysis give you?

L.O. 3

P11-3A Selected data from the financial statements of Gildan Activewear follow:

(Thousands of dollars)	2003	2002
Net sales	$630,139	$600,660
Cost of goods sold	440,293	431,996
Gross profit	189,846	168,664
Interest expense	9,463	13,342
Income taxes	8,342	7,312
Net income	$ 77,272	$ 66,492
Cash and cash equivalents	$ 92,860	$ 70,905
Accounts receivable, less allowance	86,057	87,746
Total current assets	328,953	280,307
Total assets	$575,405	$496,639
Total current liabilities	$121,423	$91,480
Long-term liabilities	100,164	135,251
Shareholders' equity		
Common shares—$1.00 par value	111,564	104,925
Contributed surplus	323	323
Retained earnings	241,932	164,660
Total shareholders' equity	$353,819	$269,908
Total liabilities and shareholders' equity	$575,405	$496,639

Required:

1. Calculate the following ratios for Gildan Activewear for 2003 and 2002:
   (Total shareholders' equity at September 30, 2001, was $198,853 thousand and accounts receivable were $125,525 thousand.)
   a. current ratio
   b. acid-test ratio
   c. working capital
   d. accounts receivable turnover ratio
   e. debt-to-equity ratio
   f. times interest earned
   g. return on equity
   h. gross margin percentage
2. Suppose the changes from 2002 to 2003 in each of these ratios were consistent with the direction and size of the changes for the past several years. For each ratio, explain what the trend in the ratio would indicate about Gildan Activewear.

L.O. 3

P11-4A The following information was taken from the annual report of Presentations, Inc.:

(In thousands)	At December 31 2006	2005
Assets		
Current assets		
Cash	$ 1,617	$1,220
Accounts receivable	1,925	3,112
Merchandise inventory	2,070	966
Prepaid expenses	188	149
Total current assets	5,800	5,447
Plant and equipment		
Buildings, net	4,457	2,992
Equipment, net	1,293	1,045
Total plant and equipment	5,750	4,037
Total assets	$11,550	$9,484

(In thousands)	At December 31 2006	2005
Liabilities		
Current liabilities		
Accounts payable	$ 1,817	$1,685
Notes payable	900	1,100
Total current liabilities	2,717	2,785
Long-term liabilities	3,500	2,000
Total liabilities	6,217	4,785
Shareholders' equity		
Common shares	3,390	3,042
Retained earnings	1,943	1,657
Total shareholders' equity	5,333	4,699
Total liabilities and shareholders' equity	$11,550	$9,484

Presentations, Inc.
Income Statement
For the Year Ended December 31, 2006
(In Thousands)

Sales revenue		$12,228
Cost of goods sold		8,751
Gross profit on sales		3,477
Operating expenses		
Amortization—Buildings and equipment	$ 102	
Other selling and administrative	2,667	
Total expenses		2,769
Income before interest and taxes		$ 708
Interest expense		168
Income before taxes		$ 540
Income taxes		114
Net income		$ 426

Required: Calculate the following ratios for 2006:

1. Return on equity
2. Debt to equity
3. Gross profit percentage (of sales)
4. Current ratio
5. Acid-test ratio
6. Times interest earned

What interpretation can you give this set of ratios for 2006 for Presentations, Inc? What additional information would be useful to you?

L.O. 3

P11-5A The financial statements of For the Kitchen, Inc. include the following items:

	At June 30, 2008	At June 30, 2007
Balance sheet		
Cash	$ 17,000	$ 12,000
Investments (in trading securities)	10,000	16,000
Accounts receivable (net)	54,000	50,000
Inventory	75,000	70,000
Prepaid expenses	16,000	12,000
Total current assets	$172,000	$160,000
Total current liabilities	$140,000	$ 90,000
Income statement for the year ended June 30, 2008		
Credit sales	420,000	
Cost of goods sold	250,000	

Required:

1. Compute the following ratios for the year ended June 30, 2008.
   a. current ratio
   b. accounts receivable turnover
   c. inventory turnover ratio
   d. gross margin percentage
2. Which financial statement users would be most interested in these ratios?
3. Suppose the industry average for similar retail stores for the current ratio is 1.7. Does this information help you evaluate For the Kitchen's liquidity?

L.O. 3

P11-6A You are interested in investing in Reese Company, and you have obtained the balance sheets for the company for the past two years.

Reese Company
Balance Sheet
June 30, 2008 and 2007

	2008	2007
Current assets		
Cash	$198,000	$ 90,000
Accounts receivable, net	210,000	116,000
Inventory	270,000	160,000
Prepaid rent	15,000	16,000
Total current assets	693,000	382,000
Equipment, net	280,000	260,000
Total assets	$973,000	$642,000
Total current liabilities	$306,000	$223,000
Long-term liabilities	219,000	117,000
Total liabilities	525,000	340,000
Common shares	150,000	90,000
Retained earnings	298,000	212,000
Total liabilities and shareholders' equity	$973,000	$642,000

Net income for the year ended June 30, 2008 was $80,000.

Required: Compute as many of the financial statement ratios you have studied as possible with the information from Reese Company. Do you want to invest in Reese Company? What else do you want to know to help you evaluate the company?

Problems—Set B

P11-1B Each of the following items was found on the financial statements for Logan Company for the year ended December 31, 2004:

L.O. 1

Loss from operation of discontinued segment, net of taxes of $2,500	$ (32,500)
Loss from sale of discontinued segment	(136,500)
Taxes saved from the loss on the sale of discontinued segment	14,000
Extraordinary loss from earthquake	(140,000)

Required: For each item, give the financial statement and section and where the item would appear. Explain what the item is, and give as many details of each item's financial statement presentation as you can.

P11-2B The following income statements are from the annual report of Gildan Activewear:

L.O. 2, 3

		Years ended	
(In Canadian Dollars)	October 5, 2003	September 29, 2002	September 30, 2001
Sales	$630,139,018	$600,660,380	$504,867,353
Cost of sales (Note 10)	440,293,451	431,996,459	398,566,740
Gross profit	189,845,567	168,663,921	106,300,613
Selling, general, and administrative expenses (Note 10)	71,153,448	63,926,673	76,074,745
Earnings before the undernoted items	118,692,119	104,737,248	30,225,868
Depreciation and amortization (Note 10)	23,614,704	17,591,885	16,208,560
Interest	9,463,475	13,341,823	13,628,350
	33,078,179	30,933,708	29,836,910
Earnings before income taxes	85,613,940	73,803,540	388,958
Income taxes (recovery) (Note 9)	8,342,000	7,312,000	(427,000)
Net earnings	$77,271,940	$66,491,540	$815,958

Required:

a. Calculate the gross margin percentage and the times interest earned ratio for each of the years given. Explain what the ratios tell you about the company's performance.
b. By using 2001 as the base year, prepare a horizontal analysis for operating income, income before taxes, and net income. What information does this analysis give you?

P11-3B The financial statements of Compass Company contained the following:

L.O. 1

	At December 31		
(Thousands of dollars)	2005	2004	2003
Cash and cash equivalents	$ 19,380	$ 21,866	
Accounts receivable, less allowance	35,640	32,232	
Total current assets	187,899	194,731	
Total assets	433,123	427,784	$395,981
Total current liabilities	73,612	63,310	
Total liabilities	118,803	162,350	175,688
Common shares—$0.01 par value	296	294	
Contributed surplus	262,462	257,684	
Retained earnings	85,312	17,896	
Net sales for the year	679,321	571,838	
Cost of goods sold	363,746	323,600	

Required:

1. Calculate the following ratios for Compass Company for 2005 and 2004:
   a. current ratio
   b. acid-test ratio
   c. working capital
   d. inventory turnover ratio
   e. accounts receivable turnover ratio
2. Suppose the changes from 2004 to 2005 in each of these ratios were consistent with the direction and size of the change for the past several years. For each ratio, explain what the trend in the ratio would indicate about Compass Company.

L.O. 3

P11-4B The following information was taken from the annual report of ROM, Inc.:

	At December 31	
(In thousands)	**2005**	**2004**
Assets		
Current assets		
Cash	$ 1,220	
Accounts receivable	3,112	
Merchandise inventory	966	
Prepaid expenses	149	
Total current assets	$ 5,447	
Plant and equipment		
Buildings, net	$ 2,992	
Equipment, net	1,045	
Total plant and equipment	$ 4,037	
Total assets	$ 9,484	$8,980
Liabilities		
Current liabilities		
Accounts payable	$ 1,685	
Notes payable	1,100	
Total current liabilities	$ 2,785	
Long-term liabilities	2,000	
Total liabilities	$ 4,785	$4,535
Shareholders' equity		
Common shares	$ 3,042	
Retained earnings	1,657	
Total shareholders' equity	$ 4,699	$4,445
Total liabilities and shareholders' equity	$ 9,484	$8,980
Sales for the year	$10,200	
Cost of goods sold	6,750	

Required: Calculate the following ratios for the year ended December 31, 2005:

1. return on equity
2. debt to equity
3. gross profit percentage
4. current ratio
5. acid-test ratio

What interpretation can you give this set of ratios for ROM, Inc? What additional information would help you?

P11-5B The financial statements of Builder Bob's, Inc. include the following items: L.O. 3

	At September 30, 2008	At September 30, 2007
Balance sheet		
Cash	$ 27,000	$ 22,000
Investments (in trading securities)	15,000	12,000
Accounts receivable (net)	44,000	40,000
Inventory	85,000	75,000
Prepaid rent	6,000	2,000
Total current assets	$177,000	$151,000
Total current liabilities	$120,000	$ 80,000
Income statement for the year ended September 30, 2008		
Credit sales	$320,000	
Cost of goods sold	$150,000	

Required:

1. Compute the following ratios for the year ended September 30, 2008, and September 30, 2007. For each, indicate whether the direction is favourable or unfavourable for the company.
   a. current ratio
   b. quick ratio
   c. accounts receivable turnover (for 2008 only)
   d. inventory turnover ratio (for 2008 only)
   e. gross margin percentage (of sales) (for 2005 only)
2. Which financial statement users would be most interested in these ratios?
3. Suppose the industry average for similar retail stores for the current ratio is 1.2. Does this information help you evaluate Builder Bob's liquidity?

P11-6B You are interested in investing in Apples and Nuts Company, and you have obtained the balance sheets for the company for the past two years. L.O. 3

Apples and Nuts Company
Balance Sheet
December 31, 2006 and 2005

	2006	2005
Current assets		
Cash	$ 98,000	$ 90,000
Accounts receivable, net	310,000	216,000
Inventory	275,000	170,000
Prepaid rent	10,000	6,000
Total current assets	693,000	482,000
Equipment, net	180,000	258,000
Total assets	$873,000	$740,000
Total current liabilities	$206,000	$223,000
Long-term liabilities	219,000	217,000
Total liabilities	425,000	440,000
Common shares	250,000	190,000
Retained earnings	198,000	110,000
Total liabilities and shareholders' equity	$873,000	$740,000

Note: Net income for the year ended December 31, 2006 was $100,000.

Required: Compute as many of the financial statement ratios you have studied as possible with the information from Apples and Nuts Company. Do you want to invest in this company? What else do you want to know to help you evaluate the company?

Issues for Discussion

Financial statement analysis

L.O. 3

1. Use the CoolBrands financial statements to compute for the two most recent years all the ratios given in Exhibit 11–6. Comment on what your analysis reveals.

Business risk

2. Which financial ratios give you information about the riskiness of investing in a company? Comment on those ratios from CoolBrands, which you computed in the preceding item.

Ethics

3. Atlantis Company sells computer components and plans on borrowing some money to expand. After reading a lot about earnings management, Andy, the owner of Atlantis, has decided he should try to accelerate some sales to improve his financial statement ratios. He has called his best customers and asked them to make their usual January purchases by December 31. He has told them he would allow them until the end of February to pay for the purchases, just as if they had made their purchases in January.
   a. What do you think are the ethical implications of Andy's actions?
   b. Which ratios will be improved by accelerating these sales?

Internet Exercise: Papa John's International, Inc.

Papa John's has surpassed Little Caesar to become the number three pizza chain, behind only number one, Pizza Hut, and number two, Domino's. Papa John's 2,800 restaurants (about 75 percent are franchised) are scattered across the United States and 10 other countries. Let us examine how Papa John's compares with its competition.

IE11-1 Go to Papa John's website, http://www.papajohns.com/, and explore "Papa John's Story" and "Our Pizza Story." What differentiates Papa John's from its competition?

IE11-2 Go to http://moneycentral.msn.com and get the stock "Quote" for PZZA, the stock symbol of Papa John's International. Identify the current price-to-earnings ratio and dividend yield. What do these market indicators mean for Papa John's?

IE11-3 Select "Financial Results" and then "Key Ratios."

a. Select "Financial Condition." Identify the current ratio and quick (acid-test) ratio for Papa John's and the industry. Who would find these ratios of primary interest? Identify the debt-to-equity ratio and interest coverage (another name for the times interest earned ratio) for Papa John's and the industry. Is Papa John's primarily financed by debt or equity? How can you tell? Does Papa John's have the ability to pay its interest obligations? Explain why or why not.
b. Select "Investment Returns." Identify return on equity and return on assets for Papa John's and the industry. What do these ratios measure?
c. Select "Ten-Year Summary." Review the information provided for return on equity and return on assets. What additional information is revealed about Papa John's financial position? Is this information helpful?

IE11-4 Review the information recorded earlier. Does Papa John's compare favourably with industry averages? Support your judgment with at least two observations.

Please note: Internet websites are constantly being updated. Therefore, if the information is not found where indicated, please explore the website further to find the information.

Appendix A

Annual Report of CoolBrands International

(In thousands of dollars, except share data)

Selected Financial Data

Year Ending	8/31/03	8/31/02	% Change
Revenues	357,273	242,222	47
Net Earnings	31,704	20,984	51
Earnings Per Share - Basic	0.61	0.44	39
Earnings Per Share - Diluted	0.59	0.42	40
EBITDA	58,575	40,064	46
Return On Average Shareholders' Equity	17.7%	13.8%	28
Price/Earnings (P/E) Ratio	29.7	17.6	69
Weighted Average Number Of Shares Outstanding	51,746	48,050	8
Working Capital	85,734	57,354	49
Total Assets	313,850	283,662	11

Table of Contents

1 Introduction
2 Shareholder Letter
4 5 Point Strategic Plan
6 Better For You
10 Super Premium
12 Classic Brands
14 Direct Store Delivery
16 Franchise Operations
18 Manufacturing
21 Management's Discussion & Analysis
25 Auditors' Report
26 Consolidated Financial Statements
Inside Back Cover Directors and Officers
Corporate Information
Manufacturing Plants

INTRODUCTION

Better for You

Ice cream is the food more people want to eat more of than any other. The best way to increase consumer purchases in today's growing health-conscious environment is to make products that combine the rich, creamy flavor people love with "healthy lifestyle" benefits. That is why *Better for You* frozen desserts form the fastest-growing segment in the ice cream category.

CoolBrands International is the leader in *Better for You* frozen desserts, a position that has helped make us the fastest-growing ice cream company and one of the overall category leaders in the United States. Last year we launched a new five point growth strategy to make CoolBrands *Better for You*, our shareholders, by targeting strategic opportunities for vertical integration and expanded market penetration to increase profitability and create new revenue streams.

In the very first year of implementing our plan, we made dramatic progress. We now have three new *Super Premium* brands, a direct-store-delivery (DSD) distribution network that reaches retailers' shelves at sales outlets across America, new franchise offerings that promise renewed growth in that high-margin segment, and new production capabilities that enhance our ability to innovate and grow sales and profits.

Our goal is to make CoolBrands *Better for You* – better for each retailer and franchisee, for each consumer to whom they sell our products and, thereby, better for each of you, our shareholders. In 2003, we made great strides toward that goal. And we enter 2004 fully committed to advance on our goal more rapidly than ever.

Dear Fellow Shareholders,

CoolBrands International had an outstanding 2003. We achieved unprecedented growth, realizing the highest revenues and earnings in our history. Despite an uncertain economy in which many companies struggled, we continued to be one of the fastest-growing companies in any industry. Most important, our achievements in 2003 set the stage for continued success in 2004 and beyond.

Financial Highlights

Our financial results for 2003 demonstrate the soundness of our strategy and its execution.

Revenues increased by 47% to $357.3 million, primarily driven by increased sales of our prepackaged consumer products. In fact, 2003 saw the most aggressive program of new product introductions and distribution gains in our history.

Net earnings increased by 51% to $31.7 million. Earnings per share increased by double digits each quarter for the third year in a row and finished the year up 40%.

Cash flow from operating activities before changes in working capital increased by 44% to a very robust $40 million, which was sufficient to provide internal funding for the increases in working capital, mainly increased receivables and inventory related to our fourth quarter acquisitions.

Selling, general and administrative expenses declined as a percentage of total revenues to 26.6% from 32% last year, reflecting diligent cost management during our rapid growth.

Our balance sheet, always strong, grew even stronger, as current assets to liabilities increased by a ratio of 2.1 to 1.

These outstanding results were the work of a talented and committed team of managers, a strong business model and a focused strategy, all of which we will bring to bear on the even greater opportunities that are before us in 2004.

Better Positioned For Growth

In 2004, there remain three keys to continued growth for CoolBrands: great brands, great products and great distribution. Going into 2004, we are stronger on each count than ever before.

Atkins® Endulge™ joins our brand portfolio as a significant addition to our already category-leading lineup of *Better for You* frozen desserts. Atkins is far and away the leading brand for foods intended for "low carb" dieting, the fastest-growing approach to losing weight. And our new Atkins Endulge *Super Premium* ice cream pints and frozen novelties promise to secure leading market share for CoolBrands in an important new *Better for You* segment.

The addition of **Dreamery®** Ice Cream, **Whole Fruit™** Sorbet, and **Godiva®** ice cream – three brands that account for approximately 25% of all *Super Premium* pints sold in U.S. supermarkets – establishes CoolBrands as one of just three major competitors in the *Super Premium* segment. Together with Atkins

Endulge pints, these brands give CoolBrands the most varied and effectively segmented lineup of *Super Premium* frozen desserts.

Eskimo Pie Frozen Distribution, our new name for the direct-store-delivery (DSD) distribution system acquired from Nestlé, dramatically enhances our control over downstream distribution of our products. DSD enables us to keep the optimal flavor assortment in stock at all times in each store to maximize sales. DSD also increases our speed to market with new products and the market penetration of all our brands. And, as one of only two major DSD systems operating in most of the major markets coast to coast, Eskimo Pie Frozen Distribution creates a new revenue stream from the distribution of our partner brands, such as Unilever and M&M/Mars, who have chosen us to take their products to market in many areas. Finally, DSD gives us direct access to the out-of-home distribution channel, which includes convenience stores, gas stations and other difficult-to-reach points of sale.

Americana Foods provides us with the capability to produce high quality, innovative products using state-of-the-art manufacturing technology and develop our brands in ways that competitors will find hard to duplicate. Americana Foods also creates a new revenue stream from the manufacture of products for our partner brands and private label products for retailers.

Tropicana Smoothies, Juices and More!, our exciting new franchising concept, promises renewed growth in the high-margin franchising and licensing segment.

We reaped great rewards in 2003 from our work in previous years establishing leading brands with high-margin products. We also laid the foundation – in particular, through the addition of the license for Atkins Endulge and the acquisitions of Americana Foods, the Dreamery, Godiva Ice Cream and Whole Fruit Sorbet brands and our new DSD distribution system – for continued increases to our revenue and profit-producing potential as we go forward.

David J. Stein
President, Co-CEO and Director
of CoolBrands International Inc.

Chief Operating Officer & Director David M. Smith (left) and President, Co-CEO & Director David J. Stein (right) proudly display many of CoolBrand's exciting new and existing products.

A Better Approach to Increasing Value

In 2002, CoolBrands International saw an emerging opportunity to capture superior returns for our shareholders. We launched a 5 Point Strategic Plan to seize that opportunity. During 2003, as we implemented our plan, we made remarkable progress toward achieving our goal of becoming a dynamic and highly profitable contender in the global frozen dessert industry.

CoolBrand's 5 Point Strategic Plan

Our plan focuses on establishing a franchise with consumers based on brand superiority in high-growth segments of the ice cream category, then organizing and diversifying to maximize profits through vertical integration of manufacturing and distribution operations. This is our blueprint for capturing increasing market share and generating higher profitability than almost every other company in our industry.

1. Control a portfolio of powerful brands that command leading market shares in key high-growth segments.

Accomplished in 2003: Continued growth of Weight Watchers® - Acquisition of Dreamery® and Whole Fruit™ and the license for Godiva® Ice Cream – Licensed Atkins® Endulge™ for low-carbohydrate frozen desserts.

The engine that powers CoolBrands is our portfolio of high-performance brands, each one commanding the brand strength and selling power to be the segment leader.

Today our brands include some of the world's most respected names in consumer products, among them:

- **Weight Watchers** - The worldwide leader in weight management.
- **Atkins Endulge** - The creator of the "low-carb" lifestyle.
- **Tropicana**® - The best-selling fresh juice brand.
- **Eskimo Pie**® - The pioneer in no-sugar-added frozen desserts.
- **Godiva** - The world's best chocolate, now the best chocolate ice cream.
- **Whole Fruit** - The U.S. leader in fruit sorbet in pints and bars.
- **Dreamery** - The flavor innovator in *Super Premium* ice cream.
- **Yoplait**® - The leading brand for nutritious, indulgent, great-tasting yogurt.

2. Control risk and maximize growth through diversification across every major product category and distribution channel.

Accomplished in 2003: Extended Weight Watchers into the foodservice channel – Launched Tropicana in the franchising segment – Finalized plans to introduce Yoplait in the frozen breakfast category.

CoolBrands is quickly making inroads in food-service and out-of-home channels with fresh initiatives that leverage our brand strength in new ways. Weight Watchers Nonfat Soft Serve Ice Cream now delivers rich, creamy flavor with only 1 FlexPoint® per serving in foodservice outlets: cafeterias, theme parks, and other out-of-home venues.

Anchored by one of the most powerful food brands anywhere, our new Tropicana Smoothies, Juices & More! offering is drawing new franchise investors. Yoplait Frozen Breakfast Bars and Sandwiches will offer a breakthrough solution to the age-old search for a complete and truly convenient nutritious break-fast *that kids will eat*.

5 POINT STRATEGIC PLAN

3. Control quality and costs through vertical integration while capturing additional revenue and profit from related operations.

Accomplished in 2003: Acquisitions of Americana Foods and Nestlé's DSD distribution system.

CoolBrands captures more profit from a wider range of related operations than any other ice cream company. Two major acquisitions in 2003 made CoolBrands even more vertically integrated.

Americana Foods, one of the largest, best-equipped production facilities in the U.S., brings us state-of-the-art technology for making a wider variety of innovative, value-added ice cream products than ever before, including extruded novelty forms that consumers increasingly prefer.

Eskimo Pie Frozen Distribution, the former Haagen-Däzs® distribution system, is the second-largest full-service DSD ice cream distribution network in the U.S. With access to all distribution channels – supermarkets, club stores, convenience stores, drug stores and foodservice outlets – CoolBrands now can deliver our products and partner brand products directly to retailers' shelves.

With our other vertically integrated operations – **Value America** Flavors & Ingredients, **Sam-Pak** Flexible Packaging and **Eskimo Pie Foodservice** – CoolBrands captures profits often left for third-party distributors and creates new revenue streams by manufacturing and distributing partner brand products. Most importantly, CoolBrands now has the highest measure of control over product manufacture and distribution, helping to ensure that our brands realize full sales potential.

4. Control unique production capacity that will enable us to manufacture the innovative, value-added products that drive our brands.

Accomplished in 2003: Dramatically enhanced R&D capabilities - Developed innovative manufacturing technologies to improve quality and efficiency – Expanded total production capacity to facilitate growth.

Our technical teams at Americana Foods and Value America developed state-of-the-art R&D and custom manufacturing methods, allowing us to formulate new products including Weight Watchers Giant Sundae Cones and Giant Cookies & Cream Bars, already big hits with consumers. These new products are real breakthroughs in the art and science of making deliciously indulgent yet good for you frozen treats. We are expanding plant capacity substantially to make Americana Foods capable of making every variety of frozen dessert product.

5. Control the downstream distribution of our products.

Accomplished in 2003: Marketwide coverage of all distribution channels in U.S. major markets.

With a rapidly consolidating industry and warehouse distributors (including those operated by chain retailers) increasingly taxed for space to handle an ever-growing number of frozen food products, direct control over the distribution pipeline is critical to build market share and profitability.

CoolBrands now controls one of just two major DSD systems in the U.S. This acquisition gives us access to out-of-home retail outlets (where the majority of all frozen treats are purchased each year) and offers our new ice cream products a significant advantage in reaching store shelves. CoolBrands is positioned to use this advantage to drive growth for our brands and partner brands using our DSD system.

Our vision at CoolBrands International is to be the premier innovator in the global frozen desserts industry. Our portfolio of leading brands and expanding range of capabilities and revenue streams manifest this vision. We have come so far in so short a time. As the pages that follow make clear, we are moving forward faster than ever before.

Better Choices for Healthier Lifestyles

The *Better for You* segment of the ice cream category is by far the fastest-growing, increasing at an annual rate of more than 30% in recent years. That makes the *Better for You* segment the greatest area of opportunity in our industry. And no other ice cream company has seized this opportunity more successfully than CoolBrands.

CoolBrands is the leader in *Better for You* frozen treats. In 2003, we commanded 26% of the market, beating the closest competitor by 5 share points. We pioneered this segment with Eskimo Pie No Sugar Added frozen treats, and we have continued to lead the way with our complete lineup of Weight Watchers® Smart Ones® frozen dessert products.

The Weight Watchers® Smart Ones® Phenomenon

Weight Watchers is the world's leading weight management system. More people around the world turn to Weight Watchers than to any other system for help in achieving a lifestyle that helps them stay fit and healthy. The ranks of loyal Weight Watchers followers are vast and growing dramatically every year. They have helped make Weight Watchers Smart Ones the growth leader in the ice cream category in each of the last two years. Our success in satisfying the needs of Weight Watchers members (and an even larger number of consumers who have never attended a Weight Watchers classroom session) is driven by our products: deliciously decadent frozen treats that offer fat-free and low-fat snacking options with only 2 FlexPoints or less in each truly *giant* serving size.

In 2002, Weight Watchers Smart Ones Giant Round Ice Cream Sandwiches were the best-selling new frozen treat in the entire category. Weight Watchers Smart Ones Giant Sundae Cones achieved the same feat in 2003, leading every other new product introduction. These category leaders, together with Weight Watchers Smart Ones Giant Sundae Cups and Giant Fudge Bars, have established Weight Watchers as the leader for low-fat and fat-free frozen treats that are *Better for You*.

In 2004, CoolBrands is adding two new Weight Watchers Smart Ones Giant frozen treats to retailers' shelves: Giant Cookies & Cream Bars, loaded with delicious chocolate cookies on the inside and outside; and Peanut Butter Fudge Giant Sundae Cones, creamy peanut butter ice cream with luscious chocolate fudge and chocolate chips inside a crunchy cone, and each, incredibly, has only 2 FlexPoints. With these new offerings from CoolBrands, things keep getting better and better for the millions of consumers managing their weight by watching their intake of fat and calories, especially those using Weight Watchers FlexPoints as their guide. But, as we all know, what works for one group may not meet the needs of another. And in the world of weight management, new ideas for healthier eating are always news...

The Atkins® Revolution

Better for You means many different things to the wide cross-section of consumers striving to eat – and snack – in better, healthier ways. And CoolBrands is keeping up with the latest trends in the *Better for You* segment.

Millions of consumers around the world have embraced the Atkins Nutritional Approach™, an alternative nutritional plan for weight control developed by Dr. Robert C. Atkins. In 2003, Atkins spurred a virtual revolution in consumer attitudes toward healthy dieting, producing shock waves that have affected almost every company in the food industry.

Unlike plans that stress the need to reduce the dietary intake of fat and calories, the Atkins Nutritional Approach focuses instead on controlling carbohydrate intake, with a minimal allowable amount of fats. The switch in emphasis from controlling fat and calories to controlling carbohydrates profoundly changes - for consumers who subscribe to the Atkins Nutritional Approach - the types of foods one may eat while following the plan.

These changes are especially dramatic for dessert options, allowing an even richer, creamier texture and fuller flavor. Our new lineup of Atkins® Endulge™ Super Premium Ice Cream is deliciously indulgent proof of this. *Better for You* has never been better tasting than with Atkins Endulge.

Atkins Endulge Super Premium Ice Cream has the rich, indulgent flavor and texture consumers expect in a *Super Premium* ice cream. Yet each serving contains 3 or fewer net carbs (carbohydrates affecting blood sugar levels). For those living a low-carb lifestyle, it's a fabulous new treat that meets their nutritional needs. For consumers watching their weight or just trying to eat healthier, it's one choice that lets them have it all.

Atkins Endulge is available in eight indulgent flavors in pints:

- Vanilla
- Chocolate
- Butter Pecan
- Chocolate Peanut Butter Swirl
- Mint Chocolate Chip
- Swiss Chocolate Almond
- Chocolate Fudge Brownie
- Vanilla Fudge Swirl

Atkins Endulge also comes in seven outrageous ice cream bar varieties:

- Vanilla with Milk Chocolate Coating
- Chocolate Fudge Swirl with Dark Chocolate Coating
- Peanut Butter Swirl with Dark Chocolate Coating
- Caramel Turtle Sundae with Dark Chocolate Coating
- Butter Pecan with Dark Chocolate Coating
- Vanilla Fudge Swirl with Dark Chocolate Coating
- Chocolate Fudge Bar

Atkins Endulge Super Pre-mium Ice Cream first reached freezer shelves at supermarkets, club stores, and natural food stores following the end of fiscal 2003. Early indications are that the brand could approach the top of the category in record time. For CoolBrands, Atkins Endulge is the latest in a long line of successes in keeping pace with the rapidly changing tastes and preferences of consumers looking for *Better for You* frozen treats, which started with our flagship brand, Eskimo Pie®.

Eskimo Pie® No Sugar Added

Eskimo Pie® No Sugar Added was the first success on the *Better for You* frontier, combining the legendary flavor of the Eskimo Pie chocolate-coated ice cream bar with the benefits of reduced fat content and no added sugar. We succeeded in launching the no-sugar-added frozen novelty segment by offering a *Better for You* treat that did not compromise on flavor. That formula for success has never changed.

And Eskimo Pie, the first national ice cream brand in *Better for You* is still going strong, with new line extensions that enhance the brand's franchise with consumers of no-sugar-added products. In 2003, we introduced Eskimo Pie Slender Pie™ No Sugar Added Round Ice Cream Sandwiches in three enticing flavors, scoring solid success in supermarkets across the U.S. We are following up in 2004 by introducing Eskimo Pie No Sugar Added Cookies & Cream Ice Cream Bars, the first-ever cookies & cream bars made with no sugar added. They're loaded with chocolate cookies and the "no compromise" flavor that has long made Eskimo Pie the leader in no-sugar-added frozen treats.

Better for You for Breakfast

Yogurt is a core product for consumers of *Better for You* foods, and the No. 1 brand of yogurt in the U.S. is **Yoplait**®. Yoplait became number one by combining the healthy goodness of yogurt and it's creamy, indulgent taste and texture with an innovative approach to bringing more consumers – especially kids – into the market with breakthrough products like Yoplait® Go-GURT®. CoolBrands is poised to continue the line of Yoplait breakthroughs with Yoplait Frozen Breakfast Bars and Sandwiches, the first-ever frozen breakfast novelties. They combine the complete, wholesome nutrition of a bowl of vitamin-fortified cereal, fruit and yogurt in a frozen novelty. They're complete, balanced breakfasts in a sandwich or on a stick for "on the go" convenience. Best of all, because they're frozen treats like ice creams bars or sandwiches, but pack the vitamin-fortified goodness of yogurt, fruit and cereal, they're healthy breakfasts that *kids will really eat*. Yoplait Frozen Breakfast Bars and Sandwiches will first hit supermarkets in the Baltimore-Washington D.C. area in February 2004. Another *Better for You* breakthrough for Yoplait . . . and CoolBrands!

Naturally Better for You

Better for You frozen snacks include frozen fruit bars that offer great fruit flavor and nutrition in a naturally fat-free, nondairy treat. In **Tropicana**® and **Welch's**®, our portfolio includes two of the world's outstanding brands for fruit juice – brands that surpass in consumer appeal any competitor in the ice cream category.

Brand power like that has helped us make Welch's Fruit Juice Bars a winner in supermarkets across the U.S. and Tropicana frozen treats a success in the U.S., Canada, France, Belgium and the United Kingdom.

CoolBrands topped off the year with the addition of **Whole Fruit**™ Sorbet in pints to our family of fruit based *Better for You* frozen treats. Whole Fruit - one of three *Super Premium* brands divested to CoolBrands by Dreyer's in connection with the merger of Dreyer's and Nestlé – uniquely combines the hallmark *Better for You* benefits of fat-free and nondairy with *Super Premium* quality and value perception. Whole Fruit dominates the sorbet segment in supermarkets, leading such brands as Haagen-Däzs in total sales by better than 2 to 1. The presence of Whole Fruit Sorbet in our portfolio points to the next focal point of brand strength for CoolBrands.

GODIVA
BELGIAN
DARK
CHOCOLATE
DREAMERY

The Best, with No Compromises

The *Super Premium* segment is second only to *Better for You* in annual rate of growth. In the past year, we became one of only three major *Super Premium* competitors by acquiring from Dreyer's the Dreamery® Ice Cream and Whole Fruit™ Sorbet brands, and the license for Godiva® Ice Cream from Godiva Chocolatier. These brands combine to account for 25% of all *Super Premium* pints sold in U.S. Supermarkets.

The simultaneous growth in the *Better for You* and *Super Premium* segments demonstrates the importance of market segmentation and the need to focus on satisfying the diverse preferences of distinct groups of consumers. CoolBrands is focused on seizing opportunities in emerging growth segments. That's how we've grown so quickly: by staying firmly on trend.

Today, people are working harder and for longer hours than ever before. Millions of these consumers prefer to spend their precious time and hard-earned money on nothing but the best, from gourmet coffee to fine wines and chocolates. And for such consumers, ice cream is no place to compromise.

CoolBrands enters 2004 with a complement of superbrands to drive sales of *Super Premium* ice cream and sorbet to these demanding consumers.

Superbrands in Super Premium

Each of our superbrands speaks to a distinct sub-segment of the overall *Super Premium* market. **Dreamery**® Ice Cream, ranked the best vanilla ice cream on the market,* is known to consumers as a flavor innovator, helping to expand segment sales with unique flavors like Coney Island Waffle Cone,™ Black Raspberry Avalanche and Chocolate Truffle Explosion. New innovations in 2004 include Hot Fudge Sundae, Give Me S'Mores and Blue Ribbon Berry Pie.

For many consumers, ice cream and chocolate are the most desirable foods. And **Godiva**®, maker of the world's finest chocolate, is now also rated the best chocolate ice cream.* Godiva Belgian Dark Chocolate Ice Cream is the best-selling chocolate ice cream in U.S. supermarkets and anchors a lineup of sophisticated chocolate-inspired flavors (including, new for 2004, Chocolate Covered Cookies & Cream) that outclasses any other *Super Premium* brand.

Super Premium and Better for You Brands

The best and the best for you. Imagine the ultimate in guilt-free indulgence: *Super Premium* frozen treats that deliver *Better for You* benefits. That's the unique positioning of **Atkins**® **Endulge**™ *Super Premium* ice cream and **Whole Fruit**™ Sorbet.

With Atkins Endulge *Super Premium* ice cream (with only 3 net carbs per serving) and Whole Fruit *Super Premium* fat-free and nondairy sorbet, in refreshingly cool flavors filled with luscious chunks of real mangoes, blueberries, boysenberries, peaches, strawberries and raspberries, CoolBrands is zeroing in on a new growth segment that taps the twin energies of the *Better for You* and *Super Premium* segments. And that's what consumers have come to expect from CoolBrands: leading the way through innovation and a commitment to excellence.

* *Consumer Reports Magazine, June 2003.*

Chipwich
ESKIMO PIE
The Original
Chipwich

CLASSIC BRANDS

Better Brands for More Choices

More than ever before, today's busy shoppers favor brands they know and trust. When consumers select frozen treats for themselves and their families, they look for products they know will meet their taste expectations and quality standards. They rely on brands that do not disappoint. That's why brands are so important, and why our brands are second to none.

Every CoolBrands product whether new or a time-tested favorite is made to live up to the expectations inspired by the brand name it bears. Each of our brands speaks uniquely to an important market segment, and each product must be true to – and carry forward – that priceless brand heritage. It all began years ago with Eskimo Pie.

Eskimo Pie® - An American Original

In 1920 Christian K. Nelson, owner of a confectionery store in Iowa, created a new ice cream treat by coating ice cream with chocolate. The next year, he and chocolate maker Russell C. Stover gave it an improved chocolate coating. They named it "Eskimo Pie," and the frozen novelty industry was born.

More than 80 years later, Eskimo Pie remains one of the best loved and most widely distributed ice cream novelties. Eskimo Pie is still pleasing consumers with a growing line of *Better for You* and traditional frozen treats. Eskimo Pie No Sugar Added frozen treats still set the pace in a growing segment that satisfies rising numbers of diabetic consumers and others moderating their sugar intake.

In 2004 we'll introduce an entirely new line of premium ice cream novelties for supermarket and club stores, including traditional favorites such as Strawberry Shortcake Bars, Chocolate Eclairs and Toasted Almond Bars made for the first time using extrusion technology, and classics such as Premium Vanilla Ice Cream Bars covered with Milk Chocolate, and even a new Premium No Sugar Added Reduced Fat Vanilla Ice Cream Bar covered with Dark Chocolate. Better yet, we're also launching a whole new line of single-serve Eskimo Pie frozen treats, including new premium flavors, packaged for out-of-home consumption and for distribution through convenience stores, gas station food marts, drug stores and other small-format food retailers.

Chipwich® - First and Still the Best

Before the invention of the Chipwich® sandwich, ice cream novelties – though consumed by people of all ages – were made mainly with children in mind. Chipwich changed things forever in 1981 by sandwiching premium vanilla ice cream between two gourmet chocolate chip cookies and then rolling it in pure chocolate chips, creating the first frozen treat good enough to satisfy the most discriminating tastes among adults and children. It was so good that Chipwich created a phenomenon. Since then, adults and kids alike around the world have purchased more than a billion Chipwich sandwiches.

Smart Ones
GIANT SUNDAE CONES
VANILLA FUDGE
Smart Ones
GIANT SUNDAE CONES
CHOCOLATE FUDGE
95% FAT FREE
Smart Ones
GIANT COOKIES & CREAM
Smart Ones
GIANT FUDGE BARS
Smart Ones
REDUCED FAT ICE CREAM
GODIVA
DREAMERY
RASPBERRY
BOYSENBERRY
STRAWBERRY
Chipwich

Better Distribution for Better Brands

Industry consolidation is making direct control over the downstream distribution of our products more critical than ever. In many channels of distribution, this control can make the difference between getting on the shelf or getting locked out, especially in the many thousands of smaller format retail outlets such as convenience stores, gas station food marts and corner delis in the out-of-home channel, where more than half of all frozen treats are purchased.

CoolBrand's newest subsidiary is one of the company's most promising developments of 2003.

Eskimo Pie Frozen Distribution operates one of only two major direct-store-delivery (DSD) ice cream distribution systems in the United States, with market coverage in California, Washington, Oregon, Utah, Minnesota, Florida, Georgia, Virginia, Maryland, Delaware, Pennsylvania, New Jersey, Connecticut, the District of Columbia and the Greater New York metropolitan area.

DSD service provides critical benefits that enhance the power of our brands:

- Increased speed to market for new products
- Improved market penetration for new and existing products
- Better in-stock performance and SKU management at store level
- Superior control over product quality throughout the distribution chain
- Enhanced merchandising and display-building capabilities
- Direct access to all potential purchasers throughout the market

With Eskimo Pie Frozen Distribution, CoolBrands now controls one of the two major DSD systems in the U.S. This operation opened new, unrestricted access to the out-of-home distribution channel. Delivering directly to these stores ensures that CoolBrands products are stocked in freezers all along consumers' daily routes.

Eskimo Pie Frozen Distribution also will achieve cost-savings and efficiencies that can't be counted on with third-party warehouse distributors. Growing numbers of frozen food products are being pushed to market through third-party distributors. Freezer space is at a premium and costs are rising. Delivering our own products means CoolBrands can count on the visibility needed for rising sales. Distribution agreements with partner brands like Unilever and M&M/Mars are bringing us new revenue streams and added profitability.

Most important, CoolBrands is now closer to complete vertical integration. With greater control over – and more profits related to – our products right up to the moment consumers take them off the shelf, we can be sure that consumers will buy more and more of our products.

Tropicana
SMOOTHIES, JUICES & MORE!
SMOOTHIES 16oz $4.25 24oz $5.25
STRAWBERRY SKINNY
CHERRY PINEBERRY
STRAWBAPPLE
PEACH APPLE
TRIBANA
NON-DAIRY SMOOTHIES 16oz $4.25 24oz $5.25
ORANGERIE
BIG BANG BERRY
RAZAPPLE
ANA-BANA-BERRY
PEACH BEACH
TROPICAL STORM
JUICES
16oz $2.50 24oz $2.95
Tropicana
SMOOTHIES

Better Brands for Better Franchises

We made significant strides in our franchising and licensing business in 2003, successfully testing the Tropicana® Smoothies, Juices & More! franchise concept in several markets prior to a full-scale launch in the U.S. and Canada in 2004.

Prevailing economic conditions favor expanded opportunities for franchise growth, and Cool-Brands is well positioned to capitalize on these opportunities. In 2004, our focus for Yogen Früz, Swensen's and Bresler's will be on developing new stores in Asia, Europe and the Middle East. In North America, however, we're turning on the juice . . .

Tropicana® Smoothies, Juices & More!

Tropicana Smoothies, Juices & More! is ready for rollout after extensive test marketing. In one test store after another, in a wide variety of markets and retail formats, Tropicana® Smoothies, Juices & More! has proven its strong revenue – generating and profit – returning potential. Full-scale launch in North America is planned to commence in 2004.

The Tropicana Smoothies, Juices & More! concept combines the peerless brand equity of Tropicana – the world's leading brand for premium chilled juices - with CoolBrands' expertise in developing franchise systems and retail store locations.

Yogen Früz®

International expansion of Yogen Früz franchises continued in 2003, with new store openings in Japan, Panama and Trinidad, while the brand maintained its position as the leading frozen yogurt brand in Canada.

Swensen's®

Swensen's Ice Cream was the first national ice cream parlor to serve a premium all-natural ice cream. Swensen's began in 1949 when Earle Swensen offered ice cream "as good as father used to make," and it's still enjoyed by customers around the world. Swensen's continued to demonstrate exceptional vitality in both the Pacific Rim and Middle East, with new store openings in China, Malaysia and Vietnam. Growth in the Middle East initiated in Kuwait, and additional areas are in negotiations.

Bresler's®

The Bresler's Ice Cream marquee is a magnet for anyone who loves the delicious taste of premium ice cream, frozen yogurt, sorbets and Italian ices. Founded during the Great Depression in the American Midwest, Bresler's remains one of America's premier ice cream brands.

I Can't Believe It's Yogurt®

I Can't Believe It's Yogurt pioneered the development of nonfat frozen yogurt and, in doing so, launched an entirely new market segment. Recognized as an industry leader in product innovation, ICBY was the first to develop complete product lines featuring fat-free frozen yogurt as well as fat-free, sugar-free frozen yogurt.

Better Technology for Better Brands & Products

CoolBrands has engineered custom techniques that make us one of the fastest, most efficient ice cream producers in the world. Our vertical integration in manufacturing ingredients, products and packaging allows CoolBrands to better control costs and quality while capturing added revenue and profit by serving other customers as well as CoolBrands products.

Our drive to be the premier innovator in the frozen dessert industry isn't limited to originality in consumer products and franchises. CoolBrands also leads the industry in developing new manufacturing technologies that help us improve efficiency and create products that satisfy the needs of consumers and our competitors find hard to duplicate.

Better Through Vertical Integration

Vertical integration enables us to control costs and quality and capture more of the total profit related to our brands. Our vertical supply chain operations – ingredient and packaging supply, finished goods manufacturing and DSD distribution – also create new profit centers from relationships with partner brands and elimination of non-essential vendors. Vertical integration is central both to our brand steward-ship and to our financial imperative to maximize profits.

Americana Foods

In 2003 CoolBrands acquired controlling interest in Americana Foods, substantially enhancing our manufacturing asset base. Americana Foods, as one of the largest and most versatile of all U.S. manufacturing facilities for frozen desserts, gave CoolBrands the additional production capacity we needed to support our rapid growth. It also augmented our technical resources – in particular, our ability to produce the extruded novelty forms increasingly desired by consumers – so that we could develop our brands in exciting new ways, as evidenced by our new products for 2004.

Americana Foods operates a sophisticated pilot plant with a fully operational R&D laboratory. This gives CoolBrands a unique ability to make trial test runs of new products and samples for evaluation without impacting normal production operations, that's a luxury not available to ordinary frozen dessert plants, and it helps CoolBrands in its drive to innovate our way to category leadership.

Value America

Value America is the premier expert in the development of new flavors, ingredients, coatings and bases used in dairy products. Throughout its 75-year history, Value America has earned its reputation for quality with every product, including proprietary blends and specialty formulations. For CoolBrands' latest generation of *Better for You* products, Value America has been instrumental in developing cutting-edge solutions for formulating the very best low-carb, fat-free and no-sugar-added frozen treats. Value America is a major supplier of best-in-class flavoring powders, eggnog and sherbet bases, fruit packs, purees and stabilizers. Its customers include the very largest dairy suppliers in the U.S.

Eskimo Pie Foodservice

If you're in soft-serve ice cream or frozen yogurt, there's a very high likelihood that Eskimo Pie Foodservice supplies the high quality flavors and mixes for the tastes your customers count on every time.

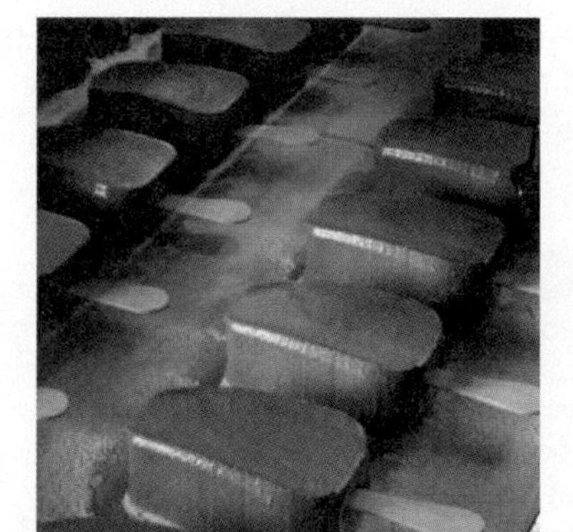

Eskimo Pie Foodservice supplies premium soft-serve mixes to customers throughout the foodservice industry all across America. We are the exclusive supplier of soft-serve mixes to some of the largest and most recognizable names in retailing and foodservice, including Sam's Club, Universal Studios, and many other leading operators throughout the United States.

Sam-Pak Flexible Packaging

In the increasingly competitive world of retail, the right packaging design is as important as the right product for the market. Impulse purchases depend heavily on what consumers see when they look in the freezer case, and what they see first isn't the product itself, it's the *packaging*. That's why Sam-Pak's expertise in creating food packaging *that sells* is so important.

Sam-Pak Flexible Packaging specializes in the design and high-speed printing and production of paper, film and foil wraps for foodservice operations, food and sterile goods manufacturers, and the pharmaceuticals industry. Sam-Pak's precision printing processes are ideal for single-portion food and pharmaceuticals flexible packaging, using the latest materials developed for light weight and durability. Sam-Pak has years of experience in the demands of regulatory agencies, just-in-time delivery, and the lightning-fast pace of retail. That experience translates into the ability to reduce industry standard turnaround times by up to 50%. Excellence in quality assurance has earned Sam-Pak the coveted *Superior* rating from the American Institute of Baking.

Ideas: the Key to Growth

Whether it's new production methods, innovative and changing novelty forms, new formulations, or ingenious ways to beat the retail clock, CoolBrands' vertically integrated production resources are fueled by our most important assets – *ideas*.

As a vigorous and innovative player in the retail marketplace, CoolBrands relies as much on ingenuity and bold new ideas as we do on the know-how to bring them to market. Without new products to power continuing growth, no company can reach its full potential.

Thanks to the people who make our manufacturing facilities *really* work, from the R&D technicians and their invaluable artistry to the indispensable men and women on bustling production lines, CoolBrands is becoming a dynamic and highly profitable contender, leading the industry to the edges of the frozen desserts frontiers and beyond.

(Tabular amounts are expressed in thousands of dollars)

Comparison of 2003 and 2002

We manage our business based on four industry segments: Prepackaged consumer products, foodservice, dairy components, and franchising and licensing.

Sales

Sales for each segment are summarized in the following table:

	Amount		Percentage of Sales	
Year Ended August 31,	2003	2002	2003	2002
	$	$	%	%
Prepackaged consumer products	255,197	156,691	76.2	66.4
Foodservice	25,243	25,067	7.5	10.6
Dairy components	38,651	34,610	11.5	14.7
Franchising and licensing	15,943	19,660	4.8	8.3
Total	335,034	236,028	100.0	100.0

Sales in fiscal 2003 increased by $99,006,000 or 41.9% from $236,028,000 in fiscal 2002 to $335,034,000. This increase was primarily related to an increase in sales of new prepackaged consumer products introduced for sale in fiscal 2003, expanded sales and distribution of our foodservice and dairy components products, sales generated by the brands and distribution assets acquired in July 2003 from Dreyer's Grand Ice Cream, Inc. and Nestlé and from the acquisition of 50.1% of Americana Foods LP which was effective July 1, 2003.

Gross profit margin

The following table presents the gross profit margin dollars by industry segment and gross profit percentage for each industry segment:

	Amount		Percentage of Sales	
Year Ended August 31,	2003	2002	2003	2002
	$	$	%	%
Prepackaged consumer products	104,594	83,030	41.0	53.0
Foodservice	9,898	10,297	39.2	41.1
Dairy components	8,921	7,135	23.1	20.6
Franchising and licensing	3,751	6,320	23.5	32.2
Total	127,164	106,782	38.0	45.2

Gross profit dollars increased to $127,164,000 in fiscal 2003 from $106,782,000 in fiscal 2002 due to the increased sales in 2003 versus 2002. However, the Company's overall gross profit percentage for fiscal 2003 decreased to 38% as compared with 45.2% for fiscal 2002, due to the impact of lower gross profit margins generated by Americana Foods' manufacturing operations and Eskimo Pie Frozen Distribution Inc's distribution operations. Franchising and licensing gross profit percentage for fiscal 2003 was adversely impacted by the losses of Company-owned stores.

(Tabular amounts are expressed in thousands of dollars)

Drayage and other income

Drayage and other income increased to $16,978,000 in fiscal 2003 from $1,007,000 in fiscal 2002 due to drayage fees received from Dreyer's/Nestlé for the delivery of their products to customers utilizing the Company's "Direct Store Delivery" (DSD) services.

Selling, general and administrative expenses

Selling, general and administrative expenses are summarized by industry segment in the following table:

	Amount		Percentage of Sales	
Year Ended August 31,	2003	2002	2003	2002
	$	$	%	%
Prepackaged consumer products	76,616	58,500	30.0	37.3
Foodservice	7,222	8,008	28.6	32.0
Dairy components	2,908	3,058	7.5	8.8
Franchising and licensing	6,639	6,981	41.6	35.5
Corporate	1,703	1,011	n/a	n/a
Total	95,088	77,558		

Selling, general and administrative expenses increased by $17,530,000 from $77,558,000 in 2002 to $95,088,000 in 2003 due primarily to the increase in selling, general and administrative expenses in the prepackaged consumer products' segment due to the increased level of sales. Prepackaged consumer products selling, general and administrative expenses increased as a result of increased spending on promotions, marketing and advertising and an increase in product introductory expenses (slotting) associated with the sale of new products introduced in 2003. The Company continues to control spending over selling, general and administrative expenses, such that prepackaged consumer products selling, general and administrative expenses declined as a percentage of sales to 30% in fiscal 2003 from 37.3% in fiscal 2002, and selling, general and administrative expenses as a percentage of total revenues declined to 26.6% in fiscal 2003 from 32% in fiscal 2002.

Interest expense

Interest expense was $1,990,000 in fiscal 2003 compared with $2,544,000 in fiscal 2002. The decrease in interest expense was primarily due to the reduction in long-term debt associated with the acquisitions of Eskimo Pie Corporation in 2001 and the assets of Fruit-A-Freeze in 2002. Interest expense will increase in fiscal 2004 as a result of the Company's fourth quarter acquisition of 50.1% of Americana Foods LP, which included U.S. $12,625,000 of secured term and revolver bank debt.

Provision for income taxes

The effective tax rate was 38.8% in fiscal 2003 and 36.2% for fiscal 2002. The effective tax rate differs from the Canadian Federal/Principal Statutory Rate primarily due to our operations in foreign countries with lower effective tax rates. Future effective tax rates could be adversely affected by earnings being lower than anticipated in countries that have lower statutory rates or changes in the valuation of our future income tax assets or liabilities.

Net earnings

Net earnings improved to $31,704,000 in 2003 as compared to $20,984,000 in 2002 and improved to 8.9% of total revenues in 2003 as compared to 8.7% of total revenues in 2002.

(Tabular amounts are expressed in thousands of dollars)

Liquidity and capital resources

Working capital at August 31, 2003 was $85,734,000 compared with $57,354,000 at August 31, 2002. The increase was primarily due to an increase in receivables of $17,806,000 and inventory of $30,243,000, offset by a decrease in cash of $16,946,000. The Company believes its working capital plus internally generated funds and the funds available from a U.S. $10 million revolving credit facility will be sufficient to meet its cash and working capital requirements for its established operations for the current fiscal year.

At August 31, 2003, the Company had $30,140,000 of cash and short-term investments as compared with $47,086,000 at August 31, 2002. The Company generated cash flow from operating activities before changes in working capital of $39,980,000 for the year ended August 31, 2003 as compared with $27,805,000 for the year ended August 31, 2002 due primarily to the increase in net earnings for 2003 as compared with 2002.

Payment requirements

In connection with the acquisition of Eskimo Pie Corporation, a U.S. subsidiary borrowed U.S. $30 million to finance the acquisition. The loan is payable in monthly installments of U.S. $250,000, which began December 1, 2000, with the remaining principal balance due on November 1, 2005. Interest on the term loan is payable monthly on the unpaid principal balance. All borrowings under the above loan agreement are guaranteed by the Company and all of its significant subsidiaries. The principal balance outstanding at August 31, 2003 was U.S. $16,250,000.

On November 19, 2002, Americana Foods LP, which is owned 50.1% by the Company, entered into a credit agreement with a financial institution that included a term loan of U.S. $10,000,000, which is secured by the Partnership's property, plant, and equipment. Principal payments are payable in fixed monthly installments of U.S. $80,739 and matures on November 19, 2007. The term of the loan bears interest at prime plus 0.5% (4.5% at August 31, 2003.)

The Partnership's credit agreement also included a revolving loan of up to U.S. $5 million, subject to a borrowing base calculation, which bears interest at prime plus 0.5% (4.5% at August 31, 2003) and is due on November 19, 2004. At August 31, 2003, approximately U.S. $2,031,000, was available to the partnership under this loan. The revolving loan is secured by the Partnership's receivables and inventory.

Impact of inflation

Inflation can significantly impact ice cream and frozen yogurt ingredients, including butterfat and packaging costs. In 2003 and 2002, the Company passed on ingredient, energy and freight cost increases by raising prices on selected product lines. In 2004, the Company believes that it will be able to pass on any cost increases, if any, in the normal course of business within a relatively short period of time. However, the ability of the Company to pass on cost increases will depend, to some extent, on whether its competitors have also done so. The Company believes that, in the past, its competitors have passed on cost increases in a relatively short period of time.

Risk factors and uncertainties

CoolBrands products are ultimately purchased by the global retail consumer, whose tastes and preferences are subject to variation and change. Although carefully monitored, these changes cannot be controlled and are difficult to predict. Management believes that CoolBrands' family of products is based on well established brand names and is easily adaptable to meet changes in consumer tastes and demands. CoolBrands operates in some countries that are subject to potential political and economic uncertainty. Such factors, beyond the control of CoolBrands, are lessened because of international diversification and the sharing of risks with Master and Sub-franchisees.

(Tabular amounts are expressed in thousands of dollars)

CoolBrands is subject to currency exchange risks since most of its subsidiaries report and transact in U.S. dollars. Risks are minimized by the subsidiaries transacting purchases and recording the related sales in the same currency. From time to time, the Company has also used forward exchange contracts to minimize exchange risk exposure.

The Corporation derives a substantial portion of its revenues from its operations in the United States. The U.S. market for frozen desserts is highly competitive. As competitors introduce new products or revise their supply or pricing strategies, the Corporation may encounter additional and more intense competition. Such competitors have greater name recognition and more extensive financial, technological, marketing and personnel resources than the Corporation. In addition, the Corporation may experience increased competition in its other markets as its competitors expand their international operations.

The Corporation is subject to risks with respect to its cost of raw materials, some of which are subject to changes in commodity prices, particularly the cost of butterfat, which is used to produce ice cream products. From time to time, the Corporation has used hedging contracts to reduce its exposure to such risks with respect to its raw material costs.

Seasonality

The ice cream and frozen yogurt industry generally experiences its highest volume during the spring and summer months and its lowest volume in the winter months.

Outlook

In the past year, the Company acted through acquisition, internal expansion and pursuit of new strategic relationships to promote future profitable growth. The Company added new brands to its portfolio, including Dreamery and Whole-Fruit acquired from Dreyer's Grand Ice Cream, Inc., and the Godiva ice cream license assigned to the Company from Dreyer's in the fourth quarter of fiscal 2003.

The Company also continued to increase its leverage and returns on its investment in brand equity through the vertical integration of our supply chain, including the acquisition from Nestlé of substantially all of the Haagen-Dazs frozen dessert direct store distribution assets in the U.S. and the acquisition of 50.1% of Americana Foods LP which owns one of the largest and most versatile frozen dessert manufacturing facilities in the U.S., both of which occurred in the fourth quarter of 2003.

Management believes that the gains in revenues and earnings realized in 2003 continued to build a foundation to support continued profitable growth in 2004. Management will continue to monitor and assess its systems, controls and personnel to execute the Company's growth strategy and maximize returns.

Auditors' Report

To the Shareholders of CoolBrands International Inc.:

We have audited the consolidated balance sheets of CoolBrands International Inc. as at August 31, 2003 and 2002 and the consolidated statements of earnings and retained earnings, and cash flows for the years then ended. These financial statements are the responsibility of the Company's management. Our responsibility is to express an opinion on these financial statements based on our audits.

We conducted our audits in accordance with Canadian generally accepted auditing standards. Those standards require that we plan and perform an audit to obtain reasonable assurance whether the financial statements are free of material misstatement. An audit includes examining, on a test basis, evidence supporting the amounts and disclosures in the financial statements. An audit also includes assessing the accounting principles used and significant estimates made by management, as well as evaluating the overall financial statement presentation.

In our opinion, these consolidated financial statements present fairly, in all material respects, the financial position of the Company as at August 31, 2003 and 2002 and the results of its operations and its cash flows for the years then ended in accordance with Canadian generally accepted accounting principles.

BDO DUNWOODY LLP

BDO Dunwoody LLP

Chartered Accountants
Toronto, Ontario
November 25, 2003

CONSOLIDATED BALANCE SHEETS AS AT AUGUST 31, 2003 AND 2002

(in thousands of dollars)

Assets

	2003 $	2002 $
Current Assets:		
Cash and short term investments	30,140	47,086
Receivables (note 3)	60,807	43,001
Receivables – affiliates (note 12)	3,185	3,792
Inventories	55,604	25,361
Prepaid expenses	9,722	6,752
Asset held for sale		3,432
Future income taxes (note 8)	1,930	2,415
Total current assets	161,388	131,839
Future income taxes (note 8)	2,977	3,433
Property, plant and equipment (note 4)	28,349	19,710
License agreements, net of accumulated amortization of $4,265 (2002 - $3,711)	12,357	13,438
Intangible and other assets (note 5)	9,084	7,332
Goodwill (note 1)	99,695	107,910
	313,850	283,662

See accompanying notes to consolidated financial statements.

CONSOLIDATED BALANCE SHEETS AS AT AUGUST 31, 2003 AND 2002

(in thousands of dollars)

Liabilities and Shareholders' Equity

	2003 $	2002 $
Current Liabilities:		
Accounts payable	27,339	24,399
Payables – affiliates (note 12)	754	978
Accrued liabilities	33,530	32,880
Income taxes payable	5,204	7,347
Future income taxes (note 8)	3,144	2,566
Current maturities of long-term debt (note 6)	5,683	6,315
Total current liabilities	75,654	74,485
Long-term debt (note 6)	38,671	29,279
Other liabilities	3,984	4,940
Future income taxes (note 8)	4,722	3,950
Total liabilities	123,031	112,654
Minority interest	2,968	300
Commitments and contingencies (notes 10 and 11)		
Capital stock (note 7)	122,406	122,378
Cumulative translation adjustment	(8,904)	5,685
Retained earnings	74,349	42,645
Total shareholders' equity	187,851	170,708
	313,850	283,662

Approved by the Board,

_______________, Director
David J. Stein

_______________, Director
Romeo DeGasperis

See accompanying notes to consolidated financial statements.

CONSOLIDATED STATEMENTS OF EARNINGS AND RETAINED EARNINGS FOR THE YEARS ENDED AUGUST 31, 2003 AND 2002

(in thousands, except for earnings per share data)

Earnings

	2003 $	2002 $
Revenues:		
Sales	335,034	236,028
Franchising and licensing revenues:		
Royalty income	2,716	3,070
Franchise and license fees	1,804	1,213
Consumer products license fees	741	904
Drayage and other income	16,978	1,007
Total revenues	357,273	242,222
Operating expenses:		
Cost of goods sold	207,870	129,246
Selling, general and administrative expenses	95,088	77,558
Interest expense	1,990	2,544
Total operating expenses	304,948	209,348
Minority interest	541	
Earnings before income taxes	51,784	32,874
Provision for income taxes (note 8):		
Current	17,536	9,715
Future	2,544	2,175
	20,080	11,890
Net earnings	31,704	20,984
Retained earnings - beginning of year	42,645	21,661
Retained earnings - end of year	74,349	42,645
Earnings per share:		
Basic	0.61	0.44
Diluted	0.59	0.42
Weighted average shares outstanding:		
Shares used in per-share calculation - basic	51,746	48,050
Shares used in per-share calculation - diluted	53,992	50,346

See accompanying notes to consolidated financial statements.

CONSOLIDATED STATEMENTS OF CASH FLOWS FOR THE YEARS ENDED AUGUST 31, 2003 AND 2002

(in thousands of dollars)

Cash Flows

	2003 $	2002 $
Cash and Short Term Investments Provided by (used in):		
Operating activities:		
Net earnings	31,704	20,984
Items not affecting cash		
Depreciation and amortization	4,801	4,646
Future income taxes	2,544	2,175
Loss on sale of asset held for sale	390	
Minority interest	541	
Changes in current assets and liabilities, net of businesses acquired		
Receivables	(5,172)	(8,156)
Receivables – affiliates	844	(927)
Allowance for doubtful accounts	(1,087)	(980)
Inventories	(9,065)	(7,500)
Prepaid expenses	(2,900)	(2,285)
Accounts payable	(7,476)	58
Payables – affiliates	(240)	257
Accrued liabilities	(2,293)	11,520
Income taxes payable	(2,292)	4,587
Other assets	364	(336)
Other liabilities	(1,023)	19
Cash provided by operating activities	9,640	24,062
Investing activities:		
Increase in notes receivable	(5)	(44)
Repayment of notes receivable	345	91
Purchase of leasehold improvements and equipment	(5,736)	(6,338)
Purchase of intangible assets	(113)	(260)
Purchase of license agreements	(1,482)	
Acquisitions, net of cash acquired	(13,409)	(8,628)
Proceeds from asset held for sale	3,283	
Cash used in investing activities	(17,117)	(15,179)
Financing activities:		
(Expense) proceeds from special warrants	(144)	13,908
Proceeds from revolving line of credit, unsecured	2,770	
Proceeds from issuance of Class A and B shares	172	2,507
Repayment of long-term debt	(9,495)	(6,662)
Cash (used in) provided by financing activities	(6,697)	9,753
(Decrease) in cash flows due to changes in foreign exchange rates	(2,772)	(3,118)
(Decrease) increase in cash and short term investments	(16,946)	15,518
Cash and short term investments – beginning of year	47,086	31,568
Cash and short term investments – end of year	30,140	47,086

See accompanying notes to consolidated financial statements.

(Tabular amounts are expressed in thousands of dollars)

1. Description of business and summary of significant accounting policies

CoolBrands International Inc. (the "Company") manufactures, markets, distributes, sub-licenses and sells a variety of branded frozen dessert products to supermarkets, grocery stores, club stores, convenience stores, gourmet shops and delicatessens in Canada, the United States and certain foreign countries and also franchises frozen yogurt and ice cream stores, dip shops and family style restaurants throughout Canada, the United States and over 80 foreign countries. The Company also manufactures and sells soft serve frozen yogurt and ice cream mixes, a variety of flavours and ingredients and flexible packaging. The Company also operates a "direct store delivery" (DSD) frozen distribution system in the United States that delivers the Company's frozen dessert products, as well as those of third party "partner brand" manufacturers, directly to retailers' store locations. The Company also manufactures frozen desserts and other food products on a contract basis, including "store brand" (private label) products for retailers.

Basis of presentation

The consolidated financial statements are prepared by management using accounting principles generally accepted in Canada and include all wholly and majority owned subsidiaries. All significant intercompany transactions of consolidated subsidiaries are eliminated. Acquisitions recorded as purchases are included in the statement of earnings from the date of acquisition. All amounts are reported in Canadian dollars unless otherwise indicated.

Use of estimates

The preparation of consolidated financial statements in conformity with generally accepted accounting principles requires management to make estimates and assumptions that affect the amounts reported in the financial statements and accompanying notes. Actual results could differ from those estimated.

Cash and short term investments

All highly liquid commercial paper purchased with maturities of three months or less is classified as a cash equivalent. Cash equivalents are stated at cost, which approximates market value.

Inventories

Inventories consist primarily of ice cream, frozen yogurt and frozen dessert products, food supplies and packaging. Inventories are valued at the lower of cost and net realizable value, with cost determined principally by the first-in, first-out (FIFO) method.

Property, plant and equipment

Property, plant and equipment are stated at cost less accumulated depreciation. Depreciation of buildings and leasehold improvements and equipment is provided by the straight-line or declining balance methods, using the estimated useful lives of the assets, principally 20 to 38 years and 3 to 10 years, respectively. Store leasehold improvements are amortized on a straight-line basis over the terms of the leases, principally 5 to 10 years.

Trademarks, license agreements and franchise agreements and rights

Trademarks, license agreements and franchise agreements and rights are stated at cost less accumulated amortization. Amortization is provided by the straight-line method using the terms of the agreements, which range from 3 to 20 years.

Goodwill

Goodwill is evaluated annually for possible impairment. The Company uses an estimate of the related reporting units' discounted future cash flows in determining if the fair value of the reporting units is recoverable. Any permanent impairment in the value of goodwill would be written off against earnings. Based on the impairment tests performed, there was no impairment of goodwill in fiscal 2003. There can be no assurance that future goodwill impairment tests will not result in a charge to earnings.

Revenue recognition

Revenue from sales of the Company's products is recognized at the time of sale, which is generally when products are shipped to customers.

Revenue from sales by Company-owned and operated stores is recognized when products are purchased by customers.

Master franchise fee revenues are recognized at the time the Company has received the deposit specified in the master franchise agreement, has substantially performed all significant services to be provided in accordance with the terms of the agreement and when collectibility is reasonably determinable.

Single store franchise fees are recognized as revenue when the franchise application is approved, cash payments are received, and the Company has performed substantially all services required under the agreement.

Continuing franchise royalties are based on a percentage of gross sales as reported by the franchisees or gross products purchased by the franchisees. These fees are recognized on an accrual basis as they are earned.

Revenue from Drayage income is recognized at the time the product is delivered for the vendor to their customer by the Company.

Advertising

The Company spends a significant amount of its advertising dollars with its supermarket customers in the form of co-operative advertising in the chains' weekly circulars. The remainder of the Company's advertising is spent on media and other direct advertising. All advertising costs are expensed as incurred. The Company spent $5,131,000 on advertising for the year ended August 31, 2003 (2002 – $5,991,000).

Product introductory costs

The Company capitalizes certain product introductory placement costs (i.e. slotting fees) paid to customers, which are incurred to develop new markets for new and existing products sold for the first time. The payment of such fees is common in the industry. These costs are expensed over a twelve month period. Product introductory expense was $11,713,000 for the year ended August 31, 2003 (2002 – $6,700,000).

Financial instruments

The carrying amount of financial instruments including cash and short term investments, receivables, receivables – affiliates, accounts payable, payables – affiliates and accrued liabilities approximates fair value at August 31, 2003, because of the relatively short maturity of these instruments. The Company is exposed to interest rate risk on its long-term debt, however, the Company mitigates some of this exposure through an interest rate swap as described in note 6.

Concentration of credit risk

Financial instruments, which potentially subject the Company to concentration of credit risk, consist principally of cash and short-term investments and receivables. The Company attempts to minimize credit risk with respect to receivables by reviewing customers' credit history before extending credit, and by regularly monitoring customers' credit exposure. The Company establishes an allowance for doubtful accounts based upon factors surrounding the credit risk of specific customers, historical trends and other information.

Earnings per share

The Company uses the treasury stock method to determine the dilutive earnings per share.

Foreign currency translation

Translation gains or losses of accounts of foreign subsidiaries considered financially and operationally self-sustaining are deferred as a separate component of shareholders' equity until there has been a realized reduction in the net investment.

(Tabular amounts are expressed in thousands of dollars)

Foreign currencies are translated into Canadian dollars using the average exchange rate for the year for items included in the consolidated statements of operations. Foreign currencies are translated into Canadian dollars using the current rate for assets and liabilities included in the consolidated balance sheets except for earnings reinvested in the business, which are translated at historical rates.

Income taxes

Income taxes are calculated using the asset and liability method of accounting for income taxes. Under this method, current income taxes are recognized for the estimated income taxes payable for the current period. Future income tax assets and liabilities are determined based on differences between the financial reporting and tax bases of assets and liabilities, and are measured using the substantially enacted tax rates and laws that will be in effect when the differences are expected to reverse.

Stock option plan

The Company has a stock option plan for directors, officers, consultants and key employees. No compensation expense is recognized in accounting for stock options in the Company's Consolidated Statements of Earnings, except for stock-based compensation expense for stock options granted to consultants which is measured at the estimated fair value at the date of grant and expensed. When options are exercised the amount received is credited to share capital. Pro forma stock based compensation expense information is included in note 7.

Derivative instruments

Under an agreement expiring April 1, 2004, the U.S. based subsidiary of the Company entered into an interest-rate swap as a derivative to modify the interest characteristics on a portion of its outstanding float rate senior unsecured term loan, in an attempt to reduce its exposure to fluctuations in interest rates. The fair value of the contract has not been reflected in the Consolidated Financial Statements. The Company does not enter into such contracts for speculative purposes.

Reclassifications

Certain 2002 amounts have been reclassified to conform with the 2003 presentation.

2. Acquisitions

a. 2003 Acquisitions

Effective July 1, 2003, the Company acquired the general partner interest and majority of the total partnership interests in Americana Foods LP, located in Dallas, Texas. Americana Foods is one of the largest and most versatile frozen dessert manufacturing facilities in the U.S., and currently supplies a wide variety of soft serve mixes, packaged ice cream, frozen yogurt and sorbet products and frozen novelties to well known national retailers, food companies and restaurant chains, including Sam's Club, TCBY Enterprises and Silhouette Brands. Americana Foods also manufactures and sells products for the food-service channel such as dairy mixes for preparing mashed potatoes which are extensively used to standardize quality and reduce labor costs in on-site food preparations.

The following is a summary of the assets acquired and the fair value assigned thereto, and the purchase consideration given:

	Fair value acquired: $	Purchase consideration: $
Current assets	22,396	
Property, plant & equipment	7,879	
	30,275	
Less: Liabilities	30,275	
	Nil	Nil

On July 6, 2003, the Company acquired the Dreamery® ice cream and Whole Fruit™ sorbet brands from Dreyer's Grand Ice Cream, Inc., as well as the right to the license for the Godiva® ice cream brand, which was assigned by Dreyer's and substantially all of the Haagen-Dazs frozen dessert distribution assets in the States of Washington, Oregon, Florida, California, Pennsylvania, New Jersey, Utah, Minnesota, Georgia, Maryland, and the District of Columbia from Nestlé Ice Cream Company, LLC.

(Tabular amounts are expressed in thousands of dollars)

The following is a summary of the assets acquired and the fair value assigned thereto, and the purchase consideration given:

	Fair value acquired: $		Purchase consideration: $
Current assets	10,971	Cash	13,409
Option to purchase City of Industry, CA. facility	2,438		
	13,409		13,409

b. 2002 Acquisitions

On June 30, 2002, the Company acquired the business and assets of Fruit-a-Freeze, Incorporated. Fruit-a-Freeze, Incorporated began making frozen fruit bars in 1977, and was a pioneer in establishing the market for frozen novelties made from whole fruit and all natural ingredients. In its home market in Southern California, Fruit-a-Freeze products are consistently top ranked sellers among frozen novelties.

The acquisition included the Fruit-a-Freeze leased frozen novelty manufacturing facility in Norwalk, CA, and Fruit-a-Freeze's frozen distribution center and direct store delivery route distribution system, operated out of a frozen storage warehouse located at the Norwalk facility. The Fruit-a-Freeze distribution system services supermarket chains, club stores, independent grocers, convenience stores and independent distributors throughout Southern California.

In addition to the $2,280,000 cash payment contingent upon sales in year one, the Agreement specifies additional payments contingent upon the sales of Fruit-a-Freeze branded products in excess of U.S. $11,173,000 in both years two and three. However, since it is unlikely that any additional payments will be required for years two and three, the Company has not recorded a liability for such additional contingent consideration payments.

The following is a summary of the assets acquired and the fair value assigned thereto, and the purchase consideration given:

	Fair value acquired: $		Purchase consideration: $
Current assets	2,814	Cash	137
Equipment	970	Future payment contingent upon year one sales	2,280
Other assets	23		
Intangible assets	153		
Goodwill	4,921		
	8,881		
Less: Liabilities	6,464		
	2,417		2,417

On August 16, 2002, the Company purchased the business and assets of Chipwich, Inc., maker of the Chipwich Ice Cream Cookie Sandwich. A Chipwich is premium ice cream sandwiched between two specially formulated chocolate chip cookies and rolled in pure chocolate chips. When it was introduced in 1981, Chipwich created the adult premium ice cream novelty category. Since then, Chipwich has established itself as one of the best-known brand names for frozen novelties.

The following is a summary of the assets acquired and the fair value assigned thereto, and the purchase consideration given:

	Fair value acquired: $		Purchase consideration: $
Current assets	379	Cash	8,491
Plant equipment	550	Cash payment, Due: January 15, 2003, subject to certain potential adjustments	391
Intangible assets	156	Warrants issued	390
Goodwill	8,187		
	9,272		9,272

(Tabular amounts are expressed in thousands of dollars)

3. Receivables

	2003 $	2002 $
Trade accounts receivable	64,217	45,502
Franchise and license fees receivable	423	2,326
Notes receivable, current maturities	167	196
	64,807	48,024
Less: Allowance for doubtful accounts	4,000	5,023
	60,807	43,001

4. Property, plant and equipment

	2003 $	2002 $
Land	1,280	1,032
Buildings	8,432	4,651
Machinery and equipment	25,290	19,438
Leasehold improvements	3,257	2,629
	38,259	27,750
Less: Accumulated depreciation and amortization		
Buildings	866	641
Machinery and equipment	8,057	6,612
Leasehold improvements	987	787
	28,349	19,710

5. Intangible and other assets

	2003 $	2002 $
Trademarks	4,421	4,857
Franchise agreements and rights	756	825
Territorial agreements	425	479
Purchase option – land and building	2,495	
Notes receivable	168	538
Other	2,715	2,374
	10,980	9,073
Less: Accumulated amortization		
Trademarks	1,203	1,103
Franchise agreements and rights	280	256
Territorial agreements	413	382
	9,084	7,332

(Tabular amounts are expressed in thousands of dollars)

6. Long-term debt

	2003 $	2002 $
Term loan, unsecured	22,518	33,516
Term loans, secured	13,292	507
Revolving line of credit, unsecured	2,770	1,052
Revolving loan, secured	4,112	
Capitalized leases	1,662	519
	44,354	35,594
Less: Current maturities	5,683	6,315
	38,671	29,279

In connection with the acquisition of Eskimo Pie Corporation, a U.S. subsidiary borrowed U.S. $30,000,000, to finance the acquisition. The unsecured term loan is payable in monthly installments of U.S. $250,000, with the remaining principal balance due November 1, 2005. Interest is payable monthly on the unpaid principal balance with interest rates fluctuating with changes in the prime lending or libor rate and the ratio of funded debt to EBITDA. The interest rates, plus applicable margins were fixed through August 31, 2001 at the lower of prime plus ½% or libor plus 2 ½% (3.125% at August 31, 2003). As of August 31, 2003, the term loan balance was U.S. $16,250,000.

All borrowings under the above unsecured term loan agreement are guaranteed by the Company. The agreement contains restrictions relating to the payment of dividends, rental obligations, liens, indebtedness, dispositions of property, change in the nature of its business, change in ownership and requires that the net proceeds from the sale (other than in the ordinary course of business) of any assets of Eskimo Pie Corporation must be utilized to reduce the then outstanding principal balance of the term loan. In addition, the Company must maintain certain financial ratios and limit capital expenditures to U.S. $5 million during any fiscal year.

The U.S. based subsidiary entered into an interest rate protection agreement on April 1, 2001 covering U.S. $15,000,000 of the then outstanding principal balance of the senior unsecured term loan with a fixed libor interest rate of 5.18%, plus applicable margin. This interest rate protection agreement terminates on April 1, 2004. At August 31, 2003, the fair value of this interest rate protection agreement was U.S. $413,000 in favor of the bank and is not reflected in the Consolidated Financial Statements.

The subsidiary also has a U.S. $10 million unsecured revolving credit facility. The revolving credit facility is available for general corporate purposes and has a maturity date of November 30, 2004. Interest is payable monthly on the unpaid principal balance of borrowings under this facility with an interest rate of libor plus 2%. The subsidiary agreed to pay a fee of ¼% per annum on the unused portion of the commitment. As of August 31, 2003, the subsidiary has U.S. $8 million of available credit under the revolving credit facility.

A U.S. $750,000 revolving line of credit with a maturity date of June 1, 2003, certain term loans and capitalized leases were assumed by a U.S. subsidiary in connection with the June 2002 acquisition of the business and assets of Fruit-A-Freeze, Inc. The secured term loans are payable in monthly installments of U.S. $21,521. Interest at prime plus 1% is payable monthly on the unpaid principal balance with interest rates fluctuating with changes in the prime lending

(Tabular amounts are expressed in thousands of dollars)

rate. The U.S. $750,000 revolving line of credit and certain term loans were paid off on December 2, 2002.

On November 19, 2002, a limited partnership, which is owned 50.1% by the Company, entered into a credit agreement with a financial institution that includes a term loan of U.S. $10,000,000, which is secured by the partnership's property, plant, and equipment. Principal payments are payable in fixed monthly installments of U.S. $80,739 and matures on February 1, 2016. The term of the loan bears interest at prime plus 0.5% (4.5% at August 31, 2003.)

The partnership's credit agreement also includes a revolving loan up to U.S. $5 million, subject to a borrowing base calculation, which bears interest at prime plus 0.5% (4.5% at August 31, 2003) and is due on November 19, 2004. At August 31, 2003, approximately U.S. $2,031,000, was available to the partnership under this loan. The revolving loan is secured by the partnership's receivable and inventory.

In April 2003, the partnership executed an amendment to the credit agreement. Pursuant to this amendment, the minimum tangible net worth requirement was raised to U.S. $6,000,000 beginning June 29, 2003. In addition, the financial institution waived all other covenant requirements for the remaining term of the agreement.

Repayments of long-term debt due in each of the next five years are as follows:

	$
2004	5,683
2005	12,426
2006	15,262
2007	10,968
2008	15
	44,354

Interest paid during the year ended August 31, 2003 was $1,980,000 (2002 – $2,472,000).

(Tabular amounts are expressed in thousands of dollars)

7. Capital stock

Authorized number of shares:

Class A Subordinate voting shares	200,000,000
Class B Multiple voting shares	200,000,000

Class A subordinate voting shares have a preferential right to receive cash dividends when, as and if declared by the Board of Directors. Class B multiple voting shares can be converted at any time into an equivalent number of Class A subordinate voting shares. The Class A subordinate voting shares are entitled to one vote per share and the Class B multiple voting shares are entitled to ten votes per share.

The Company had the following share transactions during the years ended August 31, 2003 and 2002:

	Class A subordinate voting shares #	Class B multiple voting shares #	Warrants #	Amount $
Balance at August 31, 2001	39,649	6,240		105,573
Shares issued upon the exercise of special warrants	3,750			13,908
Shares issued for cash for stock options exercised	1,894	173		2,507
Multiple voting shares converted to Subordinate voting shares	204	(204)		
Warrants issued in connection with acquisition			100	390
Balance at August 31, 2002	45,497	6,209	100	122,378
Expenses related to the exercise of special warrants				(144)
Shares issued for cash for stock options exercised	102			172
Multiple voting shares converted to Subordinate voting shares	30	(30)		
Balance at August 31, 2003	45,629	6,179	100	122,406
Paid-in-balance	$104,716	$17,300	$390	

(Tabular amounts are expressed in thousands of dollars)

The Company has granted options to purchase subordinate and multiple voting shares to directors, officers, consultants and key employees under the Company's stock option plans. A summary of the activity of the Company's stock option plans for the years ended August 31, 2003 and 2002 is summarized below:

	2002 Stock Option Plan	1998 Stock Option Plan	Integrated Brands Stock Option Plan		
	Subordinate voting shares	Subordinate voting shares	Multiple voting shares	Subordinate voting shares	Weighted average exercise price
Outstanding at August 31, 2001		4,807	300	236	2.57
Granted		55			1.24
Exercised		(1,658)	(173)	(236)	1.21
Cancelled		(28)			1.24
Outstanding at August 31, 2002		3,176	127		3.41
Granted	1,298				5.40
Exercised		(102)			1.69
Expired			(127)		5.72
Cancelled		(10)			1.25
Outstanding at August 31, 2003	1,298	3,064			3.98
Options exercisable at August 31, 2003	1,025	2,778			3.97

Stock options outstanding at August 31, 2003, aggregating 4,362,000 shares, have a weighted-average contractual life of 2.7 years and a weighted-average exercise price of $3.98 per share. Stock options exercisable at August 31, 2003 have a weighted-average exercise price of $3.97 per share. The price range was $1.15 to $1.35 (1,527,000 outstanding and 1,241,000 exercisable), $4.30 (1,000,000 options exercisable), $5.00 (1,238,000 outstanding and 1,025,000 exercisable), $7.80 (537,000 options exercisable) and $13.75 (60,000 options outstanding) at August 31, 2003. Stock options reserved for future grant at August 31, 2003 aggregated 4,048,502.

On November 1, 2002 The Company's shareholders approved The 2002 Stock Option Plan, which reserved 5.17 million options for issuance and limited the number of options that may be granted in any one fiscal year to 2.5% of outstanding shares.

The Company records no compensation expense when options are issued to employees. The Company estimates the fair value of each share option on the date of grant using the Black-Scholes option pricing model with the following assumptions: risk-free interest rate of 3.46%; expected volatility of 68.38%; expected live of 2.7 years; and no dividend payments. Pro forma net earnings and earnings per share if compensation expense had been recorded for stock options granted to employees would be as follows:

For the year ended August 31,	2003 $
Pro forma net earnings	30,351
Pro forma earnings per share:	
Basic	0.59
Diluted	0.56

(Tabular amounts are expressed in thousands of dollars)

8. Income taxes

The effective income tax rate on earnings is affected from year to year by the geographic mix of the consolidated earnings before income taxes. The following table reconciles income taxes computed by applying the combined Canadian federal/provincial statutory rate with the actual income tax provision:

	2003 %	2002 %
Combined basic Canadian Federal and Provincial income tax rate	38.00	44.62
Impact of operating in foreign countries with different effective rates	0.04	(9.63)
Permanent differences	0.74	1.18
	38.78	36.17

The Company's subsidiaries have operating loss carry-forwards for income tax purposes amounting to approximately $5,084,000 (2002 – $5,393,000). These losses expire in various amounts through the year 2019.

Significant components of the Company's future tax assets and liabilities as of August 31, 2003 are as follows:

Future tax assets	$
Non-capital loss carry-forwards	1,876
Accounting allowances not deducted for tax	1,294
Other	1,737
Total Future Tax Assets	4,907

Future tax liabilities	$
Tax amortization in excess of book amortization	2,731
Tax depreciation in excess of book depreciation	123
Product introductory costs	3,291
Other	1,721
Total Future Tax Liabilities	7,866

Income taxes paid during the year ended August 31, 2003 were $17,268,000 (2002 – $4,739,000).

9. Retirement plans

Eskimo Pie Corporation had maintained two defined benefit pensions plans covering substantially all salaried employees. Upon the acquisition of Eskimo Pie Corporation by the Company all future participation and all benefits under the plans were frozen. These plans provide retirement benefits based primarily on employee compensation and years of service up to the acquisition of Eskimo Pie Corporation by the Company. The above mentioned plans are referred to as the "Pension Benefits".

In addition, Eskimo Pie Corporation entered into an agreement with Reynolds Metals Company to indemnify the cost of retiree health care and life insurance benefits for salaried employees of Eskimo Pie Corporation who had retired prior to April 1992. Under this agreement, Eskimo Pie Corporation may elect to prepay its remaining obligation. Eskimo Pie Corporation did not provide postretirement health and life insurance benefits for employees who retired subsequent to April 1992. This indemnity agreement is referred to as the "Other Benefits".

(Tabular amounts are expressed in thousands of dollars)

The following table reconciles the changes in benefit obligations and plan assets in 2003, and reconciles the funded status to accrued benefit cost at August 31, 2003:

	Pension Benefits $	Other Benefits $
Benefit Obligation		
Beginning balance	2,973	2,834
Interest cost	196	195
Actuarial loss	171	
Lump sum purchase of obligations	(12)	
Benefit payments	(108)	(463)
Translation gain	(328)	(298)
Ending balance	2,892	2,268
Plan assets – Basic value		
Beginning balance	2,806	
Actual return on plan assets	243	
Contributions	42	
Benefit payments	(120)	
Translation gain	(305)	
Ending balance	2,666	

The funded status for the post retirement health and life insurance benefits is as follows:

	Other Benefits $
Benefit obligations in excess of Plan assets	2,268
Accrued benefit cost	2,268

The accrued benefit cost of $2,268,000 is included in Other liabilities at August 31, 2003.

The following table provides the components of the net periodic benefit cost:

	Pension Benefits $	Other Benefits $
Interest cost	196	195
Expected return on Plan assets	(243)	
Recognized net actuarial gain	43	
Net period benefit cost (income)	(4)	195

The assumptions used in the measurement of the Eskimo Pie Corporation's benefit obligations are as follows:

	Pension Benefits	Other Benefits
Benefit obligation, beginning of year	6.75%	7.75%
Expected return on plan assets, during the year	8.0%	

(Tabular amounts are expressed in thousands of dollars)

The weighted average annual assumed rate of increase in the per capita cost of covered benefits (i.e. health care cost trend rate) is 5% for 2003 and is assumed to remain at that level thereafter. A one percentage point increase or decrease in the assumed health care cost trend rate would change the accumulated postretirement benefit obligation by approximately $232,500 and the net periodic postretirement benefit cost by approximately $23,250.

10. Commitments

The majority of distribution warehouse, store and office facility leases are under non-cancelable leases. Substantially all of the leases are net leases, which require the payment of property taxes, insurance and maintenance costs in addition to minimum rental payments. Certain store leases provide for additional rentals based on a percentage of sales and have renewal options for one or more periods from five to twenty years.

At August 31, 2003 the future minimum lease payments under operating leases with rental terms of more than one year, net of sub lease rents, amounted to:

Fiscal year ending:	$
2004	8,011
2005	5,711
2006	4,760
2007	2,756
2008	2,351
Later years	2,067
Total minimum obligations	25,656

Total rental expense relating to all operating leases (including those with terms less than one year) was $2,973,000 (2002 – $1,302,000).

11. Contingencies

The Company is a party to legal proceedings and disputes with franchisees, former franchisees and others, which arise in the ordinary course of business. In the opinion of the Company, it is unlikely that the liabilities, if any, arising from the legal proceedings and disputes will have a material adverse effect on the consolidated financial position of the Company or its operations.

Several subsidiaries hold master store leases or have guaranteed store leases covering franchised locations. Such leases expire at varying dates to 2013. Where a subsidiary holds the master lease, these premises have been subleased to franchisees under terms and rental rates substantially the same as those in master leases. In a majority of these instances, franchisees make all lease payments directly to the landlords. The Company provides an estimated liability for lease terminations in the event of a default by a franchisee based on the expected costs of releasing or settlement with the landlord. The liability was $410,000 at August 31, 2003. Aggregate minimum future rental payments under these leases approximated $10,691,000 at August 31, 2003 (2002 – $11,329,000).

12. Related party transactions and amounts

Receivables – affiliates at August 31, 2002 were $266,000 in advances which are unsecured, non-interest bearing and due on demand. The affiliates include directors and officers of the Company.

Calip Dairies, Inc. ("Calip"), an ice cream distributor owned by an officer, director and shareholder of the Company, has a management agreement with Integrated Brands Inc., which the Company acquired in March 1998. This agreement terminates on December 31, 2013 and thereafter shall automatically renew December 31 of each year for an additional one year term, unless terminated under certain conditions. Under the agreement, Calip provides management services to Integrated Brands for an annual fee of U.S. $1,300,000 effective July 1, 2003, prior to which the fee was U.S. $1,000,000. Such management fees incurred for the year ended August 31, 2003 were $1,556,000 (U.S. $1,050,000) (2002 – $1,559,000 (U.S. $1,000,000)). At August 31, 2003, the $754,000 (2002 – $978,000) balance of payables – affiliates represents payables to Calip.

Integrated Brands Inc., also has a distribution agreement with Calip for distribution of the Company's products in the New York Metropolitan Area, Fairfield County in the state of Connecticut, and New Jersey. The distribution agreement continues until December 31, 2007 and thereafter shall automatically renew on December 31st of each year while the agreement is in effect for an additional one year term, unless terminated under certain conditions. The distribution agreement is terminable by either party on sixty days notice. Sales of products to Calip were $12,624,000 for the year ending August 31, 2003 (2002 – $11,709,000). At August 31, 2003, $3,185,000 of the receivables – affiliates represent receivables from Calip (2002 – $3,526,000). The transactions with Calip occur in the normal course of operations and are measured at the amount of consideration established and agreed to by the related parties.

13. Segment information

CoolBrands International's reportable segments are Prepackaged consumer products, Foodservice, Dairy components and Franchising and licensing, including Company-owned stores.

Revenues and profits in the Prepackaged consumer products segment are generated from selling a variety of prepackaged frozen dessert products to distributors and various retail establishments including supermarkets, grocery stores, club stores, gourmet shops, delicatessens and convenience stores.

Revenues and profits in the Foodservice segment are generated from manufacturing and selling soft serve yogurt and premium ice cream mixes to broad-line foodservice distributors, yogurt shops and other foodservice establishments which, in turn, sell soft serve ice cream and yogurt products to consumers.

Revenues and profits in the Dairy components segment are generated from the manufacturing and selling of various ingredients to the dairy industry and from the manufacturing and selling of flexible packaging, such as private label ice cream novelty wraps.

Revenues and profits in the Franchising and licensing segment are generated by franchising activities, which generate initial and recurring revenues and the manufacture and sale of proprietary products to franchisees and licensees and from Company-owned stores selling ice cream and soft serve yogurt out of company-owned stores and outlets.

CoolBrands International Inc. evaluates the performance of its segments and allocates resources to them based on their operating contribution, which represents segment revenues, less direct costs of operation, excluding the allocation of corporate expenses.

NOTES TO CONSOLIDATED FINANCIAL STATEMENTS FOR THE YEARS ENDED AUGUST 31, 2003 AND 2002

(Tabular amounts are expressed in thousands of dollars)

Year ended August 31, 2003

Industry Segments:	Prepackaged consumer products $	Food-service $	Dairy components $	Franchising and licensing $	Corporate $	Consolidated $
Revenues	277,134	26,234	41,594	20,890	214	366,066
Interest income	575			126	43	744
Inter-segment revenues	(5,389)	(991)	(2,943)		(214)	(9,537)
Net revenues	272,320	25,243	38,651	21,016	43	357,273
Segment earnings	45,152	2,678	6,026	2,123	43	56,022
General corporate expenses					(1,707)	(1,707)
Interest expense	(1,970)			(20)		(1,990)
Minority interest	(541)					(541)
Earnings before income taxes	42,641	2,678	6,026	2,103	(1,664)	51,784
Provision for income taxes						20,080
Net earnings						31,704
Assets	189,686	21,335	36,143	63,453	3,233	313,850
Capital expenditures	3,849	236	231	1,420		5,736
Depreciation and amortization	2,635	631	469	1,066		4,801

Year ended August 31, 2002

Industry Segments:	Prepackaged consumer products $	Food-service $	Dairy components $	Franchising and licensing $	Corporate $	Consolidated $
Revenues	157,337	26,285	37,743	24,702	286	246,353
Interest income	380			245	44	669
Inter-segment revenues	(122)	(1,218)	(3,133)	(92)	(235)	(4,800)
Net revenues	157,595	25,067	34,610	24,855	95	242,222
Segment earnings	26,101	2,289	4,077	3,867	95	36,429
General corporate expenses					(1,011)	(1,011)
Interest expense	(2,526)			(18)		(2,544)
Earnings before income taxes	23,575	2,289	4,077	3,849	(916)	32,874
Provision for income taxes						11,890
Net earnings						20,984
Assets	176,937	15,249	44,118	42,070	5,288	283,662
Capital expenditures	5,236	397	78	627		6,338
Depreciation and amortization	2,212	823	492	1,119		4,646

NOTES TO CONSOLIDATED FINANCIAL STATEMENTS FOR THE YEARS ENDED AUGUST 31, 2003 AND 2002

(Tabular amounts are expressed in thousands of dollars)

Year ended August 31, 2003

Geographic Segments:	Canada	United States	International	Consolidated
	$	$	$	$
Revenues	5,157	356,674	4,235	366,066
Interest income	103	595	46	744
Inter-segment revenues	(214)	(9,323)		(9,537)
Net revenues	5,046	347,946	4,281	357,273
Segment earnings	668	53,342	2,012	56,022
General corporate expenses	(1,707)			(1,707)
Interest expense		(1,990)		(1,990)
Minority interest		(541)		(541)
Earnings before income taxes	(1,039)	50,811	2,012	51,784
Provision for income taxes				20,080
Net earnings				31,704
Assets	7,752	296,113	9,985	313,850
Capital expenditures		5,736		5,736
Depreciation and amortization	204	4,387	210	4,801

Year ended August 31, 2002

Geographic Segments:	Canada	United States	International	Consolidated
	$	$	$	$
Revenues	6,328	235,130	4,895	246,353
Interest income	72	559	38	669
Inter-segment revenues	(316)	(4,484)		(4,800)
Net revenues	6,084	231,205	4,933	242,222
Segment earnings	1,033	33,280	2,116	36,429
General corporate expenses	(1,011)			(1,011)
Interest expense		(2,544)		(2,544)
Earnings before income taxes	22	30,736	2,116	32,874
Provision for income taxes				11,890
Net earnings				20,984
Assets	9,202	265,512	8,948	283,662
Capital expenditures	134	6,204		6,338
Depreciation and amortization	218	4,195	233	4,646

Appendix B

Present and Future Value Tables

Table 1	**The Future Value of a Single Amount ($1)**	B-2
Table 2	**The Future Value of an Annuity of $1 in Arrears***	B-3
Table 3	**The Present Value of a Single Amount ($1)**	B-4
Table 4	**The Present Value of an Annuity of $1 in Arrears***	B-5

Table 1 The Future Value of a Single Amount ($1)
$FV = P(1 + r)^n$. In this table $P = \$1.00$

Periods	0.50%	1%	2%	3%	4%	5%	6%	7%	8%	9%	10%	11%	12%	13%	14%	15%
1	1.00500	1.01000	1.02000	1.03000	1.04000	1.05000	1.06000	1.07000	1.08000	1.09000	1.10000	1.11000	1.12000	1.13000	1.14000	1.15000
2	1.01003	1.02010	1.04040	1.06090	1.08160	1.10250	1.12360	1.14490	1.16640	1.18810	1.21000	1.23210	1.25440	1.27690	1.29960	1.32250
3	1.01508	1.03030	1.06121	1.09273	1.12486	1.15763	1.19102	1.22504	1.25971	1.29503	1.33100	1.36763	1.40493	1.44290	1.48154	1.52088
4	1.02015	1.04060	1.08243	1.12551	1.16986	1.21551	1.26248	1.31080	1.36049	1.41158	1.46410	1.51807	1.57352	1.63047	1.68896	1.74901
5	1.02525	1.05101	1.10408	1.15927	1.21665	1.27628	1.33823	1.40255	1.46933	1.53862	1.61051	1.68506	1.76234	1.84244	1.92541	2.01136
6	1.03038	1.06152	1.12616	1.19405	1.26532	1.34010	1.41852	1.50073	1.58687	1.67710	1.77156	1.87041	1.97382	2.08195	2.19497	2.31306
7	1.03553	1.07214	1.14869	1.22987	1.31593	1.40710	1.50363	1.60578	1.71382	1.82804	1.94872	2.07616	2.21068	2.35261	2.50227	2.66002
8	1.04071	1.08286	1.17166	1.26677	1.36857	1.47746	1.59385	1.71819	1.85093	1.99256	2.14359	2.30454	2.47596	2.65844	2.85259	3.05902
9	1.04591	1.09369	1.19509	1.30477	1.42331	1.55133	1.68948	1.83846	1.99900	2.17189	2.35795	2.55804	2.77308	3.00404	3.25195	3.51788
10	1.05114	1.10462	1.21899	1.34392	1.48024	1.62889	1.79085	1.96715	2.15892	2.36736	2.59374	2.83942	3.10585	3.39457	3.70722	4.04556
11	1.05640	1.11567	1.24337	1.38423	1.53945	1.71034	1.89830	2.10485	2.33164	2.58043	2.85312	3.15176	3.47855	3.83586	4.22623	4.65239
12	1.06168	1.12683	1.26824	1.42576	1.60103	1.79586	2.01220	2.25219	2.51817	2.81266	3.13843	3.49845	3.89598	4.33452	4.81790	5.35025
13	1.06699	1.13809	1.29361	1.46853	1.66507	1.88565	2.13293	2.40985	2.71962	3.06580	3.45227	3.88328	4.36349	4.89801	5.49241	6.15279
14	1.07232	1.14947	1.31948	1.51259	1.73168	1.97993	2.26090	2.57853	2.93719	3.34173	3.79750	4.31044	4.88711	5.53475	6.26135	7.07571
15	1.07768	1.16097	1.34587	1.55797	1.80094	2.07893	2.39656	2.75903	3.17217	3.64248	4.17725	4.78459	5.47357	6.25427	7.13794	8.13706
16	1.08307	1.17258	1.37279	1.60471	1.87298	2.18287	2.54035	2.95216	3.42594	3.97031	4.59497	5.31089	6.13039	7.06733	8.13725	9.35762
17	1.08849	1.18430	1.40024	1.65285	1.94790	2.29202	2.69277	3.15882	3.70002	4.32763	5.05447	5.89509	6.86604	7.98608	9.27646	10.76126
18	1.09393	1.19615	1.42825	1.70243	2.02582	2.40662	2.85434	3.37993	3.99602	4.71712	5.55992	6.54355	7.68997	9.02427	10.57517	12.37545
19	1.09940	1.20811	1.45681	1.75351	2.10685	2.52695	3.02560	3.61653	4.31570	5.14166	6.11591	7.26334	8.61276	10.19742	12.05569	14.23177
20	1.10490	1.22019	1.48595	1.80611	2.19112	2.65330	3.20714	3.86968	4.66096	5.60441	6.72750	8.06231	9.64629	11.52309	13.74349	16.36654
21	1.11042	1.23239	1.51567	1.86029	2.27877	2.78596	3.39956	4.14056	5.03383	6.10881	7.40025	8.94917	10.80385	13.02109	15.66758	18.82152
22	1.11597	1.24472	1.54598	1.91610	2.36992	2.92526	3.60354	4.43040	5.43654	6.65860	8.14027	9.93357	12.10031	14.71383	17.86104	21.64475
23	1.12155	1.25716	1.57690	1.97359	2.46472	3.07152	3.81975	4.74053	5.87146	7.25787	8.95430	11.02627	13.55235	16.62663	20.36158	24.89146
24	1.12716	1.26973	1.60844	2.03279	2.56330	3.22510	4.04893	5.07237	6.34118	7.91108	9.84973	12.23916	15.17863	18.78809	23.21221	28.62518
25	1.13280	1.28243	1.64061	2.09378	2.66584	3.38635	4.29187	5.42743	6.84848	8.62308	10.83471	13.58546	17.00006	21.23054	26.46192	32.91895
30	1.16140	1.34785	1.81136	2.42726	3.24340	4.32194	5.74349	7.61226	10.06266	13.26768	17.44940	22.89230	29.95992	39.11590	50.95016	66.21177
35	1.19073	1.41660	1.99989	2.81386	3.94609	5.51602	7.68609	10.67658	14.78534	20.41397	28.10244	38.57485	52.79962	72.06851	98.10018	133.17552
40	1.22079	1.48886	2.20804	3.26204	4.80102	7.03999	10.28572	14.97446	21.72452	31.40942	45.25926	65.00087	93.05097	132.78155	188.88351	267.86355

[*FV* = future value, *P* = payment, *r* = interest rate per period in decimal form, *n* = number of periods]

Table 2 The Future Value of an Annuity of $1 in Arrears*

$$FV_a = \frac{(1 + r)^n - 1}{r}$$

Periods	0.50%	1%	2%	3%	4%	5%	6%	7%	8%	9%	10%	11%	12%	13%	14%	15%
1	1.00000	1.00000	1.00000	1.00000	1.00000	1.00000	1.00000	1.00000	1.00000	1.00000	1.00000	1.00000	1.00000	1.00000	1.00000	1.00000
2	2.00500	2.01000	2.02000	2.03000	2.04000	2.05000	2.06000	2.07000	2.08000	2.09000	2.10000	2.11000	2.12000	2.13000	2.14000	2.15000
3	3.01502	3.03010	3.06040	3.09090	3.12160	3.15250	3.18360	3.21490	3.24640	3.27810	3.31000	3.34210	3.37440	3.40690	3.43960	3.47250
4	4.03010	4.06040	4.12161	4.18363	4.24646	4.31013	4.37462	4.43994	4.50611	4.57313	4.64100	4.70973	4.77933	4.84980	4.92114	4.99338
5	5.05025	5.10101	5.20404	5.30914	5.41632	5.52563	5.63709	5.75074	5.86660	5.98471	6.10510	6.22780	6.35285	6.48027	6.61010	6.74238
6	6.07550	6.15202	6.30812	6.46841	6.63298	6.80191	6.97532	7.15329	7.33593	7.52333	7.71561	7.91286	8.11519	8.32271	8.53552	8.75374
7	7.10588	7.21354	7.43428	7.66246	7.89829	8.14201	8.39384	8.65402	8.92280	9.20043	9.48717	9.78327	10.08901	10.40466	10.73049	11.06680
8	8.14141	8.28567	8.58297	8.89234	9.21423	9.54911	9.89747	10.25980	10.63663	11.02847	11.43589	11.85943	12.29969	12.75726	13.23276	13.72682
9	9.18212	9.36853	9.75463	10.15911	10.58280	11.02656	11.49132	11.97799	12.48756	13.02104	13.57948	14.16397	14.77566	15.41571	16.08535	16.78584
10	10.22803	10.46221	10.94972	11.46388	12.00611	12.57789	13.18079	13.81645	14.48656	15.19293	15.93742	16.72201	17.54874	18.41975	19.33730	20.30372
11	11.27917	11.56683	12.16872	12.80780	13.48635	14.20679	14.97164	15.78360	16.64549	17.56029	18.53117	19.56143	20.65458	21.81432	23.04452	24.34928
12	12.33556	12.68250	13.41209	14.19203	15.02581	15.91713	16.86994	17.88845	18.97713	20.14072	21.38428	22.71319	24.13313	25.65018	27.27075	29.00167
13	13.39724	13.80933	14.68033	15.61779	16.62684	17.71298	18.88214	20.14064	21.49530	22.95338	24.52271	26.21164	28.02911	29.98470	32.08865	34.35192
14	14.46423	14.94742	15.97394	17.08632	18.29191	19.59863	21.01507	22.55049	24.21492	26.01919	27.97498	30.09492	32.39260	34.88271	37.58107	40.50471
15	15.53655	16.09690	17.29342	18.59891	20.02359	21.57856	23.27597	25.12902	27.15211	29.36092	31.77248	34.40536	37.27971	40.41746	43.84241	47.58041
16	16.61423	17.25786	18.63929	20.15688	21.82453	23.65749	25.67253	27.88805	30.32428	33.00340	35.94973	39.18995	42.75328	46.67173	50.98035	55.71747
17	17.69730	18.43044	20.01207	21.76159	23.69751	25.84037	28.21288	30.84022	33.75023	36.97370	40.54470	44.50084	48.88367	53.73906	59.11760	65.07509
18	18.78579	19.61475	21.41231	23.41444	25.64541	28.13238	30.90565	33.99903	37.45024	41.30134	45.59917	50.39594	55.74971	61.72514	68.39407	75.83636
19	19.87972	20.81090	22.84056	25.11687	27.67123	30.53900	33.75999	37.37896	41.44626	46.01846	51.15909	56.93949	63.43968	70.74941	78.96923	88.21181
20	20.97912	22.01900	24.29737	26.87037	29.77808	33.06595	36.78559	40.99549	45.76196	51.16012	57.27500	64.20283	72.05244	80.94683	91.02493	102.44358
21	22.08401	23.23919	25.78332	28.67649	31.96920	35.71925	39.99273	44.86518	50.42292	56.76453	64.00250	72.26514	81.69874	92.46992	104.76842	118.81012
22	23.19443	24.47159	27.29898	30.53678	34.24797	38.50521	43.39229	49.00574	55.45676	62.87334	71.40275	81.21431	92.50258	105.49101	120.43600	137.63164
23	24.31040	25.71630	28.84496	32.45288	36.61789	41.43048	46.99583	53.43614	60.89330	69.53194	79.54302	91.14788	104.60289	120.20484	138.29704	159.27638
24	25.43196	26.97346	30.42186	34.42647	39.08260	44.50200	50.81558	58.17667	66.76476	76.78981	88.49733	102.17415	118.15524	136.83147	158.65862	184.16784
25	26.55912	28.24320	32.03030	36.45926	41.64591	47.72710	54.86451	63.24904	73.10594	84.70090	98.34706	114.41331	133.33387	155.61956	181.87083	212.79302
30	32.28002	34.78489	40.56808	47.57542	56.08494	66.43885	79.05819	94.46079	113.28321	136.30754	164.49402	199.02088	241.33268	293.19922	356.78685	434.74515
35	38.14538	41.66028	49.99448	60.46208	73.65222	90.32031	111.43478	138.23688	172.31680	215.71075	271.02437	341.58955	431.66350	546.68082	693.57270	881.17016
40	44.15885	48.88637	60.40198	75.40126	95.02552	120.79977	154.76197	199.63511	259.05652	337.88245	442.59256	581.82607	767.09142	1013.70424	1342.02510	1779.09031

* Payments (or receipts) at the end of each period.

[FV_a = future value of an annuity, r = interest rate per period in decimal form, n = number of periods in which a payment is made or received]

Table 3 The Present Value of a Single Amount ($1)

$$PV = \frac{\text{future value}}{(1 + r)^n}$$

Periods	0.50%	1%	2%	3%	4%	5%	6%	7%	8%	9%	10%	11%	12%	13%	14%	15%
1	0.99502	0.99010	0.98039	0.97087	0.96154	0.95238	0.94340	0.93458	0.92593	0.91743	0.90909	0.90090	0.89286	0.88496	0.87719	0.86957
2	0.99007	0.98030	0.96117	0.94260	0.92456	0.90703	0.89000	0.87344	0.85734	0.84168	0.82645	0.81162	0.79719	0.78315	0.76947	0.75614
3	0.98515	0.97059	0.94232	0.91514	0.88900	0.86384	0.83962	0.81630	0.79383	0.77218	0.75131	0.73119	0.71178	0.69305	0.67497	0.65752
4	0.98025	0.96098	0.92385	0.88849	0.85480	0.82270	0.79209	0.76290	0.73503	0.70843	0.68301	0.65873	0.63552	0.61332	0.59208	0.57175
5	0.97537	0.95147	0.90573	0.86261	0.82193	0.78353	0.74726	0.71299	0.68058	0.64993	0.62092	0.59345	0.56743	0.54276	0.51937	0.49718
6	0.97052	0.94205	0.88797	0.83748	0.79031	0.74622	0.70496	0.66634	0.63017	0.59627	0.56447	0.53464	0.50663	0.48032	0.45559	0.43233
7	0.96569	0.93272	0.87056	0.81309	0.75992	0.71068	0.66506	0.62275	0.58349	0.54703	0.51316	0.48166	0.45235	0.42506	0.39964	0.37594
8	0.96089	0.92348	0.85349	0.78941	0.73069	0.67684	0.62741	0.58201	0.54027	0.50187	0.46651	0.43393	0.40388	0.37616	0.35056	0.32690
9	0.95610	0.91434	0.83676	0.76642	0.70259	0.64461	0.59190	0.54393	0.50025	0.46043	0.42410	0.39092	0.36061	0.33288	0.30751	0.28426
10	0.95135	0.90529	0.82035	0.74409	0.67556	0.61391	0.55839	0.50835	0.46319	0.42241	0.38554	0.35218	0.32197	0.29459	0.26974	0.24718
11	0.94661	0.89632	0.80426	0.72242	0.64958	0.58468	0.52679	0.47509	0.42888	0.38753	0.35049	0.31728	0.28748	0.26070	0.23662	0.21494
12	0.94191	0.88745	0.78849	0.70138	0.62460	0.55684	0.49697	0.44401	0.39711	0.35553	0.31863	0.28584	0.25668	0.23071	0.20756	0.18691
13	0.93722	0.87866	0.77303	0.68095	0.60057	0.53032	0.46884	0.41496	0.36770	0.32618	0.28966	0.25751	0.22917	0.20416	0.18207	0.16253
14	0.93256	0.86996	0.75788	0.66112	0.57748	0.50507	0.44230	0.38782	0.34046	0.29925	0.26333	0.23199	0.20462	0.18068	0.15971	0.14133
15	0.92792	0.86135	0.74301	0.64186	0.55526	0.48102	0.41727	0.36245	0.31524	0.27454	0.23939	0.20900	0.18270	0.15989	0.14010	0.12289
16	0.92330	0.85282	0.72845	0.62317	0.53391	0.45811	0.39365	0.33873	0.29189	0.25187	0.21763	0.18829	0.16312	0.14150	0.12289	0.10686
17	0.91871	0.84438	0.71416	0.60502	0.51337	0.43630	0.37136	0.31657	0.27027	0.23107	0.19784	0.16963	0.14564	0.12522	0.10780	0.09293
18	0.91414	0.83602	0.70016	0.58739	0.49363	0.41552	0.35034	0.29586	0.25025	0.21199	0.17986	0.15282	0.13004	0.11081	0.09456	0.08081
19	0.90959	0.82774	0.68643	0.57029	0.47464	0.39573	0.33051	0.27651	0.23171	0.19449	0.16351	0.13768	0.11611	0.09806	0.08295	0.07027
20	0.90506	0.81954	0.67297	0.55368	0.45639	0.37689	0.31180	0.25842	0.21455	0.17843	0.14864	0.12403	0.10367	0.08678	0.07276	0.06110
21	0.90056	0.81143	0.65978	0.53755	0.43883	0.35894	0.29416	0.24151	0.19866	0.16370	0.13513	0.11174	0.09256	0.07680	0.06383	0.05313
22	0.89608	0.80340	0.64684	0.52189	0.42196	0.34185	0.27751	0.22571	0.18394	0.15018	0.12285	0.10067	0.08264	0.06796	0.05599	0.04620
23	0.89162	0.79544	0.63416	0.50669	0.40573	0.32557	0.26180	0.21095	0.17032	0.13778	0.11168	0.09069	0.07379	0.06014	0.04911	0.04017
24	0.88719	0.78757	0.62172	0.49193	0.39012	0.31007	0.24698	0.19715	0.15770	0.12640	0.10153	0.08170	0.06588	0.05323	0.04308	0.03493
25	0.88277	0.77977	0.60953	0.47761	0.37512	0.29530	0.23300	0.18425	0.14602	0.11597	0.09230	0.07361	0.05882	0.04710	0.03779	0.03038
30	0.86103	0.74192	0.55207	0.41199	0.30832	0.23138	0.17411	0.13137	0.09938	0.07537	0.05731	0.04368	0.03338	0.02557	0.01963	0.01510
35	0.83982	0.70591	0.50003	0.35538	0.25342	0.18129	0.13011	0.09366	0.06763	0.04899	0.03558	0.02592	0.01894	0.01388	0.01019	0.00751
40	0.81914	0.67165	0.45289	0.30656	0.20829	0.14205	0.09722	0.06678	0.04603	0.03184	0.02209	0.01538	0.01075	0.00753	0.00529	0.00373

[PV = present value, r = interest rate per period in decimal form, n = number of periods]

Table 4 The Present Value of Annuity $1.00 in Arrears*

$$PV_a = \frac{1}{r}\left[1 - \frac{1}{(1+r)^n}\right]$$

Periods	0.50%	1%	2%	3%	4%	5%	6%	7%	8%	9%	10%	11%	12%	13%	14%	15%
1	0.99502	0.99010	0.98039	0.97087	0.96154	0.95238	0.94340	0.93458	0.92593	0.91743	0.90909	0.90090	0.89286	0.88496	0.87719	0.86957
2	1.98510	1.97040	1.94156	1.91347	1.88609	1.85941	1.83339	1.80802	1.78326	1.75911	1.73554	1.71252	1.69005	1.66810	1.64666	1.62571
3	2.97025	2.94099	2.88388	2.82861	2.77509	2.72325	2.67301	2.62432	2.57710	2.53129	2.48685	2.44371	2.40183	2.36115	2.32163	2.28323
4	3.95050	3.90197	3.80773	3.71710	3.62990	3.54595	3.46511	3.38721	3.31213	3.23972	3.16987	3.10245	3.03735	2.97447	2.91371	2.85498
5	4.92587	4.85343	4.71346	4.57971	4.45182	4.32948	4.21236	4.10020	3.99271	3.88965	3.79079	3.69590	3.60478	3.51723	3.43308	3.35216
6	5.89638	5.79548	5.60143	5.41719	5.24214	5.07569	4.91732	4.76654	4.62288	4.48592	4.35526	4.23054	4.11141	3.99755	3.88867	3.78448
7	6.86207	6.72819	6.47199	6.23028	6.00205	5.78637	5.58238	5.38929	5.20637	5.03295	4.86842	4.71220	4.56376	4.42261	4.28830	4.16042
8	7.82296	7.65168	7.32548	7.01969	6.73274	6.46321	6.20979	5.97130	5.74664	5.53482	5.33493	5.14612	4.96764	4.79877	4.63886	4.48732
9	8.77906	8.56602	8.16224	7.78611	7.43533	7.10782	6.80169	6.51523	6.24689	5.99525	5.75902	5.53705	5.32825	5.13166	4.94637	4.77158
10	9.73041	9.47130	8.98259	8.53020	8.11090	7.72173	7.36009	7.02358	6.71008	6.41766	6.14457	5.88923	5.65022	5.42624	5.21612	5.01877
11	10.67703	10.36763	9.78685	9.25262	8.76048	8.30641	7.88687	7.49867	7.13896	6.80519	6.49506	6.20652	5.93770	5.68694	5.45273	5.23371
12	11.61893	11.25508	10.57534	9.95400	9.38507	8.86325	8.38384	7.94269	7.53608	7.16073	6.81369	6.49236	6.19437	5.91765	5.66029	5.42062
13	12.55615	12.13374	11.34837	10.63496	9.98565	9.39357	8.85268	8.35765	7.90378	7.48690	7.10336	6.74987	6.42355	6.12181	5.84236	5.58315
14	13.48871	13.00370	12.10625	11.29607	10.56312	9.89864	9.29498	8.74547	8.24424	7.78615	7.36669	6.98187	6.62817	6.30249	6.00207	5.72448
15	14.41662	13.86505	12.84926	11.93794	11.11839	10.37966	9.71225	9.10791	8.55948	8.06069	7.60608	7.19087	6.81086	6.46238	6.14217	5.84737
16	15.33993	14.71787	13.57771	12.56110	11.65230	10.83777	10.10590	9.44665	8.85137	8.31256	7.82371	7.37916	6.97399	6.60388	6.26506	5.95423
17	16.25863	15.56225	14.29187	13.16612	12.16567	11.27407	10.47726	9.76322	9.12164	8.54363	8.02155	7.54879	7.11963	6.72909	6.37286	6.04716
18	17.17277	16.39827	14.99203	13.75351	12.65930	11.68959	10.82760	10.05909	9.37189	8.75563	8.20141	7.70162	7.24967	6.83991	6.46742	6.12797
19	18.08236	17.22601	15.67846	14.32380	13.13394	12.08532	11.15812	10.33560	9.60360	8.95011	8.36492	7.83929	7.36578	6.93797	6.55037	6.19823
20	18.98742	18.04555	16.35143	14.87747	13.59033	12.46221	11.46992	10.59401	9.81815	9.12855	8.51356	7.96333	7.46944	7.02475	6.62313	6.25933
21	19.88798	18.85698	17.01121	15.41502	14.02916	12.82115	11.76408	10.83553	10.01680	9.29224	8.64869	8.07507	7.56200	7.10155	6.68696	6.31246
22	20.78406	19.66038	17.65805	15.93692	14.45112	13.16300	12.04158	11.06124	10.20074	9.44243	8.77154	8.17574	7.64465	7.16951	6.74294	6.35866
23	21.67568	20.45582	18.29220	16.44361	14.85684	13.48857	12.30338	11.27219	10.37106	9.58021	8.88322	8.26643	7.71843	7.22966	6.79206	6.39884
24	22.56287	21.24339	18.91393	16.93554	15.24696	13.79864	12.55036	11.46933	10.52876	9.70661	8.98474	8.34814	7.78432	7.28288	6.83514	6.43377
25	23.44564	22.02316	19.52346	17.41315	15.62208	14.09394	12.78336	11.65358	10.67478	9.82258	9.07704	8.42174	7.84314	7.32998	6.87293	6.46415
30	27.79405	25.80771	22.39646	19.60044	17.29203	15.37245	13.76483	12.40904	11.25778	10.27365	9.42691	8.69379	8.05518	7.49565	7.00266	6.56598
35	32.03537	29.40858	24.99862	21.48722	18.66461	16.37419	14.49825	12.94767	11.65457	10.56682	9.64416	8.85524	8.17550	7.58557	7.07005	6.61661
40	36.17223	32.83469	27.35548	23.11477	19.79277	17.15909	15.04630	13.33171	11.92461	10.75736	9.77905	8.95105	8.24378	7.63438	7.10504	6.64178

* Payments (or receipts) at the end of each period.

[PV_a = present value of an annuity, r = interest rate per period in decimal form, n = number of periods in which a payment is made or received]

Appendix C:

Check Figures for End-of-Chapter Problems

Chapter 1

PROBLEMS

P1-2A Net income = $220,500
P1-3A Net increase in cash = $5,700
P1-4A Total assets = $36,000
P1-6A Net income = $4,700
P1-7A Ending retained earnings = $127,000
P1-8A Net increase in cash = $164,600
P1-2B Total assets = $1,231,000
P1-3B Net increase in cash = $8,100
P1-4B Net income = $28,000
P1-6B Ending shareholders' equity = $23,550
P1-7B Ending retained earnings = $155,500
P1-8B Net income = $194,700

Chapter 2

PROBLEMS

P2-1A Ending capital = $6,205
P2-2A Total assets = $1,500
P2-3A Prepaid insurance at 12/31/09 = $1,000
P2-4A Share capital at December 31, 2008 = $350
P2-1B Total assets = $15,165
P2-2B Assets increased by $3,400
P2-3B Cash from financing activities = $5,700
P2-4B Expenses = $480

Chapter 3

PROBLEMS

P3-2A Net income = $12,750
P3-3A Amortization expense = $2,000 per year
P3-4A Prepaid insurance = $3,750
P3-5A Insurance expense = $2,400
P3-6A Unearned rental income = $2,200
P3-7A Retained earnings = $33,700
P3-8A Net income = $10,425
P3-2B Net income = $29,320
P3-3B Amortization expense = $6,000 per year
P3-4B Prepaid insurance = $5,000
P3-5B Insurance expense = $600
P3-6B Unearned rental income = $3,200
P3-7B Retained earnings = $46,083.33
P3-8B Net income = $20,970

Chapter 4

PROBLEMS

P4-1A Net income = $17,000
P4-2A Total assets at 12/31/07 = $122,000
P4-3A Net effect of closing entries on retained earnings = $15,471 debit
P4-4A Ending capital = $4,200
P4-6A Total assets at June 30 = $27,069
P4-7A Total assets at December 31, 2006 = $135,900
P4-1B Total assets at 12/31/07 = $37,000
P4-2B Retained earnings at 12/31/07 = $39,000
P4-3B Net effect of closing entries on retained earnings = $15,167 credit
P4-4B Ending capital = $31,100
P4-5B Net income = $23,150
P4-6B Ending capital = $33,475

Chapter 5

PROBLEMS

P5-1A Total cost = $164,945
P5-2A Part (b), year 1, amortization expense = $65,000
P5-3A Double-declining balance, 2012 amortization expense = $2,500
P5-4A Amortization expense 2006, activity method = $1,680
P5-5A (a) $3,000 gain
P5-8A (a) book value after 2006 = $500
P5-9A (c) gain of $9,200
P5-1B Total cost = $1,876,450
P5-2B Part (b), 2007, amortization expense = $4,000
P5-3B Straight-line, 2008 amortization expense = $6,000
P5-4B Amortization expense 2011, activity method = $23,520
P5-5B (a) $2,000 gain
P5-8B (b) 2008 amortization expense = $1,000
P5-9B (a) loss of $3,000
R5-C* Net income = $23,870

Chapter 6

PROBLEMS

P6-1A (d) $11,490
P6-2A (e) $11,904
P6-3A (a) gross margin = $2,450
P6-4A (d) cost of goods sold = $3,526
P6-5A (a) cost of goods sold = $2,640,000
P6-6A (c) Net income using FIFO = $11,340
P6-7A (a) 1. cost of goods sold = $24,818

*C = comprehensive problem

P6-8A FIFO cost of goods sold = $8,180
P6-10A (a) $15,100
P6-11A (b) net income would decrease by $75
P6-12A (b) inventory loss = $1,100
P6-13A Gross margin ratio for 2008 = 0.365
P6-1B (d) $21,925
P6-2B (e) $16,822
P6-3B (b) LIFO cost of good sold = $3,797,500
P6-4B (c) Net income using weighted average = $4,567
P6-5B 2. FIFO ending inventory = $25,880
P6-6B a. FIFO ending inventory = $6,860
P6-7B a. cost of goods sold = $35,750
P6-8B (a) $7,850
P6-10B (b) inventory loss = $875
P6-11B Gross margin ratio for 2008 = 0.3618
R6-C* Net income = $95,250

Chapter 7

PROBLEMS

P7-1A Balance per bank = $97,134.23
P7-2A Correct balance = $9,354.88
P7-4A (a) net realizable value = $12,900
P7-5A (a) allowance after expense = $7,800
P7-7A (a) $600
P7-1B Correct balance = $37,773.32
P7-2B (e) deduct $18 from balance per books (ledger)
P7-4B 3. bad debt expense = $813
P7-5B 1. Warranty expense, 6/30/05 = $31,500
P7-6B (a) $5,000
P7-7B 3. net realizable value = $444,840
R7-C* Net income = $84,184

Chapter 8

PROBLEMS

P8-1A (a) payment = $6,344.14
P8-2A (1) payment = $601.14
P8-3A (1) interest rate = 9%
P8-4A Proceeds = $924,183.20
P8-5A (c) $20,464.15
P8-6A (a) $980,000
P8-7A (c) interest expense for 2007 = $8,848.16
P8-1B (a) payment = $8,700.74
P8-2B (1) payment = $977.51
P8-3B (a) interest rate = 7%
P8-4B Proceeds = $146,532.90
P8-5B (a) proceeds = $82,624.54
P8-6B (a) $980,000
P8-7B (c) interest expense for 2009 = $104,869
R8-C* Net income 2009 = $31,995
Net income 2010 = $48,846

Chapter 9

PROBLEMS

P9-1A Total shareholders' equity = $978,500
P9-2A Retained earnings = $75,000
P9-3A (a) 2,000 shares
P9-4A (b) $4.88 per share
P9-5A (c) $8.65
P9-1B Common shares = $460,000
P9-2B Common shares = $30,000
P9-3B (a) 120,000 shares
P9-4B (b) $39.20 per share
P9-5B (b) 22
R9-C* Total assets at 12/31/07 = $1,649,000
Total assets at 12/31/08 = $3,143,000

Chapter10

PROBLEMS

P10-1A Cash from operations = $10,610
P10-2A Cash from operations = $(414)
P10-3A Cash from operations = $98,900
P10-4A Cash from operations = $294,200
P10-5A Cash from investing = $50,000
P10-6A (b) cash from financing = $67,000
P10-7A Cash from financing = $341,500
P10-8A (c) operating activities
P10-1B Cash from operations = $16,900
P10-2B Cash from operations = $(1,614)
P10-3B Cash from operations = $1,168
P10-4B Cash from operations = $187,800
P10-5B Cash from investing = $30,000
P10-6B (b) cash from financing = $26,000
P10-7B Cash from financing = $326,600
P10-8B (a) financing activities

Chapter 11

PROBLEMS

P11-1A Gain on sale of discontinued segment (net) = $126,000
P11-2A Gross margin increased significantly, from 21.1 percent in 2001 to 30.1 percent in 2003.
P11-3A Current ratio for 2003 = 2.7
P11-4A Return on equity = 8.5%
P11-5A Inventory turnover ratio = 3.4
P11-6A Acid-test ratio = 1.3 for 2004
P11-1B Loss on disposal (net) = $122,500
P11-2B Times interest earned ratio of 2003 = 10.0
P11-3B Inventory turnover ratio for 2001 = 2.7
P11-4B Debt-to-equity ratio = 1.02
P11-5B Current ratio = 1.5
P11-6B Working capital for 2004 = $487,000

Glossary

accelerated amortization methods. Amortization methods that recognize more amortization expense in the early years of an asset's life and less in later years. *182*

access controls. Controls related to all business risks associated with protecting the system from unauthorized access. *70*

accounting cycle. The set of steps used to analyze, record, classify, and summarize accounting information for the preparation of financial statements. *131*

accounting period. A length of time, normally one year, used for preparing financial statements. An accounting period also can be a month or quarter. Also called ***fiscal period***. *25*

Accounting Standards Board (AcSB). An independent private organization responsible for establishing accounting rules concerning financial reporting. *47*

accounts payable. A record of all amounts that a company owes to its vendors (suppliers). A liability. *51, 56*

accounts receivable. A record of all amounts owed by customers to a business firm for items or services they purchases on credit from the firm. An asset. *16, 52*

accounts receivable method. A method of estimating bad debt expense by focusing on the balance sheet and the amount of accounts receivable expected to go uncollected. It is one way to estimate uncollectible expense using the allowance method. *293*

accounts receivable turnover ratio. Net sales divided by average net account receivables. Measures a company's ability to collect cash from its credit customers. *301*

accrual. An accounting event in which the action of a transaction is completed before the cash value of that transaction is exchanged. *59, 85*

accrual basis accounting. The method of accounting in which revenues are recognized when earned and expenses are recognized when incurred, not necessarily when cash is exchanged. *58*

accruing. Making an adjustment for a transaction in which the action has occurred but the cash has not yet changed hands. *86*

accruing salary expense. Recording and recognizing salary expense that will be paid to employees at a later date. *89*

accumulated amortization. The total amortization that has been reported as amortization expense for the entire life of a long-term tangible asset. It is a contra-asset account. *97*

acid-test ratio. The current assets easily converted into cash (cash, short-term investments, net accounts receivable) divided by current liabilities. Measures a company's ability to meet its short-term obligations. Also called the ***quick ratio***. *300*

acquisition/payment process. The group of business activities associated with acquiring and paying for goods and services. *12*

adjusted trial balance. A list of all accounts and their balances after adjusting entries have been posted to the general ledger. It shows the debit and credit balances; its purpose is to confirm that the sum of debits = the sum of credits. *138*

adjusting entries. Entries necessary at the end of the accounting period to adjust accounts for accrued revenues and expenses and deferred revenues and expenses. *52*

adjusting the books. A crucial step in preparing the financial statements when the amounts recorded for assets and liabilities are reviewed to verify that every amount accurately reflects the financial situation of the business firm on the date of the balance sheet. *52*

agents. The people involved in a transaction, representing the business firm in such roles as cashier, inventory clerk, salesperson. *13*

allowance for doubtful accounts. The amount of accounts receivable that is expected to go uncollected. It is called a contra-asset because it is deducted from the asset, accounts receivable. *292*

allowance method. A method of estimating bad debts and expensing them in the period the sales corresponding to those debts are recognized. Two ways to estimate the bad debt expense are the **accounts receivable method** and the **sales method**. Accounts receivable is reported net of the allowance for doubtful accounts in the financial statements. The allowance method is required by **generally accepted accounting principles (GAAP)**. *292*

amortization. The periodic allocation of the cost of long-term assets over their useful lives, to the income statement as an expense. *97, 174*

amortization base. Cost minus residual value. *178*

amortization expense. The amount recognized as an expense in one period resulting from the periodic recognition of the used portion of the cost of a long-term asset over its life. *97*

annual rate. The most common basis of presenting interest rates. *108*

annuity. A series of equal payments at regular intervals over a period of time. *343*

asset exchange. A transaction in which one asset increases and another asset decreases. *24*

assets. The economic resources of a business firm, resulting from past transactions; items of value to a business firm, used to generate the firm's revenue. *20, 55*

authorized shares. The maximum number of shares that a corporation is allowed by its articles of incorporation to issue. *397*

audit. An examination of a company's financial statements by a professional accountant who then gives an opinion on the fairness with which the financial statements have been presented. *19*

average cost method. An inventory cost flow method that allocates the average cost of all items between inventory and cost of goods sold. A weighted-average cost is calculated in a periodic inventory system and a moving weighted average cost is calculated in a perpetual inventory system. *228*

average cost periodic. This means that (1) the cost of all the goods available for sale for the entire accounting period is used to calculate an average cost, and (2) the cost of goods sold is calculated at the end of the accounting period. *234*

bad debt expense. The expense associated with uncollectible accounts, also known as ***uncollectible accounts expense***. When it is a significant amount, the bad debt expense is estimated with the **allowance method.** If it is not significant, bad debt expense represents the actual losses under the direct write-off method. *293*

balance sheet. Describes the financial situation of a company at a specific point in time. One of the four basic financial statements, it gives the amount of assets, liabilities, and owner's equity that a company has at a specific point in time. *20*

balance per bank statement. The company's cash account balance reported by the bank as of the bank statement date. *288*

balance per books. The cash account balance on the company's books, used to begin the cash reconciliation. *288*

bank. An institution that provides financial services to customers, such as lending money. *6*

bank reconciliation. Compares the cash balance on the company's books and the company's cash balance on the bank statement, and identifies any differences between the two amounts. It also is called a *cash reconciliation*. *288*

beginning inventory. Goods on hand (for sale) at the beginning of the accounting period. *230*

blind purchase order. A copy of the purchase order that notifies the receiving department of an expected shipment but does not indicate the quantity of goods ordered. *225*

bond. A form of long-term financing in which a company describes in a written agreement its responsibility to pay interest and repay the principal or money it has borrowed from investors. *350*

bond covenants. Restrictions placed on the bond issuer and stated in the bond agreement, protecting the interests of the bondholders. For example, bondholders have priority with respect to assets of the firm over the owners' claims on the assets in the event the company goes bankrupt. *350*

bondholder. The individual (or institution) who purchases the bond, thus loaning money to the company that issued the bond. *350*

bond market. A market that facilitates the initial selling and buying, and subsequent trading of bonds. *350*

book value of an asset. The cost of an asset minus its accumulated amortization; also called the *net book value*, or the ***carrying value***. *98, 178*

book value of a bond. Bonds payable plus the unamortized premium or the bonds payable minus the unamortized discount; also known as the ***carrying value*** of a bond. *357*

book value per share. Total shareholders' equity (minus any equity represented in preferred stock) divided by the number of outstanding common shares. *410*

bottom line. Refers to net income on the income statement. *84*

callable bond. A bond containing a call feature giving the bond issuer the right to buy back and retire the bonds before maturity. *363*

Canada Customs and Revenue Agency (CCRA). A government agency that requires business firms to report information concerning their income and expenses, and monitors the payment and collection of income taxes. *18*

capital. A business firm's financial resources, commonly meaning money. *4*

capital asset. Long-term assets, assets that will last longer than a year. *172*

capital cost allowance. An amount deducted as an expense when calculating taxable income. This deduction replaces the amortization expense that may have been deducted when calculating income. *191*

capital contributions. The owners' investments in a company; also called ***share capital***. *8*

capital expenditure. A substantial expenditure that will benefit several accounting periods, including those which improve the quality and life of an asset. *185*

capital shares. Capital shares are the units of ownership in a corporation. The owners of the corporation are called ***shareholders***. *8*

capital structure. The combination of debt and equity that a company chooses. *364*

capitalizing. Accumulating the cost of an asset in a balance sheet account until that asset is used to generate revenue, at which time the cost is expensed. *174*

carrying value. The cost of an asset minus its accumulated amortization; book value. *98, 178*

carrying value of a bond. Bonds payable plus the unamortized premium of those bonds; or bonds payable minus their unamortized discount. *357*

cash basis accounting. The method of accounting that recognizes revenues when received and expenses when paid—that is, recognizes when the cash is exchanged. *60*

cash disbursement. A payment of cash made by a company. *13*

cash flow statement. A statement listing all the cash inflows and cash outflows of a business firm for a period of time; the cash flow statement is divided into three sections: operating, investing, and financing cash flows. *27*

cash from financing activities. Cash receipts and disbursements related to a company's financing—cash transactions related to debt and equity, shown together on the cash flow statement. *28, 441*

cash from investing activities. Cash receipts and disbursements related to a company's purchase and sale of long-term assets and investments, shown together on the cash flow statement. *28, 441*

cash from operating activities. Cash receipts and disbursements related to a company's operations, shown together on the cash flow statement. This section of the cash flow statement may be prepared and presented using either the direct method or the indirect method. *28, 441*

cash from operations. This includes all cash receipts and cash disbursements for routine sales and purchases made in the course of doing business. *440*

cash receipt. Acquisition of cash by a company; cash collection. *12*

cash reconciliation. A comparison of the cash balance in the company's records and the cash balance on the bank statement. Also called a ***bank reconciliation***. *288*

chart of accounts. An organized listing of company accounts, which serves as the basis for a general ledger accounting system. *145*

***CICA Handbook*.** Statements issued by the AcSB explaining and describing the type of information required from financial reporting. *47*

claim. The legal right to a company's assets. *364*

classified balance sheet. A balance sheet that has a subtotal for current assets and a subtotal for current liabilities. *56*

closely held corporation. A corporation whose shares are owned by a small number of people. *8*

closing entries. Entries made to reduce temporary account balances to zero and to transfer the balances to permanent accounts at the end of an accounting period. *139*

common shares. Issued by a corporation, is a basic class of shares that represents general ownership in the corporation. Common shareholders have the right to vote in running the business (usually by a vote in the election of the board of directors) and the right to receive declared dividends, although the common shareholders' right to declared dividends is secondary to preferred shareholders' right to dividends. *397*

comparability. A quality of information based on the idea that it is more useful when related to the same type of information in another period, such as comparing financial statements across companies and financial statements. *49*

comparative balance sheets. Two or more balance sheets from the same company for consecutive accounting periods, shown together to reflect the company's financial situation over two or more periods. *22*

conservatism principle. An accounting principle explaining that when doubt exists between two reporting alternatives, the user of the information should select the alternative with the least favourable impact on owner's equity. *49*

consistency. A quality of useful information requiring accounting methods to be followed in the same manner from period to period, making the information comparable. *49*

contingent liabilities. Liabilities that do not currently exist but are probable and reasonably estimable, such as lawsuits and tax disputes. *247*

contra-asset. An amount deducted from its related asset account. A contra-account is used to offset (i.e., to reduce) its related account. For example, the contra-asset **accumulated amortization** is deducted from the **capital asset** to which the amortization relates. *98, 294*

contra-liability. An amount deducted from its related liability. The contra-account is used to offset its related account. For example, the contra-liability **discount on bonds payable** is deducted from the liability **bonds payable** when the balance sheet is presented. *356*

contra-revenue account. An account used to record reductions in its related revenue account. The contra- account is used to offset its related account. For example, sales discounts is the contra-revenue account to sales. *286*

contributed capital. The amount of capital (usually cash) contributed by owners to the corporation. Also called ***share capital*** or ***paid-in capital***. *57*

contributed surplus. The capital from the sale of stock that is above the par value of the shares. It is the issue price of the shares minus its par value times the number of shares issued. *398*

contribution. The resources invested in a business firm by the owners of the firm. *11*

control. An activity performed by a business firm to minimize or eliminate risk; also known as ***internal control.*** *30*

control activities. The activities intended to prevent, detect, and correct errors and irregularities relating to business risks. *102, 302*

control environment. Comprises the integrity and ethical values of the entire business organization, management's philosophy, and how the organization treats its employees. *101*

convertible bond. A bond that can be converted into shares at the discretion of the bond holder. *364*

corporation. A business firm that is a separate legal entity from its owners. Ownership is acquired through the purchase of shares in the corporation. *8*

corrective controls. Control activities directed at recovering from, repairing the damage from, or minimizing the cost of an error or irregularity. *303*

cost. The amount a company pays or agrees to pay for an item on the acquisition date; sometimes also called ***historical cost.*** For capital assets, cost includes all expenditures to get the asset up and running. *175, 177*

cost of goods available for sale. The cost of all inventory a company has on hand, available to be sold during the accounting period; includes the cost of beginning inventory and the cost of the purchases made during the period. *232*

cost of goods sold. The company's cost of goods purchased and then sold to its customers, also known as ***cost of sales.*** *237*

cost-benefit analysis. The reasoning used to determine what financial information should be included in the financial statements of a business firm. This is a general type of analysis that weighs the cost of something against the benefit from it. *48*

cost of sales. The total costs of goods made or purchased and sold; also known as ***cost of goods sold.*** *237*

cost principle. An accounting rule that requires assets to be recorded on the date of acquisition at the amount paid for them (i.e., their cost); also called the ***historical cost principle.*** *57*

credit. An entry made on the right side of an account; also means *to make* an entry on the right side of an account. *128*

creditors. Individuals, or institutions, who lend companies money with a specified rate of return. *334*

credit sale. Occurs when a customer does not pay cash at the time of the sale but instead agrees to pay later. The sale occurs now, with payment from the customer to follow at a later time. *291*

creditworthiness. Indicates whether a borrower has in the past made loan payments when due. *19*

cumulative preferred shares. Preferred shares for which dividends not paid in any given year are carried forward to the next year. *402*

current assets. Assets, such as cash and receivables, that will be converted into cash within one year or within an operating cycle, whichever is greater. Almost all businesses use a year to classify current assets. *55*

current liabilities. Obligations that will be met with current assets, usually within one year. *56*

current ratio. Current assets divided by current liabilities; measures a firm's ability to meet its short-term obligations. *67*

date of record. The date used to determine which shareholders are to receive declared dividends. Anyone owning the shares on this date will receive the dividend. *400*

debit. An entry made on the left side of an account; also means *to make* an entry on the left side of an account. *128*

debt financing. Obtaining financing by borrowing money. *334*

debt-to-equity ratio. Total debt divided by total equity. This ratio measures the ability of a firm to meets its long-term obligations. *364*

declaration date. The date on which the board of directors makes the official decision to pay a dividend. *400*

deferral. An accounting event in which the exchange of the cash related to the transaction is completed before the activity related to the transaction is completed. *59, 85, 91*

definitely determinable liabilities. Liabilities that can be exactly measured, such as bank loans and notes payable. *246*

delivery expense. See ***freight-out***. *227*

depletion. The periodic allocation of the cost of natural resources over their useful lives. *174*

depreciation. The periodic allocation of the cost of long-term tangible assets—property, plant, and equipment—to expense on the income statement, over the useful lives of those assets. The term "depreciation" is now commonly described as amortization. *174*

detective controls. Activities intended to identify when an error or irregularity has occurred. *303*

direct method of preparing a cash flow statement. Examining the income statement and converting each revenue and expense into its related cash inflow and cash outflow, comprising cash from operations. *440*

direct write-off method. A method of recognizing actual uncollectible accounts as expenses in the period in which they become uncollectible, subtracting them from accounts receivable, and expensing them through bad debt expense. *292*

discontinued operations. Part of a business firm that has been disposed of, often by selling a segment or division. The related gain or loss from disposal is shown net of taxes after income from continuing operations. *478*

discount on bonds payable. The difference between the selling price and face amount of a bond when the face amount is greater than the selling price. This difference is recorded in a contra-liability account. *354*

discount rate. Another name for the interest rate. *337, 354*

discounting a series of cash flows. Refers to calculating the value of a series of payments over a specified number of periods at a specified rate of return to today's dollars. *337*

distributions. Cash or other assets given by a company to its owners. *400*

dividends. After-tax earnings of a business firm distributed to its owners. Dividends is the specific name for the distributions of a corporation to its owners. *11, 25, 400*

dividends in arrears. Dividends due to the holders of cumulative preferred shares that a company has not declared. *402*

dividend-yield ratio. A share's dividend divided by current market price per share. *488*

double-declining balance method. An accelerated method of amortization that uses 200 percent as the percentage of the straight-line rate. *182*

double-entry system. An accounting system that uses debits and credits to record transactions to balance the accounting equation, assets = liabilities + owner's equity. *130*

doubtful accounts. The accounts that a company estimates it will not collect. *292*

earned capital. A company's accumulation of earnings since it began, reduced by any distributions to shareholders or owners; commonly called ***retained earnings***. *409*

earnings before interest and taxes (EBIT). Income from operations before subtracting interest expense and income taxes. *237*

earnings per share (EPS). Net income for the period divided by the average number of common shares outstanding. It is used by investors and analysts to evaluate a company's performance for a period. *410*

economic substance. Refers to part of a transaction that involves an activity other than the exchange of cash. Providing a service or delivering goods would be considered the economic substance of a transaction. The exchange of cash may take place before or after the exchange of goods and services. *100*

effective interest method. A method of amortizing bond premiums and discounts that calculates the amount of interest on the outstanding liability, which changes every time a payment is made. *357*

ending inventory. Inventory on hand at the end of the accounting period, shown on the balance sheet in the current assets section. *230*

enterprise. Another name for a business organization. Other similar terms are *business firm*, sometimes simply *business*, sometimes simply *firm*, as well as *company* and *entity*. *4*

enterprise resource planning systems (ERPs). Integrated information systems that capture all a company's information in a single database. *126, 147*

entrepreneur. A person who starts a business firm and takes the economic risks inherent in starting it. *11*

equity. The owners' claims to the assets of their company. *21, 56*

estimated liabilities. Liabilities in amounts that are not certain, such as warranty liability. *247*

estimated useful life. The length of time a company plans to, or can be expected to, use an asset. *177*

events. The actual transactions of a business firm. *13*

exchanges. Events in the business process that involve getting something and giving something in return. *11*

expense. The cost a business firm incurs in selling its goods or providing its services. *17, 185*

expensing. To put on the income statement as an expense; produces an immediate reduction in net income. *174*

extraordinary items. Events that are unusual and infrequent; the gain or loss related to such events is shown separately, net of taxes, on the income statement after income from continuing operations and after any discontinued operations. *479*

face value. The amount stated on bond or note; the principal; the amount of the bond that the issuer will pay back at the maturity date. *15*

financial leverage. Concept of using borrowed money to increase return on assets. *364*

financial services company. A business firm that provides services related to money, such as a bank or a mortgage company. *6*

financial statements. Reports used by a business firm to communicate information to external users. There are four basic statements: the income statement, the balance sheet, the statement of changes in owner's equity, and the cash flow statement. *20*

FIFO periodic. This means that (1) the cost flow assumption is that the oldest goods in the inventory are sold first, and (2) inventory records and cost of goods sold are updated only once, at the end of the accounting period. *232*

first-in, first-out method (FIFO). An inventory cost flow method that assigns the cost of the first items purchased to the first items sold to calculate inventory and cost of goods sold. *228*

fiscal period. See ***accounting period***. *25*

fiscal year. Describes the business year, which may or may not coincide with the calendar year. *22*

fixed assets. A term used to describe capital assets, assets that will last longer than a year. *172*

for-profit organization. An entity that provides products or services with the primary objective of making a profit. *4*

FOB destination. A condition of purchase requiring the supplier to pay for all transportation costs up to the destination point, which is when title to the purchased goods passes to the buyer. *FOB* means *free on board*. *226*

FOB shipping point. A condition of purchase in which the buyer has title to the goods when they leave the supplier and is responsible for the cost of transportation from the supplier's shipping point to the buyer's destination. *226*

free cash flow. Cash from operations minus dividends and capital expenditures. *453*

freight-in. A part of the cost of inventory. It is the transportation cost of the goods purchased. *226*

freight-out. Considered an operating expense. It is the transportation cost of goods delivered to customers. *227*

gain. The increase in net assets resulting from certain kinds of transactions, usually transactions not part of the normal operations of the firm. *189*

general ledger. A record of all accounts a company uses with the additions, deductions, and balances of each account. *127*

general ledger system. The name for a traditional accounting system, based on the recording of transactions using debits and credits. *126*

generally accepted accounting principles (GAAP). Accounting guidelines, issued by the Accounting Standards Board (AcSB), which a company must follow when preparing its financial statements for external users. *47*

going-concern assumption. An accounting assumption that allows the preparation of financial statements as if a company will continue to exist in the future unless there is contrary evidence. *57*

goods available for sale. Beginning inventory plus purchases for an accounting period. (*See* ***cost of goods available for sale***.) *232*

gross margin. Another term for ***gross profit on sales***. *26*

gross pay. The full amount an employee is paid before taxes are deducted. *247*

gross profit on sales. Sales revenue minus *cost of goods sold;* also known as *gross margin* on sales. *26*

gross profit percentage. Gross profit as a percentage of sales; also known as *gross margin on sales ratio*. *242, 245*

historical cost. The original amount a company paid for an item. *57*

historical cost principle. An accounting concept that requires companies to record assets at their original cost. *57, 175*

income before interest and taxes. The income from business operations before interest expense and income taxes are subtracted. *237*

income from operations. Income from normal business operations before any nonoperating items, including interest and income taxes, have been deducted. *237*

income statement. A statement that reports a company's net income for a period. It is a summary of all the revenues, expenses associated with those revenues, gains, and losses for the company. The income statement is also called the ***statement of earnings*** and the ***profit and loss statement***. *25*

indirect method of preparing a cash flow statement. Starting with net income and adjusting for all changes in current assets and current liabilities, resulting in the amount of cash from operations. *440*

information-processing risk. The risk associated with recording, maintaining, or reporting data or information. *147*

information systems. Computerized systems that enable companies to record, organize, and maintain information. *145*

input controls. Controls that help manage risk associated with the possibility that information will be fictitious, erroneous, or incomplete. *69*

insurance company. A business firm that provides some financial protection in the case of loss of life or property. *6*

intangible assets. Assets with value that cannot be seen or touched, such as copyrights, patents, trademarks, and franchises. *173*

interest. Payment for the use of someone else's money; the excess amount paid or received over the principal of the loan. *15*

interest expense. The cost a business incurs to borrow money. With respect to bonds payable, the interest expense is calculated by multiplying the market rate of interest by the carrying value of the bonds on the date of the payment. *357*

interest payment. The payment to holders of bonds payable, calculated by multiplying the stated rate on the face of the bond by the par, or face, value of the bond. If bonds are issued at a discount or premium, the interest payment does not equal the interest expense. *357*

interest rate. The rate applied to the principal of a loan to determine the amount of interest charged, traditionally given in terms of a year. *336*

internal controls. The policies and procedures a company uses to provide reasonable assurance as to the accuracy and reliability of its accounting records. *69*

internal control system. The framework of internal controls and security measures employed by a company. *69*

inventory. Goods purchased for sale, or for making into goods for sale. *225*

inventory cost flow. The flow of inventory costs from the balance sheet to the income statement (inventory to cost of goods sold). *228*

inventory flow. The physical movement of goods through a business. *228*

inventory turnover ratio. Sales divided by average inventory. This ratio measures how fast the company is selling its inventory. *244*

investment. Sometimes used to describe an owner's capital contribution to the company; also used to refer to the purchase of assets to make a profit (e.g., buying shares or bonds of other companies). *396*

invoice. A bill sent to a company (the buyer) by a vendor (the supplier). *15*

issued shares. The actual number of shares currently classified as *issued*—comprises all the shares given in return for ownership in the corporation less any shares that have been retired. *397*

issuer. The company that raises money from investors by issuing bonds or selling equity. *349*

journal. Book of original entry, in which transactions are recorded in a general ledger system. *126*

last-in, first-out method (LIFO). An inventory cost flow method that assigns the cost of the most recent goods purchased to the first goods sold to calculate inventory and cost of goods sold. *228*

liabilities. The claims creditors have against the resources of a business firm and the obligations of a business firm to perform services in the future. *21, 56*

limited liability. The idea that the owners of a corporation cannot be held personally liable for the actions of the corporation. Only the amounts of the owners' contributions and earnings are at risk of loss. *10*

LIFO periodic. This means that (1) the cost flow assumption is that the newest goods in the inventory are sold first, and (2) inventory records and cost of goods sold are updated only once, at the end of the accounting period. *234*

liquidity. Measure of how quickly and easily assets can be converted to cash and short-term obligations can be met. *55*

long-term assets. Assets used in the normal course of business that will *not* be converted into cash within one year. *55, 172*

long-term liabilities. Obligations that will *not* be paid within one year. *56*

long-term note payable. An obligation that occurs when a company borrows money from a financial institution, such as a bank, for longer than one year and is usually repaid with a series of payments of principal and interest over the life of the note. *334*

loss. The decrease in net assets resulting from transactions that generally do *not* occur in the normal course of business. *189*

lower-of-cost-or-market. The method for reporting inventory on the financial statements that requires valuing inventory at the lower of the cost of inventory or its market value. *243*

managerial accounting. The study of how managers use accounting information that is internal to the firm. Information internal to the firm is generally not shown on the firm's financial statements. *453*

manufacturing business. A business firm that makes the products it sells. *6*

market interest rate. The interest rate in the market for investments with similar risk. It is usually a reference to the interest rate on the date bonds are sold. *352*

market price. The price an asset could demand if it is sold on the open market. *243*

market value. The price of an asset agreed on between a willing buyer and a willing seller; the price an asset could demand if it is sold on the open market. *243*

matching principle. An accounting concept that establishes when expenses are recognized. Expenses are matched with the revenues they helped generate and are recognized when those revenues are recognized. Matching means putting the related revenues and expenses on the same income statement. *58*

materiality. Determines whether an item or transaction is significant enough to be reported in a specific way in the financial statements. *49*

merchandise inventory. All goods owned, even those in transit, and held for sale by a company, often referred to as ***inventory***. *225*

merchandising business. A business firm that buys goods, adds value, and sells the goods to other companies or consumers. There are two types of merchandising business firms: a wholesale company and a retail company. *5*

monitoring. Examining controls to ensure they are operating properly. *102*

mortgage. A note payable issued for property, such as a house, usually repaid in equal installments consisting of part principal and part interest, over a specified period. *336*

mortgage company. A financial institution that lends money to borrowers to purchase property. *6*

multistep income statement. An income statement that shows *sales − cost of goods sold = gross margin* and then shows all other revenues and expenses. *26*

net earnings. Another name for ***net income***. *84*

net income. The difference between the revenues and the expenses during an accounting period; also called ***net earnings***. *84*

net loss. Occurs when expenses are greater than revenues. *84*

net profit. Another term for ***net income***. *84*

net realizable value. A term used to refer to the amount that will be realized when an asset is converted to cash. Referring to ***accounts receivable***, it is the amount of accounts receivable less any allowances for doubtful accounts. It is the actual amount of accounts receivable expected to be collected. *292*

net sales. All sales a company has made after returns and allowances (discounts) have been deducted. *286*

noncumulative preferred shares. Preferred shares for which dividends not paid in any given year are *not* carried forward to the next year. *402*

noncurrent assets. Assets that are not used up within one year. *55*

noncurrent liabilities. Obligations that are not paid within one year. *56*

nonsufficient funds (NSF) cheque. A customer's cheque that has been returned by the bank because the customer did not have enough funds in his or her account to cover the amount of the cheque. *289*

notes to the financial statements. Information provided along with the four basic financial statements, considered to be an integral part of the statements. The notes describe the accounting methods used to prepare the statements and explain various aspects of the financial condition of the company. *489*

not-for-profit organization. An entity that provides goods and services whose motivation is other than making a profit, usually providing social services. *4*

on account. Refers to selling or purchasing goods or services on credit. *50*

open purchase order. A copy of the purchase order sent to the accounts payable department and reviewed prior to payment for the goods ordered. *225*

operating expenses. All expenses incurred in the normal operations of a business except interest and taxes. *237*

operating income. Income from operations before interest expense and income taxes are deducted. *237*

operational assets. Assets with useful lives of more than one year, purchased to generate revenue for the business firm. *192*

other receivables. Amounts owed to a company by people and companies other than customers. *87*

output controls. Controls related to the accuracy and completeness of a system's output. *70*

outstanding shares. The amount of shares issued and currently owned by investors. *397*

owners. Individuals or institutions that invest money in a business for an unspecified return. *334*

owner's equity. The amount left over after liabilities are netted out of assets; sometimes referred to as *net assets*. It is the total amount of owner's claims to the assets of the company. *26*

packing slip. A document included in the shipped order that describes what is in the order. *16*

paid-in capital. The capital owners or shareholders have invested in a corporation; also called ***share capital***. *57, 396*

par value. The face value of a security; the fixed per-share amount printed on the stock certificate. The principal amount of a bond. *398*

partnership. A business firm owned by two or more people in a legal form similar to a sole proprietorship. An LLP is a special case of a partnership, with some of the benefits of a corporation. *7*

partnership agreement. A document that defines the specific terms of a partnership or business relationship, such as how much work each partner will do and how the profits are divided. *8*

payment date. The date the assets are to be distributed to the shareholders as dividends. *401*

periodic inventory system. Record-keeping for inventory in which records are updated once, at the end of the accounting period when ending inventory is physically counted. The system can be used for FIFO, LIFO, or average cost inventory cost flow assumptions. *230*

permanent accounts. Accounts whose balances carry over from period to period. These accounts are the assets, liabilities, and owner's equity accounts. *141*

perpetual inventory system. A system that updates inventory records after every purchase or sale, providing a current record of inventory and cost of goods sold; can be used for FIFO, LIFO, or average cost inventory cost flow assumptions. *230*

picking slip. A document sent from the sales department to the warehouse requesting the goods ordered by the customer; also called a ***stock request***. *16*

positively correlated. Describes values or amounts of two items that move in the same direction. In accounting and finance, the amount of risk and the amount of return on an investment move in the same direction—when risk is high, the potential return will be high, when risk is low, the potential return will be low. *61*

postclosing trial balance. A list of all a company's accounts, each with its debit or credit balance—prepared after closing entries are posted. Only real accounts will be found on the postclosing trial balance. *143*

posting. Transferring transactions from the journal to the general ledger. *127*

preferred shares. A class of shares that gives priority for dividends and for the company's assets in the event the company must default. This class of shares is usually nonvoting (i.e., preferred shareholders do not get to vote in the election of the board of directors). *397*

premium on bonds payable. A liability account that records the difference between selling price and the face value of the bond when the selling price is higher than the face value. *354*

prepaid insurance. An asset that exists when a company pays for insurance in advance, before receiving the protective services of that insurance. *51, 92*

prepaid rent. An asset that is recorded when a company makes its rent payments in advance. *93*

present value. The current value of a future cash flow. *337*

preventive controls. Control activities whose purpose is to prevent an error or irregularity. *303*

price-earnings ratio. The market value of a company's share divided by earnings per share. *488*

principal. The actual amount of cash borrowed or loaned; sometimes used to describe the face value of the bond. *15*

proceeds. Cash collected from the sale of an asset, from issuing shares, or from selling bonds. It is a general term that indicates a cash inflow. *189*

processing controls. Controls related to the storage and manipulation of data, such as segregation of duties, documentation controls, reconciliation, and cross-checking. *70*

profit. The difference between the revenues and expenses from selling goods or providing services. *5*

profit and loss statement (P&L). Another term for the income statement. *25*

prospectus. A report detailing a future share offering containing a set of financial statements; required by securities regulators from a company that wishes to make an initial public offering of its shares. *412*

public accountant An accountant who has met certain professional requirements and has been licensed to provide accounting services to the public. *19*

purchase. A part of the acquisition and payment cycle in which the business gives up cash in return for inventory or another economic resource. *13*

purchase discount. A cash discount a company is offered by its vendors to make prompt payments. *225*

purchase order. A form on which items or services needed by a business firm are specified and then communicated to the vendor. *15, 225*

purchase requisition. A form, completed by an employee of the business firm, indicating what is to be purchased. *15, 224*

purchase returns and allowances. The cost of the inventory items a company has returned or the amount of credit given for a defective or substandard items purchased. *226*

publicly traded corporation. A corporation whose shares are traded on the stock exchanges. *8*

quick ratio. See ***acid-test ratio***. *300*

REA model. A diagram showing the relationships among the resources, events, and agents in a business exchange. *13*

real accounts. Permanent accounts, which are the accounts on the balance sheet—assets, liabilities, and equity accounts. These accounts are never closed. *141*

receiving report. A record of the actual goods received from a purchase. *15, 225*

recognition. Is considered to occur when an item is formally recorded in the accounting records and reported in the financial statements. For example, when revenue is earned, it is recognized and reported on the income statement. This term is most often applied to revenue and expenses, indicating that they are recorded on the income statement for a period. *57*

recognize. To formally record a transaction in the accounting records and report it in the financial statements. For example, when revenue is earned, it is recognized and reported on the income statement. *57*

relative fair market value method. A method of assigning cost to separate assets obtained in a basket purchase. A percentage of the total purchase price is assigned to each asset. *176*

relevant. Refers to information a business can use to evaluate past performance and predict future consequences. *48*

reliable. Refers to information that can be verified for the truthfulness and the faithfulness of the economic events it represents. *48*

replacement cost. The cost that would be incurred if a company had to replace an existing asset. *243*

residual value. An asset's estimated value that can be realized at its disposal date; also called ***salvage value***. *97, 178*

resources. Things of value, both tangible and intangible, that are exchanged in a transaction. *13*

retail company. A merchandising company that buys goods, adds value, and sells the goods to consumers. *6*

retained earnings. Equity belonging to the owners of a company as a result of earning income from business operations; also called ***earned capital***. The amount of retained earnings on the balance sheet will be equal to all the net incomes minus all the net losses and distributions paid to the owners of the company since its inception to the date of the balance sheet. *57, 409*

return on assets. Net income divided by average total assets. This ratio is a measure of how well a company is using its assets to generate income. *193*

return on equity. Net income divided by average shareholders' equity. This ratio is a measure of a company's profitability. *409*

revenue. The amount a business earns for the goods sold or the services provided. *17*

revenue expenditure. Any expenditure that benefits only the current accounting period. A simpler and clearer name is ***expense***. *185*

revenue recognition principle. Determines when revenue should be recognized. This principle allows recognition of revenue when the earnings process is substantially complete. This occurs when the economic substance of the transaction has been completed. *58*

risk. The uncertainty associated with the amount and timing of future returns; the possibility of an unfavourable outcome relating to all aspects of business. *29, 61*

sales/collection process. The business process of selling goods or providing services to consumers and, in return, receiving payment for those goods and services. *12*

sales discount. A cash discount provided by companies to encourage their customers to pay bills promptly. The difference between the selling price of the goods and the cash collected is the sales discount amount. *285*

sales method. A method of estimating bad debt expense by focusing on the income statement and the amount of the sales of the current period expected to be uncollectible. *293*

sales order. A record of a customer's order. *16*

sales returns and allowances. The account that records the amount for returned goods and allowances for defective goods; a contra-sales account. This amount is deducted from sales on the income statement. *287*

salvage value. An asset's estimated value that can be realized at its disposal date, also called ***residual value***. *97, 178*

secured bond. A bond that gives the bondholder claim to a specific asset of the company in case the company fails to pay the bondholder the interest and principal payments promised. *351*

securities commission. A government agency set up to monitor the activities and financial reporting of corporations that sell shares of ownership to the public. *10*

separate-entity assumption. An assumption in accounting that requires the financial activities and records of the business enterprise to be separate and distinct from the personal financial activities and records of its owners. *48*

separation of duties. A control used by a company to ensure the functions of authorization, recording, and physical custody are not all performed by the same individual. *249*

serial bonds. Bonds in an issue that mature periodically over several years. *351*

service business. A business firm that provides services to consumers, such as accounting and legal services. *5*

share capital. The total amount of economic resources the owners have invested in a business firm. *57, 396*

shareholder. An owner of a share or shares in a corporation. *8*

shares. Units of ownership in a corporation. *8*

short-term note payable. An obligation that occurs when a company borrows from a financial institution money to be repaid within one year, usually with a single payment of interest and principal at the end of the note. *335*

single-step income statement. An income statement that shows all revenues and then deducts all expenses. There is no subtotal for gross margin (as there is in a multistep income statement). *25*

sole proprietorship. A business owned by a single person. *6*

specific identification method. An inventory cost flow method that identifies exact items sold to calculate cost of goods sold. *228*

statement of earnings. Another name for the ***income statement***. *25*

statement of retained earnings. A statement that reports the total changes in the amount of retained earnings over a period of time. *27*

stockbroker. A business person who represents people who want to buy shares and people who want to sell shares of a corporation on the stock exchange. *8*

stock dividend. The payment of a dividend in the form of additional shares of a company. *407*

stock exchange. Marketplace for buying and selling shares of a publicly traded corporation. *8*

stock request. A document sent to the warehouse requesting the goods ordered by the customer, also called a ***picking slip***. *16*

stock split. Occurs when the corporation increases the number of shares outstanding by dividing the current shares. *408*

straight-line amortization. A method that expenses an equal amount of amortization for each year of the asset's useful life; that writes off periodic, equal amounts of bond premium and discount over the life of the bond. *178, 361*

subsidiary ledger. A record that contains detailed information in support of a general ledger account. For example, an accounts receivable subsidiary ledger contains detailed accounts of all amounts owed by customers to the business firm. *128*

supplies. Items purchased in advance, used in a firm's business activities, and recognized as an expense when used. *95*

T-account. A representation of a page in the general ledger with debits on the left side and credits on the right side. *129*

tangible assets. Refers to assets, such as equipment and vehicles, that can be physically observed and used in the firm's operating activities. *173*

temporary accounts. Account balances closed to owner's equity at the end of an accounting period. These accounts include revenues, expenses, and dividends. *139*

term bonds. Bonds that mature on a specified date. *351*

tickler file. A file that contains invoices filed in the order of the date they are due. *246*

time cards. A card used by a firm to record the amount of time worked by an employee during each day. *247*

times-interest-earned ratio. Net income before interest and taxes, divided by interest expense; describes a company's ability to make interest payments on its debt. *364*

timing differences. The difference between the time a transaction occurs and the time the cash related to the transaction is exchanged. *84*

trading. Buying and selling shares. *8*

transactions. An exchange or event between entities that has an economic impact on the business firm. *12*

treasury shares. Shares that have been issued and later bought back by the issuing corporation but not cancelled. *404*

trial balance. A list of all accounts and their balances; used to ensure debits = credits. *128, 138*

two-ten, net-thirty, or (2/10, n/30). Terms of a sales discount. Specifically, if the bill is paid within 10 days, the buyer will receive a 2 percent discount; if not, the balance is due within 30 days. *226*

unadjusted trial balance. The trial balance before any adjusting entries are prepared. *138*

uncollectible accounts. The accounts that a company estimates it will not collect. *293*

uncollectible accounts expense. An expense that recognizes the losses from uncollectible accounts and, therefore, reduces net income; also called ***bad debt expense.*** *293*

unearned revenue. A liability created when a business receives payment for goods or services before the goods are delivered or the services are rendered. *91*

unit-of-measure assumption. Assumes assets, liabilities, and equity will be measured in monetary units. *57*

units of production amortization. An amortization method based on the number of units to be produced by an asset as opposed to the years of useful life. *181*

unsecured bond. A bond that does not give the bondholder a specific claim to a company asset but, instead, is issued on the general credit of the company; also known as a ***debenture.*** *351*

unusual items. Items on the income statement that result from transactions that are either not typical of normal business activities or are infrequent in nature. *481*

usefulness. The most important quality of accounting information. How useful information is depends on how well it does what it is supposed to do. To be useful, information must be both relevant and reliable. *48*

vendor. A business firm that supplies goods and services to other business firms. *15*

warranty. An obligation of a company to replace defective goods or correct any deficiencies in performance or quality of a product. *299*

wholesale company. A merchandising company that sells goods to other companies. *5*

withdrawals. Distributions of a sole proprietorship's assets to its owner or distributions of a partnership's assets to the partners. *134*

working capital. Current assets minus current liabilities; a measure of a company's ability to meet its short-term obligations. *100*

writing off. The allocation of the cost of an asset over several accounting periods. Also, to *expense* a cost, that is, put it on the income statement as an expense. *174*

zero-coupon bond. A bond that does not make periodic payments of interest. The full face value of the bond is due at its maturity date. *362*

Index

A

accelerated amortization, 182
accountants, 30
accounting cycle
  adjusted trial balance, preparation of, 138–139
  adjusting journal entries, 134–138
  closing the revenue and expense accounts, 139–143
  financial statements, preparation of, 138–139
  postclosing trial balance, 143
  posting journal entries to general ledger, 134
  recording journal entries, 131–134
  review and summary, 143–145
  steps, described, 131
  unadjusted trial balance, preparation of, 134
accounting equation, 21–22, 24, 25*f*, 26, 56
accounting information
  see also financial statements
  business decision making, 17–18, 46–47
  comparability, 49
  conservatism, 49–50
  consistency, 49
  decision making, 17–18, 46–47
  described, 20
  flow, 18–20, 28
  materiality, 49
  others' needs, 18–19
  qualitative characteristics, 48–50, 49*f*
  usefulness, 19–20, 48, 66–67
accounting information system, 20, 70*f*, 102
accounting periods, 60–61
accounting policy changes, 480–481
accounting principles, 57–58, 59*f*, 67
Accounting Standards Board (AcSB), 47
accounts payable, 51, 56
accounts receivable
  aging schedule, 295
  allowance method, 292–297
  bad debt expense, 292
  described, 16, 52
  direct write-off method, 291–292
  disclosure on financial statements, 300
  doubtful accounts, 291–297
  factoring, 283
  management, 283
  receivables with interest, 87–88
  recording, 59, 291–297
  uncollectible accounts, 291–297, 291*f*
accounts receivable method, 293, 294–297
accounts receivable subsidiary ledger, 128
accounts receivable turnover ratio, 301–302, 485
accrual accounting, 58, 59, 59*f*, 67, 442–443
accruals
  described, 59, 85, 100, 100*f*
  interest expense, 85–87
  interest revenue, 85–87
  other revenues and expenses, 88–91
  receivables with interest, 87–88
accrued expenses, 136
accrued revenue, 135–136
accruing, 86
accumulated amortization, 97–98
acid-test ratio, 300, 485
acquisition
  of human resources, 247–249
  of inventory, 224–227
  of long-term assets, 173–175
  paying for, 245–249
acquisition costs, 175–177
acquisition/payment process
  acquisition of merchandise for sale, 224–227
  business risks, 249–250
  controls, 249, 250
  described, 12, 13–14, 14*f*
  inventory. *See* inventory
  liabilities. *See* liabilities
  merchandise inventory, 225
  objectives, 224
  purchases, 225–227
  steps in, 15–16, 16*f*, 224–225
adjunct liability, 355
adjusted trial balance, 138–139
adjusting the books, 52
adjustments
  accruals, 85–91
  accrued expenses, 136
  accrued revenue, 135–136
  cash/bank reconciliation, 288
  deferrals, 91–99
  deferred expenses, 138
  deferred revenue, 137
  journal entries, 134–138
  necessity of, 128
  under periodic inventory system, 239–240
  under perpetual inventory system, 238–239
  using Excel, 103
agents, 12, 13
allowance for doubtful accounts, 293
allowance method, 292–297
amortization
  accelerated amortization, 182
  bond discount, 356–359
  bond premium, 357, 359–361
  declining balance method, 182–183, 184–185*f*
  deferred expenses, 98*f*
  described, 174, 177–178
  effective interest method, 357
  and financial statements, 178–185
  finding and using amortization information, 192
  intangible assets, 188–189
  mortgage amortization schedule, 339*f*
  straight-line amortization, 178–180, 180*f*, 183, 184*f*, 361–362
  and taxes, 191–192
  units-of-production amortization, 181–182, 183–184, 184*f*
  vocabulary of, 177–178
amortization base, 178
amortization expense, 97
annuity
  annuity due, 343, 344–345, 344*f*
  described, 343
  future value, 343–345
  ordinary annuity, 343, 343*f*, 344, 347, 348–349
  present value, 347–349
  types of, 343
annuity due, 343, 344–345, 344*f*
annuity in arrears. *See* ordinary annuity
asset accounts, 130, 141
assets
  on balance sheet, 55–56
  capital assets, 172
  contra-asset, 98
  current assets, 55
  described, 20
  intangible assets, 173–174, 188–189

long-term assets. *See* long-term assets
noncurrent assets, 55
revaluation of, 57
tangible assets, 173
ATI Technologies, 488
audit, 19, 70–71
auditors, 18
average cost method, 228
average cost periodic, 234

B

bad debt expense, 292, 293
balance sheet
classified balance sheet, 56
comparative balance sheets, 22
described, 20–24, 23*f*
example, 54*f*
and income statement, relationship between, 60*f*, 142–143
vs. income statement, 26
preparation, 53–54
bank reconciliation, 288–291
banks, 19
basic EPS, 410
basket purchase allocation, 176
beginning inventory errors, 241–242
betterments, 186
blind purchase order, 225
board of directors, 401
bond certificate, 350*f*
bonds
book value, 357
buying and selling, 351
callable bonds, 363
carrying value, 357
convertible bonds, 364
described, 349–351, 350
discount, sold at, 354
premium, sold at, 354
price, 351
secured bonds, 351
serial bonds, 351
term bonds, 351
unsecured bonds, 351
zero-coupon bonds, 362–363
bonds payable
amortization of bond discount, 356–359
amortization of bond premium, 357, 359–361
amortization schedule, continuation of, 359*f*, 361*f*
discount, 353–359, 356
discounting a series of cash flows, 354
effective interest method, 357
issue of, as transaction, 351–352
market interest rate, changes in, 353
payment to bondholders, 352–353, 358–361
premium, 353–355
straight-line amortization, 361–362
straight-line amortization schedule, 362*f*
zero-coupon bonds, 362–363
book value, 98, 178
book value per (common) share, 410
bookkeeping, 126
books, 24
business
information needs, 17–18
organizational form, 5–6
owners, 61–63, 396
ownership structure, 6–11
purpose of, 4–5
types of businesses, 5–6, 11, 11*f*
business activities, 28
see also business processes
business description, 7
business plan, 7
business process model, 2, 5, 5*f*
business processes
acquisition/payment process. *See* acquisition/payment process
classification of steps, 11
conversion process, 12
described, 12*f*
sales/collection process, 12, 16–17, 17*f*
business risks
analysis of, 101–102
business start-up, 29–30
equity financing, 411
information processing risk, 147–148
internal controls, 69–71
inventory, 249
liabilities, 250
long-term assets, 194–195
of long-term debt, 366
purchase/acquisition process, 249–250
in sales/collection process, 356
business start-up
business plan, 7
decision making, 17
empty balance sheet, 23
first exchange, 11

C

callable bonds, 363
Canada Revenue Agency (CRA), 18
Canadian Institute of Chartered Accountants (CICA), 19, 448
capital, 4
capital assets, 172
capital cost allowance, 191
capital expenditure, 185–187
capital lease, 193
capital shares, 8
capitalized leases, 193
capitalizing the cost, 174, 175
carrying value, 98, 178
cash
need for, 439
sources and uses of, 439*f*
cash basis accounting, 60, 442–443
cash budget, 438
cash disbursement, 13
cash flow budget, 62
cash flow planning, 438
cash flow statement
accrual numbers, conversion from, 442–443
cash from financing activities, 441, 450–451
cash from investing activities, 441, 450–451
cash from operations, 440, 444–450
described, 27–28, 28*f*
direct method, 440, 440*f*, 444–447, 447*f*, 451–452, 451*f*
example, 54*f*
financial statement analysis, 452–453
financing section, 441
free cash flow, 453
historical, 62
importance of, 438–439
indirect method, 440, 440*f*, 448–450, 450*f*, 451–452, 452*f*
investing section, 441
operating section, 441
preparation, 54–55, 451
cash from financing activities, 28, 441, 450–451
cash from investing activities, 28, 441, 450–451
cash from operations, 28, 440, 444–450
cash management, 62
cash receipt, 12
cash reconciliation, 288–291
cash sales, 282–283
chart of accounts, 145
CICA Handbook, 47, 48, 50
classified balance sheet, 56
closing
under periodic inventory system, 239–240
under perpetual inventory system, 238–239
revenue and expense accounts, 139–143
Commission des valeurs mobilières du Québec, 10
common shares, 397
comparability, 49
comparative balance sheets, 22
compound interest, 340, 341*f*
conservatism, 49–50
consistency, 49
contingent liabilities, 247
contra-accounts, 356
contra-asset, 98
contra-liability, 356
contributed capital, 57
contributed (share) capital, 11
contribution, 11, 56
control, 30
control activities, 102
control environment, 101
conversion process, 12
convertible bonds, 364
CoolBrands International, A-1–A-46
corporations
advantages, 10
described, 8
disadvantages, 10–11

equity, 57
regulation, 10
corrective controls, 303
cost, 175, 177
cost allocation, 174–175
cost-benefit analysis, 48
cost flow. *See* inventory cost flow
cost of goods available for sale, 232
cost of goods sold
and inventory systems, 230, 231
in merchandising operations, 237–238
transactions, recording, 238–240
cost principle, 57, 67
CPP deductions, 248–249
credit, 245
credit card sales, 298
credit sales, 282–283
creditors, 61–63, 334
credits, 128, 129–130, 129*f*
creditworthiness, 19
cumulative preferred shares, 402
current assets, 55
current liability, 56
current ratio, 67–68, 300, 485
cutoff issues, 60–61

D

Danier Leather Inc., 68*f*, 85*f*
date of record, 400–401
debits, 128, 129–130, 129*f*
debt financing
bonds. *See* bonds
business risks, 366
described, 334
interest, 282
line of credit, 335
long-term notes payable, 334–339
mortgages, 334–339
ratio analysis, 364–365
time value of money, 339–349
debt-to-equity ratio, 364, 487
decision making, 17–18, 46–47
declining balance method, 182–183, 184–185*f*
deferrals
described, 59, 85, 91, 100*f*
expense-related deferrals, 92–99
revenue-related deferrals, 91–92
deferred expenses, 138
deferred revenue, 137
definitely determinable liabilities, 246
delivery expense, 227
depletion, 174
depletion of natural resources, 188
depreciation, 174
detective controls, 302
diluted EPS, 410
direct method, 440, 440*f*, 444–447, 447*f*, 451–452, 451*f*
direct write-off method, 291–292
discontinued operations, 478–479, 479*f*
discount rate, 337
discounting, 337
discounting a series of cash flows, 354
distributions, 11
dividend declaration date, 400
dividend-yield ratio, 488, 489*f*
dividends, 11, 25, 134, 400–403, 407–408
dividends in arrears, 402
Dorel Industries Inc., 490*f*, 491*f*, 492*f*
double-declining balance method. *See* declining balance method
doubtful accounts, 291–297

E

earned capital. *See* retained earnings
earnings per share (EPS), 410, 487
economic substance, 58
effective interest method, 357
Emerging Issues Committee (EIC), 47
Employment Insurance (EI) deductions, 248–249
ending inventory
errors, 240–241
gross profit method of estimating, 242
enterprise resource planning (ERP) systems, 146, 147, 247
enterprise-wide resource planning system (ERP), 126
equipment, 96–99, 97*f*
equity, 56–57, 130
equity financing
business risks, 411
retained earnings, 408–409
share capital, 396–404
shares. *See* shares
stock dividends, 407–408
stock splits, 408
Ernst & Young, 29–30
ERP, 126
errors
described, 302
inventory. *See* inventory errors
estimated liabilities, 246
estimated useful life, 177, 187–188
estimates, changes in, 187–188
events, 12, 13
Excel
accounts receivable aging schedule, 304
acquisition of long-term assets, 195
acquisition/payment process, 250–251
adjusted trial balance, 148
adjustments, 103
amortization schedule, 367
cash flow statement, 455
inputting transactions, 32
ratio analysis, 494
shareholders' equity, 412
statement of retained earnings, 71
exchange, 11–13
expense-related deferrals
equipment, 96–99, 97*f*
insurance, 92–93, 94*f*
rent, 93–94
supplies, 95–96, 95*f*
expenses, 17, 52–89–91
expensing, 174, 175
extraordinary items, 479–480, 481*f*

F

factor, 283
factoring, 283
Fairfax Financial Holdings Ltd., 403
FIFO, 228
FIFO periodic, 232–233
FIFO perpetual, 233–234
Financial Accounting Standards Board (FASB), 47, 480
financial information, 17
financial leverage, 364
financial management plan, 7
financial ratios. *See* ratio analysis
financial reporting. *See* financial statements
financial statement analysis
cash flow statement, 452–453
horizontal analysis, 482–484
ratio analysis. *See* ratio analysis
vertical analysis, 483*f*, 484
financial statement concepts, 47
financial statements
accounting equation, 21–22, 24, 25*f*, 26, 56
accounting policy changes, 480–481
accounts receivable information, 300
and amortization, 178–185
analysis of. *See* financial statement analysis
audited, 19
balance sheet, 20–24, 23*f*
cash flow statement, 27–28, 28*f*. *See also* cash flow statement
creditors, 61–63
discontinued operations, 478–479, 479*f*
elements of, 50
extraordinary items, 479–480, 481*f*
and flow of information, 28
income statement, 25–27
information provided by, 63–65
internal control issues, 69–71
investors, 61–63
limits of, 48
measurement, 57
notes to financial statements, 55
objective, 48
overview, 20–28
owners, 61–63
preparation of, 138–139
recognition of revenue and expenses, 57–58
statement of retained earnings, 27, 27*f*
transactions, organization of, 66–67
unusual items, 481–482
first-in, first-out method (FIFO), 228
fiscal period, 25
fiscal year, 22
flow of information, 18–20, 28
FOB destination, 226
FOB shipping point, 226
for-profit firm, 4
fraud, 29–30
free cash flow, 453
freight-in, 226, 237

freight-out, 227
future value
  annuity, 343–345
  annuity due, 344–345, 344*f*
  annuity due table, 345*f*
  financial calculator, 342
  future value of $1 table, partial, 342*f*
  future value of annuity of $1 in arrears table, B-3
  future value of ordinary annuity table, partial, 344*f*
  future value of single amount table, B-2
  of lump sum, 341*f*
  ordinary annuity, 343–344, 343*f*
  single amount, 340–342
  table, 342

G

GAAP. *See* generally accepted accounting principles (GAAP)
gain, 189
general ledger, 127–128
general ledger accounting system
  accounting cycle. *See* accounting cycle
  chart of accounts, 145
  computerized general ledger software, 145
  debits and credits, 128, 129–130, 129*f*
  described, 126
  vs. integrated information systems, 145–147
  process of recording information in, 126–128
generally accepted accounting principles (GAAP)
  allowance method, 292
  changes in, 480–481
  described, 47
  going-concern assumption, 67
  inventory cost flow assumptions, 228, 229
  revenue recognition, 284
  straight-line amortization, 361
  substance *vs.* form, 193
going-concern assumption, 57, 67
gross margin from sales, 237
gross margin on sales ratio, 245
gross margin ratio, 487
gross profit percentage, 242

H

High Liner Foods, 399*f*
historic cost principle, 175
historical cost principle, 57
horizontal analysis, 482–484
human resources, acquisition of, 247–249

I

income, measurement of, 84–85
income statement
  and balance sheet, relationship between, 60*f*, 142–143
  vs. balance sheet, 26
  described, 25–26, 26*f*
  example, 46*f*, 53*f*
  financial statement analysis, 478–481
  multistep income statement, 26
  preparation, 52–53
  single-step income statement, 25
indirect method, 440, 440*f*, 448–450, 450*f*, 451–452, 452*f*
information. *See* accounting information
information system. *See* accounting information system
insurance, 92–93, 94*f*
intangible assets, 173–174, 188–189
integrated information systems, 145–147
interest
  compound interest, 340, 341*f*
  described, 15, 336*f*
  formula, 86–87
  measurement of interest costs, 334
  payment, 357
  revenue, 85–87
  simple interest, 340, 341*f*
interest expense, 85–87, 357
internal controls
  components of, 101–102
  corrective controls, 303
  described, 69
  detective controls, 302
  financial statement-related, 69–71
  inventory, 249
  liabilities, 250
  long-term assets, 194–195
  preventive controls, 302
  for safeguarding assets, 194–195
  sales/collection process, 302–303
inventory
  acquisition of, 224–227
  acquisition/payment process, 224–225
  cost, 243
  cost flow assumption examples, 230–235
  cost flow assumptions, 228–229
  costs of purchases, 225–227
  disclosure requirements, 244
  finding and using inventory information, 244
  flow, 228
  freight costs, recording, 237
  gross profit method of estimating, 242
  lower-of-cost-or-market, 243–244
  market value, 243
  merchandise inventory, 225
  in merchandising operations, 237–238
  periodic inventory system, 230, 231–232, 239–240
  perpetual inventory system, 230–231, 238–239
  purchases, recording, 235–236
  record-keeping, 229–230
  risks and controls, 249
  transactions, recording, 238–240
  valuation, 243–244
inventory cost flow
  average cost method, 228
  average cost periodic, 234
  conclusions, 235
  described, 227–228
  earnings management, 229
  examples, 230–235
  FIFO periodic, 232–233
  FIFO perpetual, 233–234
  first-in, first-out method (FIFO), 228
  last-in, first-out method (LIFO), 228
  LIFO periodic, 234
  periodic inventory system, 231–232
  perpetual inventory system, 230–231
  record-keeping, timing of, 230–235
  record-keeping costs, 229
  selection of cost flow assumption, 229
  specific identification method, 228
  and taxes, 229
inventory errors
  beginning inventory, 241–242
  described, 240
  ending inventory, 240–241
inventory turnover ratio, 244–245, 485
investment, 56
investors, 61–63
invoice, 15
irregularity, 302

J

journal, 126, 127*f*
journal entries
  adjusting, 134–138
  closing entries, 139–143
  posting to general ledger, 134
  recording, 131–134

L

last-in, first-out method (LIFO), 228
lease, 193
leasehold improvements, 193
liabilities
  adjunct liability, 355
  on balance sheet, 56
  bonds. *See* bonds
  classification of, 245–249
  common types of, 246–247
  contingent liabilities, 247
  contra-liability, 356
  definitely determinable liabilities, 246
  described, 21
  estimated liabilities, 246
  human resources, acquisition of, 247–249
  payroll liabilities, 247–249
  recognition, 246
  risks and controls, 250
  valuation, 246
liability accounts, 130, 141
LIFO, 228
LIFO periodic, 234
line of credit, 335
liquidity, 55
liquidity ratios, 485
Livint Inc., 69

loans, 15
Loblaw Companies Limited, 410, 410*f*, 411*f*
long-term assets
  acquisition costs, 175–177
  acquisition of, 173–174
  amortization. *See* amortization
  business risks, 194–195
  cost allocation, 174–175
  described, 55, 172
  disclosure requirements, 193
  safeguarding, 194–195
  sale of, 189–191
long-term liabilities. *See* bonds; debt financing
long-term notes payable, 334–339
loss, 189
lower-of-cost-or-market, 243–244

M

management plan, 7
managerial accounting, 453
manipulated earnings, 284
market indicator ratios, 485, 488–489
marketing plan, 7
matching principle, 58, 67, 299
materiality, 49
measurement
  in financial statements, 57
  of income, 84–85
Mega Bloks, 481
merchandise for sale. *See* inventory
merchandise inventory, 225
merchandising business, 5–6
monitoring, 102
mortgage amortization schedule, 339*f*
mortgages, 334–339
multistep income statement, 26

N

natural resources, depletion of, 188
nature of business operations, 5–6
net income, 46, 84, 440
net realizable value, 293
new business start-up. *See* business start-up
noncumulative preferred shares, 402
noncurrent assets, 55
noncurrent liability, 56
not-for-profit organization, 4
notes to financial statements, 55, 489

O

on account, 50
Ontario Securities Commission (OSC), 10
operating expenses, 237
operating income, 237
ordinary annuity, 343, 343*f*, 344, 347, 348–349
other receivables, 87
output controls, 70–71
owner contributions. *See* share capital
owners, 61–63, 334, 396
owner's equity, 21
ownership structure
  corporations, 8–11
  partnerships, 7–8
  sole proprietorships, 6–7

P

packing slip, 16
paid-in capital, 57
  see also share capital
par value, 398
partnerships, 7–8
payment date (dividend), 401
payment for goods and services, 287
periodic inventory system, 230, 231–232, 239–240
permanent accounts, 141
perpetual inventory system, 230–231, 238–239
picking slip, 16
poison pill, 401
positive financial leverage, 364
postclosing trial balance, 143
posting, 127
preferred share dividend, 401–402
preferred shares, 397–401
prepaid insurance, 51, 92–93
prepaid rent, 93–94
present value
  annuity, 347–349
  described, 337
  discounting a series of cash flows, 354
  financial calculator, 347
  ordinary annuity, 347, 348–349
  present value of $1 table, partial, 347*f*
  present value of annuity of $1 in arrears table, B-5
  present value of ordinary annuity table, partial, 348*f*, 349
  present value of single amount table, B-4
  single amount, 346–347
  table, 346–347
preventive controls, 302
price-earnings (PE) ratio, 488, 489*f*
principal, 15
proceeds, 189
processing controls, 70
professional services firms, 30
profit, 5, 46
profit and loss statement. *See* income statement
profitability ratios, 485, 487
property, plant and equipment, 96–99, 97*f*
public accountants, 19
Public Sector Accounting Board (PSAB), 47
purchase allowances, 175, 237
purchase discounts, 225–226, 235–236
purchase order (PO), 15, 225
purchase requisition, 15, 224
purchase returns, 175, 237
purchases, 13, 235–236

Q

quick ratio, 300, 485

R

ratio analysis
  accounts receivable turnover ratio, 301–302, 485
  acid-test ratio, 300, 485
  book value per (common) share, 410
  common ratios, 486*f*
  current ratio, 67–68, 300, 485
  debt financing, 364–365
  debt-to-equity ratio, 364, 487
  described, 484–492
  dividend-yield ratio, 488, 489*f*
  earnings per share (EPS), 410, 487
  financial health, evaluation of, 67–68
  financial leverage, 364
  gross margin on sales ratio, 245
  gross margin ratio, 487
  inventory turnover ratio, 244–245, 485
  liquidity ratios, 485
  market indicator ratios, 485, 488–489
  price-earnings (PE) ratio, 488, 489*f*
  profitability ratios, 485, 487
  quick ratio, 300, 485
  return on assets (ROA), 193–194, 487
  return on equity (ROE), 409, 487
  shareholders' equity, 409–410
  solvency ratios, 485, 487
  times-interest-earned ratio, 364, 487
  understanding ratios, 489
  using, 489–492
  working capital, 100–101, 485
REA model, 13, 13*f*
real accounts, 141
receivables. *See* accounts receivable
receiving report, 15, 225
recognize (revenue). *See* revenue recognition
regulatory agencies, 18–19
relative fair market value method, 176
remodelling expenses, 186
rent, 93–94
repairs, 186–187
repurchase of shares, 403, 404–407
residual value, 97, 178, 187–188
resources, 12–13
retail company, 5
retained earnings, 21, 26, 57, 408–409
return on assets (ROA), 193–194, 487
return on equity (ROE), 409, 487
return on investment. *See* return on equity (ROE)
revaluation of assets, 57
revenue, 17, 52–88–89
revenue expenditure, 185–187
revenue recognition, 58, 99, 283–285
revenue recognition principle, 58–67
revenue-related deferrals, 91–92
risk, 29–30, 61
  see also business risks
risk assessment, 102
Royal Bank of Canada, 488

S

sale of long-term assets, 189–191
sales, 282
sales/collection process
  accounts receivable, 291–297
  accounts receivable management, 283
  business risks in, 356
  cash reconciliation, 288–291
  controls, 302–303
  credit card sales, 298
  described, 12, 14–15, 14*f*
  payment for goods and services, 287
  revenue recognition, 283–285
  sales discounts, 285–286
  sales returns, 287
  steps, 282–283
  steps in, 16–17, 17*f*
sales cycle, 282–283
sales discounts, 285–286
sales information, 300
sales method, 293–294
sales order, 16
sales returns, 287
salvage value, 97, 178
Sears Canada Inc., 8, 9*f*, 18, 23, 25–55, 56, 192*f*, 482–484
secondary market, 351
Securities Commission, 10
SEDAR (System for Electronic Document Analysis and Retrieval), 19
separate-entity assumption, 48, 67
service, 5
share capital, 57, 396, 408
share repurchase, 403, 404–407
shareholder, 8
shareholders' equity
  accounts, 141
  book value per (common) share, 410
  earnings per share (EPS), 410
  ratio analysis, 409–410
  retained earnings, 408–409
  return on equity (ROE), 409
  share capital, 396–408
shares
  common shares, 397
  cumulative preferred shares, 402
  described, 397
  dividends, 400–403
  noncumulative preferred shares, 402
  outstanding, 397
  par value, 398
  preferred shares, 397–401
  repurchase of, 403, 404–407
  treasury shares, 404–407
Shoppers Drug Mart, 406*f*
simple interest, 340, 341*f*
single-step income statement, 25
sole proprietorships, 6–7
solvency ratios, 485, 487
specific identification method, 228
statement of operations. *See* income statement
statement of retained earnings
  described, 27, 27*f*
  example, 53*f*
  preparation, 53
stock dividend, 407–408
stock exchange, 8
stock request, 16
stock splits, 408
stockbrokers, 8
straight-line amortization, 178–180, 180*f*, 183, 184*f*, 361–362
subsidiary ledgers, 128
substance *vs.* form, 193
supplies, 95–96, 95*f*

T

takeovers, 401
tangible assets, 173
taxes
  and amortization, 191–192
  and inventory cost flow, 229
temporary accounts, 139, 141
tickler file, 246
time value of money
  compound interest, 340, 341*f*
  described, 339
  future value, 340–345
  present value, 345–349
  simple interest, 340, 341*f*
times interest earned, 487
timing differences, 84–85
trading, 8
transactions
  accounting equation, effects on, 64*f*
  components of, 12–13
treasury shares, 404–407
trial balance
  adjusted trial balance, 138–139
  described, 128
  postclosing trial balance, 143
  unadjusted trial balance, 134

U

unadjusted trial balance, 134
uncollectible accounts, 291–297, 291*f*
uncollectible accounts expense. *See* bad debt expense
unearned revenue, 91–92, 284
unit-of-measure assumption, 57, 67
units-of-production amortization, 181–182, 183–184, 184*f*
unusual items, 481–482
useful life. *See* estimated useful life

V

valuation accounts, 356
valuation of inventory, 243–244
Van Houtte Inc., 89*f*
Veldhuis, 31
vendor, 15
vertical analysis, 483*f*, 484
virtually complete, 58

W

warranties, 299–300
weighted average cost, 228
wholesale company, 5
withdrawal, 134
working capital, 100–101, 485
writing off the cost, 174, 357

Z

zero-coupon bonds, 362–363